UNDERSTANDING
GLOBAL
CULTURES

Second Edition

This book is dedicated with fond memories
to Mr. Francis P. Long, distinguished faculty member for 44 years
at the Scranton Preparatory School, Scranton, Pennsylvania.
I was very fortunate to have Mr. Long as an instructor
in Latin, Greek, German, and English Literature.
He imbued in all of his young students a love of learning
and taught all of us to see both the beauty and the
internal contradictions in widely divergent cultures,
both ancient and modern.

Understanding Global Cultures

Metaphorical Journeys Through 23 Nations

Second Edition

Martin J. Gannon

Sage Publications, Inc.
International Educational and Professional Publisher
Thousand Oaks ▪ London ▪ New Delhi

For information:

Sage Publications, Inc.
2455 Teller Road
Thousand Oaks, California 91320
E-mail: order@sagepub.com

Sage Publications Ltd.
6 Bonhill Street
London EC2A 4PU
United Kingdom

Sage Publications India Pvt. Ltd.
M-32 Market
Greater Kailash I
New Delhi 110 048 India

Printed in the United States of America

Library of Congress Cataloging-in-Publication Data

Gannon, Martin J.
   Understanding global cultures: Metaphorical journeys through 23 nations / by Martin J. Gannon — 2nd ed.
   p. cm.
   Includes bibliographical references and index.
   ISBN 0-7619-1328-9 (cloth: alk. paper)
   ISBN 0-7619-1329-7 (pbk.: alk. paper)
   1. Cross-cultural studies. 2. Cross-cultural orientation. 3. National characteristics. I. Title.
   GN345.7 .G36 2000
   306—dc21   00-011613

01 02 03 04 05 06 07 7 6 5 4 3 2

Acquiring Editor:	Marquita Flemming
Editorial Assistant:	MaryAnn Vail
Production Editor:	Diana E. Axelsen
Editorial Assistant:	Victoria Cheng
Typesetter/Designer:	Lynn Miyata
Indexer:	Mary Mortensen
Cover Designer:	Michelle Lee

Brief Table of Contents

Detailed Table
of Contents

Preface:
A Personal Statement

If we are right in suggesting that our conceptual system is largely metaphorical, then the way we think, what we experience, and what we do every day is very much a matter of metaphor.
                            —Lakoff and Johnson (1980), p. 1

The first edition of this book introduced a new concept and method, the cultural metaphor, for understanding and comparing cultures around the globe. A cultural metaphor is any activity, phenomenon, or institution with which members of a given culture emotionally and/or cognitively identify. As such, the metaphor represents the underlying values expressive of the culture itself. Frequently, outsiders have a difficult time relating to and/or understanding the underlying values of a culture, and this book is designed to address this difficulty. Culture allows us to fill in the blanks, often unconsciously, when action is required, and cultural metaphors help us to see the values leading to action. This is probably the most interesting feature of culture (see Brislin, 1993; Triandis, in press). And, although the unit of analysis in the book is the nation or national culture, cultural metaphors can be derived for ethnic groups within and across nations (see Chapter 24, "The Chinese Family Altar").

When I first began work on cultural metaphors, I was concerned that there would be an automatic negative reaction to the concept, because metaphors are related to stereotypes. From the 1950s until about 1990, the typical reaction to any generalization about groups, particularly in many departments of American universities, was "That is a stereotype," and the clear meaning was that it was totally biased. As explained in Chapter 1, however, humans use such generalizations automatically, and some stereotypes are legitimate, whereas others are not. Clearly, one illegitimate stereotype is a generalization allowing no exceptions. Cultural metaphors, on the other hand, are probabilistic statements that apply to a group, but not to every individual within it.

As with many others, I was profoundly influenced by Geert Hofstede's (1980a) classic, *Culture's Consequences*. Hofstede identified four—later expanded to five—dimensions along which national cultures vary (e.g., power distance; see Chapter 1). But this brilliant book appeared to be incomplete, because the five-dimensional profile seemed to take away the richness and deepness of culture as I had experienced it over the years. Furthermore, this and other prominent dimensional approaches do not seem to explain or even describe the inconsistencies and contradictions that exist in any culture. For example, many ethnic and national cultures will behave in a seemingly unethical manner in some areas, but with rectitude and charity in other areas. Moreover, the profiles are difficult to remember and use when crossing cultures.

In 1988, I approached Maryann Waikart, the Director of our MBA program at Maryland at the time, and offered to teach a seminar about cultural metaphors. As I explained to her, Hofstede's work had been instrumental in my thinking, and I wanted to enrich his perspective by teaching a new seminar that would focus on the use of cultural metaphors. Other than that, I was not quite sure what I was going to do! She thought the idea was great, and so the seminar—and, eventually, books, articles, and research and training programs—began to be built around the concept of cultural metaphors.

Fortunately, a body of literature began to show that metaphors constitute the basic mechanism that allows humans to structure reality and to think; as Ortony (1975) stated the case, metaphors are not only nice, they are necessary (see also Lakoff & Johnson, 1980). About this time, cross-cultural psychologists began to use metaphors to go beyond the dimensional perspective, such as Kashima and Callan's work (1994) on the Japanese household. They also started to employ metaphorical thinking in the area of cross-cultural communication and negotiations (see Gelfand & McHusker, in press).

When the first edition of this book appeared, the response to it was largely positive, much to my relief. Several newspaper writers devoted attention to it, the professional and academic book reviews ranged from qualifiedly positive to very enthusiastic, and many people found the framework useful. For example, several cross-cultural trainers use specific chapters of the book as background reading for managers going abroad; "The Turkish Coffeehouse" served as background reading for an extended cultural sensemaking exercise at the 1998 Biennial International Meeting of the Western Academy of Management in Turkey; several professionals began to develop exercises using cultural metaphors (see Gannon, 2001); at least one doctoral dissertation and one master's degree thesis were derived from the book; translations began to appear; textbooks started to highlight cultural metaphors; several newspapers printed articles on the concept, and one article published in the *Washington Post* was reprinted in many newspapers both nationally and internationally (see Oldenburg, 1991); the methodology underlying cultural metaphors was added to the literature (see Gannon & Audia, in press); and a research program was centered around the concept (see Gannon & Associates, 1997).

However, there are obviously many areas that demand increased attention. My personal hope for the first edition was that this specific cultural perspective would be able to supplement the economic perspective, particularly in the area of economic development. In the first edition, I had great reservations about the economic reforms taking place in Russia, simply because cultural factors seemed to be of little concern. More than 6,000 firms were privatized, and citizens received shares in the new firms, but many sold their stocks to sophisticated investors for a pittance; this was the fastest and largest transformation to a market economy in history. This economic approach seemed foolhardy at the time, although it had been partially successful in the much smaller Czech Republic, and subsequent events support this view. My personal view is that the economists had largely overlooked the influence of culture and its expression in laws and customs.

When the book appeared, Mancur Olson, a well-known development economist, and I began discussions about using cultural metaphors in economic development programs. Mancur, whose economic perspective is filled with metaphorical reasoning (see Olson, 1982, 2000), challenged me by arguing that, although culture is important, it is a somewhat fuzzy concept, and that, regardless of a nation's or group's culture, monetary rewards motivate people.

Unfortunately, his untimely death curtailed our discussions but did motivate me to at least address the issue relating culture and economics more precisely. In the first edition, there was no overriding framework into which parts of the book could be divided. In this revised edition, the framework developed independently by Harry Triandis (see Triandis & Gelfand, 1998) and Fiske (1991a, 1991b) is employed; that is, there are four generic types of cultures: horizontal collectivism, or community sharing; vertical collectivism, or hierarchical ranking; horizontal individualism, or equality matching; and vertical individualism, or market pricing. In addition, I have employed

Samuel Huntington's (1996) perceptive distinction between torn and cleft cultures in two separate parts of the book. A torn national culture is one, such as Russia, that has been torn from its roots at least once; a cleft national culture is one in which the subcultures of the diverse ethnic groups are difficult to integrate. All of these frameworks allow us to gain new insight into various cultural metaphors and to begin to address the challenging issue of integrating cultural and economic perspectives.

There are two additional parts of the book. In the first, there is a description of the bullfight and its symbolic meaning to the Spanish and the Portuguese. The part's title expresses the theme: same cultural metaphor, different meanings. The second part focuses on the cultural values that unite the ethnic Chinese, who live in several different nations.

Furthermore, while accepting the bare-bones definition of culture as common values (see Earley & Laubach, in press), I have avoided the contentious issue of adding other characteristics to the definition. As an alternative, I have constructed a four-stage model of cross-cultural understanding (see Chapter 1). I have also addressed in this chapter the key issue of when culture does and does not matter.

During professional presentations on cultural metaphors, I am often asked how I became interested in culture. In fact, it was of little interest for many years, simply because high performance ultimately wins out in most cases, regardless of the cultural backgrounds of individuals, especially if the playing field is level. Generally speaking, the American organizations with which I am most familiar—research universities, federal government agencies, and business firms of all types—offer such a field. The economic perspective, after all, does have much to offer, especially if cultural conditions support it.

During the early years of my career, I focused on the issue of contingent employment, and particularly temporary help employment, at a time when only four or five researchers throughout the world were even interested in the topic to any great extent. About 1984, Ken Smith, Curt Grimm, and I began a research program on a new dynamic action framework of competitive moves and countermoves in the area of strategic management (see Smith, Grimm, & Gannon, 1992). The shift to cultural studies began, as noted above, in 1988, after several extended stays in nations other than the United States convinced me of the critical importance of this area, particularly in a global economy. Thematically, the specific research and writing programs are integrated into an overall concern about making organizations effective, both in the United States and elsewhere (see Flood, Gannon, & Paauwe, 1996; Gannon, 1988).

A long-time Maryland colleague, Hank Sims, keeps pointing out—in a very laudatory manner, I hasten to add—that I tend to deviate from the traditional academic career and keep reinventing myself in terms of research and writing programs. An alternative and kinder view is that this process is evolutionary, for the analysis of cultural metaphors has allowed me to integrate a diverse set of interests. It has also allowed me to interact with a wide-ranging group of fascinating individuals interested in culture, and these include citizens of many diverse nations; academic researchers; students at all levels (doctoral, MBA, and undergraduate); managers; and researchers from such disciplines as psychology, economics, sociology, and, of course, my favorite, management.

The specific influence on my interest in culture was preparation for extended stays in Germany (1981-1982) and Thailand (1988). In the case of Germany, presumably, I had a good understanding of the culture because my wife, Doris, was born in Germany and raised there until age 9, and we had vacationed there for several weeks in previous years. Still, I prepared for both Germany and Thailand by reading intensively about the history and culture of each nation. In both cases, the visits were pleasant, but the intensive reading and study proved to be poor preparation for understanding Germans and Thais. For instance, the "dos and don'ts," such as how to greet Thais and act in a temple, or *wat,* were easy to understand, but authors usually presented them one by one without providing an overall framework or context into which they could be placed. Typically, the visitor is assaulted with new stimuli and experiences, and it is difficult to remember these "dos and don'ts" just when they are needed! Clearly, such guidelines are important, but they are merely pieces in the puzzle when trying to understand the values, attitudes, and behaviors of any cultural group. Without a framework, the visitor can even believe that he or she is acting properly when, in actuality, he or she is violating deeply held values and customs (see De Mente, 1990; Stewart & Bennett, 1991).

There is some work in cultural anthropology that bears directly on the concept of cultural metaphors, particularly Clifford Geertz's well-known description of male Balinese society in terms of the cockfight (Geertz, 1973). However, each of the metaphors in this book uses three to six characteristics of each metaphor to describe the culture of the nation being assessed. Through the use of each metaphor, we can begin to see the society in a new and different way and, it is hoped, in the same manner as its members do. We can also compare societies through the use of these metaphors and their characteristics.

Although each metaphor is a guide or map, it is only a starting point against which we can compare our own experiences and through which we can start to understand the seeming contradictions pervasive in most, if not all, societies. Also, although we are describing a dominant, and perhaps the dominant, metaphor for each society, other metaphors may also be suitable.

In this book, we do not address the issue of suitable alternatives or supplementary metaphors. Furthermore, our descriptions do explicitly recognize and focus on the regional, racial, and ethnic differences within each nation, particularly in cleft nations. Still, the unit of analysis in this book is the nation, because a good amount of evidence suggests that there are commonalities across regional, racial, and ethnic groups within each of them that can be captured effectively by cultural metaphors. And, as pointed out in Chapter 15, "The Malaysian *Balik Kampung*," if citizens in a nation cannot identify at least one activity, phenomenon, or institution expressive of their values, the probability is high that the nation will experience difficulty and may even be rent asunder.

This book contains 23 metaphors. There are approximately 200 nations in the world. Realistically, then, the approach could be used for all or most nations, thus providing a starting point for understanding commonalities across nations and differences between them. My coauthors and I are currently working on several additional cultural metaphors, but they are not yet ready to see the light of day.

Throughout this book, I have supported the various descriptions of national cultures by reporting statistics specific to a particular nation and, when appropriate, contrasting nations to one another using comparative data. Most of these statistics and comparative pieces of information are drawn from *The Economist Pocket World in Figures, 1998 Edition* (1997).

There are two other books accompanying this one. The first, *Cultural Metaphors: Readings, Research Translations, and Commentary,* provides a variety of perspectives on metaphors and cultural metaphors. The second, *Working Across Cultures: Applications and Exercises,* contains a large number of applications and exercises that allow the user to see culture in action. Each of the three books can be used separately or in conjunction with one another.

This book could not have been written without the help of individuals who are intimately familiar with the specific cultures for which we sought to construct metaphors. They served as coauthors of the various chapters. Our basic approach was for each coauthor to use the methods for constructing metaphors as outlined in Chapter 1 when writing his or her chapter, preceded and followed by intensive discussions both among the coauthors and with other knowledgeable individuals. Each chapter was rewritten in light of the suggestions offered by these individuals. For the first edition, I wrote Chapters 1 and 18 and was responsible for restructuring and editing the other chapters. The coauthors were Diana Liebscher and Eileen Fagen, Britain; Stefania Amodio and Lynne Levy, Italy; Douglas O'Bannon and Julie Kromkoski, Germany; Peter Brown and Sharon Ribas, France; Ana Hedin and Michelle Allison, Sweden; Amy Levitt, Russia; Stacey Hostetler and Sydney Swainston, Belgium; Katherine Feffer Noonan, Spain; Daniel Cronin and Cormac MacFhionnlaoich, Ireland; Amy Levitt, Turkey; Efrat Elron, Israel; Isaac Agboola, Nigeria; Diane Terry, Japan; Amit Gupta and Jeffrey Thomas, India; Hakam Kanafani, the United States; and Pino Audia, China.

For the revised edition, we added several new chapters. Coauthors for chapters in the revised edition are Jennifer Lynn Roney, Poland; Christin Cooper and Maria Masatroianni, Brazil; Rozhan Othman, Malaysia; Louise Warberg, Saudi Arabia; and Carlos Cantarilho, Portugal. Manuel Bacerra also was added as a coauthor to the chapter on Spain.

Several of the doctoral students who were participants in my cross-cultural seminar have now become faculty members in business schools at major universities, and they are Douglas O'Bannon, Webster University; Cormac MacFhionnlaoich, University College–Dublin; Efrat Elron, University of Jerusalem; Amit Gupta, Indian Institute of Management, Indore; Jeffrey Thomas, Indiana University, Bloomington; Pino Audia, London Business School; and Manuel Bacerra, Instituto de Empresa, Spain. Others with university affiliations are Jennifer Lynn Roney, Southern Methodist University; and Roshan Othman, Universiti Kabangsaan, Malaysia.

In addition to the authors, many others contributed to this book. Some coauthors interviewed several people, and each chapter was read and critiqued by several citizens or residents of the countries being described. We would particularly like to thank our colleagues at the Robert H. Smith School of Business, University of Maryland at College Park, for their advice and suggestions, including Michael Agar, Mercy Coogan, Stephen Carroll, Edwin Locke, Sabrina Salam, Allyson Downs, and Guenther Weinrach. We also want to thank the following for providing a supportive environment: Rudolph Lamone, former Dean of the Robert H. Smith School of Business; Dean Howard Frank; Maryann Waikart, former director of the MBA program; and Mark Wellman, director of the MBA program. Michele Gelfand, Assistant Professor of Organizational and Cross-Cultural Psychology, was very helpful, particularly her understanding of the Triandis/Fiske framework and its importance in explaining the values and behaviors of ethnic and national cultures.

Furthermore, given both the scope and depth of this project, we were almost overwhelmed, not only with its complexity but also with its details. We have painstakingly attempted to eliminate any errors, however small, that would serve to detract from the general focus of the book. I accept responsibility for any inadvertent errors that might have occurred; if you encounter even a minor error, we hope that you will bring it and any suggestions for improving the book to our attention.

As usual, the staff at Sage Publications performed its work admirably, and I am especially appreciative of the help that Marquita Flemming, my editor, and others provided. These include Diana Axelsen, production editor;

Liann Lech, copy editor; Lynn Miyata, typesetter; and Maryann Vail, editorial assistant. Finally, my wife, Doris, and our two children, Marlies and Reid, offered invaluable advice and suggestions. They listened patiently and responded to my rambling thoughts and concerns over the many years during which the concepts underlying this book gradually evolved. Without their support, this book might never have made the long journey from fragmentary insights into final form.

—*Martin J. Gannon*
Mgannon@rhsmith.umd.edu
University of Maryland
College Park, Maryland

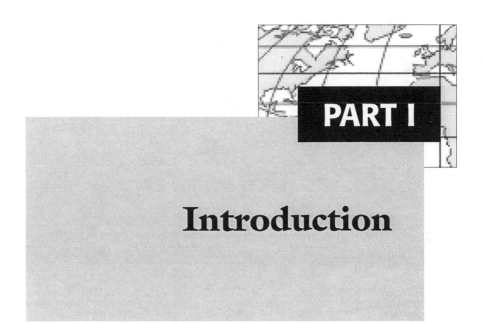

PART I

Introduction

Chapter 1 provides a description of cultural metaphors, that is, any major phenomenon, activity, or institution with which its members closely identify emotionally. This chapter also introduces a four-stage model of cross-cultural understanding. In the next section of the chapter, there is a description of when culture does and does not matter. The final section highlights the organization of the book itself, including the selection of specific chapters to illustrate the major themes of various parts of the book.

CHAPTER 1

Understanding
Cultural Metaphors

In 1990, I was privileged to attend a 10 day cross cultural training program led by Professor Richard Brislin at the East-West Center, University of Hawaii at Manoa. All 35 attendees were professionals involved in cultural studies in some way, and they included professors from a diverse range of disciplines and immigration officials of several nations. During the course of the program, a well-known cross-cultural training exercise, The Albatross (Gotchenour, 1977), was conducted that proved to be very insightful. Perhaps because of my background as a professor of management, I immediately wrote a case study about the experience and have used it more than 100 times in a variety of settings involving students and managers. The reader is invited to read this case study and answer the questions after it before I provide any additional details:

---◆---

I recently participated in a cross-cultural training session at the East-West Center, Hawaii. There were six male volunteers (including me) and six female volunteers. We walked into a room where a man was dressed in Eastern or Asian garb but in a somewhat indistinguishable manner; he could have been a king or a Buddhist monk. A woman sat beside him, and she was also dressed in a similar indistinguishable fashion.

There was no talking whatsoever in this training session, which lasted for about 10 minutes. The "king" beckoned the males to sit on chairs, after which he indicated that the females should sit at their feet. He then greeted each male silently and in standing position; he clasped each male by the arms and then gently rubbed his hands on the male's sides. The males did as the king instructed, but there was some nervousness and laughter, although no talking. The king then bowed to each female.

Next, the king presented a large vase of water to each male, and he drank of it. The King then did the same thing with each female.

The king and queen then walked before the volunteers, peering intently at the females. After a minute or two, the king put on a satisfied look and made a noise as if satisfied. He then looked at the queen, who nodded in agreement. The queen then took the hand of one female in order to lead her to a sitting position on the ground between the king and queen. Next, the king and queen tried to push the female's head toward the ground as she sat on the ground between them (they were on chairs), but she resisted. They tried once again, but she still resisted. The training session then ended.

Instructions: Each small group should appoint a recorder/secretary to report back to the larger group. Time limit is 10 minutes. Please answer the following questions:

♦ What kind of a culture is this? Please describe.

♦ How would you interpret the differential treatment of males and females in this culture?

———•———

There were about six subgroups per session over the approximate 100 sessions, so there have been approximately 600 interpretations. In 9 of 10 instances, the subgroup describes the culture in the following manner: a male-dominated traditional culture, probably Asian or African or Middle Eastern, ritualistic, and conservative. Sometimes, the subgroup tries to identify the religion involved, and Buddhism or Islam is cited frequently. And, although almost all subgroups feel that females are in a subordinate role, a few believe that females have a high status clearly separate from that of the dominant males.

In fact, this is an earth-worshipping culture in which males are clearly subordinate to females, and the only way to integrate all of the information provided is to use this framework. For example, the male leader was not being friendly when he patted the males; rather, he was checking for weapons, as males tend to have too much testosterone and too strong a tendency to engage in immature fighting. Similarly, the females were seated in the place of honor (nearest to the ground), and the males were relegated to the bleachers. The males drank first to test for poison, thus ensuring the safety of the females. Even the "king," whose ambiguous position is highlighted by the quotation marks, must ask permission of the female leader before selecting a favored female, who was placed nearest the ground for the ritual in an honored position between the two leaders. Frequently, I ask why a particular female was chosen, and rarely does anyone guess the reason: A visual inspection indicated that she had the largest feet, an obvious sign of importance in an earth-worshipping culture. In many cultures, the number three is used, and it was being used in this ritual until the favored female resisted.

This exercise is usually sufficient to make the point that having a framework is very useful in understanding any culture. If the trainees had been told that the culture was earth-worshipping, they could have integrated the various stimuli that were overwhelming them. Furthermore, the feedback session after the training proved to be insightful, as the young woman selected for the ritual was asked why she resisted. At this time, I usually profile this young woman, a very accomplished cultural anthropologist who has devoted her career to the study of village life around the world. She was in her mid-thirties, well published and tenured at a good university, attractive, and divorced but without children. Her response focused on the maltreatment that she had experienced at the hands of various men in her life and on her resolve never to allow such maltreatment to occur again. Thus, she had interpreted the ritual as a form of subservience to men, as the "king" was pushing her head toward the ground, as was the "queen," but she did not mention this fact. My pedagogical point is that this young woman, given her educational training and work experiences in different villages, was as knowledgeable as or more knowledgeable than any professional in the room, but her perspective—warped by unpleasant experiences with men—had led her to react emotionally, even to the extent that she was not able to think about an alternative framework, such as an earth-worshipping culture. I also point out that I felt overwhelmed during the training and had no idea what was going on.

As this narrative suggests, culture counts, and it counts quite a bit. To give but one example, Geert Hofstede (1991) completed a questionnaire study at the IBM Corporation involving 117,000 of its managers and employees in 53 countries, in which he demonstrated that national culture explained 50% of the differences in attitudes. In fact, culture explained more of the difference than did professional role, age, gender, or race. A comparable but earlier study of 3,600 managers in 14 countries placed this figure at 30% (Haire, Ghiselli, & Porter, 1966). Given such studies, it seems that culture influences between 25% and 50% of our attitudes, whereas other aspects of workforce diversity, such as social class, ethnicity, race, sex, and age, account for the remainder of these attitudinal differences.

But the case study also highlights other critical aspects of culture, which operates subtly, often on the unconscious or semiconscious level. Culture has been aptly compared to a computer program that, once activated by a few commands or stimuli, begins to operate automatically and seemingly in an independent manner (Fisher, 1988; Hall, 1966; Hofstede, 1991). Clearly, such automaticity occurred in the case study, but unfortunately, the stimuli were not properly matched to the cultural framework because of the negative relationships with males that this young woman had experienced.

Frequently, when a foreigner violates a key cultural value, he or she is not even aware of the violation, and no one brings the matter to his or her attention. The foreigner is then isolated and begins to experience negative feelings. As one American businessman in Asia aptly pointed out, one of the central problems of doing business cross-culturally is that once a visitor makes a major cultural mistake, it is frequently impossible to rectify it, and it may well take several months to realize that polite rejections really signify isolation and banishment. Sometimes, a foreigner makes such a mistake and eventually leaves the country without even realizing or identifying what he or she had done.

Even genuinely small cultural mistakes can have enormous consequences. Many Germans, for instance, do not like to converse too much during meals. A German will ordinarily begin the meal by taking a sip of beer or soda and then pick up the knife and fork and hold them throughout the meal, putting them down only when he or she has finished eating. For many Germans, eating is a serious business, not to be disturbed by trivial comments and animated conversation. On the other hand, many Italians tend to talk constantly during meals and wave their hands repeatedly. As a result, a German and an Italian dining with one another may feel aggrieved by each other's behavior, and much time is wasted negotiating acceptable rules of behavior that could otherwise be spent on substantive issues, including the development of trust.

Furthermore, whereas technological and societal changes have been rapid in recent decades, cultures tend to change only slowly, typically at a snail's pace, and the influence of culture persists for centuries even after mass immigrations take place. The American Irish have the "gift of the gab," befitting a cultural heritage that has a strong oral tradition, and they are disproportionately represented in fields such as trial law and politics, where this gift is an asset (see Chapter 12). The English and the French in Canada think and feel differently in large part because of their respective cultural heritages, and these differences have threatened the very existence of the country.

Individuals from English-speaking countries are at a particular disadvantage culturally because the people of many non-English-speaking countries use both English and their own native languages. It is common for

English-speaking visitors to a non-English-speaking country to assume cultural similarity when dissimilarity is really the norm. Today, approximately 800 million individuals speak English, which has become the international business language, thus creating both opportunities and pitfalls for natives of English-speaking countries.

However, it should be noted that knowing a country's language, although clearly helpful, is no guarantee of understanding its cultural mind-set, and some of the most difficult problems have been created by individuals who have a high level of fluency but a low level of cultural understanding. Glen Fisher (1988), a former foreign service officer, describes a situation in Latin America in which the American team's efforts were seriously hampered because of the condescending attitude of one member whose fluency in Spanish was excellent. Fortunately, another member of the team helped to save the day because she showed a genuine interest in the culture and its people, even though she was just beginning to learn how to speak Spanish. Moreover, members of a culture tend to assume that highly fluent visitors know the customs and rules of behavior, and these visitors are judged severely when violations occur.

Americans are at a particular disadvantage in trying to understand the mind-sets of other cultures because, at least until recently, they did not travel abroad in great numbers. Even today, American travelers follow a frantic schedule, sometimes visiting Hong Kong, Thailand, Japan, and Taiwan within the space of 2 weeks. To expect these American travelers to understand these cultures in such a short period of time is unrealistic. Even fewer Americans spend any time residing in foreign countries, and when doing so, they tend to isolate themselves from the natives in their "golden ghettoes." By contrast, Europeans speak two or more languages, including English, and they experience great cultural diversity simply by traveling a few hundred miles from one country to another. Many Asians, because of their knowledge of the English language and education in Europe and the United States, are similar to these Europeans in terms of cultural sophistication.

This book describes a new method, the *cultural metaphor,* for understanding easily and quickly the cultural mind-set of a nation and comparing it to those of other nations. In essence, the method involves identifying some phenomenon, activity, or institution of a nation's culture that all or most of its members consider to be very important and with which they identify closely. The characteristics of the metaphor then become the basis for describing and understanding the essential features of the society.

For example, the Italians invented the opera and love it passionately. Five key characteristics of the opera are the overture, spectacle and pageantry, voice, exteriority, and the interaction between the lead singers and the chorus (see Chapter 18). We use these features to describe Italy and its cultural mind-set. Thus, the metaphor is a guide, map, or beacon light that helps the foreigner understand quickly what members of a society consider very important. This knowledge should help him or her to be comfortable in the society and to avoid making cultural mistakes. However, the cultural metaphor is only a starting point, and it is subject to change as the individual's firsthand knowledge increases.

Constructing Cultural Metaphors

Countless social scientists, particularly cross-cultural psychologists and cultural anthropologists, have devoted their lives to the study of culture. Our cultural metaphors are based partially on the work of cross-cultural psychologists and cultural anthropologists who emphasize a small number of factors or dimensions, such as time and space, when comparing one society to another.

The first of these dimensional approaches was described by two anthropologists, Florence Kluckholn and Fred Strodtbeck (1961), although Kluckholn is generally given credit for developing the original ideas. They compare cultures across six dimensions. However, they emphasize that philosophers, social scientists, and commentators interested in understanding cultural differences have focused attention on these dimensions for hundreds of years. These six dimensions are as follows:

- What do members of a society assume about the nature of people, that is, are people good, bad, or a mixture?

- What do members of a society assume about the relationship between a person and nature, that is, should we live in harmony with it or subjugate it?

- What do members of a society assume about the relationship between people, that is, should a person act in an individual manner or consider the group before taking action (individualism vs. groupism or collectivism in terms of such issues as making decisions, conformity, and so forth)?

- What is the primary mode of activity in a given society, that is, *being,* or accepting the status quo, enjoying the current situation, and going with the flow of things; or *doing,* that is, changing things to make them better, setting specific goals and accomplishing them within specific schedules, and so forth?

- What is the conception of space in a given society, that is, is it considered *private,* in that meetings are held in private, people do not get too close to one another physically, and so on; or *public,* that is, having everyone participate in meetings and decision making, allowing emotions to be expressed publicly, and having people stand in close proximity to one another?

■ What is the society's dominant temporal orientation: past, present, and/or future?

Kluckholn and Strodtbeck note that each society has a dominant cultural orientation that can be described in terms of these six dimensions, but that other, weaker orientations may also exist simultaneously in its different geographical regions and racial and ethnic groups.

Another well-known anthropologist, Edward T. Hall, has spent more than 40 years developing and writing about a similar dimensional classification system (for a good summary of it, see Hall & Hall, 1990). Basically, he focuses on the communication patterns found within cultures, and he emphasizes four dimensions along which societies can be compared:

■ Context, or the amount of information that must be explicitly stated if a message or communication is to be successful

■ Space, or the ways of communicating through specific handling of personal space (e.g., North Americans tend to keep more space between them while communicating than do South Americans)

■ Time, which is either *monochronic* (scheduling and completing one activity at a time) or *polychronic* (not distinguishing between activities and completing them simultaneously)

■ Information flow, which is the structure and speed of messages between individuals and/or organizations

Hall then arrays societies along an overarching high-context/low-context dimension. In a high-context society, time tends to be polychronic, and there is a heavy investment in socializing members so that information does not need to be stated explicitly for it to be understood. Members of such a culture have known one another for long periods of time, and there is strong agreement as to what is expected and not expected. In the high-context Japanese society, there is even an aphorism that expressly addresses this issue: He who knows does not speak; he who speaks does not know (see Chapter 3). Hence, verbal communication frequently is not necessary and may well impede the transmission of the message. Also, members of high-context societies tend to have less physical space between them when communicating than do those in low-context societies.

As Hall notes, high-context societies tend to require a strong leader to whom everyone else expresses submission or at least great respect. In the Arabic countries, such a leader will sit in his office surrounded by people seeking his help and advice. He will not address the issues and people sequentially, as would tend to happen in monochronic countries such as the United States and Germany. Rather, he will deal with several issues and people as conditions seem to warrant, going from one group to the other in a seemingly haphazard fashion that takes into consideration their sensitivities and need to save face or avoid embarrassment.

Hall tends to array societies he has studied in the following way, going from high-context to low-context: Japan, the Arab countries, France (approximately in the middle of the continuum), the United States, and Germany. Clearly, Hall has a bias against low-context societies, even though he recognizes that it is much easier to interface with a low-context society because information about rules and permissible behaviors is stated explicitly. To him, such societies tend to be too mechanical and lacking in sensitivity to the needs of individuals. However, he does not analyze critically some of the problems found in high-context societies, particularly the overwhelming power of the leader that can be used indiscriminately, or the in-group bias that hinders relations with anyone outside of the culture. Hall's system begins to break down when he talks about the low-context way that the Japanese interact with foreigners but the high-context way in which they interact among themselves. Thus, he seems to be describing the classic in-group/out-group phenomenon rather than an overarching dimension along which societies can be arrayed. Triandis, Brislin, and Hui (1988) have argued that the major dimension separating societies is that of individualism and collectivism, in which the in-group and out-group distinction is critical, and it really seems to be this dimension that Hall is describing. Furthermore, as described in the various chapters of this book, there are many specific kinds of individualism and collectivism.

Still, Hall's work has been significant and insightful, particularly his treatment of time and space. Throughout this book, we will use some of his basic concepts, especially the monochronic-polychronic distinction and that between a high-context and a low-context communication.

The third major dimensional approach was developed by Geert Hofstede, whose work is cited above. Although there are other, similar frameworks, Hofstede's has proved to be the most robust and useful. (For examples of such frameworks, see Schwartz, 1994, and Trompenaars & Hampden-Turner, 1998.) Hofstede is a prominent organizational psychologist whose research is based on a large questionnaire survey of IBM employees and managers working in 53 different countries. Hofstede's work is especially significant because the type of organization is held constant, and it is the only large-scale, cross-cultural study in which the respondents all worked for a multinational corporation that had uniform personnel policies. He develops empirical profiles of these 53 countries across five dimensions of basic cultural values:

- Power distance, or the degree to which members of a society automatically accept a hierarchical or unequal distribution of power in organizations and the society

- Uncertainty avoidance, or the degree to which members of a given society deal with the uncertainty and risk of everyday life and prefer to work with long-term acquaintances and friends than with strangers

- Individualism, or the degree to which an individual perceives him- or herself to be separate from a group and free from group pressure to conform

- Masculinity, or the degree to which a society looks favorably on aggressive and materialistic behavior

- Time horizon (short term to long term), or the degree to which members of a culture are willing to defer present gratification in order to achieve long term goals

The three-dimensional approaches developed by Kluckholn and Strodtbeck, Hall, and Hofstede have become enormously influential and, at the same time, controversial. Although they rely upon a small number of dimensions so that profiles of various societies can be constructed, by necessity, they leave out many features of the cultural mind-sets that are activated in daily cultural activities, and they neglect the institutions molding these mind-sets. These dimensional approaches are an excellent starting point for understanding cultures and providing an overall perspective on cultural differences, but an individual will experience great difficulty in applying them to daily interactions. In effect, these dimensions are instructive but somewhat lifeless and narrow, in that they leave out many facets of behavior.

The metaphoric method highlighted in this book supplements and enriches the three-dimensional approaches so that a visitor can understand and, most importantly, begin to deal effectively with the flesh and blood of a culture. Although the metaphor itself cannot encompass all of the reality that is found within each society, it is a good starting point for understanding and interacting effectively with it. At the same time, the various chapters of the book are linked together through the use of the three dimensional approaches.

Throughout this book, we have attempted to identify metaphors that members of given societies view as very important, if not critical. However, we needed to identify metaphors that would be relatively complex so that we could make several direct comparisons between the metaphor and the nation being represented by it. Also, we wanted to have a metaphor for each society that would have several suitable features that we could then use to describe it. In addition, we sought to include numerous factors or variables such as religion and small group behavior when using the metaphor to describe the society, recognizing that some of them are important in some societies but not others. For each society, we used all of the dimensions of the three-dimensional approaches described above. In addition, we focused on all of the following:

- Religion

- Early socialization and family structure

- Small group behavior

- Public behavior

- Leisure pursuits and interests

- Total lifestyle: work/leisure/home and time allocations to each of them

- Aural space, or the degree to which members of a society react negatively to high noise levels

- Roles and status of different members of a society

- Holidays and ceremonies

- Greeting behavior

- Humor

- Language: oral and written communication

- Nonoral communication, such as body language

- Sports as a reflection of cultural values

- Political structure of a society

- The educational system of a society

- Traditions and the degree to which the established order is emphasized

- History of a society, but only as it reflects cultural mind-sets, or the manner in which its members think, feel, and act; not a detailed history

- Food and eating behavior

- Social class structure

- Rate of technological and cultural change

- Organization of and perspective on work, such as a society's commitment to the work ethic, superior-subordinate relationships, and so on

- Any other categories that are appropriate

Using all of these categories initially, we studied each society in depth and interviewed several of its natives. After an initial draft of a chapter was written, it was presented at seminars and reviewed by natives and long-term residents of the society being described. The chapter was then rewritten in light of the suggestions that were offered, and additional comments were solicited. This iterative process typically led to rewriting the chapter five or six times, and sometimes nine or ten times.

A Four-Stage Model of Cross-Cultural Understanding

For the revised edition of this book, we have developed a four-stage model of cross-cultural understanding that we employed to frame the analysis of each nation more precisely. The first stage centers on a four-cell typology of process/goal orientation and degree of emotional expressiveness. The two major dimensions of the typology are defined as follows:

■ The degree to which process such as effective communication and getting to know one another in depth should precede discussion of specific goals

■ The degree to which a culture fosters and encourages open emotional expression

There are many cultures where process must be emphasized before any meaningful collaboration around specific goals can occur. Other cultures, such as the American and German, tend to emphasize goals over process. As some American managers express the point, it is not necessary to like one another in order to do business, presumably because a written contract will keep everyone honest. Furthermore, in some cultures, emotional expression is not only acceptable but also important, whereas in other cultures, such expression is discouraged. As Figure 1.1 indicates, the visitor to a nation can obtain a general orientation to it by using this typology and its key dimensions.

In the second stage, the visitor needs more specificity, particularly in the relationship between culture and economics or business practices. For the past several years, Harry Triandis (in press) and Alan Fiske (1991b) have independently developed frameworks linking culture and economics more tightly. There are minor differences between the two frameworks, and sometimes, Fiske does not clearly demarcate the cultural level from the individual level. For our purposes, however, the two frameworks can be treated as identical.

FIGURE 1.1.
Process, Goals, and Expression of Emotions

Open Expression of Emotions and Feelings

		Lower	Higher
Degree to Which Process Must Be Emphasized Before Goals Can Be Discussed	**Lower**	England, Ireland, and Scotland	United States and Germany
	Higher	China, Japan, and India	Mexico, Spain, and Italy

Both authors seek to identify generic types of cultures. They begin their analyses with the cultural dimension of individualism-collectivism, which has been the dimension of most interest to researchers because of its obvious importance. Also, they emphasize the degree to which there is a large amount of inequality or power distance in the culture. Thus, there is a four-cell typology of cultures emphasizing individualism-collectivism and power distance (see Figure 1.2). There are two generic types of collectivism (horizontal and vertical) and two generic types of individualism (horizontal and collectivistic). Horizontal collectivism reflects community sharing in which members of the in-group share all of their goods, as in a small village, even to the extent that there is no such phenomenon as theft. There is not much differentiation between individuals, and ethics are based on group membership: in-group or out-group. In essence, members of out-groups are viewed as nonpersons.

Vertical collectivism, or authority ranking—found in large parts of Asia, Africa, and Latin America—involves a psychological relationship between the leader or leaders and all others in the culture. Frequently, such a culture is symbolized not by the handshake, which reflects equality, but by different forms of bowing. Only a few Americans and Europeans have even experienced such a culture in depth, because the relationship between superior and subordinate in most American firms is instrumental and focuses only on work-related goals. In contrast, there is a dynamic, two-way relationship between subordinates and leaders in authority ranking cultures: Although the leaders receive more rewards, they are responsible for safeguarding the livelihoods of subordinates, even to the extent of finding them new positions

FIGURE 1.2.
Four Generic Types of Cultures

		INDIVIDUALISM	COLLECTIVISM
	low (horizontal)	Equality Matching	Community Sharing
POWER DISTANCE	high (vertical)	Market Pricing	Authority Ranking

when bankruptcy occurs. In turn, the subordinates are expected to be committed to the leader and the organization. Letting people go to save money is anathema. Ethics is still determined in large part by group membership (ingroup and out-group), but status as signified by family background, position at work, and so on is also critical.

Horizontal individualism, or equality matching, is dominant in Scandinavian nations such as Sweden and Norway. All individuals are considered equal, even when some are taxed heavily, and it is expected that those who cannot make individual contributions to the common good will do so at a later time if possible. Finally, vertical individualism, or market pricing, is found in the United States and other market-dominated nations. Although individualism is emphasized, so, too, is the free market, and inequality resulting from its operation is deemed acceptable. There is equality of opportunity and a level playing field, but not equality of outcomes. Ethics revolves around the operation of such a market.

Fiske, in particular, relates these concepts to the four types of statistical scales: nominal, ordinal, interval, and ratio. His argument is that individuals have difficulty making decisions and use these scales as rough approximations for determining how to interact with others. Thus, community sharing represents nominal scaling, because only names are given to entities (in-group vs. out-group). In an authority ranking culture, Individual A may be more important than Individual B, and Individual C may be more important than Individual B, but there is no common unit of measurement. The scale is ordinal in nature. Hence, we cannot say C is twice as important as A. In equality matching, the culture does have a common unit of measurement, but it does not make value judgments about individual worth, because there are too many dimensions along which individuals can be measured. In this sense, the scaling is interval. Finally, in market pricing, there is a common unit of measurement and a true zero point (zero money), which allows members of the culture to transform every other dimension and compare them monetarily. In this case, the scaling is ratio.

Fiske provides an insightful example of these four types of culture in his discussion of a small town's decision about the purchase of an expensive fire truck. The issue becomes, Who should receive the new fire protection? The reader may want to stop at this point to consider the matter. The answers are as follows: (a) community sharing, or only members of the in-group; (b) authority ranking, or all members of the in-group, but the leaders receive more attention and monitoring of their homes; (c) equality matching, where everyone is protected; and (d) market pricing, or only those who can pay the taxes. This example is not farfetched. In the United States, there have been several recorded instances when fire trucks did not respond, sometimes because a home is just outside of the fire department's district, and sometimes because the owners of the homes did not contribute monetarily to the fire department's upkeep.

In Hofstede's original analysis of 40 nations, he divided them at the median score on both individualism-collectivism and power distance (Hofstede, 1980b). No nation is in the community sharing quadrant, probably because this form of collectivism is not appropriate for such large entities as nations. The interested reader can find the dispersion of the 40 nations into the other three quadrants by consulting the original work.

The model's third stage revolves around the other etic or culture-general dimensions along which specific cultures have been shown to vary. Osland and Bird (2000) provide an excellent summary of most of these dimensions, such as achievement motivation, and the remaining three dimensions developed by Hofstede (uncertainty avoidance, time horizon, and femininity or assertiveness). Triandis has recently highlighted another key dimension: the tightness or looseness of rules (Triandis & Gelfand, 1998). In this way, it is possible to compare cultures in a novel manner. Thus, whereas Japan is collectivistic and Germany individualistic, both are characterized by a large number of rules governing behavior (high degree of tightness).

In the fourth stage, cultural metaphors are employed for understanding a culture. They build upon the etic understanding provided by the approaches used in the first three stages. During this stage, the specific types of individualism and collectivism are related to each cultural metaphor, such as competitive individualism in the United States and proud and self-sufficient individualism among the Spanish.

It is possible to sensitize individuals to cultural differences and similarities through the use of the four-stage model. For example, there are several applications, such as marketing and advertising exercises, that help the trainee apply this model to actual problems (Gannon, 2001). Also, this model integrates the etic (culture-general) and emic (culture-specific) approaches in a dynamic manner rather than treating them as separate.

When Culture Does, and Does Not, Matter

The next important issue that we address in this chapter is, When does culture matter? There are times when culture is not important and other times when it is critically important. In this book, we emphasize culture but do caution the reader to consider other factors.

Frequently, occupational similarities neutralize culture. For instance, when two medical doctors are working jointly on a problem, their medical backgrounds can help them to work together smoothly regardless of cultural backgrounds. Also, similarity of social class can diminish the importance of culture. For example, throughout the world, middle-class families tend to use positive reinforcement in raising their children and provide them with opportunities to develop skills and a strong sense of self-esteem. These families may provide their children with music lessons and ask them to perform in front of guests, who respond enthusiastically. Conversely, blue-collar families throughout the world tend to emphasize negative reinforcement and punishment, which negatively influence skill development, opportunities to function in a public or leadership role, and feelings of self-esteem (see Kagitcibasi, 1990).

However, sometimes, powerful groups will exclude others from opportunities and then stereotype them negatively, thus consigning them to permanent inferior status. This clearly happened in Ireland, when the English ruled the nation for centuries. Apartheid, now outlawed in South Africa, began as a reaction to scarcity of jobs and led to the stigmatization of native Africans for nearly a century (see Olson, 1982). If the playing field is level, as is more probable when markets are genuinely competitive, this outcome is mitigated.

At times, social class or occupational similarity and culture become confused in the minds of visitors. Some Americans, for example, complain about the rudeness of Parisian shopkeepers, whereas other Americans describe wonderful relationships with their occupational peers in France. Presumably, what is occurring is just as reflective, if not more reflective, of social class or occupational similarity than of culture.

Sometimes, the nature of the problem minimizes the importance of cultural differences. For example, when companies from two or more nations are working together on a joint project that their top managements support strongly, organizational members are more likely to forget cultural differences, especially when ample rewards for goal attainment and punishments for nonattainment are available.

When trust is present, culture decreases in importance. Jarvenpaa, Knoll, and Leidner (1998) studied 75 virtual work teams throughout the world that were integrated via the Internet. The major finding was that if trust can be established quickly, culture is not a major issue.

One of the most controversial issues is the degree to which technological changes such as the Internet influence culture. As Wallace (1999) points out, the Internet has not resulted in a global village, as the case is so often stated. Rather, individuals with similar interests—including crime, in the case of the ever-expanding crime syndicates—seek out one another on the Internet. As such, the Internet has led to more differentiation than integration. But any indirect form of communication, such as e-mail, presents special difficulties. For example, a high-context and high-level manager in Indonesia became angry when he received a terse message from his American counterpart, not because of the content but because of the manner in which the message was phrased. Furthermore, it seems that any major technological change has a greater influence on culture in the later stages of maturation than in the earlier stages, and the Internet is in the early stage of maturation (Hughes, 1994). As a general rule, technological and economic changes do matter, especially when they are disruptive of cultural patterns. Still, problems are minimized when changes are introduced gradually and are not directly injurious to deep-seated values.

As suggested in the preface, perhaps the most interesting feature of culture is that it triggers unconscious values leading to action. Thus, it is not surprising that culture is important when individuals must communicate directly. If individuals expect that outsiders will follow their cultural rules and are unwilling to facilitate the relationship by developing new rules acceptable to all, communication is likely to break down. Rebecca Mark, Senior Vice President of International Operations at Enron, a large, multinational energy company, openly downgraded the importance of culture when she was responsible for a $3 billion joint venture in India. However, she changed her behavior after the conservative Indian government stopped her firm's activity. At that point, she followed the advice of an Indian friend, who gently suggested that she begin to show appreciation for Indian culture by wearing saris rather than her favored miniskirts and by showing an interest in Indian cuisine. These actions signaled that Rebecca wanted to facilitate communication and recognized the importance of Indian culture (see Karp & Kranhold, 1999). Similarly, a Texas businesswoman was having difficulty in China until she started wearing dresses that were red, a favorite color among the Chinese.

Such small changes tend to trigger positive reactions, even at the unconscious level.

As shown in numerous research studies, culture is particularly important in cross-cultural negotiations. Understanding both the similarities and the differences of the cultures represented by the negotiators is a good way to facilitate interaction and goal attainment. Americans, for example, have a reputation for being direct and low context when communicating information, and this becomes a problem when the communication is phrased in terms of "take it or leave it." Billion-dollar deals have died on the table because of such behavior.

Culture is also important when individuals move to another nation or culture for an extended period of time. The well-known phenomenon of culture shock does occur and, if not handled properly, can lead to major problems. In this regard, it is not surprising that managers from a firm's headquarters who are sent to work in a subsidiary for an extended period cling to the values and ways of behaving found in their base culture, even to the extent of isolating themselves in "golden ghettoes."

Culture is also relevant if distorted stereotypes are present. There is some confusion surrounding the definition of a stereotype, but at a minimum, it represents a distorted view or mental picture of groups and their supposed characteristics, on the basis of which we tend to evaluate individuals from each group. Stereotypes can be erroneous and can lead to unwarranted conclusions, particularly if no exceptions are allowed. In this sense, a stereotype is a universal syllogism. Ironically, in-group members frequently use universal stereotyping as a form of humor, but react very negatively if out-group members employ it. A few years ago, my wife and I were visiting Northern Ireland and met a group of Northern Irishmen who presented such a stereotype. Such a description would have been offensive coming from an American, Asian, or African:

> The Welsh pray on Sunday and prey on their neighbors the rest of the week; the Scots keep the Sabbath and anything else they can lay their hands on; the Irish are not sure what they want, but they are willing to fight to the death to get it; and the English are all self-made, which relieves God of a most onerous responsibility.

However, all human beings use stereotypes because they are a shorthand and easy way of classifying the multitude of stimuli to which we are exposed. The issue is not stereotyping itself, but whether the stereotypes are accurate.

Most of us take an extremely negative position on stereotyping. It can be very embarrassing to be accused of stereotyping, especially because it is often so difficult to refute the charge. In today's world, the accusation is raised frequently, and as a result, it has become very difficult to discuss genuine differences. However, many social psychologists now take the position that there are real differences between groups and societies and that the negative connotations associated with stereotyping have led us to deemphasize these legitimate differences. From this perspective, a stereotype represents only a starting point that is to be evaluated rigorously and changed as experience with groups warrants. Nancy Adler (1997) argues persuasively that it is legitimate and helpful to use stereotypes if they are descriptive rather than evaluative, are the first best guess, are based on data and observation, and are subject to change when new information merits it.

Metaphors are not stereotypes. Rather, they rely upon the features of one critical phenomenon in a society to describe the entire society. There is, however, a danger that metaphors will include some inaccurate stereotyping, and we have attempted to guard against this possibility by having the various chapters of this book reviewed by natives of the societies being described or by long-term residents of them. In some instances, we were unable to construct a metaphor that satisfied natives, residents, or ourselves. Hence, this book includes only metaphors about which there is a consensus.

Admittedly, it is very difficult to test the validity of these metaphors empirically, at least at this point in time. Our tests are two in number: (a) consensus, and (b) whether a metaphor other than the one we have selected increases our understanding of a particular society. Also, we have noted in many instances that not all members of a society adhere to the behavioral patterns suggested by the metaphor by using such phrases as "Some Germans," "Many Italians," and "the Irish tend to . . ." In effect, we are highlighting patterns of thought, emotion, and behavior that a society manifests and that are portrayed clearly and concisely by means of a simple and easily remembered metaphor. In this way, the visitor can use the metaphor as a guide, map, or beacon light to avoid cultural mistakes and to enrich cross-cultural communications and interactions.

In sum, culture frequently does not matter, but at other times, it is very influential. We have described only some of the instances when culture does and does not matter. Culture probably counts the most when there is scarcity of resources, opportunities, and feelings of inequity (perceived or real). It is comforting to cluster with others similar to oneself, especially when rejected by dominant groups. As Huntington (1996) argues persuasively, the major threat to world security is the increase in ethnic wars that has accompanied globalization and privatization. Cultural differences are especially exacerbated when accompanied by extreme religious and ideological viewpoints. Many cultural problems are solved in the long run through intermarriages and increased social and business contacts, all of which are hindered by religious and ideological differences.

All of the factors described above, and some others not described because of space limitations, are important for evaluating when culture does or does not matter. The position taken in this book is that culture is important and is of critical significance in many situations, but not all of them. Culture also interacts with political, social, and economic forces and is, in that sense, a fuzzy concept. But clearly, it is possible to understand cultures and use this understanding to enhance relationships between individuals and groups. Throughout the remainder of the book, we will be employing the methodology described in this chapter, including the four-stage model of cross-cultural understanding, to demonstrate how cultural metaphors can strengthen understanding and to show how they are related to the core values, attitudes, and behaviors of various nations.

Organization of the Book

The observant reader may wonder why specific nations have been assigned to specific parts of the book, because some nations could fit easily into two or more parts. Figure 1.2 served as an initial screening device. It reflects Hofstede's (1991) fourfold table of 53 nations profiled in terms of low (horizontal) or high (vertical) power distance and individualism or collectivism. This figure also mirrors three parts of the book: authority ranking national cultures (vertical collectivism), equality matching national cultures (horizontal individualism), and market pricing national cultures (vertical individualism) (see also Hofstede, 1980a, Figure 5.2). It is important to note that no nation fell into the cell "community sharing," which suggests that this form of cultural organization (horizontal collectivism) may not be appropriate for large entities, such as nations.

Next, I explored in depth those nations that are cleft. According to Huntington (1996), a cleft nation is one whose ethnic groups are so different culturally that they have difficulty integrating into a common national culture. This definition clearly applies to Malaysia, Nigeria, and Belgium. I expanded on Huntington's definition by including two additional nations: Israel and Italy. There are so many ideological groups and political parties in Israel that it resembles a nation of tribes with radically different viewpoints and ways of living (David, 1998). Similarly, southern and northern Italy have been radically different from one another for hundreds of years in terms of basic institutions and cultural predilections, and these differences have persisted into the modern era (Putnam, 1991).

According to Huntington (1996), a torn nation is one that has been ripped from its cultural roots at least once, in the sense that many of the basic cultural values guiding it have been destroyed. Both Russia and Mexico fit into this category and together constitute a separate part of the book.

There is also a part of the book that explores the same metaphor reflecting different values and meanings in different nations: the Portuguese bullfight and the Spanish bullfight. Finally, we move beyond the nation as the unit of analysis in the final part of the book, which uses the Chinese family altar to describe and analyze the behavior and values of the expatriate Chinese living in several nations.

Although I have arranged the eight parts of the book in this manner, the reader can pick and choose chapters as desired or required. Also, I have noted when a nation fits into more than one category or part of the book within the chapter devoted to it. The parts serve as the major categorizing mechanism, but the reader must be sensitive to the fact that a specific nation may well fit into two or more parts.

PART II

Authority Ranking Cultures

I n this part of the book, we focus on authority ranking cultures in which there is a high degree of collectivism but also a high degree of power distance. Unlike market pricing cultures, in which the relationship between the superior and subordinate is primarily one-way, these cultures emphasize that superiors and subordinates have obligations toward one another transcending job descriptions. This is particularly true of such nations as Japan and Thailand and, to a lesser extent, nations such as Poland and Brazil. Ordinal statistical scaling dominates relationships, that is, Person B is more important than Person A, and Person C is more important than Person B, but there is no common unit of measurement. Thus, it is impossible to say that C is twice as important as A.

CHAPTER 2

The Thai Kingdom

Thailand, with its population of approximately 58 million and a land mass about equal to that of France or the states of New York and California combined, is a Southeast Asian nation that is at the crossroads of Asia. Various peoples from China and India and the bordering nations of Laos, Myanmar, Malaysia, and Cambodia originally populated it. All of these peoples have influenced the development of Thai culture in one way or another.

The nation itself is divided into several distinct regions. Low-lying Bangkok, one of the largest cities in the world, represents one such region. Southern Thailand borders Malaysia, whereas northern Thailand borders Laos and Myanmar. Northern Thailand includes the city of Chiang Mai, Thailand's second largest city, and is home to the hill tribes, some of whom move periodically from mountainous area to mountainous area. The Thai government is trying to stop this practice, because these tribes frequently cut down trees that are hundreds of years old for firewood. It is also trying to put curbs on the logging companies in the northeast for the same reason. Excessive cutting of trees has led to erosion and, sometimes, mudslides that kill the villagers living below the mountains.

About 48% of the workforce is still involved in agriculture, and Thailand is one of only seven or eight food-exporting nations in the world. Although the food is abundant and the Thai cuisine world famous, agriculture contributes only about 11% to the GNP, industry 39%, and services 50%. There are wide disparities in income, both within and between regions (such as Bangkok and the northeast). Thailand's growth rate has been extremely high for the past several years, and it has become the Fifth Tiger of Asia. However, public and private expenditure on education is less than 4% of the GNP, the lowest in the region, and the educational system is centralized and cumbersome. Furthermore, the educational system emphasizes the arts and humanities; only about 15% of university students graduate each year in science or technical subjects ("South-East Asia's Learning Difficulties," 1997). To become a modern, high-tech nation, Thailand must increase investments in education stressing science, engineering, business, information systems, and related areas.

Americans and Thais share many similarities but also are quite different from one another. When Americans visit Thailand, they are frequently entranced by the friendliness of the people; its many Buddhist temples, or *wats*; and the contrast between rural and urban life, particularly urban life found in Bangkok, the nation's capital. Officially, Thailand is a constitutional monarchy that is modeled closely on the English system (see Chapter 14). Thailand was influenced strongly by England because until recent years, Thais tended to be educated in England rather than in the United States or continental Europe.

Perhaps the most distinctive symbol in Thailand is King Bhumibol, who has been in power since 1947. The Thai kingdom was in decline until his ascension, and he became king when his older brother, King Mahidol, was killed in 1946. Since 1947, the king has created what is arguably the most powerful and workable kingdom in a world that increasingly views kings as anachronistic. He is a talented and sophisticated man known for his love of the arts, and he is a noted jazz composer. Most importantly, he symbolizes critical features of Thai culture and, it can be reasonably argued, is the glue that is holding the nation together. In this chapter, we will not speculate on the issue of succession to his rule. Rather, the focus is on the Thai kingdom and why it is consonant with the underlying core values of all or most Thais. The characteristics of this cultural metaphor are a loose vertical hierarchy, freedom and equality, and the Thai smile.

Loose Vertical Hierarchy

Thailand is an authority ranking culture in which vertical collectivism is emphasized. However, probably because it is at the crossroads of many competing cultures, the Thais follow far fewer rules than do most authority ranking cultures. As Triandis and Gelfand (1998) have shown empirically, the Thais are at the extreme end of the cultural dimension of looseness-tightness of rules. This means that there are probably more contradictions and tensions in Thai culture than in most other cultures.

The visitor to Thailand is confronted immediately with some of these contradictions. There are numerous Buddhist *wats,* or temples, in Thailand, but most Thais do not frequent them except for scattered ceremonial days. Still, the Buddhist values are ingrained in the Thais, as discussed below, both in the culture in general and in the schools.

During the Vietnam War, the Americans used Thailand as a recreational area, which helped to promote the well-known and widespread prostitution found in Thailand. This has had some very unfortunate consequences, because it is estimated that more than 1 million Thais are infected with HIV. However, upper-middle-class Thai women can be Victorian in their attitudes. It is not unusual for a young man to visit a girlfriend's home for a date for many months and, when they are outside the home, for them to be escorted by an older sister or aunt.

The king has been particularly effective at using vertical hierarchical rules to manage the nation. Although the king does not involve himself in daily governmental affairs, he will become active during times of crisis and has requested that prime ministers and generals vacate their positions of power voluntarily. Nothing more needs to be said, and there is no additional discussion.

Similarly, until recent years, the king or members of his family handed out individual diplomas at all university graduations. Each proud graduate wanted to have his or her picture taken with the king, and so two cameras were used for each photo in the event that one of them failed to record this moment. The king also appears at prominent *wats* for Buddhist ceremonies.

As these activities suggest, the king is very involved in the lives of Thais, and they revere him for it. Thais can become infuriated when the king is insulted in any way. One unfortunate visitor to Thailand became angry with a waiter in a restaurant, threw his cash payment of the meal on the floor, and stomped on it. He failed to realize, however, that Thai money contains the king's picture, and an enraged Thai attacked him mercilessly because of the desecration. Another unfortunate visitor ripped up his Thai money as a sign of dissatisfaction at the airport, only to be arrested and jailed for 6 months.

The essence of an authority ranking culture is that there is a dynamic and two-way relationship between a superior and others. *Kreng cai,* or taking the other person's feelings into account, is a key concept in Thailand. All of the actions of the king reflect this orientation. It is quite similar to the Japanese concept of *amae,* or looking to others for security and assurance. Thais are very sensitive to feelings and clearly recognize nuances of behavior that the typical American does not even see dimly. Similarly, Thais are adept at sorting themselves out in a reception line by status, even though they may not have met previously.

As might be expected in an authority ranking culture, the military also is an important player. Many generals have business interests. There is a large amount of corruption in Thailand, at least in part because the social class structure involving the competing interests of businesspeople, the military, the politicians, the king, and others is so complex.

Thais tend to *wai* to one another rather than shake hands, although the handshake is becoming more common, particularly in international business. They hold both their hands together as if in prayer and bow their heads when greeting one another. Bowing lower than the other person signifies lower social status, and bowing at the same level signifies equality in social class ranking. Sometimes, a superior will not even *wai* but just nods his or her head, and at other times, he or she will complete an attenuated *wai* that is scarcely noticeable. Supposedly, this pattern of *wai*-ing and relating it to social class structure emerged when a person conquered in battle would show the victor that he was totally subservient; his bow to the victor exposed his head to any blow that the victor wanted to administer. If a blow was not administered, the victor was signaling that a two-way relationship of fealty had been born, but one in which there was a clear superior and a clear inferior. Thus, it is not surprising that, at public ceremonies such as university graduations, anyone who wants to leave before the king must do so in an unobtrusive manner, making sure that he is lower than the king. In relationships within families, this vertical ranking also prevails. Many Chinese Thai families, for example, live in a compound in which there are several homes, one for the father and mother and one each for married family members. There is a common area in the center where they meet at night and other times. Typically, there is at least one night per week when there is a large family gathering and dinner. The oldest son usually is the major decision maker in the family business if the father has retired, and the younger sons serve as vice presidents. If one of the sons is not very effective, he will retain the title but be assisted by either an in-law or an outsider who will be the real decision maker in that part of the business. Similarly, although the royal family is important, it is clearly the king who dominates.

Furthermore, each family emphasizes this hierarchical ranking. One young woman, who received her MBA in the United States, did not want to return to Thailand and marry a man she had known since childhood, but she did so when her mother said: "If you don't return and marry him, I never want to see you again." However, she and her mother did follow the dictates of loose authority ranking and agreed that she would not have children for 5 years; if the marriage did not live up to expectations, she would divorce her husband and remarry, which, in fact, she did. In another situation, a Chinese Thai family met to discuss an emergency problem: A younger female member of the family was very unhappy in the United States at a new university. In this instance, a family member was immediately dispatched to the United States to bring her home.

This form of vertical ranking is exemplified in the Flower Ceremony, which is held in universities once a year. For decades, Buddhist monks were the educators in Thailand, and the ceremony originated in their schools. An American Fulbright professor (George, 1987) was so startled by this ceremony that he wrote the following description:

> Today, students paid homage to their professors—a symbolic celebration of rather common significance to them. I found it an astonishing phenomenon.
>
> In a large auditorium, representatives from each department within the Faculty crawled up, in the manner of Asian supplication, and gave beautiful floral offerings to their "Aacaan" [professors]. Their choral chants asked for blessing and showed gratitude. Their speeches asked for forgiveness for any disrespect or non-fulfillment of expectation. They promised to work diligently.
>
> In a moment of paradox, I remembered I must not forget to pay the premium on my professional liability insurance this year. (p. 5)

Still, Thais recognize implicitly both the humor in this ceremony and the loose nature of authority ranking. Although many students make such declarations, they have difficulty honoring them.

Education in Thailand, as in other authority ranking cultures such as Japan, has stressed memorization and the taking of copious notes in lectures. Discussion is not emphasized. If a student asks a professor a question and the professor does not know the answer, he or she may well give an incorrect answer that the student will record dutifully, even though the student is aware that the answer is incorrect. In this way, face is saved for both people. A similar pattern of behavior involving managers and employees can be found in some traditional Thai firms, but it is less common in the multinationals and larger firms now operating in Thailand.

One positive feature of the looseness of rules involves the ethnic groups in Thailand, particularly the Chinese and the ethnic Thais. About 80% of the population is composed of ethnic Thais, almost all of whom are Buddhist, and they are powerful in politics and the military. Another 10% of the population is composed of the ethnic Chinese, who generally believe in Confucianism and, to some extent, Taoism. The ethnic Chinese tend to own prosperous, family-run firms, most of which are relatively small in size. There is a good amount of intermarriage between these two groups, and some Thais will argue that they are more liberal and accepting than their counterparts in other nations, even those in Southeast Asia.

One reason for the high rate of intermarriage is that these two groups are compatible in terms of religious and ethical perspectives (see Chapter 24, "The Chinese Family Altar" for a discussion of Buddhism, Confucianism, and

Taoism, and how they are compatible with one another). However, this argument should not be taken at face value, because discrimination and hostility do exist, but seemingly to a much smaller extent than in most nations.

In short, the king's actions are quite consistent with the core values of the authority ranking Thais. He does, however, respect the loose nature of the rules, as evidenced by his hands-off policy on daily governmental affairs and related issues.

Freedom and Equality

Thailand means "land of freedom," and the name is apt, because it is the only nation in Southeast Asia—and one of the very few in the world—that has never been conquered. In the 1700s, the Thai army was in grave danger during a war with Myanmar, but its leader—Taksin—reorganized the remaining 500 soldiers and led a brilliant counterattack. Although he became king and established the capital in Bangkok, he went insane and was replaced by a king from whom the current king traces his lineage directly.

Bordering several nations, the Thais have always been concerned about their military strength, and the Thai soldiers are well trained. Many of them receive training in America and Australia. In the past, the military has been involved in governmental affairs, even to the extent of overthrowing the elected governments. However, this issue has not surfaced in recent years, and the king's word is followed by all, including the military. It would be difficult for Thailand if the military were weak, but the issue is always the balance between civilian and military rule.

The king himself jogs daily with a general assigned to protect him. He has always been physically fit, and some of the rapport he enjoys with the military may stem from this fact. His only son, in fact, served in the military for many years, although the Thais are not fond of him, probably because of the carefree lifestyle he chose rather than the ideal lifestyle exemplified by his father.

Westerners are frequently perplexed by the contradictions of Thai behavior. On one hand, it reflects authority ranking. But it also reflects the pride stemming from this tradition of freedom from foreign domination. Even during World War II, Japan did not invade Thailand because of a diplomatic agreement motivated in large part by the Japanese fear of a drawn-out and costly confrontation with the fabled Thai military.

Also, Thais see themselves as equal to Westerners because of this tradition and expect to be treated accordingly. Thus, both freedom and equality are key components of Thai culture. In fact, in the relationship between superiors and subordinates, there are obligations on both sides, and the Thai subordinates expect to be treated with respect. The Thais, as Buddhists, believe in karma, or the concept that one's behavior leads to consequences. Thus, Thais believe that behavior in this life determines the life form an individual will assume in the next life, and that there will be many life cycles. Behaving inappropriately toward others, including subordinates or superiors, will help to determine the life form.

Thai fighting, particularly Thai boxing, is a unique manifestation and expression of freedom, equality, military prowess, and even the relationships between males and females. The roots of Thai boxing can be found in experiences of the Chinese immigrants to present-day Thailand 800 years ago, who were forced to fight marauding tribes with a formless type of combat using head, teeth, fists, knees, ankles, and elbows (*muay Thai*). This hand-to-hand combat is still part of the military training.

Modern Thai boxing, as practiced in the two major stadiums in Bangkok, is something to behold. Light gloves are worn, and kicking is permitted. There are typically 10 fights per night, each of which lasts five rounds of 3 minutes each. Each stadium is small, holding only about 1,000 customers, almost all of whom are males, but many other Thais stand outside of the stadium and follow the action intently by radio and, in some cases, television. Before each fight, each fighter performs a small ritual indicating the school or philosophy of fighting in which he has been trained. An Asian band plays throughout each round, but slowly in the first two rounds. In the third round, however, the band increases its sound and speed, thus exciting the crowd, and many fans rise excitedly and begin to place bets through the use of hand movements. In some ways, this behavior is very similar to that surrounding the Balinese cockfight (see Geertz, 1973).

About 50% or more of the fights do not go the full five rounds, because the fighting is bone chilling; knockouts are common. Although some people are repelled by Thai boxing, the Thais have excelled at it and have produced many Olympic champions. As an expression of military prowess, it is outstanding. Thai boxing also symbolizes how far Thais are willing to go to preserve freedom and equality. Even the separation of sexes, which can be Victorian at times, occurs during Thai boxing matches.

The Thai Smile

Anyone who has visited Thailand even for a few days can be dazzled by the friendliness of the Thais, and the Thai smile is legendary. Some of this demeanor comes directly from the Thai practice of Buddhism. There are two general streams of Buddhism, one of which—Theravaden Buddhism—emphasizes an internal focus and meditation more than the other (see Smith, 1991). Thailand is representative of Theravaden Buddhism.

We have described Buddhism elsewhere (see Chapter 4). Thai Buddhism, given its inward focus, stresses the key concept of the Middle Way, that is, keeping emotions and even body movements under control. The Thais believe that anger and even emotionality leads to more anger and more emotionality, which restricts freedom because individuals engage in activities that they would otherwise avoid. They tend to be sophisticated diplomats and negotiators because of these beliefs. Similarly, the king's public appearances are reserved. He does not use emotional approaches and arguments that many of his counterparts throughout the world favor.

Furthermore, as might be expected in a face-saving culture, Thais hate to say no directly. They use statements such as, "We'll need to think it over" and "That may be a problem" as proxies for no. Many Westerners spend months negotiating a particular issue only to realize belatedly that a slight movement of the shoulder is the equivalent of saying no.

No matter what happens, however, Thais will keep smiling. Thus, a smile should not be interpreted as deep friendship but as a mechanism for making life pleasant and avoiding difficulties that might lead to the dreaded expression of negative emotions. Thais, in fact, genuinely dislike complainers, including demanding Western tourists, and will avoid them. In contrast, Israelis complain about many things at parties but still have a good time (see Chapter 17).

However, the Thai smile can be genuine and, as is common in collectivistic cultures, must be evaluated in terms of the context or situation. For example, Thais love to have *sanuk,* or fun, and they punctuate the workday with periods of group activity stressing it. If work is boring and monotonous, the Thais are likely to quit, especially if the periods of *sanuk* are denied. Japanese firms, for example, sometimes pay the Thai workers less than the American firms do and work them longer hours, but they ensure that the workday is broken by such periods of respite.

As this discussion suggests, the Thais have a different conception of time than do Westerners. Being Buddhist, they do not make sharp distinctions between the past, present, and future. In Buddhism, time is only one circle, not three. In my first MBA class at Thammasat University, I arrived at 5:50 p.m., or one-half hour before the class period, to make sure everything was prepared, but the first Thai student did not appear until 7 p.m. Naturally, I complained about this behavior, but one smiling Thai student confided that "We love to start class on Thai time and quit on American time." I had difficulty responding to this comment.

There is another related Thai belief that is captured in the virtually untranslatable phrase, *mai pen rai*. Essentially, it means that humans have little, if any, control over nature, technology, and many other forces. Carol Hollinger (1967/1977), an American high school teacher in Thailand, fell in love with Thai culture, particularly this aspect of it, and titled her book *Mai Pen Rai Means Never Mind*. This phrase does not signify the acceptance of a fatalistic view of life that is sometimes found among conservative Muslims or Christians. Rather, it is an acceptance of things as they are and the willingness to make life as pleasant as possible regardless of life's circumstances. When Thais use this phrase, they tend to flash their distinctive smiles, and even that small action immediately lessens the magnitude of the problem, whatever it is.

The royal family, and particularly the king, follows similar patterns of behavior. Although serious, the king does enjoy parties and will perform his own jazz compositions at them. Clearly, he is happy interacting with all types of people and will smile through boring ceremonies that other international leaders would not even think of attending. As indicated previously, throughout his life, he has maintained excellent physical conditioning. Given the many onerous duties that he must perform while smiling, such conditioning has probably been critical.

John Fieg (1976; Fieg & Mortlock, 1989) has captured the essence of Thai culture and the three characteristics highlighted in this chapter (loose authority ranking, freedom and equality, and the Thai smile) in his classic study comparing Thais and Americans. In both cultures, there is a love of freedom, a dislike of pomposity, and a pragmatic outlook. But the differences are significant, and Fieg uses the image of a rubber band to highlight Thai values, attitudes, and behaviors. When the rubber band is held loosely between the fingers, its looseness is comparable to the manner in which most Thais interact with one another during the day. However, as suggested previously, Thais also have a complex status system in which relationships are vertical and hierarchical. Once this status system is activated in any way—for example, a superior giving a direct order to a subordinate—Thais tend to respond immediately to its dictates, and so the rubber band tightens. As soon as the demands of the status system have been met, Thais can return to looser and more liberated behavioral patterns.

In contrast, Fieg uses a string held tightly between the fingers for most of the day to describe Americans. Periodically, the string is loosened, but Americans do not enjoy the same degree of behavioral freedom that Thais experience—that is, the string can never be as loose as the rubber band. In the United States, there are many internal and external controls that motivate individuals in this achievement-oriented society. Examples of external control include the numerous legal, accounting, and governmental forms that

Americans fill out routinely. Imbuing children with the desire to work hard and to respond enthusiastically to the demands of the Protestant work ethic reflects internal control. Such internal and external control is present in Thailand to a much lower degree than in the United States.

In sum, Thailand is a fascinating nation, and its core values overlap with those of the United States. But it is clearly different from the United States, and the Thai kingdom is an apt metaphor for capturing the essential features of this land of freedom.

CHAPTER 3

The Japanese Garden

We can become more international, but still honor the rules of our society.

—A banner in Japanese at Narita Airport, Tokyo

Each group is entitled to loyalty from its members, and these various loyalties essentially define a Japanese life. The groups you belong to make up who you are. Your group is your identity.

—Reid (1999), p. 74

Japan is an island nation of 125 million citizens. There are 331 people per square kilometer, making Japan the 17th most densely populated nation in the world. Compared to the United States, it is relatively small in size: 377,727 square kilometers versus 9,372,610. Japan ranks 15th among nations in terms of the oldest populations, with 14% over age 65. Its economy is the second largest, right behind the United States.

Reading articles about Japan in Western newspapers and magazines can easily confuse an American. There are many articles suggesting that the Japanese are becoming totally American in outlook and culture. For example:

In July, 1998, Toshiki Kawasaki had a choice: become an American-style capitalist or else . . .

So on a muggy July day, Mr. Kawasaki says, Malox ousted the "wimps" who ran the trucking subsidiary and eventually sacked 100 of its 440 employees. (Shirouzu, 2000, p. 1)

Many Japanese recoil from such extreme measures and tend to see them as violating cultural norms. Although they think favorably about American economic success, they question the cultural values leading not only to success but also to social pathologies. Whereas the United States had 7.53 murders per 100,000 in 1996, Japan had only 0.97; robbery, 255.8 versus 1.75; rape, 37 versus 1; arson, 46 versus 1; aggravated assault, 440 versus 5.4; and burglary, 1,099 versus 187 (see Reid, 1999, p. 23).

Furthermore, there are countless heartrending stories painting a contrasting portrait to Malox's actions against wimps. Japanese companies declaring bankruptcy frequently attempt to place their employees with other companies, and the shame associated with failure has led to many suicides among managers. There were 478 such cases documented in 1997, and probably many more that were not reported. It is hard to imagine comparable action by managers in the United States, who supposedly are motivated more by guilt than by shame. Nobuo Shibata, the 48-year-old president of a small metal sheet company, and his brother took their own lives but left this plaintive note: "We apologize to all our employees for the slump in our business" (Sugawara, 1998).

In the early 1980s, almost all of the American writings on Japan praised this country wholeheartedly and tended to highlight only its positive features (e.g., William Ouchi, 1981, in his best-selling book, *Theory Z*). Ezra Vogel (1979) even titled his best-selling book *Japan as Number One*. By 1990, many American writers and citizens had radically altered their view of Japan from one of uncritical admiration to one of "fear and loathing of Japan," as the title of a *Fortune* article so aptly expressed the viewpoint (Smith, 1990). Some reasons for this perspective were the economic success of Japan at the time and the difficulty American firms had in penetrating Japan's markets. Since that time, Japan has experienced 10 years of recession, and now Americans seem contemptuous: These wimps must accept American-style capitalism or suffer disgrace and economic failure.

However, the reality of the Japanese situation and culture seems more complex than Americans can imagine. Even the concept that Japan is a collectivistic nation needs to be qualified. In Hofstede's (1991) classic study of 53 nations, Japan and Argentina tied at rank 22 on individualism, which indicates that there are many more collectivistic nations than Japan. Still, Japan is a classic authority ranking nation, and to expect it to become a market mechanistic or vertically individualistic nation overnight is unrealistic. The fact that it has accepted recession for 10 years without attempting major changes reflects this viewpoint.

To gain some perspective on Japanese culture, it is useful to compare the basic metaphors or mind-sets through which the Americans and the Japanese see the world. Whereas American football reflects the American perspective, most, if not all, Japanese would immediately identify the Japanese landscape or wet garden as an appropriate, if not the most appropriate, metaphor for understanding the Japanese culture.

There are two general types of Japanese gardens: The wet or landscape garden, and the dry Zen Buddhist or religious garden. The major difference between them is that the dry garden does not have water or a pond but, rather, raked pebbles to simulate water. Hence, the wet and dry Japanese gardens are functionally equivalent to one another, and both are designed to create a sense of integration between the observer and nature and an atmosphere in which meditation can take place. In this chapter, the focus is on a wet Japanese garden.

Like the water flowing through a Japanese garden, Japanese society is fluid, changing yet retaining its essential character. Alone, each drop has little force, yet when combined with many others, has enough force to form a waterfall, which cascades into a small pond filled with carp. The pond appears calm, but beneath the surface, a pump constantly recirculates water back to the top of the waterfall. A rock tossed into the pond causes a ripple, then sinks to the bottom, always to remain separate. Undoubtedly, the scene is designed to replicate nature and to capture its true essence, and the sound of the gently flowing water amid this small re-creation of beauty evokes feelings of harmony, oneness with nature, and perhaps even timelessness.

The garden itself serves as a reminder of the centrality of nature to the development of Japanese society, religion, art, and aesthetics: not just nature, but the way in which the Japanese perceive nature. Just as the garden is part of nature, the Japanese tend to view themselves as integral with it. In contrast to the Western view of nature as something to be confronted and subdued, the Japanese generally see it as something to be accepted.

The Japanese, an agricultural people, developed a passionate love of nature and a keen awareness of the beauties inherent in it. No part of Japan is more than 70 miles from the sea, and the mountains, which cover four fifths of the land, are in view from any vantage point. Japan's temperate climate and abundant rainfall contribute to a view of nature as a friendly blessing and source of growth and fertility. Thus, it is not surprising that the earliest Japanese literature manifests a deep appreciation of the beauties of the sea, mountains, and wooded glens.

The three basic elements of the Japanese garden are stone, plants, and water. Usually, these are combined to form larger elements common to Japanese landscape gardens, such as flowing water; a pond; and groupings of stone, trees, and shrubs, each in as natural-looking a state as possible to evoke the feeling of artlessness.

Japan, like the water in a Japanese garden, is seldom still. It is a complex, dynamic society that has undergone enormous change in the past 125 years, transforming itself from a feudal state into a modern, industrialized nation that has fought two world wars, the latter of which resulted in utter defeat. Since then, the country has risen to become a major economic power. In the process, the Japanese have absorbed Western technology, science, education, and politics while retaining their unique cultural identity.

Still, underlying this profound change is the perspective that is mirrored in the Japanese garden. To see how the elements of such a garden are manifested in Japanese society, we focus on four topics: *wa,* or harmony, and *shikata,* or the proper way of doing things, with emphasis on the form and order of the process; combining droplets or the energies of individuals into group activities; *seishen,* or spirit training; and aesthetics.

Wa and Shikata

To understand Japan, it is important to know its history, which can be viewed as a continual search for *wa,* or harmony, or, in the Japanese garden, the harmonious relations among elements so as to create a feeling of the effective interaction between human beings and nature. The Japanese are a remarkably homogeneous people who have lived in relative isolation for centuries. Prior to the end of the previous ice age, about 11,000 years ago, Japan was connected by land to the rest of Asia. Because those groups who wandered into it could go no further, they remained and mixed with those who came later. Historical records show that a considerable number of people flowed into Japan from the Korean peninsula until the eighth century A.D. By that time, the mixing was nearly complete, and for the past 1,000 years, immigration has been infinitesimal.

Virtually devoid of natural resources such as iron and oil, the Japanese borrowed the technique of rice farming from the Chinese sometime around the year 1,000 B.C. Each of its villages became self-sufficient, but the complexity and interrelatedness of the tasks associated with rice farming led the Japanese to emphasize the importance of group activities and group harmony without which there would be starvation.

In the seventh century B.C., this emphasis on harmony was expressed in the country's first Constitution, written by Prince Shotoku. The first of the 17 Articles made harmony the foundation for all of the others. This is in marked contrast to the Western conception of the importance of life, liberty, and the pursuit of individual happiness.

Furthermore, the Japanese have always had a distinct awareness of the difference between things foreign and native, and early on recognized the value of borrowing from others while maintaining their Japaneseness. After

A.D. 552, when Buddhism was formally introduced to the Yamato court from China, the Japanese increasingly became conscious of the superior continental civilization of the Chinese. From the 7th to the 9th century A.D., they made a conscious effort to vigorously borrow Chinese technology and institutions; they studied the philosophy, science, literature, arts, and music of China in depth, and these, in turn, deeply influenced Japanese thought, culture, and habits. The Japanese even adopted the Chinese writing system, which had a unique character for each of the thousands of Chinese words. However, even though the Japanese wrote in Chinese, they spoke only Japanese, which is as different from Chinese as it is from English. Japan's island location was far enough from China to escape invasion but close enough to benefit from interacting with this nation, which, at that time, was the most technologically advanced and powerful one in the world. From the 9th to the 12th centuries, the Japanese blended these new elements with their own culture to form a new synthesis.

In the 12th century, Yoritomo Minamoto first used the title of shogun or Generalissimo of Japan and established his headquarters in Kamakura, which is 1 hour's drive from Tokyo, or Edo, as it was called at that time. Although the Imperial Family living in Kyoto was still allowed to perform ceremonial activities, the real power rested with the shogun, and clan lords reported directly to him. This shogun era lasted until 1868, at which time the Imperial Family's power was restored (Meiji Restoration).

During the shogun era, the emphasis on harmony continued, but in a distinctly different manner. Surprisingly, the shogun system was similar to European feudalism. About 10% of the population consisted of samurai, or warriors, who pledged absolute loyalty to the shogun. Thus, this system is quite different from that of the Chinese Confucian system, in which loyalty to the family is the overriding value, and the subjugation of the samurai to the shogun paved the way for the transference of loyalty to the ultimate family, the nation. Also, unlike Europe, the Japanese did not have a cult of chivalry. In addition, the samurai were also men of learning, and they prided themselves on their fine calligraphy and poetic skills.

However, most of the population had only limited rights, and a samurai could kill any commoner on the spot if he failed to abide by the many rules and practices pervasive throughout the society. Under such conditions, it is little wonder that the Japanese sought to achieve harmony and to protect "face," which is an unwritten set of rules by which people in society cooperate to avoid unduly damaging each other's prestige and self-respect. Even today, the Japanese tend to apologize in advance before making a critical comment on another person's project so as to avoid the loss of face for either party; many of them begin a formal speech in a comparable manner. In a similar vein, Japanese baseball games are scheduled to end after 3 hours and

20 minutes, and ties are common, which is fine with the face-saving Japanese interested in preserving *wa*.

Japan's sense of isolation was heightened during the reign of Shogun Ieyasu in the 16th century, when he banished Jesuit missionaries, cut off the ears of Christians, and mandated that only coastal vessels not fit for ocean travel be built. With the exception of a small Dutch trading area in the Kyushu port of Nagasaki, relations with the outside world were cut off.

In 1853, Japan was forced to end its self-imposed seclusion when Commodore Perry and a quarter of the U.S. Navy arrived off the shores of Edo. It had no choice but to sign unequal trade treaties with the United States and principal European powers. These developments led to a weakening of the shogun system and its replacement by the Imperial Family in 1868.

Furthermore, it is extremely difficult, if not impossible, for a foreigner, or *gaijin*, to be accepted fully in Japan, because to do so would upset harmonious relations between and among groups that have taken years to develop. A foreigner is like the rock tossed into the garden's pond that disturbs the harmony momentarily but disappears quickly from sight. However, many visiting Americans misperceive the extreme care and attention given to them as genuine friendship, or at least genuine acceptance. Why this occurs leads us naturally to *shikata,* which is necessary if *wa* is to be maintained.

Because of the subsistence-level economy that developed in the rice-growing villages and the emphasis on nature, the Japanese came to believe that there is an inner order (the individual heart) and a natural order (the cosmos), and that these two are linked together by form (see De Mente, 1990). *Shikata* is the way of doing things, with special emphasis on the form and order of the process; in compound forms, the term is *kata*. Thus, there is a *kata* or *katas* for eating properly, for using the telephone, for treating foreigners, and so on. To the Japanese, the process or form for completing an activity is just as important as completing the activity successfully, whereas Americans historically have been concerned with the final result rather than the process for achieving it. The Japanese emphasis on total quality management (TQM) and *kaizen* (continual improvement) is consistent with *shikata,* because they tend to feel that doing something in the proper manner ultimately will lead to doing it in the most successful manner.

Katas were developed within this hierarchical society because it was assumed that everyone has specifically categorized and defined life roles (*bun*) in which obligations are spelled out in detail. Edwin Reischauer (1988, p. 146) has termed the Japanese the most punctilious, if not the most polite, people on earth because of such explication. At 2 a.m., one may see several older Japanese standing at a street corner patiently waiting for the light to change before crossing the street, even if no cars are in sight for miles. A person's outward conduct, as manifested in the obeyance of rules, is a reflection of one's inner character. There are even *katas* associated with Japanese base-ball, and visiting American baseball players frequently find it difficult to adjust because they must hold the bat in a particular way and observe other rules that they consider irrelevant.

The importance of *katas* cannot be overemphasized, and there are specific *katas* for activities that Americans tend to handle in many different ways, such as greeting visitors and exchanging business cards. When a *kata* for a new activity does not exist, the Japanese may have difficulty completing it. Thus, some Japanese officers who wanted to discontinue fighting in World War II bemoaned the fact that no *kata* for surrender had been developed simply because it was so unthinkable. As they stated, "We don't know how to surrender" (De Mente, 1990, p. 68).

When a Japanese violates a *kata,* the reaction may be harsh. In one instance, five 14-year-old girls bullied a classmate into committing suicide because she failed to show enough sincerity when attending a funeral ceremony for the mother of one of the five girls.

Seishin Training

To live comfortably in such a rule-ordered society, an individual needs a great deal of self-control, and he or she is socialized from birth to acquire it. In the Japanese garden, the carp symbolize masculinity, valor, endurance, and te-nacity. Analogously, the concept of *seishin,* or spirit, which is an integral part of the Japanese philosophy of life, stresses the importance of self-discipline and devotion to duty. Through discipline and adversity, a person achieves self-development and, most importantly, self-mastery. *Seishin* training has been most commonly applied to the study of martial arts, flower arrangements, and the tea ceremony. In the case of martial arts, physical training is seen as a means to a spiritual end of attaining inner balance and harmony. Mastery of skill requires self-control and self-discipline; this leads to the development of inner strength.

Perhaps the best way to understand Japanese behavior is to take part in such martial arts as karate and swordplay. Karate (meaning "empty hands") was introduced to Japan by Buddhist monks both as a form of self-defense against marauders and as spiritual training. Once again, forms, or *katas,* constitute much of the training that a karate student receives, and he or she will practice these forms by him- or herself for hours before engaging in any kind of combat. Eventually, the karate student is taught to "think through" an obstacle, and one of the most difficult challenges facing a parent is to see a 9-year-old son or daughter trying to think through, or break, a 1-inch-thick plywood board with an open-handed blow. Sometimes, the karate instructor will have the unsuccessful student repeat the exercise three or four times so as to exhibit self-control and learn to handle adversity, and some young students have broken their hands while engaged in this activity.

Although, theoretically, the ultimate result of *seishin* is an improved state of personal spiritual growth and freedom, many Japanese use it to attain practical ends, such as better performance in school or work. Large Japanese firms appeal to this element of Japanese thought in their training programs. These training programs have been called "hell camp" because the trainees are allowed to sleep only a few hours per day and must undertake physically demanding activities designed to instill a sense of self-discipline and devotion to the company. In many modern transformations of the philosophy, the central emphasis is on the development of a positive inner attitude by means of which external constraints can be overcome and difficulties resolved. Japanese tend to believe that any obstacle can be overcome provided one tries hard enough. Conversely, Americans emphasize ability as much as, or more than, effort.

Seishin helps an individual not only to stand on his or her own and endure personal hardship, but also to live in a group-oriented society. Serving the group's interests often involves self-sacrifice. To the Japanese, social conformity is not a sign of weakness but of strong inner self-control that has helped the individual to overcome his or her more antisocial instincts. Endurance for this conformity is made easier through character training and self-discipline.

Manifestations of *seishin* abound in Japanese society. One often sees Japanese elementary school children dressed in shorts, the school uniform, in the middle of winter. Junior high school students are not allowed to wear jackets, sweaters, or any other garment over their school uniforms in the winter, although Japanese classrooms are rarely heated. During the first few weeks of January, the junior high school students are required to begin the day with a 30-minute jog around the school grounds. Most junior high schools also hold weekly, schoolwide meetings outside. If it is sweltering hot, the Japanese student does not ask to be excused; he or she stands at attention as long as he or she can before fainting. This practice helps develop a toughness of character and an ability to endure hardship at a young age.

Seishin training tends to be associated with Zen Buddhism, which is a unique form of Buddhism that has enjoyed a resurgence of interest in Japan since the 1970s. Whereas Hinduism incorporates the belief in many personal gods, Buddhism rejects them. However, it does accept the Hindu emphasis on meditation as a major vehicle for achieving nirvana, or salvation. Buddha emphasized four Noble Truths: Suffering is inevitable; it occurs because of selfish or self-centered desires; such desires can be overcome; and the method of overcoming them is to follow the Eight-Fold Path, which is the Buddhist version of the Ten Commandments.

Zen Buddhism continues the emphasis on meditation, and most of the Zen training occurs in a large meditation hall. The trainees and monks frequently meditate in the lotus position for hours on a cold stone floor in a room in which the temperature is 40 degrees, and one monk will prod and hit the trainees or students with a bamboo stick if their attention begins to wander. About twice a day, each student will meet with a monk, who will ask him to respond to *koans*, or riddles, which are designed to help him attain an open mind or to see things as fresh and new. Zen Buddhism proposed that one can free oneself from his or her self-centered world by perceiving the timelessness and oneness of the universe. Likewise, in a Japanese garden, the whole of nature can be seen despite the individual parts. Also, each part of the garden can capture the essence of nature in its own way. The garden depicts a freed world that has been reduced physically and enlarged spiritually to suggest the size and grandeur of nature. Japanese who recognize that they are part of nature and, hence, mortal essentially stop time by allowing it to have its own way. In the same manner, although the seasons may change the appearance of the Japanese garden, the stones, trees, and water in it are always visible and unchanged.

Combining Droplets or Energies

Achieving harmony through *kata* and *seishin* training leads naturally to the topic of combining energies of individuals in groups or, analogously, combining droplets of water in the garden to form a waterfall. This emphasis on the group begins at birth, for the mother tends to shower an excessive amount of love and attention on the child, especially a boy. In Japan, infants and children are constantly in contact with their mothers, are treated permissively, are seldom left alone, and often sleep with their parents until the age of 7 or 8. For the first 2 years of life, the child is swaddled and carried by the mother in a special device attached to her body. All of these practices result in a high degree of dependence on the mother and an attitude defined as *amae* in Japanese, which means to look to others for affection. As the child grows up, this dependence on the mother as the source of gratification is transferred to the group, particularly the person's mentor, or *senpai*.

During the first few years at a business firm, an employee may be assigned to an older individual or *senpai*, who will show him or her how to perform the job and help him or her adjust to the new environment. More commonly, *senpai-kohai* relationships develop informally. The *senpai* offers advice and encouragement, and may play an important role in the socialization of the youngest employees.

The Japanese emphasis on the group is quite apparent and permeates practically every aspect of Japanese life. It can be seen in the educational system, the structure of business organization and work, and the political system, to name just a few.

At school, the children are identified by their class. For example, in junior high school, a student might say, "I belong to *ichinen ni kumi*," or Year 1 Class 2. (Each grade is composed of approximately six classes.) For the next 3 years, that student will spend every day with the other 40 to 50 students in his or her class and will identify himself or herself with that group. A well-known Japanese proverb, "The protruding nail will be hammered," aptly explains the behavior of individual students. Adhering to this proverb does not pose a problem for most students, who have learned that security, acceptance, and love flow from the group. In fact, most students display a sense of belonging that would be envied by many of their counterparts in the West, who often feel alienated and alone.

On the other hand, life can be intolerable for the rare student who does not fit comfortably in a group. Fellow students relentlessly bully, pick on, tease, and persecute this individual. This phenomenon, *ijime,* usually translated as bullying, leads to several deaths every year. If the nonconforming student has any friends, they quickly desert him or her for fear of being excluded from the group, which is the worst fate that can befall a Japanese child or adult.

Students achieve group identification not only with their class but also with their school, particularly at the college level. The university one attends frequently determines one's future career prospects, because the top businesses hire primarily, if not exclusively, from the top universities. Ties made in college days are important in Japanese life, and throughout their lives, Japanese will identify themselves with the university they attended.

In Japan, a job means identification with a larger entity, through which one gains pride and the feeling of being part of something significant. An individual's prestige is tied directly to the prestige of his or her employer. The company is not typically viewed as an entity trying to take advantage of its employees in order to make profits, but as a provider of individual security and welfare. When a Japanese person is asked what he or she does, he or she usually responds with the name of the company for whom he or she works, and not the job he or she performs. By contrast, Americans will normally respond to the question of what they do by mentioning the occupation or job first, and they may not even divulge the name of the company. The Japanese worker or manager usually perceives his or her company and other institutions with a strong sense of "we" versus "they." Approximately 30% of the Japanese managers and workers, primarily those working for the larger firms, actually are guaranteed lifetime employment until the age of 55, after which they can work for the larger firm's subcontractors until age 70, but at a reduced salary. This guarantee strengthens the feeling of identification with the firm. And even when a firm is not financially able to make such a guarantee, which is occurring much more frequently in recent years, its owners tend to feel far more obliged to their employees than do their American counterparts. Even in the United States, Japanese firms will frequently retrain their American employees during an economic downturn rather than lay them off or fire them, as is the norm among American-owned firms.

Also, the distinctive structure of the business firm that is found in Japan supposedly fosters group identification. Prior to World War II, much of Japanese industry was organized into six huge *zaibatsus,* or family-owned companies, each of which consisted of approximately 300 companies and their suppliers. Each *zaibatsu* combined the activities of many subcontractors with whom it had long-term contracts, a manufacturing organization, a major financial institution, and an export-import organization. Such a form of organization is outlawed in the United States and other developed countries, and it was actually forbidden by law in Japan after World War II. However, a nonfamily variant of the *zaibatsu,* the *keiretsu,* has emerged and become prominent.

American and European managers frequently complain bitterly about the operations of the *keiretsus,* because they have a great amount of power over many activities in the marketplace, and they can persuade Japanese distributors not to carry the products of the foreign companies. Ironically, however, the most dynamic and prosperous companies in the Japanese economy tend to be those that are not members of *keiretsu* (Tasker, 1987). Similarly, although foreign executives have argued that the Japanese Ministry of Trade and Industry (MITI) has unfairly supported rising industries such as personal computing and high-definition television through its various policies and regulations, some of Japan's most profitable corporations, such as Honda and Sony, have become successful without its help; MITI actually advised Mr. Honda, the car company's founder, to go into another line of business.

Since 1990, there has been an increase in entrepreneurial activities among younger managers, some of whom have started their own firms rather than accept employment in established firms. Such entrepreneurial efforts will increase as the world economy becomes more global. But identification with the company will probably remain much stronger in Japan than in the United States.

Furthermore, the organizational structure and work allocation in Japanese firms also emphasize the group. Work is often assigned to various office groups and is viewed essentially as a group effort. Frequently, there are no formal job descriptions existing separate from work groups. A company will sometimes reward the office group, and not the individual, for work well done. Even the physical arrangement of the office emphasizes the group mentality: The manager will sit in front of the workers in a classroom-style setting, and they will work in subgroups with their own supervisors. If the workgroup is small, everyone will sit around a table, with the most senior members closer to the manager. As a general rule, the Japanese do not allow a manager to have his or her own office and, even if the work requires that he or she be given one, tend not to prefer this arrangement.

Japanese groups abound in society—women's associations, youth groups, PTA, and hobby groups, to name just a few. Political parties and ministerial bureaucracies often divide into opposing factions. The new charismatic religions, such as *Soka Gakkai,* are composed of small groups that meet together. In sightseeing, the Japanese tendency to perform activities in a group is particularly evident, because they tend to wear the same types of clothes and behave as if they were one.

Decision making in Japan also reflects this emphasis upon the group. For example, in a Japanese company, a business proposal is usually initiated at the middle or lower levels of management. The written proposal, called *ringi-sho,* is distributed laterally and then upward. Each person who reviews it must impress his or her personal seal of approval. Making decisions requires a great deal of time, largely because a good amount of informal discussion has preceded the drawing up of the *ringi-sho.* In spite of its time-consuming nature, the consensus approach to decision making does have important merits. Once the decision is made, it can be implemented quickly and with force because it has the backing of everyone in the department. By contrast, American managers frequently make decisions quickly, but a great amount of time and effort is required for implementation, often because only a few key people have actually been involved in the decision-making process itself.

A particularly telling contrast occurred when Travelers Group and Nikko Securities were contemplating a joint venture. After Sandy Weill of Travelers and his Japanese counterparts agreed on the basic issues, Mr. Weill placed a conference call to New York to obtain board approval, which he secured in 30 minutes. Conversely, the Nikko board required 12 days of briefings and discussion to approve a decision that had been resolved in their favor.

Just like the water droplet, the individual is significant only insofar as he or she represents the group. If individuals disagree with one another, the overall interest of the group comes before their needs. Cooperativeness, reasonableness, and understanding of others are the virtues most admired in an individual. Harmony is sought, and conflict is avoided if at all possible.

The extent to which the individual is responsible to the group, and the group responsible for the actions of the individual, is illustrated by the following incident. An American teacher was accompanying an eighth-grade Japanese class on its annual field trip to Kyoto when one of the Japanese teachers kindly informed her that the students would be required to sit in the school auditorium for 1 hour upon returning from Kyoto. When the American teacher inquired as to why, he responded that one of the students had been 10 minutes late to the school meeting earlier this morning; therefore, all would be punished.

Like the water that flows in the garden, the Japanese people prefer to flow with the tide. In contrast to the West, observers have noted the relative absence among the Japanese of abstract principles, moral absolutes, and definitive judgments based on universal standards. The Japanese think more in terms of concrete situations and complex human relations; therefore, whereas to Westerners, the Japanese may seem to lack principle, to the Japanese, Westerners may seem harsh and self-righteous in their judgments, and lacking in human feeling.

As Ellen Frost (1987) points out, many Japanese refer to this difference by saying that the Japanese are "wet" people, whereas Westerners are "dry." She elaborates as follows:

> By "dry" they mean that Westerners attach more importance to abstract principles, logic and rationality than to human feeling. Thus, Westerners are said to view all social relations, including marriage, as formal contracts which, once they no longer satisfy individual needs, can be terminated. Their ideas of morality are generalized and absolute, with little regard for the particular human context. . . . By contrast, the "wet" Japanese are said to attach great importance to the emotional realities of the particular human circumstances. They avoid absolutes, rely on subtlety and intuition, and consider sensitivity to human feelings all-important. They notice small signs of insult or disfavor and take them deeply to heart. They harbor feelings of loyalty for years, perhaps for life, and for that reason are believed to be more trustworthy. (p. 85)

The term *naniwa bushi* exemplifies this wet quality. In modern use, the term is applied to people who are open-minded, generous, and capable of appreciating another person's position, even when that position is neither logical nor rational. A negotiator who adopts a rigid position, recites a familiar catalog of grievances, and appears to have no understanding of Japanese concerns is said to lack *naniwa bushi*. Such a person is judged to be neither effective nor trustworthy. Some Japanese feel that many Westerners adopt such a negotiating style, which seems to be one of the reasons why difficulties occur between them. Thus, it seems logical that Japan does not have clearly identifiable political parties, as in the case of the United States, but a loose arrangement of powerful interest groups that negotiate their differences using *naniwa bushi*.

Some see the Japanese identification with nature as the explanation for the origin of the relativism of Japanese attitudes. Others point to the influence of Chinese thought, with its situational approach to applying principles. Whereas in the West, the division was between good and evil, in China the division was between yin and yang, two complementary life forces. Thus, the Japanese tend to see situations more in terms of tones of gray, whereas Americans see them as black and white. However, others suggest that this relativism stems from child-rearing techniques discussed previously. Probably all of these explanations are interrelated and have some validity.

The emphasis upon situational ethics is illustrated in the Japanese legal system. If the convicted shows that he or she is genuinely repentant for what he or she has done, then it is highly likely that the person will receive a more lenient sentence. Furthermore, the laws passed by the Japanese Diet or Central Government are structured loosely so that the courts can interpret them in ways that different situations demand. By contrast, the American Congress attempts to write laws in such a way that all possible issues are spelled out carefully, and, as a result, judges must operate within relatively strict limits. Furthermore, the Japanese orientation toward harmony and group loyalty means that conflict resolution is valued, not the individualistic assertion of legal rights. For example, in the hamlet of Kurusu, conflict over the building of a factory received national attention from the media, and 2 years later, shame still pervaded the community. Consequently, the legal system and Japanese values reinforce the emphasis on group consensus or solutions prior to coming to court. The opposite situation exists in the United States, because individuals involved in legal disputes are aware that judges must interpret laws that are already delineated finely.

This practice does not mean that the Japanese do not have a sense of right and wrong. It is simply that they place greater emphasis on the particular situation and human intentions than Westerners do. Lacking a Judeo-Christian heritage, Japanese do not possess a feeling that certain areas of life are obviously sinful. The major issue is whether an action harms others and has a disruptive effect on the group and community. Many experts assert that the Japanese are motivated primarily by a sense of shame to correct a problem when such disruption occurs, whereas individualistic Westerners are motivated mostly by a sense of guilt at their failure to fulfill responsibilities. Such an orientation is particularly evident in their attitudes toward sex and drinking.

As Diana Rowland (1985, p. 115) explains, sex is viewed not as sinful but as just one of the more pleasurable necessities of life. In Japan, sex is not associated with love as strongly as it is in Western culture but, rather, is seen as being related more to desire. Traditionally, marriages were arranged, and even today, both families and companies act as intermediaries. Hitachi, for example, has a "Tie the Knot" Office that matches their male and female employees, many of whom eventually marry (Jordan, 1997). For many Japanese, marriages were not designed to be the sole means of satisfying sexual needs. Therefore, extramarital affairs were not censored. In practice, however, a double standard existed; men were free to keep a mistress (or mistresses) and seek sexual pleasure in any way they chose, whereas women were supposed to toe the line of marriage. One Japanese wife explained to an American friend:

> Why should the wife care if her husband goes off to "play"? It doesn't mean anything. She knows he will never leave her. In fact, I think the bond in a Japanese marriage is much stronger than that in the West. A Japanese woman would not consider divorcing her husband over such a trivial matter.

However, this attitude may be changing because of the rise of AIDS. Also, the divorce rate is increasing, and many women are marrying later in life. Still, this attitude confirms the fact that situational ethics is important to the Japanese.

Drinking and even drunkenness are good-naturedly tolerated, and even encouraged. In fact, almost anything one does while drunk, except driving, is considered forgivable. Intoxication allows the Japanese to express themselves freely without fear of repercussion, and it is normal for members of a Japanese workgroup to spend several hours after work drinking and eating as a group before catching a late bus home. However, Western women sometimes find this behavior difficult to accept, even when a Japanese man is very polite when not drinking. In one celebrated instance, a British female high school teacher finally lost patience with a Japanese co-worker who had repeatedly harassed her while he was drinking, and "decked" him at an office party. However, although Japanese may indulge in unruly behavior while drinking, they rarely engage in displays of hostility and violence.

Like the natural order of the Japanese garden, the Japanese believe in a natural order in society. Therefore, as reflected in the history of hereditary power and aristocratic rule in feudal Japan and in modern Japanese organizations, different ranks and status are considered natural. Within an organization, a person's rank is usually more important than his name. For example, the principal of a school is often addressed simply by the Japanese word for principal, *kocho sensei*. This emphasis on title establishes an individual's rank within an organization while also serving to reinforce group identity.

The Japanese are great believers in establishing a person's status as quickly as possible so that the proper interaction and communication can take place. When meeting for the first time, Japanese businessmen follow the *kata* or form of immediately exchanging business cards, *meishi,* largely to establish each man's specific position and group affiliation. This exchange is not to be taken lightly, and the recipient of such a card is expected to read the card carefully and even repeat the person's name and title before putting the card away. To immediately put the card away, as many Americans do, would be insulting to the giver.

Language is also used to reinforce the natural order of ranks and statuses. Various endings arc added to words of introduction that subtly indicate the status of a person, particularly in the case of a foreigner, or *gaijin.* The Japanese language is famous for such subtlety. Even at work, honorifics are used to address higher-status managers, but they are frequently dropped during the later stages of a working day as these managers indicate by their language and behavior that everything is going smoothly.

Even slight differences in seniority establish rigid status differences. Although two individuals may be merely 1 year apart of each other, this fact determines who will be senior and junior for the rest of their lives.

A good part of personal self-identification derives from one's status. Furthermore, one is expected to act according to his or her status. To do otherwise would be unbecoming. Because they serve as role models and are addressed by the honorable title *sensei,* teachers in Japan must pay particular attention to their behavior outside of school. For example, if caught driving while under the influence of alcohol, a teacher would lose face and probably have to resign his or her position.

A hierarchy exists not just within the group, but between different groups. Most Japanese have a clear idea of the informal rank among universities, business firms, and even countries. This latter ranking helps to explain the Japanese attitudes toward people from different countries. For example, those from developed countries, such as the United States, England, France, and Canada, are considered to possess higher status than are those from developing Asian countries. Even within Japan, certain groups suffer discrimination, particularly the 600,000 Koreans. At one time in history, the Japanese had a caste system similar to that of India, and, although it is outlawed, the "outcastes" who work on slaughtered animal products in any way are considered inferior by many Japanese, and private detectives are hired before most marriages to ensure that one's child does not marry into one of these families. Reportedly, some Japanese firms go to excessive lengths to ensure that only "pure" Japanese will be offered positions with them.

One of the great dangers of overemphasizing the uniqueness of being Japanese and group harmony is that a destructive groupthink may occur.

Some prominent Japanese have openly criticized minority groups in the United States in ways that many Americans consider racist, and Dr. Tsunoda of Tokyo Medical and Dental University has even argued that the Japanese are unique because they have an unusual brain structure. According to Dr. Tsunoda, the Japanese brain mixes rational and emotional responses in the left hemisphere, whereas the Western brain is divided into the rational left and emotional right sides. As indicated previously, the political parties are not parties per se but representative of powerful interest groups, and political scandals that would not be countenanced in other developed countries have occurred in Japan at least in part because of their existence. These examples should suffice to demonstrate that there are some downside risks associated with the emphasis on Japanese uniqueness and group conformity.

Contrary to expectation, this emphasis upon status and rank coincides with a lack of class consciousness. Ninety percent of the Japanese population considers itself to belong to the middle class. In Japanese society, ties are vertical; loyalties overwhelmingly tend to lie with the immediate group. For example, a Japanese factory worker for Toyota identifies himself as a Toyota man and has little solidarity or identification with a factory worker for Honda.

Promotion is based significantly on seniority in Japan, although this is not the only consideration, and today, firms are emphasizing individual performance. An individual may not jump a rank and must serve a prerequisite number of years in the previous rank in order to be eligible for promotion. However, only a limited number of positions are available for a much larger number of eligible employees. Therefore, the company promotes a certain percentage of eligible employees from each group until a person reaches a specific age, at which time it is unlikely that one will be promoted further.

It is important to note that hierarchy in Japan is not directly associated with clear authority and clearly delineated roles, as it is in the West. For example, senior but less competent employees may be given relatively high titles that entail minimal responsibility, and an extremely able young individual may be given more responsibility than his or her title indicates. Also, although the Japanese emphasize group consensus and harmony, in fact, Japanese managers tend to share information with their subordinates and delegate decision-making authority to them less than do American managers. As these examples suggest, appearance does not always reflect reality in Japan, just as the water in the garden's pond appears to be quite calm, even still. Yet the architect of this garden knows that beneath the surface, the water is continually being sucked into a horizontal pipe and pumped back to the top of the waterfall.

Like the pond, from the outside, the Japanese appear to be an extremely harmonious people. However, this appearance does not take into account the intense competition that exists in Japanese society. Firms compete fiercely for market share, rival political parties compete for power, and individuals compete ferociously to enter the top universities. On the individual level, conflict occurs between family members, between friends, and between co-workers. However, individuals often suppress their true feelings, and, if open conflict erupts, it is kept within the confines of the group.

In general, Japanese usually express the group opinion, *tatemae,* although it may differ from what he or she really thinks, *honne.* They associate this duality with the legitimate needs of the group and the reinforcing role of each person within it. Ellen Frost (1987) explains this dichotomy as follows:

> *Tatemae* . . . is used in connection with a view made from an accepted or objective standpoint. *Honne* has the meaning of one's true feelings or intentions. . . . This doesn't mean anyone is lying. There is a delicate but important difference between tatemae and honne which comes up in any situation where a person must consider more than one's own feelings on the matter. (p. 92)

To Westerners, this lack of frankness smacks of insincerity. However, to many Japanese, the failure to observe *honne* and *tatemae* shows insensitivity and selfishness. Japanese tend to appreciate foreigners who outwardly conform to certain rules of behavior. Whether they actually respect these rules is not relevant; observance of them is a sign of appropriate and, hence, sincere conduct on their part.

However, this suppression of the self may have some negative effects. Dean Barnlund (1989) conducted a comparative study of Americans and Japanese on the issue of the private and public self that was well-received by both Japanese and American experts. He basically argues that because Americans tend to expose their private selves much more than the Japanese, they have a much better understanding of their private selves and are able to cope in an active manner to threatening interpersonal experiences. He concludes with the following:

> The Japanese appear to be more socially vulnerable and to cultivate greater reserve, are more formal and cautious in expressing themselves, and communicate less openly and freely. Americans, in contrast, appear more self-assertive and less responsive to social context, are more informal and spontaneous in expressing themselves, and reveal relatively more of their inner experience. (p. 64)

A recent study of shyness among several nations confirms this portrait. Bernardo Carducci developed a questionnaire measuring the degree to which people feel shy in the following nations: the United States, Germany,

Mexico, Israel, Japan, and France. Japan proved to be the shyest nation: Six of ten believe they fall into this category. In contrast, the least shy nation was Israel, at 31% (see Morin, 1998).

Some Japanese respond that Americans say and do things that they later regret. The aphorism, "He who speaks does not know; he who knows does not speak," relates directly to this issue, because frequently, the most powerful member of a group is the last to speak, if he or she deigns to speak at all. What matters, however, is that the Japanese emphasis on the group is protected by the use of *honne* when the Japanese interact among themselves and with foreigners.

Aesthetics

The Japanese aesthetic sense is well developed and distinctive, and, in fact, it may be this culture's most important contribution to the world. As with most, if not all, of the activities discussed previously, this aesthetic sense is based heavily on the natural interaction between human beings and nature.

Japan has only one indigenous religion, Shintoism, which is nature-based and animistic; even the word for God is translated as "up the mountain" in Japanese. Joseph Campbell (1962) captures the aesthetic sense of this religion in the following passage:

> Such a place of worship is without images, simple in form, wonderfully rooted, and often painted a nice clear red. The priests, immaculate in white vesture, black headdress, and large black wooden shoes, move about in files with stately mien. An eerie music rises, reedy, curiously spiritlike, punctuated by controlled heavy and light drumbeats and great gongs; threaded with the plucked, harplike sounds of a spirit-summoning kot. And then noble, imposing, heavily garbed dancers silently appear, either masked or unmasked, male or female. These move in slow, somewhat dreamlike or trancelike, shamanizing measure; stay for a time before the eyes, and retire, while utterances are intoned. One is thrown back two thousand years. The pines, rocks, forests, mountains, air and sea of Japan awake and send out spirits on those sounds. They can be heard and felt all about. And when the dancers have retired and the music has stopped the ritual is done. One turns and looks again at the rocks, the pines, the air and the sea, and they are as silent as before. Only now they are inhabited, and one is aware anew of the wonder of the universe. (p. 475)

The importance of nature can be seen not only in Shintoism but also in Japanese painting, literature, and language. Long before it was considered acceptable in the West, landscape painting was a major theme of the *sansui-ga* painting introduced from China at the end of the Kamakura period (1185-1333). Nature is often the subject of the seasonal references in *waka* and haiku poetry, and in the seasonal introductions that the Japanese customarily use in correspondence. The Japanese language is full of references to nature; it even has a special word to describe the sound of cherry blossoms falling.

But the Japanese are acutely aware that nature can wreak havoc. In 1923, the Great Tokyo Earthquake resulted in the loss of 140,000 people, and there is a one-in-five chance that a similar occurrence will happen in the next few years ("The Flowers of Kobe," 1995). In 1995, the Kobe Earthquake resulted in 3,500 deaths. Although the Japanese are trying to make their buildings earthquake resistant, they realize that their efforts may prove futile.

Aesthetically, the water in the Japanese garden, and the garden itself, tries to represent nature as it is, not to order and impose a visible form on it as a Western garden may, but to capture its intrinsic being. The gardener does not create the beauty, but merely allows it to express itself in louder and plainer terms. In doing so, he or she considers not only the placement of the rocks and trees, but also the effect that time, namely the change of the seasons, will have on the garden. He or she observes the laws of *mujo,* or mutability, and *sisei ruten,* or perpetual change of the universe. For example, the garden may be designed in such a way that in winter, the bare branches will have their own particular appeal. Given this emphasis on the natural impermanence of things, it is not surprising that the three great nature-watching rituals in Japan are snow-gazing in February or thereabouts, cherry blossom viewing, and viewing the ninth moon of the year or the harvest moon, all of which activities preferably occur in a Japanese garden.

The gardener also observes another Japanese aesthetic theory that developed from the Japanese acceptance of nature—that of uniqueness. No two trees are alike. Therefore, the gardener does not search for the perfect rock, for such a rock cannot exist in a world characterized by uniqueness, but looks for a tree or rock that expresses its own individuality. The gardener also does not seek to perfectly order a garden that is made of imperfect and unique objects. To insist upon a harmony other than the underlying, naturally revealed one would be unnatural.

Zen Buddhism's influence on the development of Japan and the Japanese garden, not just the religious garden but the landscape garden, has been enormous. As suggested previously, Zen Buddhism proposes that one can free oneself from this world by perceiving the timelessness and oneness of the universe. Likewise, in a Japanese garden, the whole of nature can be seen despite the individual parts. Also, each part of the garden can capture the essence of nature in its own way. The garden depicts a freed world that has been reduced physically and enlarged spiritually to suggest the size and grandeur of nature. Japanese who recognize that they are part of nature and, hence, mortal essentially stop time by allowing it to have its own way. In the same manner, although the seasons may change the appearance of the garden, the stones, trees, and water in the Japanese garden are always visible and unchanged.

In Japan, the Buddhist concept of transience has been integrated into the indigenous concept of nature as an extension of oneself. This integration can be seen in the oneness with nature and the Buddhist feeling that worldly display counts for nothing. For example, Zen teachings gave rise to the principles of *wabi* and *sabi* inherent in the tea ceremony, Japanese garden, and flower arrangements. *Wabi* is the aesthetic feeling of discovering richness and serenity in simplicity; it is an emotional appreciation of the essence of things, including the ephemeral quality of life. *Sabi* bespeaks of a feeling of quiet grandeur enjoyed in solitude, and it normally involves the beauty that comes from the natural aging of things. To the Japanese, something old is to be respected, even its imperfections. Clearly, the Japanese garden is an ideal setting for experiencing *wabi* and *sabi*.

In *The Global Business,* Ronnie Lessem (1987) discusses two principles that explain the Japanese aesthetic, *shibui* and *mono-no-aware*. *Shibui* refers to a quality of beauty that has a tranquil effect on the viewer; the object, whether natural or manmade, clearly reveals its essence through perfection of form, naturalness, simplicity, and subdued tone. *Mono-no-aware* refers to the merging of one's identity with that of object or mood, especially one tinged with recognition of the impermanence of things. He suggests that this aesthetic awareness leads to a sensitivity to man and nature that is rare in Europe or the United States.

A Japanese person may stroll in the garden, or perhaps just sit on its edge, listening to the water and soaking in its beauty. The garden provides a place of escape from society, both physically and spiritually, just as many Japanese seek refuge through their hobbies.

This refuge usually takes the form of some kind of identification with nature, as in the case of cultivating one's own tiny landscape garden or arranging flowers. Millions of Japanese express themselves through the traditional arts, dancing, music, and literature. In developing their individual skills, they practice self-control and self-discipline. In Japan, pursuit of a hobby, called *shumi*, which literally means "tastes," is important to one's self-identity and even self-respect.

Except for the sound of the flowing water, all is quiet near the Japanese garden. Likewise, silence is an important value to the Japanese. As mentioned previously, a common Japanese proverb is, "Those who know do not speak; those who speak do not know." Conversation is often punctuated by long stretches of silence. The Japanese say that it is during these silent intervals that real communication takes place, and that they can sense others' feelings and thoughts. Westerners should not feel compelled to fill in the gaps with conversation, which may only annoy Japanese, who already perceive Westerners as talking too much.

To return to Hofstede's (1991) research on the five dimensions of culture, the Japanese tend to avoid uncertainty and seek comfort in familiar situations. In one celebrated instance, a Japanese manager typed up the complete minutes of a forthcoming meeting devoted to a possible Japanese-German joint venture, but faxed them by mistake to the German side. In addition, Japan ranked first on masculinity, thus indicating that its people are aggressive in the pursuit of worldly success and material possessions. As indicated previously, the carp in the Japanese garden symbolically represents this aggressiveness or masculinity. Unlike the Chinese, who are hampered by their excessive devotion to the past and ancestor worship, the Japanese historically have been great borrowers from other cultures and are quick to change when conditions warrant such action. In this sense, the Japanese are similar to the individualistic Americans.

But the Japanese are clearly different from Americans, as our metaphor of the Japanese garden indicates. Still, worried Japanese elders are concerned that the water in the garden will not continue to flow smoothly because the "new humans" may have lost their appreciation of things Japanese. Iwao (1990) argues that there have been three major changes in the Japanese character over the past decade: a tendency toward diversity and individuality, a need for swift results and instant gratification, and a desire for stability and maintenance of the status quo. It is true that young Japanese seek more leisure time and are more likely to devote themselves to personal goals than in the past. As Iwao suggests, consumer behavior reflects a movement toward diversity and individuality. Female roles, attitudes toward marriage, and work are also changing. A survey conducted by the Dentsu Institute of Human Studies in 1999 seemed to confirm all or most of these trends, for 52% said that their nation should opt for a society of equal opportunity but more risk (Neff, 1999).

The water in the Japanese garden is flowing quickly and with force. It may even cause the shape of the pond to alter somewhat. The change of the seasons will also bring changes to the garden. Yet the basic design and elements of the Japanese garden will always remain, for this island nation of homogeneous people relies heavily on its groups to maintain stability and ensure change and progress within the framework of a high-context culture emphasizing the natural ordering of individuals, groups, and activities.

CHAPTER 4

India:
The Dance of Shiva

Sex may drive the soap operas in America. But in India, what really moves the dishwashing liquids are serials based on ancient myths of Indian gods.

—Karp and Williams (1998), p. A1

India is a country bursting with diversity—virtually every writer describes it as one of the most culturally and geographically diverse nations in existence. It is the second largest country in the world, with a population of 950 million, and it is about one third the size of the United States.

India is the world's most populous democracy. It became a modern nation only in 1947, after the British ceded control. At that time, neighboring Pakistan, which is Islamic, was also created. India is a poor nation, but on many measures, it has achieved substantial success since 1947. Life expectancy has increased from 32 to 62 years; adult literacy from 14% to 52%; and income, adjusted for purchasing power, from $617 to $1,230. This nation also has the largest number of college-educated scientists and computer specialists in the world and a middle class that is estimated to include 100 to

150 million, although 53% of the population lives on less than one dollar per day. It has surpassed Pakistan on most measures of economic and social success, but its success is limited when compared to that of the Five Tigers of Asia. A major reason for India's limited success is its dramatic increase in population.

In 1991, *The Economist* published an influential survey of India whose cover included a picture of a caged tiger with the title "caged" (Crook, 1991). The basic message was that India was too bureaucratic and centralized. For example, international firms seeking to establish Indian subsidiaries waited approximately 500 days for approval of their applications, whereas Indian businesspeople waited only about 50 days. Manmohan Singh, India's Finance Minister at the time, and others were influenced by this negative depiction and began efforts to privatize the economy and streamline the government. Although still highly bureaucratized by Western standards, the Indian government has made significant efforts since that time to modernize its operations.

Religious diversity is a major feature of India, and it is fitting that our image of, and cultural metaphor for, this country should be based on religion. As Swami Vivekananda so succinctly stated, "Each nation has a theme in life. In India religious life forms the central theme, the keynote of the whole music of the nation."

For 2,000 years of its history, India was almost completely Hindu. But for the past millennium or more, Indian culture has been a synthesis of different racial, religious, and linguistic influences; Hinduism itself has undergone many changes owing to the impact of other faiths. Therefore, it is incorrect to contend that Indian culture is solely Hindu culture. However, to begin to understand India, we must start with Hindu traditions. The overwhelming majority of Indians are still tradition oriented, and changes in their culture and society cannot be understood without reference to that tradition.

There are numerous deities or gods in the Hindu religion, each being different manifestations of one supreme being. The most important gods are Brahma (the Creator), Vishnu (the Preserver), and Shiva (the Destroyer). Among the greatest names and appearances of Shiva is Nataraja, Lord of the Dancers. The Dance of Shiva has been described as the "clearest image of the activity of God which any art or religion can boast of" (Coomaraswamy, 1924/1969, p. 56), and it also reflects the cyclical nature of Hindu philosophy. Through this metaphor, we will begin to explore Indian culture and society.

Among Hindus, dancing is regarded as the most ancient and important of the arts. Legend attributes to it even the creation of the world: Brahma's three steps created earth, space, and sky. Every aspect of nature—man, bird, beast, insect, trees, wind, waves, stars—displays a dance pattern, collectively called the Daily Dance (*dainic nrtya*). But nature is inert and cannot dance until Shiva wills it; he holds the sacred drum, the *damaru,* whose soundings set the rhythms that beat throughout the universe. Shiva is like a master conductor, and the Daily Dance is the response of all creation to his rhythmic force.

Shiva is seen as the first dancer, a deity who dances simply as an expression of his exuberant personality (Banerji, 1983, p. 43). His dance cannot be performed by anyone else, because Shiva dances out the creation and existence of the world. But just as the mortal dancer gets tired, so, too, does Shiva lapse periodically into inactivity. The cosmos becomes chaos, and destruction follows the period of creation. This concept of the Dance of Shiva is innate in the Eastern ideas of movement and history—it is continuous and both constructive and destructive at the same time (Gopal & Dadachanji, 1951).

The Dance of Shiva represents both the conception of the world processes as a supreme being's pastime or amusement (*lila*), and the very nature of that blessed one, which is beyond the realm of purpose or understanding (Coomaraswamy, 1924/1969). The dance symbolizes the five main activities of the supreme being: creation and development (*srishti*); preservation and support (*sthiti*); change and destruction (*samhara*); shrouding, symbolism, illusion, and giving rest (*tirobhava*); and release, salvation, and grace (*anugraha*).

Considered separately, these are the activities of the deities Brahma, Vishnu, Rudra, Mahesvara, and Sadavisa, respectively. Taken together, the cycle of activity illustrated by the Dance of Shiva encapsulates Hinduism as the main driving force of Indian society. The idea of cycles is a common thread in traditional Indian philosophy and is the theme that will run through our discussion of its culture.

Two distinctive variants of basic Indian culture spring from the people's Dravidian and Aryan ethnic origins. The Dravidians probably came to India from the eastern Mediterranean coasts, forming the highly developed Indus Valley civilization 3,000 years before Christ. About 1500 B.C., this civilization fell into decline, and the people migrated to the southern part of the Indian subcontinent. At approximately the same time, Aryans arrived in India from Persia, settling almost all of the Indo-Gangetic Plain. Today, 72% of the population is of Aryan origin, whereas Dravidians account for 25%. The remaining 3% is made up of a myriad of other groups, including Mongoloids (Culturegrams, 1991). India's most populous cities—all ranking among the 40 largest in the world—are Bombay (10 million) to the west, Calcutta (4 million) to the east, Delhi (7 million) to the north, and Madras (4 million) and Bangalore (3.5 million) to the south.

Religion and language separate the people far more than ethnic background or geography. Although more than four fifths of the Indian population is Hindu, sizable numbers belong to other religious groups: Muslim

(11%), Christian (3%), Sikh (2%), Buddhist, Jain, and aboriginal animists. Hindus are spread all over the country, with smaller concentrations at the southern, northeastern, and northwestern extremities. The minority populations (the term is relative, because Muslims alone number 100 million) actively resist being dissolved into a Hindu melting pot. Muslims are in the majority in Kashmir, and Sikhs are concentrated in Punjab. Buddhism claims some 5 million adherents in its homeland (and more than half a billion worldwide), including more than 50% of the population in western Kashmir and in Sikkim. Mixed religious groups are found in the northeastern and southwestern parts of the country.

The four major religions—Hinduism, Islam, Christianity, and Sikhism—are all associated with specific languages in which their original scripts were written: Sanskrit, Arabic, Latin, and Gurumukhi, respectively. The first three are not spoken languages in India, and the fourth, in a modernized form, is a state language of Punjab. In addition to Arabic, the Muslims in India evolved a language of their own, Urdu, and a number of other regional languages. There are at least 300 known languages in India, 24 of which have at least 1 million speakers each.

After India's independence from Britain in 1947, Hindi, a north Indian language, was proclaimed the national language. Hindi was spoken at that time by only about 25% of the people, but it was the single most prevalent language in the country. The South had virtually no Hindi speakers, and the southern people opposed starting the process of learning an "alien" language. As a result of these objections, the original Constitution recognized no fewer than 15 official languages (three more were added in 1992), and English was designated as an additional official language as a compromise. Even today, Hindi is the native tongue of fewer than half of all Indians, and English is often the language of national communication. English is spoken throughout the country, an enduring legacy of colonial days that is increasingly important for India as the globalization of markets and communications continues.

India's history reflects the cycles of chaos and harmony epitomized by the Dance of Shiva. Time after time, India has recovered from episodes that would have ended the existence of any other nation. In fact, Shiva's son, Ganesh, is the symbol of good arising from adversity. According to the legend, Parvati, the consort of Shiva, would spend hours bathing, dressing, and adorning herself. This often meant that Shiva was kept waiting, so Parvati set their son Ganesh on guard to prevent Shiva bursting in on her unannounced and catching her in a state of unreadiness. One day, Shiva was so frustrated by Ganesh's actions that he cut off the child's head. Distraught, Parvati completely withdrew from her lord, and Shiva realized he would have to restore the child to her if he was to win her back. He resolved to use the first available head he could find, which happened to be that of a baby elephant. The boy regained his life and now had the added advantage of the elephant's wisdom. Similarly, India's past and present contributions to art, science, and the spiritual world of the unknown are immense, despite periods of turmoil and apparent anarchy.

The estrangement of North and South India, illustrated by the debate over language, has historical roots that reach long into the past. The South has enjoyed calm and relative tranquillity throughout most of its history, whereas the North has been subjected to a series of foreign invasions, often on a grand scale. Consequently, the northern culture is more a product of a mixed heritage. Among the most significant modifying influences in the North were the various Muslim invasions beginning about A.D. 1000. As a result of these, the administrative structure of northern India was destroyed repeatedly, society often deprived of leadership, and religious faith shaken.

Muslim rule of North India began early in the 13th century and lasted until the middle of the 19th century. Muslim rulers were harsh on Hindus. It is against Muslim beliefs to worship any idol or image of God, so the invaders destroyed many thousands of Hindu temples and replaced them with mosques. A discriminatory tax was imposed on non-Islamic subjects, and Hindus were given low-level positions, if employed at all. Forceful conversion of Hindus to the Islamic faith was carried out widely. Hindus in their own land were turned into second-class citizens and never shown the beautiful side of Islam. The confrontation between two virtually incompatible religious systems led to implacable mutual hatred between their respective followers. The echoes of this conflict resound even today. For instance, in 1992, more than 200,000 Hindus stormed and destroyed a 450-year-old Muslim mosque erected by the Mughals to replace a Hindu temple on the site that marks the birthplace of the Hindu god Rama, and hundreds of people were killed in the ensuing bedlam. Such instances are relatively common.

Unlike the North, southern India enjoyed a stable, almost uninterrupted regime of Hindu kingdoms until 1646, when the Muslims succeeded in conquering and unifying all of India. The Muslim Mughal empire began to disintegrate during the 18th century, with independent regional kingdoms springing up all over. The influence of the British East India Company rose as Britain ousted rival western colonial powers in the South. During those days of weakness, plundering invaders came from Persia and Afghanistan. North India entered a state of anarchy from which it did not emerge until the British gradually extended their control, leading to the establishment of the British Raj (Rule) in the 19th century.

The British government instituted direct rule over India in 1858 following the Sepoy (Indian) Mutiny. Many Indians think of this event as the first war of independence. The Sepoys—Indian soldiers in British employ—

mutinied over a rumor that animal fat was being used in the cartridges they had to bite in order to load their rifles. Hindus heard it was beef fat, whereas Muslims heard pig fat, thereby violating the taboos of both. British troops barely put down the insurrection—the British garrison at Kanpur, with its women and children, was slaughtered, and Kanpur became a rallying cry for British vengeance (Arden, 1990, p. 133).

Early expressions of nationalism first crystallized in the Indian National Congress in 1885 and the All-India Muslim League in 1906. Following the infamous massacre of more than 400 unarmed demonstrators at Amritsar by General Dyer's troops in 1919, Indian leaders put aside their previous faith and hope in the good intentions of the British Empire. Inspired by M. K. Gandhi, the Indian National Congress began a program of peaceful non-cooperation (*satyagraha*) with British rule. Tragically, just months after India's independence was finally granted, Mahatma ("Great Soul") Gandhi was killed by a Hindu extremist who had denounced him as an appeaser of the Muslims.

The British granted independence in 1947, but the country was partitioned into a largely Hindu India and a Muslim Pakistan. Overnight, partition created great communal strife, and 12 million refugees moved across the new India-Pakistan border during 1946-1947—Hindus into India, and Muslims into Pakistan. More than 200,000 people were killed in the accompanying riots, giving the world a lasting image of a modern India seemingly at war with itself. In fact, except for times of crisis, India has managed to accommodate and contain the destructive forces latent in group differences. But it is also true that today, the political and social compromises that have permitted the country to deal with its diversity are under extreme pressure.

Faced with threats of succession, caste warfare, and sectarian violence, India's central authorities have sometimes adopted stern measures. The army has been called on more frequently to restore order to the country's troubled provinces than to defend the country from external threats.

Jawaharlal Nehru, the head of the Congress party, became India's first prime minister in 1947. He was unwaveringly loyal to the basic concepts of freedom, democracy, socialism, world peace, and international cooperation and emerged as an eloquent statesman for the world's nonaligned, less developed nations. Two years after Nehru's death in 1964, his daughter, Indira Gandhi (no relation to Mahatma Gandhi), succeeded to her father's office. Mrs. Gandhi struggled to modernize India and make it an economic power, but perhaps she lacked her father's devotion to "the spirit of man." She invoked the emergency provisions of the Constitution in 1975 and suspended civil liberties, citing the need to address some of the nation's persistent problems "on a war footing." When elections were called in 1977, the Indian people expressed their resentment against the methods of "the Emergency" and voted Gandhi out of office. After full democracy was restored, an apparently chastened Indira Gandhi returned to power in 1979, where she remained until she was assassinated 5 years later.

Rajiv Gandhi, Indira's son, became prime minister on her death, but, amid claims of widespread corruption in the government, his Congress (I) party lost a general election. The succeeding government was short-lived, unable to sustain a parliamentary majority for their policies. During the next campaign, Rajiv Gandhi was also assassinated, and the Congress (I) party was swept back to power on a huge sympathy vote.

It appears that the Nehru-Gandhi dynasty that has dominated India's modern political system is now at an end, or at least suspended. The family's journey—its sequence of evolution, power, death, return, creation, destruction, and, perhaps, ultimate salvation—epitomizes the actions of the Dance of Shiva and the cyclical nature of Hindu philosophy.

Currently, India really has no dominant political party. The BJP party, a conservative Hindu-Centric party, has risen in stature and has won major elections; the Congress party is regrouping and is still very powerful; and there are several other parties contending for power.

Cyclical Hindu Philosophy

The Indian perspective on life tends to differ most sharply from that of Europe and the United States in the value that it accords to the discipline of philosophy (Coomaraswamy, 1924/1969, p. 2). In Europe and America, the study of philosophy tends to be regarded as an end in itself—some kind of mental gymnastic—and as such, it seems of little importance to the ordinary man or woman. In India, philosophy tends to overlap with religion, and it is regarded as the key to life itself, clarifying its essential meaning and the way to attain spiritual goals. Elsewhere, philosophy and religion pursued distinct and different paths that may have crossed but never merged (Munshi, 1965, p. 133). In India, it is not always possible to differentiate between the two.

In Hindu philosophy, the world is considered illusory, like a dream, the result of God's *lila*. According to one interpretation, *Bharata Varsha,* the ancient name of India, literally means "land of the actors" (Lannoy, 1971, p. 286). In an illusionary world, people cannot achieve true happiness through the mere physical enjoyment of wealth or material possessions. The only happiness worth seeking is permanent spiritual happiness as distinguished from these fleeting pleasures. Absolute happiness can result only from liberation from worldly involvement through spiritual enlightenment. Life is a journey in search of salvation (*mukti*), and the seeker, if he or she withstands all of the perils of the road, is rewarded by exultation beyond human experience or perception (*moksha*). In the same way that the Dance of Shiva leads the cosmos through a journey, Hindu philosophy directs each individual along a path.

There are basically four paths or ways that lead to the ideal state: intense devotion or love of God (*bhakti yoga*), selfless work or service (*karma yoga*), philosophy or knowledge of self (*jnana yoga*), and meditation or psychological exercise (*raja yoga*). The four ways are not exclusive, and an individual may choose or combine them according to the dictates of temperament and circumstance. Whatever path is followed, every Hindu is aware of the difficulty of reaching the ideal state in a single lifetime. This is the point at which the concept of reincarnation, or the cycle of lives, becomes important.

Individual souls (*jivas*) enter the world mysteriously; by God's power, certainly, but how and for what purpose is not fully explainable (Smith, 1958, p. 100). They begin as the souls of the simplest forms of life, but they do not vanish with the death of their original bodies. Rather, they simply move to a new body or form. The transmigration of souls takes an individual *jiva* through a series of complex bodies until a human one is achieved. At this point, the ascent of physical forms ends, and the soul begins its path to *mukti*. This gives an abiding sense of purpose to the Hindu life—a God to be sought actively and awaited patiently through the cycles of many lives.

The doctrine of reincarnation corresponds to a fact that everyone should have noticed: The varying age of the souls of people, irrespective of the age of the body ("an old head on young shoulders"). Some people remain irresponsible, self-assertive, uncontrolled, and inept to their last days; others are serious, friendly, self-controlled, and talented from their youth onward. According to Hindu philosophy, each person comes equipped with a highly personalized unconsciousness, characterized by a particular mix of three fundamental qualities: *sattva* (clarity, light); *rajas* (passion, desire); and *tamas* (dullness, darkness). Their relative strength differs from one person to another, but in the Hindu idea of destiny, the unconscious has an innate tendency to strive toward clarity and light (Kakar, 1978).

The birth of a person into a particular niche in life and the relative mix of the three fundamental qualities in an individual are determined by the balance of the right and wrong actions of his or her soul through its previous cycles. The rate of progress of the soul through this endless cycle of birth, life, and death—the soul's karma—depends on the deeds and decisions made in each lifetime. One way of mapping the probable karma of an individual is to consult astrological charts at the time of his or her birth, and this is an important tradition in Indian society.

The Dance of Shiva portrays the world's endless cycle of creation, existence, destruction, and re-creation, and Hindu philosophy depicts the endless cycle of the soul through birth, life, death, and reincarnation. We will now turn to examining the cycle of individual life within that greater series of lifetimes.

The Cycle of Life

According to Hindu philosophy, a person passes through four stages of life, the first of which is that of a student. The prime responsibility in life during this stage is to learn. Besides knowledge, the student is supposed to develop a strong character and good habits, and emerge equipped to produce a good and effective life.

The second stage, beginning with marriage, is that of a householder. Here, human energy turns outward and is expressed on three fronts: family, vocation, and community. The wants of pleasure are satisfied through the family, wants of duty through exercising the social responsibilities of citizenship, and the wants of success through employment.

The third stage of life is retirement, signifying withdrawal from social obligations. This is the time for a person to begin his or her true education—to discover who one is, and what life is all about. It is a time to read, think, ponder over life's meaning, and to discover and live by a philosophy. At this stage, a person needs to transcend the senses and dwell in harmony with the timeless reality that underlies the dream of life in this natural world.

The Hindu concept of retirement is exemplified in a story told by a traveler in India (Arden, 1990, p. 132). The traveler saw a white-bearded man seated on a blanket, writing in a notebook. The man looked up and smiled as the traveler walked past. "Are you a Buddhist?" the traveler asked, to which the man shook his head. "A Hindu? A Muslim?" Again, he shook his head, and replied, "Does it matter? I am a man." The traveler asked what the man was writing. "The truth," he said, "only the truth."

The final stage is one of *sannyasin,* defined by the *Bhagavad-Gita* as "one who neither hates nor loves anything." In this stage, the person achieves *mukti* and is living only because the time to make the final ascent has not come. When he or she finally departs from this world, freedom from the cycle of life and death is attained.

A person can pass through the four stages of life in a single lifetime or stay at each stage for many lifetimes. Even Buddha is reputed to have passed through several hundred lives. Progress is determined in light of the activities and inclination of the person at each stage of life. For example, Indian religion is replete with rituals, the primary purpose of which is to receive the blessings of God. Each ceremony involves the singing of religious songs (*bhajans*) and discourses by priests and other religious people (*satsang*). The sincerity with which people indulge in these activities and apply the tenets of the philosophy in their practical life determines their progress through the cycle of life and death. A person may expound philosophy at great length, go to the temple every day, and offer alms to saints and the poor, yet indulge in all sorts of vices. These contradictions in life are resolved on death by karma, which dictates that upon reincarnation, each person will receive rewards or punishment for his or her accumulated good and bad deeds.

The Hindu desire for positive outcomes of daily activities, resulting in positive karma, leads us to a brief discussion of the importance of astrology. With so much at stake, almost everyone in India consults the stars, if not on a daily basis, then at least on important occasions. Matching the horoscopes of a bride and groom is as much a part of planning a marriage as choosing the flower arrangements. It is routine for Indians to consult the stars about the best day to close on a house or sign an important contract. When it was revealed that an astrologer helped former President Ronald Reagan's wife, Nancy, set her schedule, Americans hooted with derision. In contrast, no one in India batted an eye when India's former prime minister, Narasimha Rao, delayed naming his cabinet because an astrologer warned that the intended day was not auspicious enough.

Like Hindu philosophy, the Indian concept of time is cyclical, characterized by origination, duration, and disappearance ad infinitum. This is reflected in the dramatic structure of a traditional Sanskrit play. These plays are typically based on the themes of separation and reunion, and they tend to end as they begin. Various devices are used—the dream, the trance, the premonition, and the flashback—to disrupt the linearity of time and make the action recoil upon itself (Lannoy, 1971, p. 54). Similarly, the Dance of Shiva is a repetitive cycle of creation, existence, and destruction; constant change within a period of time, but ultimately, time itself is irrelevant.

In an attempt to neutralize the anguish of impermanence and change, the carved religious images that every village home possesses are made of permanent materials, such as clay or metal. This also reveals the functional role of the image in a materially restricted environment. The practice of religion at home is one of the main reasons Hinduism was able to survive the invasion of foreign powers over the centuries. And just as religion is important to the family, so, too, the family plays a dominant factor in Indian society.

■ The Family Cycle

Most Indians grow up in an extended family, a form of family organization in which brothers remain together after marriage and bring their wives into their parental household or compound of homes. Recent migration to cities and towns in search of economic opportunities has contributed to the weakening of many traditions, including that of extended families. In this section, we describe family traditions that exist most strongly in the India of about 400 million people that continues to be affected marginally by industrialization. While weakened in some parts of society, many aspects of the family cycle are still important to all.

The preference for a son when a child is born is as old as Indian society. A son guarantees the continuation of the generations, and he will perform the last rites after his parents' death. This ensures a peaceful departure of the soul to its next existence in the ongoing cycle of life. The word *putra*, or son, literally means "he who protects from going to hell." In contrast, a daughter has negligible ritual significance. She is normally an unmitigated expense—someone who will never contribute to the family income and who, upon marriage, will take away a considerable part of her family's fortune as her dowry. Although formally abolished, the institution of dowry is still widespread in India, but it is becoming increasingly fashionable among educated Indians to not indulge in the practice.

A striking reflection of this gender preference is the continued masculinization of the Indian population, particularly in the north. There are 108 males to 100 females. The main reasons for this outcome are the higher mortality rate of female children and the tendency to limit family size once there is a sufficient number of sons. Also, the recent availability of sex determination tests has allowed women to ensure that their firstborn is a boy, because they can abort unwanted female children.

Just as the Dance of Shiva represents preservation, overlooking, and support, parents tend to nurture their children with great care. A Hindu child grows up in the security of the extended family and has few contacts with other groups until it is time for school. Although the mother is chiefly responsible for the care of the child, there is also close contact with other females and mother-surrogates, and this continues for much longer than in many other cultures. A child is usually breastfed for at least 2 years (although significantly less in the case of a female child) and will be fed any time that it cries. Consequently, most infants are virtually never left alone.

The strong ties of home life do not conflict with the Hindu belief in the liberty of the soul removed from worldly concerns. Love of family is not merely a purpose in itself but a way to the final goal of life. Love will not yield the rewards of *mukti* when it remains self-centered; that is why the Hindu try to diffuse their love over sons, daughters, guests, and neighbors (Munshi, 1965, p. 115).

Children in India are considered sacred, a manifestation of God, but if the Hindu ideal is a very high degree of infant indulgence, reality is somewhat different in the poorer areas of India. Here, there are typically many young children under one roof, and 1 in 10 will die in infancy, so babies are not regarded as extraordinary creatures. Except for the firstborn son, they tend to be taken for granted. This is reinforced by the belief in rebirth; because an individual is not born once and once only, he or she cannot be regarded as a unique event. The mother has probably witnessed the birth of several babies and may have seen them die, too. When her child cries, falls sick, or is accidentally hurt, she is not beset with feelings of intense guilt. A mother's work may be long and hard, both in the home and in the fields, so she is unable to give her child undivided attention.

Even as the Dance of Shiva leads the world through the joys of existence, an element of chaos is inherent in the world's Daily Dance. Similarly, nature in India has been full of threats to a child's safety—famine, disease, and chronic civil disorder. As a rule, until modern times, more than half of all deaths befell children in their first year of life. But as the nation got a grip on its affairs, and as campaigns against diseases such as malaria and smallpox took hold, mortality rates fell. By 1981, nearly three out of four newborns could expect to survive to age 20 (Narayana & Kantner, 1992, p. 26). The cultural importance of children is derived from the need to carry on the cycle of life. This continued importance is reflected in statistics that show that although death rates since 1921 have fallen, birth rates have declined much more slowly.

Government attempts to regulate the birth rate have become synonymous with its sterilization programs. Resentment against coerced sterilization in India helped defeat Indira Gandhi's government in 1977. As a result of the political fallout, birth control was set back as a popular cause. Middle-class Indians, influenced by education and the desire for an improved standard of living, are increasingly adopting family planning methods. But when the formidable psychic barrier of traditional Hindu beliefs in the life cycle is considered, it seems clear that rapid population growth will continue in the poorer, rural areas.

An Indian father is frequently remote, aloof, and a much feared disciplinary figure, just as Shiva is distant from the world he nurtures. But there are also special bonds between father and son, and the relationship is one of mutual dependence. A son must obey his father unquestioningly, pay him respect, and offer complete support in every need both in life and after death. The father owes his son support, a good education, the best possible marital arrangement, and inheritance of property. One Indian proverb reads, "A son should be treated as a prince for five years; as a slave for ten years; but from his sixteenth birthday, as a friend."

The son learns that women are lower in status than men very early in life. The position of any woman in this hierarchical society means that she must constantly be making demands and pleading with superiors for one thing or another. The son soon develops an attitude of superiority. A female's authority can seldom be absolute, except for the unchallengeable position that the senior grandmother may inherit. A son finds out that anger may be productive; violent outbursts of anger are often effective if directed against someone of uncertain status. Similarly, the destructive powers of the Dance of Shiva are effective in creating new opportunities and patterns.

The relative position of men and women is clear in Indian society, and the question of competitive equality is not customarily considered. The Hindu marriage emphasizes identity, not equality. Generally, women are thought to have younger souls, and therefore, they are nearer to the world than men and inferior to them. Girls are trained to be submissive and docile, and to fulfill culturally designated feminine roles. The ideal of womanhood in Indian tradition is one of chastity, purity, gentle tenderness, self-effacement, self-sacrifice, and singular faithfulness. Throughout history, Indian women have had dual status—as a wife, she seduces her husband away from his work and spiritual duties, but as a mother, she is revered.

Among the crosses women have had to bear in Indian society are female infanticide, child marriage, purdah (feminine modesty and seclusion), marital mistreatment, and the low status of widows. Until the mid-19th century, the voluntary immolation of the widow on her husband's funeral pyre (*sati*) was not uncommon; the widow believed her act would cleanse her family of the sins of the three generations. Poor families are more likely to be fearful of not being able to scrape together enough money to find their daughters husbands and may resort to killing infant girls. Generally speaking, however, the lower down the economic hierarchy, the more equal are the relations between the sexes. Of course, there are many factors that can bring about or alleviate hostile feelings toward women, but the various forms of mistreatment suffered by women are often viewed by them as part of their destiny as a woman. The Dance of Shiva is not destined to lead to joy throughout the world, and if the corresponding experience of humankind includes some unhappiness for women in society, that is simply the way things are.

A man's worth and recognition of his identity are bound up intimately in the reputation of his family. Lifestyle and actions are rarely seen as the product of individual effort, but are interpreted in the light of family circumstance and reputation in the wider society. Individual identity and merit are enhanced if the person has the good fortune to belong to a large, harmonious, and closely knit family, which helps to safeguard a child's upbringing and to advance a person in life. The family contributes to decisions that affect an individual's future, maximizes the number of connections necessary to secure a job or other favors, comes to aid in times of crisis, and generally mediates an individual's experience with the outside world. For these reasons, the character of the respective families weighs heavily in the consideration of marriage proposals.

Arranged marriage is still the norm in India. Advertisements regularly appear in European and American newspapers for the purpose of identifying potential candidates. The Western concept of romantic love arises from the Western concept of personality and, ultimately, from the un-Indian concept of equality of the sexes. Still, the concept of life as an illusion makes the idea of loveless marriage easier to understand.

Marriages are usually for a lifetime, because divorce is considered socially disgraceful. The average age for Indian women to marry is 18 to 19, whereas only about 13% of U.S. women of this age are married. The percentage of Indian women aged 15 to 19 who are married ranges from 14% in states where a high value is put on female education, to more than 60% in less developed states (Narayana & Kantner, 1992, p. 31). In the case of child marriage, the girl lives at her parents' home until she is about 15 or 16 years of age, after which she moves to the home of her husband's family. A newly arrived daughter-in-law is sometimes subject to varying forms of humiliation until she becomes pregnant. This treatment originated historically from the urgent need to ensure the early birth of a son in times of low life expectancy. Also, the size of the dowry that a girl brings with her can also determine how she is treated or mistreated in her husband's home. The husband's family may keep making demands upon her for additional support from her family, and, if it is not forthcoming, she may be tortured or even burned alive, although the outcry against such treatment seemingly has diminished such illegal practices.

The restricted life of women in the conservative atmosphere of India does not prevent them from developing a strong sense of self-respect. Their ultimate role is to preserve unity and continuity in the chain of life, and there is pride and dignity in their sense of identity with the family and their role as wife and mother. Indian society seems to have given women, rather than men, resilience and vitality under the difficult circumstances of life in that country. But ultimately, all respond to the Dance of Shiva, and whether that brings great joy or unhappiness to the current life is irrelevant compared to the ongoing search for salvation, or *mukti*.

Since the beginning of time, dancing has been a rite performed by both men and women; Shiva and his wife, Parvati, are often depicted in ancient sculptures as one composite figure, half male and half female. Typical figurines of Shiva are four-armed, with broad masculine shoulders and curving womanly hips. Similarly, there is a place for both genders to contribute to Indian society today. In this century, Indian women have undergone a social revolution more far-reaching and radical than that of men. While this process has been going on, women have attained positions of distinction in public and professional life. The political dominance of Indira Gandhi is one example of how women can be held in high esteem by all Indians.

In summary, it can be seen that the extended family unit is still a strong feature of Indian society. Just as the Dance of Shiva wills all nature to respond to its rhythm, so, too, each member of the family fulfills a role dictated by family tradition.

The Cycle of Social Interaction

A sense of duty (dharma) is the social cement in India; it holds the individual and society together. Dharma is a concept that is wider than the Western idea of duty, because it includes the totality of social, ethical, and spiritual harmony (Lannoy, 1971, p. 217). Dharma consists of three categories: universal principles of harmony (*sanatana dharma*), relative ethical systems varying by social class (*varnashrama dharma*), and personal moral conduct (*svadharma*). Among the prime traditional virtues are leading a generous and selfless life, truthfulness, restraint from greed, and respect for one's elders. These are principles that are consistent with a virtual global idea of righteousness. Hinduism has progressed through India's moments of crisis by lifting repeatedly the banner of the highest ideals. The image of the Dance of Shiva is strongly evoked by the following passage from the *Bhagavad-Gita:*

> Whenever the dharma decays, and when that which is not dharma prevails, then I manifest myself. For the protection of the good, for the destruction of the evil, for the firm establishment of the national righteousness, I am born again and again. (Deutsch, 1968, p. 31)

The oldest source of ethical ideas is the *Mahabharata,* or Great Epic (of Bharata), the first version of which appeared between the seventh and sixth centuries B.C. It is a huge composite poem of 90,000 couplets, in 18 books, that traces the rivalry between two families involved in an unrelenting war. The story is interrupted by numerous episodes, fables, moral tales, and long political and ethical discourses, all of which serve to illustrate the illusory nature of the world and encourage the reader to strive for God. This sacred book, a repository of Hindu beliefs and customs, is based on the assumption that dharma is paramount in the affairs of society. The epics took at least 1,000 years to compose and are still the most widely read and respected religious books of the Hindus. The most popular and influential part of the epics is the *Bhagavad-Gita* ("Song of the Blessed One"), a book Gandhi once said "described the duel that perpetually went on in the hearts of mankind."

A recent European traveler in India gave this illustration of the power of dharma. Sitting precariously among local people on top of a bus during a long journey, the traveler was astounded when a sudden shower of money fell into the dusty road behind them. An Indian alongside the traveler began shouting and pounding on the roof of the bus for the driver to stop. At some distance down the road, the bus pulled over and the man rushed away. All of the passengers disembarked and waited for the Indian to return, laughing at his comic misfortune and manic disappearance. Eventually the man reappeared, clutching a big handful of notes, including Western money. It was then that the traveler realized his own wallet was gone from his back pocket; it had come loose and blown away from the top of the bus, scattering the equivalent of a year's income for the average native (about $350). The Indian, a total stranger, had run back and convinced the poverty-stricken locals to hand over the money they were gathering ecstatically from their fields. The traveler began to thank his new friend for his troubles, but with the comment "It was my duty," the Indian declined to take any reward.

It is generally believed that social conflict, oppression, and unrest do not stem from social organizations, but originate in the nonadherence to dharma by those in positions of power. It is their actions that have created the cycle of disharmony. Hindus see a quarrel as a drama with three actors—two contestants and a peacemaker—and it is not one of the protagonists but the peacemaker who is seen as the victor in the dispute, because it is he or she who has restored harmony (Lannoy, 1971, p. 198).

Individuals who head institutions are believed to be the sole repositories of the virtues and vices of the institution. Traditionally, social reform movements focused not so much on abolishing the hierarchical organizations or rejecting the values on which they are based, but on removing or changing the individuals holding positions of authority in them (Kakar, 1978). For example, during the declining years of both the Mughal and British Indian Empires, the ruling classes enjoyed lives of luxury and extravagance in India. Conspicuous consumption by the aristocratic elites at the expense of the productive classes still exists in the India of the early 21st century. The identity may have changed, but the attitude remains.

The issues behind the social and political ferment in India today are not rooted primarily in economic deprivation and frustration, although these make the mix more volatile (Narayana & Kantner, 1992, p. 2). Rather, it is the widespread feeling that the institutions on which the society was founded no longer work. In a reflective piece written shortly after the assassination of Rajiv Gandhi, the New Delhi correspondent of *The Economist* ("Death Among the Blossoms," 1991) wrote that

> The state is seen as corrupt and callous, incapable of delivering justice or prosperity to the people. . . . The police and civil servants are seen as

oppressors and terrorists. The law courts are venal and can take decades to decide a case. The rule of law does not seem to be working in settling people's grievances. What seems to work is violence and money, and all political parties are engaged in a mad race to maximize the use of both. . . . Amid this moral decay, religious, ethnic and caste crusades have a growing appeal. People find a purity in them which they do not find in secular, national parties. And an increasing number of people are willing to kill in the name of causes which they find holier than the discredited law of the land. (p. 40)

The tragic recourse to mob violence by religious followers at different times in the country's history is a contradiction that astounds casual observers of India. How can such terrible things happen in a country where everyone believes in harmony and awaits the ultimate consequences of good and bad deeds in reincarnation? Hindus believe that *sila*, character or behavior, has its roots in the depths of the mind rather than in the heat of the action (Lannoy, 1971, p. 295). Because all worldly acts are transient, part of the illusion of life, they can have no decisive moral significance. Within the Dance of Shiva, destruction exists as strongly as creation and preservation; so it is with India.

This is not to say that violence is condoned by the Hindu faith; just the opposite applies. However, Hindus avoid the theological use of the terms "good" and "evil," and they prefer to speak of "knowledge" and "ignorance"—*vidya* and *avidya*. Destructive acts done by people who are ignorant are not regarded as sins, but those acts committed by people aware of their responsibilities are counted against them in their seeking of *mukti*.

Bathing in the holy water of the Ganges is believed to wash away all the sins of the person, and it is required of every Hindu at least once in his or her life. Indians tend to synthesize or integrate with nature because they assume that this is the natural relationship of human beings with the world, unlike Westerners, who tend to exploit the physical environment for their own purposes. But the belief in the spiritual purity of the Ganges is so strong that government attempts to clean up the badly polluted waters have little chance of being effective. Many people simply do not accept that anything can spoil the Ganges's perfection. As a consequence, rotting carcasses of both animals and partly cremated people are a common sight along the river banks. The image of death among life, decomposition next to creation, and pollution mixed with purity is evocative of the Dance of Shiva.

Another pervasive social dimension in India is the caste system (*verna*), which is now officially outlawed but is still a source of constant tension. Following the assumed natural law that an individual soul is born into its own befitting environment, Hindus assume that an individual belongs to a caste by birth. There are four main castes, each of which contributes to society in specific ways: Brahmans, seers or religious people; administrators; producers such as skilled craftspeople and farmers; and followers or unskilled laborers. Each of these natural classes has its appropriate honor and duties, but as privilege has entered the scale, with top castes profiting at the expense of those lower down, the whole system has begun to disintegrate. Below the system is a fifth group, the untouchables, who lie outside of the major activities of society. Its members are engaged in work that is considered socially undesirable and unclean. Untouchability, as it exists today, is often described as a perversion of the original caste system.

Within each caste or group, there are numerous subcastes, or *jati*, that influence the immediacy of all daily social relations, including work. About 3,000 *jati* exist, and they are further divisible into about 30,000 sub-*jati*, with unwritten codes governing the relationships between *jatis*. Friendships with members of the same *jati* tend to be closer and more informal than do those with members of other *jatis*. As a general rule, a person's name provides information not only about his or her *jati* but also about the region of the country from which the person's family originated. For example, Gupta is a family name from the trading class, although many have gone into the professions, especially teaching. Most Guptas come from the North Indian states of Haryana, Uttar Pradesh, and West Bengal.

The *jati*'s values, beliefs, and prejudices become part of each individual's psyche or conscience. The internalized *jati* norms define the right actions, or dharma, for an individual—he or she feels good or loved when living up to these rules, and guilty when transgressing them.

When society was divided strictly by caste, there was no attempt to realize a competitive equality, and within each caste, all interests were regarded as identical. But that also meant that equality of opportunity existed for all within the caste—every individual was allowed to develop the experience and skills that he or she needed to succeed at the caste's defined role. The castes were self-governing, which ensured that each person was tried and judged by his peers. Central authorities viewed crimes committed by upper-caste members more severely than those of the lower caste. Because it was simply not possible to move outside of the caste, all possibility of social ambition, with its accompanying tension, was avoided. This suits the Hindu belief in harmony. The comprehensiveness of the caste system, together with holistic dharma, contributed to the stability that prevailed among the vast mass of people for much of India's history. Preservation of order, interspaced with disorder, is a characteristic of the Dance of Shiva.

The worst facet of the caste system falls on the untouchables. This caste has come to be the symbol of India's own brand of human injustice, victims of a system that kept people alive in squalor. Of course, social hierarchy is universal, found not only among the Hindus but also among the Muslims,

Christians, Sikhs, Jains, and Jews (Srinivas, 1980). There is also a prevalence of pollution taboos in all civilizations, including the most advanced and modern; eliminating dirt is an attempt to introduce order into the environment (Lannoy, 1971, p. 146). But Hindu society pays exceptional attention to the idea of purity and pollution, and historically, this has resulted in the virtual ostracism of the untouchables from the rest of society.

By way of historical explanation, Hindus believed that proximity to the contaminating factor constitutes a permanent pollution that is both collective and hereditary. Therefore, they had a dread of being polluted by members of society who were specialists in the elimination of impurity. Hindu society was more conscious of grading social groups according to their degree of purity than of a precise division of castes into occupations. The untouchables—traditionally, society's cleaners, butchers, and the like—were at the bottom of the Hindu hierarchy because they were considered irrevocably unclean. A similar caste system was developed in Japan, and it, too, has been outlawed, although its effects are still being felt.

Although India's traditional social structure was based on institutionalized inequality, today the government, and supposedly the nation, too, is committed to social equality. Beginning with Mahatma Gandhi, public figures have tried to reform the attitudes of Indian society toward the untouchables. Gandhi named them Harijan, literally, "Children of God." The entire caste system was declared illegal by the Constitution, and today, untouchables are guaranteed 22.5% of government jobs as compensation for traditional disfavor. These policies have met with some success, but such a deep-rooted prejudice cannot be eliminated by a mere stroke of the pen.

The ambiguity of caste in occupational terms is another wedge by which the lower castes push their way upward on the scale. However, ambiguity is not so great as to render the system inoperative. Violations of caste norms, such as intercaste marriage, still evoke responses of barbaric ferocity. Educated Indians look upon such incidents as throwbacks to the inhumanity of feudal times that must be dealt with sternly by the authorities. But efforts to create greater equality of opportunity for members of the traditionally disadvantaged castes meet stiff resistance from these same ranks (Narayana & Kantner, 1992, p. 5).

Additional reforms remain problematical, as recent history suggests. In 1990, the government introduced policies reserving 27% of central and state jobs for these castes and Christian and Muslim groups that were socially backward. In protest, dozens of upper-caste students burned themselves to death. The upper-caste Brahmans, a mere 5.5% of the population, have traditionally run government departments, but the struggle for jobs in India is so intense that the students saw themselves as victims of injustice, not historical oppressors. The prime minister at the time, V. P. Singh, was forced to resign when the government's coalition partner withdrew its support of the government, mainly over caste reform issues.

The Harijan quickly realized their ability to assert their democratic rights as equal citizens through organized political activity. The effect of politicization of caste in modern times has made it clear that power is becoming ascendant over status. Modern education also acts as a solvent of caste barriers. These factors hold out the best hope for the disappearance of caste over the longer term.

The hierarchical principle of social organization has been central to the conservatism of Indian tradition. Among the criteria for ordering are age and gender. Elders have more formal authority than younger people, and, as we have already related, men have greater authority than women. Many times, women are not involved in social functions or conversations and are required to cover their heads in front of elders or mature guests. Most relationships are hierarchical in structure, characterized by almost maternal nurturing on the part of the superior, and by filial respect and compliance on the part of the subordinate. The ordering of social behavior extends to every institution in Indian life, including the workplace, which we will examine shortly.

It is clear that the traditional social structure of India is undergoing change and reform. This is consistent with the evolutionary aspects of the Dance of Shiva. But any change requires the destruction of old ways, and pressure is beginning to build within the old system. It may be that before those changes are complete, Shiva will rest, and chaos will rule for a time. Or, perhaps a new rhythm is beginning for the dance of the 21st century, and the Daily Dance of Indian society will quietly adjust in response.

The Work and Recreation (Rejuvenation) Cycle

There are several different perspectives on the importance of work: to earn a living; to satisfy the worldly interests of accomplishments, power, and status; and to fulfill the desire to create and care for the family. An aspect considered more important in India is that work enables, prepares, and progresses the individual through the cycle of life toward the ultimate aim of achieving *mukti*. The Indian approach to work is best defined by the *Bhagavad-Gita*: "Both renunciation and practice of work lead to the highest bliss. Of these two, the practice of work is better than its renunciation" (Deutsch, 1968, p. 60).

Work was prescribed originally as duty (dharma) without any concern for material outcomes. Castes were occupational clusters, each discharging their roles and, in turn, being maintained by the overall system. But meeting the obligations to one's relatives, friends, and even strangers, as well as maintaining relationships, constituted the ethos of the system. Even with the rapid expansion of industrial activity in the 20th century, requiring large-scale importation of Western technology and work forms, Western work values have been internalized only partially by Indians. Today, with government-mandated affirmative action, it is not unlikely that someone from a higher caste may work for someone from a lower caste. Many Indians have developed a state of mind that allows them to put aside caste prejudice in the workplace but, on returning home, to conduct all of their social activities strictly according to caste norms.

We have already seen how family life develops an acute sense of dependence in the individual that serves to fortify the participative and collective nature of society. Similarly, most Indian organizations have numerous overlapping in-groups, with highly personalized relationships between the members of each group. They cooperate, make sacrifices for the common good, and generally protect each other's interests. But in-groups often interfere with the functioning of formally designated sections, departments, and divisions, and they can lead to factionalism and intense power plays within an organization. Just as disorder within order is a characteristic of the Dance of Shiva, so, too, is incompetence often overlooked because work performance is more relationship oriented than contractual in nature. A competent person may be respected but not included in a group unless he or she possesses the group characteristics.

Family, relatives, caste members, and people speaking the same language or belonging to the same religion may form in-groups. Typically, there are regionally oriented subgroups, formed on the basis of states, districts, towns, and villages from which people's families originated. Within the group, Indians are very informal and friendly.

Geert Hofstede's attitudinal survey of the cultural differences between some 53 countries is especially helpful in the case of India, which tends to cluster with those countries where there is a high degree of uncertainty avoidance (Hofstede, 1980a). Indians tend to work with lifelong friends and colleagues and minimize risk-taking behavior. This orientation is consistent with the Hindu philosophy of life as an illusion, Indians' preoccupation with astrology, and their resignation to karma. India also falls with those countries characterized by large power distances. However, India ranks 21st of the 53 nations on individualism. Although we might expect a more collectivistic orientation, this ranking may reflect the influence of British rule. Finally, India has a high score on masculinity, which is consistent with the emphasis on male domination in Hinduism. Generally, the values described by Hofstede reflect a historical continuity and resilience of the Indian social system, despite the onslaught of foreign invasions, colonial rulers, and economic dislocations.

The hierarchical principle continues to be a source of stagnation in modern Indian institutions. Younger people have a limited, or no, say in decision making. Persistent critical questioning or confrontations on issues necessary to effect change simply do not occur. Any conflict between intellectual conviction and developmental fate manifests itself in a vague sense of helplessness and impotent rage. Gradually, the younger workers resign themselves to waiting until they become seniors in their own right, free to enjoy the delayed gratification that age brings with it in Indian society. The apparent lack of control and ambition displayed by the participants at work is similar to the resignation of the world to the will of Shiva. The world responds to Shiva's rhythm, captive of its pace, and is unable to influence it.

The importance of honoring family and *jati* bonds leads to nepotism, dishonesty, and corruption in the commercial world. These are irrelevant abstract concepts; guilt and anxiety are aroused only when individual actions go against the principle of primacy of relationships, not when foreign standards of ethics and efficiency are breached. This gives rise to legendary tales of corrupt officials that are shared widely among travelers and businesspeople who have spent time in India.

Indian organizations have been shaped by colonial experiences that have bureaucratized them and polarized the positions of the rulers (managers) and the ruled (workers). As a consequence, the role of the manager tends to be viewed as that of an order-giver or autocrat. In "Going International" (1983), a popular management training videotape, there is a telling vignette involving an American manager and one of his Indian subordinate managers. As a general rule, American managers perceive their role to be that of a problem solver or facilitator and attempt to involve subordinates in routine decisions (Adler, 1997). The American manager in this videotape attempted to use this style with his Indian subordinate, who wondered about his superior's competence and held him in some contempt for not being autocratic. The clear implication is that American managers must act more authoritatively in India than in the United States.

In the areas of rejuvenation and recreation, one of their sources for the Indian people is participation in the many religious festivals held throughout the year. These festivals are usually associated with agricultural cycles or the rich mythology of India's past. In some regions, community festivals involve the active participation of not only Hindus, but also members of other religions. Family bonds are emphasized and strengthened repeatedly through the joint celebration of religious festivals. The Indian sense of fun and play is given free rein during the festivities, which often include riddles, contests of strength, role reversals, and rebellious acts. Just as the Dance of Shiva is an expression of his joy and exuberance, festivals give Hindus an opportunity to express their feelings of devotion and happiness.

Religious raptures, possessions, and trances are common during Indian seasonal festivals. This is a structured and, in some cases, highly formalized phenomenon that enriches the consciousness of the individual and the group. There are also the attendant dangers of degeneration into hysterical mob psychology, which Indian history has witnessed many times. Festivals allow the discharge of intense emotion that is otherwise submerged in a network of reciprocity and caste relations, but they also can be used to reestablish order. In this sense, festivals mirror the activity, relapse, and reordering of the cosmos that is the result of the Dance of Shiva. But just as the dancer cannot help dancing, the celebrant is not always capable of restraining his or her religious fervor.

Memorials to the grand line of India's "modern gods"—Mahatma Gandhi, Jawaharlal Nehru, and now Indira Gandhi—are as much the objects of pilgrimages as any temple or festival. Indira Gandhi was killed by her own trusted Sikh bodyguards just 5 months after she ordered the storming of the Golden Temple at Amritsar by the Indian army to dislodge Sikh rebels. Her home in New Delhi is now a museum and shrine visited by thousands daily. The spot in her garden where she was gunned down is bracketed by two soldiers; her bullet-ridden sari (dress) is on display inside. Crowds gather before these, many weeping. Another Indian example is that of N. T. Rama Rao, a former movie star and chief minister of the state of Andhra Pradesh from 1983 to 1989. Rama Rao acted in leading roles in more than 320 films with mythical, historical, and folklore themes. Among the masses, Rama Rao was associated with the qualities of the gods he played, and when he gave up his movie career to establish a new political party, he was voted into office immediately. The fact that his party's radical Hindu fundamentalist policies sometimes caused strife within society is not inconsistent with the concurrently constructive and destructive nature of the Dance of Shiva.

The favorite pastime of Indians is watching movies, either at movie theaters or through renting videos from the shops that have sprung up all over the country, and today, India's "Bollywood" is the second largest producer of films in the world. Movies that draw on images and symbols from traditional themes are dominant in popular Indian culture. They incorporate but go beyond the familiar repertoire of plots from traditional theater. Films appeal to an audience so diverse that they transcend social and spatial categories. The language and values from popular movies have begun to influence Indian ideas of the good life and the ideology of social, family, and romantic relationships. Robert Stoller's (1975) definition of fantasy, "[the] protector from reality, concealer of truth, restorer of tranquility, enemy of fear and sadness, and cleanser of the soul" (p. 55), includes terms that are equally attributable to the illusory nature of the Dance of Shiva, and it is easy to understand why films play such a major role in Indian recreation and rejuvenation.

■ Summing Up

India is the heart of Asia, and Hinduism is a convenient name for the nexus of Indian thought. It has taken 1,000 to 1,500 years to describe a single rhythm of its great pulsation, as described by the *Mahabharata,* or Great Epic. By invoking the image and meaning of the Dance of Shiva, and drawing parallels between this legendary act of a Hindu deity and many of the main influences of traditional Indian life, we have attempted to communicate the essence of India's society in this chapter.

It is not always possible to identify a nicely logical or easily understandable basis for many of the contradictions that exist in Indian society, just as it is difficult to explain the existence of racism, sexism, and other forms of intolerance and injustice in Western countries. In India, the philosophy of life and the mental structure of its people come not from a study of books but from tradition (Munshi, 1965, p. 148). However much foreign civilization and new aspirations might have affected the people of India, the spiritual nutrient of Hindu philosophy has not dried up or decayed (Munshi, 1965, p. 148); within this tradition, the role of the Dance of Shiva, described below, is accepted by all Hindus (Coomaraswamy, 1924/1969):

> Shiva rises from his rapture and, dancing, sends through inert matter pulsing waves of awakening sound. Suddenly, matter also dances, appearing as a brilliance around him. Dancing, Shiva sustains the world's diverse phenomena, its creation and existence. And, in the fullness of time, still dancing, he destroys all forms—everything disintegrates, apparently into nothingness, and is given new rest. Then, out of the thin vapor, matter and life are created again. Shiva's dance scatters the darkness of illusion (*lila*), burns the thread of causality (karma), stamps out evil (*avidya*), showers grace, and lovingly plunges the soul into the ocean of bliss (*ananda*). (p. 66)

India will continue to experience the range of good and bad, happiness and despair, creation and destruction. Through it all, its people will continue their journey toward *moksha,* salvation from the worldly concerns of mankind. Hindu philosophy is the key to understanding India and how a nation of such diversity manages to bear its immense burdens while its people seem undeterred and filled with inner peace and religious devotion.

And through it all, Shiva dances on.

CHAPTER 5

Bedouin Jewelry and Saudi Arabia

"This is the twist in this country," said a wealthy Saudi business-man who is close to the royal family. "The government is pushing toward modernization, and the culture is going backward."

—Lancaster (1996), p. A26

As is the case with many nations, Saudi Arabia is confronting the tension between traditional and modern beliefs, values, and life-styles. The Saudi royal family is the official guardian of the Muslim holy shrines of Mecca and Medina, but it is supporting modernization, at least partially because the economy is too dependent on oil, and there is only a limited supply of it. For example, the family is encouraging tourism, even to the extent of permitting the building of an artificial ski resort. But, whereas the Saudi royal family erected a modern concert hall completed in 1989, no symphonies or operas have been performed because of the conservative opposition's insistence on strict Islamic standards. *Mutaween,* or the religious police, routinely punish immodestly dressed women or merchants who do not close their shops during the five daily prayer periods. Similarly, the government executed 90 people in 1997, up from 71 in 1996, by ritual decapitation with a sword.

This tension between modernization and conservatism is likely to increase in all of the Gulf Arab states. More than half of their collective populations is under 20 years old. In Saudi Arabia, about 42% of the 18.5 million population is under 15. The tension was particularly acute in Saudi Arabia during the early to mid-1990s because of the 1990 Gulf War with Iraq, in which Saudi Arabia and other Arab nations were allies of the Western powers; 24 Americans were killed in Saudi Arabia. More recently, the Islamic traditionalists have muted their criticisms and seem to accept the need for modernization, or at least some aspects of it. But, as suggested by the figures on population growth, it is easy to imagine a return to traditions and a rejection of modernization. Given this tension between tradition and modernization, Bedouin jewelry is an appropriate cultural metaphor for Saudi Arabia.

Saudi Arabia became a nation in 1932, when Ibn Saud united disparate tribes into one nation and named himself as king. Oil was discovered 10 years later, but the country remained fairly isolated until the 1970s. Then, suddenly, Saudi Arabia was slaking the world's thirst for oil, and the country was yanked into the 20th century. It is still stumbling, struggling to reconcile deeply held traditional values with disconcerting new realities. By examining the ancient art form of Bedouin jewelry, we can address the values and beliefs of Saudi culture. Who the Saudis are today began with the Bedouin of the Arabian desert.

Saudi Arabia stretches across three fourths of the hot, dry, rugged Arabian Peninsula. Its land mass is about 24% of that of the United States. The country's borders are the Red Sea on the west; Jordan, Iraq, and Kuwait on the north; the Arabian (Persian) Gulf, Qatar, and the United Arab Emirates on the east; and Oman and Yemen on the south. Small, jagged mountains rise in western Saudi Arabia near the Red Sea. From there, the land gradually slopes down to the Arabian Gulf in the east. Three major deserts lie in between. The largest is the Rub al-Khali, or the "Empty Quarter." It is the greatest continuous sand area on earth. Although several oases spring out of this harsh landscape, the country has no natural rivers or lakes. But Saudi Arabia does have one enormous consolation. Beneath this austere terrain are the largest reserves of oil in the world.

Several million years ago, this area was covered by shallow seas filled with mollusks, brachiopods, and plankton. When they died, they sank to the floor of the sea. Eventually, the waters receded, and the sea floor compressed at high temperatures under layers of sedimentary rock. The organisms were transformed into oil and natural gas.

Much later, the Arabian Peninsula was a grassy savanna. Until about 18,000 years ago, ample rainfall supported vegetation and wildlife. But the end of the previous ice age caused a prolonged drought. Rivers evaporated, leaving dry valleys called wadis. The fertile land turned into desert. Now, rainfall averages 0 inches to 4 inches per year. When a rare downpour does occur, the wadis are briefly filled with water once again before soaking into the ground or evaporating away. During much of the year, temperatures are 90°F to 120°F. However, strong winds and cooler temperatures can make winter days quite cold. These raging winds also generate the stinging sandstorms common to the Arabian desert. Surviving in this environment takes skill, courage, and fortitude.

For centuries, the Bedouins of Saudi Arabia have made the desert their home. Their way of life is a highly sophisticated adaptation to an extremely harsh environment. The fact that they have been successful at it for so long is a source of fierce pride. Bedouins feel far superior to townspeople, and they present a certain arrogance for having braved the deserts and won. Surely theirs is a purer, worthier life.

The word Bedouin means "desert dweller." They live in extended family groups, moving when they need new pasture or water. The only animals that can live comfortably in the desert are goats, sheep, and, most of all, camels. Goats supply milk, as well as hair for tents. Sheep give meat, and wool for carpets and blankets. Camels provide milk, meat, hair for tents, dung for fuel, urine for shiny hair, and transportation, all of which almost makes up for their nasty tempers. In addition, camels can go many days without food or water. Raising and selling camels to townspeople has always been a traditional source of income for these desert dwellers.

Because the desert provides scant food for the livestock, Bedouin camps must move often. Usually, this is every couple of weeks. Camps consist of tents, 2 to 30 of them. Probably, most camps have fewer than 10. Each tent houses a nuclear family, plus perhaps an unmarried uncle, mother, sister, or brother. A Bedouin tent is a long, low, black structure made of camel and goat hair, with a wide front opening. The shape is ideal for protection against wind and sandstorms. Each tent is divided into two sections: one side is for the mother and daughters, the other is for the father and sons. The tents and all possessions can be packed up and on the way within 2 hours.

Bedouins pay little attention to national borders. Saudi Arabian borders are poorly defined, but the Bedouin need for pasture and water takes precedence over any arbitrary lines. The families camp on the edge of the desert, occasionally visiting towns for supplies. Their habit is to live in the higher areas during the hottest part of the year so they can escape the worst heat and sandstorms. Later, they move back to the lowlands to avoid cold temperatures and winds. Bedouins are continuously on the alert for chance thunderstorms that mean lush pastures are sprouting, flowers are blooming, and wadis are filling.

Camel raiding has always been a traditional pursuit of Bedouin men. Although it is now outlawed, the raiding rules are still important for illustrating the strict code of Bedouin honor. First, the hostility must be declared explicitly; using the element of surprise is shameful. Therefore, raiding is not done at night. Second, no women or children may be harmed. Third, sunrise raids are fairer, so that victims have a better chance to track and retrieve their camels before nightfall. Breaking these rules brings shame to the perpetrators, tarnishing their honor severely.

Bedouins are known throughout the world for their great generosity. A guest, even an unexpected stranger, will be fed and housed for 3 days. In fact, if those raiders arrived at the opposing camp, they would receive the same welcome. And they would not be harmed during their stay. Whereas an ordinary meal consists of milk and milk products, dates, flat bread, and perhaps rice, the guest's feast also includes fresh meat and pine nuts. Pale green coffee with cardamom, as well as tea, is served. Afterwards, poets and dancers (always male) provide entertainment. Poets, or storytellers, are important to Bedouin culture. Because few Bedouins can read or write, poets function as historians and educators, as well as entertainers. Poets are highly esteemed in desert culture, and they also possess certain persuasive powers.

Bedouin loyalty goes first to the extended family. No one can survive the hard desert life alone. Other people are essential for shared chores and protection. Yet the meager desert offerings cannot support whole clans, let alone tribes, in the same spot at once. The family unit is large enough, yet small enough, for safety and survival in the desert. Intense feelings of loyalty and dependence are fostered and preserved in this unique family group setting. Home is viewed as people, not place.

One way of strengthening the Bedouin extended family is by consanguineous marriage (marriage to a close relative). A Bedouin girl marries while young, around 14 years of age. For several reasons, her ideal spouse is a first cousin: She is already familiar with her cousins after having grown up in the same camps; a husband cannot mistreat her with fathers and brothers nearby; she can remain near her mother and sisters; her future children will enhance and perpetuate the group; and the dowry she acquires upon marriage will remain within the family. For centuries, intermarriage has bound Bedouin families to each other and to their culture. Thus, it is not surprising that Saudis are much more collectivistic and denigrating of out-group members than Americans (Al-Zahrani & Kaplowitz, 1993).

Bedouin life remained constant for many hundreds of years until oil was discovered. The discovery of the marine treasure trove beneath the desert has affected every Saudi citizen, and that includes even these inscrutable, self-sufficient nomads. The wandering Bedouin lifestyle that withstood the severity of the desert is succumbing to the forces of progress.

What are these forces? First, camels were once the main source of Bedouin income. But Saudi preferences have changed as beef has become more available through international trade, modern domestic transportation systems, and improved refrigeration methods. Camels are now an expensive hobby rather than a primary source of food. Second, more Bedouins are taking permanent jobs in towns for a steady income, requiring them to settle nearby. Third, they like the conveniences that make life easier—products such as canned tomato paste for rice, flashlights, portable radios, insulated coolers, sewing machines, and trucks. These possessions are cumbersome to haul to a new camp every few weeks. Fourth, some of their locales have been breached by oil pipelines, highways, storage tanks, and industrial sites. Fifth, the Saudi government wants them settled.

The government considers the Bedouin a disruptive element. They do not pay taxes, their trucks are unlicensed, the women do not always veil and often drive, they can disappear at will into the desert, and their loyalties are to the tribe rather than to the government. Basically, they refuse to be controlled, which is threatening for an absolute monarchy like the House of Saud.

Some governmental efforts to settle the Bedouin have failed. Housing for Bedouin has been built in major population centers, but most of it does not meet their needs. It remains empty. The desert dwellers feel cramped in the stationary rooms, and they are baffled by appliances. They prefer carpets spread on sand rather than on hard concrete floors. Most of the housing units are small and designed for nuclear families, with high privacy walls between houses. Because there is no place for their animals, sometimes Bedouin families will camp outside their new walls and keep the animals inside the house.

A more appropriate governmental attempt to encourage settlement is to bring necessities to the desert. Water trucks and nurses visit the more permanent camps. Sometimes, cash grants are distributed. Special hospitals that have campsites right outside the rooms treat Bedouin patients. The government recruits young men for Bedouin National Guard units, where their strength, agility, and desert skills are highly valued. These transitional measures are somewhat successful, and increasing numbers of Bedouin are settling permanently.

Wandering Bedouin now comprise about 5%-10% of the Saudi population (Mackey, 1992, p. 22; Wilson & Graham, 1994, p. 12). They have never made up more than half of the population (Alotaibi, 1989, p. 36).

Most Saudis feel ambivalent about the Bedouin. The nomads are envisioned as simplistic, dirty, and crafty—in general, uncivilized. They are both ridiculed and feared. Yet they are admired for their virtues of generosity, boldness, and courage. Bedouin are idealized, much as knights and cowboys are in other places. But no matter how far Saudis are removed from the desert, the Bedouin ethos is the bedrock of their culture.

Silver Bedouin jewelry is one of the few art forms of the desert dwellers, made all the more beautiful by their spartan surroundings. But it is more than adornment; it is also a woman's personal wealth. Usually, a lady acquires her first jewelry as part of her dowry. Later on, family savings are invested in either jewelry or livestock. The designs are similar from one woman to the next, although the cost varies depending on the silver content. It is impossible for an amateur to determine the amount of silver in a particular piece. In this way, all women can own similar types and amounts of jewelry, regardless of financial status. A woman will choose to wear certain pieces every day, and then add other pieces for special occasions.

Traditional Bedouin jewelry is purchased from either settled artisans or itinerant silversmiths. Sometimes, a craftsman will live among a tribe, if it is a large one. His workmanship ranges from exquisite to crude, but all of it is eye-catching. Necklaces, bracelets, rings, belts, earrings, nose rings—whatever kinds of jewelry are worn by women everywhere are worn by Bedouins, too. The artisan incorporates multiple silver beads, chains, bells, and cylindrical pendants into his basic designs. Then, he adds filigree, heavy granulation, and gemstones. The stones can be amber, coral, carnelian, garnet, or turquoise; sometimes, they are only colored glass or plastic. Many pieces have tiny objects placed inside of bells and pendants that rattle melodiously with movement. Others have Koranic verses sealed permanently within cylindrical charm cases. Craftsmen add one item that is unique to Bedouin jewelry: coins.

Progress now threatens the popularity of Bedouin silver jewelry, just as it does the Bedouin lifestyle itself. Townspeople prefer gold jewelry, and as the Bedouin people leave the desert, they are also beginning to choose gold. In addition, many of the silversmiths are retiring, and younger people are not interested in pursuing the trade. Still, traditional silver jewelry can be studied as a metaphor for Saudi culture. Salient features of Bedouin jewelry are its bold form, handcrafted appearance, traditional design, and female ownership.

Bold Form

To an outsider, Bedouin silver jewelry is overwhelmingly ostentatious. Westerners would feel garish and conspicuous wearing the favorite Bedouin styles—multiple chains, pendants, bells, and coins, decorated with knobs of thick granulation and strands of filigree, and inlaid with colored stones, all of which are in the same piece! One, called a *kaff* (glove), has a ring for each finger, a section for the back of the hand, and a bracelet, all connected with chains and bells. Sometimes, a piece will have only one type of decoration, such as a ring with just filigree, but it will be used very liberally for an exotic effect.

Likewise, the Saudi personality is lavish, too. The Saudis' generosity is legendary. When entertaining, they overwhelm the guests with abundance. Saudis are proud to serve two or three times the required amount of food, and they insist that guests consume preferably more than their fill. The host typically does not eat along with his guests. He walks around checking on everyone's intake, urging them on and plying them with additional courses.

Good personal relationships are valued professionally and individually. Saudis will do almost anything for even a casual friend. They like to be helpful and endeavor to fulfill expectations. But an oral promise has its own value as a generous response, even if action does not follow. Results can be a separate thing altogether. For themselves, they do not hesitate to ask for special favors, for rules to be bent, or to be treated as special cases (Nydell, 1987, p. 17).

Just as the silver jewelry of the Bedouin imbues an aura of opulence on the owner, the Arabic language surrounds Saudis with its mystique of extravagance and vitality. Saudi Arabia is the birthplace of Arabic, and Saudis are secure in the belief that their language is superior to all others (Khalid, 1979, p. 130). Arabic has phonetic beauty, rich synonyms, rhythmic cadences, and majesty. The structure of the language encourages repetition and exaggeration. But thoughts themselves are often vague, and sometimes, only general meanings are inferred. The language overemphasizes the significance of words as such, and underemphasizes their meaning. This unbounded medium has far-reaching effects.

In the first place, eloquence and verbosity are equated with knowledge. Like the jewelry with low silver content, an effective speaker can appear prudent and rational by using only his verbal skills. Poets are held in high esteem, and they frequently function to mesmerize and motivate audiences to action. Advanced education and sophistication do not reduce an Arab's susceptibility to a good sermon or a political harangue. The grace and fluency of the words count more than the logic and veracity of the argument (Khalid, 1979, p. 131). Therefore, oral testimony is considered superior to circumstantial evidence, businessmen often get bogged down in language as they trail off from the main point, and students are better at memorizing coursework than in using it.

Bedouin jewelry is bold in design, but the individual components of each piece are often flamboyant as well. Perhaps this is related to the Saudis' characteristic generosity and feeling of superiority. More must be better. Or, possibly, it is proxemics, which Edward T. Hall (1966) describes as "man's use of space as a specialized elaboration of culture" (p. 1). Certainly, they love ample space in their homes. Ideally, ceilings should be high and views unobstructed. A sitting room may have 25 chairs arranged around the edges, with what seems like a cavernous speaking distance between them. But in public, Saudis do not mind being crowded.

In fact, Hall (1966) concluded that Saudis do not have any sense at all of privacy in a public place. They find it difficult to understand that privacy can exist while being surrounded by other people. No zone of privacy surrounds Saudis in public. Consequently, they are not bothered by the jostling and noise of public places in the Middle East. Lack of public privacy zones explains their aggressive behavior at accidents, where Saudis surround the scene, yell advice, and shake their fists—even if they did not witness the incident. It is not unusual for them to join haggling sessions they happen to come across. They nonchalantly cut off other drivers, perhaps because no one has a right to claim the public space into which he is about to travel.

Rarely do these situations lead to physical confrontation. Actual violence is almost unheard of here. Likewise, as a country, Saudi Arabia does not invade enemy territory, although it often engages in strong rhetoric. The fact is, they are premier mediators. Saudis aim for consensus, although their initial position may be extreme. They willingly make concessions and expect others to reciprocate (Adler, 1997, p. 180).

So, the idea that someone could have privacy in a public space confuses Saudis. There is not much of a concept of personal privacy, either. The Arabic word closest to "privacy" means loneliness. Saudis feel that friends should see each other often, and there is no compunction against dropping in unannounced. Greetings are effusive and extensive: "Praise be to Allah," "Welcome to you," "Hello, friend." Common inquiries center on the state of one's health or the cost of a recent purchase, but never on the female family members. Saudis are quick and generous with praise for others, and they like to highlight their own accomplishments as well (Samovar & Porter, 1994, p. 290).

Geert Hofstede (1991) concluded that Arab countries scored 53 out of 100 on the masculinity scale, giving them a rank of 23 out of 53. This average score might seem surprising, but feminine societies stress solidarity, emotional displays, relationships among people, and resolution of conflicts by compromise. Masculine cultures stress achievement, competition, and resolution of conflicts by violence. Their culture incorporates several of Hofstede's feminine characteristics.

Handcrafted Appearance

The second feature of Bedouin jewelry is its handcrafted appearance. Whereas some of the jewelry shows intricate and precise workmanship, other pieces are crude and casually made. This does not diminish or detract from it, however. Both kinds are considered legitimate, just as the Saudi considers the

Bedouin to be the embodiment of deep cultural values and desert riffraff at the same time. Cursory examination of the jewelry leaves no doubt that both types are handmade: Bells are often mismatched, pendants have irregular shapes, stones are slightly jagged, granulation is lumpy and uneven, fasteners are often simple hemp strings, and cheap cloth backings are attached to prevent the wearer from burning her skin. These raw aspects of the jewelry mirror the harshness of desert life.

Saudis believe in fate, that there is not much control over one's life. Bedouin jewelry reflects this acceptance in several ways. The jewelry itself represents an adaptation to life in the desert. The cloth that protects from the hot sun, the gemstones that are found locally, and the coins from the trade caravans and pilgrimage routes all demonstrate improvisation using what is at hand.

Saudis have traditionally felt "Subjugated to Nature," as defined by Kluckholn and Strodtbeck (1961, p. 13), living at the whims of their natural environment (and Allah). Fate decreed that they accept these natural forces, but economic advancement has meant leaping ahead to "Mastery over Nature." Now, desalinization plants process drinking water, irrigation systems water crops, and drilling equipment extracts oil and natural gas. Creeping sand dunes are still a problem. Saudis are becoming expert at mastering nature, but their mind-set is still fatalistic.

"Being" is more important than "doing" in Saudi culture. Adler (1997) defines a Being orientation as people, events, and ideas flowing spontaneously within the moment. The future is not nearly as important as the past and the present; present gratification is not delayed for future gain. One could say that they live for today. Fate and Allah are in charge of the future.

Edward T. Hall (1983) suggests that time is not fixed or segmented for polychronic people. Time is considered loose and fluid rather than compartmentalized. Therefore, occasions do not have definite beginnings and endings, and schedules are not as important as people. Saudis are polychronic and are irreverent about time boundaries. Consequently, guests may be kept waiting, deadlines are often missed, and appointments are broken. Polychronic people are able to carry on many activities simultaneously. For example, several customers may be helped at the same time, or different business negotiations might be managed at once in the same office. This behavior exemplifies the Being orientation.

Traditional Design

The Bedouin favor traditional styles of jewelry that are decorative and valuable. Styles worn today are the same ones that ancients wore, and they are always silver. New and unusual designs are seldom crafted. Individualism and creativity are discouraged in both Bedouin silversmithing and Saudi culture. This country ranks 26th of 53 nations on Hofstede's (1991) scale for individualism, which places it on the collectivist side of the spectrum. Collectivism is having a "we" consciousness, belonging to a cohesive in-group from birth onward, and taking the group's opinions as one's own. Private opinions and individual achievement are not valued highly in this setting.

One of the strongest manifestations of Saudi collectivism is the family. The extended family is the norm, although with new prosperity, more nuclear families are living alone. But even then, other members are either close by or in the same walled compound—the Bedouin camp replicated in modern times. These families collectively form clans, tribes, and the nation of Saudi Arabia. Like a piece of Bedouin jewelry that has several different components, the country has distinct segments as well.

For Saudis, family is paramount. It determines how they think, whom they marry, and where they work. Familial involvement is not viewed as interference but, rather, is welcomed as support. Loyalty to one's family takes precedence over work or friends, and it is rewarded with protection by the group. In the workplace, relatives receive preferential consideration in hiring and promotion opportunities. Families never leave a member in need. There are no day care centers or nursing homes. The oldest male member is honored as head of the family. Children are reared not only by their own parents, but also by all adults in the family. In fact, even friends will feed, care for, and discipline others' children. This results in a remarkably homogeneous upbringing for the country's youth. Like the desert nomads, people with this background cannot live alone comfortably. To be separated from the family is the ultimate punishment.

Honor and shame figure very largely in modern Saudi culture, just as they did in camel-raiding days. When a person's honor is tarnished, he feels shame and loses face. So does his family, which, by association, is also shamed. Members of collectivist cultures place importance on fitting in harmoniously and saving face. Honor can be lost through stinginess, poor treatment of the old and weak, fathering only daughters, being passed over for special favors, yielding in traffic, and immoral sexual conduct of female family members.

Understanding the importance of honor and shame in Saudi culture provides insight to certain behaviors. Mackey (1987) maintains that shame is a factor in Saudi generosity. She even argues that hospitality is provided to add to the *giver's* reputation, not necessarily to benefit the recipient (Mackey, 1987, p. 116). Fear of making a mistake and suffering the resulting shame may explain excessive delays in the business world. Many Saudis drink or gamble when outside of their country, even though these acts are forbidden by Islam. In fact, Westerners flying into Saudi Arabia are often surprised by the Clark Kent-Superman behavior of returning Saudis, who quickly take off makeup and don traditional Arab clothes before departing from the airplane. Perhaps Saudis feel that honor is not lost if no one is there to bestow shame. It could be that Saudis rarely resort to violence because they feel that the worst harm comes from the shame of grievous verbal insults.

Another cohesive force, besides family and honor, is marriage. The marriage model is the same for modern Saudis as for the nomads. Partners are chosen by elder family members. Marriage is such a momentous undertaking that young people welcome the group's opinion. Although it is rarely invoked, both the man and the woman have the right of refusal and can ask for another choice when selecting a mate. Marriage to first or second cousins is common. The benefits of keeping money and people in the family supersede any genetic concerns. Most marriages take place before age 20, and the new couple usually lives with the husband's family (Mackey, 1987, p. 150). However, larger dowries and college educations are pushing this age higher. New marriages are not based on romantic expectations, but on a desire for companionship, children, and, later, love. Although Muslims may have up to four wives, most men have only one at a time. An old proverb states, "A man between two women is like a lamb between two wolves" (Peters, 1980, p. 24).

Religion is like the hemp that draws all the parts of a Bedouin necklace together. All Saudis are Muslim. The king is not only their political leader, but their religious leader as well, and the Koran is the framework for running the country. Piety is honorable for a Saudi, and religion is not separated from daily life. Fatalism is exemplified by the frequent use of the qualifier *inshallah,* or God willing. A Muslim's greatest joy comes from performing the *huj,* or pilgrimage to Mecca. The charm cases incorporated into silver jewelry contain verses that praise Allah and ask for daily protection. Permeating the cohesion of family, honor, and marriage are the inviolate religious beliefs of Saudi Muslims.

Saudi Arabia ranks seventh out of 53 nations on power distance (Hofstede, 1991), which is the extent to which the less powerful citizens accept that power is distributed unequally. It is also a high-context culture, which means that only a small amount of information must be stated explicitly in order for understanding to occur, because so much information is implicit. In short, Saudi Arabs adhere to many written and unwritten rules, tolerate hierarchies, follow formalities, practice obedience, and encourage conformity.

Female Ownership

Custom and tradition play prime roles in the acquiring and wearing of Bedouin jewelry. What is striking is that it is wholly female. Not many other joys of Saudi culture belong entirely to women. Their reasons for wearing adornment are universal: vanity, superstition, sentiment, and pleasure. Ownership bestows honor on her as a woman of property, as well as guarantees her the security of having negotiable assets. Her wealth also adds beauty to an austere desert life.

Like the serendipitous nature of Bedouin jewelry, the role of Saudi women contains surprises, too. The world disdains the limitations under which Saudi women live, but perhaps outsiders are not qualified to pass judgment. What do Saudi women themselves think?

Saudi females do not necessarily see themselves as repressed. They think of themselves as protected and are frequently shocked at the crimes, such as rape and physical beatings, that their Western female counterparts suffer. Neither men nor women want to subject females to the stress, temptations, and indignities of the outside world. Most women feel satisfied that the present system provides them with security and respect, and they pity the rest of the world's women. Besides, even though males head the family, women have enormous influence inside their own homes. And through their extended family, they have wonderful support systems. Their husbands do not receive the same deference in private that they do in public. As elsewhere in Saudi life, there is much discussion between a husband and wife when they have a difference of opinion. This, then, has been the world of Saudi females for centuries.

Those old mollusks and brachiopods and plankton are now wreaking havoc. The long black abaya and veil, the separate entrances for men and women, the inability to use university educations, and the prohibitions against driving soon might seem a little less protective and a lot more restrictive than they once did. The possibilities for change are daunting, although it has occurred in other Arab countries. Some Saudi women have already started pressing for greater personal and social freedom, while at the same time realizing what they will be losing. Like the flamboyant desert jewelry that has adorned Bedouin women for centuries, the traditional life of Saudi women will slowly lose its luster.

Saudi Arabian culture is rooted deep in the desert, where the Bedouin people developed an incredible ability to survive under extreme conditions. Most Saudis feel they are of this desert, even if they have no Bedouin ancestry. For hundreds of years, Saudi values and beliefs were safe, sheltered from the outside world. For hundreds of years, Bedouin women proudly wore their distinctive jewelry, with its bold form, handcrafted appearance, traditional design, and female ownership. By using Bedouin jewelry, we can create a metaphor for modern Saudi Arabian culture. The perception of the jewelry has undergone radical change in recent years. There may soon come a time when the country's values and culture are challenged at their cores as well.

CHAPTER 6

The Turkish Coffeehouse

Turkey is a remarkable land of contrasts that joins the continents of Asia and Europe. It has elements of old and new, Islam and Christianity, mountains and plains, modern cities and rural villages. Often referred to as the cradle of civilization, Turkey is filled with archaeological remnants of the ancient Greeks and Romans, along with treasures of the sultans and caliphs of the Ottoman dynasty. Perhaps most interesting of all are the people of Turkey, rich in emotions, traditions, and hospitality. Turkish origins can be traced to the Mongols, Slavs, Greeks, Kurds, Armenians, and Arabs. Like the Thais, the Turks have never been conquered or colonized by other peoples. This distinction, along with a geographic boundary straddling the two continents of Europe and Asia, makes Turkey unique. Turkish culture today is a marriage of Turkish traditions and Western ideologies.

Turkey is a mountainous peninsula slightly larger than the size of Texas that shares borders with Bulgaria, Greece, Iran, Iraq, and Syria. Considered a strategic location because of its control of the straits linking the Black and Aegean Seas, Turkey is the only NATO country other than Norway to border the states of the former Soviet Union. The western portion of Turkey, Thrace, is located in Eastern Europe, whereas the larger eastern section, Anatolia, is part of Asia. Of 61 million people, 85% are Turkish and 12% Kurdish, and its population is the youngest in Europe, with 73% below 35 years of age. More than 10 million agricultural workers endure hot summers and cold Turkish winters. Literacy estimates at more than 83% are higher than ever, and the average life expectancy is 70 years of age. Unlike other Islamic societies, the Republic of Turkey was established in 1923 as a secular, democratic nation. There is, however, a small but growing minority that would like to see Turkey become a theocratic nation once again. The Turks are proud of both their achievements as a modern state and their rich heritage.

An appropriate metaphor for understanding Turkish culture is the coffeehouse, a part of everyday life in Turkey. What the Turkish coffeehouse represents is quite different from its counterparts in other countries. An emphasis on both Islam and secularity is the first of four characteristics of the coffeehouse that mirror Turkish culture. Coffeehouses also provide an important forum for recreation, communication, and community integration. Moreover, the customers who frequent coffeehouses reflect a male-dominated culture. Finally, the Turkish coffeehouse found in villages and towns is modest in comparison to exotic taverns, distinguished pubs, and chic cafés that are found in the larger cities.

Before we can understand how these four characteristics of the coffee-house reflect Turkish culture, we need to know something about the unique history of Turkey. Ancient Anatolian civilization dates back to 6500 B.C. As early as 1900 B.C., the Hittites occupied Turkey. Seven hundred years later, the Phrygians and Lydians invaded the land. These early Anatolian groups ruled until the Persian Empire took hold in the sixth century B.C. Then, the Greek-Hellenistic rule emerged, followed by the Romans in 100 B.C. Influences of each succeeding group left their mark on the people by contributing customs, language, and trade practices.

In the year 330, Constantine the Great named Constantinople the capital of the Byzantine Empire. Arabs relocated westward, and by 700, the empire included Anatolia, Greece, Syria, Egypt, Sicily, the Balkans, most of Italy, and some areas of northern Africa. Turkish tribes began to migrate from central Asia to Anatolia in the 11th century. The Oguz Turks, who embraced the new religion of Islam, occupied a vast part of Anatolia during the eleventh century. After their setback in the Crusades, Turkish *gazi*s, or Islamic warriors, fought against the Byzantine Empire and initiated the construction of the Ottoman dynasty. The Ottomans conquered the region and expanded their reign to the Christian Balkans. In 1453, the Ottomans conquered Constantinople, which was virtually the last stronghold under Byzantine rule. Constantinople, which is known today as Istanbul, was then rebuilt as the capital of the Ottoman Empire and the center of Sunni Islam.

The Ottoman Empire reached its peak of wealth and power under the rule of Suleyman the Magnificent in the 1500s. He controlled all or part of states including present-day Turkey, Iran, Iraq, Egypt, Israel, Syria, Kuwait, Jordan, Saudi Arabia, Albania, Algeria, Libya, Tunisia, Greece, Bulgaria, Sudan, Romania, Hungary, Yugoslavia, Czechoslovakia, Ethiopia, Somalia, and the Soviet Union. His vast empire covered three continents and was noted for its system of justice and expansion of the arts, literature, architecture, and craftwork. For almost six centuries, the Turks lived in or near Europe and interacted with Europeans, assimilating parts of European culture over time. Sultan Suleyman's death in 1556 marked the end of a wonderfully creative era. The empire began its decline with the loss of Hungary and the Crimea in the 1700s. In the next century, the Ottomans lost control of Egypt and most of the Balkans, and this was followed by the loss of Serbia, Romania, Cyprus, Algeria, and Tunisia.

In 1908, the Young Turks attempted to restore power to the empire. Instability in the region brought about drastic territorial changes and reduced the Ottoman holdings even further. The shrunken empire entered World War I on the side of the Central Powers in 1914. By the end of the war, the Arab provinces were lost, and a Nationalist movement began. These events led to both the proclamation of a new nation and additional contributions to Turkish culture.

In 1923, the Treaty of Lausanne established the Republic of Turkey as we recognize it today. Mustafa Kemal, also known as Atatürk, renounced all prior conquests and introduced widespread reforms to guide the country. Atatürk means, literally, "father of the Turks." His deliberate reforms transformed the diverse empire into a nation while shaping daily lifestyles for every Turkish citizen. Along with the internal modernization of the country, the Republic turned toward Western principles and conventions. Turkey became a member of NATO in 1952 and an associate member of the Common Market in 1963.

Turkish coffee was first introduced during the Ottoman Empire. In the 15th century, merchants from the Far East traveled along the Silk Road to trade their exotic spices and other wares in European markets. In an effort to encourage trade and offer hospitality, hostels for travelers called caravansaries were built. As they passed through ancient Turkey, the merchants bartered along the way and offered their products in exchange for hospitality. According to the strictest rule of the Koran, the sultans forbade the drinking of coffee because it is a drug. In spite of the restriction, coffee drinking became so popular that the palace rescinded the rule and allowed its consumption. Today, Turkish coffee is as popular as ever.

Islam and Secularity

One of Atatürk's most important reforms was the adoption of a constitution that encouraged secularism. Although an overwhelming number of Turkish citizens are Muslims (about 96%), other religions such as Greek Orthodoxy and Judaism are tolerated in Turkish society. During the rule of the Ottoman

Empire, religion, as well as culture, was totally integrated with government, and Islamic world power was concentrated in Turkey. Atatürk and his followers felt strongly that adherence to the caliphate was an obstacle to the country's attempts to Westernize. Major changes resulting from secularism included a shift from Islamic to European legal codes, closing of religious schools and lodges, and recognition of the Western calendar rather than a religious one. Despite these sweeping changes, Islam still thrived, and in the 1950s, religious education was reintroduced. Today, the Turkish government still oversees a system in which children are exposed to a measure of religion in schools, and the clergy receive salaries from the government.

The distinction between Turkey and the other Islamic nations is noteworthy. Unlike other Islamic countries, Turkey is a secular nation. Governments, schools, and businesses are operated independent of religious beliefs. Even traditional clothing, such as veils for women and fezzes for men, was abandoned in the shift from Islam to secularity. Consequently, Islam does not affect daily Turkish life as much as it would in an Arab nation. Religious power over Turkish institutions is nonexistent, and this fact reflects a preference for association with other Western cultures.

However, as noted above, a small but growing political movement has evolved around the issue of making Turkey a theocracy comparable to that found in Iran and other Arab nations. Although Turkey has a Western-style system of government in which there are free elections, the military is extremely influential and will intervene if a political party seems to be too theocratic in orientation. In 1998, the Supreme Court, prodded by the military, forbade the operation of the Islamic Welfare Party. However, the Islamic politicians have regrouped under a new but similar political party, the Virtue Party. (Political parties frequently have colorful names in Turkey, such as the Motherland Party.) Prosperity has witnessed the growth of a prosperous middle class, which has become a new center of power and influence, and it staged the first modern protest against military and political corruption in 1997. Hence, there are three major centers of power and influence in Turkey: the military, the middle class, and the Islamic Movement (Pope, 1997a).

Although Islam is separate from state matters, its traditional practices, such as that of women wearing headscarves in public, has generated controversy. In 1999, Merve Kavakci, a Texas-educated politician in the Virtue Party, created an uproar by appearing in parliament in a headscarf. Almost immediately, an appeal was filed with the Supreme Court to outlaw the Virtue Party for this and other assumed infractions. Furthermore, Mustafa Karaduman has become a very successful businessman by establishing an Islamic-style clothing chain for women. One of his creations is the *nesrin,* which is an ankle-length skirt with a long jersey to which a hood is attached. Conservative Islamic women can easily take off the hood in places such as Parliament, where they are banned (Zaman, 1999).

The growing importance of the middle class and international business, however, has challenged traditional fashions. Western-style clothes are common. More tellingly, the highly popular male mustache is now more reflective of social class and political and religious leanings than national identification. Whereas 77% of Turkish men had mustaches in 1993, the percentage was still only 77% in 1997, and it is declining, especially in large firms. But mustaches still reflect ideological differences between leftist (bushy) and rightist (drooping to the chin). Beards, found on 19% of the men, can be short and trendy, Marxist, long and religious, or clipped and politically Islamic (Pope, 1997b).

Islam is also evident in the five times for prayer spread throughout every day. Turkish Muslims do not necessarily converge on the mosque when the call to prayer is sounded the way that Catholics in such nations as Poland and Ireland flock to church for Sunday mass at specified times. Islam is a religion for individuals to communicate directly to God, without a need for intermediary spokesmen. Consequently, those who pray at mosques do not need to coordinate their visits, although many arrange their visits to coincide with the five daily prayer periods. Afterwards, Turks may head to the coffeehouse for refreshments and socializing.

Five well-known pillars embody the essence of Islam. The first is acceptance of the creed, "There is no God but Allah and Muhammad is his prophet." The second pillar comes from the Koran, or Holy Book, and involves keeping life in its proper perspective. This can be done through prayer, five times a day, to submit one's self to God's will. Third is the observance of the holiday of Ramadan by fasting during daylight hours for 1 month as determined by the lunar calendar, and fourth is giving to charity. Fasting underscores man's dependence on God, teaches self-discipline, sensitizes compassion, and forces one to think. The final pillar is a once-in-a-lifetime pilgrimage to Mecca for those who are able. It is understood that those who reach the holy city where God revealed Himself have demonstrated their devotion to Him.

In Turkish towns, the two most important places for social gathering, the mosque and the coffeehouse, are located in the town square. The coffeehouse is often adjacent to the village mosque and may even provide a small operating fund or rent for the general upkeep of the mosque. Throughout the world, inhabitants of small towns tend to be more conservative than do city residents, and Turkey is no exception. As a result, the Turkish townspeople tend to follow their faith more strictly than do their urban counterparts. Also, eastern and central Turkey are more religious than western Turkey, in part because of the diversity of the people living in the western parts. Although there has been a resurgence of religious practices since the 1950s, Islamic fanaticism remains a minor but vocal influence today, and even moderate Muslims have tried to revive some traditions that were eliminated with the arrival of a secular nation.

In addition to rent, many of these coffeehouses occasionally collect donations from patrons to pay for the mosque's water and cleaning. As noted above, Muslims are called to prayer five times each day, although the frequency of prayer for contemporary Muslims is a function of both the level of piety and the availability of time. Thus, a visit to the coffeehouse can also be considered a ritual, ironically linked with the daily ritual of prayer. Furthermore, cleanliness is an important related Islamic value, and the owner of a coffeehouse typically squirts a bottle of water on the floor from time to time to keep the dust from rising. Even some of the original popularity of coffeehouses was due to the Islamic prohibition of alcohol and the use of coffee as a substitute and acceptable beverage.

There are many other Turkish cultural values and beliefs derived from the Islamic faith, some of which are not directly related to the operations of the coffeehouse. In particular, Muslims believe that the future will be better than the past. The village parents who struggle to support their children may rely on this optimism for decades. Also, the ideas that the soul lives forever and that every man is responsible for his actions are also important considerations for Muslims in their acceptance of their lot in life.

The Ottoman Empire governed the people by *seriat,* or Islamic law. Turks also adhered to moral and social rules, such as respect for one's father, on a daily basis. These ideas persist in modern Turkey. Unlike in purely theocratic Islamic nations, however, Turkish legal decisions are not judged by one code alone. Likewise, civil marriage ceremonies must be conducted, irrespective of religious ones, to obtain recognition under Turkish law. Civil code based on European models was introduced in 1926. Still, basic customs from the Ottoman days, just like the survival of the coffeehouse, have been carried over into modern Turkish society. Some Turks, such as Mustafa Karaduman (see above), still refuse to accept interest accrued from savings accounts because such profits are prohibited in the Koran. Widely used Turkish phrases derived from Islam include *Salaam,* a friendly greeting that literally means, "Peace be upon you," and *Masallah,* which means, "God protect you from harm." Both phrases are used in everyday language, in much the same way that Americans respond with "God bless you" when someone sneezes. Other examples include abstinence from or moderation in drinking alcohol, fulfilling oral promises, and using the catchall phrase, *Bismillahir-rahman-irrahim.* This translates to "I am starting this in the name of merciful Allah" and is said when starting a task, be it a journey, a test, a wedding, or a meal.

Among Turkish traditions, the household extends beyond the nuclear family, and individuals are loyal to the entire family or kinship group. Women especially are expected to offer hospitality to all guests. If a visitor knocks on the door before or during mealtime, he is almost always invited to join the family in the dining room or at the kitchen table. It is considered common decency to offer the visitor food and drink, and a hearty appetite is a compliment for a Turkish host or hostess. Sitting with crossed legs can be disrespectful to Turkish elders. As in mosques, Turkish guests offer to remove their shoes as a gesture of cleanliness upon entering someone's home. Marriage decisions are influenced by families in rural areas, and in some instances, dating is not permitted. One should keep in mind that these are merely generalizations about Turkish customs and do not apply to all Turkish citizens. Turkish compassion and hospitality come from the ethical aspects of the Islamic faith, as do racial equality and religious tolerance. Islam acknowledges the legitimacy of other Semitic religions that preceded it, but recognizes both Judaism and Christianity as incomplete. Finally, part of the greatness of the Ottoman dynasty is attributable to Islam, which brought together different peoples and united them through spiritual means.

The concept that every event in an individual's life is predetermined has its roots in the religion of Islam. Like many other religions, Islam attributes circumstances beyond one's control to a supreme being. Muslims believe that a person will act according to his or her own decisions under a given set of circumstances. For example, much of the younger population is migrating toward cities to obtain jobs and better schooling. This trend does not reflect anyone's fate in particular, but the individual who decides to change his or her lifestyle by leaving the village subjects himself or herself to kismet, or chance. In other words, God meant for that person to move on and start a new way of life. If the person eventually relocates back to his or her own village, then that, too, is kismet. This belief allows an individual's shortcomings to be accepted more easily.

The Turkish orientation toward time goes hand in hand with the belief in destiny. It is easy to say that most Turks are not very conscious of time, and one of the attractions of the coffeehouse is that customers can linger there if they so choose. Hosts and hostesses are concerned if their guests do not arrive promptly at the time given for an invitation to a social event, but they are very understanding. Delays at airports and train stations are not a cause for alarm. "Polychronism" best describes the Turkish ability to concentrate on different things simultaneously, whether at work, at home, or in the coffeehouse. Although schedules and appointments are important, especially in Western-oriented firms, people and relationships are also valued. To the polychronic Turks, time is intangible and supports the development and maintenance of long-term relationships. Elements of the past, present, and future tend to merge, and they permeate Turkish values and norms.

If a Turk were asked to ponder the ideal position of his country in international dealings, he would probably refer to the halcyon days of the Ottoman Empire. The historic aspect of the country is crucial to understanding the Turkish mind-set, and a comparison of today and yesterday is absolute. Conversely, Turks place much emphasis on what future generations will accomplish. This explains why it is important that children are given optimal educational opportunities irrespective of costs and degree of parental sacrifice. Personal savings take the form of real estate or gold reserve investments. Kismet and time orientation are inextricably linked together in Turkish culture.

Understanding the idea of destiny helps us to comprehend why time is relatively unimportant. In the United States, if a business project falls behind schedule, a firm risks embarrassment and scrutiny by consumers, investors, shareholders, and the government. In Turkey, the same type of delay is attributed to God's will and is forgiven more easily. Thus, the phrase *Inshallah*, "if it is God's will," is heard quite often. A famous Turkish joke about a fellow named Hodja illustrates the degree of time and urgency in daily business:

> One day, a fellow named Hodja brought some material to a tailor and requested that he measure him and make a shirt from the material as soon as possible. The tailor measured him and said, "I am very busy, but your shirt will be ready on Friday, *Inshallah*." Hodja returned on Friday, but the tailor apologized that the shirt was not ready and said, "Come back Monday and, *Inshallah*, it will be ready." On Monday, Hodja went back to the tailor only to find out that the shirt was still not finished, and he was told, "Try again Thursday, *Inshallah*, and I promise it will be ready." This time, Hodja wisely answered, "How long will it take if we leave *Inshallah* out of it?!"

Recreation, Communication, and Community Integration

Coffeehouses became popular during the 16th century. The coffeehouse has always been a source of information, especially when illiteracy rates were high. In those days, one person would read the newspaper to an eager audience. Throughout the reign of the Ottoman Empire, defense strategies were discussed and developed there. Coffeehouses had battery-operated radios before they were introduced in homes, and the same was true when television arrived. Today, a patron enjoys camaraderie when viewing a soccer match at the coffeehouse instead of watching it on his television set by himself at home, and this pattern fits the group-oriented lifestyle of the Turks.

Turkish men go to the modern-day coffeehouse to become part of a group. They feel very comfortable when surrounded by friends and family, and they prefer the stability of belonging to an organization to individualism. And, as an old Turkish proverb states, one cup of coffee is worth 40 years of friendship. According to Bisbee (1951),

The prime ingredients of the Turks' idea of fun and amusement seem to be relaxation, imagination, sociability and humor. Sitting is almost, if not quite, the most popular recreation of all. Turks sit at windows, in gardens, at coffeehouses . . . anywhere and everywhere they can see a pleasing view and relax in conversation. (p. 145)

In Turkey, there is a relationship between collectivism and accomplishing the goals of the group. In small villages, the coffeehouse is often the setting in which important village decisions are made. Prior debate of the issue also takes place at the coffeehouse. A custom, *imece,* describes a Turkish social gathering at which everyone pitches in to help a neighbor undertake a large task, such as building a new home. In many instances of *imece,* the initial request for assistance and plans for the event are proposed at the coffeehouse. Turks prefer to approach problems in a logical but personalized manner, and they will discuss practical solutions at length in the coffeehouse. In small Turkish towns, the mayor can frequently be found at his second, unofficial office, the coffeehouse. It is not uncommon to find community notices tacked onto a coffeehouse bulletin board. Typical examples are government announcements that crops will be sprayed with pesticides on a particular date, or that a public hearing to discuss a new water project will be held. Messages are left there for others who will eventually show up; it is the information center in which most communication takes place, including political discussions and gossip. Being a member of the coffeehouse is considered important, regardless of the topic under discussion.

Likewise, women have a need for affiliation; they get together at weekly coffees or teas at the homes of friends. The weekly coffee presents an opportunity to show some hospitality and become involved with others. Traditional Turkish hospitality extends to strangers, particularly in rural areas. The group itself is highly valued, and individual identity is determined on the basis of group membership. Conformity to group norms and traditions is expected; trust and reliance within the group is important (Dindi & Gazur, 1989, p. 17). In Geert Hofstede's (1991) 53-nation study of cultural values, it is not surprising that Turkey clusters with those nations emphasizing collectivism rather than individualism.

Even at work, collectivistic values are expressed in unusual ways. At McDonald's, the "Employee of the Month" is not selected for outstanding work. Rather, the selection is made on a rotational basis. Furthermore, because Turkey also clusters with high-power-distance nations in Hofstede's 53-nation study, there is little, if any, two-way discussion or participation with subordinates in many firms. However, Turkish managers link collectivism and power distance—and, by extension, a distinctive concept of employee participation—by telling the employees that they are an essential part of the organization, and that as long as loyalty is shown, they will not be fired, even if performance is substandard.

As might be expected in a collectivistic culture, communication tends to be high-context in nature. For example, if someone says, "It is very hot," you must assume that the person wants a ride in your car. This indirect form of communication is common, even among very close family members.

Family gatherings are very important, as are deep friendships. Turks are nostalgic when it comes to family traditions and special occasions. Just as a man can stop by the coffeehouse whenever he wants, so, too, it is not considered impolite to drop in at a friend's home without an invitation. This is true regardless of one's economic, social, or educational status. Fostering good relationships requires time, and Turks feel that such time is always well spent.

Coffeehouses open early in the day, and for many Turks, they are the place to stop in before beginning the day's work. In the late afternoon, workers stop in prior to going home to their families. After dinner, various men visit the coffeehouse to catch up on the latest news. In the summertime, customers sit outside, on sidewalks or patios, to escape the oppressive Turkish heat and catch an occasional cool breeze. In the winter, everyone gathers around the warmth of a stove or furnace in the coffeehouse. Just as the Italian piazza is the place in which to stroll to see others and be seen, the village coffeehouse provides a place for social gathering. As in bygone eras, the village coffeehouse remains a center for everyone, regardless of income, education, or social status.

A traffic accident illustrates what Hofstede, in his 53-country study, might call the "feministic" nature of the Turks. According to Hofstede, femininity expresses the extent to which societies value caring for others, quality of life, and people. Within moments of the accident, everyone who witnessed the collision, along with those who did not, is on the scene. No one present would dream of minding his or her own business. Each stranger then offers help, comments, and interpretations of the accident, and chaos results! If a vehicle breaks down at night, Turkish passersby generally do not hesitate to stop and offer assistance to the driver. To ignore someone in distress would be considered indecent. By contrast, many Americans would not dare to stop for fear of their own personal safety. In Turkish culture, involvement and interdependence are the ideal. Turks care about others, and they show their concern by stopping to help perfect strangers. People are important in Turkish culture, and most Turks will sympathize with those who are less fortunate. Above all, Turks pride themselves on hospitality and being helpful to strangers.

However, these customs are decreasing in importance in urban areas, particularly Istanbul, which are suffering from all of the problems that are associated with rapid migration from rural areas. As is the case elsewhere, residents of rural areas are drawn to the cities because of opportunities for work and diversity of experiences. Pockets of extreme poverty, many times in and around downtown areas, have arisen. Militant Islam, which was previously strongest in the rural areas, is on the increase in urban areas, at least in part because of such conditions.

Feministic values are also exhibited in the way Turks show interest in others through conversation. Whether sharing small talk at the coffeehouse or within the hospitality of one's home, the Turkish people tend to be curious by nature. Consequently, very little in one's life is a real secret. Communication is the essence of Turkish existence. When one Turkish stranger meets another, he typically asks where the first is from. What he is more interested in is who his parents are and where they are from. The next few minutes are spent quizzing the other person with questions like, "Oh, my brother-in-law's uncle is from there, do you know Ahmet?" or "Surely you must know Ali." "Turkish geography" is really a game played to discover to which clan the stranger belongs, as happens in other countries, such as Israel and Ireland. Thus, identifying relationships displays the collectivist orientation of the Turks, whereas the interest in others demonstrates the bias toward femininity.

A Male Domain

A Turkish coffeehouse is a place where men assemble throughout the day and throughout the year. Regardless of age, men gather at the coffeehouse to play backgammon, share gossip, or just enjoy company. Young boys accompany their fathers and play alongside the tables until they are old enough to join discussions. Old men sit on wooden chairs and sip coffee while reminiscing, offering words of wisdom, and solving the world's problems.

A visit to the Turkish coffeehouse is a favorite pastime for male Turks of all ages. In recent years, the city coffeehouse has decreased in popularity when compared to its counterpart in smaller towns and villages. One can draw a correlation between the prominence of coffeehouses and cultural values in cities versus rural areas. In the larger cities of Istanbul, Ankara, and Izmir, life is hectic, and people have little time to sit and chat. However, Turkey is still an agrarian society in large measure; 48% of the workforce is in agriculture. People working outside of industrialized areas are often limited by weather conditions and daylight. With extra time on his hands, a farmer may visit the coffeehouse, and it is a welcome diversion for a man out of work. Coffeehouses remain popular in rural areas, where Turkish traditions and male roles are strong. The popularity of the city coffeehouse has declined as a new generation places less emphasis on traditional values and a greater emphasis on earning a living. Within the city, the older citizens tend to be more devout and frequent the coffeehouse more than younger Turks, who often spend their free time on self-improvement. Turkish city dwellers today spend most of their leisure time on other activities, such as cinema, theater, and concerts, as alternatives to the coffeehouse. As cities become more cosmopolitan, urban coffeehouses are less likely to attract clientele in comparison with coffeehouses in less populated locales. The coffeehouse remains a cherished institution outside of the cities where lower- and middle-class customers enjoy good coffee and good conversation, and city dwellers recognize its historical importance and speak of it fondly even when they do not frequent it.

There is no question that Turkey has a male-dominated culture, and the nature of such domination is always present at the coffeehouse. Although women are welcome, the coffeehouse has always been considered a male domain. This is true of other public places in Turkey, even today. The Islamic origins of the population still influence the role of women. For example, most women pray at home rather than at the mosque.

Even in Western-oriented Istanbul, which accounts for about 40% of Turkey's gross national product, the separation of sexes is evident. Even during the day, there always seems to be eight men to every two women in public places, and at night, the number of females decreases significantly.

A long tradition of men as breadwinners, leaders of the family unit, and decision makers in local politics and matters of national concern exists in Turkey. As heads of the families, men in rural areas decide which crops will be planted and at which market crops will be sold. Village coffeehouses often become a market where brokers trade farm commodities. Within the clan structure, it is understood that sons will be in charge of the family and daughters will marry into their husband's family. As in other Western cultures, sons carry on their family name. Within the traditional family, a father's request is always obeyed, and Turkish fathers are especially protective of their daughters.

A Modest Environment

The simplicity of the coffeehouse itself is noteworthy. The furniture is basic, and the chairs are uncomfortable. A typical coffeehouse in a small village may consist of one small room, a kitchen, and several small wooden or aluminum tables and chairs. A smoky atmosphere from cigarettes or *nargile*, the traditional waterpipe, is unmistakable. Although each coffeehouse differs, the sounds are always familiar; steady chatter, heated discussion, and hearty laughter can be heard above the clatter of cups and saucers, and Turkish music comes from a radio. Likewise, the Turkish people are concerned more with substance than with form. The true draw of the coffeehouse is the opportunity for release and self-indulgence. The release is only temporary, allowing escape from the stress or monotony of the moment, and the indulgence reflects the element of Turkish culture that says, "experience life."

As noted earlier, Turkish life in the city is very different from that in the village. In the cities, neighborhood coffeehouses abound. However, the middle and upper classes tend to spend time at various elite establishments, such as bars or cafés, instead of being loyal to a particular coffeehouse. Apartment living is very popular in Turkish cities. Turks are less transient than Americans and tend to live in the same building for years, where they are surrounded by family and friends. Simply put, people are valued in Turkey. Respect for others is important; however, like other Mediterranean peoples, Turks have little fear of consequences for failing to respect laws. Along with liberal interpretations of traffic signals, patience is not a Turkish strong suit. A prime example is the early morning scene when workers try to catch a bus. It is "every man for himself" as people struggle on the downtown streets of Ankara to get on the crowded buses. In most other situations, however, Turks have considerable respect for the rights of others.

Coffeehouses are family-run establishments. It is often the owner's son who takes orders and delivers teas and coffees to the table. One should not expect to be served a meal there; however, patrons are more than welcome to bring in food. Many hungry patrons will first stop at a local carry-out for a freshly baked snack. *Simit,* a round, flat bread topped with sesame seeds, is a familiar sight at coffeehouses. As expected, a coffeehouse owner does not mind food being brought into the coffeehouse because he knows that the more food eaten, the more drinks will be ordered. Unlike at Turkish restaurants, a customer is welcome to remain at the coffeehouse as long as he wishes. The coffeehouse is not a high-profit enterprise. By the same token, it is rare that a coffeehouse folds. The reason is that coffeehouses provide an incredible service to the community as a meeting place and information center.

Turkish coffee is always made in a special way; first, the grains are ground into a fine powder. Next, water and sugar are blended with the powder, and, finally, the mixture is boiled over a flame. The three possible versions of Turkish coffee are *sade, orta,* and *sekerli,* which mean "no sugar," "some sugar," and "more sugar," respectively. At the coffeehouse, the waiter will call out the orders to the kitchen so that fresh pots can be made. When he returns, the waiter never seems to remember who ordered what. A running joke is that one day, Atatürk, who is greatly respected by the Turks, went to a village coffeehouse with his entourage. The waiter took everyone's order and brought the coffees to the table. Atatürk was amazed that the waiter had gotten the order correct and told him so. When asked by Atatürk how he remembered, the waiter responded, "Yours is the only order that counts!"

Life Outside the Coffeehouse

Many activities occur outside of the coffeehouse, and we need to understand them and the manner in which they reflect cultural values. For example, observance of Islam in Turkey today has led to popular misconceptions about the role of women. Since the adoption of this religion more than 1,000 years ago, conservative ideas, including the seclusion and submission of women to men as a form of protection for them, evolved. At one time, it was expected that women retreat to the harem out of deference to men. However, even in the harem, women had some degree of power in terms of training daughters and young sons in household management, arts and crafts, and religion. The harem was highly political; concubines were selected for sultans by their mothers, and royal marriages were arranged there in those days. In 1925, the wearing of veils by Turkish women was officially discouraged. In the following year, Atatürk, the founder and first president of modern Turkey, introduced civil marriage codes that abolished polygamy and established divorce and child custody rights for both men and women.

As in earlier times, Turkish women have always been subtly capable of influencing their husbands' way of thinking. In Turkey, women are brought up to show respect for their husbands, and they do not openly flaunt any power they may hold over their men. Turkish women rarely make firm denials of a husband's decision, yet they may quietly oppose decisions with which they are unhappy. In either case, the wife recognizes the needs of her husband's ego and is typically shrewd enough to offer small suggestions rather than demand compliance with her wishes. Many Turkish women possess an emotional inner strength and maturity that developed from the burdens of maintaining a stable family life under harsh economic conditions. This is particularly true for those who live in remote areas. In rural villages, women are responsible for meals, housework, and child care. Turkish kitchens are busy all day long as women prepare delicious meals of roasted lamb, rice *pilav*, or other specialties. Throughout Turkey, women take pride in a cooking style that intermingles Arabic, Greek, and European influences. An important development for women in the villages is that they have become responsible for working outside the home, too. The unemployment rate tends to be very high, and many men have difficulty finding work. Inflation as high as 60% and above also puts a strain on the availability of jobs. Lack of employment opportunities for men in small towns and villages has sustained the appeal of the coffeehouse. External employment is often a necessity for women, who will work outside of their homes on local farms and in factories, or will sell handmade items to support their families. Beautiful woven carpets, ceramic pottery, mosaics, and other items handcrafted by Turkish women are appreciated throughout the world. The women's determination in taking care of daily life affords them some measure of power over their husbands' behavior. Women who work in the fields cook, eat, clean, and even sing together. Urban wives who may be on a more equal educational footing with their husbands may also affect their behavior and decisions that can be as trivial as recommending what clothes a husband should wear or as monumental as deciding to risk a new business venture. Finally, career-oriented women reflect modern Turkish societal norms, which recognize joint decision making and cooperative patterns of husband-wife authority, along with traditional respect for the husband. It should be noted that families still supervise closely the activities of unmarried women, and strong attitudes prevail about the proper conduct for women.

Furthermore, respect for one's parents is absolute. In turn, a parent is expected to be concerned about his or her child's future. The extended Turkish family is proof of the respect afforded to elders. Grandparents, aunts, uncles, and cousins often live in or near the same dwellings as core family units. The notion of an old-age home is nonexistent. Likewise, hired baby-sitters are unusual because family members care for children. Parents are willing to stretch the family budget in order to provide a tutor or send a child to better schools. Most parents feel obligated to give their children a moral education as well. Children are a continuation of a family's reputation, and famous children are an even greater source of pride for doting parents.

Boys and girls are brought up similarly with a few exceptions. Prior to reaching 7 years of age, a boy is circumcised in a religious ceremony that symbolizes his ascent to manhood. Upon graduation from high school, there is a mandatory 18-month period of military service. Men who attend a university have the option of deferring their service until they reach 32 years of age. There is no compulsory service for women, although they are allowed to enlist for noncombatant positions if desired. Traditionally, the new bride became part of her husband's family only after she had produced an heir. Except in rare circumstances, this is no longer true. Today, Turkish daughters-in-law are accepted immediately into the family household. The family structure is important, and the divorce rate is relatively low. In Turkey, it is unusual for a person to live on his or her own, unless he or she is a dormitory student.

Another significant reform, the right to education for the masses, took place in 1924. Atatürk believed that education was an essential element of

Westernization. Today, education is seen as the legitimate discriminator for the social classes in Turkey. Elementary school is mandatory for all children. As in the United States, the school year begins in September and ends in June. In keeping with national policy, secularity is practiced. Although *laik,* or separation of church and state, is understood, school vacations coincide with the Islamic holidays Ramadan and Kurban. In addition to monitoring regular schools, the Turkish Ministry of Education also controls religious schools to limit their influence. For those schools that have limited resources, the school day is taught in half-day shifts. Wearing of uniforms is required for the young children. A dress code also requires neat grooming, such as conservative haircuts for boys and hair ties for girls with long hair. Children learn respect for teachers at an early age. In the classroom, students normally stand whenever a teacher enters the room. It is considered disrespectful to disagree with the teacher.

The curriculum includes math, science, history, Turkish language, art, music, physical education, and morals. After fifth grade, similar to what happens in Germany, children study for a placement exam that determines their future path of study. In larger towns and cities, tutors are often hired to complement formal school instruction. For those who score well, the next year is spent at a private secondary school to learn a second language, most often English, French, or German. The language study is followed by 2 years of preparation for high school. These students attend high school for 3 years, and upon graduation, those who wish to continue their studies at a university take a difficult entrance examination. Students who do not score as well on the placement exam attend a general secondary school followed by entry into a vocational or technical school to learn a trade. Those students interested in entering a university are also invited to take the entrance exam.

The competition for attending universities is very keen because of the limited number of universities in the country. Approximately one fifth of the 900,000 students who test are accepted into the universities annually. There is an obvious inequity in this system. Those who are privileged enough to have access to higher quality academic resources have a better opportunity for admission to a university. The selection process is highly competitive; within the 29 universities in Turkey, many disciplines have a limited number of student spaces available. Thus, a university student may aspire to a profession for which he or she is effectively barred, unless he or she is able to study that profession abroad. While selection to an institution is competitive, interaction among students is cooperative. It is common practice for students to work together on homework and studying. Students tend to take studying seriously and to appreciate their learning opportunities.

Furthermore, humor is an important mechanism in Turkish culture and is a good way to make friends and maintain friendships, both in the coffeehouse and outside of it. Turkish humor is distinctive; Turks do not mind making fun of themselves. When things become too serious, a joke is welcomed to strike a balance and provide relief. The coffeehouse itself provides a similar relief from life's predicaments. Whether in political satire, television shows, or the coffeehouse, humor is used frequently. For example, Turkish coffee is served in a small cup and has a thick, almost muddy, consistency; it is usually served with a glass of water. A popular joke involves differentiating between a Turk and a foreigner. The difference? A Turk drinks the water first, to clean his palate; the foreigner takes the water after the coffee, to wash it down!

In Turkey, humor takes on many forms. Weekly comedy magazines have a wide readership, particularly among university students. Stories that center around a former prime minister named Akbulut are popular; it seems that this gentleman was underqualified for the job, and he is used as the butt of many good-natured jokes unrelated to politics. The Laz of northern Turkey are also figures in jokes throughout Turkey. Anecdotes about this minority from the coastal region by the Black Sea evoke laughs even in that area. Laughter provides recreation and reminds Turkish citizens that they should stay humble.

Humor is taught early on, and folk heroes like Nasreddin Hodja are loved by children and grown-ups alike. As a boy, Hodja always had something clever and humorous to say in every situation. Hodja stories are well known and relate to everyday life in Turkey. A favorite story goes as follows:

> Hodja was walking down the street when he noticed something glittering in the gutter. He ran over to pick it up and noticed it was a small metal mirror. He looked in it and said to himself, "No wonder they threw this thing away. I wouldn't keep something as ugly as this either!"

What makes Hodja special is that he always expresses a note of encouragement and tries to live a happy life of honesty and simplicity. His jokes run the gamut from religion to mothers-in-law to sultans and even to his own hearty appetite. Not only are his jokes retold at the coffeehouse, they often begin with "One day, when Hodja was at the coffeehouse . . ." The proof of this character's popularity is that most people, if not all, in Turkey like to claim that Hodja was born in his or her village!

Humor is an effective communication technique and can even serve as a way to avoid confrontation and conflict. Turks are generally quite modest about their accomplishments. This makes sense, because besides being impolite, self-boasting would tend to separate an individual from his or her group. Instead, it is perfectly acceptable for good friends or family members to brag about others. Modesty complements the Turkish values of tactfulness and diplomacy. Turks prefer to avoid confrontation and to handle disputes indirectly whenever possible. Being direct is considered rude and insulting; directness goes against the respect Turks feel for other people (Dindi & Gazur, 1989, p. 19). Respect for authority is regarded very highly, and it is unconditional in many instances. In his 53-nation study, Geert Hofstede (1991) showed that uncertainty avoidance epitomizes Turkish culture. For example, the strong need for consensus, the undesirability of conflict and competition, and the strong belief in experts and their expertise are understandable when examining the face-saving nature of Turkish culture.

Turkey faces considerable challenges in the very near future. High unemployment and inflation have left the economy unstable, and past government corruption and military coups cast doubt over true Turkish democracy. The question of Kurdish independence still needs to be addressed for the 7 million Kurds who live in Turkey. Although the Turks prefer further integration with Western Europe, Turkey has not yet been offered full membership in the European Union. At the same time, in their attempt to discourage Westernization, Islamic fundamentalists point to a growing economic gap between rich and poor. Disputes over Cyprus continue to strain Greek-Turkish relations, terrorism exists within Turkish borders, and Turkish minorities in the Balkan states are persecuted.

On the other hand, the future holds promise for Turkey. The end of the Cold War, support for the destruction of Saddam Hussein's regime during the Persian Gulf War, and important Turkish energy resources provide hope for increased stability in the region. Water projects on the Tigris and Euphrates Rivers will help provide better irrigation of Turkish farmland when completed. Trade with the republics of the former Soviet Union now totals several billion dollars each year. Despite inflationary problems, economic reforms of the 1980s have caused a steady average growth of 5% per year in the gross domestic product of Turkey. Together, these events demonstrate that Turkey possesses a good amount of strength and resilience.

This, then, is our portrait of Turkey, a traditional agrarian nation that is seeking to modernize rapidly. The coffeehouse reflects many of the important values and behaviors of the Turks, particularly the relationship between Islam and secularity, recreation, communication, community integration, male dominance, and the importance of substance over form within such a modest environment. And, although Turkey is changing, its citizens still recognize the historical and cultural importance of the coffeehouse, even when they frequent it only periodically. Thus, there will always be a place for the coffeehouse in Turkey, especially in the rural areas and small towns that still dominate life in this country.

CHAPTER 7

The Brazilian Samba

The next great civilization will emerge, like a serpent, from the Amazon. Look at the geography. You see, Brazil is shaped like a big heart. Brazil provides the heart for the world. But what happens when you turn a heart upside down? It becomes a big bunda [rear end]. We can't seem to get away from the rear perspective.

—Krich (1993), p. 102

The ambivalence expressed in the quote above, from the director of a samba school, reflects the general feeling found in the Brazilian population. This large population, numbering 159 million in 1998, is extremely diverse and spread across several distinct regions and 26 states. In land area, Brazil is almost equal to the entire United States: 8,511,965 square miles versus 9,372,610 square miles. Brazilians have tremendous spirit in the face of adversity, particularly economic, which has plagued the country for decades. The well of this spirit is continually replenished by the Brazilians' passion for life. Metaphorically, the samba encapsulates this passion and serves to replenish the well in both good times and bad.

The samba has truly become a national symbol. For example, at a beauty pageant for Italian-Brazilian young women, held in Brazil, all contestants were asked what they first thought of when hearing the word "Brazil."

Immediately, all of the young women began to samba. The samba's technical definition is "a binary, percussive rhythm in which the 1st beat is never sounded, causing a continual, hesitant urgency" (Krich, 1993, p. 73). This idea parallels the Brazilians' polychronic nature and seemingly constant movement. A Brazilian is naturally uncertain about his or her future when the first indication of the direction in which he or she is going cannot even be heard. This notion of not having a clear sense of direction dates back to the founding of this country. The settlers from Portugal did not have a definitive plan of action for such issues as the assimilation or destruction of people from different races. But the Portuguese allowed for the societal absorption of the Indian population and the Black slaves, thus facilitating the formation of Brazilian culture.

The very existence of the samba is, in fact, due to the musical talent of the plantation workers. It was on the plantations that the first whispers of what is now known as the samba were heard. Decades later, the samba predecessors appeared in civil society in the form of elegant tangos as Blacks rose in social status in Brazil's bigger cities. The initial characterization of this dance as the samba occurred at free slaves' dance parties in Bahia in the 1870s. Bahia was and is a center of the vibrant and rich Black culture in Brazil. As the story goes, a woman from Bahia named Tia Amelia took the samba further south to the slums of Rio de Janeiro. It was her son, Donga, who composed the first recorded samba in 1916. As early as 1923, samba schools were born. It is these schools that flourish today and symbolize the spirit of the samba to most of the outside world, especially during Carnival. Although part of the spirit of the samba is captured in the glorious dancers and floats in the samba school parades during Carnival, the samba is much more complex. Its physical characteristics and musical qualities weave an intricate web over Brazilians and affect many facets of life.

The samba takes on many forms, such as "samba pagode, samba raiado, samba de partido alto, samba do morro, samba de terreiro, samba cançao, samba enredo, samba choro, samba do breque, sambalero, sambalanço, and samba" (Krich, 1993, p. 73). Many of these various sambas are appropriate for specific situations and social levels. For instance, the *samba enredo* is composed and used in the samba schools. The *samba de terreiro* is less sophisticated and likely to be danced in more rural areas. Other sambas are simply musical innovations. For instance, the *samba do breque* incorporates a rhythmic spoken part, much like rap, in the middle of the traditional samba music.

The lyrics of the various types of sambas are numerous as well, although all have a common theme, for the words center around the common man's trials and tribulations across history and in daily life. Popular subjects include corruption, poverty, historical events, and local heroes. The number of samba songs that have been composed is enormous, especially if you consider that samba schools produce an average of 2,000 new songs per year for Carnival.

There are five characteristics of the samba that, when explored in detail, delineate the culture of this country with respect to its people, their behavior, and their manner of conducting business. We have chosen to discuss primarily the physical attributes of this dance, as opposed to the musical and lyrical aspects, for the sake of brevity, although there is an obvious overlapping. These characteristics are small-step circularity, physical touch, undulation, spontaneous escape, and the paradox of dancers.

Small-Step Circularity

When dancing the samba, one moves in small, somewhat controlled steps in a circular pattern while holding the upper torso still. This notion of small steps and circularity has been present in Brazil since its discovery in April 1500. Brazil was literally, but accidentally, run into by Pedro Alvares Cabral, a Portuguese trying to find an oceanic passage to Asia. Because Columbus ran into land along the same parallel, Cabral was presumably hoping to do the same. But earlier, in 1494, Spain and Portugal had divided the New World in the Treaty of Tordesilhas, and undiscovered Brazil was given to Portugal, even though no one was aware of its vast size. In other words, this land became part of the Portuguese empire largely through default and not through competition or war.

In general, "Brazil's development as a nation has been essentially evolutionary with few sharp breaks or drastic discontinuities" (Schneider, 1996, p. 35). Brazil grew amid small steps that were often circular, for example, from military to civilian rule and back. In the early 1800s, the Portuguese emperor, Dom Joao VI, moved to Brazil because he feared Napoleon's power in Europe. It was under his rule that growth truly began. After the situation in Europe stabilized, he returned to Portugal and left his son, Dom Pedro I, to rule Brazil. It was this ruler who realized Brazil's need to officially separate itself from Portugal; on September 7, 1822, he declared Brazil's independence. Several years later, he, too, returned to Portugal but left his son, Dom Pedro II, in charge of this nation. During his rule, while he was away on business, his daughter signed a document freeing the slaves. Soon thereafter, two army generals took the initiative to oust Dom Pedro II from Brazil. Hence, in 1889, the monarchy was dead, and the Republic of Brazil was formed. This transition from monarchy to republic demonstrates how Brazilians move in small steps. It took them 67 years after their country was declared independent to fully remove the Portuguese monarchy from power.

The existence of several different forms of government over time, as well as the vacillation between these forms, also supports the notion of small steps and their circularity. It is significant that the republic was proclaimed by two generals, because military dictatorship has been prevalent in Brazil for most of the nation's history. Many presidents have been military officers, thus further confusing the issue between military and democratic rule. In 1985, civilian rule and elections supplanted military rule, although the generals are still key players.

Furthermore, there are nine different political parties in Brazil: the National Reconstruction Party, the Social Democratic Party, the Party of the Brazilian Democratic Movement, the Democratic Worker's Party, the Worker's Party, the Brazilian Labor Party, the Liberal Front Party, the Popular Socialist Party/Brazilian Social Democratic Party, and the Liberal Party. It seems there is much circularity, overlay, and repetitiveness in the ideologies and activities of these various parties. But this phenomenon also shows how individuals are given significant freedom in expressing their beliefs and forming organized groups representing these beliefs. Again, this notion dates back to Brazil's founding, where different groups were not forced to assimilate fully to the Portuguese culture. This liberal attitude extended to the practice of interracial unions, resulting in a myriad of mixed marriages and mixed children. All types of Brazilians integrated themselves into a unified society through the small steps of increased racial integration. In fact, Krich (1993) believes that "a new generation of blacks is finding the samba one of the handier means of advancement" (p. 82) in Brazilian society. Although practiced more devoutly in particular regions, the samba has been pervasive throughout the country, and knowing how to samba is part of being Brazilian. Hence, this dance is a vehicle through which all of the diverse peoples and regions of this vast country can seek some degree of unity.

Still, the issue of race is extremely complicated in Brazil. There is a good amount of income inequality, and much of it is concentrated among those with darker skin pigmentation, even though Brazilians of all types tend to interact more easily in daily life than their American counterparts. Eugene Robinson (1995, 1999), an African-American journalist, attributes the difference between Brazil and the United States to the "one-drop" theory prevalent in the United States, that is, one drop of African blood leads to a classification as black. Thus, there is a wide gap between Blacks and whites in the United States. Demographers have substantiated this gap in the United States: African Americans represent the only ethnic or racial group that has not had a significant increase in out-group marriage in recent years, which typically leads to cultural integration.

However, in Brazil, the opposite theory was prevalent, that is, one drop of white blood lightens, making the person white. Hence, it is popular to use the term "Brazilian Rainbow" but not "American Rainbow," even though gradation of skin color is a point of discussion among African Americans. Because of this indeterminacy of skin color, some observers argue that social class is much more important than race in Brazil, and even more important in Brazil than in class-conscious England (Bond & Smith, 1998). Ironically, scientists now argue that race is a useless and superficial classification, given the high rates of miscegenation throughout the world. To complicate matters, it should be noted that there are large numbers of other ethnic groups in Brazil. In fact, few nations have a population more diverse than Brazil, which includes people of American Indian, European, African, and East Asian origin of both pure and mixed blood. Brazil has the largest concentration not only of Blacks and their descendants outside of Africa, but also of Japanese and their descendants outside of Japan. But all or almost all of them identify primarily with Brazil. For example, 100,000-plus Japanese Brazilians work in low-level jobs in Japan because of the lack of jobs in Brazil, but virtually none speaks the Japanese language, and they are shunned by the Japanese. Similarly, German Brazilians celebrate Oktoberfest in the traditional German manner until midnight, when Brazilian music such as the samba transforms the event. Commenting on such phenomena, *The Economist* ("Eine Kleine Samba," 1995) argues that the Brazilian Rainbow, even with its defects, should be studied in depth: "Brazilians are remarkable more for what brings them together than for what keeps them apart" (p. 49).

Furthermore, the monetary and educational systems also demonstrate evolution and small-step circularity. Since 1940, Brazil has used five different currencies: the mil reis, the cruzeiro, the cruzado, the new cruzeiro, and, currently, the real. Hesitant to bring about sweeping change, the Brazilians attempted to keep the cruzeiro by devaluing it many times over. In the early 1990s, the yearly rate of inflation reached a mind-boggling 2,500%, but it has since been reduced to low double digits. When it was finally apparent that the situation was hopeless, a move was made to introduce the cruzado. However, when this did not work, a move back to the cruzeiro was made, and the currency was declared to be the new cruzeiro; again, the notion of circularity is evident.

The educational system in Brazil is quite interesting because it is both lax and controlled at the same time. As with most educational systems, there are levels of education such as grade school, high school, and college. However, in order to enter a university, one must take an exam called the *vestibular*. One's entrance to the university is based solely on his or her performance on this exam; high school grades and extracurricular activities are not important. Thus, there tends to be a lax attitude toward school work in high school. Before the exam, however, there is a big push, and strong efforts are made to pass this exam. Of significant interest is the fact that one takes this exam in a particular subject area, such as history, physical education, and so on. Hence, at the age of 18, one must already commit to a college. Once students are accepted into a university for this field, they study only subjects related to this field.

A typical university campus has separate buildings for each subject matter; those studying history spend all of their time in the history building. Once accepted, there is not much danger of failing, and a relaxed atmosphere is reached once again. In addition, there are no core courses that each student must take in order to graduate. However, if one decides that he or she does not want to continue studying a subject, he or she may not simply transfer into another department; the student must take the *vestibular* over again in a new subject matter. Hence, the student loses valuable time spent studying subjects. In this manner, the educational system is rather rigid, as symbolized in the tight control of the torso and movement found in the samba. However, it is also clear that many steps must be taken in order to reach a degree in one's preferred field.

Education is an area in which the conflicts and contradictions in Brazilian culture become apparent. Whereas the average years of schooling have increased from 2 to 6 since 1970, comparable figures for fast-growing Asia are 4 and 9. Many of the schools are decrepit and underfunded, thus putting Brazil at a disadvantage in a globalized economy in which an educated workforce is critical. Sometimes, the conflicts are startling. For example, in the early 1990s, the Bulhones family exerted incredible power and influence over all aspects of life in the state of Alagors, where the people suffered from the highest infant mortality rate in the region, the lowest child vaccination rate, the lowest rate of prenatal care, and one of the lowest rates of schooling—1.8 years per adult. But in contrast, the local elite looked forward to the inauguration of cellular telephone service in January 1994. Wearing designer clothes, Mrs. Bulhones, the governor's wife, roamed among the shantytown dwellers and peasants, proclaiming, "Poor people have just the same right to see me pretty as people in society." About that time, she chartered an executive jet three times to fly to São Paulo and back, with the state treasury picking up the $24,000 tab. Meanwhile, the state's public schools were closed for 7 months because teachers were protesting salaries of $80 a month. The person taking the hard line with the teachers was the Secretary of Education, who was also the governor's brother. Thus, this family represents a pointed example of the political oligarchy that blurs lines between public and private consumption and responsibilities.

Small steps and circularity are characteristics that are found in a Brazilian's personal life as well. Although it is quite easy to make acquaintances, or *colegas,* in Brazil, it takes some time to cultivate deep and lasting friendships. A typical pattern for a foreign student is to establish a network of *colegas,* and to socialize outside of school and create friendships with a few individuals who become more than *colegas.* Next, this student may be invited to the homes of his or her friends and eventually be treated as a member of the family. Similarly, business is typically conducted in restaurants, and it is a sign of honor and trust to be invited to a businessperson's home.

A Brazilian's transition from his or her parents' home to his or her own home also consists of many small steps. Family is the most important institution and, hence, greatly influences the individual. For instance, the dating process is greatly regulated by the family. It is not uncommon for a man to court a woman on the porch for a time before being allowed in the house. Once welcomed into the home, many couples spend time together in the living room in the presence of the family. After a relatively long courtship, couples may marry. Although times are changing, most young adults leave their parents' home only when they marry. Hence, it is unlikely that many individuals live on their own; instead, they live first with their parents and siblings and then immediately with their spouses and children.

This notion of extended courtship is found in business relationships as well. When conducting business in Brazil, one must first establish a solid friendship. Only after a committed relationship is in place can a deal be struck. A typical piece of advice is to "be prepared to commit long-term resources of time and money to establishing strong relationships in Brazil. Without such commitments, there is no point in attempting to do business there at all" (Morrison, Conaway, & Douress, 1995, p. 44). Hence, it is clear that patience and the willingness to cultivate solid personal ties, through the small steps, are crucial to the success of business negotiations in this country.

Brazil is generally a patriarchal society where the father of the family is deferred to in many important decisions. Older members of the family also are accorded respect and are well taken care of by younger family members as they age. Hence, it is not surprising that in Hofstede's (1991) study of 53 countries, Brazil ranks 14th in power distance. In terms of business dealings, there are many layers of authority, and often, a foreigner must take many steps in order to find the person who can make things happen.

Also, compared to Americans and Japanese, Brazilians are much more likely to use commands and to say no in negotiations (Adler, 1997, p. 215). The use of commands can be traced back to the extensive military rule experienced by the people of this country. Thus, this behavior is a small step away from the historical political system. The excessive tendency to say no is also a way of keeping negotiations from forging ahead too quickly, behavior that again demonstrates the need to proceed in small steps.

Physical Touch

Through the on-again, off-again military rule, there is a definite feeling of control that is held by the elite over the general population. In fact, modern-day society contains strong vestiges of colonial times, when the elite group controlled nearly all of the wealth. It has been estimated that 10% of the Brazilian population controls 90% of the national wealth. The uncertainty about the future brought about by the small steps and circularity of this country's history also places stress on Brazilians. Brazil has been termed a "big emerging market" for quite some time. The long wait for the awakening of this sleeping giant has instilled a sense of tension in the population, which has developed means to deal with this oppression and uncertainty on a daily basis. A dominant means is the reliance on personal relationships and human warmth. This idea can be explored further by analyzing the samba with regard to its characteristic of physical touch.

The samba is normally danced in close proximity to other people, and the movement is quick and continuous to keep up with the samba beat. The very history of the samba is quite indicative of the importance of physical touch. It is said to be the descendant of an Angolan fertility rite that comprises the "violent bouncing together of belly buttons" (Krich, 1993, p. 73). The *Umbigada* ritual is thought by some to be another influence on the modern samba. This ritual is conducted in a circle where people are granted the chance to dance by a thrust of the pelvis. The word *Umbigada* is derived from the word *umbigo,* meaning belly button. Hence, the connection between this ritual and the former is clear. Also, the Ngangela word *kusamba* can be defined as "to skip, to gambol, to express uninhibited joy" (Krich, 1993, p. 73). Thus, the importance of physical touch and human warmth is well captured in the metaphor of the samba.

This necessity of human contact is best exemplified through the Brazilian family. As noted earlier, family ties are of paramount importance in this country. Because children often do not leave their parents' home until they are married and then frequently establish their new home close by, family members are usually found within a defined geographic area. This living arrangement allows family members to communicate with each other in person on a regular basis. The most common way to reaffirm family ties is the Sunday meal. Normally, the head of the clan hosts this meal, and all of his children and grandchildren congregate at his house to share conversation and good food. This idea is conveyed through the following quote: "We can't forget that with the Portuguese cooking we inherited the taste for a plentiful table, for varied foods, and the pleasure of eating with company, friends and family—the basis of Brazilian hospitality" (História do Brasil, 1971, p. 121).

A natural progression of the strong unity within the family is the extensive use of nepotism in the business world. Family members take special care to make sure that all relatives are provided for. Unfortunately, many employment opportunities are given to family members regardless of their ability to perform the job correctly.

However, if the family structure is weak or nonexistent, the Brazilian is at a great disadvantage given the importance of social networks that are based largely on family ties. An extreme example is the killing of orphans and selling their body parts, a practice that was common a few years ago. Similarly, the police sometimes act in a corrupt fashion, even to the point of killing civilians with little or no justification. A few years ago, there was public outrage when a judge did not punish two upper-class young men who poured kerosene over a lower-class Indian demonstrating on behalf of his people. The judge argued that the young men were sensitive to others, as shown by the treatment of their dogs. Such practices horrify many seasoned reporters, who bring these practices to the public's notice.

Still, it is important to remember that individual Brazilians have a sense of equality and the freedom to pursue their dreams. Throughout history, people from different races were allowed some degree of religious freedom and had the right to procreate with whomever they chose. In business negotiations, for example, Brazilians are much less likely than Japanese or Americans to use a normative appeal, where one uses societal norms to prove his or her point (Adler, 1997, p. 215). Hence, the Brazilian has a definite sense of self within the close-knit group. This notion of collectivism in face of the general liberties granted to the individual is well represented by Hofstede's rating of Brazil along this dimension. Because Brazil is precisely in the middle of the individualism-collectivism continuum, it is not surprising to see such a contrast in ideals. Similarly, Pearson and Stephens (1998) showed that Brazilians expressed much more concern for the outcomes of others than did Americans.

When conducting business, it is important for an American to remember that although his or her Brazilian contact may seem to be similarly individualistic, he or she is linked to many groups and often places the needs of those groups, particularly his or her family, ahead of personal goals. It is not uncommon for a businessperson to cancel a meeting or arrive late to a meeting because he or she needed to take care of a family issue.

Similarly, when negotiating with Brazilians, one must not simply forge ahead to discuss the business at hand. Getting to know one another is very important to the Brazilian. Because personal relationships are so important, asking after the well-being of family members is generally a good place to start. Like any other relationship where personal time and care are important, a carefully cultivated business relationship with a Brazilian can yield long-term benefits to both parties.

This notion of physical contact is also evident in more specific negotiating behaviors. Brazilians have a much higher tendency than Americans and Japanese to engage in facial gazing and touching (Adler, 1997, p. 218). Facial gazing is probably due to the desire of the Brazilian to read the expressions of his or her business partner and gain knowledge about his or her personality, and the use of physical touch is often simply a reaffirmation of the relationship and a transfer of concern for the other person. A very concrete example of this physical contact is in the typical Brazilian greeting, which involves kissing one another on the cheek. It is practiced between women, between women and men, and sometimes between men as well. Normally, two people kiss each other once on each cheek. If a person is not married, he or she may receive a third kiss for good luck in getting married; again, the reference toward family is evident. It is also crucial for a foreigner to note the proximity with which conversation occurs in Brazil. "A normal conversation between two Brazilians generally takes place somewhere between 6 inches and 12 inches apart" (Morrison et al., 1995, p. 34). In the United States, the typical space between two people is 2 feet or more. Again, the idea of closeness and human warmth is apparent in the Brazilian culture.

Undulation

The characteristic of the samba described as undulation, a distinctive moving of the hips, also enables one to gain insight into the Brazilian culture. This notion of undulation is an extension of the idea of circularity described earlier. Where circularity may result in traveling a lengthy path to a solution or reaching a dead end, undulation most often results in taking a shortcut to a solution.

In Brazil, it is common to get things done by circumventing rules and obstacles. Accomplishing a task in the face of the huge amount of bureaucracy found in this country is literally done through the art of dancing around things, as the metaphor of the samba suggests. This art dates back to the founding of this country. As Krich (1993, p. 169) points out, many of the original Portuguese were underdogs or bandits who were suddenly given land and titles. The behavior of these people who were now in high places remained entrenched in what they knew best—how to survive on the streets. More often than not, this survival depended on personal connections and navigating one's way around societal norms.

It is particularly interesting to note a popular myth in Brazilian culture that exemplifies this ideal of ignoring rules. The protagonist of this myth is the *Saçi,* a short black man with one leg who smokes a pipe and dons a red cap. There are many stories about this *Saçi,* all with the same central theme of mischief. This character generally plays pranks on people and gets away with it. For example, in one story, he goes to a farm, and, because of his presence, the milk sours. According to Solomon (1996), a myth is "a story containing symbolic elements that expresses the shared emotions and ideals of a culture. In this way, a myth reduces anxiety because it provides consumers with guidelines about their world" (p. 543). Hence, it is not surprising that in many social circles in Brazil, an individual who succeeds through mischief is seen as a hero.

The Brazilian penchant for breaking rules and reaching goals outside of proper procedures is evident at traffic lights, which are frequently disregarded. However, stopping at a red traffic light can be dangerous, especially at night, because drivers are frequently accosted.

Another way to find one's way around the rules is through using one's status. Because Brazil has a hierarchical structure, respect must be paid to those of a higher status, as evidenced by a standard response: "Do you know to whom you are speaking?" This is intended to point out the status the individual wishes to invoke as justification for contending that the law was not intended for such a special person (Schneider, 1996, p. 193). Again, the importance of personal relationships and who you know is demonstrated. An effective personal network frequently gets a person much further in accomplishing his or her goal than does following the law.

This type of behavior, when *not* invoked by rank, is called a *jeitinho*. To give a *jeitinho* is loosely translated as enlisting a fellow human being to help one circumvent the rules because of one's personal circumstance. In general, this notion is closely connected to the Brazilian belief in the equality of individuals and in preserving the human relationship in face of the extensive bureaucracy and the rigidity of military rule. "From this perspective, the 'jeitinho' is a flexible way of dealing with the surprises of daily life, a way of humanizing the rules that takes into account the moral equality and social inequalities of persons in the society" (Hess, 1995, p. 40). In this instance, pulling rank when asking for a *jeitinho* will surely backfire on the individual asking for a special exception.

For instance, in dealing with the Brazilian embassy, a person can ask the clerk if he or she could make a *jeitinho* and process the paperwork sooner. The traveler can say that he or she needs to return to Brazil as soon as possible to be with a relative who is seriously ill. This appeal to the clerk's compassion for humanity and strong family values will tend to facilitate the process. Engaging in the *jeitinho* ritual allows the Brazilians to both bypass impersonal rules and exert a certain amount of control over their daily lives that is difficult in a nation with an uncertain future.

In pure business transactions, asking for a *jeitinho* may not be enough. In this case, you would hire a *despachante* to aid you in the navigation of Brazil's numerous and complicated bureaucratic rules. Fifteen years ago, the extensive bureaucracy inherited from the Portuguese was simplified, to a certain extent, and the need for such a service has diminished somewhat. There are, in fact, whole offices comprised of *despachantes* whose work is devoted to wading through regulations for their clients.

One Brazilian has used a *despachante* on a number of occasions. Although this woman was a Brazilian citizen, she had permanent residence in the United States. She visited Brazil frequently during the American summer months. In Brazil, before a citizen is allowed to leave the country, he or she has to prove that his or her taxes are in order. Hence, each time this relative left Brazil to return to the United States, she had to prove that she lived in the United States year round and that she did not have to pay Brazilian taxes. Ordinarily, one may accomplish this task by filling out a form once and filing it with the appropriate government agency. In Brazil, however, nothing is this simple. The fact that this woman's residence status had to be reaffirmed every time she left Brazil is indicative of the inefficiency of the bureaucracy. Determining the appropriate government office with which to interact is also quite difficult. Furthermore, Brazilians have such little faith in the written word—and particularly personal signatures—that every conceivable document has to be notarized. Thus, the usefulness of the *despachante* becomes evident. This relative would hire such a person within a day of arriving in the country in the hope that the paperwork would be completed by the end of her 2-month stay in Brazil.

The structure of the *despachante* business is also somewhat complex. There is often a head *despachante* who takes leadership over your individual request. However, he or she then has several layers of people below him or her who perform the more tedious tasks. One such task involves waiting in line for hours in order to get a particular document signed by the appropriate person. Hence, the very system that has evolved to aid an ordinary citizen in navigating the Brazilian bureaucracy has become quite cumbersome in its organization as well.

The notion of circumventing rules can also be found in issues that affect international relationships. In the area of intellectual property rights (IPR), Brazil has a very poor record, even though it is a signatory to the Paris, Berne, and Universal Copyright conventions on IPR and is in agreement with the GATT Trade Related Aspects of Intellectual Property accord. In fact, in terms of software piracy, for every legal copy sold, four illegal copies are made. This instance is typical of an underdeveloped nation that has an inefficient bureaucracy. Here, again, the degree of collectivism in the Brazilian culture, coupled with the importance of personal relationships, encourages this behavior. Whereas some outsiders may view Brazil's emphasis on humanity in a positive light, others think otherwise, as demonstrated by a French president, Charles de Gaulle, when he said of Brazil, "This is not a serious country." It is evident that Brazil must alter its behavior so that it can be seen as a legitimate business partner in the global environment. Dancing around the obstacles that numerous and complex regulations create has become so ingrained in this culture that seemingly only the need to conduct international business will result in Brazilians conforming to more universal norms.

▪ Spontaneous Escape

Spontaneous escape represents the fifth characteristic of the Brazilian samba. As might be expected, Brazilians tend to get lost in this notion of escape and lose track of time. Frequently, they do not strive to avoid the uncertainty of their lives, and when they feel uncertain, they escape through the music and dance of the samba. For all Brazilians, the samba represents this notion of a spontaneous escape from their everyday reality of unemployment, low standard of living, and poverty that affects about 90% of the Brazilian population.

Yet if one looks closely, the country is still smiling. Why? Perhaps it is because they can dance the samba and, for a brief moment, be the center of attention in a world full of freedom. For a country that had been under military rule for many years and plagued with a distrust of government and widespread bribery and corruption, this need for escape is something every Brazilian craves. The samba is an escape because its music and dance sweep you away, and you lose track of time and the environment. It is no wonder that Brazilians are described as being polychronic and tend to lose track of time when deeply involved in an activity.

As noted earlier, the samba came to be seen as synonymous with carnivals, the most well-known of which occurs in Rio de Janeiro. Throughout the world, most carnivals last 1 day, but in Rio, Carnival extends over 4 days. Each of the 16 samba schools works steadily over the year preparing its float for various parades and competitions, and the final parade occurs in the Sambodromo, a one-of-a-kind parade stadium that can hold 60,000 people. Various theories are used to explain the uniqueness and popularity of the Brazilian carnivals. One prominent explanation emphasizes the escape from daily drudgery and the spontaneous and unexpected activities during which members of different social classes mingle easily with one another at parties and parades.

Also, spontaneity of the Brazilian culture can be seen in many of the activities within its institutions. In the Brazilian educational setting, an everyday classroom can become a musical spectacle at any moment in time. One Brazilian described her college years in Brazil by citing the many times during her classes that the students would just spontaneously take whatever was in their reach and start invoking the samba beat. For example, a pencil may be tapped on a desk or a ruler slapped on a chair. She further described many instances when students would jump out of their chairs and begin dancing samba to the beat. During many of these samba sessions, the teacher would not object to the disruption as long as it was brief.

Most Brazilians can describe their school days with stories much like the one mentioned above. For this reason, the idea of samba as a cultural representation of Brazil becomes even more evident. This idea of spontaneity and escaping one's reality through the dance and motions of samba is taught to all Brazilians from their early years of education through their university graduation.

Another frequently cited example is the number of times in a university setting that teacher and students will stop their lessons and take a cigarette break together. This is as natural for a Brazilian as playing soccer. Soccer is yet another cultural aspect of Brazil that reflects the spontaneity of the samba, and the Brazilian style of play is called samba soccer.

This overwhelming need for escape among the people of Brazil is evident when one looks more closely at the economy. Despite significant displays of prosperity, Brazil's largest cities are overpopulated and account for some of the poorest people in the world. In fact, it is the country with the most *favelas*, or ghettos, in Latin America, and the need to escape this ironic twist of fate for the Brazilians is essential to their endurance and survival.

This idea of escape is very much a part of the Brazilian culture and language. One of the most famous phrases that Brazilians use that best sums up the Brazilian civilization is *tudo bom*, or everything about life turns out to be good in some way or another. This phrase is very illustrative of the Brazilians' attitude toward life and the negative twists and turns that are encountered in daily life. They are a people that has endured much political and economic hardship, but has always emerged from difficult situations dancing the samba. One Brazilian demonstrated this phenomenon daily at the office, when she would use the phrase *tudo bom* even when she was having a bad day. It was her belief, as with most Brazilians, that disappointment is a fact of life; only by maintaining a positive attitude will everything eventually work out.

In terms of business practices, the American manager trying to do business in Brazil must be aware that meetings will not always start or finish on time, that agendas may not be followed, and that requests may not be granted right away. As mentioned earlier, time is less important to Brazilians than to Americans, and schedules are frequently viewed simply as a formality.

Conventional American rules of behavior in business settings like negotiations are virtually nonexistent. One of the strongest differences between Brazilian communication behavior and the United States is the number of silent periods and conversational overlaps (Adler, 1997, p. 218). Brazil is a polychronic and being society, and Brazilians tend to be a spontaneous people who do what they feel and desire at a given moment without thinking about the others around them. Typically, everyone feels that his or her opinion is most important and speaks when he or she feels like doing so, even to the point of interrupting others abruptly.

Furthermore, when negotiating with a Brazilian, being aware of the culture's relative rankings in terms of collectivism-individualism is important in understanding why Brazilians have many conversational overlaps in their negotiations. Brazilians tend to interrupt each other constantly, perhaps reflecting the need for individual expression for the good of the whole. The Brazilians are very open to negotiations, and nothing is considered absolute. This concept reflects the need of Brazilians to be individualistic and to not conform.

In addition, given the collectivist orientation of Brazilian society, it is not uncommon to see a high correlation between people's personal and work lives. For example, major firms in Brazil help their employees with their financial problems and are very accommodating to family illnesses and other personal needs.

Another aspect of conducting business in Brazil relating to the spontaneous escape characteristic of the samba is the need that Brazilians have to socialize at lunch with potential business partners. Specifically, as in most Latin cultures, the Brazilians do not feel that life is all work and no play. The lunch setting is the typical Brazilian businessperson's escape from an often frustrating work environment. So, when attending a business lunch with a Brazilian, accept small talk and non-business-related conversations. The manager should also be open to spontaneous questions about his or her hobbies and family; the business lunch in Brazil is an opportunity for potential business partners to get to know each other and not necessarily to talk about the bottom line. The Brazilians take their meal times very seriously and cherish the chance to get away from business issues. Typical business lunches in Brazil can last anywhere from 1½ to 3 hours. For Americans hoping to form alliances in Brazil, it is important to recognize and respect this need to escape as part of the Brazilian culture.

Moreover, people hoping to conduct business in Brazil must realize and appreciate that Brazil is a country with no clear-cut rules. For example, in Brazil, unethical behavior, such as reneging on a contract, is treated as ethical if dependency relationships or face is not upheld properly. For many Westerners, this type of behavior would be considered unethical and unacceptable. When doing business with the Brazilians it is important to understand their way of going around things instead of confronting them—literally dancing around things. Thus, for most Brazilians, the samba represents a stable factor over time, amid changing currencies, inflation, and political parties.

Paradox of Dancers

It is not unusual for a Brazilian factory worker to spend a month's salary on the costume he will wear at the carnival parade. With friends from his samba school, with whom he has been rehearsing the entire year, he will dance on top of a gigantic dragon during the parade, and he will experience a short but heavenly sense of existence. Such experiences portray very well the influence and impact of samba in Brazil. Samba schools in Brazil started more than 70 years ago and are as much a part of regional identity as soccer teams. This anecdote, however, best illustrates the paradox of the dancers of the samba.

As the story demonstrates, in Brazil, the dancers (people) of the samba are full of contrasts. When preparing to compete with their samba schools or to dance the samba in the carnival, Brazilians escape to another world where they can be anything they want. For that one moment, the samba is their ticket to paradise. For example, samba costumes can cost up to $3,500 (a year's savings for slum dwellers). For these people, however, "their investment pays off by bringing to life a daydream appropriate to the ancestors of slaves . . . they for a day become a friend of the king" (Krich, 1993, p. 69). This paradoxical way of living is seen in many aspects of the Brazilian culture.

As Krich (1993, p. 80) points out, whole samba parades are constructed as a tribute to an obscure, bygone composer; a forgotten slave revolt; the history of rice cultivation; or even the glory of the banana. This contrast between pleasure and pain can be seen throughout the Brazilian countryside. Eugene Robinson (1997) identified the city of Salvador da Bahia as being the pulse of Brazilian music. In this city, the contrast of images that Brazilians carry within them becomes most evident because of the activities taking place in the central plaza in Salvador. The plaza is a tourist mecca where travelers pose for pictures and dreadlocked entrepreneurs sell local crafts; years ago, this same plaza was the site of the public torture of slaves.

Historically, Brazil has been a country of contrasts and paradoxes. As noted earlier, Brazilian people come from various social and economic backgrounds and races, and few nations can match its diversity. Although many experts believe that the people of European descent have made the greatest contribution to the physical formation of Brazil, they also believe that the extensive interracial marriages throughout the history of Brazil have created a population so genetically complex that Brazilians constitute a new and distinct people.

The people of Brazil can easily confuse an outsider. Whereas most Brazilians look black, at least to North American eyes, only about 5% tell census takers that they consider themselves black. This contrast of the people of Brazil is also illustrated through an excess of common terminology describing *mestiços,* or mixed races. They use very creative metaphorical names for describing the various skin types found in Brazil. For example, they refer to very dark African types as *cor do carvão* (color of coal) and to dark-skinned people occupying an important position in society as *branco da terra* (white of the earth). This may seem surprising because the Brazilian society has been very successful in combining many racial and ethnic elements in its art, food, and music. Although these differences in social status exist, there are times, such as when dancing the samba, that the overall feeling of the people is "We are all Brazilian." This slogan identifies the overarching feeling of Brazil as a culture and perhaps even an ethnic unit.

This ironic unity is also reflected in the Brazilian cuisine. Many traditional dishes, such as seafood stews, replete with palm oil and coconut milk, have been influenced heavily by the Africans. The arts and crafts, particularly the wood carvings, look as though they could have been produced in Senegal or Ghana. These examples illustrate the everyday surroundings of Brazil.

The contrast between rich and poor can be seen in almost every aspect of Brazilian culture. For example, many cities in Brazil are a paradox of modern-day skyscrapers and industry, and historical pathways as represented by colonial churches and villages. It is not uncommon to see luxury apartments and houses at the foot of slum hills, or *favelas*. The government also reflects this paradox of dancers in that it is half privatized and half government-run, again placing Brazil in the middle of the individualism-collectivism continuum.

In addition, religion illustrates the paradox or contrasts of the Brazilian people. The pervasive religion is a syncretism of Roman Catholicism and African cult worship, featuring a pantheon whose origins can be traced directly back to the continent of Africa. In Brazil, there is great tolerance for contradiction. The many religions of Brazil reflect this paradox also in that numerous witchcraft and cult religions have borrowed symbols, such as the crucifix and various saints, from Catholicism. Hence, there is an intermingling of religious components where conservative traditions of the Catholic faith are adapted to ideas of witchcraft and supernatural powers. Between 80% and 85% of the population is baptized Roman Catholic, making Brazil the largest Catholic country in the world. However, most of these Brazilians are Catholic in name only and believe in folk Catholicism, spiritualism, or one of the Afro-Brazilian cults.

In Latin America, the estimated number of evangelical Protestants has increased from 5 million in 1960 to 60 million in 1997. To counter this trend, Brazilian Catholic priests now rely on rap music, sambas, and related music as a means of attracting Catholics back to the fold (Faiola, 1997).

As a final statement on the paradox of Brazil and its people, we can look to the Brazilian flag, which has a large yellow diamond on a green background. The color green stands for the lush fields and forests of Brazil. The color yellow represents its wealth in gold, which is found in many areas of the country. In the center of the yellow diamond, there is a blue sphere that symbolizes the usual navy blue sky that one finds in the tropical areas of the Earth. In that sky, there are the stars that represent the capital of the country and its federal states. Actually, there are 26 states and the capital (27 stars). In the middle of the sphere, there is a white banner with a legend, *Ordem e*

Progresso, which means "Order and Progress." This description of Brazil by the Brazilian people is a paradox in itself. Although Brazilians take pride in their abundant national resources, these resources are actually being eroded by current business practices. Furthermore, the notion of order and progress is quite contrary to how the country has been run in its colorful history.

The paradox of the dancers of the samba has very important implications for businesspeople wanting to work with Brazilians. As we have illustrated above, Brazilians are a melting pot of people with characteristics that are not easily categorized or, for that matter, understood. When trying to work with the Brazilians, it is important to remember their rich history and cultural triumphs. Brazilians are not quick to trust foreigners and need time, as mentioned earlier, to consider a *colega* a true friend. Patience is the key virtue in forming business partnerships in this country. Sensitivity to class differences and various special interest groups is necessary when forging political alliances and creating strategic advantages. Brazil is a country of many differences, but it can be united through dancing the samba for a common cause. For this reason, it is important to understand which units comprise the Brazilian population before you can become comfortable with its economy, society, and culture (people).

The importance of the samba is encapsulated in the words of a diehard Brazilian in the following quote:

> [Without samba,] there's an emptiness that could never be filled. It's the pill for our sickness, a medicine for the heart. There is no substitute, whether you're happy or sad, you remember a big passion and that makes you suffer. Instead of fighting in the streets or hitting one another, we make a song. Take away the samba and we're nobody. (Krich, 1993, p. 75)

This quote best describes the sentiment in the Brazilian country about the dance that unites them and identifies them and their people as the heart of the world.

Looking toward the future, Brazil must change in order to operate effectively in the worldwide economy and abide by its agreements with organizations such as GATT, WTO, and NAFTA. It must continue to reduce its trade barriers, although tariffs have decreased significantly since 1990, from 150% to 20%. Brazil, however, can make these social and economic changes much more quickly than it can convince its people and its culture to change. Despite the significant changes that must be made in the Brazilian infrastructure and regulatory environment, Brazil will continue to be diverse, complex, and mysterious, and the samba will continue to express these cultural themes in new and exciting ways.

CHAPTER 8

The Polish
Village Church

*Swept by converging streams of economic, political and social
events, Poland has been affected by all. Yet she has remained stub-
bornly unique . . . she has absorbed much, resisted much, and
remained very much herself. In many respects, Poland presents a
remarkable example of continuity not often met within history.*

—Benet (1951), pp. 26-27

The first-time visitor to Warsaw, Poland, is frequently surprised by
its modernity, as exemplified by its buildings in the central business district, many of which could be mistaken easily for buildings in American cities. At the very modern Marriott hotel, businesspeople are constantly
on their cell phones or in intense discussions making deals. There are a few
older buildings left over from the Communist era, but not many. Although
Warsaw was largely destroyed in World War II, the visitor would have a difficult time finding remnants of this destruction and even of Poland's past.

Yet Poland, with its population of 39 million, is still very much a traditional society consisting mainly of small towns and villages. This central
European nation is making the exhilarating but disquieting and rapid transition from traditional to modern society. Given Poland's long and torturous

history, described briefly below, it is understandable why the Polish people can be described as contradictions that are held together by a strong social system and a sense of shared adversity and experience. The Polish people are guarded in their manner of dealing with each other and outsiders, as well as in their trust of institutions and people. Despite this guardedness, they possess a richness and depth of spirit that has helped them persevere through their many shared adversities. Poland, in the years following Communism, is struggling successfully to find a place in the world as a free country and a people of self-determination. The path Poland is now taking is influenced very much by the nation's peasant roots, a history of foreign power domination (including Communism), and Catholicism. These three forces shape how the Polish people see themselves, their behaviors, and their institutions.

The village church, found in virtually every Polish town, stands as a symbol of these three forces and presents a particularly appropriate metaphor for Polish culture. In each village, a church sits in a prominent location and serves as the focal point of town activity. The churches are the beneficiaries of much of the village money and attention. Some are as old as 500 years, and others were built since the collapse of Communism. Church events are considered compulsory, and failure to attend is not viewed favorably. During holy periods, such as Christmas and Easter, residents attend the many church services held every day of the week. Services such as the Easter Resurrection ceremony, held on the night before Easter, pack the church, and the people overflow into the street. Men often congregate outside the church as the women, children, and the elderly find seats inside. The men and older boys gather around the entrances to listen. Church personnel have adapted to these circumstances by sending a priest outside the church to administer the Communion rituals at the appropriate time. Similar to the Malaysian *balik kampung,* the village church is important as a focal point for Poles because pilgrimages back home for religious holidays are common. The church represents a safe haven from the forces of history that have shaped and, at times, attempted to destroy Poland.

Whenever a Pole wants to explain some aspect of his or her work, he or she starts by talking about Polish history. History has played an important role in shaping the Polish way of thinking. The history of Poland is largely the history of peasants who were dominated by exterior groups (e.g., wealthy landowners, foreign powers, and Communist leaders).

From the medieval period (sixth century) through the late 19th century, the people farming the land were predominantly serf labor. Emancipation and refeudalization occurred several times throughout this period, which witnessed a continuing struggle between peasants who sought rights and freedom, and landowners who secured legislation to force the peasants to stay on their land so that the landowners could exploit their labor for immense profits. The Polish bourgeoisie was perceived as a threat to these wealthy landowners. Therefore, landowners encouraged Jews, Germans, and Armenians to immigrate to Poland and to assume needed technical positions, because the foreigners' economic prosperity did not pose a political threat. As the bourgeoisie diminished in size, the population of Polish towns declined, and the power and tax base of the king fell. Landowners during this period became increasingly tied to specific German and Dutch bankers for capital. This left the landowners relatively powerful while they developed an increasing dependence on the core of the European economic system (north-western European states). Some peasants did own the land they worked during this period, but they remained primarily subsistence farmers. To a great extent, the technology used in Polish agriculture remained primitive because of the ample supply of serf labor.

During the 16th century, Poland was very large and powerful. But the Polish state during the 16th through 18th centuries was run by a parliament that consisted of members of the Polish gentry, who selected the king. These wealthy landowners were successful at maintaining their independence and wealth through their employment of the "liberum-veto," a procedure giving any member of the parliament the power to defeat any legislation with a single vote. Needless to say, few meaningful actions occurred. This procedure helped to maintain a balance in Polish politics and defined the strong, individualistic values of the Polish gentry. It did, however, prevent Poland from amassing strong collective behaviors required to fend off foreign invaders through political means.

This weakened state and dependence on foreign capital allowed for Poland's relatively stronger neighbors—Russia, Prussia, and Austria—to partition Polish land beginning in 1772 and to assimilate it into their own borders. By 1795, Poland had vanished. Then, the 1815 Congress of Vienna officially decreed that the Kingdom of Poland still existed, but that legally, it was governed by the Russian czar. In effect, the Polish state as a separate entity ceased to exist, and there was constant friction between the Russian Orthodox Catholics and the Polish Roman Catholics. Also, from 1772 onward, the power and wealth of the landowners was greatly weakened. In addition, pressure throughout Eastern Europe forced the abolition of serfdom and redistributed land to foreign parties and to the peasants themselves. It was not until 1918 that Poland again emerged as a separate nation, but without serfdom.

From 1918 until 1936, Poland was a free country after defeating the Russian Army in 1918, and the distribution of land ownership to the peasants (land reform) was a primary political objective. A soaring population growth rate, coupled with the tradition of partible inheritance, through which land was divided among all living children upon the father's death, prompted the economic failure of land reform. The process resulted in lower production and lower profits from agriculture during the interwar period. Germany invaded Poland in 1936 and ruled the nation until the end of World War II.

The aftermath of World War II brought a division of the spoils between the victors, the Western allies and Russia. Devastated by war, during which it lost about 30% of its population, Poland became a pawn in this process. Communism was adopted as the official state ideology in 1948, and despite its lack of general support among the Polish populace, Soviet government support made it impossible to sustain significant resistance. Economic rebuilding and a change in governmental priorities prompted the postwar Polish leaders to divert resources from traditional sectors, such as agriculture, to industry (manufacturing, mining, service, and construction). Inadequate and unsupported reforms, however, produced a worsening economy and growing social discontent.

Collectivization of farming, a key tenet of Communism, took place in Poland in the years 1949 to 1956. At its height, however, only 8.6% of total cultivated land was collectivized. A powerful peasant commitment to the land, and often to a specific plot of land, proved to be the reason for the failure of collectivization.

For the peasant, the farm was as much a social as an economic unit. Its output was produced for the satisfaction of family needs. Market pressures running counter to family consumption needs and demanding production increases were often perceived as oppression. The reaction to these pressures was often to reject increased production and to produce only enough for family subsistence. Government agricultural policies had succeeded in reinforcing the essential features of peasantry. This fact gave the peasants power that could significantly disrupt the government systems, and they were seen as a threat.

As the state required greater and greater levels of agricultural production, the peasant farmers tended to resist through delaying tactics. This tactic highlighted their power over the government system, which initiated greater pressure from the state to collectivize, thus creating a vicious downward spiral of lower levels of production. In the 1950s, this process hit a crisis point where peasants lost their pride of ownership in their farms and became reluctant to improve or even to maintain them, resulting in low productivity and workforce apathy. Eventually, the Polish government repealed its policy to collectivize farming in Poland.

Other policies were also met with strong resistance. The Poles' basic distrust of government systems produced an unwillingness to make sacrifices to turn around the economy. In addition, the socialist ideology on which the Polish social and political system was built altered the outlook of traditionally hardworking Poles to believe that it was the states' responsibility to provide for the household. When the state could not provide adequately for the Polish people, they became resentful. To compensate for the growing unrest, the government increased the workers' wages fivefold in the years 1979 to 1986. The Polish government was close to proclaiming state bankruptcy when it declared martial law in 1981 to quell the growing unrest and the calls for reforms by the Solidarity movement.

In 1989, spearheaded by the Solidarity movement and prompted by the weakening political and economic position of the Soviet Union, the round-table meetings in Warsaw resulted in the peaceful overthrow of the Communist state in Poland and the beginning of significant economic, political, and social reforms that continue today.

It is against this backdrop that we explore Polish culture. The village church resides in the center of most Polish villages, exemplifying the central place that Catholicism occupies in Polish life. In addition, the church's austere exterior and plush interior represent the contrasting nature of Polish identity, produced partially by the many years of foreign power domination and the partitioning of the Polish state. Finally, the village church endured and flourished during a period when religious worship was banned in Poland. Poles are very proud of this fact, and the village churches stand as a symbol to the ability of the Polish people to survive during extreme adversity.

Central Place of the Catholic Church

The village church sits in the middle of the village, often in a place of particular prominence, such as the crest of a hill. This placement signifies the preeminence of the church in Polish life, both in the past and in the post-Communist period. Although the power and influence of the church are decreasing among some citizens, it is difficult to overstate the importance of the Catholic Church in the public and private lives of the Polish people. Hann (1985) goes as far as to say that "Polish has come to mean Catholic" (p. 100). Virtually every major holiday is religious in post-Communist Poland. Public processions of clergy and laypeople carrying religious banners and relics are the primary rituals in many of these celebrations. In these rituals, neighborhoods, the youth, and Easter baskets are blessed. This is coupled with full masses, sometimes lasting as long as 3 hours. In addition, Polish youth and adults celebrate "name days" rather than birthdays. These name days are set aside to celebrate the saints after whom many Poles are named.

The Catholic Church has played an important role for the rural citizens in modern Poland. These parishioners continue to be a particular focus for the Church. During the period of peasant emancipation at the end of the

19th century, the Church played an active role in acquiring freedom and land for the peasants, even though the Polish state was not an independent entity. This championing of the peasant cause positioned the Church perfectly to play an active role in the creation of national sentiment, and it bound the Poles even more closely to the Church. The result was that the parish became the focus for a collective Polish peasant identity.

The collectivizing influence of the Catholic Church is naturally accompanied by moral codes of conduct, including the belief in equality and fair division of resources and in promoting the church's sense of social justice. Also, the Church placed importance on collectivity over individuality and on suffering over short-term gratification of personal needs. Sacrifice is seen as the best means by which a Catholic can find salvation. This belief has spread beyond religious life in Poland and has permeated Polish views of national identity. It has given solace to a people that has suffered long periods of political and economic domination for centuries, including the relatively recent horrors of World War II. The search for explanations as to why they have had to suffer so terribly has generated a natural connection between Poles and the Catholic Church.

After World War II, Poland was unique among Communist nations in that the Catholic Church and the symbols of Catholicism were not outwardly diminished by the Communist attempts to condemn and destroy them. In fact, commitment to Catholicism was probably strengthened by the condemnation, as were other aspects of Polish life. Polish peasants continued to abstain from meat on Fridays; to name their children after saints; and to marry, baptize, and administer Communion in religious ceremonies. The Catholic Church also occupied an active role in the political life of the peasant. It openly sanctioned much of the opposition to government policies in Poland. In addition, the Church provided the structure to aggregate and articulate peasant interests, as a result of which the devout Polish peasants were able to oppose Communism collectively through their religious affiliation.

This peasant-church connection is further manifested in the almost spiritual link that the Polish people have with their land, as demonstrated by the All Saints Day commemoration celebrated every November 1st. This commemoration is an amazing cultural demonstration of respect for the dead that has turned into an event. Its religious meaning serves to connect the Polish people both symbolically and literally to their roots and to the land, as demonstrated by the actions of many Poles who have moved to the cities within the past few generations. Many of them travel back to their villages for this commemoration, and some of them to the villages of both sides of the family. City dwellers who have these agrarian roots usually choose to be buried in the village from which they came, further preserving the connection and the importance of family lineage and agrarian heritage. In addition, the family plots establish a permanent link of generations to generations in the village, a lineage that is literally "planted in the ground."

The Partitioning and Polish Identity

The exterior architecture of the old and new churches alike is simple. New churches are large, bearing brick or lightly painted stucco exteriors. The old churches are rustic, made from meticulously matched split logs with steeply curved metal roofs. They are simply adorned with wooden crosses and rose-bud-shaped steeples. The inside of these old churches is like the inner light of the Polish people: filled with color, attention to detail, wealth of spirit, and surprise. But the church exterior hides the riches of golden altars, antique wooden carvings, and hand-painted walls. Still, the inside of these village churches is not gaudy, but simply elegant and rich with years of protecting the unfulfilled souls of the peasant people.

Like the contrast between the austere exterior and the rich interior of the village churches, the public and private lives of the Polish people are remarkably different and separate. This separation is in great part a result of the partition of the Polish state in 1772 and the resulting lack of control over the Poles' own official business. Communism also contributed to this lack of control. It promised "social peace" and "welfare security" in exchange for social control and private ownership of property. Poles desiring certainty and security after the perils of years of foreign power invasions and rule, and the harsh consequences of World War II, entered into a social contract with the Communist government. The Polish people, however, chose to focus on the welfare of close family and friends as opposed to a larger group, as the Communist system required. The result of this social contract was an abdication of responsibility for much of the state of affairs that touched them directly. One example of this mentality is the upkeep of public property. In the socialist state, theoretically, public property was the responsibility of everyone, but in practice, it was neglected badly. In this system, responsibility simply disappeared.

This does not mean that Poles do not care for their property. They do, in fact, take great pride in their simple possessions. Most Polish homes and apartments have a room where visitors are welcomed and in which they display prized possessions, special glassware, and religious symbols in glass-enclosed display cases. But exterior spaces are not viewed with ownership or pride and thus do not elicit particular care.

Poles value private ownership of property, and many village homes are works in progress. Young men will begin building a home whenever money is available. They will build in steps, and when a section is completed that is habitable, they will move their family into this space. Other floors may remain as open shells until more money is available to complete them or until the expanding family needs the space. Grandparents and even siblings are likely to work together on a house, sharing their money and efforts and, eventually, the finished home. Extended family cohabitation is common in the Polish villages as well as in the cities. Despite the strong influence of the Catholic Church, Poles in the cities such as Krakow and Warsaw tend to limit their families to one or two children, whereas village families are likely to have three or more.

Poles are proud people who value appearances, particularly as they relate to their clothing. During the Communist period, the Poles did not have a good selection of apparel and had to settle for drab colors and poor styles. Today, the individuality of Poles is reflected in their choice of apparel and the pride they take in wearing it. Young men and women in the cities wear designer fashions. Although they may own only one or two such outfits, they will wear them frequently and care for them meticulously. Older women can be seen on city streets in winter wearing a drab Communist-era coat with a brightly colored (purple or pink) hat. Village women wear traditional scarves over their heads that differ in design depending upon the region of Poland. They are also frequently colorful.

Despite the attention to their appearance, the face that Poles present in public is guarded and private, with smiles reserved for more informal and private moments between friends and family. Individuals tend to mind their own business. In the cities, Poles are reluctant to get involved in the affairs of others. For example, if an individual falls in the street, it is unlikely that Poles will intervene unless it appears that there is serious injury. Older women are the rare exception to this norm. Women who reach the status of grandmother are only too willing to render advice, particularly to younger women with children. Children are considered public domain, and Poles easily give advice on appropriate attire and discipline, as well as offers of candy or fruit. In addition, in the villages, involvement in the private matters of neighbors is quite common but is highly resented by those who are the subject of the attention. Still, offers of assistance when made without invasion of privacy are welcomed and usually serve to generate a strong bond between the parties that will be remembered and reciprocated.

Ironically, Poles identify strongly with Poland but feel that the Polish people tend to be lazy and quarrelsome (Bond & Smith, 1998). Poles' suspicions about their neighbors' intentions are based on a strong and pervasive distrust within Polish society, which is often connected to accusations of bribery or favoritism. Bribery is an ever-present phenomenon in Polish life. It is a source of jokes, folklore, and resentment and is often the explanation for the way things are. Side payments are still necessary to receive adequate medical services and even entrance into universities. For example, to get into many prestigious universities in Poland, an individual must pass a particular entrance exam. To pass these exams, one must obtain special tutoring from the university professors, because the contents of the exams are a closely guarded secret. Some Poles call this a bribe to the university professors, whereas others see it simply as payment for services.

Bribery permeates many aspects of Polish life, including the workplace.

For example, Polish workers often use the expression "we came here on a rabbit" when bemoaning their particular lack of benefits or poor working conditions. This expression refers to their choice or likely inability to make some form of payment to their supervisor. They conversely refer to those who are favored and receive benefits or privileges as "arriving on a calf." The reference is that the calf is the bribe to the new employer.

Bribery is just one manifestation of a system of privileges, power dispersal, and political access that is called *kumoterstwo* in the Polish language. *Kumoterstwo* comes from the word *kumo* for friend, chum, or crony. *Kumoterstwo* is translated into English as favoritism, but it tends to encompass a great deal more in the Polish experience. A Polish system of networks supports a heavy reliance on social contacts for a number of official or unofficial services or products. These relationships are based first on familial ties and second on economic or social standing, as opposed to occupation. These networks have become a necessary organizational tool for rural Poles, but they tend to generate resentment and suspicion among those who do not have them. Often, the networks that are associated with power are accompanied by these monetary payments for favors, or bribes. Generally, these relationships are not viewed as right or good but only as necessary or a fact of life. Their specific existence is kept very hidden under layers of denial, but they are fair game for general discussion and ridicule.

This form of social organization is a response to the difficulties associated with the Communist state. At the end of World War II, Poles were subjected to a government that was ineffective and illegitimate in their eyes. They needed to find a way around the system. They relied on their traditional individualistic values and their dogged determination to guide their approach to dealing with their environment.

In brief, Poles live a dual life between public and private. Behaviors that are considered appropriate to get things done in the public sphere, such as bribery or deception, are not acceptable within the small private spheres of Polish life. Poles have learned to expect different rules for different situations and are able to compartmentalize their lives into these different spheres. The village church stands as a symbol of the divided lives that Poles live and their attempts to pull these two worlds together. Similarly, the internal and external appearances of these churches also represent compartmentalization, a survival mechanism that has ensured the longevity of the Polish identity and the Polish spirit.

The Survivor—Transition

The Catholic Church survived and even flourished during the Communist period in Poland but not in other Communist states. Like the Catholic Church, the Polish people have survived under great adversity. The changing economic and political context of democracy and a market system today presents new challenges and opportunities for the Polish people. But this new world leaves Poles without a clear enemy and with a great deal of uncertainty.

Resistance to a common enemy is a key feature in Polish self-identity. During the two-century partition of Poland, the foreign powers—Russia, Prussia, and Austria—were viewed as enemies to be resisted. This resistance pulled Poles together for a common purpose and helped maintain their unique cultural heritage. During the post–World War II period, the enemy was Communism and the Soviet influence over the political and economic system. Poles are proud of their history, which is marked by these dramatic periods of resistance to external enemies. Most notably, Poles have resisted much larger and stronger armies with great valor. For example, Polish underground resistance during World War II was instrumental in providing the allied forces with critical information, and the Poles were able to thwart many Nazi efforts through sabotage. Resistance to collectivization of farming during the Communist era is another key example. Finally, the efforts of the Solidarity Union and others were instrumental in hastening the collapse of Communism. These collective efforts were encouraged by the doctrine of the Catholic Church, which supported resistance to Communism and earlier had championed land reforms during the period of the partition of the Polish state. The Poles have always adapted and resisted, and it is precisely because of their ability to adapt well to their environment that their unique culture has survived.

One way that Poles have adapted to adversity is through humor. Polish humor is a black humor that often pokes fun at the Polish condition. For example, the Polish winters can be very harsh, with bleak gray skies and extremely cold temperatures. One joke goes as follows:

> When the Germans were about to invade Poland during World War II, one Polish farmer was bemoaning to his friend the integration of Poland into the German state. The friend said to the farmer, "Well, I don't think it is all that bad." The farmer looked at his friend in amazement. "How

can you find good in this situation?" His friend replied, "Well, at least we won't have any more long Polish winters."

A second joke speaks to the lack of support Poles give to each other:

> Satan was showing a reporter around Hell. The reporter saw many deep pits with guards around the top of each. The reporter asked what they were. Satan said that there was a pit for each nationality of people. "Here are the Germans, over there are the Americans, and here are the Poles." The reporter noticed that the Polish pit did not have any guards around it. When he asked Satan why this was, Satan replied, "Well, the guards are stationed at the mouth of each pit to keep people from crawling out. In the Polish pit, we don't have to worry about that, because whenever anyone tries to get out, a Pole from inside pulls him back in again."

These jokes are a common and necessary form of social interaction in Poland, but it is not acceptable for foreigners to tell these same jokes. Rather, these jokes are reserved for Poles to turn the hardships of their lives into humor that they can share.

As these examples imply, Polish people communicate in a high-context manner, especially when compared to Americans. A good example is the hugely successful commercial of Pollena 2000, a laundry detergent. This commercial advertising of a product made by the Polish company Pollena-Bydgoszcz (later acquired by Unilever) was based on the novel by Henryk Sienkiewicz, *The Deluge*. This novel, in the form of a trilogy, is still the most loved novel in Poland. Action in the novel occurs during the Swedish invasion of Poland in 1655, called the deluge. Characters of twin brothers were employed in the commercial. These brothers were pretty good warriors but only because of their physical strength and not their mental capabilities. Therefore, before getting involved in any fight, they would always ask their father, "*Ociec prac?*" meaning "Father, should we fight?" However, in direct translation, *prac* means also "to wash." So, in the commercial, the father would answer, "Yes, but only in Pollena 2000!" On the other hand, German low-context detergent commercials focusing on the physical attributes of the product, typically discussed by two housewives who explicitly compare the quality of the wash, were perceived by the majority of Polish TV viewers as dull and boring.

The collective efforts that so define the Polish people are usually followed by periods marked by extreme difficulties in managing and operating as a unified people. Factions split off, and individual interests take precedence. Poles refocus quickly on the issues of their own families, leaving a process of disunity that often appears like anarchy. But it is also in these periods that the ingenuity of individual Poles is unleashed.

However, the opportunities of a market system have divided modern Poland along generational and geographical lines. Opportunities abound for young Poles, particularly in the cities. These Poles had less exposure to the Communist ideology, and thus, employers can mold them more easily. In fact, when Marriott was recruiting for workers in Warsaw, one ad was tailored to avoid such Communist indoctrination: "No experience wanted."

In addition, these younger Poles tend to be willing to take the risks associated with entrepreneurial activities. They have traveled internationally more and are much more comfortable using the English language, now generally recognized as the dominant language in international business, than their older counterparts. But change is slow. For example, between 1984, when Solidarity won the elections, and 1989, there was a slight but insignificant move from autocratic to participative leadership styles among Polish managers (Jago, Maczynski, & Reber, 1996). Also, Polish and Czech managers tend to be more autocratic than do French, German, Swiss, and American managers (Jago et al., 1993). This latter study was conducted in the early 1990s and may confirm the Russian influence on Polish and Czech managers, which should decrease over time.

Entrepreneurship is at the heart of the Polish spirit, and it has flourished since 1989. They can fix virtually anything by recycling parts from other items, often using their vast networks to procure or barter needed parts. Poles deal with their economic challenges by establishing small, sometimes one-man or one-woman businesses to sell products of every kind. The roads into Poland from Germany have become makeshift markets, and Western Europeans travel along them to buy products of every kind from Polish entrepreneurs. Likewise, the grounds of the Communist-era Palace of Culture and Science, in the heart of the Polish capital, Warsaw, have become a flea market with rows and rows of concession stands. Many Poles now dream of being their own bosses, just as their forefathers dreamed of owning a farm.

The changing role of the Church in Poland today is both positive and negative in the eyes of many Poles. Former Communist leaders, particularly in the Polish villages, now attend church regularly, thus uniting the village people under the church's steeple after many years of division. But the Catholic Church faces great difficulty in defining its new role in the lives of Poles. It has embarked on large-scale church development in Poland, and new churches are being built throughout the countryside. Many Poles resent this expansion of expensive churches when the needs of people are not being met as a result of changes in social services, such as guaranteed employment or welfare, health care, and education.

While the Church continues its role as a haven of resistance, it now serves as a moral barometer to the temptations of greed and selfishness, which capitalism represents. This message has found some degree of acceptance, but many Poles, particularly the young, find that taking advantage of the opportunities that the market economy presents is alluring and key to their survival. Finally, many Poles feel that the Church has lost touch with the Polish people. For example, in 1995, they elected the former Communist Kwasniewski as president, voting out of office the incumbent and the once-popular leader of the Solidarity Movement, Lech Walesa, who was strongly supported by the Catholic Church. The win was accomplished with heavy support from the Poles in the countryside, who voted against the Pope's wishes because they felt that the Church just did not understand the issues they faced on a daily basis.

And yet the Polish people do not want to forget the past. In 1999, movies based on Polish history proved to be surprising box office successes, whereas American blockbusters faltered. Similarly, Poles love the opera *The Haunted Mansion,* by Stanislaw Moniuszko, not only because of the Polish mazurkas danced in it but also because of its explicitly favorable treatment of rural Polish life. This opera, written in the Polish language, was considered so subversive that it was banned during the partition period. Frederic Chopin, the 18th-century romantic and nationalistic Polish pianist and composer, is revered.

To understand Poland in its entirety, it is important to comprehend the transition to modern economic life as represented by Warsaw, its modern buildings, and its modern hotels, such as the Marriott. Just as importantly, however, it is critical to understand the traditional culture of Poland that has withstood centuries of attack. There is no better way to understand this culture than to examine the traditional village church using the features of the church's central plan in the village, the partitioning of Poland and its influence on Polish identity (particularly in terms of public and private behavior), and the survivor's adaptations during periods of abrupt social change and transition.

CHAPTER 9

Kimchi and Korea

Throughout its long history, Korea suffered terribly at the hands of many nations—China, Japan, Russia, England, and France—whose armies invaded and ravaged it over several centuries. After being occupied by British troops in 1860, the Koreans tried in vain to close off their borders to foreigners and, in the process, earned the epithet "the Hermit Kingdom." In 1910, Japan annexed Korea, which then suffered 35 years of severe mistreatment until becoming independent in 1945. Although the Koreans were supposed to enjoy equal status with their Japanese counterparts, they were governed as a conquered people. For the first decade of Japanese rule, Koreans were not allowed to publish newspapers or develop any type of political organizations.

During the 1920s, Koreans were granted much greater latitude in voicing their opinions as a result of several large student demonstrations. The people gradually asserted themselves through various activities and organizations, including labor unions.

In 1937, the official policy of separate but equal treatment for Koreans came to an abrupt end, in large part because of the war between Japan and China between 1937 and 1945. Korea was mobilized for war, and hundreds of thousands of male Koreans were conscripted to help the Japanese army both in Korea and China. The Koreans were required to communicate both publicly and in private homes in Japanese; they had to worship at Shinto temples; and Korean children were encouraged to adopt Japanese names. All of the Korean-language newspapers ceased production. In effect, Japan was trying to assimilate Korea in every way imaginable, with the intent of destroying Korean culture and identity.

Fortunately, Japanese rule of Korea came to an end in 1945, and Koreans reasserted their culture with full force. Even so, their freedom would not be ensured for more than a decade because Chinese and U.S. troops occupied the country as part of the Korean War (1953-1957) between North and South Korea.

This chapter concerns only South Korea, which became separate from North Korea because of the Korean War. At that time, North Korea was the industrial powerhouse, whereas South Korea was much more of an agricultural society. Today, however, years of Communist rule have virtually destroyed the economic base of North Korea, whereas South Korea has flourished. It is probable that reunification will occur, given the parlous condition of North Korea ("A Survey of the Koreas," 1999).

In comparison to most nations, Korea is one of the most pure and unified cultures in the world. Admittedly, this purity is under attack because of globalization, but it is still recognized as the most Confucian nation in the world.

South Korea today is a small country about the size of Indiana with a population of about 45 million. It is mountainous, and the country possesses few natural resources. Similar to many developing nations, its cities have become very crowded. About 25% of the people live in the very crowded city of Seoul, and if the suburbs are included, this figure rises to 35%. Economic growth in the past 20 years has been incredible, and Korea is known as one of the Five Tigers of Asia. Although the 1997 Asian financial crisis highlighted problems in the economy (especially in the financial sector), the recovery has been outstanding, and the future seems promising.

Kimchi represents Korea in the same way that hamburger reflects the United States. Other than steamed rice, kimchi is the most popular food in Korea. Kimchi comes from a Chinese word translated as "immersing vegetables in a salt solution." There are literally hundreds of versions of kimchi.

Early forms of kimchi have been traced to the seventh century and King Shinmun's great wedding feasts. He ruled the country between 681 and 692. Koreans may have created kimchi out of necessity. As mentioned above, Korea is a small country with few natural resources. The long winters made the farming of fresh vegetables very difficult. As a result, families would spend weeks in the fall harvesting their crops and pickling them in salt solutions (with other spices added for taste) to ensure that they would ferment and be preserved for the winter, providing food for the family all year long. Kimchi includes Chinese cabbage, sea salt, sugar, crushed red chili, chopped ginger, garlic, and green onions. Koreans simply buy ready-made kimchi in jars and cans. They still eat it with almost every meal, although fresh vegetables are readily available at any time of the year.

Koreans sometimes express emotions using kimchi as a metaphor. For example, a Korean may express excessive anger or the feeling of wanting to kill someone by comparing it to the hot, roiling kimchi he or she digests. There is even a national museum in Seoul, the nation's capital, dedicated only to kimchi. Given such facts, it is appropriate that kimchi serves as our cultural metaphor for Korea.

The 60th Birthday

A Korean's 60th birthday is important. Whereas many Americans detest growing old and stop celebrating birthdays, Koreans tend to rejoice when reaching 60. Presumably, all major life goals have been attained, and it is now time to relax and enjoy life to the fullest. The Chinese Zodiac cycle is 60 years long, and Koreans believe that life runs in accordance with that cycle. Also, until recent generations, the estimated life of those born in Korea was approximately 60 years. Thus, the 60th birthday signifies that family and friends should gather to celebrate.

Often, the birthday party is held at the *K'unjip*, or "big house," which is the eldest son's household, where he lives with his wife, children, and parents. It is through the eldest son that the family genealogy is traced from one generation to the next. He is responsible for caring for parents and conducting rituals in their honor, and his wife is expected to produce the male heir for the next generation.

Korea owes much of its values and culture to Confucianism, which was first introduced to Korea late in the Koryo Dynasty, which ended in 1392. The succeeding Choson Dynasty, which ruled until 1910, adopted Confucian philosophies as the state ideology.

Confucianism is built on five relationships defining a hierarchical system in which there is a very high degree of power distance. These relationships are as follows:

- Father and son: governed by affection
- Ruler and minister: governed by righteousness
- Husband and wife: focused on attention to separate functions
- Old and young: organized on proper order
- Friends: faithfulness

These relationships are reflected in most activities in Korean society. Importantly, four of the five relationships are based on authority and subordination. Even the father-son relationship is not governed primarily by mutual affection but by the ability and willingness of the son to carry out his father's will. Thus, Confucianism tends to create a very particularistic culture in which each person's behavior is motivated by his or her relationship with a specific individual. A Korean can ethically be comfortable using different values in different relationships, and he or she may be very uncomfortable with universalistic cultures, such as the United States, where the general rules of behavior apply to all, regardless of the situational relationships at hand.

If the son carries out his obligations successfully, which include hosting the 60th birthday party, he will be rewarded upon his father's death: He inherits the house and a greater portion of his parents' estate than his siblings. Naturally, he becomes the family patriarch.

At dinnertime during the 60th birthday party, each of the five relationships is activated. The food is placed in the center of the table for all to share in a communal manner. When members of the family are seated on the floor cushions and begin to eat, the son's hard-working wife will fill the father's plate first, and kimchi will definitely be on it.

Confucian relationships demand that the father begins to eat first, followed by others in order of age. Ranking by age is critical and governs so much of Korean life that, upon meeting a stranger, one of the first topics of conversation is each person's age, so that each of the strangers can immediately assume his or her role in the relationship as the leader or the subservient. In comparison, asking a person's age in many Western cultures is considered intrusive.

With the exception of those who are friends, nobody at this party (or anywhere in Korea) refers to others by name. Rather, titles are used to highlight hierarchical rankings. For example, the eldest son will be referred to alternatively as "son," "big brother," "husband," "father," "elder," or "young one" throughout the day, depending on circumstances. The titles are so important that many at the party may not know the names of others. Supposedly, some families separated during the Korean War could not reunite because the brothers and sisters did not actually know one another's names, making a search impossible.

Strangers by Day, Lovers by Night

There are many aphorisms that mirror the Confucian perspective on male-female relationships, including the one above, which is focused specifically on husbands and wives. Given the subordination of the wife, it is logical to expect that the wives and their daughters prepare the birthday feast and clean up. Men are expected to be good workers and represent the family in public. The women are to provide children (in particular, at least one male), care for the family, and be subservient in public.

First and foremost, the relationship between a husband and wife is functional. Romantic love is an afterthought that is nice but not critical, because the purpose of marriage is to carry on the family lineage by producing a male heir. Even today, but less so, marriages are often arranged, frequently by matchmakers. As might be expected, the husband and wife may hardly know each other, if at all, at the time of marriage.

Because of the importance assigned to the functions of husband and wife, Korean families still want to approve or veto any potential union. These families tend to believe that successful unions are created when both husband and wife are of similar social and economic status. Also, ancestral heritage is usually critical when evaluating potential partners, because members of the same family clan, or *tongjok,* cannot marry. A *tongjok* includes families that share a surname with a similar heritage or source dating back for several generations.

A newly married woman leaves her parents' household permanently to join her husband's family, where she ranks at the bottom, below all of the other siblings. If she marries the eldest son, she is required to care for both her husband and his parents. Her standing improves if she delivers a male heir.

In public, women enter and exit elevators after men, help men with their coats, and follow dutifully behind them as they walk down the street. However, as is represented by the yin and yang of the Korean flag, wives do possess power, especially at home.

Korean men's status is a function of their occupation and the company employing them. The strong Confucian work ethic requires that the men work long hours, which means that they are often absent from home. At home, the wife has more power than the husband: She manages the family finances, runs all of the activities in the home, and takes care of the children. Some men become helpless at home. Hence, Korean widowers will often remarry almost immediately after a wife dies, just to keep the household operating effectively.

Korea is noted for its strong work ethic, as we might expect in a Confucian culture. Also, it is quite common for men at all levels of business to attend nightly functions with their coworkers and business counterparts. These functions often include not only dinner, but late evenings of drinking and karaoke-style festivities.

Similarly, the women work very hard to fulfill their many duties. Because their functions revolve around the home, Korean women tend to be evaluated on their ability to run a tight ship. The Korean home is almost unfailingly well maintained. Some Korean wives who have immigrated to Western nations do not like returning to Korea too often because of the onerous family responsibilities that are asserted automatically when they arrive.

Korean children also possess the strong Confucian work ethic. They help out at home and are expected to work hard at school. Korean children attend school 6 days a week, and even the younger students will have 2 to 3 hours of homework. Similar to Japan, Korea's literacy rate is more than 99%.

Kimchi's Public Role

The history of kimchi serves to highlight Korea's collectivist nature. As noted earlier, Korea has suffered many periods of foreign occupation, and during them, kimchi reflected the collectivist nature of Koreans that was critical for survival. Food often had to be hidden by families to protect it from foreign soldiers. Kimchi proved to be perfect for these resourceful people. Because it is a preservable food, Koreans would bury the kimchi underground to protect it from soldiers until the family was ready to eat it.

When first introduced to one another, Koreans, like those in other Asian cultures, tend to ask "What company do you work for?" rather than inquire about a person's title or occupation, which is of much more importance in the West. Also, people use their surnames first, followed by their individual names. Given such collectivism, it is easy to understand why Koreans have traditionally deemphasized individual stars in favor of team effort.

In Korea, what is good for the group is viewed as more important than what is good for the individual. This is a high-context society in which loyalty and the party line are valued more than the truth. Koreans are often very uncomfortable with the direct Western communication styles. Instead, from the highest levels of government to the household level, people are expected to tell the "truth," which is not facts per se, but rather the thoughts and feelings conforming to traditional ideals and norms. Thus, the message delivered lies not in what was said, but in the implicit message underlying the spoken words.

Men and women are expected to control their thoughts and emotions and express only that which serves society best, as we might expect in a Confucian culture. For example, when asked to lie under oath to save a friend, greater than 90% of people in Western cultures such as the United States and Canada, but only 37% of the Koreans, would refuse (Trompenaars & Hampden-Turner, 1998).

The Irish of Asia

Koreans can be compared to the Irish because they tend to be more emotional than their Asian neighbors. A good amount of this emotional expressiveness can be traced to their collectivism and long periods of domination by

foreign powers, during which they spasmodically arose in fierce and open rebellion. But some of it is an outgrowth of Buddhism, which 25% of the population practices. The principle of the Middle Way that the Buddha advocated—
keeping emotions under control, even to the extent of holding the body as
quiet as possible under all conditions—is still dominant in South Korea. As
discussed in Chapter 3, "The Japanese Garden," such practices, in combination with traditional Confucian ideals, tend to result in suppressed emotions
that periodically flare up. Given this perspective, it is easy to understand why
Catholicism, with its emphasis on rituals, collectivism, and shared emotional
expressiveness, has been much more successful in Korea than in other Asian
nations; 25% of the population, particularly the younger generation, practice
it. Also, Christianity is viewed as less restrictive than Confucianism in terms of
onerous family obligations, as exemplified by the activities at the 60th birthday party.

Collectivism and repressed emotional expressiveness are both related to
kibun, or the sense of well-being and harmony among people, that is central
to the Korean way of life. The concept of *kibun* is closely related to "face."
Taken literally, losing face means losing an eye, a nose, and, ultimately, the
entire face and the person's life. Losing face is a very serious matter, and even
minor criticisms in public are serious issues. Unlike the Western concept of
winning at all costs, face is the set of unspoken rules by means of which everyone's dignity and group harmony are preserved. Negotiations are frequently
long and drawn out, simply to avoid losing face. They also involve a great
deal of high context behavior, including an abhorrence of saying no directly
Palliatives such as "perhaps we can consider this proposal at another time" or
"that would be difficult" really may be the equivalent of no. Like the context-
specific Chinese, the Koreans tend to study an actual situation at great length
before agreeing to a course of action, and that includes getting to know the
prospective business partner well before doing business with him. Unlike
Westerners, who tend to start negotiating by taking a position right from the
start and then modifying it as they proceed, the high-context Koreans are frequently comfortable with an ambiguous position at the start that gradually
coalesces into a position or conclusion near the end of the negotiations.
American managers listening to an audiotape of Chinese managers making a
decision reacted incredulously to this pattern of behavior, as did the Chinese
managers when they listened to the American managers making decisions
(Twitchin, n.d.).

If Koreans like a person, they are prone to express this feeling more
openly than their Asian neighbors. It is not unusual for a Korean businessman
to take off his gold watch and give it to a Western visitor who has just said in
passing that he likes the watch. Such actions are also rooted in Buddhism, which
says that it is the gift giver and not the recipient who is the main beneficiary.

Just as kimchi reflects collectivism, it also mirrors the Korean trait of emotional expressiveness. Positive emotions tend to occur not only during the 60th birthday party, but also at any meal where kimchi is served. But when the high-context nature of Korean communication is violated, especially when kimchi is on the table, the affront is serious and may well lead to an unpleasant and jarring emotional confrontation.

Business in Korea is a direct reflection of the cultural values highlighted by kimchi. The South Koreans have organized their business activities in a manner very similar to that of the Japanese, who resurrected the outlawed *zaibatsus* after World War II into the modern *keiretsus*. A *keiretsu* is a large consortium of about 300 companies that has overlapping boards of directors, one large bank, an import-export arm, and subcontractors (e.g., Matsushita). In South Korea's case, these groupings, which are heavily family-based in terms of ownership, are called *chaebols*. After World War II, the Japanese introduced lifetime employment for workers and managers in the larger companies within the *keiretsus* because of labor unrest. South Korea has experienced such unrest since World War II but has not formally adopted the system of lifetime employment, which covers about 25% of the workforce in Japan. However, the operations of the *chaebols* are more reflective of Chinese culture than Japanese culture, because the Japanese stress employee participation to a greater extent. Like the Chinese, the Koreans tend to believe that power flows from the top down, and they act accordingly. This may be one reason why management and labor are more separated in Korea than in Japan (see Carroll & Gannon, 1997). Also, ownership in the *chaebols*, as noted above, is less dispersed among nonfamily members than in the Japanese *keiretsus*. Because of the Asian crisis of 1997, Korea has become a more open economy, but the *chaebols* are still critical.

At work, Koreans experience difficulty in taking a risky position or making an individual decision. Nearly all action is taken by committees, which provide a buffer to prevent any one person from drawing attention for decisions gone bad.

This aversion to risk combines with the Confucian hierarchies and relationships to add another dimension to Korea's high-context society. In the public arena, Koreans provide others with very little personal space. Although some of this behavior occurs because of the crowded living conditions, it is also caused by uncertainty avoidance. The respect for relationships and their governance of action applies only to known relationships. If a relationship has not been defined clearly, then Koreans act as if the relationship, or other person, does not exist.

When a relationship does not exist, Koreans will avoid taking any action because they do not know the correct response. Instead, they will treat other people as if they do not exist, leading to no personal space. For example, unlike in America, where lines are universally honored, in Korea, there is no respect for public lines. Instead, people will push and jostle to get to the front of the line. In grocery stores, strangers will bump into each other with their carts, and they do not even notice this slight inconvenience. By comparison, a fistfight could easily occur in the United States.

Also, Hofstede's (1991) research indicated that Korea is a less assertive and feminine society than the United States. This feature, in combination with the Confucian reverence for the past and collectivism, influences the Korean perspective on time and nature. Western countries tend to act in a future-oriented manner and believe that they control time and nature much more than Koreans, who are not as goal driven even though they have a reputation as hard workers. They focus more on the present than the future and tend to believe that they are controlled in large part by fate and nature, especially when compared to Americans. Because goals are less important to Koreans than to Americans, they will spend more of their time on multiple, concurrent activities instead of single actions that lead to the next step in achieving a goal, as we would expect from such a high-context culture.

In sum, kimchi's preservative nature and its historical role in safeguarding families in times of strife make it an excellent proxy for the Confucian and collectivist nature of Korean society. Kimchi spotlights the Confucian ability to let time stand still, revere tradition, and create the hierarchical rules surrounding relationships. The use of kimchi to protect families reflects the importance of putting the good of the country and family ahead of the individual, protecting against risk, and understanding the value of the present moment.

However, this perspective on Korean culture may be oversimplified. As globalization runs rampant, Koreans have tried mightily to preserve their heritage, but new international Korean superstars in sports, the increasing respect accorded women in the workplace, and the weakening of the financial system created by the *chaebols* in the face of the global economy and markets are slowly making Korea a new place.

Perhaps a supplementary cultural metaphor for Korea is the national flag, whose symbol is the *taeguh,* representing unity and harmony, or what Korea essentially values. Still, the *taeguh* has two parts, the yin and the yang. In combination, yin and yang connote harmony, but separately, they represent opposites. Possibly, the opposites define modern Korea better, because the contrasts and tensions in the culture have become more pronounced, including the subordination of women in the family relationships versus their hidden power in the household; the need for self-control balanced against the explosive volatility of individual emotions; and the hierarchy of power created by the five relationships vis-à-vis the collectivism that preaches equality of the group. The final, but perhaps the most potent, contrast is the pull of history and tradition and the push of globalization. Still, kimchi and its symbolic meanings capture a large part of Korean culture and behavior, and a visitor to this nation would be remiss in overlooking its importance.

PART III

Equality Matching
Cultures

I n equality matching cultures, there is a high degree of individualism but a low degree of power distance (horizontal individualism).
This type of culture emphasizes interval statistical scaling, that is,
there is a common unit of measurement so that it is possible to say that Individual B is 100% more important than Individual A; that Individual C is 100%
more important than Individual B; and therefore that Individual C is twice as
important as Individual A on a particular dimension. But this type of culture
does not recognize a true zero point, such as zero money. Hence, it is possible to compare individuals on one dimension at a time but not on several
dimensions, because there is no way of transforming values to one common
unit of measurement and arriving at a final score for each individual.

CHAPTER 10

The German Symphony

ermans, much like the Japanese, represent a major challenge to American understanding, even though the largest group (about 30%) of Americans is of German descent. When Americans discuss Germans, they frequently describe them in terms of an excessive emphasis on rules and order. Such descriptions have some basis in fact. For example, in 1997 alone, the German government passed nearly 5,000 federal laws and ordinances containing some 85,000 provisions (Grimond, 1999). Each of the 16 states, or *Lander,* also has its own set of laws and regulations.

But rules in and of themselves provide only a very limited and stereo typical view of German culture. To gain substantial insight into the culture, it is important to understand the essentials of German history. Germany was not even a nation until 1871, whereas many other European nations, such as Spain, England, Poland, Sweden, and France, had achieved this distinction several hundreds of years earlier. The Romans, whose empire was all-encompassing, feared and detested these "uncouth" peoples and left them alone after tribes led by Hermann the Great defeated them in 109 B.C. When other nations used the name *deutsch,* or German, the connotation was pejorative (Schulze, 1998). Even the German mercenaries who fought in the American Revolution were a source of derision and were considered ill-disciplined and lacking in courage. Finally, through the efforts of Frederick the Great and his father, a strong Prussia emerged between 1740 and 1780, and its military and governmental leadership led to the integration of the many small king-doms into the Germany of 1871.

However, given its lack of an illustrious history, some Germans roman-ticized the rule of Charlemagne in the eighth century as leader of the Holy Roman Empire into what they called the First Reich. Such romanticism is found in most, if not all, nations as they seek to explain their past and the manner in which it relates to the present, but the grandiosity of the German perspective became distorted during Hitler's time. Although Charlemagne ruled almost all of Europe, his influence was brief, and his three sons began the division of Europe that led indirectly or directly to the creation of several European nations. Germany, being part of Western Europe but bordering Eastern Europe, became host to a large number of ethnic groups that settled within its boundaries.

The Second Reich began in 1871. This period was marked not only by militarism but also by rapid economic growth, an emphasis on education and culture, and the development of the first modern welfare system. Several German universities were recognized as among the best in the world; there was ample governmental support of the arts, including the symphony; and even Bismarck, the Iron Chancellor, demonstrated his generosity by champi-oning the first modern social security system for retirees by ensuring that they would receive a government pension. However, Bismarck selected the age of 65 for pension eligibility because almost all citizens died before that time.

Furthermore, although all schoolchildren know about World War I, few of them realize that the Versailles Peace Treaty of 1918 imposed ex-tremely difficult conditions upon Germany that resulted in great hardship and inflation in the 1920s. Alfred Keynes, the great English economist, resigned from the Peace Commission because he foresaw the consequences of these conditions. A famous cartoon in the 1920s highlighted the eco-nomic breakdown by showing a man with a wheelbarrow full of money pur-chasing a loaf of bread with it. The depression of the 1930s only worsened the situation, and there were numerous political parties vying for power. Eventually, the struggle involved the Communist Party and the National Socialist Party led by Adolf Hitler. Ironically, Hitler was elected to office in a democratic election in large measure because most Germans at that time saw him as a source of stability and a counterforce to Communism, which was spreading rapidly throughout the world. This was the beginning of the pre-sumptive 1,000-year Third Reich, whose atrocities and brief history have been documented abundantly elsewhere.

Modern Germany began in 1945, when the Allies took control of Germany. The Anglo-American influence on Germany became evident in government, and a flourishing democracy with a small number of parties began to vie with one another in open and free elections. This influence was also evident in the support of labor unions built in terms of Anglo-American collective bargaining. Finally, the Marshall Plan of 1947, which provided the financial base for effective business and commerce, secured the nation's future. For the first time in modern history, a defeated nation was not subjected to undue hardship but the possibility of recovery. By the 1980s, Germany, although consistently portrayed as militaristic by the Western press, was, in fact, antimilitaristic. The standing joke in the 1980s in Germany was that it had already won World War III—The Economic War. There was a basis in fact for this assertion, because Germany far outstripped both the United States and Japan in terms of export sales per capita, although the American press focused almost all of its attention on Japan during the 1980s, as evidenced by the well-known phrase "Japan as Number 1." Today, NATO, led by the United States, openly criticizes Germany for its lack of interest in military preparedness and low level of involvement in European military matters, such as the struggles involving Serbia, Croatia, and Bosnia.

In Hofstede's study of 53 nations, the rankings of Germany were as follows, with 1 being the highest value: 43 on power distance; 15 on individualism; 9.5 on masculinity, or aggressiveness and materialistic behavior; 29 on uncertainty avoidance; and 11.5 (out of 22 nations studied) on long-term time orientation, or the willingness to defer present gratification for future success. Similarly, several surveys indicated that about 25% of Germans desire high social status, versus 2% of Swedes and 7% of Americans (Triandis, in press). These findings are consistent with the cauldron of history out of which modern Germany emerged.

■ Explaining the Symphony

As it was developing economically and politically into a nation, Germany was attentive to its culture and arts, and particularly the symphony. The essence of Germany can be experienced through the eyes and ears of the symphony, which was created in the German territories in the 16th century. Its origins can be traced to the early Italian opera (Copland, 1939/1957). What originally started as chamber music or operatic accompaniment, with a few musicians and a relatively uncomplicated score, has matured into full sections of woodwinds, brass, strings, and percussion; the occasional piano; and a long list of creative sound effects. Certainly, the most enduring achievements of composers from all stripes of music have been accomplished in the symphony. Analogously, this endurance is reflected in the staying power of the German society and culture.

It was through the efforts of Haydn and Mozart that many of the features of the symphony originated. Beethoven, however, single-handedly created a colossus that he alone seemed able to control (Copland, 1939/ 1957). The symphony lost all of its connection to its operatic origins. The form expanded, the emotional scope broadened, and the orchestra stamped and thundered in a completely new and unheard-of fashion. The composers following Beethoven added important innovations, including a cerebral emphasis and an atonal perspective. Today, the symphony is established as firmly as ever, but it was and will remain unfinished as innovations enrich it.

As for the musical instruments, single instruments had been played for centuries. However, prior to the 16th century, musicians had not mastered the art of playing together (Schulze, 1938). Since then, there is nothing to match the capacity of the greatest of all musical instruments, the symphony orchestra, which includes about 100 instruments and uses about four fifths of the range of human hearing (Schulze, 1938). The symphony's power emanates through the sound of musical instruments collected from all over the world. Schulze (1938) captured the historical significance of the symphony's musical instruments in the following summary:

> Snake charmers from the Orient contributed the oboe. Ancient Greeks before Homer developed the primitive clarinet. Horns were probably first used in the religious ceremonies of the God-fearing Israelites. Conquering and militaristic Rome brought trumpets to a high point of favor, while fifty generations later this same land took pride in its superb violins. At a late date, tubas sprang from Europe, and still later the saxophone and sarrusophone. Africa is famed for its drums and Greece for its pipes of Pan. (p. 5)

The music and the performers are brought together by the conductor. A skilled baton unites the disparate personalities and talents of the musicians so that they perform as one, at the literal level of the meaning of the term "in concert." The various musical divisions of style and perspective, such as those between entire sections of strings and the brass, and between the individual flutist and percussionist, are melded and molded by the conductor to produce a unified sound.

The orchestra, like the society, is made up of individuals, each with his or her own likes and dislikes. However, for the greater good that is the music, individual preference is subdued to the wants of the conductor and the needs of the symphony. Everyone cannot be a soloist, nor do all wish to be. In any event, the soloist's time of improvisation is brief, and the conductor soon signals that it is time to return to the history of the piece. It is this discipline or subordinated individualism—the voluntary submission of the individual to the whole, the guidance of the conductor, and the shared meaning of the music—that allows the symphony orchestra to flower and flourish.

Germans love symphonic music. Much like in the past, descendants of the aristocracy living in the old castles along the Rhine still arrange concerts of baroque and chamber orchestra music that are played in secluded rooms illuminated only by the intimacy of candlelight. These concerts are peaceful affairs that mentally transport the listener to an idealized Germany of old. Germans also frequent the symphony on a regular basis; the former West Germany, with its population of about 62 million, boasts *80* symphony orchestras. Frequently, the visitor to small German towns and villages will be able to attend symphonic concerts given by local musicians in churches, typically on Sunday afternoons and weekend nights, and particularly during and around religious holidays, such as Easter and Christmas.

This societal and cultural love of music has produced many of the world's great composers, including Haydn, Mozart, Schubert, Schumann, Bach, Handel, Strauss, Beethoven, and Brahms. It has also produced several world-class conductors, including Herbert von Karajan and Rudolf Kempe.

As a people, many Germans play musical instruments as a hobby, and of those, many belong to informal musical groups that carry forward the tradition. From the horns of the Alps to the brass polka bands, and up to the apex of the magnificent operas of Wagner, music is an integral part of German life. German music is not only integral, it is serious; it is not generally an outlet for emotion and craziness, as it is in the United States and other societies. Music is foreground, not background. It is meant as a collective experience intended to enrich life. Even the audience at German symphonies reflects this seriousness; typically, its members dress formally; listen intently to the music; and are silent until a major movement of a symphony is completed, at which time they tend to respond enthusiastically but with decorum.

In this chapter, we emphasize the following features of the symphony as reflective of German culture and values. These are the diversity of the musical instruments, positional arrangements of the musicians, the conductor or leader, precision and synchronicity, a unified sound, and the unfinished nature of the genre.

Diversity of the Musical Instruments

Prince Metternich, a 19th-century Austrian statesman, once remarked that the characteristic feature of the Germans was not unity, but multiplicity (Cottrell, 1986). This observation still has considerable validity today. Germany is divided into an astounding array of ethnic groups. Historically and culturally, each of these ethnic groups evolved separately, and each continues to have its own characteristics. Since the 1950s, the population of

Germany has become more diverse. Millions of foreigners have immigrated to Germany, seeking employment, citizenship, or asylum. About 7.37 million foreigners, or 9% of the population, live in Germany.

One fact is fundamental to understanding this varied array of ethnicity—throughout its long history, Germany rarely has been united (Solsten, 1996). Charlemagne's 9th-century Holy Roman Empire was more symbolic than real within a generation. Medieval Germany was marked by division. The Peace of Westphalia of 1648 at the conclusion of the Thirty Years War left an exhausted Germany divided into hundreds of states. In fact, until the unification of West and East Germany on 3 October 1990, Germany had known only 74 years (1871-1945) as a united nation with one capital. As noted earlier, for most of the two millennia that central Europe has been inhabited by German-speaking peoples, the area called Germany was divided into hundreds of states. Like the musical instruments of the symphonic orchestra, the people of modern Germany can trace their ancestral lineage to a multitude of past and present countries and cultures.

Historically, immigration has been a primary force shaping demographic developments in Germany (McClave, 1996). Upon the first unification in 1871, a significant source of population growth was an influx of immigrants from Eastern Europe. Adding to an already ethnically diverse population, these immigrants came to Germany to work on farms and in mines and factories. This wave of immigrants was the first of several that would occur over succeeding decades, thereby increasing an already diverse population.

Foreigners began arriving in West Germany in large numbers in the 1960s after the construction of the Berlin Wall. Since then, partly because of unification, the foreign population in Germany has increased substantially. Several million ethnic Germans from Eastern European countries, especially the former Soviet Union, began migrating to Germany with the end of the Cold War in Europe. As of 1998, Turks made up the largest group (2.2 million) of registered foreigners living in Germany, followed by immigrants from the former Yugoslavia (721,000) and Italy (608,000). Because of the higher birth rate of foreigners, about 1 of every 10 births in Germany is to a foreigner. Likewise, Germany's Basic Law offers liberal asylum rights to those suffering political persecution. From 1990 to 1992, nearly 900,000 people sought refuge in a united Germany. Although only 5% of requests for asylum are approved, slow processing and appeals may mean that many refugees remain in Germany for years (McClave, 1996).

Compared to America and Americans, Germany is not a melting-pot society, and Germans are not mobile. Many have stayed in the same geographic region and even the same house for generations. They are not accustomed to meeting and interacting with strangers at home, partially because most people live in apartments and/or small homes. As a result, they treat foreigners with a certain amount of wariness (Hall & Hall, 1990). Still, Germany's foreign residents remain vital to the economy, parts of which would shut down if they were to depart. Also, as McClave (1996) notes, "The birth rate among native Germans is so low that some studies have estimated that Germany will require approximately 200,000 immigrants a year to maintain its population into the next century and support its array of social welfare benefits" (p. 160).

Recently, Germany relaxed its citizenship laws. All children born in Germany automatically receive citizenship at birth, provided that at least one parent was born in Germany or arrived before the age of 14 and has a residence permit.

Geographically, Germany is also distinct. West Germany's absorption of East Germany enlarged its area by approximately 30%. The territory of the former East Germany accounts for almost one third of united Germany's territory. Now roughly the size of Montana, Germany is Europe's sixth largest country.

Germany has had difficulty integrating East and West Germany since they were reunited in 1990, because the costs were greatly underestimated, and there has been a persistently high level of unemployment of about 10% or above, particularly in the East. This has led to tensions between the West and the East. Incorporating more diversity into the new nation automatically created complexity, much like the addition of musical instruments does in the symphonic orchestra.

Various parts of the nation are also quite diverse. Sunny Bavaria, for instance, seems to be worlds away from the colder north both in temperament and culture. Frankfurt, the financial capital of the nation, is more like an American city than a German city. And there are several other large cities, each with its own character. However, this diversity is muted in many ways, including the preference for *dorfs*, or small villages, surrounding the cities in which large numbers of citizens live.

But it is not to be denied that the large number of instruments in the orchestra creates complexity, in about the same way that the many forms of diversity (ethnic, geographic, etc.) do in German society. The need for controlling this complexity is addressed by the other features of the symphony.

Positional Arrangements of the Musicians

When a symphonic orchestra is seated in front of the audience, the stage is crowded. To solve the problem of having large numbers of musicians onstage, and to make it easier for the musicians to play their instruments, the conductor arranges the seating so that there are four separate sections: strings, woodwinds, brass, and percussion. This compartmentalized arrangement of seats helps to maximize the musical instrumentation and the quality of the sound, as does the seating of musicians within sections in terms of skills and responsibilities (e.g., first violinist, second violinist, etc.).

Such crowdedness is mirrored in German society. Germany is only about 66% of the size of France, the largest nation in Western Europe, and only 4% of the size of the United States. More importantly, it is the world's 29th most crowded nation: 229 residents per square kilometer versus only 29 for the United States. Viewed from the perspective of both the symphony and crowded conditions, it is easy to empathize with the compartmentalization of German society that is represented by their affection for privacy and respect for others. Apartment dwellers are wont to leave polite but anonymous notes asking their noisy neighbors to scale back the sound. And, just as the positional arrangement of the musicians in the orchestra separates them from one another, the home separates the individual from the outside world. Throughout the year—and most especially at Christmas—Germans greatly cherish the privacy and security of the home. In Christian Germany (about half of the population is Catholic and half Protestant), Christmas remains a very dutifully observed religious holiday, a time when gemütlichkeit strongly prevails over the people. This word translates simply "as 'comfort' or 'coziness,' but it has wider connotations—of the hearthside and deep content, of home cooking and family security" (Cottrell, 1986, p. 123).

The home (*das heim*) is at once a haven from the bustle and stress of the working world and a place where personal status may be more solid and unthreatened. It is a castle and a refuge from the outside world. Homes are protected from outsiders by a variety of barriers: fences, walls, hedges, solid doors, blinds, shutters, and screening to prevent visual and auditory intrusion (Hall & Hall, 1990). Front yards, although beautifully maintained, are used only rarely. Outside activities, such as sitting in the sun or visiting with family, are restricted to the backyard, away from the street and the eyes of others. The home is the most important possession to a German, and life in the home with one's family is treasured. Similarly, it is remarkable to see some Germans vacationing on the seashore of the North Sea as they shovel sand on three sides to a height of four feet in order to define the space or sand home that they will occupy for only a few hours.

Like the home, the door "stands as a protective barrier between the individual and the outside world" (Hall & Hall, 1990, p. 40). Germans tend to keep doors closed. Doors are often thick and solid, their hardware heavy, tight-fitting, and built to close tolerances. The closed door preserves the integrity of the room, provides a boundary between people, and minimizes interruptions and accidental intrusions.

A related issue is the physical distance between individuals when talking to one another on a face-to-face basis. Germans keep more space between them than do individuals in nations such as France, Italy, and Thailand. Supposedly, this distancing is a protective barrier and psychological symbol that operates in a manner similar to that of the home. In addition to physical distance, many Germans also possess a distinctive sense of aural distance. German law actually prohibits loud noises in public places during certain days and times of the week. In one town, some residents filed suit against parents who allowed their children to play in the local playground during lunchtime and early evening. As noted above, Germany, particularly in the western part, is a crowded country, and the emphasis on both physical and aural distances may be a reflection of this fact.

The compartmentalization in German society also is actualized in the German penchant for formality. Within the German home, family members abide by formal rules of behavior designed to give one another distance and privacy (Hall & Hall, 1990). These patterns of formality extend in adulthood to relations with friends and coworkers in the office. Germans tend to introduce themselves by their family name, as opposed to their first name. The use of formal and informal pronouns in the German language indicates the nature of this relationship. The familiar *du* (you) and first names are reserved for close friends and family. The difference between close friends and acquaintances is distinct. Those people at work or school whom an American would label as friends usually are referred to as colleagues by the more conservative Germans. This sharp distinction may be related to the socialization process throughout the German life course. Most Germans develop two or three close friends during their early years. In turn, these relationships often are maintained for life. It usually takes a German much longer to categorize someone as a friend, but once this determination is made, he or she will treat this individual in a very special manner.

Although the following illustration is extreme, it helps to bring these concepts into perspective. An Irish professor and a German professor worked side by side for 3 years at an international agency in Brussels. Although they were of equivalent social status, their relationship was impersonal. In Germany, the professor was formally addressed as "Herr Professor Doctor" followed by his last name, whereas in Ireland, the Irish professor was called "Professor" or even by his first name. Over beer one night, the German professor indicated that they could now be more informal and friendly with one another, and that the Irish professor should feel comfortable addressing him as only "Doctor" in the future.

A similar emphasis on compartmentalization is found in the degree of politeness that Germans extend to acquaintances and strangers. Germans are careful not to touch accidentally or to encourage signs of intimacy (Hall & Hall, 1990). Gestures and smiling are restrained. On the other hand, Germans do maintain eye contact in conversations to demonstrate that they are paying attention. At times, Germans may appear stiff, distant, and forbidding. However, this reserved nature should not be misinterpreted as a lack of friendliness.

These elements of compartmentalization, much like the positional arrangements of the orchestra, also extend to German business practices. Although Germans place a great deal of emphasis on promptness, delays in such areas as deliveries do occur because of the compartmentalization of German life and business. It is possible for a salesperson to take an order and then leave on vacation without asking a coworker to follow up on the order (Hall & Hall, 1990). Likewise, problems in the shipping division of a German business may not be conveyed to the retailer and the customer.

Typical German business organizations tend to be more compartmentalized than American organizations, most probably because of the high value attached to respecting status and power within the hierarchy. The owner of an insurance company constructed a building in Frankfurt in the form of a hierarchy that is symbolic of this perspective. Each level of the building contained fewer people per square kilometer. The owner, surrounded by a few key staff people, occupied the top floor. The building itself looks like a line drawn at a 45% angle and is called "the ladder of success."

In recent years, German business organizations have emphasized the use of cross-functional teams. Still, in Germany, information flows from one department to another less easily than it does in the United States, as we might expect when privacy is valued so highly. As a result, quick decisions on business issues are difficult to reach. Inevitably, decisions are often made without the benefit of current information gleaned from fast-changing markets.

The importance of the German executive's office cannot be overemphasized. As in the United States and many other nations, the size of the office, having a personal secretary right outside of it, and related factors are key markers of status and hierarchy. But what is distinctive about the German office is that the manager sees it as inseparable from and as an extension of his or her personality (Hall & Hall, 1990). Hence, the importance of closed doors, which a visitor should generally avoid opening without permission.

Furthermore, once inside the office, the visitor should be careful not to violate the norms of physical space found in Germany by moving a chair too close to the manager. One German manager became incensed that visiting American salespeople would invariably move the visitor's chair closer to his desk, presumably to establish a physical sense of intimacy in trying to finalize a sale. This executive took the extreme measure of bolting the visitor's chair to the floor, thus frustrating any movement that a visitor might attempt.

As Hofstede's (1991) study confirmed, Germans tend to be risk averse and are less comfortable with strange situations and newcomers than many other peoples. Just as the symphonic orchestra tends to be compartmentalized, so, too, the German penchant for analyzing projects in depth leads to a situation in which their levels of risk are reflected accurately. This risk aversion may account for the extreme lengths to which German executives will go when analyzing business opportunities before committing to them.

Conductors and Leaders

Like the general direction provided by the symphonic conductor in the creation of the single, powerful sound of the orchestra, German leaders have provided direction and guidance to an often fragmented state. Historically, with the notable exception of Adolf Hitler, Germans have not reacted favorably to charismatic leaders who are intent on leading them to a new world order without any questioning of their authority (Hall & Hall, 1990). Rather, Germans have preferred a visionary leader who is mature and strong enough to delegate responsibility and decision making to competent subordinates throughout the hierarchy.

Frederick the Great, who ruled Prussia from 1740 until 1780 and was largely responsible for creating the base of the German nation, epitomizes the classic German ruler whose modern embodiment was incorporated in the figure of Konrad Adenauer, a long-time president in Germany after World War II who was one of the leading figures in establishing the European Union. Frederick survived the rigors of his Prussian military education to become a philosopher-king, famous for his taste in art, music, and literature. He wrote poetry and scholarly essays, played the flute, composed concertos and sonatas, and maintained a regular correspondence with Voltaire. To this day, this ideal of leadership is emulated throughout German society. Corporate executives, for instance, tend to be more well-rounded than their American counterparts, and many of them are members of book clubs that favor the serious study of science, literature, and philosophy; about 75% of the CEOs of German industrial companies hold a doctorate. Clearly, the visionary leadership provided by Frederick resulted in reforms that transformed a previously fragmented state into a major European power.

Similarly, the expectation is that the corporate leader will approximate such a visionary but mature profile of leadership and, because of it, be able to provide the direction that organizational members desire. The German CEO will generally tell a foreign marketing executive to see his or her counterpart responsible for making decisions in this area. German managers expect a great deal of their subordinates and test them by pushing them to perform, but they do not hover (Hall & Hall, 1990). Adler (1997) describes Germany as a "well-oiled machine," with a small power distance and strong uncertainty avoidance. German businesses reduce uncertainty by defining roles clearly. In contrast to high power distance cultures—where employees want their managers to act as decisive, directive experts—Germans expect their managers to delegate responsibility and decision making to competent subordinates throughout the hierarchy.

There are, of course, some drawbacks to this style of leadership. Martin Gannon attended several briefing sessions in Germany focusing on the DaimlerChrysler merger. Some of the differences between the German and American companies, even after the merger in 1997, were noteworthy. Daimler had only four organizational levels, which is consistent with its emphasis on low power distance and delegation of responsibility, whereas Chrysler had nine. However, it was much more difficult for Daimler executives to take action, because their subordinates demanded the right to participate in the decision and, at times, to veto it. Also, the Daimler hierarchy was much more rigid, even to the point that a middle manager would not even dare to jump organizational levels, which were to be respected if one wanted to be viewed favorably. But the American middle managers had no difficulty offering their suggestions and ideas to upper-level managers; even Robert Eaton, the Chrysler CEO who was largely responsible for the dramatic success of this company in the 1980s and 1990s, could be easily approached without fear of consequence.

As indicated previously, the Allies strongly influenced Germany after World War II, and this influence can be seen in the area of leadership. Germany developed a unique and democratic form of corporate governance termed "co-determination." Unlike the single board of directors in American corporations, German firms, by law, must have two boards: a management board (*Vorstand*) and a supervisory board (*Aufsichtsrat*), the second of which must include some employees and labor union representatives. There is also a workers' council (*Betriebsrat*), which has the right to monitor and approve all corporate plans and actions. The *Vorstand* initiates an action, such as downsizing, but it must be approved by the *Aufsichtsrat* and *Betriebsrat,* and finally by the national union. Needless to say, making decisions is slow and complicated. But once decisions are made, they are implemented quickly because of the consensus. Still, large corporations feel that this system is too cumbersome and complex, and many of them have begun to relocate operations abroad because of this governance structure and other factors such as the high cost of labor and government regulations.

However, the German system of corporate governance is changing. German labor organizations have lost 3.5 million members since 1991; the proportion of workers in unions was 1 to 3 in 1991, but only 1 in 4 in 1999, and additional losses are anticipated. And although the total cost of labor was far higher in Germany than in most other nations, it has declined from $31.85 per hour in 1995 to $27.81 in 1997, and additional reductions are forecast. During the same period, the American figure rose from $17.19 to $18.17.

Perhaps the business leaders who have proved to be particularly visionary in conducting the activities of their firms are those in the *Mittelstand*. These are 2.5 million small to medium-sized companies that account for 80% of employment in the private sector and two thirds of the GNP. About 40% of their sales come from exports, which is about 25% of total export sales ("The Mittelstand Takes a Stand," 1995). These companies are frequently located in small towns. Although they emphasize long-term employment, they have been particularly adept at identifying markets and employing technology to cut total costs.

Precision and Synchronicity

Perhaps the most critical features of the symphony are precision and synchronicity. Given the complexity of the music and performance, the conductor stresses these two related characteristics. Everything must be done perfectly, and everyone must be willing to participate within the boundaries of the performance. There are individual soloists, and they are given ample opportunity to show their skills and abilities. But for the greater good of the orchestra, their time is short, and they recede into the orchestra, once again merging their identities and personalities with other orchestra members. Unlike the opera, during which great singers clearly separate themselves from the chorus through their memorable performances of arias, the symphonic performers must willingly subordinate their individual selves to the greater good. Similarly, Germans tend to be individualistic, but their subordinated individualism is different from the competitive individualism found in the United States or the egalitarian individualism of Sweden.

There are countless examples of precision and synchronicity in German business. Most Germans are quite conscious of time and how to allocate it efficiently. To many Germans, there is no such thing as "free time." In one survey, the German respondents had difficulty with the category "I had free time on my hands" when asked to indicate why they were seeking a part-time position. They believe that there is a sharp distinction between work and leisure, but in both cases, they prefer that the time be used rationally and efficiently.

In both social and business life, tardiness is frowned upon. It is expected that everyone will arrive at least on time for a meeting, and preferably 5 minutes early. Just as the soloist who comes in off cue may lose his or her position with the orchestra, the businessperson who comes late for a meeting may lose a client or miss important information. German meetings and negotiations are also long and tend to have well-marked stages. Unlike Americans, who like to get to the bottom line as soon as possible and follow the dictum "Keep it simple, stupid," Germans love historical background and charts. One American executive who was raised in Germany recalls his presentation before an American board of directors when he was unconsciously using the German perspective. He originally had planned to give a historical overview of a project for about 25 minutes, but he stopped short after 5 minutes when he noticed the vacant and bored looks on the faces of board members. Similarly, a German executive who has lived in the United States for many years likes to point out how Americans and Germans would approach the study of elephants, and we leave it to the reader to decide the national identity of the authors:

- The Elephant: A Short Introduction in 24 Volumes

- The Elephant: How to Make It Bigger and Faster in 20 Minutes

Precision and synchronicity also tend to influence communication. Germans communicate in a low-context manner, that is, they directly express their ideas in both written and oral form. Many American negotiators far prefer to deal with Germans than with members of high-context cultures, who present their initial ideas indirectly and vaguely. But Germans tend to use a deductive way of thinking that relies upon past history and theory, in contrast to the Anglo-American style, which tends to use cases and examples to back up an argument. The basic German approach to problem solving is to deduct from a theory or small number of principles, whereas the American approach focuses on the issue of operationalizing a solution as soon as possible. American businesspeople are frequently surprised when their initial ideas are met with a seemingly hostile response: You are wrong. In reality, the German must be convinced that he or she is incorrect, and he or she is open to such an approach, but the solution must be backed up by logic, data, and consistency. Similarly, an American must be not only well-prepared but also willing to discuss seemingly insignificant details. Precision and synchronicity must be honored, and one case study that is used casually to justify a course of action, or even a few of them, is not ordinarily persuasive.

Similarly, words should mean exactly what they are intended to mean. An American might say "I'll call you for lunch" without really intending to do so, but the German preference for precision and synchronicity will require that this statement be honored. Failing to do so will mark the American as insincere, careless in thought and habit, and culturally insensitive. An extreme example of miscommunication occurred in the Daimler plant in Alabama, when German workers assigned to it showed up at their supervisor's home after the first day of work because they had interpreted the statement "Let's have dinner" in a very literal manner.

One distinctive feature of the German language is that the verb tends to be at the end of the sentence. Similarly the main point is often made at the end of a talk, meeting, or negotiations. Much like classical symphonies, meetings start slow, can last for hours, and ultimately build to a climax. At meetings and in negotiations, there is a slow but steady progress through easily recognizable stages during which timing, intonation, and control of voice, speech, and emotions are critical. Thus, in business as in music, sound, tone, modulation, and timing are key to a successful performance.

It is also helpful to demonstrate efficiency in communication, as this reflects precision in the manner in which the relationship will be established. For example, an American will tend to greet a German with "Hello, Tomas, how are you?" It is probably better to say, "Hello, Tomas, what can I do for you today?"

Finally, the emphasis on precision and synchronicity also includes attire and dressing. Given their relatively conservative perspective, Germans dress more conservatively than Americans, and it is helpful for Americans to look professional and act accordingly. Sitting at ease but upright, wearing clothes that are fashionable but do not take attention away from the matter at hand, and politely listening and contributing insight without constantly interrupting the precision and synchronicity of the discussion are all techniques that can help to enrich the communication process and relationship.

Germany's unity is also expressed through its educational system, which begins with the *Grundschule,* or elementary school, where one teacher is sometimes assigned to the same group of children as the children progress from Grades 1 through 4 or, in some states, Grades 1 through 6; our discussion will assume Grades 1 through 4, although the total number of years of school is identical whether the *Grundschule* extends through Grade 4 or Grade 6.

After graduating from the *Grundschule,* students are assigned to one of three different types of school. In some German states, the teacher makes this assignment, whereas in other states, it is based on the results of a standardized examination. Given the importance of this assignment, it is quite common for German elementary students to have tutors as early as first grade so as to improve their chances of success. This assignment largely determines each student's career, and no other society separates its children at such an early age. It is possible, but somewhat difficult, to change from one type of school to another after the fourth grade.

The first type of school is the gymnasium, or academic school designed for those who want to pursue university education. Students attend the gymnasium from Grades 5 through 13, but they can leave after Grade 10 for a non-college-oriented career. If they pursue this option, their degree is equivalent to that of a *Realschule* graduate, as described below. Students in the gymnasium are required to pass a very difficult exam, the *Abitur,* before they can be considered for admission to the university, which is not automatic but dependent on the number of available slots. Even those who pass the *Abitur* and are admitted are not granted admission to the entire university, but only to one of its faculties. Thus, even these students have fewer opportunities than their American counterparts.

After Grade 4, other students continue their education at the *Realschule,* or "real-world" school, through Grade 10. Some of these graduates then serve as apprentices for 2½ to 3 years while attending school 1 day a week. German industry subsidizes these apprentices and hires most of these students after they have completed the apprenticeships. Other *Realschule* students attend *Fachoberschule,* or middle school, for 2 more years after the 10th grade and obtain a middle school degree, during 6 months of which they serve as apprentices. These students can attend the traditional universities if either they pass the *Abitur* or attend the *Fachhochschule* (specialized universities) for at least 1 year. Normally, these graduates do not attend the traditional universities but continue to pursue a university degree in these specialized universities, which emphasize four different concentrations: technical, social sciences, science, and business.

After the *Grundschule,* some students attend the *Hauptschule* (capitol school), and they can leave after Grade 9 without a degree. Most of them, however, leave with a degree and then serve as apprentices for 2½ to 3 years while attending school 1 day a week. These students also have the opportunity to attend the traditional universities or the specialized universities (*Berufsoberschule*) by going to school for 2 additional years and passing the *Abitur* examination.

In recent years, this system, although logically consistent and unified, has become strained. German parents want their children to graduate from the gymnasium, much like American parents want their children to be in programs for the gifted and talented. Today, 50% of the students graduate from gymnasia, but many of them cannot achieve the career success historically associated with such graduation because of their overwhelming numbers vis-à-vis available opportunities. Also, there are far too many graduates from traditional universities that specialize in the professions.

Clearly, this educational system reflects the German penchant for order and unity. The sequence of schools mandates particular steps for a student in order to attain the necessary education for whatever he or she prefers to do occupationally in support of the German effort. In a sense, Germans subordinate some individuality to this system so that all of society may benefit. As with orchestra members, the order imposed by this educational system allows Germans to do their individual parts to make the German effort successful.

Presently, there is a great debate over the relative merits of the German educational system when compared to the American approach (Carroll & Gannon, 1997). About 66% of the German workforce has completed the apprenticeship programs that are available in the *Realschule* and *Hauptschule,* and there is an easy transition between school and work (Prewo, 1993). This is not true for many Americans. Likewise, the United States has a population in which approximately 20% of its citizens are substandard in reading and writing skills; almost all Germans are at least adequate in these skills. The American system, however, seems much more responsive to changing needs, and it is much easier to change career directions in the United States than in Germany.

The subjugation of the individual for the good of the whole also is evident in the German military personnel procurement policies. Even in light of geopolitical changes in post–Cold War Europe, Germany continues to maintain a military force structure based on a policy of conscripted service. Although conscription has long been rejected by a majority of the younger generation, the Army (*Bundeswehr*) is accepted by the majority of Germans as an instrument for defense and maintaining peace (Fleckenstein, 1999). This is largely due to the right of conscientious objection and civilian alternative employment. National military service and civilian alternative service are both regarded as valid options open to conscripts.

Although it is a constitutional duty to render service involving the use of arms for public good, German law also guarantees the right to object to service on grounds of conscience. Conscripts granted conscientious objector status are required to do civilian alternative service, performing tasks that are primarily social service benefiting the community. These tasks contribute substantially to maintaining the social safety net. Although conscientious objectors engaged in civilian alternative service were at first considered to be shirking their duty, their approval ratings now "are on par with those for doctors" (Fleckenstein, 1999, p. 36). In fact, one of the many arguments for the continuation of conscription is that German society would not be able to sustain the loss of the social contributions provided by these objectors. Clearly, this ability of German youths to engage in a form of national service for the public good is analogous to the subjugation of the separate instruments to the unified sound created by the symphonic orchestra.

Given Germany's history, it is ironic that this nation is viewed as a "wimp" because its citizens are so reluctant to participate in war (Fisher, 1993). Several surveys suggest that many Germans would like their nation to become neutral or Swiss-like in matters of war.

Germans even manifest their unified sound or unity in their love for flowers and gardens. Most houses in Germany are lined with flowers in windowsills. German gardens often contain a complete variety of vegetable plants and fruit trees that are displayed and placed in a systematic way. Germany as a whole is dotted with thousands of small villages and sprawling urban centers that are separated by fields or grasslands plowed and maintained in a systematic and orderly manner (Cottrell, 1986). The same can be said of the vineyards that dominate much of the land in southern Germany. This ordered beauty and sense of unity are most appreciated throughout Germany.

Furthermore, the extremely efficient rail and road networks tend to emphasize this sense of unity. There is a clear parallel between the efficiency and unity of these networks and the predictability, regularity, and unified sound of the symphony. Chronometer-like timing, precision, and conformity underlie both music and transportation activities. On seeing these German transport systems—more than 4,500 miles of high-speed highways (autobahn) and the nationalized railroad (*Deutsche Bundesbahn*), with its luxurious Trans-European expresses and fast, reliable intercity services—it is difficult to believe that, for centuries, German transporation systems lagged far behind those of its Western European counterparts (Cottrell, 1986). In addition, in terms of rail travel, the foreign traveler to Germany will find that trains rarely leave their originating station late or do not arrive at their destination on time.

Just as the symphonic orchestra unites the individual musicians, the old tradition of folk festivals unites the German population. There are literally thousands of festivals in Germany each year. They range from village feast days to "elaborate civic displays of organized chaos" (Cottrell, 1986, p. 118). Typical of festivals held all over Germany is beer drinking, abundant food, brass bands, dancing, and colorful parades. Although at first, it may seem that carefree festivals run counter to the dour and serious German stereotype, such communal activities are actually among the most popular and oldest of traditions, and they reinforce the feelings of group solidarity.

Most German festivals have a religious origin. *Karneval* is a Catholic celebration, a period of frivolity and deliberate self-indulgence before the time of Lenten fasting. In the 15th century, when ascetics criticized Germany's wild and unrestrained pre-Lenten celebrations, a churchman reasoned in defense that "a wine barrel that is not tapped will surely burst" (Cottrell, 1986, p. 118). To this day, his comment remains as good an explanation as any of the extraordinary way in which millions of Germans can suddenly cast aside inhibitions and everyday formalities once a year and throw themselves wholeheartedly into the madcap fun of *Karneval* (also known as *Fasching*). Although not directly traced to religious origins, there is nothing else in Germany to compare with the sheer overindulgence of *Oktoberfest*. This festival and many of the wine festivals celebrate the earthly yield of crops. Throughout the wine-growing districts, there are concerts, fireworks displays, dances, and nonstop pouring of wine. Clearly, Germans cling fondly to old traditions designed to give the season a truly magical air, and thus, they are reminded of their unity as a people.

Similarly, festive events that bring Germans together regularly are sporting activities. In contrast to America, interscholastic sports are neither sponsored nor organized by the schools. Instead, completely independent of schools, individuals must join sports clubs for such competition. Soccer and tennis attract millions of participants and spectators. There are hiking trails and maps for trails all over the country. One of the more enjoyable activities in Germany is to hike up to a mountaintop restaurant. Even traditional American sports, such as football and basketball, are beginning to attract more participants. However, two common elements run through all of these activities. First, they are enjoyed at all levels of society; second, they tend to be organized into, or at least enjoyed in, groups. These aspects of sport may provide relief from workplace stresses while providing the Germans the sense of group identity that they tend to enjoy. Unlike his or her American counter-part, the average German worker has ample leisure time to enjoy these many activities; the average number of hours devoted to work is much lower in Germany, and holidays are much more frequent and longer.

The Unfinished Symphony

Many of the great German composers, such as Beethoven and Brahms, bequeathed to posterity unfinished symphonies, and scholars love to debate what the composers intended and how they planned to realize their intentions. Similarly, Germany is a work in progress.

Because of the unification of East and West in 1990, one of the chief aims of the constitution, national self-determination for all Germans, had been achieved. However, Germans of the now-enlarged Federal Republic felt as if they had inherited a huge estate that was proving to be more of a liability than an asset. Unification may be described as an expected marriage of two partners from totally different backgrounds who started with a short honeymoon followed by a period of recriminations (Kettenacker, 1997). West Germans are said to expect gratitude, East Germans a sense of charity and caring. Both, however, are unreasonable propositions. Thus, Germans have embarked on a search for a new national identity that will shelter them from their worries and anxieties and overcome their loss of direction. Soul-searching, always a favorite German pastime, can no doubt be recognized as more justified than ever.

Germany's comparatively short history as a nation-state since 1871 is the master key to understanding its political culture, from which a new identity must be distilled (Kettenacker, 1997). Clearly, World War II and its aftermath changed Germans in some very material ways, as we have seen. Almost all of these changes have been positive, including German leadership in the European Union (EU), its economic prosperity, and its successful implementation of new organizational approaches in government and business. But like many European nations that are now part of the EU, Germany has dual allegiance, both to the nation and to the EU. At least a few surveys have suggested that proportionately fewer Germans identify primarily with the EU than do their counterparts in other nations. There is nothing wrong about such identification, provided that Germany continues to maintain its expected leadership role in both the EU and NATO. Otherwise, the peace and prosperity of the world could be jeopardized.

Looking through the lens of the characteristics of the symphony, we can speculate on the nature of German culture and changes within it over the next several years. Although the population will continue to diversify, other factors will be critical as well. There are clear generational clashes in Germany, as in many European nations confronting an aging population crisis. Currently, the proportion of Germans over 60 years of age is 21%, but this proportion will probably rise to about 34% by 2040. Also, there are clear ideological conflicts that are reflected in the platforms and even the names of the Christian Democratic Party, the Democratic Socialist Party, and the Green Party. And the issue of Germany's leadership role in both the EU and NATO will probably be a continuing source of tension.

Still, it seems safe to predict that Germany will continue to emphasize the characteristics of the symphony, such as positional arrangements, compartmentalization, subordinated individualism, precision and synchronicity, and unity or a unified sound. Although parts of Germany are changing, and other parts still cling to the past, we can expect that there will always be a symphony.

CHAPTER 11

The Swedish *Stuga*

The pillars of the country's economy—its system of interlocking,
closely held companies and its generous welfare state—are being
rocked by the forces of global competition and rising investor de-
mands for better returns. . . . Mergers worth more than $52 billion
swept Sweden last year . . . $6 billion more than in Germany,
where the economy is 10 times as large.

— "Busting Up Sweden, Inc." (1999), p. 52

There are few, if any, nations that have manifested as firm a commitment to cultural values as Sweden. But as the quote above indicates, economic forces are causing a reevaluation of these traditional values, which are effectively symbolized by the *stuga,* or summer/weekend home.

Sweden is one of the "three fingers of Scandinavia," located between Norway and Finland. In size, it is just larger than the state of California. There are thousands of islands lining the coast, and mountains form much of the northwest. Many rivers flow from the mountains through the forests and into the Baltic Sea. Sweden is dotted with lakes, and more than half of the country is forested.

Although it rarely snows in the southern part of the country, the northern part has more than 100 snow days each year. The unique culture of the Swedes has been a result of the struggle to deal with and control harsh surroundings, and the outcome has been a stable society that, although it has experienced some difficulties in recent years, is economically and socially the envy of many others.

The population of Sweden is 8.8 million. At least 85% of the people are ethnic Swedes. A small, indigenous minority (approximately 15,000), the Sami, lives in the north. Known to some as the "Lapps," the Sami are nomadic and herd reindeer for a living.

In Sweden, approximately four out of every five couples are unwed. Under Swedish law, couples have the same rights to property and inheritance whether they are married or not. If Swedes marry, it is generally upon the birth of a child, and yet the divorce rate is more than 50%.

Sweden is a highly secular society. Although 95% of Swedes belong to the Evangelical Lutheran Church, most people rarely, if ever, attend church.

The standard of living is very high in Sweden, as indicated by the high ownership of telephones, television sets, and cars. Slums do not exist, and the crime rate is very low. Free, compulsory education has served to raise the literacy rate to 99%. Swedes tend to be avid readers. The number of book titles published in Sweden is 158 per 100,000 population, making Sweden the seventh leading nation in this area.

Sweden has a constitutional monarchy, and the head of government is the prime minister. Members of parliament are elected for 3-year terms.

An appropriate metaphor for Sweden is the stuga or summer/weekend home. Before showing how this metaphor accurately reflects modern Swedish society and its cultural mindset, we need to provide some background about its history and form of government.

Sweden's recorded history begins around A.D. 500, with a series of unending minor wars and feuds. The Svea tribe, the largest at the time, gave its name to Sweden, or *Sverige,* which means the Realm of the Sveas. Around A.D. 1000, the famous Vikings formed a tribe of superb seamen known for their violence and success at ravaging Europe. But the Swedish Vikings soon turned their attention toward the East, setting up principalities in Russia and trading relationships with the Byzantine Empire.

German domination of Sweden began in the Middle Ages. Missionaries from Germany arrived in Sweden during the ninth century but were not successful in converting the Swedes to Christianity until the middle of the 11th century. German merchants conquered through commerce and gained almost total control over Swedish trade and politics in the 13th century. During the next few centuries, Germany ruled Sweden using a modified form of European feudalism. Still, Swedish farmers held tightly to their ancient rights and privileges under Norse "village ordinances" and Viking democracy, where the chief was only the first among equals.

Sweden, Norway, and Denmark were united in 1397 as the Union of Kalmar, which was formed because their leaders felt that all of Scandinavia should be ruled by the same monarch, Queen Margareta of Denmark, to fight against German domination. The union was successful in defeating the Germans in battle and stripping some of their power, but German political and commercial influence continued for several centuries.

During the early 1500s, Sweden took the first steps toward parliamentary government. A national assembly (the *Riksdag*) was formed, consisting of four estates: nobles, clergy, burghers, and peasants. Gustav Vasa accepted the Swedish throne in 1523 and began the Vasa dynasty, which still continues to rule the country. Gustav Vasa's achievements were remarkable and long-reaching. He supported the Swedish Reformation to the Lutheran religion, succeeded in separating church and state for the first time, and strengthened the monarchy by making it hereditary. During the early years of the Vasa dynasty, Sweden became a major military power and sought to expand in trade and territory. The following years were filled with battles. Sweden became a formidable military power, and Sweden took over various parts of Europe.

The 17th century ushered in the Age of Enlightenment, a time of scientific discovery, growth of the arts, and freedom of thought and expression. In 1769, Englishman Joseph Marshall, commenting on his travels through Sweden, reported that one could search "in vain for a painter, a poet, a statuary or a musician," but admitted that "they were unrivalled" in the natural sciences (Jenkins, 1968, p. 63). Swedish leadership in the sciences extended beyond the Age of Enlightenment because of the Swedish talent for orderly classification and systematization. The world's first systematic registration of population statistics was begun in Sweden in 1749, and the census is still taken every year rather than every 10 years, as happens in the United States. In 1819, traveler J. T. James commented, "On the whole, with regard to science, there is no country in Europe which, in proportion to her numbers, has contributed so largely to its advancement as Sweden, and none where it is still so steadily and successfully pursued" (Jenkins, 1968, p. 78). Scientists today visit Sweden to gain access to her remarkable compilations of data.

The Age of Freedom followed in the 18th century, during which the *Riksdag* introduced a constitution limiting the power of the monarchy. This Age of Freedom witnessed the start of a transformation of Sweden from an agriculturally based nation to a trading nation. In 1809, the Treaty of Fredrikshamn was signed with Russia, resulting in the loss of Finland as part of Sweden. Norway separated into a sovereign state in 1905. In 1912, the three Scandinavian countries of Sweden, Norway, and Finland declared their agreement on a policy of neutrality, even during world wars. Movement toward equality came fairly late in Sweden, but Swedes were much more progressive than their European or American counterparts after the movement began. In 1842, the *Riksdag* introduced compulsory education and elementary schools. Universal suffrage, including women, was proclaimed in 1921. In 1971, the *Riksdag* became a single chamber, and in 1974, a new constitution gave the ruling monarch purely ceremonial functions.

Sweden's late Industrial Revolution in the early 1900s contributed to its swift rise from poverty to prosperity. The country had already established solid educational and transportation systems that supported industrialization. There was also money for expansion into new industries because of Sweden's valuable timber and iron that were in great demand in Europe. Sweden had discovered early that a partnership of private and public interests was the best combination for both achieving economic success and benefiting as many people as possible. The evolution into a social democratic system had started.

To understand modern Sweden, it is imperative to understand Swedish social democracy, which is quite different from the socialism or Communism practiced until recently in the Eastern Bloc countries; it is a merging of the ideals of socialism and capitalism. This form of government is the hallmark of the Social Democratic Party, which dominated the nation from 1921 until recent years. In the early 1990s, the Conservative Party won the national election, but as of this writing, there is a Social Democratic prime minister. However, he must share power, because the Social Democratic Party is now in a minority position. Still other political parties—including the more capitalistic Conservative Party—accept many of the traditional ideas of social democracy within the framework of a more capitalistic and privatized economy.

Furness and Tilton (1979, p. 38) stress six fundamental values of Swedish social democracy: equality, freedom, democracy, solidarity, security, and efficiency. This form of democracy in Sweden is often called the "Swedish model" and sometimes "humane capitalism," and it relies heavily on the close collaboration between business, government, and labor. Social democracy has created a society free of the inequalities of capitalism and many of the inefficiencies of authoritarian central planning.

The Swedish word *lagom* is key to understanding the rationale behind social democracy. *Lagom* is untranslatable but essentially means both "middle road" and "reasonable." This word is representative of the foremost characteristic of the Swede: unemotional practicality. Swedes tend to believe that all problems can be solved rationally and satisfactorily through the proper application of reason. The Swedes have shown unusual thoroughness and ingenuity in translating their beliefs into social reality. The result of their efforts is a uniquely sensible way of life: a calm, well-ordered existence that is part welfare, part technological advance, part economic innovation, and part common sense.

Still, because Sweden has experienced some economic difficulties in recent years, it has been reevaluating its unqualified commitment to social democracy, under which there is tight central control of the economy. Today, Sweden has begun to move toward a more competitive economy, a less generous welfare state, and lower rates of taxation for individuals and business firms. The forces of globalization, as noted earlier, are causing many of these changes. Swedes seem to understand the necessity of these measures if the country is to remain prosperous and internationally competitive. Even the high rate of foreign aid per worker, of which the Swedes are justifiably proud, has been adjusted downward. Nevertheless, the social welfare guaranteed to every Swede is far higher than that found in most countries, an outcome that is reflective of the model of social democracy, or combining socialism and capitalism. One extreme example is that a person working part-time can quit working and receive more money for being unemployed.

One advantage to this pursuit of *lagom,* or rational thought and behavior, is that arguments erupt less frequently than in most, if not all, other nations. When the rational Swedes begin the decision-making process, there is a strong tendency to find agreement. This allows the Swedes to reach a consensus quickly and act to solve the awaiting problem. In fact, Swedes are so zealous and efficient at attacking perceived problems in their society that they will often import not only ideas to solve problems, but problems as well! Thus, John Kenneth Galbraith's (1984) *The Affluent Society* led the Swedish government to bigger and better spending programs to eliminate "public squalor," although it would be difficult to find anything in Sweden to fit Galbraith's image of American conditions.

Social democracy has been dubbed "The Middle Way" because it is a reasonable middle road between capitalism and socialism. Because social democracy is so consistent with the Swedish value of *lagom,* it has become much more than simply a model for economic planning. Social democracy is a functioning social system in Sweden as well as a political party. Thus, even when the Social Democratic Party is not in power, Sweden is still a social democracy. As Kesselman et al. (1987) explained,

> Anyone who visits Sweden will quickly recognize that the influence of Social Democratic thinking extends beyond the 45 percent of the adult population who vote for the Social Democrats. To a remarkable extent, the Swedish Social Democrats have been able to define the problems on the political agenda and the terms in which these problems have been discussed by all major political parties. It is in this sense that social democracy might be described as the hegemonic force in postwar Swedish politics. (p. 529)

The interesting paradox in Swedish social democracy is the seemingly contradictory goals of equality and efficiency. Modern Sweden, though, is a society that has found a viable mean between equitable distribution of profits and economic performance. Milner (1989) believes that the "institutionalized social solidarity around them enables Swedes to feel secure and thus prepared to follow the market in the promising directions it opens up" (p. 17).

The ability to achieve equality and efficiency may be a result of certain circumstances in Sweden conducive to a successful social democracy. Sweden's small size and relative cultural homogeneity allow for social and cultural consensus. International competitiveness is valued universally but is also seen as the means to secure the cultural value of equality.

The Swedish Summer Home

The dream of most, if not all, Swedes is to spend the summer in the family *stuga,* or the summer home. The typical summer home is a small wooden house, painted the traditional reddish-brown color that is a by-product of copper mining; there are white trimmings around the door and windows; the facilities are modest; and the furniture is plain and simple. Only the necessities are found in the summer home. Often, there is an outhouse, but otherwise, there is no disturbance to the surrounding area.

More than 600,000 *stugas* are scattered everywhere, around the lakes and in the countryside. There are no fences or "no trespassing" signs to be found. Usually, you cannot see another house from your *stuga,* but sometimes, there are clusters of homes making a small community. Most Swedes are only a generation or two away from the farm, so many can go back to the old family home. Some Swedes must rely on the summer homes of friends or relatives, and others may have access to a *stuga* owned by their company.

The ideal vacation is spent at the *stuga* in the months of June or July, communing with nature. Outdoor activities range from river rafting to walking, or just sitting underneath a tree and reflecting on life. Swedes usually like to spend time alone or in small family groups at the *stuga*. The idea is very different from the American "the more the merrier" vacation or the German vacation during which activities take place on a regular and predictable basis so that no time is wasted. Swedes want to use this time to get away from it all, be alone with their thoughts, rejuvenate themselves, and refresh their ties to nature.

One Swedish graduate student in the United States began to wax enthusiastically about her upcoming vacation in Sweden to her American friends. She planned to spend an entire month by herself at her family's *stuga,* taking along only a few small necessities, a radio, a small rowboat, and numerous books she wanted to read. The Americans were incredulous, and one of them expressed the unspoken but unanimous group opinion when she said that the month sounded more like a prison term than a vacation. Whereas many Americans react this way, Swedes generally nod knowingly and approvingly when another Swede offers such an enthusiastic description of an upcoming vacation.

Sweden's best-known artist, Carl Larsson (1853-1919), focused primarily on the *stuga* and the informal country style it represents. As *The Economist* ("Where Ikea Got Its Style," 1997) points out, Larsson's art reflects the admired lifestyle highlighted in Swedish magazines today and the simple lines of Swedish design that have made firms such as IKEA world-famous.

As this discussion intimates, Swedish culture and values are mirrored in the metaphor of the Swedish summer home, or *stuga*. The following characteristics of the *stuga* clearly reflect Swedish culture: love of untrammeled nature and tradition, individualism through self-development, and equality.

Love of Untrammeled Nature and Tradition

The national hymn in Sweden is *Du gamla du fria,* which does not concentrate on glory, honor, or warfare, but on a land of high mountains, silence, and joyfulness. Gustav Sundberg (1910), in his book on Swedish national culture, discussed this issue in the following manner:

> The most deeply ingrained trait in the Swedish temperament . . . is a strong love of nature. . . . This feeling is equally warm among both high and low—albeit not equally conscious—and this strong attachment to nature, which in some cases may produce wild unruly emotions, is on the other hand the most profound explanation of the indestructible power and health of the Swedish nation. (p. 104)

The Swedes' love and respect for nature is a strongly held value that has led to many laws that protect wildlife, parks, and waterways. The country has been termed a "green lung"—a place where you can breathe and enjoy the untouched countryside. Swedes had been environmentalists long before it became fashionable, probably because of their intense love of nature and the desire to preserve it as it was when families lived on their farms. Ironically, Rachel Carson's (1962) *Silent Spring* caused an uproar in Sweden, in large part because of the Swedish love of untrammeled nature. In contrast, the Germans prefer a controlled nature, as represented by the flowers that adorn their homes (see Chapter 10, "The German Symphony"). In the United States, there are fierce debates over the utility of environmentalism that, to many Swedes, seems irrational.

This preoccupation with nature stems in large measure from a centuries-long battle against the hostile elements in a vast, damp, cold, and sparsely settled land. It is not surprising that the engineer is held in high esteem in Sweden, because his or her efforts are directed toward combating and controlling the forces of nature. Similarly, the Nordic invention of orienteering is a result of this desire to combat the forces of nature. The orienteer is set down in a remote, unfamiliar location and challenged to find his or her way out with the help of only a map and a compass.

One of the least densely populated countries in Europe, Sweden has the space to provide ample outdoor activities, whatever your pleasure. Walking is a favorite pastime of the Swedes, and a long walk on the lakeshore or in one of the many national parks is a preferred way to commune with nature. Fishing and picking flowers, berries, or mushrooms are also on the back-to-nature agenda. It is very fashionable to return to Stockholm on Monday morning with the stain of berries on your hands. For those more daring, a variety of water sports is abundant at the many lakes in Sweden. River rafting and canoeing are very popular, as is sailing.

For a true back-to-nature experience, Swedes like to go up north with a backpack and walk in the mountains for days. Some hikers follow well-established trails and stay overnight in cabins provided for them. Other hikers prefer to stay overnight in tents that they carry with them, and these hikers use only a map and compass to guide them. In effect, they orienteer. Another back-to-nature experience that Swedes love is rafting. The journey starts at one end of a lake, where there are many logs from the huge timber industry in Sweden. For a fee, you make your own raft from the logs and make your way downstream to where the logs are returned for use in the timber mills. The trip takes several days, and the riders stop the raft at the side of the lake at night and make camp. This experience is the essence of the idea of getting back to nature and of living off the land.

Until relatively recently, Sweden was an agriculturally based society. Ninety percent of the families lived on farms until the Industrial Revolution in the early 1900s brought workers to the cities. Sweden has moved very quickly into an industrialized, city-based country, with only 2% of the population employed on the land. Thus, many Swedes remember life on the farm or have certainly heard many stories about it. The ties to the farm are very strong and deeply personal. Regardless of the everyday city life, most Swedes are still peasants at heart who could easily return to the ways of their ancestors, because the past is not too distant. Back-to-the-farm and nature romanticism constitutes a major part of Swedish culture. They long for an escape to the country where they can remind themselves of a simpler time.

Furthermore, Swedes generally value tradition and still have a village culture. The Swedes deal with this paradox by spending the summer back in the traditional village setting of the old family home. As Arne Ruth (1984) relates,

> The [Swedish] model presents the paradoxical spectacle of a nation possessing more of the outward trappings of modernity than any other society, yet at heart remaining the incarnation of Tonnies's mythical *Gemeinschaft*. With the cushions of tradition gone, the brutally modern forces of *Gesellschaft* throw the society's delicately balanced social structure out of gear. (p. 63)

Geert Hofstede's (1980a) 53-nation study of cultures indicated that Sweden clusters with those countries emphasizing a small power distance between individuals and groups in society, a pattern that is typically found in a village setting. Swedes tend to be horizontal individualists who favor norms of equality over equity, in sharp contrast to the United States (see Tornblom, Jonsson, & Foa, 1985). Their individualism is manifested by their extreme self-reliance and avoidance of long-term relationships outside of the family. For example, Swedes will tend to pay for a cigarette on the spot if they ask for one; living by oneself is common, even among the elderly; and if staying overnight at a friend's home, a Swede will bring his or her own sheets (see Daun, 1991). Thus, it is not surprising that about 90% of Swedes regularly report that they like to live "as they please."

Traditionally, the Swedes have had the characteristic of practicality and rationality. When there is a conflict between practicality and other values, practicality tends to win. This can be seen repeatedly in the setting of national policy. Staunchly neutral since her last war in 1814, Sweden can be said to avoid war largely because she views it as impractical and, in the long run, not beneficial to any of the participants. Likewise, although the Social Democrats ruled Sweden for more than 70 years and built a gigantic welfare system during that time that would be the envy of any socialist country, they never nationalized industry simply because it is not rational, and being rational is obviously more important than being strictly socialist.

◼ Individualism Through Self-Development

The summer home is a place to go for solitude and quiet individualism. A Swede will escape into the nature surrounding the summer home to spend some time reflecting on life and getting in touch with the inner self. In the untouched countryside, a person can stroll for miles without coming across another human being. Great value is placed on this time for self-development. Managers complain about the unwillingness of workers to put in overtime so that they can pursue such activities. Currently, most Swedes are entitled to 5 weeks of vacation per year, which they generally prefer to take in the summer. Absenteeism and excessive use of sick leave are problems for Swedish managers. Workers in Sweden take an average of 27 sick days per year, compared to an average of 5 sick days per year in the United States.

Swedes must work to afford to pay the high national sales tax, and a dual income is essential in order to maintain the quality of life desired. Although Sweden is a "doing" culture and Swedes are achievement-oriented, they tend to prefer a job where they can develop as a person, and they frequently look for jobs that are intrinsically interesting or that allow them to spend more time away from work. Decentralized decision making is valued and consistent with the ideals of equality and independence. Swedes are highly committed to quality of life and thus tend to value private time alone or with family more than, or at least equal to, work.

Much of the emphasis on self-development is motivated by individualism. There is a common misperception that Sweden is a collectivist society because it is a welfare state. Swedes pay high taxes in order to fund a system where education, housing, health care, and many other programs are available to all. It is true that Swedes value equality, but they have come a long way from the farm. Modern Swedes tend to place individual interests before collective interests. Gustav Sundberg, a Swedish statistician, observed in 1912 that "we Swedes love and are interested in nature, not people" (Jenkins, 1968, p. 154).

In Hofstede's (1980a) study of cultural values, Sweden clusters with those nations emphasizing individualism, but it is obviously more collectivistic than the United States, which ranks first on this measure. Swedish individualism is different from American individualism, though, because Swedes desire individualism in order to develop as a person (horizontal individualism), whereas American individualism is more competitive in nature (vertical individualism).

The emphasis on community and family has eroded with the increased industrialization of Sweden. As a visiting American observed (Heclo & Madsen, 1987),

> Officially Swedish ideology is very good. Their attitude toward society as a whole and the world is generous. But the funny thing is that people don't care much about their neighbors. Swedes are so insular, self-contained. It's easy to be lonesome here. (p. 4)

This American experienced the process during which visitors to Sweden are welcomed cordially and generously, but then the enthusiasm ends quickly. At heart, Swedes are basically loners who are not accustomed to thinking in terms of other individuals. After the original courtesies are over, it is usually difficult to pursue the relationship on a deeper level.

Ironically, the success of the social welfare programs has fueled the move toward individualism. Many Swedes feel that paying taxes absolves them of responsibility to other generations and to the needy. Likewise, teenagers in Sweden are encouraged to be independent, and they frequently travel outside of the country with friends. As a result, Swedish teenagers tend to be much more mature than the typical American teenager. Thus, a weaker bond between the generations has resulted. As Hans Zetterberg (1984) explains, "The milk of human kindness therefore flows less frequently from one human being to another; instead, it is dispensed in homogenized form through regulations and institutions" (p. 91).

There is an amazingly large number of organizations in Sweden that exist to promote the interests of their members in a variety of areas. Close to 200,000 membership organizations create a dense social network of 2,000 associations per 100,000 people. An apparent contradiction exists between a Swede's preference for working toward a goal as a group and the individual isolation that is typically characteristic of him or her. The organizational system is accepted only because it is seen as the most practical and efficient way to get things done. Interactions between members are generally kept on a formal basis, thus preserving the individual's isolation.

Because the views of a single person are seldom voiced without first being digested by a group, organizations tend to promote conformity. It has even been argued that the end result is a lack of individual initiative and creativity. Indeed, the generally placid temperament of the Swedes might be offered as proof of this hypothesis. However, it is a difficult jump in logic to state that organizations preceded the typically reserved affect of the average Swede. Rather, it is more likely that the organizations have allowed the natural temperament of the Swedes to be retained while satisfying the practical need for a public voice for their concerns.

Swedish individualism is further supported by the insistence on individual rights, which seem to extend even to trivial levels. If it is raining and a passing car splashes you, the rules give you recourse. You take down the license number, go to the police station, and file a complaint, indicating that your suit was damaged. If the court finds that the driver did not take appropriate precautions, he or she would be ordered to pay damages (in this case, to have your suit cleaned). Sweden has a form of legal welfare that allows even those who cannot afford court costs to pursue a civil case.

Equality

The summer home brings into focus most of the important values in Sweden, including equality. The ancient tradition of *Allemansratt,* or Everyman's Right, permits anyone, within reason, to camp anywhere for a night, or to walk, ski, or paddle a canoe anywhere. Fishing is generally free, but licenses, permits, or papers are frequently required. Everyman's Right also allows Swedes to pass over any grounds, fields, or woods regardless of their ownership. Swedes are careful not to abuse this right, and generally, they do not disturb the areas close to an individual *stuga*. They use common sense, but it is not illegal to pick berries, mushrooms, or flowers from any source. There are no laws of trespass, and "keep out" or "private" signs do not exist. Equal access to the greatly loved nature in Sweden is representative of the value of equality in other aspects of Swedish life.

The egalitarian passion that has been almost as important as moral force is termed *jamlikhet*. Success in the creation of an egalitarian society hinged upon rapid economic growth and social democracy, and the national wealth resulting from the Industrial Revolution was distributed to all citizens through the guidance of Social Democratic policies. The goal was to organize society much as the Swedes would construct a machine. In pursuit of this goal, Swedes are constantly looking for new approaches or ideas that will make the societal machinery run better.

However, the Swedish machinery designed to achieve such goals is quite complicated. Sweden could not be described as a simple and efficient machine. Rather, it is more like a Rube Goldberg invention: highly complicated and inefficient in the sense that there are many unnecessary steps and processes that must be followed, but nevertheless, the goals are eventually achieved.

The expression *krangel-Sverige* roughly means "red-tape Sweden," and it connotes a bewildering assortment of complications, regulations, procedures, and channels of authority. This does not imply that the system has broken down, merely that it is inconvenient for the person who must deal with it. Swedes feel that the main function of the system is to operate; whether it gives pain, irritation, or pleasure to someone along the way is irrelevant to the main reason for its existence. Thus, the Stockholm tramways regularly pass would-be passengers if the tramway is behind schedule, because the function of a tramway is to meet the established timetable, and serving the public is only secondary. Similarly, the medical care system is intended to deliver medical care. Because waiting in line does not seriously interfere with this goal, long waits to obtain medical care are not viewed as worthy of discussion.

In the past, the legendary Swedish *titelsjuka*, or title-sickness, resulted in telephone listings that included the Swede's title. Today, about 50% of the listings have titles following the names, but this is done for the practical reason of distinguishing people. The fact that the practice has declined is evidence of the desire for a society of strict equality. Comparable opinion polls indicate that only 2% of Swedes desire high social status, versus 7% of Americans and 25% of Germans (Triandis, in press). Almost everyone now labels himself or herself middle class. The principle of universality means that all Swedes, regardless of social position, rely on the same network of services. Thus, all have a stake in the quality and accessibility of services.

Historically, Sweden has had very high tax rates, and the resulting taxes are used not only as a leveling device, but also to pay for the extensive social welfare system. The government provides programs to make jobs available to all who wish to work, pensions for the elderly, sickness benefits for all workers, housing allowances, free education through college and university, almost-free medical care, and part-free dental care. Unemployment benefits are generous, but they are not designed to encourage laziness.

Family benefits, a current issue of debate in the United States, are abundant in Sweden. A year or more of parental leave is available to both parents upon the birth of a child. In Sweden, men's attitudes have changed much faster than in other parts of the world, and some 20% of men take some parental leave. The government provides general child allowances for all children and gives advance payments for child support. Day care centers, called *dagis,* are provided by local authorities. These benefits are very important in Sweden because approximately 90% of all Swedish women of working age are employed outside of the home.

Equal pay for equal work is another feature of egalitarianism in Sweden. Still, many occupations are clearly divided by sex. Swedish women face the same problems as those in the United States in trying to move up the corporate ladder. Sweden is also struggling with providing equality to immigrants. There are more than 1 million immigrants, mostly for political and humanitarian reasons, who have difficulties achieving the same standards of living as native Swedes. The government has made tremendous attempts to integrate the immigrants and to offer equal opportunity, but Swedish racism has surfaced and is growing despite public disapproval.

On Hofstede's masculinity-femininity scale, Sweden is extremely feminine when compared to other nations in that 53-nation study. Femininity is defined as the extent to which the dominant values in society emphasize relationships among people, concern for others, and the overall quality of life. The characteristic of femininity is descriptive of the Swedes, but in some respects, the society is changing. Relationships among people are becoming more distant, and concern for others is eroding because of increased individualism.

As the election of a Conservative prime minister after decades of rule by the Social Democrats suggests, there has been a change in ideological climate, although not in the moral content of Swedish social policies; the issue is really the extent of the state's prerogatives versus individual and family rights. As early as 1984, Arne Ruth pointed out that the ideals and policies espoused by the Social Democrats needed to be updated and reinforced by new models:

A rationalistic futurism took the place of religion; social and technological change was felt to be not only unavoidable, but morally imperative.
Antitraditionalism became, paradoxically, the dominant tradition. . . .
Industrial organization and technological innovation are among the oldest and most formidable currents in Swedish culture. . . . There will need
to be a new source for the cultural myths necessary to release once again
the social energy that has for so long characterized the Swedish model.
(p. 93)

However, the change in cultural values appears to be more superficial
than substantive. It is true that there is opposition to the Swedish model
among some Swedes, and there has been some loss of a sense of community
and heritage because of rapid industrialization. Sweden is now preoccupied
with such domestic problems as high taxes to support the welfare system,
energy sources, a declining work ethic, the physical and social environment,
globalization, and the purchase of Swedish firms by non-Swedish firms. A
few prominent Swedish firms have even moved their company headquarters
outside of the country to avoid taxes and excessive regulation.

Still, because of caps on government spending, the government is now
enjoying a small budget surplus after 30 years of deficits. Moreover, it is planning to support a $2 billion national high-speed data network that will con-
nect even the remotest Arctic villages to the Internet, thus reinforcing the
basic Swedish value of equality. Entrepreneurial activity is high, and Stockholm is now called the Wireless Valley. Although the average worker pays
64% of his or her salary in taxes, the benefits seemingly outweigh the costs.
Even many entrepreneurs defend the tax system and actively participate on
government task forces designed to bolster Sweden's position in information
technology and other areas. The nation, as a whole, is benefiting. For example, the government financially supported a mobile standard in wireless technology in the 1990s that has brought the nation to a leading position in this
area. More than half of Swedes use the Internet, and more than 70% have
mobile phones.

Such actions suggest that the unity of the Swedish mind-set is remarkable, as is the Swedes' devotion to untrammeled nature. Although change
will occur, it will occur sensibly and in the Swedish way. In sum, we can
expect that the Swedes will continue to emphasize the values and attitudes
associated with their summer homes, particularly those of love of nature and
tradition, individualism expressed through self-development, and equality.

CHAPTER 12

Irish Conversations

The three pillars of Irish culture are its language, its rural heritage, and the Catholic Church. For hundreds of years, Ireland was essentially an English colony, and this domination significantly influenced how these three pillars interacted with one another. Even as late as the 1950s, most of the Irish lived on farms or in small communities, and even Dublin was a provincial city in comparison to other European capitals. But today, Ireland is a Celtic Tiger whose economy has experienced explosive growth. In 1950, the gross domestic product (GDP) per capita was only $2,500; today, it is about $20,000 (Norton, 1999). This transformation has occurred in large part because of Ireland's entry into the European Union (EU). As one Irish visitor to the United States explained to an American who had lived in Ireland 40 years ago but had not returned, "We are European now."

The decline of the rural heritage is especially pronounced in and around Dublin, where 40% of the 3.5 million citizens live. Crime, drug use, and other urban ailments are now prevalent. Similarly, the Catholic Church, although still strong in that about 90% of the population attends Sunday Mass regularly, no longer has the power and prestige that it flaunted for generations. Only the Irish language, Gaelic or *Gealige,* is increasing in importance after becoming nearly extinct. There now is an Irish-language TV station, and one survey indicated that 1 million citizens claimed some proficiency in it, whereas market researchers for the new station estimated the figure to be 500,000 ("A Modern Vogue for More Than a Brogue," 1996, p. 52). Unlike most nations, Ireland has two official languages, English and

Irish or Gaelic, and studying Irish is required in the school system. Thus, the hope for sustaining Irish culture may be vested in its language.

It is a truism that the use of language is essential for the development of culture, and most, if not all, cultural groups take great pride in their native languages. Thus, it is not surprising that voice is one of the four essential elements of the metaphor for Italy, the opera (see Chapter 18, "The Italian Opera"). In the case of Ireland, it was the brutal English rule over the nation, extending over several centuries, that essentially made the Irish an aural people whose love of language and conversation was essential for the preservation of her heritage. More specifically, the *intersection* between the original Irish language, Gaelic, and English has made the Irish famous for their eloquence, scintillating conversations, and unparalleled success in fields where the use of the English language is critical, such as writing, law, and teaching.

The Celts, or Gaels, conquered Ireland and its native inhabitants, the Firbolgs, several centuries before Christ. They split Ireland into various kingdoms whose petty kings usually ruled over a local group of clans. During this period, the belief in magical powers was the guiding force of the civilization, and even today many of the landmarks and traditions in Ireland can be traced back to this time of magical creatures.

Ireland escaped the rule of the Roman Empire because of its far distance from Rome. St. Patrick, who had previously been captured and enslaved, returned to Ireland in A.D. 432 and had great success in Christianizing it. When the Roman Empire fell in A.D. 756, Europe plunged into its Dark Ages, but Ireland's Golden Age of learning and scholarship began and lasted until the 11th century. As Thomas Cahill (1995) showed in his best-selling history, the Irish essentially saved European civilization through this emphasis on scholarship and its preservation. In A.D. 795, the Vikings from northern Scandinavia started to invade Ireland, and they founded settlements along the coasts and established Dublin as their capital. Eventually, the Irish united under the high king, Brian Boru, and defeated the Vikings at Clondarf in A.D. 1014. The Vikings were allowed to remain in their seaport towns; intermarried with the Irish; and, in time, were absorbed by Irish culture.

Starting about A.D. 1160, the English, sometimes at the invitation of the petty kings or rulers, became increasingly involved in Ireland's affairs. However, the English who settled in Ireland were quickly absorbed by the culture through joint business ventures, intermarriage, and a perception that England was too distant from Ireland to have the ability to control it. In 1366, the English passed the infamous Statutes of Kilkenny as a defensive reaction against this absorption, and they outlawed intermarriage and concubinage between the English and Irish and the use of Gaelic by both the English and "the Irish living among the English" (Beckett, 1986). The English were even forbidden the use of Irish names and dress, and laws excluding the

Irish from positions of authority were passed. Although many of these statutes were strictly enforced in later centuries, they tended to be disregarded in Ireland when first passed.

In 1534, Henry VIII began to exert strong English control over Ireland. His successors initiated a "plantation policy" by seizing Irish lands and encouraging Protestants to settle in the country in an attempt to make the nation Protestant. There were several Irish revolts, but they were beaten down. The 10-year revolt that started in 1641 was particularly important because 600,000 people died during it, and eventually, Oliver Cromwell, the Puritan leader, put it down mercilessly and brutally. Cromwell kept a diary describing the joy that he experienced at inflicting so much pain on the Irish for the greater glory of God. Although some of the Irish still resent the English, they hate Cromwell. Ironically, today, the English and Irish are working together amiably in the EU, and the Irish GDP per capita is higher than that of England.

The Irish eventually sided with James II, a Roman Catholic who became King of England but was forced from the throne in A.D. 1685, at least in part because he had abolished many anti-Catholic laws. Although he tried to regain his throne, he and his Irish supporters were defeated in the Battle of the Boyne in A.D. 1690. For the next two centuries, conditions among the Irish Catholics, which had been deplorable, worsened. Additional land was seized by the English, and by 1704, the Irish held only about one seventh of the land in Ireland. A series of penal laws was passed so that Catholics could not purchase, inherit, or even rent land; they were also excluded from the Irish Parliament and the army, and were restricted in their rights to practice Catholicism. Also, Catholics were barred not only from the one university, Trinity, but even from most of the schools in which English was the language of instruction.

To counteract the assault on their culture, the Irish employed illegal schoolmasters who taught in Gaelic in "hedge schools," or schools hidden from sight behind hedges; sometimes, the classes convened in the homes of the students. Because the schoolmasters did not have access to many school materials or even to classrooms, almost all of this education was oral in nature, involving memorization, oral presentations, and debates.

Between 1782 and 1798, the all-Protestant Irish Parliament ruled the country, and it did restore to Catholics their rights to hold land and lifted the restrictions on the practice of Catholicism. However, the Irish still did not have political rights, and the wretched lot of most of the Irish did not change. Moreover, the Irish Parliament was dissolved in 1801, and from that time until 1922, when Ireland attained independence, the nation was ruled from Parliament in London in which there was a small number of Irish MPs. In 1828, largely through the efforts of one Irish MP, Daniel O'Connell ("The

Great Liberator"), Catholic emancipation did occur, and the penal laws governing the Irish were relaxed.

Throughout this period, there were rebellions in 1798, 1803, 1848, and 1865. Although unsuccessful, they helped to lay the foundations for final independence in 1922, sparked largely by the Rebellion of 1916. Although all of these rebellions were unsuccessful, they reflect the Celtic trait of accepting nobility in death for a righteous but doomed cause.

In 1831, the English established a national school system in Ireland in which only English could be used. Irish children had to wear a wooden baton around their necks. If they were heard talking in Gaelic, the teacher would make a mark on the baton, and their parents usually beat them at home, because the parents' opportunities to work, and thus even to live, were completely in the hands of the English. Many of the Irish began to discard Gaelic, at least openly. Patrick Pearse, an Irish patriot who was later executed because of his leadership of the 1916 uprising, characterized the educational system as a "murder machine" designed to stamp out Irish language and culture. Furthermore, Britain had set up an agricultural system that made the Irish dependent upon one crop, potatoes. When that crop failed, the Great Potato Famine of 1845-1849 occurred. The English refused to provide any major assistance to the Irish because of their belief in the workings of a free market economy, and they allowed approximately 1 million people to starve to death out of a population of 9 million. This event has often been compared to the Holocaust during World War II. Even before the Famine, the conditions among the Irish had become so deplorable that the Irish satirist, Jonathan Swift, argued eerily in "A Modest Proposal" that the Irish babies would be better off if they were killed and eaten, and some of his modest proposals closely resembled what actually happened in the Holocaust.

Ireland as we know it today began to emerge in 1916, when a small group of Irish patriots commandeered the General Post Office Building in Dublin on Easter Sunday. The English executed the 15 leaders of the rebellion, which sparked a war against the English that led to the modern division of Ireland into two parts—the Protestant north, with a minority Catholic population, and the Catholic south. The focus of this chapter is the Catholic south, which occupies five sixths of the land.

It is said that everybody knows everybody else's business in a country village. Ireland and its culture still reflect this village-like perspective and mentality. Whenever the Irish meet, one of the first things they generally do is determine one another's place of origin. The conversation usually helps to identify common relatives and friends. Given the wide circle of friends and acquaintances that the Irish tend to make in their lives, it is usually not difficult to find a link.

Ireland's size is little more than one one-hundredth of that of the continental United States. It lies to the west of Great Britain and is economically tied to this country. Ireland does have the four major cities of Dublin, Cork, Limerick, and Galway. In the early 1970s, more than 60% of the workforce was employed in agriculture, but today, only 12% can be found in that line of work; 27% of the workforce is in industry, and 61% in services. Ireland is a high-tech leader in the EU, and its workforce is young. More than 50% of the population is under 30 years of age, and 24% is under 15.

The importance of conversation to the Irish makes it a fitting metaphor for the nation. However, to understand the metaphor fully, we need to explore the intersection of Gaelic and English, after which we can focus on an essential Irish conversation, praying to God and the saints. The free-flowing nature of Irish conversation is also one of its essential characteristics, as are the places where conversations are held.

Intersection of Gaelic and English

The Irish are a people who tend to enjoy simple pleasures, but the complexity of their thought patterns and culture can be baffling to outsiders. Generally, they have an intense love of conversation and story telling and have been accused often of talking just to hear the sound of their own voices. The Irish use the English language in ways that are not found in any other culture. They do not just give a verbal answer; rather, they construct a vivid mental picture that is pleasing to the mind as well as the ear. When the transition from Gaelic to English occurred, the Irish created vivid images in Gaelic and expressed them in English; the vivid imagery of many Irish writers originated in the imaginative storytelling that was historically a critical part of social conversation. Gaelic was, to the Irish, a graphic, living language that was appropriate for expressing the wildest of ideas in a distinctive and pleasing manner. Frank McCourt's (1996) very popular *Angela's Ashes,* his description of growing up in extreme poverty during the Depression in Limerick, is a perfect example of this use of language. Almost everyone who has read this book comes away with one major impression of this unique book: You feel as if you are actually with McCourt as he goes through his dire and seemingly hopeless experiences.

As indicated previously, Ireland remained relatively bucolic until recent years. Eamon DeValera, the prime minister for seemingly endless years, was an advocate of rural life, and he and his colleagues resisted efforts to industrialize and modernize Ireland. Given this situation, it is easy to see how the talent for conversation as an art form was maintained. And although the Irish cuisine has improved markedly in recent years, for many Irish, conversation is at least as important as, if not more important than, the food being served. A visitor sometimes notices that the Irish seem to forget about their food until it is almost too cold. However, if an Irishman admonishes a countryman for eating too much and/or too quickly, the witty reply is frequently to the effect that one never knows when the next famine will occur. Such "slagging matches," in which a comment is made at the expense of another person, and a witty retort is made, followed by a series of such interactions, are much loved by the conversational Irish. Moreover, this emphasis on the primacy of conversation is in contrast to the practices found in some cultures, such as the Italian and French, where the food is prized.

If the size of the population is taken into account, it seems that Ireland has produced many more prominent essayists, novelists, and poets than any other country since approximately 1870. This prominence reflects the intersection of the Gaelic and English languages and the aural bias of the Irish. They have also produced great musicians who combine music and words in a unique way. Conversely, the Irish have not produced a major visual artist equal to those of other European countries, and their achievements in science are modest.

There are countless examples that could be used to illustrate this intersection, but the opening words of James Joyce's *Portrait of the Artist as a Young Man* (1964), in which he first introduced the technique of stream of consciousness, aptly serve the purpose:

> Once upon a time and a very good time it was there was a moocow coming down along the road and this moocow that was coming down along the road met a nicens little boy named baby tuckoo. . . .
> His father told him that story; his father looked at him through a glass; he had a hairy face.
> He was a baby tuckoo. The moocow came down the road where Betty Byrne lived: she sold lemon platt.
> O, the wild rose blossoms
> On the little green place.
> He sang that song. That was his song.
> O, the green wothe botheth. (p. 1)

There are several points about this brief but pertinent passage that deserve mention. It expresses a rural bias, befitting Ireland, and it reflects the vivid Gaelic language in which Joyce was proficient. Also, it immediately captures the imagination, but leaves the reader wondering what is going to happen: He or she must read further if he or she wants to capture the meaning, and it seems that the meaning will become clear only in the most circuitous way. Furthermore, although the essence of the passage is mundane, it is expressed in a captivating manner. The reader is pleasantly surprised by the passage and eagerly awaits additional pleasant surprises. In many ways, this passage is an ideal example of the manner in which Gaelic and English intersect. And although some of the modern Irish and Irish Americans may not be aware of these historical antecedents, their patterns of speech and thought tend to reflect this intersection.

Perhaps the most imaginatively wild of the modern Irish writers to incorporate the intersection of the Gaelic and English languages in his work is Brian Nolan, who wrote under the noms de plume Myles na gCopaleen and Flann O'Brien. Nolan wrote some of his novels and stories in Gaelic and others in English. Even the titles of his books are indicative of this imaginative focus, such as *The Poor Mouth: A Bad Story About the Hard Life* (O'Brien, 1940/1974). "Putting on the poor mouth" means making a pretense of being poor or in bad circumstances in order to gain advantage for oneself from creditors or prospective creditors, and the book is a satire on the rural life found in western Ireland. His masterpiece, *At Swim-Two-Birds* (O'Brien, 1961), sets the scene for a confrontation between Mad Sweeny and Jem Casey in the following way (O'Brien, 1961):

> *Synopsis, being a summary of what has gone before,* **FOR THE BENEFIT OF NEW READERS: Dermit Trellis,** an eccentric author, conceives the project of writing a salutary book on the consequences which follow wrong-doing and creates for the purpose
>
> **The Pooka Fergus MacPhellimey,** a species of human Irish devil endowed with magical power. He then creates
>
> **John Furriskey,** a depraved character, whose task is to attack women and behave at all times in an indecent manner. By magic he is instructed by Trellis to go one night to Donnybrook where he will by arrangement meet and betray . . . (p. 1)

The remaining characters are sequentially introduced in the same imaginative way.

In the area of music, the Chieftains, who have been performing together for more than 25 years, represent the distinctive approach of the Irish to music. Their songs, played on traditional instruments, are interspersed with classic Irish dances and long dialogs that sometimes involve the audience. Similarly, Thomas Moore (1859), who lived in the 19th century, is sometimes cited as the composer who captured the essence of the intersection of the Gaelic and English languages in such poetic songs as "Believe Me If All Those Endearing Young Charms," which he wrote for a close friend and beautiful woman whose face was badly scarred in a fire:

> Believe me, if all those endearing young charms
> Which I gaze on so fondly today
> Were to fade by tomorrow and fleet from my sight
> Like a fairy gift fading away.
> Thou woust still be adored
> As this moment thou art
> Let thy loveliness fade as it may.
> And upon the dear ruins
> Each bough of my heart
> Would entwine itself verdantly still.

A reminder that the Irish are different from the English and Americans is their brogue. When the conversion from speaking Gaelic to speaking English was occurring, this brogue was an embarrassment for many Irish. The English looked down upon these "inferior" people who were unable to speak "proper" English (Waters, 1984). Today, the brogue is prized by the Irish and appreciated throughout the world.

Given that Ireland is a nation in which unhurried conversation is prized, it is logical that there is a balance between the orientations of "being" and "doing." Although the Irish have enthusiastically accepted change in recent years, they still express astonishment at the "doing" entrepreneurial activities of their 44 million Irish American counterparts, who have made St. Patrick's Day, a holy day in Ireland, into a fun-loving time for partying that embraces all people (Milbank, 1993). The Irish generally take life much more slowly than the Americans, who tend to watch the clock constantly and rush from one activity to another. No matter how rushed the Irish may be, they normally have time to stop and talk.

The Irish also tend to place more importance on strong friendships and extended family ties than do Americans. Nothing illustrates this emphasis more than the behavior of many early Irish immigrants when they first arrived in the United States. They settled near other friends or relatives who had preceded them to the United States and developed a reputation for being very clannish. But slowly, the Irish love of conversation and curiosity about all things led to their interaction with others and their Americanization.

Prayer as Conversation

Prayer, or a conversation with God, is one of the most important parts of an Irish life. More than 95% of the population is Roman Catholic, and regular attendance at Sunday mass is estimated at 87% of the population, which is the highest percentage of any country in the world. Many Catholic households contain crucifixes and religious pictures. These serve as outward reminders of the people's religious beliefs and duties.

Furthermore, this prayer is accompanied by acts of good works that stem directly from the strong ethical and moral system of the Irish. They are recognized as having made the highest per capita donation to relief efforts in countries such as Ethiopia, and they are quick to donate their time, energy, and even lives to help those living in execrable conditions. The extent of the crisis in Somalia, for instance, was first reported to the United Nations by the president of Ireland, Mary Robinson, and an Irish nurse was killed after arriving in Somalia to help out.

The state relies upon the works of the Catholic Church to support most of its social service programs. For example, most of the hospitals are run by the Catholic Church rather than by the state. These hospitals are partially funded with state money and are staffed with nuns whenever possible. The state has very little control over how the money is spent, especially because it lacks the buildings and the power to replace the Church-run system that was in place when the state was formed.

The national school (state) system is also under the control of the various religious denominations in Ireland. It is the primary source of education for primary school children. The state funds the system, but the schools are run by local boards that are almost always controlled by the clergy. There is a separate national school for each major religion. The local Catholic national school is managed by the local parish priest, whereas the Protestant vicar has his own separate school. Many of the instructors in these schools are nuns or brothers who work very inexpensively and keep the costs much lower than the state could. Conversely, in the United States, it is no longer lawful even to pray in public schools. In exchange for these lower costs, the state has relinquished control. This is really the Church's last line of defense, because it has the ability to instill Catholic morality and beliefs in almost every young Irish child in the country.

Sunday mass is a special occasion in Ireland, and the entire family attends. It is a family affair. On this occasion, everyone wears his or her Sunday best. One Irish woman tells the story of returning home for a visit from the United States and, on Sunday morning, being asked by her mother if she did not have a better dress to wear to church; she had become lax in her church dress after spending several years in the United States.

Many Irish begin and end their day with prayer. This is their opportunity to tell God their troubles and their joys. One of the more common prayers is that Ireland may one day be reunited. This act of talking to God helps to form a personal relationship between the Irish and their God. It is difficult to ignore the dictates of God because He is such a personal and integral part of the daily Irish life. God is also present in daily life in the living personification of the numerous priests, brothers, and sisters found in Ireland. They are not shut away in cloisters but interact with the laity throughout the day.

Entering the religious life is seen as a special calling for the Irish. In the past, when families were very large, it was common for every family to give at least one son or daughter to the religious life. It was the greatest joy for an Irish mother to know that her son or daughter was in God's service, which was prized more highly than a bevy of grandchildren. Vocations to religious life have decreased in recent years, but Ireland still has many more priests per capita than most, if not all, other Catholic countries.

In the Republic of Ireland, there are few problems between the Catholics and other religious groups, unlike the situation that exists in Northern Ireland. In fact, the Catholics enjoy having the Protestants in their communities, and they treat them with great respect. In one rural area where the Protestant congregation had dwindled, the Catholic parish helped the Protestants with fund-raising to make repairs to their church. This act of charity illustrates the great capacity for giving that the Irish possess, because generally, they are not greatly attached to material possessions and are quite willing to share what they have with the world.

A Free-Flowing Conversation— Irish Hospitality

Conversations with the Irish are known to take many strange turns, and you may find yourself discussing a subject and not knowing how it arose. Also, it is not only what is said that is important, but the manner in which it is expressed. The Irish tend to be monochronic, completing one activity before going on to another one, yet they cannot resist divergences and tangents in their conversations or their lives. They often feel that they are inspired by an idea that must be shared with the rest of the world regardless of what the other person may be saying. The Irish tend to respect this pattern of behavior and are quite willing to change the subject, which can account for the breadth of their conversations as well as for their length.

Like their conversations, the Irish tend to be curious about all things foreign or unfamiliar, and they are quick to extend a hand in greeting and to start a conversation, usually a long one.

It is not unusual for the Irish to begin a conversation with a perfect stranger, but for most of the Irish, there are no strangers—only people with whom they have not had the pleasure of conversing. The Irish do not usually hug in public, but this in no way reduces the warmth of their greeting. They often view Americans as too demonstrative and are uncomfortable with public displays of affection. They tend to be a very hospitable, trusting, and friendly people. Nothing illustrates this outlook more than their national greeting, *Cead mile failte,* or "One hundred thousand welcomes," which is usually accompanied by a handshake.

In addition, the Irish are famous for their hospitality toward friends as well as strangers. As Delany (1974) points out, "In the olden days, anyone who had partaken of food in an Irishman's home was considered to be secure against harm or hurt from any member of the family, and no one was ever turned away" (p. 103). This spirit of hospitality still exists in Ireland. In the country, the Irish tend to keep their doors not only unlocked but open. Whenever someone is passing by or asking for directions, he or she may be invited into a home to have something to eat or drink. It is not unusual for the Irish to meet someone in the afternoon and invite him or her to their home for supper that evening, and this happens not only in the country but also in the cities. Meals are accompanied by great conversation by both young and old.

Many of the Irish do not believe in secrets, and even if they did, it would be hard to imagine them being able to keep one. They seem quite willing to tell the world their business and expect their visitors to do the same. However, the Irish and other nationalities feel that Americans are much too willing to divulge information. As the Irish saying goes, "You can get a lift with an American, and by the time you separate, you know much more about the person than you care to know."

However, the Irish are often unwilling to carry on superficial conversations. They enjoy a conversation that deals with something of substance, and they are well-known for breaking the often-quoted American social rule that one should not discuss politics or religion in public. The Irish enjoy nothing more than to discuss these subjects and, it is hoped, to spark a deep philosophical conversation.

▪ Places of Conversations— Irish Friends and Families

There really is not a place where the Irish would find it difficult to carry on a conversation. They are generally quite willing to talk about any subject at any time, but there are several places that have a special meaning for the Irish. Conversation in the home is very important for an Irish family. It is also one of the major social activities of an Irish public house, or pub.

The typical Irish family is closely knit, and its members describe their activities to one another in great detail. Meal time is an event in the Irish household that should not be missed by a family member, not so much because of the food but because of the conversation. Supper is the time of day when family members gather together to pray, eat, and update one another on their daily activities. The parents usually ask the children about their day in school and share the events of their own day.

Education and learning have always been held in high regard by the Irish. Teachers are treated with great respect in the community, and their relatively high salaries reflect their worth to the community. Ireland has a literacy rate of 99% because of compulsory national education. College education is available to all through government grants for those who cannot afford university fees.

A frequent topic of conversation at family dinners is news of extended family, friends, or neighbors. The Irish have an intense interest in the activities of their extended family and friends, but this interest is not for the sake of pure gossip. Generally, they are quick to congratulate on good news and even quicker to rally around in times of trouble or need. When someone is sick, it is not unusual for all of the friends and family of the person to spend almost all of their time at the hospital. They help the family with necessary tasks and entertain one another with stories and remembrances. Many of the Irish have a difficult time understanding the American pattern in which the nuclear family handles emergencies and problems by itself.

This practice also holds true whenever there is a death in the community. Everyone gathers together to hold an Irish wake, which combines the viewing of the body with a party that may last for 2 or 3 days. There is plenty of food, drinking, laughing, conversation, music, games, and storytelling. Presumably, the practice of a wake originated because people had difficulty traveling in Ireland due to poor roads and nonmechanized means of transportation, and the wake afforded an opportunity not only to pay respect to the deceased but also to renew old friendships and reminisce. Although the problems of travel have been solved, the Irish still cling to this ancient way of saying goodbye to the deceased and uplifting the spirits of those he or she has left behind.

An event that is as important as the wake is a wedding; it is a time of celebration for the entire family and neighborhood. There is customarily a big church wedding followed by a sit-down dinner and an evening of dancing and merriment. Registry office weddings are very rare in Ireland, as might be expected in this conservative and Catholic-dominated nation.

Irish parents tend to be strict with their children. They set down definite rules that must be followed. Irish children are given much less freedom than American children, and they usually spend all day with their parents on Sunday and may accompany them to a dance or to the pub in the evening. Parents are usually well acquainted with the families of their children's friends and believe in group activities. The tight social community in which the Irish live makes it very difficult for children to do anything without their parents' knowledge. There is always a third cousin or kindly neighbor who is willing to keep tabs on the behavior of children and report back to the parents, some of whom have even managed to stretch their watchful eyes across the Atlantic to keep tabs on their children living in the United States. This close control can sometimes be difficult for young people, but it creates a strong support network that is useful in times of trouble.

A frequent gathering place for men, women, and children is the local pub, given that the drinking age is not enforced throughout most of Ireland. There are two sections in most pubs: The plain, workingman's part, and the decorated part where the cost of a pint of beer is slightly higher. In the not-too-distant past, it was seen as unbecoming for a woman to enter a pub; there are still some pubs in which women are comfortable only in the decorated part, and they typically order half-pints of beer, whereas the men order pints. Normally, the pubs do not serve food, which may reflect the Irish deemphasis on food noted previously.

Pubs tend to be very informal, often without waiters or waitresses and with plenty of bar and table space. Young and old mingle in the pub, often conversing with one another and trading opinions. The Irish are raised with a great respect for their elders and are quite comfortable carrying on a conversation with a person of any age or background. They tend to be a democratic people by nature and, although they may not agree with a person's opinion, they will usually respect him or her for having formed one.

Irish pubs are the sites of probably the liveliest conversations held in Ireland. Ironically, the number of pubs per capita has declined dramatically in recent years, in large part because of the movement against excessive alcohol consumption and the powerful association of pub owners that lobbies against new licenses (Zachary, 1999). The Irish tend to be a very sociable people who generally do not believe in drinking alone. This pattern of behavior has often resulted in their reputation for being alcoholics. In fact, the Irish consume less alcohol per capita than the average for the EU, but there are at least two distinctive groups: those who do not imbibe at all and those who do so, sometimes to excess. Admittedly, many Irish do drink more than they should, but the problem often appears worse than it is, because almost all of their drinking takes place in public. Furthermore, co-workers and their superiors frequently socialize in pubs, and they tend to evaluate one another not only in terms of on-the-job performance but also in terms of their ability to converse skillfully in such a setting. The favorite drink of the Irish is a stout ale, Guinness. It is far more popular than the well-known Irish whiskey.

Even more important than a good drink in a pub is good conversation. The Irish are famous for their storytelling, and it is not unusual to find an entire pub silent while one man holds sway. It is also not unusual for someone to recite a Shakespearean play from memory in its entirety, or to quote at length from the works of such Irish writers as James Joyce and Sean O'Casey.

Besides stories, many a heated argument can erupt in a pub. The Irish seem to have a natural love of confrontation in all things, and the conversation does not even have to be about something that affects their lives. They are fond of exchanging opinions on many abstract issues and world events. It is during these sessions at the pub that the Irish sharpen their conversational skills. However, although these conversations can become heated, they rarely become violent.

Irish friends, neighbors, and families visit one another on a regular basis. As indicated above, rarely, if ever, is one turned away from the door. Family and friends know that they are always welcome and that they will be given something to eat and drink. It is not unusual for visitors to arrive late in the evening and stay until almost morning. Such visits are usually not made for any special purpose other than conversation, which is the mainstay of the Irish life no matter where it is held.

Ending a Conversation

A conversation with an Irish person can be such a long and exciting adventure that a person thinks it will never end. It will be hard to bring the conversation to a close because the Irish always seem to have the last word. Ireland is a country that welcomes its visitors and makes them feel so comfortable and accepted that it is hard to break free and return home after an afternoon or evening of conversation.

Geert Hofstede's (1991) research profiling the value orientation of 53 nations includes Ireland, and his analysis confirms many of our observations. Ireland is a masculine-oriented society in which sex roles are differentiated clearly. However, it is not an acquisition-oriented society, as Hofstede's classification might suggest, but a society in which there is a balance between being and doing.

Furthermore, Ireland clusters with those countries emphasizing individualism, as we might expect of people who are willing and eager to explore and talk about serious and conflict-laden topics. Individualism is expressed through conversation and views on issues that affect society; it is also expressed in other talents, such as writing, art, and music. As suggested previously, music offers its own means of conversation, and Ireland reportedly has one of the highest number of musicians per capita of all countries. Still, the Irish tend to be collectivistic in their emphasis on the family, religion, a very generous welfare system, and the acceptance of strong labor unions.

Ireland also falls into the category of countries emphasizing a strong desire to meet new people and challenges (low uncertainty avoidance). Also, the Irish cluster with those countries that attempt to diminish social class and power differences as much as possible.

In short, the Irish tend to be an optimistic people who are ready to accept the challenges that life presents, although there is a melancholy strain in many of the Irish that is frequently attributed to the long years of English rule and the rainy weather. They usually confront things head-on and are ready to take on the world if necessary. They can be quite creative in their solutions, but can also be quite stubborn when asked to compromise, and they tend to be truly happy in the middle of a heated but stimulating conversation. Given their history and predilections, it is not surprising that the Irish prefer personal situations and professional fields of work where their aural-focused approach to reality can be given wide rein, even after they have spent several generations living in countries such as the United States and Australia.

PART IV

Market Pricing
Cultures

Market pricing cultures assume that it is possible to compare individuals using ratio statistical scaling, that is, there is a common unit of measurement but also a true zero point. In this way, it is possible to compare individuals on several dimensions simultaneously and even to transform all of the scale values into one final score for each individual. The true zero point is zero money, that is, everything is judged and evaluated in terms of this point.

CHAPTER 13

American Football

*Indeed, the growing complexity of business makes many corporate
managers shy away from baseball as a metaphor. Baseball, more
than most other major sports, is structured in ways that promote
the emergence of improbable heroes. . . . Many business leaders see
their game as more like football, with its image of interdependent
players with multiple skills cooperating to move the ball down a
long field 10 yards at a time.*

—Kaufman (1999), p. A8

A few years ago, two international MBA students at Maryland, a male from Russia and a female from South Africa, came into my office on a Monday morning in autumn. They had attended their first football game over the weekend when Maryland was playing North Carolina at home. I asked them what they thought about the game. One responded vehemently: That is the dumbest, the most stupid game in the world. I asked for some elaboration, and the description went something like this: Gigantic men, many of whom seemed unduly heavy, were dressed up in padded suits; they ran furiously and mindlessly against one another, and then milled about for a few minutes before running furiously and mindlessly at one another again; they repeated this action all afternoon, and once in a while scored a touchdown or a field goal; a band was playing; and there were some cheerleaders. I gave them a copy of the first edition of this book and told them to read the chapter on American football. The two students returned with a much better appreciation of football, but more importantly, they understood the intent of the chapter: If you do not understand American football, you will have difficulty understanding American culture and the manner in which business is practiced by Americans. Social critic Camille Paglia (1997) suggests that women should study football rather than attend feminist meetings for the same reason.

Apparently, both American males and females are in agreement, because football is the most popular sport in America: 68% of the nation's sports fans, and 57% of female sports fans, love football (Conty, 1999). Football Sunday has replaced Christmas as the national holiday in which families and friends gather together for parties. Even the O. J. Simpson trial was billed as the Trial of the Century in large part because it involved a football idol.

However, not everyone is enamoured. George Will declared that football manages to combine two of the worst aspects of national life: violence and committee meetings. Alistair Cooke described it as a cross between medieval warfare and chess (see "Punctured Football," 1993, p. 83).

But come with us as we describe an actual professional football game. Typically, it starts with a tailgate party, a uniquely American phenomenon. Some fans drive hundreds of miles to attend the game, whereas others drive for only a few minutes, but everyone arrives at the parking lot fully prepared for an outdoor party. They quickly unpack their heating grills, food, beer, and soda. Friends may cluster together, but they are sure to share their food and thoughts about the home team with other fans in the vicinity. After the party, everyone is ready to attend the game.

And the game is spectacular! There must be at least 300 performers on the field, each with a flag and a lavish smile, all synchronized to the slightest move. The sun is glittering on the dancers' shiny clothes, and the wind is dancing with the flags to the beat of the drums and the sounds of the horns. The sky is clear except for a Goodyear blimp circling high above the stadium where the Minnesota Vikings play their home football games. The fans are so responsive that they react spontaneously to anything and everything that occurs. They cheer the cheerleaders! They cheer the announcer! They cheer other fans! They even cheer the beer vendors! These fans are seriously committed to having a good time at the football game this Sunday afternoon. The crowd seems to be homogeneous; fans are wearing the same colors, supporting the same team, and hoping for the same outcome. Yet every fan has added his or her own personal touch to this weekly extravaganza. That man over there has painted his face with the team's colors. This younger guy in front has a huge banner with a witty message that indicates his frustration with the coach. A couple on the left are dressed as Vikings, manifesting their appreciation and relish for the team's name. Everybody is eating, yet no one is particularly rapt in this food feast. They are just continuously munching and crunching while essentially doing something else.

The cheerleaders gather on one side of the field and intensify their dance routines. The music is suddenly blasted, shaking one's body. A bomb—yes, a bomb—explodes on the field, igniting a thunderous roar from the crowd. Smoke fills the air, and the middle part of the field becomes virtually concealed. As the smoke clears, one seems to detect a car on a podium right on the 50-yard line. Yes, it is a car. Now that the view is unclouded, one can see a Honda standing gallantly on a wide podium surrounded by dancers and models. The Honda jingle is played on the stadium's loudspeakers, the crowd is singing along, and then the announcer proudly proclaims Honda as a sponsor of this week's game. Just as the announcer ordains, the reliable Honda Civic is driven away, followed by the dancers, who are still frolicking and prancing persistently in a marketing celebration.

After the sponsor of this game is announced (and never before), the stage is set for the actual game of football. A sport that captures many of the central values of American society, football has steadily become an integral component of the community: The Friday night high school football games played throughout the United States, the Saturday afternoon college games, and the professional games watched avidly in person or on television are part of the American landscape. Even becoming a cheerleader is highly valued, and the actions taken to influence such an outcome are legendary, including those of one Texas mother who planned the assassination of the mother of her daughter's rival for a coveted position on the junior high cheerleading squad.

Football is not only a sport in the United States but also an assortment of common beliefs and ideals; indeed, football is a set of collective rituals and values shared by one dynamic society. The outlandish speed, the constant movement, the high degree of specialization, the consistent aggressiveness, and the intense competition in football, particularly professional football, all typify the American culture.

Football is a team sport, yet the individual is glorified and celebrated. The extent of individualism in football seems to be unsurpassed in any other team sport. All the major trophies in football are named after individuals who have contributed to the sport. There is the Heisman Award, the Vince Lombardi Bowl, and many other trophies that extol the individual. In professional football, every player has a particular role to play. The play's success depends on how well all of the players perform, yet there is frequently one player who exerts extra and unusual effort. This distinguished player is seen as making the play happen and receives most of the accolades for doing so.

Professional football teams are actually multi-million-dollar corporations subdivided into departments and divisions, each with a large, highly specialized staff. Each member of this football organization has one very specialized task. Each squad has its own coach or coaches, and there are also the medics, the trainers, the psychiatrists, the statisticians, the technicians, the outfit designers, the marketing consultants, and the social workers, all with specific duties and assignments. There is even a person assigned to carry the coach's headphone wire throughout the game so that he will not trip on it! Professional football epitomizes perfection for many Americans. The plays in football are complex and precisely executed athletic routines; the players' movements and maneuvers are designed to achieve a high level of physical perfection; and the National Football League (NFL), in general, embodies all that is impeccable and optimum in the American mind: profits, fame, and glory.

There is a certain mystical appeal to professional athletes that frequently compels Americans to fantasize about becoming football players, who are judged to have it all by the community. Some Americans view football players as icons possessing superhuman traits. Sportswriter Thomas Boswell has made the following comments about the centrality of sports to American life, and these are particularly appropriate for football (Boswell, 1990):

> These days, sports may be what Americans talk about best. With the most knowledge. The most passion. . . . Not so long ago, such discussions . . . were couched in specifically religious terms. . . . Today, where would we reach first for material or metaphor to make such points to our children? Probably to sports. . . . In fact, sports has become central to what remains of our American sense of community. . . .
>
> In sum, great athletes in late 20th-century America have—without knowing it or wanting it—been put in something akin to the position of mythic or religious figures occupied in other cultures and times. . . . They play the role of surrogates in our thinly-veiled ethical conversations. (pp. 24, 26, 28)

Success or failure in football is a direct result of a team's efforts. In other words, failure can be avoided, and it is up to the individual team to acquire success. Fans do not usually feel sorry for losing teams. Losers are generally forgotten and ridiculed, whereas winners are glorified and praised. Such reactions are in sharp contrast to those found in other countries (e.g., see Chapter 3, "The Japanese Garden").

Football is a ceremonial celebration of perfect movement. The finesse of the wide receiver who dances through space in a dramatic way to catch the ball and the delicacy of the running back's movement when avoiding tackles suggest that the football player is also a dancer and not merely an athlete. In fact, dancing is the ceremonial countenance of football: The cheerleaders are joyfully dancing on the sidelines; the players are dancing gracefully on the field, particularly after scoring a touchdown; and the fans are dancing to the music played over the loudspeakers during halftime.

Professional football also embodies deep religious sentiments and a profound belief in the family. In the NFL, teams sometimes bring priests to conduct prayers before each game and after each victory; religious functions are frequently encouraged and planned by the teams' management; and coaches talk frequently about religion, how it has affected their lives, and how it relates to football.

The "families" within a single football team are the different groups of players forming a squad, each of which is one family that includes a group of players with similar attitudes and traits. Each player relates primarily to his squad. There are three squads on every football team, each with its own distinguishable characteristics and values: The defensive squad is usually the most aggressive and violent; the offensive squad includes the higher-profile, higher-paid players; and the special-team squad is characterized by big plays and high intensity. It is amazing how players try to fit into each of the particular squads' cultures, even to the extent of using outlandish nicknames such as "the Hogs" to describe a squad.

Professional football, therefore, is a metaphor that describes and explains various critical aspects of the American culture. In this chapter, the focus is on three fundamental aspects of football that form the basic components of the metaphor, namely individualism and competitive specialization, huddling, and the ceremonial celebration of perfection.

Individualism and Competitive Specialization

Even though football's rules and regulations are constantly changing from one season to the other, the basic values and ideals of the sport have changed very slowly over the years. In American society, innovation and modification are encouraged and sought, but usually not when it comes to values and ideals. American values, like those of football, have developed rather slowly, and few radical shifts in ideals have taken place over the past two centuries. Equality of opportunity, independence, initiative, and self-reliance are some of those values that have remained as basic American ideals throughout history. All of these values are expressive of a high degree of individualism. In fact, in Hofstede's (1991) 53-nation study of cultural values, the United States ranked first on individualism. Those same ideals are elementary in professional football and have been so over the years.

Furthermore, competitive specialization, both for each individual and for the groups in which he or she participates, appears to be the most evident feature of America. Generally speaking, the notion of "specializing to compete" is the principal ideological ideal that Americans adhere to, practice, safeguard, and promote worldwide. Competitive specialization is the tool with which Americans tend to tackle life's main challenges. This tool is often serviced and maintained with high levels of emotional intensity and aggressiveness. From this perspective, it is not surprising that most Americans, when asked what they do, immediately describe their occupation or profession, unlike the Japanese, who tend to respond with the name of the company in which they work (see Chapter 3).

The similarities between real life in the United States and a professional football game are astounding, especially within the warlike atmosphere that pervades this sport. Football closely parallels the actions that take place in the extrovertic, and sometimes even belligerent, American society. According to the Myers-Briggs Type Indicator®, which is the most widely used personality scale in the United States, 75% of American males and females are extrovertic and aggressive in personal relations. Although such extroversion is in large measure a positive feature of American life (Barnlund, 1989), the United States leads most other countries in terms of indicators that profile the negative aspects of extroversion and aggressiveness. For example, the United States, in comparison to all nations, ranks third on serious assaults and sixth on theft per 100,000 population.

Americans recognize instinctively the link between life in America and what happens on the football field. Violence and aggressiveness are part of football's appeal to American society, and they both relate football to actual life. Aggressiveness, which is often interpreted as energy and intense motivation, is encouraged in America. Analogously, aggressiveness is a celebrated characteristic in football. The teams compete with one another, players on the same team compete for starting positions, and even the fans compete for better tickets.

This type of individual competition and aggressiveness seems to be particularly suited to America. Richard Hofstadter (1955) graphically describes why Social Darwinism, or the survival of the fittest individual, was a social philosophy that appealed to Americans at the turn of the 20th century:

With its rapid expansion, its exploitative methods, its desperate competition, and its peremptory rejection of failure, post-bellum America was like a vast human caricature of the Darwinian struggle for existence and survival of the fittest. Successful business entrepreneurs apparently accepted almost by instinct the Darwinian terminology which seemed to portray the conditions of their existence. (p. 44)

This viewpoint was cogently and persuasively championed by Russell H. Conwell, the first president of Temple University and a minister of the Methodist church. Starting in 1861, he delivered his famous "Acres of Diamonds" speech, linking Social Darwinism to religion, more than 4,000 times (quoted in Burr, 1917):

> I say you ought to be rich; you have no right to be poor. . . . I must say that you ought to spend some time getting rich. You and I know that there are some things more valuable than money; of course, we do. Ah, yes. . . . Well does the man know who has suffered that there are some things sweeter and holier and more sacred than gold. Nevertheless, the man of common sense also knows that there is not any one of those things that is not greatly enhanced by the use of money. Money is power; money has powers; and for a man to say, "I do not want money," is to say, "I do not wish to do any good to my fellowmen." It is absurd thus to talk. It is absurd to disconnect them. This is a wonderfully great life, and you ought to spend your time getting money, because of the power there is in money.
>
> Greatness consists not in holding some office; greatness really consists in doing some great deed with little means, in the accomplishment of vast purposes from the private ranks of life; this is true greatness. (pp. 414-415)

Perhaps the best contemporary indication of this emphasis on individualism and competition can be found in the area of CEO compensation. In 1960, the average CEO made 41 times what a factory worker made; by 1992, the comparable figure was 157, and it has risen since that time. Moreover, a study of 13 industrial nations indicated that the disparity among incomes is much greater in the United States than in the other industrialized nations (Burtless & Smeeding, 1995). Periodically, journalists write articles such as "Gross Compensation: New CEO Pay Figures Make Top Brass Look Positively Piggy" (1996), but the trend continues.

As this discussion implies, competition seems to be more than a means to an end in America, and has apparently become a major goal in and of itself. Just as more than half of the rules and regulations in professional football deal with protecting and enhancing competition in the NFL, so, too, were American antitrust laws and regulations created essentially to safeguard competition and equality of opportunity for individuals and groups, and these are deeply rooted in American ideals and values that trace back to the European immigrants who came to America. These immigrants represented diverse groups who were basically at war with each other in Europe: The English did not like the Irish, the Germans had problems with the Poles, and so on. Although these hostilities and negative feelings were intense when the immigrants came to the United States, they were not usually displayed violently because the immigrants were tired of wars and bloodshed. Rather, these feelings manifested themselves in competition, specialization, and the division of labor. Each geographical area in the United States specialized in a particular category of production: The Northeast in manufacturing, the Midwest in agriculture, and the West in raising cattle. Even within parts of the country that specialized in agriculture, there was further specialization. The more fertile northern region of the United States (such as Idaho) specialized in farming crops different from those of the less fertile (but more populated) southern region. The distinct, highly specialized immigrant communities were still competing with each other economically, but their use of the law of comparative advantage propelled each of them to focus their efforts on one particular domain of production in which they excelled.

Thus, the communities were involved in a new kind of war, one that once and for all was designed to settle the score between Protestants and Catholics, Poles and Jews, English and Irish, and Germans and Danes. Competition prevailed, and the battles of the Middle Ages were refought in America but with new specialized weapons and for new competitive endowments. Each community frequently believed that it carried the burden of proving its own superiority through bigger dams, larger statues, more crops, and greater wealth. The legacy of competition continues to flourish in American society today, but with more legitimacy.

The European immigrants, although distinct and dissimilar, shared deep suspicions of authority. They assumed that authority impedes competition and foils specialization for both individuals and groups. Their main reason for fleeing Europe in the first place was corrupt and oppressive authority and/or government. Systems of checks and balances were developed in the United States primarily to protect the people from rulers who might control the economy, dictate religion, or dominate political power. Similarly, the NFL is the only league in the world that uses a system of checks and balances during a sporting match. There are two sets of referees, one on the field equipped with whistles and flags, and the other in the review booth equipped with a video cassette recorder and a color television. If one team does not like a call that a referee on the field makes, it can appeal to the review judges, who watch the play on video and make a final judgment.

Technological development is a catalyst to competitive specialization. Technology is the ingredient that provides competitive specialization with the efficiency required in an intensely capitalist society such as the United States. Similarly, technological development plays a key role in the NFL. The weight machines that professional football players use, the cameras and satellites that follow them, and the specialized equipment that they wear are integral to the American fascination with tools and machines.

The reason behind this fascination with tools is quite simple: America has historically been "short" on labor and "long" on raw materials. In order to use the abundance of raw materials, Americans had to substitute machinery and equipment for unskilled labor. Influenced by the success of their highly mechanized industry in the late 1800s, Americans were induced more and more shrewdly to use the power of machines and technology. To Americans, technology was empirically proven to stimulate growth and success, and their dependence on machines grew deeper and deeper with every increase in the number of American-patented inventions.

Today, it seems as if every American carries around a gadget of some sort to aid him or her to do some kind of task, and in this way, Americans are quite similar to the Japanese. Look at the football player! He wears a helmet, shoulder pads, neck pads, shin guards, ankle pads, and thigh guards to protect himself; he wraps antistatic, nonadhesive tape around his wrists and fingers for support; and he wears state-of-the-art, astro-rubber shoes for artificial turf or evenly spiked, fiber-saturated shoes for grass fields. Then, each type of player has his own distinctive equipment: The receivers wear grip-aligned synthetic gloves to catch the football; the linebackers wear tinted-glass face masks (shatterproof, of course) to protect their eyes from the glare; and the cornerbacks wear ultralight, reinforced plastic back pads to maximize their speed. Even the coaches have their own specialized gadgets: They use sensitive cellular devices to communicate with the statistician. And even though some sports traditionalists find it hard to believe, some teams are researching a cellular microheadphone to be installed in the quarterback's helmet so that he can hear the coach's instructions.

Americans are typically not influenced greatly by extended kinship or family groups; it is the nuclear family that is the locus of activity and identification. In many ways, American families are like the three squads in football mentioned earlier. A football player relates primarily to his squad and only secondarily to the team. Similarly, Americans relate to society through nuclear families and not kinship groups. As a general rule, American children are taught to relate essentially to their nuclear family at a young age; they learn through the example of their parents that the nuclear family is the integral part of their lives. Americans normally encourage independence, self-reliance, and initiative in their children. A child is raised to believe that a rich, healthy, happy, and fulfilling life can be attained by almost anyone as long as one is willing to follow certain steps and procedures. The American egalitarian spirit is nourished in a child's spirit and accentuated in his or her mind by his or her eager-to-make-the-child-successful parents. As a result, when that child has matured into the adult stage, he or she tends to believe that success (wealth, health, and happiness) is an individual's responsibility and duty. Any individual who is poor, unhealthy, or unhappy is viewed frequently by

American society as a person who failed in availing himself or herself of the opportunities offered.

As Stewart and Bennett (1991) show, Americans believe in equality, but only equality of opportunity; personal successes and failures are attributed directly to the individual. Many, if not most, Americans tend to see poverty and misery as self-induced, at least to a large extent. Stewart and Bennett also point out that this makes life difficult for the average American, because he or she must achieve constantly in order to meet such high expectations. Americans are not honored for past achievements but for what they are accomplishing currently; in this sense, their personalities tend to be constantly in a state of flux and evolution.

One of the major results of this orientation is that American managers are generally very open to change and are constantly introducing new programs with which they can identify and for which they can claim much of the credit; it is not sufficient for them to build only on the programs of their predecessors (Kanter, 1979). However, they tend to jettison programs just as quickly, and the United States is famous for both the fads that it introduces and the short-term orientation of its managers.

Huddling

There is another characteristic that differentiates football from any other sport in the world: the huddle (how offensive teams group before each play to call a certain plan into action). There is no other sport in the world in which planning is accorded such importance. In the huddle, there are different players from diverse backgrounds and with various levels of education. All have agreed that the only way to achieve a certain goal is to put differences aside and cooperate objectively. After the game, every player returns to his own world, living his own life in his own unique way. That is the essence of the melting pot, a diversified group of people that forgets its differences temporarily in order to achieve a common goal. As early as 1832, Alexis de Tocqueville drew attention to this facet of the American perspective (as quoted in Miller & Hustedde, 1987):

> These Americans are the most peculiar people in the world. You'll not believe it when I tell you how they behave. In a local community in their country a citizen may conceive of some need that is not being met. What does he do? He goes across the street and discusses it with his neighbor. Then what happens? A committee comes into existence and then the committee begins functioning on behalf of that need. And you won't

believe this but it is true. All of this is done without reference to any bureaucrat. All of this is done by the private citizens on their own initiative. (p. 91)

And this melting pot is becoming even more diverse: Between 1980 and 1997, the percentage of the population from Hispanic origin increased from 3% to 11%; the comparable figures for Asians were 1.5% to 4%; and for blacks, 11.7% to 12.1%. The figures for whites decreased from 83.1% to 73% (Booth, 1998).

Can a football team afford the luxury of eliminating the huddle? In most cases, no. However, the 1991 Super Bowl, possibly the best Super Bowl of all, featured the Buffalo Bills, who did not huddle after each play, and the New York Giants, who did. It was a very close game that was decided only in the last minutes. The no-huddle Bills were able to use this approach only because of the expertise of their outstanding quarterback, Jim Kelly. Once again, an individual was able to shine within the group context. Still, the final result was that the huddling Giants won. Although the final verdict on this issue has not been made, it seems that all teams, including the Buffalo Bills, will take advantage of the huddle, at least in many, if not most, instances. Similarly, most, if not all, groups and organizations in America employ huddling to handle their problems and achieve their objectives.

The American concept of huddling to coordinate activities is quite different from that of the Japanese sense of community within the organization. The Japanese normally socialize with coworkers after work, and if a major problem occurs, they will sometimes go off-site for an evening of drinking, dinner, informal camaraderie, and, finally, the discussion of the problem at hand and how to address it. Periodically, they will repeat such sessions until the long-term problem is solved. Americans, on the other hand, tend to huddle together in a business meeting specifically to address and solve the problem at hand, after which they scatter to complete their other work-oriented activities. If additional meetings are necessary, they are normally conducted in the same fashion.

As Daniel Boorstin (1965) has so persuasively shown, the lone cowboy or lone frontiersman is a poor metaphor for the United States. Rather, as adventuresome Americans moved westward to pursue a better life, they came together frequently to form temporary associations or teams to solve specific problems. However, given the rapid mobility of American society—a characteristic still dominant today—relationships among members of these groups tended to be cooperative but only superficially friendly; there was no time to develop deep friendships. The United States is the classic "doing" society whose members are primarily interested in building and accomplishing goals.

The focus in America is on accomplishing present goals to ensure a safe future, and little attention is given to past activities and history. Europeans and Asians frequently complain that it is very difficult to establish deep, personal relationships with Americans. As a general rule, Americans commit themselves intensely to a group effort, but for only a specified and frequently short period of time. Unlike many Europeans, who live, work, and die within 30 miles of their birthplaces, Americans frequently huddle in temporary groups as they change jobs, careers, geographical areas, and even spouses throughout their lives.

In football, the huddle divides the game into smaller sets of tasks that, when accomplished, successfully lead to the fulfillment of victory. The game itself is divided into independent jobs that are separated by short periods of position reassessment and fueled by continuous tactics. The huddle phenomenon in American culture—meeting together to subdivide a large task into smaller, related jobs that are accomplished one at a time—is illustrated in the way that Americans tackle problems. Any intricacy is broken down to smaller issues addressed one at a time. Americans tend to believe that any problem can be solved as long as the solution process is composed of a specific number of steps to follow and questions to answer. Likewise, in football, no matter how complicated a situation may be, teams are convinced that they can overcome the complexities through a standardized planning process.

The American System of Manufacturing (ASM), a system that developed as a result of Frederick Taylor's work on time and motion study at the end of the 19th century, is the "huddle" of American economic history. It reflects how the American mind is tuned. Just as the huddle in football allows a standardized planning process for a specific situation, the ASM allows a standardized manufacturing process for different products.

The ASM emphasizes the simplicity of design, the standardization of parts, and large-scale output. Americans introduced the concept and use of mass production as a direct consequence of the intense use of machinery. Whereas it took a group of German workers 1 week to masterfully produce 10 high-quality shotguns in the 1800s, the same number of American workers, with the help of standardized parts and ready-to-assemble components, produced in 1 day many more shotguns at a cheaper price. American products throughout history have not generally been known for their elegance but for their utility, practicality, and inexpensiveness. The American culture is one that respects machines and considers them critical to civilization. In fact, one of America's major contributions to the development of society has been its emphasis on ingenious tools and giant machines.

American society directly relates standardization to ranking of individuals. There is a great dependency on ranking via a standardized process (often based on statistical analysis) in America. Usually, there is no time to judge people subjectively. Stewart and Bennett (1991) point out that many "being" or high-context societies rank or rate employee performance in an absolute sense so as to save face; for example, Jones is a superior or good performer. However, Americans, in their "doing" mode, typically disagree with this approach and compare individuals to one another when evaluating performance. Standards are relative and not absolute, and an employee may well be replaced when someone else ranks higher than him or her. Even in an academic setting, students in the United States are evaluated and compared relative to each other. The students' grades are plotted as a curve of relative performance (usually a bell curve). This curve determines each of the students' final reported grade.

As might be expected, Americans normally want to know what the bottom line is so that they can make a decision objectively. This perspective is particularly disconcerting in American schools and colleges, where many students want to know only what will be on the final examinations. The egalitarian character of America, together with the fast pace of life, necessitates one form of standardized ranking or another when assessing a certain situation.

Although many Americans consider mathematics boring and tedious, all forms of standardized ranking that involve figures and numbers are used. When ranking the quarterbacks, for instance, the NFL standardizes the ranking process by defining different numerical categories, often called "numbers," that cover all aspects of the position. Each quarterback has certain numbers and figures ranging from "percentage of pass completions" to "interceptions over touchdowns" to "number of yards passed per game." The quarterback's livelihood depends on those numbers. In order to negotiate a raise, a quarterback has to improve his numbers, and when a quarterback is benched, it is often because of unsatisfactory numbers.

Numbers have an immense impact on the decision-making process in American society, whether it is a financial market analysis, a college recruitment program, or a political decision. American politicians are very sensitive to polls (which are nothing but bottom-line numbers), even to the extent that there is always a statistician on any major political staff. Similarly, the dependence on aptitude tests is crucial in the American education system. Academic institutions normally require that students take one kind of standardized test or another. Even though the admission decision is based on a larger number of criteria, the aptitude test score is still extremely influential. Just as a college football player's numbers are the arguments upon which he is judged for professional recruitment, so, too, are a student's aptitude test scores frequently the decisive factors for college acceptance or rejection.

This whole notion of standardized ranking evolves from the American perception of time. Time is not thought of as a continuous and abundant commodity. There is frequently no time for conducting any specialized or personalized tests when judging recruits. There is only one standard test, to be taken once every so often because, naturally, time is limited. Analogously, the sport of football is based on the notion that time is limited, and teams are continuously trying to beat the clock, particularly near the end of the game when the 2-minute warning is given.

There is almost always a time limit in America, and the huddle phenomenon in football reflects this time shortage. There is a specific time limit for the huddle before each play. One often watches football players rushing into or out of the huddle in a quick attempt to conserve time. Similarly, Americans constantly have a stressful feeling that time is running out, and therefore, they must talk quickly, walk quickly, eat quickly, and even rest quickly. When eating, Americans sometimes attempt to consume the largest quantities of food in the shortest time possible. Where else in the world can a mere human being eat a double cheeseburger, accompanied by massive amounts of potatoes and a cup of soda so big one cannot lift it, in less than 10 minutes?

When talking, an American has mastered the art of developing acronyms for time-consuming words like "economics" (econ for short)! The concept of extended formal names, such as "Herr Professor Doktor," is not only anathema to egalitarian Americans, but it also runs against the grain of their time-saving efforts. Any combination of words that form a name or a title of some sort is promptly diminished to a fewer number of letters so as to save time when saying them. The National Football Conference and the American Football League are never referred to as such, but rather, they are efficiently called the NFC and the AFL! The Grand Old Party is GOP; madam is ma'am; President Kennedy is JFK; the federal bank is the "fed"; an amplifier becomes amp; and, best of all, "howdy" is the time-conscious way to say "How do you do?"

Because of the American notion affirming scarcity of time, when improvident news events occur, especially scandals such as the O. J. Simpson trial, they are vigorously discussed and energetically debated in American society, but not for long. Americans do not have much time to dedicate to one news event. As Edward and Mildred Hall (1990) have shown, Americans are monochronic, doing one activity at a time rather than several activities. After intensely analyzing one major event for a short period, Americans become distracted and begin to focus on a new event.

Time is also limited in America because there are so many things to do in one's lifetime. The society develops technologically at horrendous speed, and it is difficult to keep up. One has to be continuously on the move. This is America; there is little time for contemplating or meditating. Ideally, one succeeds at an early age, and success in America is often impersonal and lonely. Football provides that sense of belonging and the brotherhood/sisterhood atmosphere that success lacks, and the huddle is the ideal, time-efficient approach for handling problems either in football or at work. The popular belief that the top is often lonely, however, does not inhibit most Americans from pursuing higher levels of achievement, because life, they believe, is a test of self-reliance and independence.

Ceremonial Celebration of Perfection

The new immigrants had a utopian vision for America. The ideals that America symbolized were, and still are, considered sacred and perfect. Unlike other major societies, the sources of American values are man-written materials that are believed to be inviolate and perfect, namely, the Constitution and the Declaration of Independence. American history is an ongoing battle designed to preserve these perfect values and utopian ideals incarnated in the Constitution and the Declaration of Independence.

With that in mind, one can understand why the portrait of America in the minds of the immigrants was actually a utopian image. Charles Sanford (1961) encapsulates the essence of this image in the following way:

> The Edenic image, as I have defined it, is neither a static agrarian image of cultivated nature nor an opposing image of the wilderness, but an imaginative complex which, while including both images, places them in a dynamic relationship with other values. Like true myth or story, it functions on many levels simultaneously, dramatizing a people's collective experience within a framework of polar opposites. The Edenic myth, it seems to me, has been the most powerful and comprehensive organizing force in American culture. (p. vi)

For centuries, America was "utopianized" by people fleeing persecution, subjection, tyranny, and oppression. America, the concept, was actually an attempt to create utopia. America, the value, encompassed all that is perfect: strength, wealth, philanthropy, family, children, and glory. This is *utopia*. Analogously, football personifies that unblemished portrait of utopia. Professional football is a symbol of that perfect American utopia.

It is very important to note that the Declaration of Independence and the Constitution, the basic written sources of American values, were authored by individual human beings, not gods, prophets, sacred apostles, or holy emperors. From this fact, one can understand why America ceremonially glorifies the individual. The common belief in America is that the individual is capable of doing anything that he or she wants to accomplish. Individual achievements, whether earning a degree or scoring the highest number of field goals for one game, are considered precious human deeds and are entitled to commemoration in one type of ceremony or another. Ceremonial celebrations of more significant accomplishments of American individuals, such as winning the Democratic Party's presidential nomination or the Super Bowl, become automatically a reflection of the American pursuit of perfection and utopia.

When retired NFL players are selected to the Football Hall of Fame, the most prestigious honor in professional football, the induction ceremonies celebrate both the individuals selected and the country that bestowed such perfection. There is a high sense of nationalism in professional football that is reflected ceremonially before the start of each football game. The national anthem is played and sometimes sung by a celebrity, and the fans proudly sing along with him or her. The flag procession precedes every football game, and representatives from the Army, Navy, and Air Force carry the American flags and assemble on the field. Apparently, there is nothing worth celebrating more or nothing more perfect than America. In the United States, sporting events in general, and professional football games in particular, are, in essence, ceremonies that celebrate how perfect teams can be, how spectacular the nation is, and how well the system works.

The celebration of nationalism is evident not only in football but in most, if not all, areas of socializing in America. On television, which Americans watch while socializing, many commercials are tied directly to nationalism, and innumerable marketable products or services are related to America. In general, Americans perceive the United States to be young, successful, and prestigious. By associating products with America, marketers aim to relate the youthfulness, beauty, and sex appeal of the United States to their own products. For example, here are the words to a Miller beer commercial:

> Miller's made the American way,
> Born and brewed in the U.S.A.,
> Just as proud as the people . . .
> Who are drinking it today,
> Miller's made the American way.

The jingle is accompanied by pictures of smiling American faces and happy American children, all of whom are joined in a dramatic celebration of the perfect beer brewed by the perfect country. In the background, and throughout the commercial, the American flag is flying gracefully, symbolizing flawlessness. There is basically nothing stated about this beer other than that it is pure American, but that is enough for many American consumers. The utopian American character rubs on success, popularity, and prestige.

Sometimes, nationalism generates ethnocentric behavior in America. In football, for instance, the Super Bowl is referred to as the world championship in spite of the fact that only American teams compete in it. To many Americans, the United States is the world, or at least the best part of it. The globe revolves around America, and the poorer members of the international community are protected by and fed with American remittances. Therefore, nations of the world must follow the American course and act the American way or else suffer the consequences of failure.

Consequently, the economic success and military might of America often induce egotistical reactions to international events among its citizens. These narcissistic feelings are evoked frequently by the media's persistent portrayal of, and fascination with, the world's disasters and mishaps. To the American media, "no news is good news," and therefore, the outside world is often reported as volatile, violent, and miserable. The positive features of foreign countries are highlighted only rarely by the American media. Because the average American is bombarded continuously with news of famines, wars, violence, and political turmoil from the outside world, he or she is frequently not aware of the pleasant and fascinating features of other nations. This ethnocentrism is so extreme that many Americans believe that the United States is the safest and most prosperous country in the world, even when the facts do not support such a conclusion, as we discussed earlier.

The American utopia is not complete without the practice of religion. More than half of the American population attends church regularly. Only Ireland, where 87% of the population regularly attends church, and possibly a few other countries, such as Poland, surpass the United States on this measure. There are more than 400,000 churches in the United States appealing to all different types of religious beliefs. Although the country is primarily Christian, with 30% of the population Protestant and 20% Roman Catholic, there are numerous other denominations. Also, billions of dollars are spent on church-related activities. For example, it is often said with some justification that the Vatican would be in grave financial difficulties if American Catholics decreased significantly their level of financial support.

In football, the ceremonial pursuit of perfection is blessed by priests who pray for individual teams before and after matches, as we have already discussed. Just as team managers try to relate to and identify with the society through religious ceremonies, so, too, Americans participate in religious activities in order to belong socially to a group. For the early immigrants who left their families and possessions, religion became the basic element that reestablished their social life in America. To these new immigrants, moving to a different society entailed a weakening ethnic identification and rootlessness. Thus, religion became a means of identification and belonging for

Americans, and churches and religious organizations frequently formed political pressure groups to achieve goals that helped their members and were compatible with their beliefs.

By way of summarizing this discussion of American culture, it is possible to relate this football metaphor to Hofstede's (1991) five dimensions of culture described in the first part of this book. As indicated previously, of the 53 countries in Hofstede's original study, the United States ranked first on the importance that its respondents attached to the belief in individualism. The United States also clustered with those countries that accepted and even relished a high degree of uncertainty and risk in everyday life, and that manifested a high degree of masculinity or an aggressive and materialistic orientation to life. Also, Americans demonstrated a preference for informality, low power distance between individuals and groups, and weak hierarchical authority. These findings are not surprising and help to confirm the generalizations put forth in this chapter.

The United States is still viewed by many throughout the world as far better than the countries in which they live, if not as a utopia. It still attracts large numbers of immigrants who are willing to put up with the glaring problems of American cities because of the opportunities that are available to those who work hard and strive for success. When they arrive, they tend to experience a distinctive form of culture shock that occurs because of the interplay among individualism and competitive specialization, huddling, and the ceremonial celebration of perfection. Much of this culture shock is encapsulated in American common sayings and aphorisms, and we end this chapter by highlighting some of them:

- Life is just a bowl of cherries.
- Let's get together and work on this problem.
- It's not violent. It's energetic, dude!
- It's lonely at the top.
- Get out of my face!
- Gotta run, man, maybe we'll talk later.
- America . . . love it or leave it, buster!
- Where there's a will, there's a way.
- One step at a time.
- It's never too late.
- You're from Nigeria? Is that a city in Germany?
- Hi! How are you? (as he or she walks by, not really wanting or expecting an answer)

CHAPTER 14

The Traditional
British House

We shape our dwellings, and afterwards our dwellings shape us.
—Winston Churchill, speech on rebuilding
the House, October 28, 1944

In the early 1990s, there was an extended discussion about a possible cultural metaphor for Britain in Martin Gannon's MBA class on cross-cultural management and behavior. Try as they might, two students— one American who had lived in Britain for 10 years and one Brit married to an American—had been unable to identify even one possible metaphor, even after a semester's work on the topic. Finally, the American started to compare her experiences in the United States and Britain. She likened Americans to independent atoms that periodically come together to accomplish a specific goal, and the British to individuals connected together through some sort of "invisible glue." According to the American, the British appear to understand the manner in which their destinies are inextricably linked; there is little, if any, need to be explicit about their basic values and why they behave as they do. The British student immediately saw how this invisible glue was closely associated with the traditional British house, and serious work on this cultural metaphor then began.

Britain's long and illustrious history lends credence to this cultural metaphor, and the heroic manner in which the British people rallied in World War II when the nation was bombed and damaged heavily tends to reinforce it. Britain is the only major industrial nation that does not have a permanent written constitution; it does not even have an official flag. Supposedly, everyone knows what to do, and they do it. But there have been some critical changes. Britain, once the most centralized of European nations, is going through a devolution of power, as evidenced by the fact that a parliament in Scotland and an assembly in Wales were created recently. Also, membership in the House of Lords is no longer a matter of heredity. And Margaret Thatcher, who became prime minister in the late 1970s, led a movement toward privatization that is still continuing.

Robert Cannadine (1998) depicts three models of Britain, the first of which supports the invisible glue concept: It is a nation whose people are linked closely together by shared values and expectations. However, the second model focuses on a nation divided sharply along three class lines: the upper class, the perpetually striving middle class, and the lower class. Cannadine's third model is the bleakest: Britain is really two nations, one very privileged and one oppressed. In this chapter, we touch upon all of these models, because all of them possess a kernel of truth.

But first, we need some understanding of a traditional British house, which is built to stand the test of time. It is almost always brick, but it can also be made of stone or concrete. Houses hundreds of years old and a few buildings thousands of years old are still standing and functioning in their original capacity. These houses were not built overnight, nor are they meant to last just a short time.

Much of the essence of Britain and her people can be sensed from the fortitude and long-lasting style of their buildings. The design of a British house is traditional and blends with the others around it; the foundations are deep and strong; and the floor plan does not vary and is unchanging over time. The walls have their own firm, fixed foundations so that the floor plan of the house is visible before the internal walls even go up.

Like the British people, there are few, if any, surprises in their traditional house. A British person could find his or her way around a three-bedroom "semi" (semi-detached house, or duplex) anywhere in the country. They are all based on the same tried and tested design. Thus, based on the outside of a house, the British know what the inside layout of the house is like—just as they know what to expect from one another.

The British way of life is reflected in their traditional houses. They are unchanging except for some slow chipping away or eventual weathering over the years. There is only one right way to do things, and most, if not all, citizens know what it is—no one has to be told.

Putting up a very modern California-style wood house with an open and unusual floor plan surely does not meet this need. In fact, a timber frame house of any sort would not tend to meet with approval and would make financing and insurance difficult to get. Some of the British would derisively term this type of house "ticky tacky," and a true British family would hesitate to rely on such methods for such a serious business as building a home. In fact, even when the population was sparse and forests abounded, houses were made of stone, not wood. A house, like a way of life, should have strong foundations, be familiar, be unchanging, and be built in tried and tested ways.

For this reason and many others, the British seem to mystify Americans, and vice versa, although the sense of identification between them is very strong. Margaret Thatcher, former Prime Minister of England, was fond of referring to Americans as her first cousins, and Americans reacted positively to this and similar statements. In fact, this strong sense of identification is justified, because surveys focusing on many countries show that the British and Americans tend to cluster together in terms of basic values and attitudes. This is not terribly surprising, because American law, government, and social mores are rooted in their British antecedents. However, there are significant cultural differences that surprise and confuse us when we consider our "cousins," the British.

It will be helpful to examine the British culture in terms of the metaphor of the British house. We will examine the "laying of the foundation of the house" evident in their history, as well as the political and economic climate of today. Next, we will look at the "building of the brick house," which naturally includes the various elements of growing up British. Finally, we will describe "living in the traditional brick house," including some of the cultural patterns in business and social situations.

History, Politics, Economics— Laying the Foundations

First, let us identify Britain geographically. There are a number of terms that are used when discussing this area, such as the British Isles, Great Britain, Britain, and the United Kingdom. We will be discussing Britain, which is synonymous with Great Britain, consisting of England, Scotland, and Wales. These make up the larger of the two islands that lie off the northwestern coast of Europe. The smaller island is made up of the Irish Republic (a separate country) and Northern Ireland, which is still under British rule. Britain reluctantly increased its control over Northern Ireland in the early 1960s because Catholics and Protestants were openly fighting and killing one another. Recently, some of the animosity has declined, and Northern Ireland now has a government in which Catholics and Protestants share power. The term "United Kingdom" refers to England, Scotland, and Wales (Britain), and also includes Northern Ireland.

Britain's earliest history is a succession of invasions and immigrations from tribes such as the Celts, Romans, Anglos, Saxons, and Jutes, many of whom were warriors, barbarians, and pirates. The date at which Britain was first inhabited is unknown, but parts of a woman's skull were found at Swanscombe in Kent and dated at about 250,000 years ago.

However, Britain's history from the middle 1500s to the 1950s is a story of domination that many have tried to emulate, and none has succeeded. For many years, their empire was so vast that "the sun never set on the British empire."

The British have left their mark in a variety of ways in many of the foreign lands over which their flag has flown. One of the most obvious is the fact that the accepted international business language across the world today is English. Many of their former colonies set up their parliamentary and legal systems to emulate the British system, including freedom of the press, and still look to the British for advice and consent in their own affairs.

The rate of immigration into the "home country" of Britain from former colonies is about 1 million people per year, approximately offsetting the same number of emigrations each year, and one quarter of the population of central London is of African, Asian, or Caribbean origin. Britain has lagged behind the United States in equal opportunity laws and job opportunities for ethnic minorities. However, cross-cultural marriage is far higher among Whites and Blacks in Britain than in the United States. Approximately 40% of Afro-Caribbean men between the ages of 16 and 34 have a white partner in Britain, and for women, the figure is 21%. The corresponding figures for the United States are 4% and 2%. A large part of the explanation seems to lie in the highly segregated residential patterns in the United States, because Blacks live primarily in the inner cities and Whites in the suburbs. Seemingly, many Brits do not mind living closely to others of different social classes and frequently marrying them, a result supportive of the "invisible glue" perspective (see "Integrated but Unequal," 1997).

For most of the 19th century, Britons were better educated, better behaved, and incredibly richer than most other Europeans. Across Europe, people set out to dress like the British, talk like them, and imitate their good graces. Even the fashion of wearing black, which survives in our contemporary evening wear, came from the British style in the 1830s. "It's their confidence," Aldous Huxley (1951) said of them in *Antic Hay*, "their ease, it's the way they take their place in the world for granted, it's their prestige, which the other people would like to deny but can't" (p. 38) that made them admired models. The adoption of British ways was so universal that it was unquestioned. People automatically chose the best, and the best was British (Barzini, 1983, p. 36).

For hundreds of years, there was a tacit admission of British supremacy in almost every regard. Furthermore, there was universal admiration and envy for their wealth, power, sagacity, and brutal ruthlessness, whenever necessary. There was a certainty that Britain knew best; that its overwhelming power and wealth would take care of most of the world's military, political, and economic problems; that private problems could be controlled by the British moral code and rules of good manners; that Britain could prolong the status quo indefinitely; and that there was nothing to worry about (Barzini, 1983, p. 37). This is the heritage of the British people—the foundation on which the rest of the traditional house is built.

As noted in Chapter 1, culture can vary along several dimensions, including time, or whether a society is past, present, or future oriented. It is easy to see why the British would emphasize the past far more than would Americans (Trompenaars & Hampden-Turner, 1998, p. 130). The antique pageantry and ceremony of her political structure is built right into the walls and shell of the house—without it, the house certainly would not stand as tall and proud.

Britain's government is considered one of the world's most efficient, and it is based on acts of Parliament. There is a written constitution, although it is quite different from the permanent U.S. Constitution in that it is the acts of Parliament existing at any one time that are its basis. Within Parliament, the House of Lords basically acts as a review body and can delay, but not veto, acts passed by the House of Commons. Thus, the real power rests with the House of Commons. Precedent or common law is used only when there is no legislation concerning a major issue or no clear legislative intent. Common law, however, is widely used. It is frequently assumed by the British that everyone knows the rules, and so the application of common law is received positively by most citizens. Contrary to the fundamental American assumption that supreme authority must never be vested in a single institution, the British Parliament exercises supreme power over both the figurehead monarchy and the courts. Like a load-bearing wall, it accepts full responsibility for governing in Britain.

In a very different way, the monarchy is a vital part of the political scenario; panoply and pageantry distinguish every ceremonial phase of royal processions. This enduring display of pomp simultaneously manifests the people's unity and strengthens it. The official opening of Parliament involves a ceremony over which the queen presides, and each week, she meets with the prime minister to discuss current national issues. The past, present, and future are united in the crown and the monarch. It is one of the things that makes Britain unique, and even many of its former colonies welcome the royal family with open arms and a unique respect. Without the presence of the royal family, some of the mortar that holds the traditional British house together would surely decay. Periodically, the monarchy is criticized, particularly in terms of being a feudal institution not appropriate in modern times, but the public supports it strongly.

There are two main political parties in Britain—Labour and Conservative (Tory). From time to time, a third party emerges, such as the Liberals or, more recently, the Social Democrats. Britain has a representative form of government. In a national election, people vote for their constituency MP, and that person represents them in Parliament. It is quite possible, and has happened, that the majority of votes is for a party that has a minority of seats in the House, and so it does not win the election, because winning is determined by the number of party-affiliated MPs elected. Elections can be called by the government at any time within 5 years of the previous election. This policy gives the party in power a political edge, because it can, within limits, arrange for an election to take place when public support for the government is greatest. To offset this, a vote of "no confidence" in the prime minister and his or her party can force a reelection at any time.

Voting is along party lines, and personalities are less important. Voting is also very much allied to social class, and so it is common to vote the way your parents did, and the way your neighbors do. In addition, the political parties are farther apart ideologically than are American parties, and changes in government can result in noticeable changes throughout the country. For example, the election of a Conservative government led by Margaret Thatcher resulted in nationalized industries being privatized, reduced income taxes, and "reforms" of trade union legislation.

In addition to the elected officials, there exists a whole matrix of official and social relations, within which power is exercised, called "The Establishment." This elite web includes such diverse interests as Oxford and Cambridge Universities; the British Broadcasting Corporation (BBC); and wealthy, high-society individuals known as "the Great and the Good." It is a difficult network to break apart because of the different forms it may take under different circumstances. Some say that this network has lost some of its clout, whereas others feel that it just keeps changing shape.

Economically, Britain can be divided into two parts. The south (the area within a few hours' drive of London) is considered by those who live there to be superior in sophistication, wealth, and social status. This is somewhat accurate because of the predominance of service, high-tech, and other growth industries there. The rest of Britain, in the north, is associated with heavy industry, engineering, mining, and unemployment. High unemployment has been the result in some parts of the north, where traditional industries such as steel, coal mining, and textiles have contracted in size.

Long after their empire was dissolved by granting independence to former colonies, the British were still considered the moral leaders of Europe. In World War II, they felt they had earned the right to be the third superpower in the world because the country had paid so dearly in terms of human life, physical destruction of property, and courage. However, in 1955, they stood aloof from, or outright objected to, attempts at unifying Europe. Although British opposition has softened in recent years, there is still resistance to the idea of a unified Europe. Britain is a member of the European Union, but it has not accepted the use of the Euro, the common currency.

Evidently, the British could have collaborated on many occasions to formulate the recommendations for a unified Europe in their own interest, but many of its leaders found it unthinkable to join with other nations and risk losing their full identity. Britain has tended to be a jealous guardian of its freedom of action, proud of its solitude. The British preferred to be victims of their own mistakes rather than to trust the judgment of other people (Barzini, 1983, p. 61).

But in many of the areas discussed above, rapid change is occurring. A national survey indicated that 67% of the British feel that they have too little say in the way they are governed. Also, 36% identified the United States as the nation from which Britain could learn the most about governing; the next highest percent was 23% for Germany (David, 1999). The British tend to admire the balancing of power in the United States, and they especially point to the American Congress, in which there are two strong entities, the Senate and the House. It is no longer possible to be a member of the House of Lords because of heredity, but this body is still of very minor importance. Furthermore, this national survey indicated that although only 22% of the British feel that Parliament will continue to have the most influence on their lives and those of their children, 44% felt the same way about the European Union. It was particularly noteworthy that 46% of the Scots believed that the Scottish Parliament would exercise the most influence over their lives, and 26% of the Welsh viewed the Welch Assembly similarly.

We have taken a look at the British character as exemplified in their traditional, rigid, but long-lasting brick houses, and have suggested that the Britons' strong sense of history is the foundation on which society rests today. Some of the traditions and shared beliefs represent the mortar that binds people in a national identity. Now we will look at the social mechanisms—socialization processes and the educational system—that sustain these feelings.

◼ Growing up British—Building the Brick House

Because of the prestigious foundations of British history, foreigners still expect the British to show something of their ancient firmness, resourcefulness, diplomacy, leadership, and, certainly, their good graces. How do the British continue to instill some of these admired virtues into their society? How do they put the bricks together atop the foundation to grow up British?

It has been said that all Britons have a few ideas embedded firmly in their heads that exactly and universally give them the answers about how to be perfectly British. This has allowed them, throughout history, to know exactly what their fellow citizens would expect them to do and how to go about doing it. For the most part, there is only one right way to do just about anything—from greeting guests to waging war.

Above all else, the British bring up their children to behave. Inquiries about children will often be about whether they are well behaved rather than whether they are happy. It is assumed that they need to be controlled and not spoiled. A great importance is placed on learning proper manners.

The British are taught at an early age to control spontaneity, and because children can be embarrassingly spontaneous, the emphasis is on keeping them quiet and not bothering adults. For example, it is rare to see children in a restaurant—most restaurants are just not set up to deal with them, and other diners would not approve because children do not yet know how to mind their manners. Children who do not know their place are thought to be precocious. Precociousness, equated with showing off or boasting, meets with disapproval. After all, children are meant to be seen and not heard. This emphasis on manners, and knowing one's place, continues as one grows.

A result of this restraint is in the well-known British reserve in adults. Most, if not all, Britons have at least one thing in common: a respect and a strong desire for privacy. This sentiment is so strong that they often appear to others as distant and aloof. It is as if they are building walls between themselves and others to create their own space within the brick house.

This need for privacy is a defining factor and one of the dimensions along which cultures differ. The phrase "We like to keep ourselves to ourselves" is particularly British (Glyn, 1970, p. 176). Glyn notes that even in the case of child care, baby-sitters need to be hired because relatives generally will not help or interfere. He also observes that even on trains, the British will frequently not sit near someone when a more secluded seat is available. In a crowded fast-food restaurant, if people are forced to share a table, they will often act as though the other party is not even present. Striking up a conversation with a seatmate would generally be considered an invasion of personal space.

There are very practical reasons for the British insistence on private, personal space. Britain is a crowded country, and space must be used efficiently. Britain is about half the size of California, but its population of 58 million people exceeds that of California by about 30 million people. In the European Union, the average population density is approximately 146 people per kilometer, but in Britain, it is 235. Although the British prefer houses and are not great flat (apartment) dwellers like other Europeans, their houses are small by American standards and closer together than in America. And just as there are partitions of rooms within the house, the British also grow hedges around their gardens to separate their space from neighbors and to keep out the eyes of the passerby.

A good neighbor is one who is friendly at a distance—who does not intrude. Because physical distance is not possible, the only available protection of personal space is psychological distance. One should always phone ahead before visiting a British home—dropping in unannounced would generally be unwelcome. Also, frequent social telephone calls tend to be regarded as an intrusion.

Emotional outbursts (except at times of genuine crisis) are seen as "soppy" or as evidence of an unstable personality. From childhood onward, the British are admonished to keep a "stiff upper lip"—referring to pursing the lips to prevent an outburst. Even good friends may never be as intimate as in many other cultures. However, this may apply differently to the different classes, with genteel restraint being seen as definitely more upper-class than lower class British.

John Cleese (of Monty Python fame) made this point entertainingly in the film *A Fish Called Wanda* (Shamberg & Crichton, 1988) when he said to his American girlfriend, Jamie Lee Curtis:

> Wanda, you make me feel so free. Do you have any idea what it's like being English? Being so stifled by this dread of doing the wrong thing, of saying to someone "Are you married?" and hearing "My wife left me this morning," or saying "Do you have children?" and being told they all burned to death on Wednesday.

There is a lot of weight from their lofty heritage that the British must endure. Although the foundation is strong and deep, the walls and especially the exterior of the British house and personality must seem to be effortlessly indestructible and imperturbable.

Inside the house, private space is also cherished. The British do not generally like open-plan living areas. Instead, rooms are separated and divided by walls and doors that close. Although houses are relatively small, family members are thus ensured private space. Still, Edward T. Hall (1966) points out that the smallness of the houses effectively precludes children from having their own rooms, as is the norm in the United States. He argues that, as adults, the British do not have as great a need for separate offices as do members of some other cultures. Even members of Parliament do not always have their own separate offices.

All of this talk of privacy and reservedness should not be taken to mean that British people are unfriendly. By and large, they are friendly people and make the most gracious hosts. If you ask people for help, even on the street, most will give it cheerfully. Americans, on the other hand, are often seen by the British as coming on too strong and too gushing, as being insincere, and as getting too personal too soon. The British need time to size you up, because you could be as untrustworthy as an aluminum-sided house.

Although the British enjoy the privacy of their own small homes, they also enjoy the camaraderie of the local pub. Nearly every large and small town throughout Britain has at least one pub, many of them hundreds of years old. This is where many British do most of their socializing with co-workers and friends. It is a favorite pastime to share a few beers together after work, even with their bosses. In fact, pubs can almost be thought of as a substitute for the living room in a traditional house, because Britons do not entertain as frequently as Americans in their own homes.

Pubs generally serve various kinds of beer—ale, stout, lager (the British equivalent of American-style beer) or bitter—by the pint or half-pint. Women should note that ordering a pint is unladylike; a half-pint is better. Beers are served at room temperature and never cold, which would disguise the flavor. Most other drinks are served without ice and, true to the British ideal of what is right, you will be given only a single ice cube when asking for ice.

Orderliness, patience, and unexcitability are hallmarks of British behavior. They prefer to see each task through until completion, regardless of the priority one might assign to it. For example, if you approach a hotel desk where a clerk is alone attending to some paperwork, he or she will finish the current task unhurriedly before attending to you. There is nothing between the ordinary and a true state of emergency for most British.

There is a wide spread of living standards in Britain, ranging from some of the worst slums in Europe to very grand estates. Roles and status are generally well defined. Still pervading this stratified society are distinctions between the working class, the middle class, and the elite upper class. In numerous surveys over the past decades, the British themselves reinforce these divisions by assigning themselves more than 90% of the time to one of these classes without prompting. In a 1991 survey published in *The Economist*, 29% said they were middle class and 65% working class ("The Little Class Game," 1992). By contrast, most Americans, including many who would be considered working class in Britain, describe themselves as middle class.

One is born into a class, and it is difficult to move from one class to another. Once again, tradition rules, whether it be in one's house plan or social class. Family background, especially the accent and use of the language, will tend to determine the type of education and, hence, the qualifications earned for a career.

Although real disposable income overall has increased in recent years, so, too, has income inequality. In 1979, the top 20% of British households had 43% of all earned income, whereas the poorest 20% had only 2.4%. In 1996, the corresponding figures were 50% and 2.6%. Similarly, the middle 60% of the households experienced a decline of eight percentage points. And, although the proportion of students getting a university degree increased from about 14% in 1985 to 31% in 1996, a survey of those receiving their first university degree in 1992-1993 indicated that only 33% had been in continuous employment. Also, more than 50% felt that their skills were underutilized on the job (see "Degrees of Dissatisfaction," 1996). Such facts reinforce Cannadine's third model, in which Britain is divided into two separate nations: the haves and the have-nots. Even Cannadine's second model focusing on a three-class nation seems to have some support. If anything, the distance between the top 20% and everyone else seems to have increased.

The British are experts at classifying each other by tiny details of speech, manners, and dress. George Bernard Shaw wrote (in *Pygmalion*) that "The moment one Englishman speaks, he makes another Englishman despise him." This statement was made so beautifully clear in the adaptation of this work into the musical comedy "My Fair Lady." Immediately after hearing just a few words from any Brit, another Brit generally can classify him or her as to social class and where he or she grew up.

Although Shaw's writing was done in the 1800s, the British can still identify regional accents and, therefore, where the speaker is from and his or her class. The discrimination that this once produced may be fading, because regional accents can now be heard in professions and walks of life that were once reserved for the upper class only. For instance, although there was a time when only "proper" upper-class English would be heard on the airwaves, particularly the BBC, regional accents are becoming more acceptable and are heard in all areas of broadcast. This may be indicative of a broadening and deepening of the middle class in society, raising the level of some of the working class.

Even so, the use of the language (and other behavior) can still be telling of class. Alan Ross (1969) published a popular version of his article "Linguistic Class Indicators in Present Day English" under the title "U and Non-U," referring to upper-class and non-upper-class language. Many of the distinctions have faded with time, but some are as true today as ever. For example, "I worked very hard" is U, but "I worked ever so hard" is non-U. "Half past ten" is U, but "half ten" is non-U. Rugs or a plain carpet are U, but wall-to-wall patterned carpet is non-U; putting milk into tea cups first is non-U, but offering it after the tea has been poured is U. Another non-U "Britishism" that tends to puzzle foreigners is saying "He wasn't half angry," which means he was extremely angry; or "He isn't half handsome," which means he was exceedingly handsome (Braganti & Devine, 1992).

In this regard, T. R. Reid has pointed out that the British admire American pragmatism and hire American firms such as Bechtel for very difficult projects, such as rebuilding the Royal Opera House at Covent Garden. But Reid also points out that Americans possess a distinctive advantage: The British cannot classify them by their speech, which tends to cut across class distinctions. As he states, "In Britain, the way you talk speaks volumes about you—your economic status, your school, your ancestry, your career prospects" (Reid, 1999, p. A26).

Still, it is becoming increasingly difficult for outsiders to identify a Brit's social class. *The Economist* ("The Little Class Game," 1992) asked a knowledgeable but anonymous Italian to describe how he makes such identification, and, after admitting to the increased difficulty of doing so, he offered the following advice:

> So if you are in doubt, and you do not feel ready to play the Little Class Game with the professionals, go for the obvious. Some items of clothing still speak volumes about their owner. When you see somebody dressed as if he has stolen the trousers from an Italian two sizes bigger than he is, you assume he is middle-class, probably an estate agent. . . . And if you meet a girl with no stockings on in winter and navy-blue legs, you can still safely bet she is working-class. Some things, thank goodness, never change. (p. 64)

Of course, the British seem to believe that Americans do not speak English at all and find their language a sloppy adaptation of it. Other Europeans might tend to agree, because they learn British English and sometimes find Americans more difficult to understand. Apart from the strict use of grammar and pronunciation, the British and Americans can confuse each other with their use of different words. For example, in Britain, you will not hear apartment, but flat; not drug store, but chemist; not elevator, but lift; not attorney, but solicitor; not call (which means to visit in person) or phone, but ring up; and not trunk (of a car), but boot.

There are some segments of the population that have developed entirely different speech patterns that may not be understood easily by other British (or other English speakers). The most well-known is the working-class Cockney population—officially, those born within hearing distance of the Bow Bells that ring from the Church St. Mary le Bow in the east end of London. These people have developed Cockney rhyming slang, some of which has passed into general usage. If a man talks about the "trouble and strife," he is referring to his wife. To say "I didn't say a dicky bird" means "I didn't say a word." Understanding Cockney rhyming slang is yet more difficult when the conversion is one step further removed. For example, "loaf of bread" stands for head, but the whole phrase is not used, just "loaf." So, if someone tells you to use your loaf, you are being told to think clearly, or to use your head. Another popular expression is "Blimey!" which means "God, blind me if I tell a lie," and is used throughout Britain as a common exclamation.

British people also do not tend to move too far away from their family home and would most likely strive to live in a house very similar to the one in which they grew up. They are not inclined to make changes simply for the sake of change, but prefer to stick with familiar and comfortable surroundings. Moving across town is not treated lightly, and one would need a good reason to move to another part of the country. Lack of work is often not considered to be a strong enough motivator to move away from one's home and roots. The British tend to keep work and leisure completely separate, much as the living areas and bedrooms of the traditional two-story house are separated by downstairs and upstairs. Therefore, they are not likely to let their lives be dictated by their jobs or careers.

British educational policies have changed considerably over the past 25 years, but the old system and its influence are still evident. Tenure has been abolished at the universities, which are ranked on a series of criteria used for determining future funding. As noted above, the number of university graduates has increased, but it is still extremely difficult to get into the top-rated universities, and many graduates are dissatisfied with their jobs.

Today, many children attend American-style "comprehensive" high schools or secondary schools for children of all abilities. But the nature of the secondary schools is still very important. Whereas Americans tend to identify a person's social standing at least in part by the prestige of the college attended and rarely think about the secondary school, the British give approximately equal weight to the college and secondary school attended. Public secondary schools (which, in the United States, are private schools) existed and still exist for children of the financially able, or those able to win scholarships. These were often founded by trades organizations—for example, the Merchant Taylors boys' school in London and both girls' and boys' schools founded by The Worshipful Company of Haberdashers. Others, including Harrow and Eton, are well known, and they provide more than their share of entrants to the prestigious Oxford and Cambridge Universities. The reputation of the school attended accompanies one through later life, and the more prestigious it is, the more doors it opens. These more prestigious schools often have ties or scarves with certain colors or patterns associated with them. Wearing them is considered an earned honor, and it would be a major faux pas to wear a tie or scarf to which one is not entitled. In fact, some pubs forbid the wearing of scarves after sports contests because fights are likely to break out, especially if scarves are flaunted or if some patrons denigrate other patrons' scarves.

Although there has long been a strong connection between church and state, outside Northern Ireland religion plays little part in the everyday lives of the British. Even though Henry VIII declared himself the equivalent of the Pope when he created the Church of England, 35% of the British population claims to have no religion, which is the second highest number in Europe (after the Netherlands). The rest of the population, if pressed, would probably say that they are C of E (Church of England, or Anglican). The church services generally do not inspire enthusiasm, being rather serious.

Just as the mortar holds the solid British house together, so, too, do the socialization processes, class distinctions, and educational system described above represent the floor plan or design of the traditional British house. It is within this framework that the British people live, work, and play. But once any house has been built, people live in it in their own way. We will now look at some of the dimensions of British everyday life, such as work habits, etiquette, humor, social customs, and leisure activities.

■ Being British—Living in the Brick House

Most travelers expect to find the British stuffy and starched. Indeed, that is one side of the coin: the gentleman wearing pinstripes and a bowler hat, carrying a furled umbrella, greeting another with "I say, old chap" and the like; and the oh-so-proper lady shopping at Harrods and having afternoon tea with dainty little cups and rich pastries. Flip the coin, however, and you may find orange- and green-haired punks with spike hairdos, as well as other, less noticeable eccentrics.

Furthermore, you may offend the Scottish (or Scots) or the Welsh if you do not respect their differences, even though Britain encompasses England, Scotland, and Wales. Many of the variances appear superficial, such as food preferences and specialties, but others are more substantial. For instance, Scotland has its own legal and educational system that is patterned after the German system (see Chapter 10, "The German Symphony"), and Wales finds its identity in its own language.

Despite this wide spectrum, the British are considered a relatively homogeneous group of people. We will focus here on the similarities between them, not their differences. For instance, they all share the same constantly wet weather. The benefit of this is that it produces some of the lushest, greenest land in the world. Perhaps to enjoy this aspect of life, the Scottish invented the game of golf in the 14th century and still have some of the most desirable courses in the world. At one point, the Scottish king outlawed golf because the citizens were devoting too much time to it and not enough time to archery and preparation for battle.

Maybe this constant wet weather is what the British mean by "making the best of a bad lot." If things go wrong (or the weather happens to be lousy), the right thing to do is to make the best of it. This will be admired. The British tend to think highly of anyone who suffers setbacks and perseveres; whether success comes is less important.

"It is not whether you win or lose that is important, but how you play the game." The British really mean this, and will even applaud the opponent for making a good play in a cricket match. Another expression in Britain is that "it's just not cricket" when something is handled unfairly. It is true that draws (ties) are quite acceptable, and sometimes preferable, in British soccer and cricket matches. This is something that is totally disheartening and very rare in America, where the rules are often such that tie-breaking is essential. Also, the heart of the British tends to go out to the underdog, the player who is in a lost and hopeless position such as that of the man playing for a draw in cricket, who must stay at his post until the close of play to deny the opponents their victory.

Again, however, these generalizations must be tempered. In recent years, the British have not won many international events; it has been more than 60 years since an Englishman won the men's singles at Wimbledon. And the loutish behavior of some English soccer fans caused *The Economist* to identify them as "England's Shame" (1998). Still, most of the British follow the pattern set by their ancestors when it comes to fair play.

Whereas cricket tends to be a middle- and upper-class sport, and very popular in public schools, soccer (it is called football in Britain) is a working-class sport. And just as elite public schools, clubs, and universities have their own scarves or ties associated with them that are earned and worn with pride, so, too, are scarves available in soccer team colors. These scarves may not be earned, but they can be seen trailing from car windows on Saturdays as enthusiastic fans travel to watch "away" matches.

Regarding sports as a leisure activity, the British tend to be keener spectators than active participants. They invented many of the sports that the world plays today: football (soccer), golf, tennis, badminton, and rugby. Indeed, the all-American sport of baseball is based upon the old British city game of "rounders." The British tend to be loyal fans and as sport mad as the Americans. They talk about it, read about it, gamble on it, and turn out in the worst weather to watch their local teams.

One major difference is that the British do not appreciate individuals who stand out; they prefer a well-trained team that works together in sportsmanlike fashion (Glyn, 1970). Glyn also notes that when games reach the international level, the British tend to lose interest; when things get that big and remote, the spirit of playing for pleasure is compromised. Perhaps this is why their international performance has been less than stellar.

Those who have the financial resources spend much of their leisure time in the country. It is considered the utmost luxury to have a house in the country, and most Britons yearn for this. In the smallest towns and villages throughout Britain, houses may still be addressed by their names instead of street numbers. These names are usually descriptive and may include the name of the original owner. Examples might be Hawthorne's End or Cadbury's Cottage. This is a quaint carryover from the days when people referred to addresses this way and streets were unpaved and unnamed.

An important leisure priority for the British is a respect for nature in the form of the countryside and gardens. The British generally like to walk, sometimes around the block, but in a garden or country setting is better. Another way of getting close to nature is to create your own garden. However modest the patch of ground in front or back of the brick house, there is another traditional element—the English garden. It is not called a yard, which signifies a dusty concrete patch like a school yard, but a garden, which implies flowers and grass. The British are renowned for their beautiful gardens, which may be elaborate or small, but usually consist of a patch of lawn surrounded symmetrically by colorful flowers and shrubs. Of course, these gardens do not suffer from lack of water and tend to be wonderfully lush.

Ceremonies and holidays offer an interesting example of how the past-oriented British hold on to age-old attitudes and traditions. A large proportion of Britain's oldest surviving customs come from towns and cities, and they are bound with a long and complex history (Kightly, 1986). The celebrations are widespread; there are more than 7,000 fairs annually, and each village has a yearly festival celebrating the day of the patron saint to whom its parish church is dedicated. Founder's days are common as well, with institutions such as schools, hospitals, and alms houses honoring their benefactors annually. Such celebrations reinforce the same conservative traditions that the British house embodies.

One favorite tradition is Guy Fawkes' Day, which is recognized each November 5th and is dedicated to the memory of the fate of a traitor who tried to blow up the houses of Parliament. Bonfires are set, a straw doll to symbolize Guy Fawkes is set atop, and spectators cheer as it burns to ashes. At a Guy Fawkes bonfire, people chant the rather morbid poem: "Penny for the Guy, poke him in the eye, stick him in the fireplace and watch him die."

British humor seems to run the spectrum of possibilities. Despite their well-recognized reserve, the British have a basic aversion to seriousness and prefer to lighten most events with humor. On one hand, there is the dry, satirical humor that one would associate with Noel Coward. At the other end of the spectrum, the British love the broadest slapstick, replete with rude jokes and outrageous behavior, such as in *The Benny Hill Show* and Monty Python. Even in dignified settings, such as Parliament, high-spirited bantering finds its way into many otherwise dull negotiations. In one celebrated instance, an MP had to apologize to the Parliament after its members voted that he must retract the statement "Half the members of Parliament are asses." He apologized by saying that "half the members of Parliament are not asses," and then sat down. This skillful display of biting humor disarmed his adversaries.

Perhaps this love of humor comes directly from their culture, where a direct display of feelings is suppressed. Humor distracts from embarrassing or tense situations that might otherwise be difficult for the British to handle. Just as the windows in a traditional home bring in light and fresh air, humor changes the atmosphere and relieves tensions.

In recent years, one of the most popular British sitcoms is "Keeping Up Appearances," both in Britain and in the United States, where it is carried on public TV. This sitcom focuses on only one topic, with variants thereof: social class differences. Some commentators, both British and American, have heaped unqualified praise on this show, and the reader is encouraged to see it not only for its great humor but also for its incisive depiction of social class differences.

In social and business situations alike, one should be right on time or up to several minutes late, but never early! The British institutionalized the idea of being "fashionably late"—usually interpreted as being 10 to 20 minutes late. If the British arrive early for an appointment, they will often wait in their cars or outside until the agreed upon time.

The old notion of the British being unable to relate to you unless you have been properly introduced by a third party is out of date. Increasing informality in this area is becoming more common, but the British reserve may still shine through, giving the impression of coolness or indifference. Nevertheless, first names are used almost immediately in business and social situations among people of the same level. People of a much lower status in business or social class will usually address their superiors by an appropriate title and surname. In some cases, men may be heard calling each other by their last names only, but this is simply a carryover from public school days and need not be imitated.

The phrase "How do you do?" is a very common greeting in Britain. It is not an inquiry, but expects the same response, "How do you do?" and nothing more. To avoid sounding obviously American, say "Hello," not "Hi." Also, the British think the phrase "Have a nice day" upon leaving someone is strange and see it as a form of command. The British tend to be more circumspect in their conversation than others. They avoid being direct for fear of offending someone. In fact, they often phrase definite statements as questions. For instance, they may say, "It gets dark in the evening, doesn't it?" No one is expected to answer the question. These examples confirm the oft-quoted adage that the British and the American share a common culture separated by language.

Politeness and modesty are the hallmarks of the British in social conversation. Do not be surprised if, after you pontificate at length about the history of Poland to a new acquaintance, you find out much later that he or she is an expert scholar in this area. It would be impolite and immodest for the acquaintance to point that out to you at the time. Most likely you will have to learn these facts from another mutual acquaintance.

In all forms of communication, whether verbal or written, subtlety, imprecision, and vagueness are typical. Exact facts and figures are avoided. Anyone can find obvious examples of this in the local newspapers, where trends are expressed in terms of "more" or "less," but do not answer the question, "How much more or less?" Such exacting details are seen as trivial, unnecessary, and somewhat distasteful.

The British view of work tends to be pragmatic, but less so than Americans. They prefer "muddling through," which usually results in finding the most expedient rather than the most innovative solutions. The French, who prefer to emphasize pure theory, sometimes experience difficulty understanding this "muddling through" perspective that their more empirically inclined British counterparts manifest.

Paradoxically, the average Briton will obey any rules that are spelled out or stated in exacting detail. Their strong sense of order and tradition dictate that they do what is right, and written instructions and legal signs are an indication of what is right. Unlike many other countries, where rules and laws may or may not be obeyed depending on the circumstances, it is a common sight in Britain to see lines of people and cars waiting patiently in a way that would make members of other, more hurried and anxious cultures cringe. It is understandable, then, that the British would shy away from having too many rules and written laws because they would tend to obey them strictly.

Most Britons prefer to work for other people rather than themselves. Only about 10% of the population is self-employed. Overall, in the business environment, there is more formality between different levels in the hierarchy, which is more rigid than in America, and formality in dealings between employee and superior is greater. Adler (1997) gave an example of an American executive who went to London to manage the company's English office. This executive noted with annoyance that visitors had to go through several people—the receptionist, the secretary, and the office manager—before seeing him. The English explained that this was usual procedure, and without it, the executive's status would be compromised.

Similarly, Laurent (1983) studied diversity in concepts of management among businessmen in 12 Western countries. Twice as many British as American managers felt that hierarchical structures exist so that everyone knows who has authority over whom, and twice as many thought that there was an authority crisis. The British were also more in favor of well-defined job descriptions, roles, and functions. This is consistent with living in the traditional British house, with its floor plan divided into many small rooms, each with a designated purpose.

Trade union membership has declined in recent years, but about 35% of the British workforce is unionized; the corresponding figure is 16% in the United States. The relationship between unions and management tends to be adversarial, but in recent years, the unions have deemphasized the use of the strike weapon.

The most important abilities of managers are seen as conducting meetings efficiently and having good relations with subordinates. It is a convention that instructions should be disguised as polite requests. Combined with British reserve, this makes for a distant relationship in which both sides are constantly on their guard. Fairness is the most important arbiter of management style.

In general, meetings are a significant part of the workday in Britain. Business decisions are typically made jointly and are usually discussed, ratified, or implemented at a meeting. These meetings are generally informal, beginning and ending with social conversation, and individuals are expected to make a contribution, even if it is only in the form of questions. Ideas and opinions are normally encouraged, but their value to the group depends heavily on the status or seniority of the person stating them.

In addition, Hofstede's (1991) study points out that the British accept only small power distances between individuals and believe that all people should have equal rights. However, because there is a great emphasis on status and deference, subordinates are fairly comfortable being told what to do and are less likely to think of questioning an order from a superior of any type than are their American counterparts. For example, some people would not consider questioning a doctor's advice or a teacher's wisdom.

Although the British are seen as being more individualistic than collectivist in Hofstede's study, "individualism" in the British sense tends to find its form in eccentricity and nonconformity rather than self-initiative and competition. For example, because fox hunting is difficult in crowded Britain, some enthusiasts hire a jogger to dress up as a fox who, when cornered by the dogs, is lovingly licked rather than bitten.

Also, the British are often uncomfortable and unwilling to take a stand unless they know that the group consensus will support them. A concern to avoid disharmony among the group members will smooth over all but the most fundamental disagreement. For this reason, even as consumers, the

British will frequently accept indifferent treatment from businesses with little complaint. Such acceptance may reflect social class differences. If a customer does complain, the response will quite likely bring a patient explanation of why the customer is wrong, and how the business's actions are justified.

They also normally prefer to work in the security of a group within an established order with which they can identify. Motivation comes when they see the work as useful to themselves and others, and as striving toward a common goal. The basis of social control in Britain, as in most Western nations, is persuasion and appeal to the individual's sense of guilt at transgressing social norms and laws. Indeed, this works particularly well in Britain because of the strong sense of tradition, the right way to do things, and "not letting the side down."

Most British will identify hard work, education, ambition, ability, and knowing the right people as the methods used in getting ahead. However, these factors often must be accompanied by regular company moves to achieve successful results. This is due to the fact that in many organizations, one must still wait for someone higher up to be promoted, move on, or pass away to make space for an employee promotion.

Women make up approximately 50% of the workforce in Britain, which is much higher than in other European countries despite low maternity benefits and little or no child care support. Economic necessities have driven women into the workforce. Because they are paid less than men, and many are willing to work part-time, companies are happy to have them. Do not expect to find a significant number of them in the higher levels of management or in technical careers. However, one of Britain's strongest leaders in modern history, Margaret Thatcher, was a woman who was known throughout the world as the "Iron Lady." Women who find themselves in positions of authority can and do demand respect.

Speaking of respect, no one draws more than the Queen. There is a magical and mystical quality about the royal family, and especially the Queen, that makes one stop and take notice. As might be expected in a tradition-bound society, the most glamorous and somber events involve royal processions. The Queen's coronation was complete with decorative pomp and pageantry, the ritualistic anointment with oil, and crowning.

More recently, however, the scandal pages and gossip newspapers have been captivated by the less noble actions of various members of the royal family. This is nothing new, because throughout the history of the royals (or any family examined so unrelentingly), there have been some demonstrations of less-than-perfect behavior. However, in a democratic society, it is also no surprise to find that there is a constant questioning of the necessity and future of the monarchy—should the throne continue to exist, should they pay taxes, and so on. In answer to these charges, one must remember that in the Queen are embedded notions of history, tradition, civility, and national pride, and one third of the British population still dream of meeting her (Michon, 1992). However, the royal family did begin paying yearly taxes in 1992, which implies a narrowing of the gap between the royal family and the ordinary citizen.

The royal family and the tradition of the monarchy are held very dearly in the hearts and minds of the British people, and the Queen and her nobility are constant reminders of the brilliant past of the British empire, the world-wide respect and awe afforded her throughout the world, and the hope and dignity of the future. The untimely death of Princess Diana in 1997 reinforced the popularity of the monarchy. It also caused many British to display their emotions much more than they normally do, and commentators are still trying to discover why. By and large, this emotional display was probably more of the exception than the rule.

This concludes our discussion of the British. As it suggests, the British tend to be steadfast and traditional in orientation, and the traditional British brick house is an apt metaphor for understanding the country and its people. Change does not come rapidly, and it must not do violence to the traditional, favored ways of the past. Because of this, there is a strong adherence among the people to a set of cultural values that is uniquely British, that have served them well in the past, and that—with modification—should help them adapt successfully to a rapidly changing world.

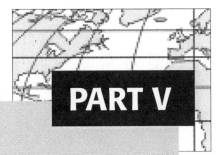

PART V

Cleft National Cultures

I n some nations, the ethnic groupings are strong and identifiable. Moreover, the groups tend to be insulated from one another, particularly if they do not share the same or similar religions and value systems. In some cases, a cleft nation may have difficulty identifying a cultural metaphor expressive of the major values of all of the ethnic groups living there. However, it was possible to identify cultural metaphors for all of the nations treated in this part of the book.

We have categorized Italy as a cleft national culture not because of ethnic groupings but rather because the North and South are radically different from one another in terms of value orientations such as collectivism and individualism. Similarly militant ideological differences separate many of the groups in Israel. Thus our definition of a cleft nation includes not only ethnic groups but also geographically separate and rigidly ideological groups.

CHAPTER 15

The Malaysian
Balik Kampung

In a 1996 faculty seminar at the Universiti Kabangsan in Malaysia, I was explaining the concept of the cultural metaphor, that is, an activity, phenomenon, or institution with which all or most individuals of a cultural group closely identify and that reflects underlying values. In the case of a nation or national culture, these individuals would be its citizens. As explained in Chapter 1, ideally, the activity, phenomenon, or institution should be unique or very distinctive, and preferably difficult for outsiders to understand how it expresses underlying values. Some faculty members imme diately observed what many foreign visitors to Malaysia also experience, namely, that the three cultural groups—the native Malays (about 59% of the approximately 20 million population), Indians (9%), and Chinese (32%)— seem to be so different from one another that it is nearly impossible to iden- tify such a national cultural metaphor. Indeed, Samuel Huntington (1996) has argued that a national culture such as that in Malaysia is cleft: Its various ethnic groups are so separate that it is difficult to unite them into a common culture. Gannon pointed out that if a nation's citizens could not even identify

Professor June Poon, Chew Kok Wai, Chow Sook Woon, Syamala Nairand, and Kalaimar Vadivel provided valuable comments on this chapter. June Poon is Associate Professor of Human Resource Management at Kabangsan Universiti, and the other commentators are graduate students.

one cultural metaphor about which there was general agreement, the possibility that the nation would survive in its current form is highly uncertain. From this perspective, Prime Minister Mohammed Mathadir's emphasis on Asian values, although sometimes anti-Western in tone, represents a search for cultural metaphors.

After a spirited discussion, Rozhan Othman suggested that the *balik kampung,* the periodic return to the village, would probably be representative of a cultural metaphor. As he stated, the patterns of behavior associated with it tend to be very defined and predictable across all three cultural groups. For instance, police in search of Communists when the nation was waging war with them a few decades ago would wait outside a village and allow a prominent Communist to have the festival dinner during *balik kampung,* after which they immediately arrested him.

Malaysia gained independence from the British in 1957. It is similar to many developing nations undergoing rapid industrialization, particularly those in Southeast Asia in which ethnic groups are so sharply delineated. Even though almost half of the nation's population lives in the urban areas, many of these city residents are newly arrived or have lived there for only a relatively small number of years. Hence, their attachment to traditional and rural values is understandable. In fact, the capital city of Kuala Lumpur, with a population of 5,000,000, has been described as a city whose sections loosely represent groups from specific rural areas and even villages.

Moreover, Malaysia's history greatly influenced the occupational structure and separation of groups. The British, as part of their divide-and-rule policy, brought in the Chinese to work as laborers in the tin mines, and they were not allowed to acquire land. The most promising alternative was to engage in trading, and today, the Malaysian Chinese are part of the worldwide group of expatriate Chinese who reside in many nations. Most of the Chinese are both Confucian and Buddhist. In contrast, the Indians were recruited to work either as laborers in the rubber plantations or as laborers and clerks in the railway service. Indians working on the plantation live in villages in estate housing apart from the Malays; those in the railway service tend to live in towns. Hinduism is their main religion. As a general rule, the Malays live in villages and work in the agricultural sector as either rice farmers or fishermen. Almost all of them are Muslims.

Thus, these three ethnic groups were separated not only by their languages, religion, and traditions, but also by their occupations and geographical concentrations. These separations were magnified by the British practice of opening up English schools mainly in the town; rural schools tended to be Malay and Indian in which the native languages—Malay and Tamil—were used. Before 1957, only those who had gone through an English education had the opportunity to advance to tertiary education. This requirement restricted further the possibility of achieving social mobility through education for these two groups.

As might be expected, these sharp divisions facilitated the race riots of 1969 against the Chinese, who had, over time, achieved more financially than the Malays, the poorest group. In response, the government devised a system of equal opportunity called *bumipatra,* or "sons of the soil," to help the Malays. This policy seems to be working, at least partially, although cronyism is a major problem in the awarding of government contracts. Companies seeking a listing on the local stock exchange are required to have a *bumipatra* shareholding of at least 30%. In 1970, *bumipatra* companies accounted for about 2.4% of corporate equities, but by 1998, about 20% (Glain, 1998, p. A15). In contrast, 5% of the population (mainly Chinese) control about 95% of the GNP in nearby Indonesia, where deadly and widespread ethnic riots directed against the Chinese occurred in 1965 and 1998. It is hoped that such riots can be avoided not only by government policies but also by an understanding of common values or cultural metaphors with which all or most citizens closely identify.

There are three characteristics of the *balik kampung* that we highlight, namely, returning to the nearby roots, authority ranking, and reinforcing basic values and behaviors. We treat each of them in turn.

Returning to the Nearby Roots

Immigration takes many forms, such as physically separating individuals from their root culture by thousands of miles. This can be a heart-wrenching situation, as the plaintive songs of immigrants to the United States and other nations during the 19th century attest. For almost all such immigrants, there was no hope of ever returning to the root culture, and so they were forced to adopt new values and behaviors to meet the demands of the new situations. In contrast, Malaysia represents a nation undergoing rapid industrialization, but one in which the immigrants to the cities are from the nearby rural areas. This pattern is widespread in many developing nations throughout the world. Thus, describing a cultural metaphor for Malaysia should prove helpful for such nations as they modernize.

Returning periodically and regularly to the nearby rural roots is our first characteristic of *balik kampung,* for ironically, it is in the diversity of Malaysia's ethnic groups that we find a metaphor apt enough to describe the Malaysian culture. In many societies, differences in religion and tradition are sources of divisiveness. But in Malaysia, the religious and traditional celebrations provide rituals common across all ethnic groups. During such festivals, *balik kampung* is very prominent, although it obviously occurs at other times.

For example, in 1996 through 1998, the major Muslim celebration, *Hari Raya,* and the Chinese New Year fell on consecutive days, and cities were deserted in favor of the villages for several days. During the Hindu *Deepavali* festival, or Festival of Lights, a similar pattern emerges. *Balik kampung* is more than just traveling away from the hectic city to enjoy a few days in a serene village. It represents a critical integrating element of the Malaysian value system, that is, the attachment that Malaysians have with their origins and families. The rituals performed during the religious festivals help to shed light on the importance of *balik kampung* and the values associated with it. A significant feature of *balik kampung* is that it provides an occasion for the entire extended family to get together, and the family will typically gather under one roof for the celebration. In most Malaysian families, this means three generations: grandparents, parents, and their children. For some families, the living room is transformed into a huge bedroom.

Religious rites play a critical role in the celebrations of the three ethnic groups. The festivals provide a time for reflection, atonement for past sins, and personal reformation. Among the Malays, the *Hari Raya* represents a victory over self and temptations after fasting during the whole month of Ramadan. As Muslims, the Malays pay the *zakat,* a form of alms, to purify their wealth and property; they will also seek forgiveness from each other on this day. Among the Indians, the *Deepavali* Festival commemorates the success of Lord Krishna, one of the three main Indian gods, in killing the devil Naragasuran. Indians begin this festive day by taking a bath of oil as a symbol of cleansing away their sins.

A ritual common to all three ethnic groups during these festivals is the audience with the elders. Among the Malays, the children will take turns kneeling before the parents to pay their respect and seek forgiveness. The Chinese will take turns bowing before the parents and wishing them a happy new year. In some traditional Chinese families, each child will present the parents with a small cup of tea and will wish them good health. Among the Indians, the children will kneel before their parents and seek their blessing. In all three traditions, the eldest child will begin the ritual, and the other children will then join. Age is important in determining one's status and position in the family. Similarly, in all three traditions, children are given gifts of money. The Malays and Indians have adopted the Chinese practice of putting the money in small paper envelopes called *ang pow.* Gifts are also exchanged among relatives, neighbors, and friends. Among the Malays and Indians, the gifts are usually in the form of food and special delicacies made by the family during the festival. Among the Chinese, a favorite gift is mandarin oranges. Even the deceased parents and grandparents are remembered explicitly.

After going to the mosque, many Malays will stop at their parents' or grandparents' graves to clean them and offer prayers. Among the Chinese and Indians, family members will pray for the departed ones at the family altar in the home.

After performing the prayers, having breakfast together, and greeting the elderly, the three ethnic groups will begin visiting others in quite a similar manner. On the first day of the celebration, they will mainly visit their relatives and neighbors. It is only then that they will visit friends, and the Malays generally do not do such visiting until the second day.

A common practice across all ethnic groups is having an open house during the festivals, at which Malaysians from all ethnic groups and walks of life are welcome. Anyone can come for a visit without making a prior appointment and be assured that he or she will be welcomed. In many instances, the festival dinner becomes a multiethnic celebration involving friends, colleagues, and business acquaintances from all three ethnic groups. The *Hari Raya* celebration lasts 1 month, the Chinese New Year 15 days, and the *Deepavali* 1 week. Although some Malaysians have adopted the practice of having visitors on specific days during these periods, visitors are welcomed at any time. Even the king, prime minister, and ministers will have open houses on specific days.

Although we have been emphasizing the festivals, many Malaysians *balik kampung* monthly and even weekly, because it is relatively easy to return to the nearby roots. Parents use these periods to remind their children of their humble origin and teach them the courtesies of traditional Malaysian culture.

Authority Ranking

As indicated previously, Huntington (1996) identifies nations such as Malaysia as cleft in that no one ethnic group is so dominant that it can dictate required behaviors. However, he fails to point out that there are at least two kinds of cleft nations: those whose ethnic groups have values that significantly overlap, and those where the overlap is not large. Malaysia represents the first type, and a nation such as Canada, with its sharp divisions between English, French, Chinese, and Native Indians, represents the second. From a cultural perspective, the probability of Malaysia surviving as a nation is much higher than that of Canada.

Using Alan Fiske's typology, we can describe the three ethnic groups as cultures emphasizing authority ranking (Fiske, 1991a); Triandis and Gelfand (1998) employ the term "vertical collectivism" in a similar fashion. According to Fiske, members of authority ranking cultures are able to rank individuals in terms of power and prestige, but there is no common unit of measurement, that is, the data points are ordinal rather than interval. For example, 2 is greater than 1, and 3 is greater than 2, but 3 is not twice as great as 1. This tends to give rise to powerful leaders whose orders are accepted without question, because the power of leaders becomes exaggerated in the minds of followers, who have difficulty calculating the exact amount of power that a leader possesses. However, such leaders are required to take care of group members in return for such unquestioned loyalty. Behaviorally, authority ranking cultures manifest themselves in elaborate bowing in which the lower-ranked person bows lower than the superior. There is a much stronger psychological relationship found in authority ranking organizations than in Western organizations, where only rational-legal authority bonds individuals to one another (Weber, 1947).

Thus, Malaysians are very conscious and sensitive to status and position in an organization's hierarchy. This is consistent with Hofstede's (1980a, 1991) finding that Malaysia is a high power distance nation. In business dealings, it is customary to send someone of equal rank to deal with the counterpart from another organization. Failure to do so will normally be interpreted as not showing proper respect to authority and will tend to vitiate future business dealings.

Similarly, the importance of age as an authority-ranking device is reflected in the honorary title *Dato* that accompanies an award bestowed by the king; it literally means "grandfather." In Malaysia, this indicates that the person is wise and honorable. Even when the person is relatively young or middle-aged, Malaysians are expected to call him by this honorary title. It is difficult to imagine a Western middle-aged person who would be comfortable with such a title.

Also, other phrases tend to emphasize the importance of age. Among the Malays, the elders are considered as *lebih awal makan garam,* which translates as "having tasted salt earlier." The Chinese say *wo' che' yen tuo' kuo ni che' fan,* which translates as "I have eaten more salt than you have eaten rice." Furthermore, it is expected that the younger members of a family will not start eating until the elders have begun. There are even rules for order of movement when walking, although these are not enforced as strictly today. For example, younger Malays should not walk in front of a sitting older person without seeking his or her permission first, and then he or she should bend slightly from the waist with the right hand extended (Craig, 1979, p. 92). In all three communities, politeness also requires that a person should never sit with the feet pointed directly toward someone, especially someone older.

Even within the extended family, all three ethnic groups employ specific titles for family members according to ranking and position within it. These titles are much more complicated than those used in Western nations. For instance, the Malays do not refer to their uncles and aunts by name but by rank: The eldest uncle would be termed *Pak Long,* the second uncle *Pak Ngah,* and so on. These and similar terms tend to reinforce the concept of authority ranking.

◼ Reinforcing Common Values

As countless immigrants have discovered, it is difficult to maintain the values of the root culture if thousands of miles separate the immigrant from the root culture. It is important to reinforce these values, at least on a periodic basis. As our discussion has already indicated, such reinforcement is possible with the *balik kampung,* particularly in the area of authority-ranking symbols. However, the *balik kampung* goes far beyond authority ranking, because it is a dynamic forum in which common values and behaviors are reinforced. Some of these are family-focused collectivism, maintaining harmony and preserving face, reaffirming religious traditions, and adjusting to other cultural groups.

The individual's relationship with the family is considered critical in all three groups, and this translates into a close relationship between the family and community. Among the Malays, living harmoniously and cooperating with other families in the village are important, for in the easily remembered past, the only way that families could work the rice fields was by sharing and pooling their labor and resources. Such working together is known as *gotong royong* among the Malays, and it is also practiced during weddings and funerals. Neighbors will work together to prepare the food and setting for the wedding celebration. Likewise, during funerals, neighbors will help one another prepare the grave and make funeral arrangements. This is one reason why there are so very few professional funeral services in Malaysia. As migrant communities, the Chinese and Indian families tend to emphasize the importance of their relationships with the clan and trade association (see Chapter 24, "The Chinese Family Altar"). In the recent past, it was only through such self-help organizations that these two groups were able to pool their capital to help each other start their businesses. Thus, events such as weddings and funerals tend to reinforce basic values common across all three groups and constitute a major reason for periodically completing a *balik kampung.*

The importance attached to collectivistic values is particularly highlighted by the *pok chow* system found among Chinese laborers. *Pok chow* literally means "gang contracting," and it represents a group of workers that gets together by mutual consent. A *pok chow* group is essentially a work group whose members decide on their own rules, division of work, the remuneration given to each worker, and even the election of the leader (Sendut, Madsen, & Thong, 1989, p. 61). It is only in recent years that Western firms have employed a similar system, self-managed work teams, that such collectivistic systems have emphasized for centuries, and it is little wonder that Hofstede's (1980a, 1991) study of 53 nations indicated that Malaysia is highly collectivistic.

Most Chinese and Indians in Malaysia are third- or fourth-generation Malaysians and cannot be described as classic, first-generation immigrants. Likewise, many Malays today live in the urban areas and no longer rely on agricultural activities. Still, a recent study indicated that there is still a great emphasis on collectivism in all three groups (Md. Zabid, Anantharaman, & Raveendran, 1997). Thus, it is not surprising that Malaysians tend to prefer a participative approach to decision making both at work and outside of it. In negotiations, compromise and seeking collaboration are preferred to confrontation and a winner-take-all approach that seems to be common in the United States (see Frank & Cook, 1995). This emphasis on moderation is called *chung* among the Chinese (Wang, 1962, p. 12), and it reflects the Koranic concept of *ummatan wasata* among the Malays. As indicated previously, authority ranking reinforces collectivism, and all of the age-related rituals during *balik kampung* tend to keep it alive.

One of the most interesting results of collectivism in Malaysia is that Malaysians have a tendency to hold an entire group, and sometimes a nation, responsible for the misconduct of a person or a few people from that nation. As such, criticism by the media or nongovernmental groups from a foreign country on human rights or environmental issues is attributed to the country as a whole. Westerners tend to classify such behavior as bordering on paranoia. To Malaysians, the experience of being exploited and humiliated during colonial rule has made them wary about the loss of face from the criticisms meted out by foreigners.

Although *balik kampung* reinforces family-focused collectivism, it also serves as a means for maintaining harmony and preserving face. In a highly collectivistic culture, there is great importance attached to maintaining harmony and building relationships, and self-centered individualism that would detract from these activities is normally viewed in a negative manner. One of the important ingredients in building harmony is to avoid doing anything that can disgrace and humiliate others. Preserving respect and dignity is fundamental to understanding Malaysians. Among the Malays, this is termed *maruah,* whereas the Chinese refer to it as "face," and the Indians use the closely related term *thanmanam*. As indicated in Chapter 24, face is the unwritten set of rules that everyone is expected to follow in order to preserve individual dignity and group harmony.

Importantly, the *balik kampung* provides a venue in which this can be accomplished. If a personal offense or slight has occurred, an individual can attempt to correct it on a face-to-face basis during *balik kampung,* as happens during family meetings involving younger adults and their elders. At the very least, the individual can offer prayers and alms as a way of alleviating a sense of shame. Members of collectivistic cultures tend to respond more to a sense of shame at having hurt others than to a sense of guilt, which seems to be more important in Western nations. Malaysians are very sensitive about maintaining face and will try to avoid disgracing others, particularly in public. In extreme situations, some Indians consider suicide preferable to accepting a loss of face, which motivates others to protect them from experiencing it. Similarly, it is common for a Chinese businessman to withdraw from negotiations if he feels that the outcome will make him lose face.

In decision making, given that all three ethnic groups value age, Malaysians frequently defer to the more senior or elderly member of the organization, who will generally be the first to speak at a meeting. As suggested above, however, the most senior person is expected to be responsible and should respect his juniors. At least partially for this reason, heated debates tend to be uncommon, and differences are typically stated in a tactful and polite manner. The most senior member is expected to consult with subordinates, although he may withhold critical information if he feels it is in the best interests of the group.

To maintain harmony and preserve face, Malaysians have developed elaborate courtesies and rituals. During the *balik kampung,* and before and after it, the Malays seek forgiveness from one another, yet they are not expected to mention, and usually avoid mentioning, any specific mistake or error. In this fashion, harmony is maintained, and debating over specific issues is avoided. A Malay leaving his or her village or hometown for a long time will usually seek such forgiveness from parents, relatives, and friends. Sometimes, this is also done when someone is returning home during the *balik kampung.*

All three ethnic groups emphasize the need to be polite even when disagreeing. An abrasive and confrontational style is problematic. Speaking with a raised voice, shouting, and swearing are inexcusable, because the person subjected to this kind of behavior will suffer a loss of face, and the instigator will experience a loss of respect that is difficult, if not impossible, to recover.

Thus, Malaysians engage in a great deal of high-context communication, and this includes avoiding the word "no" when disagreeing with another person (Hall & Hall, 1990). To a Westerner, this is commonly believed to be dishonest and annoying, but the Malaysian is simply trying to avoid damage to a relationship. Likewise, Malaysians sometimes use very subtle and indirect words to convey their meaning, for example, using proverbs and idiomatic expressions. It is little wonder that Westerners frequently employ third parties to clarify the meanings involved in communication and negotiations.

Malaysians also use third parties, but they do so when they expect that the outcome of a particular negotiation can be potentially embarrassing. Among the more traditional Malays, it is common for arranged marriages to occur, and the man's parents will send the third party to the girl's parents to inquire about her availability. If, for some reason, the girl does not want to consider the man as a potential groom, both families have avoided an embarrassing situation. Only after the girl's parents have responded positively will the parents from both sides meet so that his parents can propose that a wedding take place.

An anecdote may help to highlight the elaborate and complex ways in which Malaysians communicate. A hostess was entertaining her guest at a dinner at home. The guest was hungry and was hoping to have another helping. However, she noticed that there was no more food at the table. Rather than asking for another helping directly, she complimented the hostess on the beauty of the plate that had been used to serve food. The hostess noticed that the plate was empty but did not want to say that there was no more food. Rather, she showed the pot used to cook the food to the guest. She then explained to the guest that she had cooked the food in the equally beautiful pot, thus showing the guest that the pot was empty. This enabled the guest to understand that the food was finished without the hostess being forced to say so. Of course, this anecdote is exaggerated but does indicate the lengths to which Malaysians will go to maintain harmony and preserve face.

Similar communication patterns can be found in many situations. For example, during *balik kampung,* both the visitor and host know that serving food is part of the festival. Yet the visitor will always make it a point to tell the host not to trouble himself or herself with preparing something. Likewise, the host will always apologize for not making adequate food preparations, even though the meal is elaborate and sumptuous.

We have already suggested that the *balik kampung* is particularly important during religious festivals, and religious practices tend to reinforce common values. Malays will offer special prayers on the morning of the *Hari Raya,* as will the Chinese on the eve of the Chinese New Year and the Indians on the morning of *Deepavali.* All generations of a family will participate in these religious rites.

As Muslims, Malays pray five times each day, and this practice is continued during *balik kampung.* Malays engage in prayer services when someone moves into a new house or when a firm occupies a new building. Likewise, a Malay organization usually celebrates its success by having its employees offer a thanksgiving prayer to Allah. Many Chinese shops and offices will have an altar for the owners to offer prayers and, as indicated in Chapter 24, Chinese homes frequently have family altars. At some work sites, some Chinese workers will build their own altars.

Among the Indians, the same attachment to religion is evident. In some factories, a Hindu altar featuring several prominent Indian gods is erected so that Indian workers can pray at work. The Indians are similar to the Chinese in that they tend to offer prayers in the morning and evening, and they are similar to the Muslim Malays in that Friday is a special prayer day. Many Indians either fast or observe a vegetarian diet on Fridays, even during *balik kampung.*

We have already described gift-giving practices during the festivals. Westerners are frequently surprised by the degree of gift giving that occurs in Asia, and many Western businesspeople have belatedly contacted their home offices to airmail a large number of gifts that they can give to their counterparts at various ceremonies and dinners held while they are staying in Asia on a short-term or long-term basis. All three ethnic groups engage in a great deal of gift giving, because it is viewed as an ideal way to maintain harmony and save face. As described earlier, gift giving is a common practice among Malaysians during *balik kampung,* at least partially for these two major reasons.

There is, however, an element of reciprocity in this relationship. The person given the gift cannot refuse it, because this would involve a loss of face. At the same time, he or she is now obligated to the person giving the gift. Among the Malays, this is called *hutang budi,* which roughly translates into a debt of deed. The person receiving the present need not reciprocate immediately but is expected to remember his or her *hutang budi* when the giver asks his or her assistance at a later date.

This custom of reciprocating is important in building long-term relationships. Non-Malaysians may find this practice exploitative, especially when practiced by some Malaysian businesspeople seeking favors. However, refusing a gift is ill-advised. Rather, the person should reciprocate immediately by giving a gift of similar value, which signifies that the *hutang budi* has been paid.

Of course, religious sensitivity and custom should be observed when giving gifts. Malays do not appreciate alcoholic beverages as gifts or food containing pork. Meat should come from animals slaughtered in accordance with Islamic rites. Similarly, the Chinese give gifts in even numbers, for example, a pair of pens rather than a single pen. However, the Indians prefer their gifts in odd numbers. Among the gifts that should not be given to the Chinese is a clock, which is considered a bad omen, because the Cantonese word for clock also means "to go to a funeral" (Craig, 1979, p. 37). There are other "dos and taboos" that can be learned easily by consulting books specializing in this area that are available in almost all bookstores (e.g., Axtell, 1990).

Thus far, we have been emphasizing practices and behaviors that reinforce common values and behaviors across the three groups but that occur only within each group. But *balik kampung* also displays a certain paradox about the Malaysian culture, for each of the three groups reinforces its identity but also the larger identity of being Malaysian. Malaysians of all groups and religions will join their fellow Malaysians to celebrate the respective festivals. There is even evidence that certain customs that were formerly practiced by one ethnic group during the festivals have now been adopted by the others. In a similar fashion, a Malaysian comfortably switches between more than one language in one sentence. For example, the first two words may be Tamil, the next three English, the next three Malay, and the last one Chinese.

In employment, more organizations that formerly hired from only one ethnic group have expanded to include two or three of the groups. Partly this is due to the governmental *bumipatra* policies, but also partly because a nation undergoing rapid industrialization needs to employ its citizens as productively as possible. Although Southeast Asia as a whole has experienced difficult economic times in the past few years, the general trend for the past 25 years has been very positive, suggesting that Malaysian firms will need workers with valuable and scarce skills for the foreseeable future regardless of ethnic background.

The approach taken by Malaysia in nation building also reflects an emphasis on the mutual adjustments of the three ethnic cultures so that harmony is preserved. Since independence in 1957, a coalition government consisting of political parties representing the major ethnic groups has ruled the nation, which is forging a national identity by accommodating and allowing for diversity. Malaysia is avoiding the path that some nations have taken when they have expelled ethnic minorities or forced them to abandon their religious and cultural identities. For example, although the Malay language has been adopted as the national language, Tamil and English are still widely used. Mandarin and Tamil vernacular schools continue to operate, and many are funded by the government. The state-owned TV station has regular news broadcasts in Malay, Mandarin, Tamil, and English. Although Islam is the state religion, freedom to embrace other religions is guaranteed by the Constitution. Anyone traveling through Malaysia will come across mosques, temples, and churches spread throughout the entire nation. And unlike some nations, in which only the festivals of the majority are public holidays, the following are classified as public holidays: the Muslim *Hari Raya* celebrations, Chinese New Year, Buddhist *Wesak*, Hindu *Deepavali*, and Christmas.

This, then, is Malaysia, whose underlying values are expressed in the *balik kampungs* of the three major ethnic groups. In many ways, Malaysia and, to a lesser extent, other Southeast Asian nations such as Thailand and Singapore represent ideal laboratories for demonstrating that ethnic groups seemingly radically different from each other can be forged into a common identity over time. The *balik kampung*, with its emphasis on returning to nearby roots, authority ranking, and reinforcing common values is critical in this endeavor. Thus far, the *balik kampung* has helped to integrate rather than separate the three groups and aided Malaysia in its pursuit of what John Berry (1990) has identified as ideal—allowing individuals to maintain their own cultural identities and simultaneously to adopt new values supportive of the cultural identity of a larger group, such as a nation.

CHAPTER 16

The Nigerian Marketplace

Nigeria represents both the hope and the despair of Africa, a continent ruled by European colonial powers until recent years. Nigeria itself was ruled by Britain until 1960 and has been an independent nation for only 40 years. Nigeria's ruling classes have squandered the country's rich natural resources irresponsibly and are, as the title of a recent article in *The Economist* states forthrightly, "out of control" ("Out of Control," 1999, p. 44). Corruption is widespread; in 1996 and 1997, Transparency International, an organization dedicated to the elimination of corruption in international business, ranked Nigeria as the most corrupt nation among 85 in its survey, but in 1998, Nigeria moved from 85th to 81st on the list. Nigeria's 112 million people constitute about 25% of the total African population. As a percent of gross domestic product (GDP), Nigeria has the lowest education spending in the world and the second lowest health spending. GDP per person has fallen significantly and is about $300 per year, less than 10% of South Africa's.

Still, there is hope. For almost all of its 40 years, the nation was ruled by the military. When he became president in 1998, General Abdulsalam Abubakar forthrightly described the nation's plight in the following way: "Currently, we are the world's 13th poorest nation. Given our resource endowments, this sorry state is a serious indictment." In 2000, he handed over power to a democratically elected president, Olusegun Obasanjo. Ironically, it was Obasanjo who, as military ruler in 1979, supported the first democratically elected government in Nigeria's history. Unfortunately, it was short-lived, and military rule returned after 1983. Although too early to tell, it appears that Nigeria is now on the right track.

As a modern political entity, Nigeria came into existence in 1914 when the British amalgamated three of their West African colonial territories: the Colony of Lagos, the Southern Nigeria Protectorate, and the Northern Nigeria Protectorate. Each of the three territories was previously consolidated by the British out of a diverse collection of indigenous kingdoms, city-states, and loosely organized ethnic groups through treaties or outright conquest. Thus, Nigeria as a geopolitical entity was, in effect, a creation of British imperialism. Nigeria remained a colony of Britain before gaining independence in 1960.

Archaeological evidence attests to millennia of continuous habitation of parts of what is now Nigeria. One of the earliest identifiable cultures is that of the Nok people, who inhabited the northeastern part of the country between 500 B.C. and A.D. 200. The Nok were skilled artisans and iron-workers whose abstractly stylized terra-cotta sculptures are admired for their artistic expression and high technical standards (Burns, 1963, p. 25). High-quality bronze art at Ife and Benin City in the southwestern parts of the country also predated the arrival of Europeans in the region. Over the centuries, successive waves of migration along trade routes into Nigeria from the north and northeastern part of the African continent swelled the population, which eventually became organized along tribal lines into kingdoms, emirates, city-states, and loosely organized ethnic groups. This was the setting that the early European adventurers, notably Portuguese navigators, found when they first made contact with the people of the coastal regions in the 14th century A.D.

The marketplace is an appropriate metaphor for understanding the culture of the people of modern Nigeria. In this context, the marketplace refers to the physical areas of a city, town, or rural village where the indigenous commercial activities are concentrated. This metaphor has a special significance because the bulk of the history of the region up to modern times can be summed up in one word: trade. Many of the ancestors of modern Nigerians first migrated to the region along trade routes; the slave trade was primarily responsible for the arrival of Europeans in large numbers; and after the abolition of the slave trade by the British in 1808, the need to enforce the abolition and to replace the trade with legitimate commerce was a primary motivation for the British to maintain a presence.

For centuries, before the arrival of the Europeans, the marketplace was the community center for a town and the surrounding settlements. It was the center of commerce, the local town hall, and the main social center all rolled into one. This characterization is still true in the rural areas, where about 70%

of the Nigerian population still lives. Market networks link many towns and villages together. The networks consist of major markets that meet on specific days and attract traders for miles around. In the past, such networks were the conduits through which new commodities, outside influences, and immigrants reached local communities.

The characteristics of the Nigerian marketplace that stand out are its diversity, its dynamism, and the balance between tradition and change. Each of these characteristics strongly reflects modern Nigerian society.

Diversity

The typical Nigerian marketplace, especially in the bigger towns, is a sprawling, usually bustling place where virtually every commodity is available. As a general rule, the market is divided into rows of covered stalls, with a narrow aisle separating each row. Each row of stalls is assigned to a specific commodity, ranging from perishable foods to household electrical appliances. The marketplace is where the vast majority of the people shop for their daily needs. This is the case even in the urban centers, where there are modern department stores. Commodities in plentiful supply include fresh meat and fish, vegetables, household goods, electrical appliances, jewelry, building materials, clothing, and traditional medicinal herbs.

Sellers of similar commodities often unite to form market associations to look after common interests. Nearly everything is available either wholesale or retail. The major marketplaces are usually centrally located, with a network of roads linking most parts of the town to the market. In addition to commodities, the marketplace offers services, which include privately operated taxi and bus services to any part of town, heavy hauling, appliance repair, custom tailoring, and secretarial services. Intercity transportation hubs are also usually located in close proximity to the main markets. Diversity refers not only to the wide range of goods and services available but also to the size, relative importance, and modernness of the market compared to others in the area.

The diversity of the Nigerian culture is one of its hallmarks. In a country just about the size of Texas and New Mexico combined, there are about 300 ethnic and subethnic groups, with as many distinct languages and dialects. Often, a dialect is clearly understandable only to the inhabitants of a town and its immediate environs. Just as the marketplace is clearly divided into sections by commodity and into subgroups by market associations, so, too, is the Nigerian society clearly delineated by ethnic and language differences. But just as the separate commodity sections form an integral whole to serve a common clientele, so, too, does the Nigerian society try to forge a national identity out of the widely diverse ethnic groups artificially joined together into a nation by the British.

The heterogeneity of Nigerian society is physical, social, religious, and linguistic. Each ethnic group is concentrated in clearly defined geographical areas that they have occupied for centuries. The same is true of the subethnic groups. Two large rivers, the Niger (from which the name of the country was derived) and the Benue, form a "Y" that divides the country into three parts. Each of the three parts is dominated by one of the three main ethnic groups: the Yoruba, the Hausa-Fulani, and the Ibos. The Yoruba are the only major ethnic group with a traditional aristocracy. Although the power and influence of the aristocrat class has diminished over the years, they are still a major social force in Yoruba society. Yoruba-speaking ethnic groups also extend beyond the Nigerian border into the Benin Republic.

The Ibos are located primarily to the east side of the Niger. Although they are concentrated more densely in their primary geographical area, they are more fragmented politically than the Yoruba or the Hausa-Fulani. The Ibos are notable for their business acumen and strong work ethic. The Hausa-Fulani occupy most of the area to the north of the Niger and the Benue, which is more than twice as large as the southern regions combined. In most cases, differences in physical features among ethnic groups are not significant enough to reliably distinguish a member of one ethnic group from another.

In the past, permanent facial markings were used to distinguish members of one ethnic group from the others. Their primary purpose was to identify friend or foe in warfare rather than to serve as bodily decoration. The practice of facial markings has been largely abandoned in modern times. Today, names and attire are more reliable indicators of ethnic belonging than are physical attributes.

With so many different ethnic groups and languages, it would seem that defining the contours and structures of this highly heterogeneous society is impractical. Admittedly, it is difficult, but it is not impossible. There are several reasons for this. First, despite the great number of ethnic groups, four of them—Yoruba (20%), Hausa (21%), Fulani (9%), and Ibos (17%)—comprise more than 65% of the Nigerian population (1991 census). In addition, the Hausa and the Fulani have so intermixed over the centuries that they are now commonly regarded as a homogeneous group.

Second, the correspondence between language and ethnic group varies. Several groups may speak essentially the same language and have similar cultural characteristics, but prefer to identify themselves as separate entities in terms of differences that span centuries. For instance, the Yoruba have at least 20 subethnic groups, each of which protects its separate identity vigorously.

However, modernization and the federal government's adoption of policies that promote a sense of national identity have gradually resulted in the emergence of some common national characteristics. Examples of such government intervention include the establishment of English as the official language of government and commerce throughout the country, the practice of posting some federal employees to states other than their own, and the requirement of an immediate 1-year national youth service of all graduates of postsecondary institutions. In recent years, the influence of the mass media, especially television, has also helped to break down cultural barriers among ethnic groups.

But Nigeria has a long way to go in terms of interethnic harmony. Interethnic mistrust is deep and is a primary reason for the repeated failure to establish a viable Western-style democracy in Nigeria since independence, giving the military an excuse to establish authoritarian regimes for 50 long years. Although most Nigerians are patriotic and genuinely want their country to work, deep-rooted ethnic allegiance often takes precedence over national allegiance. As a typical example, the Egba are among the 20-odd subethnic groups of the Yoruba, but when the chips are down, an Egba considers him- or herself an Egba first, a Yoruba second, and a Nigerian last. In the distant past, members of the subethnic groups have fought bitter fratricidal wars among themselves. Territorial expansionism, control of trade routes, and the desire to cash in on the lucrative slave trade were among the reasons for these wars.

Geert Hofstede (1991), in his landmark analysis of the cultural differences across 53 countries, did not include a single black African nation in his study. This was not because the multinational corporation in which the analysis was completed (IBM) had no subsidiary in any of them, for there was one in Nigeria during the period of the study. But IBM, along with several other multinational corporations, later chose to leave the country rather than comply with a new federal decree requiring 40% Nigerian equity in certain classes of foreign business investments in Nigeria. This is brought up to illustrate an important aspect of the Nigerian psyche: a strong sense of national honor and self-worth. In general, although Nigerians admire and actively attempt to emulate Western economic and social development, they are quick to take offense at real or perceived condescension on the part of Western expatriates.

Even though Hofstede's study did not include a black African nation, it is not difficult to estimate where many of them, including Nigeria, would fit in his five major dimensions. Traditionally, there is a large power distance between social classes and between superiors and subordinates in most Nigerian ethnic groups except the Ibos. If the four major ethnic groups are ranked in order of power distance, the Hausa-Fulani would probably score the highest, followed closely by the Yoruba, and trailed by the Ibos. The

Hausa-Fulani are overwhelmingly Sunni Muslims who have adopted much of the Islamic world's rigid social order and way of life. The Yoruba's high power distance is tempered considerably by opportunity for upward mobility based on individual achievement. The Ibos were noted for their egalitarian society for centuries and have largely remained so.

Collectivism and high uncertainty avoidance are more evenly applicable to the bulk of Nigerian society regardless of tribal affiliation. Virtually all of the disparate ethnic groups believe in the extended family system. Home-town associations are formed with the expressed purpose of improving the infrastructure and facilities in the community. For example, during the early years of national development, it was not unusual for a community to sponsor the overseas studies of a promising local student in the hope that he or she would return to serve the community. Nigerians also score high on uncertainty avoidance, preferring to deal with people and situations with which they are familiar.

However, some research suggests that the business-oriented Ibos are more individualistic than the other major ethnic groups. That is, they explain their success or failure in terms of their own abilities, whereas their ethnic counterparts emphasize luck and/or the situation (see Bond & Smith, 1998). Given this research, we would expect that the Ibos would have a longer-term time orientation than their ethnic counterparts and would be more willing to sacrifice short-term enjoyment to attain long-term goals.

Also, masculinity or aggressive masculine behavior in the pursuit of dominance over others can most probably be attributed to the Nigerian society as a whole. However, with regard to the role of women, there are notable differences among the three major ethnic groups. The Hausa-Fulani, true to their Muslim religion, tend to consider women as quite subordinate to men in virtually every respect. This is not the case among the Ibos and the Yoruba, where women have traditionally faced little opposition to their entrepreneurial spirit.

Social Dynamism

Nigerians have often been characterized as resourceful, pragmatic, entrepreneurial, and energetic (Aronson, 1978, p. 137). In this context, social dynamism refers to the energy, vigor, and adaptability of the Nigerian society. These qualities are readily observable at the Nigerian marketplace, which bustles with activity, especially on Saturdays, when most families do the weekly grocery shopping. Traders hawk their wares in sing-songs particular to their commodity. The bargaining is energetic, with the burden on the customer to negotiate a fair price. Although many items have fixed prices, most do not. This means that the smart shopper must come to the market fully armed with a knowledge of the latest fair prices for the commodities of interest. The shopper must also be savvy about the various shady characters who are attracted to the marketplace. The typical seller, in turn, has perfected the art of keeping a poker face in order to extract as much profit from the sale as possible without antagonizing the customer.

Many shoppers have favorite stalls that they patronize repeatedly. Such repeat buyers are often taken care of quickly, with the minimum of negotiating necessary to arrive at a mutually acceptable price. In recent years, sellers seem to have concluded that the time and effort spent on haggling are not worth the extra profits and have started to place a fixed price on as many items as possible. Prices are usually set by market or trade associations, and changes in them are frequently communicated by word of mouth several times a day.

Doing things quietly is not the Nigerian way, whether it be an argument, a political discussion, a celebration, or a sad occasion. Just as the market bustles with a cacophony of sights and sounds, so, too, do Nigerians complete most activities with gusto. The dynamism of Nigerian society is reflected in the business and political landscape, the attitude toward education, the manner in which the people celebrate holidays and family events, and their favorite leisure pursuits.

At independence, Nigeria's economy was engaged almost exclusively in the production of food for home consumption and commodities (e.g., cocoa, groundnut, and palm oil) for export. The vast deposits of oil and natural gas were not yet discovered. Since then, successive governments, including the military regimes, have made the development of the industrial sector of the economy a priority.

Just as the local marketplace bustles from dawn to dusk with activity, so, too, does Nigeria's more formal economic scene bustle with complicated deals and contracts. Nigeria has considerable crude oil and natural gas resources and has been a member of the Organization of Petroleum Exporting Countries (OPEC) since the 1960s. This natural wealth has provided the resources to modernize the economy, especially during the boom years of the 1970s, when vast amounts of new crude oil deposits were being discovered in the coastal areas at the same time that prices of crude oil were rising steadily in the world market. In the 1970s, the federal government took steps to ensure greater Nigerian participation in such key economic activities as banking, insurance, manufacturing, and oil production, which were then dominated by foreign companies or their local subsidiaries. The policies have achieved considerable success. Nigerian interests in key aspects of economic activities now exceed 70% (Schatz, 1987).

Unfortunately, only a small fraction (less than 10%) of the population controls much of this wealth. The wide gap between the rich and the poor is a major concern for Nigeria's economic planners. For many years, the federal government dominated and closely controlled the economy, but in recent years, it has recognized the detrimental effects of meddling too much in the economy and has moved toward the establishment of a freer market.

The Nigerian political arena is not for amateurs or the faint-hearted, just as the marketplace is not for amateurs who are not versed in the fine art of haggling. Politics in Nigeria is a rough-and-tumble game, and only the fittest survive. Politicians, including ex-presidents, are sometimes put into jail for questionable reasons.

However, unlike the situation in many African countries, no Nigerian political leader has ever tried to impose a single-party state. The electorate is too sophisticated for that. Modern Nigeria is a federation of 23 states and a new federal capital, Abuja, which is located near the geographical center of the country. The political framework is similar, by design, to the federal system of the United States, but the institutions and requirements reflect the needs and experience of the country. The federal government consists of an executive branch, a legislative branch, and a judicial branch. Each of the 23 states is similarly organized.

Officially, Nigeria is a Western-style democracy, but the threat of authoritarian rule is never far away, and there have been several military coups. Nigerians are accustomed to waking up to a brand new government that has suddenly taken shape overnight, and they have learned not to let the political instability interfere too much in their daily lives and business activities.

Many of the traders and craftsmen in the marketplace are graduates of apprenticeships in their specific areas. In the same manner, Nigerian society believes that a sound educational system will provide the energy that will propel the country into the industrialized age. Parents who have the means hire private tutors, send their children to prestigious schools that may be far away from home, and give up their own comforts so that their children can do better than themselves. Like the political system, the education system is patterned after that of the United States. One reason for this is that many of the policymakers in government were educated in the United States. However, as noted previously, Nigeria's federal government performs abysmally in the area of education.

Education is free and compulsory up to the sixth grade, but most choose to go further if they have the means. English is the official language of instruction. It is introduced at the primary school level and used exclusively at the secondary and postsecondary levels. The government, recognizing the value of a high level of literacy to rapid development, has tried to take advantage of the oil wealth to implement a free education policy at all levels. It has not been able to achieve this objective partly because of the sheer size and cost of the educational system, which is controlled by the government at all levels. Admission to postsecondary institutions is limited and extremely competitive. Although these institutions continue to expand, they are currently not capable of admitting all of the students who qualify for admission.

Furthermore, Nigerians are not shy about making a public scene when the need arises, just as the haggling in the marketplace is sometimes done with rancor whenever either party steps over the line of decorum. Arguments are typically carried on in a loud and animated manner, but they rarely lead to physical combat. Bystanders eagerly offer their own loud opinions about the ongoing dispute. The urban centers, especially in the south, are overcrowded, and there is a constant influx of students and job seekers from the rural areas. Competition is intense for nearly everything. Jobs, housing, transportation, and other daily necessities of life are in scarce supply in the cities, even though the cities receive a disproportionate share of federal development budgets.

So, believing that it is a jungle out there, the smart urbanite steps out each morning prepared to survive another hectic day. Western expatriates are usually, but not always, untouched by all this hustle and bustle of daily life because they tend to live in the quieter, wealthier neighborhoods that had their origins in colonial times, when the government and the larger foreign companies built residential reservations for their expatriate staff.

For example, in "A Tale of Two Cities" (1993), the magazine *Business Traveler* describes the schizophrenic life that expatriates live in the largest city, Lagos:

> One described an average week in the city: "We've had two machine gun attacks on neighboring factories—bodies were littered across the road. The insurance guesthouse next door was ransacked and one driver's brother lost his car to kidnappers. A friend of a friend is hobbling around after being robbed and then shot in the legs so he could not chase the thieves. They shot him even though he had calmly handed over his money.
>
> "Every day is different in Lagos and you just have to adapt. Most of us have clubs where we can retreat and laugh over the latest mishaps with friends. They are also vital for making contacts to have a chance of getting things done." (p. 25)

However, not everyone goes to the market with the intention of shopping. Some go to take in the scene, browse, or meet friends. Nigerians take their leisure seriously and try to find the time to indulge in their favorite leisure activities. They are keenly interested in sports, and their preferred sporting activities reflect their dynamism. Wrestling was a popular sport in many parts of the country before the arrival of the Europeans. It is still popular, as is boxing. But neither comes close to the interest in soccer, as both a participatory and a spectator sport. Nigerians are generally not interested in nonphysical sports.

Checkers is popular among the lower working class, and the game is typically accompanied by friendly banter and bets (nonmonetary). The favorite way to relax is to be in the company of friends who can trade war stories about the vagaries of daily life, pass on the latest social gossip, and solve the country's problems. In general, Nigerians do not seek isolation and solitude; they avoid them as much as possible.

Holidays and ceremonies are an important aspect of Nigerian culture. Both the Christian and Islamic holidays are nationally observed, as are local community festivals, some of which have been observed for centuries. Some of these local festivals were of a pagan nature but are now largely stripped of religious significance. Common ceremonies include weddings, the naming of a new child, and funerals. Often, such ceremonies are very lavish affairs, depending on the wealth of the celebrants. Ostentatious display of wealth is the norm, and the rich often welcome the opportunity to do so. The ostentatious display is typically overdone. It is a brash, bold, in-your-face statement to the world that the celebrant is rich and is not ashamed to show it. Everyone knows what the status symbols are—the big wedding or funeral, the chauffeured car, the expensively tailored suits, and the big houses complete with servant quarters. There was even a time, during the oil boom years, when owning your own jet was added to the list.

Holidays provide a respite from what many in the populace regard as the rat race of daily life. Even the marketplaces are silent and empty on the major holidays. The favorite way to spend a holiday is to hold a feast or to attend one. Either way, it is an opportunity to congregate and socialize with good friends.

Recreation and leisure in the Western sense is practiced by only a small percentage of the population, mainly the wealthy elite. They may play tennis or golf, or go for a swim. There are exclusive country clubs where admission is usually based on wealth, connections, and social status. The vast majority do not have the means or the time to indulge in Western-style leisure, and the average Nigerian does not go on a road trip just to see the country or go for a hike in the woods just to commune with nature. In the cities, there are plenty of nightclubs, movie houses, restaurants, and private clubs that Nigerians tend to frequent. As noted above, watching sports is also a favorite pastime.

Balancing Tradition and Change

Modern Nigerian society is markedly different from that which existed before outside influences began to take hold in the early 19th century.

Nowhere is this more noticeable than in the way the center of political and economic power has shifted from local traditional rulers and their council of senior chiefs to the educated elite, business magnates, politicians, and the military. No country wants to be an island, isolated from all outside influences. But if outside influences threaten to engulf aspects of the society that are cherished by its members, then it is necessary to take action to preserve them. This is true for modern Nigeria, where the trick is to modernize without sacrificing cherished traditional values.

Among the daily facets of life that were tightly controlled by the traditional rulers in precolonial times were the local marketplaces, especially the most important ones. Among the Yoruba, for instance, the largest and most influential markets were situated in front of, or in close proximity to, the king's official residence, and they were called *oja oba* ("the king's market"). In some areas, the official title of the local head chief was *loja* ("owner of the market"). Virtually all markets are now administered by local government councils, which are popularly elected bodies. Although control of the markets has shifted from the traditional rulers to the people, these rulers are still regarded in many places as the titular heads of the markets, especially in the rural areas. The changes in market administration are indicative of the changes that have occurred in Nigerian society as a result of modernization.

Other notable aspects of culture and tradition that have changed considerably over the years include religious preferences, the traditional family compound, dating behavior, language, sports, and leisure pursuits. However, the changes are not universal. As a general rule, the rate of change in the urban centers has far outpaced that in the rural areas.

In precolonial days, power was heavily concentrated in the hands of local kings and their chiefs. Palace intrigues and territorial expansionism through intertribal warfare were common features of life. Again, a noted exception to this situation were the Ibos, whose egalitarian social structure did not allow for the concentration of power in any one individual or a small group of rulers.

Although their power and influence have been curtailed largely by the establishment of more democratic political systems, traditional rulers still play an important role in their communities. They are regarded as the custodians of their people's legacy and identity, and they are usually at the forefront of the fight to defend traditional values against the unrelenting onslaughts of Western values. In addition, some senior local traditional rulers, especially in the north, have learned to exert influence behind the scenes. Moreover, northern Muslim traditional rulers also tend to be their community's religious leaders. This pragmatic approach has resulted in some senior traditional rulers becoming even more powerful than they would have been if they still had direct political power. But they are no longer referred to in English as "king." The most common English term used is "traditional ruler."

When a traditional ruler dies, the eligible candidates still campaign vigorously to win ascendancy to the throne, for there is almost never an automatic line of succession. Candidates are drawn from traditional ruling families, and only the adult male members are eligible. In some areas, the chieftaincy is rotated, by tradition, from one ruling family to another.

Traditional rulers are selected by a council, whose members are invariably called "kingmakers," consisting of the senior chiefs in the community. The selection process varies from community to community. It is worth noting that while the selection process has remained largely unchanged, the criteria for selection have changed markedly over the years. In modern times, candidates with adequate formal education who have distinguished themselves in some fields are favored.

An important area where major changes have occurred is religion. The first religious incursions came from the north, when the Fulani, under Usman Dan Fodio, overran the Hausa and other northern states in the 18th century. The conquerors forcibly established Islam in the city-states that dotted the region. Usman Dan Fodio would have carried out his vow to expand his jihad, or holy war, all the way down to the sea if the British, who were then establishing a presence in the south, had not put a stop to his ambition (Burns, 1963, pp. 50-51). The early European explorers and traders entering the country from the south were followed quickly by Christian missionaries. Today, only a small percentage of Nigerians still adhere exclusively to indigenous animist religions. About 47% classify themselves as Muslims, nearly 38% as Christian, and about 15% as other.

Nigerians are generally a spiritual and religious people. Before Christianity and Islam were imported into the region about two centuries ago, most ethnic groups had developed a set of common spiritual beliefs ranging from seemingly mindless superstitions to the concept of a supreme being (Burns, 1963, p. 264). Before the arrival of the Europeans, some religious priests had acquired extraordinary social powers that rivaled those of the local king through the manipulation of the peoples' fears about the supernatural. It took years to convert the majority of the populace to the imported religions.

Even then, many did not find the spirituality they needed in what they considered the sterile form of worship of the European Christian sects. Some were also turned off by the perceived condescension of the Christian missionaries. Indigenous Christian sects founded and led by Nigerians soon began to proliferate, especially in the Yoruba-dominated western region. Notable sects include the Cherubim and Seraphim sect, the Apostolic Church, and the African Church. What these indigenous sects have in common is a form of worship that is more reflective of the Nigerian society: less formality in worship; singing and dancing to lively indigenous Christian music; spontaneous audience participation during worship services; and a deeper, personal relationship with God. Today, some of these sects are increasing their memberships at a very rapid rate.

Although many of the inevitable changes that have come with modernization have been welcomed by the general population, others have been perceived as socially regressive. An example of this is the way in which the traditional family compound has changed. In the past, as the male children in a family became adults, they were given plots of land adjacent to the family home on which to build their own houses in preparation for starting their own families; female members of the family were expected to get married and become members of their husbands' families. Today, the young adults are more likely to move to the cities, first to further their education, then to work or engage in business. In the cities, the relative scarcity of land and the high cost of building construction make the idea of family compounds impractical. The end result is that there has been a decline in the allegiance to the larger kinship group. Urban centers continue to grow in size and population, whereas the rural areas stagnate or shrink.

Courting behavior has changed in some ways and remained the same in others. Traditionally, there was no such thing as dating in a Western sense. Once a couple was seen together in public, they were expected to marry eventually. Few Nigerian ethnic groups use go-betweens to get young couples together; most couples choose each other independent of parental or other interventions, even in the rural areas. The vast majority still prefer to marry within their own ethnic group, but that is changing among young, college-educated professionals. Today, Western dating behavior has become prevalent in the cities, where anonymity has helped to throw off some of the taboos of courting that continue to be observed in the rural areas. As a result, young bachelors, having experienced freedom of choice in the cities, often return to their hometown in the rural areas to look for a bride.

Weddings are usually major events, with members of the extended family on both sides in attendance. Alternatives for weddings include the local magistrate court, a church or mosque, or a traditional wedding. Many couples choose a combination of the traditional wedding with one of the other alternatives. Most brides take their husband's surname immediately after marriage. At one time, divorce was rare, but it is becoming a common occurrence, partly because of the pressures of modern life and the decline of the family compound.

Like courting behavior, linguistic patterns have changed considerably. Because of the waves of migration of the young from the rural areas to the urban centers, many of the 300-odd ethnic languages now may be spoken by as few as 10,000 people. The three main languages—Hausa, Yoruba, and Ibo—are spoken by more than 65% of the population. It is telling that after

40 years of nationhood, very few Nigerians are interested in learning to speak another ethnic group's language.

Also, urban versions of the major languages have developed. For instance, "Lagosian" is the term given to the style of Yoruba spoken in Lagos, the former capital, which is in Yorubaland. Lagosian is a stylized version of spoken Yoruba that is peppered with English words, and it is considered by the young Yorubans to be the most sophisticated version of the language. Another urban language is pidgin English, which is spoken chiefly within the lower working class. It cuts across ethnic lines, providing a means of communication among the disparate ethnic groups that live and work side by side in the large urban centers.

Just as some markets have remained in the same location for centuries, selling many of the same traditional foodstuffs that the ancestors of modern Nigerians ate, so, too, have some beliefs, practices, and social norms endured the onslaught of centuries of outside influence. Aspects of the Nigerian culture that have survived colonialism and modern influences largely intact include seniority and authority relationships, social roles and status, a rigid class structure (where it existed), orientation to time, view of work, early socialization, the extended family system, and traditional festivals.

A strict system of seniority governs normal interpersonal relations. A child, for instance, is not expected to look his or her parents or an elder directly in the eye while being scolded. This expected deference applies to any interaction where one party is significantly senior to the other. The prerogative to use first names is granted only to close friends and superiors. It is considered an insult for a younger sibling to address an older sibling casually by the first name unless they are very close in age. An age difference of just 1 year is enough for an older individual to expect to be addressed respectfully.

A common way to address a superior respectfully is to precede the first name with a respectful salutation. Among the Yoruba, one way to do this is to precede the first name of the older sibling with *buroda* (derived from "brother") or *anti* (derived from "auntie"). Both terms have English origins, and it is not clear how they began to be used by the Yoruba as a means of conveying deference. Parents are invariably addressed using the local equivalents of the Western "dad" or "mom."

This seemingly stratified ordering by age group and seniority reflects the high power distance discussed previously. But there is only a weak stratified class structure per se except among the Hausa-Fulani in the northern states. The larger the age difference or seniority, the greater the amount of deference expected. Methods of greeting seniors, parents, and other adults vary among ethnic groups, but they generally involve some bowing of the head, if the greeter is male, or bending of the knees, if the greeter is female.

In return for deference, the seniors are expected to guide, lead by example, and be generally supportive of their subordinates. Although the major criterion for determining seniority in social situations is age, there are instances where the senior in a situation is the younger person. In the workplace, for instance, a supervisor may be senior to much older workers, from whom he or she may expect the deference accorded to seniors.

In business situations and among the educated, Western greeting behavior is more prevalent than traditional greeting behavior, but traditional greetings are still expected where the age or seniority gap is significant. This requirement does not extend to subordinate expatriates, who are routinely excused from traditional greeting requirements in favor of Western ones. Superior expatriates are not accorded traditional greetings either, not because they are not considered worthy, but perhaps because they know it is not expected.

The Nigerian's attitude toward work is a study in contrasts and points to a deep-seated social problem that retards economic progress. On one hand, the entrepreneurs operating firms of various sizes work prodigious hours to build and maintain their businesses. On the other hand, the average salary or wage earner wants to put in as little effort as possible. Because the first group often must hire the second, a conflict of goals results. This attitude is not a manifestation of an inherent laziness; it seems to be a manifestation of a lack of faith in the system. Many workers simply do not believe that advancement on the job is based on job performance. They have been conditioned to believe that favoritism, nepotism, and other unfair methods are the usual means of advancement. This attitude is further reinforced by the fact that seniority (length of service) rather than performance is a common criterion for advancement, especially in the civil service.

The effect of this attitude on national productivity is not difficult to fathom. The same deep distrust of the establishment is the reason why Nigerians of all stripes dislike paying taxes. Salary and wage earners cannot avoid having their taxes withheld, but entrepreneurs can, and do, work around the tax system without feeling the least bit guilty. The widespread incidence of official corruption and mismanagement is often cited as justification for cheating the government out of taxes. Quite a few entrepreneurs convince themselves that they can best use the money for the public good rather than let the bureaucrats decide how to spend it.

The role of women has also not changed significantly over the years. Women continue to bear the brunt of child care and household responsibilities, in addition to holding down a job or running their own businesses. The typical Nigerian husband considers it beneath his dignity to perform household chores. There is often a clear delineation between the kinds of tasks, commercial activities, and jobs that men and women normally do. This delineation of tasks and activities is very much in evidence in the Nigerian marketplace, where women far outnumber men as both traders and customers. The casual observer might infer from this that the marketplace is a female domain, but this perception is inaccurate. Although women have always outnumbered men in the marketplace, the men have wielded the real power behind the scenes.

In this regard, it was noted above that the marketplace was formerly administered by the local head chief, and more recently by elected local government councils. Both the head chieftaincy and the councils are male-dominated institutions. The true picture is that whereas women dominate at the retail level, men dominate at the production, wholesale, and administrative levels of the market structure. In addition, some commercial activities are perceived to be either male-oriented or female-oriented. Sometimes, there appears to be no logical reason for the distinction other than the mere fact that the activity has been a male or female preserve for as far back as anyone can remember. For instance, butchers are almost exclusively male, whereas fishmongers are almost exclusively female. Female-oriented activities are purposely avoided by men, whereas male-oriented activities are often closed to women, either overtly or covertly.

This distinction between which activities are proper for males and females is much sharper in the rural areas than in the cities, where the educated younger generation has learned to compromise. A woman raised in the city is far more likely to be assertive with men than is a woman raised in the rural areas. The city woman is also more likely to derisively dismiss the male view that a man's home is his castle. She is also more likely to abandon an untenable marriage, especially if she is among the thousands of enterprising women who have achieved financial independence in their own right. Education and personal achievement tend to be social levelers when it comes to sex roles.

Women have been active in local and national politics for years, dating from the early colonial periods, when market women rioted to protest the imposition of taxes on women. Politics in Nigeria is still largely male-dominated, but women are making steady progress.

The one area where women have distinguished themselves is in commerce. This is also just about the only area where society has given them wide latitude. The homes, streets, and markets of Nigeria are alive with women trading, and many have built large-scale trading enterprises with little outside aid. In the workplace, Nigerian women have as much opportunity for advancement as their counterparts in any Western country, including the United States.

Overt or covert discrimination against women persists, however, because the typical Nigerian man, in the final analysis, was not raised to regard women as equals. Polygamy is legal, but it is neither encouraged by the authorities nor tolerated by the women. It is no longer fashionable among the educated class and has been declining steadily in recent years, except in the Muslim north.

Furthermore, the decline of the family compound has not resulted in a parallel decline in the extended family system. The extended family system is a cherished aspect of African societies. Simply put, this concept means the embracement of near and distant relatives as full members of the nuclear family. The extended family is the African parallel of Western social welfare systems. Members of extended families take care of one another, find jobs for young members, band together to help members in times of sorrow or hardship, intervene to solve marital problems, and come together to celebrate one another's successes. When a member gets married or otherwise has a reason to celebrate, there is no need to send out formal invitations to extended family members because everyone is invited and expected to attend.

In addition, Nigerians have always tended to be conscious of status differences. In the Nigerian marketplace, some retailers achieve prominence and become unofficial deans of the market or leaders of the market associations. Social status is very important to Nigerians, but status consciousness is not the same as supporting a rigid social stratification system. In the past, the highest status was accorded to the king, followed by his chiefs. Other people conferred with high status may include war heroes, successful traders, or great farmers. Today, as in the past, Nigerians, especially men, aspire to be recognized by their community as people of "timber and caliber," which is a popular term connoting high status and integrity. Status can be earned through education, success in business, philanthropy, exemplary character, leadership qualities, or any combination of these. However, wealth by itself does not automatically confer status. A wealthy man of dubious character and negligible philanthropy may be shunned by the community.

In modern Nigeria, one of the most sought-after status symbols is a chieftaincy title, which is considered to be higher in status than an earned doctoral degree. When an individual with an earned doctorate becomes the chief of his hometown, he may use the title "Chief," followed by the title "Dr." in brackets, as in "Chief (Dr.) XYZ." A chieftaincy is highly valued because it is an affirmation by the community that the conferee has been recognized as a community leader.

Although chieftaincies are of various ranks and importance, all conferees are eligible to use the title "Chief." There are separate title lines for men and women, for women can be chiefs as well. Traditional rulers see two clear advantages in the modern chieftaincy system. It encourages successful citizens to be philanthropic, because that is an important criterion for becoming a chief. Furthermore, it promotes the preservation of traditional culture and values because it co-opts the conferee into the traditional structures of the community.

Ironically, the increasing popularity of chieftaincy titles has threatened the integrity of the institution. Many successful Nigerians feel incomplete without being recognized by their hometown with a chieftaincy. As a result, rumors of payoffs, favoritism, and award of chieftaincies to ineligible individuals sometimes surface.

The desire for status also carries over into the workplace. Prestigious job titles and impressive offices are prized. People are often defined by what they do for a living and how high they have risen in their profession. However, most people work simply as a means of earning a livelihood; the concept of work for its own sake is not widely valued. And, as suggested previously, evidence of large power distance is prevalent throughout the workplace. Subordinates are expected to show deference, but it is not uncommon for superiors to have strong, informal relationships with some immediate subordinates. The size of the power distance is roughly proportional to the vertical distance between the two parties on the organizational chart.

Another area that highlights the balance between change and stability is that of time. There is a common misconception among Westerners that Nigerians, like many Africans, do not pay much attention to the clock. Nigerians are quite capable of going by the clock, and they are pragmatic enough to recognize when they should do so. In senior-subordinate relationships, the subordinate is expected to be prompt, and he or she usually shows up at the appointed time. Despite their attitude toward work, workers usually report to work on time. Schoolchildren are routinely punished for arriving late to school. Nearly everyone who can afford a watch has one. Westerners apparently came up with the practice of being "fashionably late," and Nigerians merely raised it to an art form.

However, certain economic and social aspects have contributed to the relaxed approach to time. In the rural areas, there is usually no need to watch the clock because the pace of life is slow. In the cities, severe traffic congestion and an unreliable public transportation system make it difficult to foresee how long a trip across town will take. Although city dwellers readily start off early in order to arrive at their jobs or schools on time, they do not feel pressed to do the same for casual social engagements. Everyone understands the difficulties of being on time, so they are not offended when appointments are missed. Just as the trader at the market patiently waits for the next customer when business is slow, so, too, does the Nigerian host wait patiently for the guests to arrive. Thus, Western hosts should not be surprised if their Nigerian guests show up hours after the appointed time without apologizing profusely for the delay. However, when the issue is business, Nigerians will try their best to be prompt and apologize for being late.

There is a significant contrast in culture and values between the younger, college-educated generation and the older generations, which, as a rule, are less educated. The older generations are more conservative in their views and are alarmed that traditional values are eroding rapidly among the younger generations. They fully support economic and social progress, but not at the expense of cherished traditional values.

In trying to strike a balance between tradition and change, perhaps the greatest difference is between the Muslim north and the largely Christian south. Most of the values, culture, and traditional institutions in the Muslim north have survived intact; it is ultraconservative compared to the Christian south. The typical northern Muslim, regardless of age group, is not impressed by Western manners, culture, and values. He or she is more likely to identify with the culture and values of the Islamic world. Thus, a Muslim community leader in the north is more likely to address a community meeting in either Hausa or Arabic rather than English, even if both he and his audience speak English fluently.

Sometimes, observers characterize the southern educated elite as trying to be more Western than Westerners. There is an element of truth in this characterization. For instance, it is not unusual for English to be the first language of the child of an educated southern elite rather than the parents' ethnic language.

Since October of 1999, eight mainly Muslim Northern states have adopted *sharia*, strict Islamic law. This has been accompanied by religious-based riots in which hundreds have died. Many Christians and other non-Muslims living in the North have started to emigrate to other parts of the nation, although Muslim leaders publicly stress that *sharia* will apply only to Muslims.

Throughout this chapter, we have attempted to offer an accurate portrayal of the people and culture of Nigeria. Like a portrait, it is a snapshot of the nation and does not include all of the detailed nuances of this highly diverse society. Still, the image of the marketplace is critical for understanding traditional and modern Nigeria. It is an appropriate metaphor for many African nations that face the gigantic task of integrating their diverse ethnic groups as they seek to modernize without losing the cherished aspects of their traditional cultures.

CHAPTER 17

The Israeli Kibbutzim and Moshavim

In one sense, Israel is a classic cleft culture in which various ethnic and religious groups experience great difficulty living comfortably with one another (Huntington, 1996). Although citizens are Jewish, the nation seems to be a nation of tribes with radically different viewpoints and lifestyles (David, 1998, p. 5). Psychologically, it is more difficult to live in Israel than in many nations that have resolved or at least minimized their ethnic and ideological differences, and various estimates indicate that 1 million Israelis and possibly more have either emigrated permanently or live outside of it on a semipermanent basis. However, many of these exiles will not openly admit that they are reluctant to return to Israel on a permanent basis, or perhaps have no intention of ever doing so. Many Israelis would view such an admission as traitorous, at least.

A perfect example of this psychological conflict and identity crisis is the comedy routine of a famous Israeli trio, HaGashash HaChiver. An Israeli couple goes on a tour of the United States and stops to visit a relative's friends, who had moved to the United States several years ago. When the visitors ask their hosts when they plan to return to Israel, the host says, "You have caught us literally sitting on our suitcases, all packed and ready to go; we are just waiting until our son finishes college, and then we will hurry back to our beloved Israel." When the visitors inquire about the son's age, they are astonished to learn that he is "already 3 years old."

Even the short history of Israel, founded in 1948, is as complicated or more complicated than that of many older nations. And it is even difficult to identify a cultural metaphor that is expressive of the nation's basic values and, as suggested above, its conflicts. We have chosen the kibbutz because it is so intertwined with the nation's history and values. Also, the debates about the viability of the kibbutz in a globalized economy reflect the intense debates among the various tribes of modern Israel, as we will see. Probably no other institution is as uniquely Israeli as the kibbutz—the collective farm that played a critical role in the Jewish settlement of Palestine, and later in establishing and developing the Jewish state. As Lawrence Meyer (1982) describes it, "The Kibbutz is the ultimate symbol of pioneering Labor Zionism, the institutional embodiment of the dream of returning to the land, working it, receiving sustenance from it, and reviving an ancient culture in the process" (p. 327).

The first kibbutz was founded in 1909, and today, there are more than 260 of them. While many of them are still engaged in farming, others are involved in several different types of industrial activities. Although they contain less than 3% of a population of 6.1 million, the influence that the kibbutzim (plural form of kibbutz) and their democratic and egalitarian character have had on Israeli society is vastly disproportionate to their modest numbers.

The basic principles of kibbutz life are community ownership of all property, absolute equality of members, democratic decision making, the value of work as an end as well as a means, communal responsibility for child care, and primacy of the group over individuals. However, there are many pressures on the kibbutzim, and a variant of it, the moshav (moshavim is the plural) allows for private ownership of some property by its members and for more individual freedom for its members; the moshavim now account for 30% of all kibbutzim. In this chapter, we will describe the kibbutzim and include some final remarks about the moshavim.

Members of the kibbutz receive no pay for their work. All of their essential needs—food, shelter, clothing, medical care, and education—are provided by the community. Children are raised with their peers, meals are usually eaten in the kibbutz dining hall, and members convene once a week to discuss and vote on issues. Jobs rotate among members. All positions of authority—such as those of the chief executive of the kibbutz, plant managers, and supervisors—change every 2 or 3 years. Power is not permitted to accumulate in the hands of individuals. The kibbutzim range in size from 100 to 2,000 members and are small enough so that the individual's role in the community is visible and tangible.

Because of the kibbutz's relative success as a social, innovative, political, and economic enterprise, it has attracted worldwide attention. Also, the kibbutz is a vehicle for obtaining insight into the Israeli character and the mythology from which the Israelis draw their self-identity. The perception of the kibbutz as an ideal existence stems from the initial goal of the founders—that the kibbutzim would be the core of society, rather than only an alternative.

To understand the kibbutz, we need some historical background. Israel's place in history is directly related to its geography. It is a very small country lying on the coast of the eastern Mediterranean. It is only 260 miles from north to south and averages 60 miles from east to west, but it shares borders with the Arab nations of Lebanon, Syria, Jordan, and Egypt. Still, the country's landscape is marked by abrupt changes from mountains to plains, and from fertile green areas to harsh deserts. The diversity of the scenery is immense—there are more than 15 distinct geographical regions.

The history of Israel has been characterized largely by uniqueness and oppression, and at various times, it has been ruled by Christians and Muslims. In their early history, the Israelites, in opposition to the tribes surrounding them and their belief in polytheism, worshiped only one God. For this belief, they suffered persecution and enslavement, thus creating the condition for their flight from Egypt under Moses' leadership. Christianity and Islam trace their origins to Judaism and this belief; Muslims hold that Muhammad ascended to heaven from Jerusalem, and Christians maintain the same belief about Jesus, making the city sacred for all three religions. What sets Judaism apart from other major religions is its search for *meaning* in all aspects of life, and the kibbutz is a reflection of such uniqueness (Smith, 1958).

The opening of the Suez Canal in 1869 significantly increased the geopolitical and economic importance of the Middle East, and Jewish immigration began to grow significantly. Most of the newcomers immigrated to Israel not for religious reasons, but because of a unique modern national and ideological movement—Zionism.

Zionism, born in the second half of the 19th century, was the movement for the redemption of the Jewish people in the Land of Israel. It derives its name from the word "Zion," the traditional synonym for Jerusalem and the Land of Israel. The movement gained strength because of the continued oppression and persecution of Jews in Eastern Europe and increasing disillusionment with their formal emancipation in Western Europe. Emancipation had neither put an end to discrimination nor led to the integration of Jews into their local societies. The Zionist movement aimed at attaining an internationally recognized, legally secured home for the Jewish people in their historic homeland. Inspired by Zionist ideology, increasing numbers of Jews immigrated to Palestine at the end of the 19th century. These early pioneers drained swamps, reclaimed wastelands, founded agricultural settlements, and revived the Hebrew language for everyday use. It was at this stage that the kibbutzim became intertwined with the history of Israel, because they were founded by the Zionists seeking to create a new society for the Jewish people.

After the Ottoman Turks were defeated in World War I, Britain took control of Palestine. Until World War II, consecutive waves of immigrants arrived, and an infrastructure of towns and villages; industry; culture; and health, educational, and social systems was developed. Meanwhile, immediately before and during World War II, Jews in Europe suffered immensely, and the Holocaust was the most brutal form of genocide ever practiced by any culture. Renewed calls for an independent state were raised.

In 1947, the United Nations General Assembly adopted a resolution calling for the partition of the land into two states, one Jewish and one Arab. On May 14, 1948, the state of Israel was declared. On the very next day, a combined Arab force attacked the new state, and although it was badly outnumbered and suffered the loss of 1% of its entire population, Israel won 6 months later.

In 1948 and immediately thereafter, the new state of Israel faced the daunting task of turning the Zionist ideological dreams into reality. Immigrant absorption was an immediate priority. In its first 3 years, Israel welcomed 678,000 immigrants, many from the Arab countries, and, in the process, doubled its population. The nation's economic growth over the next decade was truly remarkable, especially in light of the fact that Israel has few natural resources and does not even have water in some major areas of the country. With the development of modern and sophisticated farming and irrigation techniques, orchards and groves were blooming even in the most arid regions of the country. Tens and hundreds of new towns and agricultural settlements came to life, modern industrial plants were built, roads throughout the country were paved, and a modern army was equipped virtually from scratch.

This success could not have occurred without outside help, which has continued to this day. By 1991, Israel had become the single largest recipient of charity, grants, and assistance per capita in the world, the bulk of it from America.

In both 1956 and 1967, Egypt moved aggressively against Israel, both wars resulting in Israel's victory. The 1967 war, also known as the Six Day War, resulted in a devastating defeat for Egypt, Syria, and Jordan, because Israel gained possession of the Sinai Peninsula, Gaza Strip, the Golan Heights, the West Bank of Jordan, and East Jerusalem. For the first time in 2,000 years, Jerusalem was again under Jewish sovereignty. However, the country relaxed its military posture, and the Egyptians and Syrians attacked again in 1973, this time on Yom Kippur, the holiest day on the Jewish calendar. Israel was caught by surprise, and although it won the war, the losses were significant.

Today, Israelis are in the awkward position of living in a cramped geographical area within which the Palestinians also live, but separately. There are great tensions between these two groups, and Israel has been cited frequently by Amnesty International for violating the basic rights of the Palestinians. Even Israelis are divided on the issue of the poor treatment accorded these Palestinians. In this chapter, the focus is on the Israelis, although clearly, their troubled relationship with the Palestinians at least needs to be mentioned.

With the understanding of both Israel and the kibbutz's origins in mind, it is possible to see how the kibbutz reflects many of the essential features of Israeli society and the Israeli character. First, the explicit social and ideological values to which the kibbutzim adhere are also manifested in the Israeli society, although to a lesser degree. Also, the small size of both Israel and the kibbutz are related to specific behavioral outcomes, and the traumas that the Israelis have experienced have led to the evolution of a distinctive worldview and personality profile in both the kibbutzim and Israeli society. It is these points of comparison between the kibbutz and Israeli society that we will highlight.

Explicit Values

Most, if not all, societies possess explicit values that their members share, at least to some degree. In Israel, these values are very explicit in the kibbutz and, correspondingly, in Israeli society. They include democracy, egalitarianism, socialism, a group-oriented mixture of socialism and individualism, and a deep connection to the land.

One of the main features of the kibbutz is the direct and total democracy it practices. Almost every decision and rule are voted upon by all kibbutz members, and no major decision can be made by only one or a few individuals. Analogously, democracy is a deep-rooted Jewish value. Having to confront many perilous situations as a group rather than as atomistic individuals, the Jews developed a self-deprecating sense of humor that deflated pretentiousness and heightened a feeling of social democracy, out of which evolved political democracy. Both social and political democracy were brought to Israel by the immigrants from Western countries, but mainly by the Eastern European immigrants who founded most of the kibbutzim before the establishment of the state. The successful preservation of political democracy occurred in part because of the disproportionate influence of kibbutz members in Israeli politics.

Formally, Israel is a parliamentary democracy consisting of three branches. The executive branch (the government) is subject to the confidence of the legislative branch (the Knesset—Israel's parliament), but the judiciary branch has an absolute independence that is guaranteed by law. The 120-member

Knesset is elected every 4 years. The entire country is a single electoral constituency, and Knesset members are assigned in proportion to each party's percentage of the total national vote. In this way, even very small parties who succeed in gaining only 1% of the votes can be represented. This system of voting was a result of a preference for a government that would not reflect only one party, but the consensus of at least half a dozen—a preference not to follow the policy of having one party but to accept the lowest common denominator of many. Hence, the system lends greater leverage to small and even minuscule factions and interest groups, and a good amount of bargaining occurs among the parties, some of it quite dishonorable.

Bargained deals often result in undemocratic concessions to religious splinter groups, who hold the balance of power between the main political blocks. Such concessions have led to strict Sabbath laws and laws such as those prohibiting the raising and selling of pork, civil marriage, and divorce. Many of these laws are unacceptable to a large portion of the Israelis. Electoral reform is often spoken of, but action has been minimal.

Although Israel is not a theocratic state, there is a significant overlap between the government and Judaism. For example, rabbinical law prevails in such matters as marriage, divorce, and the Sabbath. The Labor Party, which ruled Israel from 1948 until 1977, lost to the Likud Party, which advocated keeping the West Bank as a permanent part of Israel. In 1992, the Labor Party returned to power; its leader, Yitzhak Rabin, signed the Oslo Accord in 1994 that promised a Palestinian state on the West Bank. However, he was assassinated in 1995, and the Likud Party returned to power, nearly destroying the Oslo Accord. By this time, the warring tribes were many: There are more than 10 political parties in the 120-person Knesset representing all political stripes. In 1999, a weakened Labor Party (now renamed One Israel) returned to power, but only as the major partner in a coalition of political parties.

A prominent example of how important democracy is to Israel is the status of the army within the society. Although necessity has turned the army into a very important and essential part of Israeli life, Israel is far from being a military society. The average Israeli man spends a large portion of his adult life in the army, both during his compulsory 3 years and then during at least 30 days a year as a reserve, but he remains very much a civilian. The Israeli army is highly professional, with a basic discipline similar to that of many other armies, but it is always the first preference to train the soldier by example, not by order and punishment. Amos Elon (1971), the Israeli author, points out that

> The army is not an aristocratic institution, as it continues to be in some democratic countries. There is no deliberate attempt to break the will of

recruits. It is a citizen army, and the gap between officers and men is minimal. There are few privileges of rank. The Israeli military code bluntly states that officers have no privileges whatsoever, only duties. Officers are usually addressed by their first names. There are no fancy uniforms. . . . Military titles are used in writing, but rarely in verbal address. The use of such titles in civilian life, after retirement is frowned upon. . . . Job turnover among officers is unusually rapid and the army is almost never a lifelong occupation. Most officers are weeded out soon after they reach forty. This practice has helped to prevent the establishment of a military class. (p. 252)

Hence, it is an army that exists out of necessity, not out of choice. It combines the needs that evolve out of Israel's memories of its tragic past of persecution, the state of war, and its small size with the wish to maintain a democratic society that will not be controlled by any elite. Thus far, Israel has been successful in maintaining that combination.

The kibbutz is close to the ideal of an egalitarian society. The equality of all people within the small, enclosed society of the kibbutz is one of its most fundamental principles, and the periodic rotation of critical and powerful roles is one very effective way of preserving egalitarianism.

Likewise, the egalitarian principle is basic to Israeli society. In Hofstede's (1991) study of cultural values across 53 nations, Israel had the second lowest score on the dimension of power distance, or the belief that inequality among members of a society should be emphasized; Austria had the lowest score. The roots of the idea of the equality of all people are historical as well as ideological.

Twenty centuries of oppression have made Jews skeptical of the indiscriminate use of power. Many Israelis find the mere striving for power to be objectionable. This has caused a basic disrespect for authority, which is a main characteristic of Israeli society. Also, the anarchist strain that is found in Israel has its origins in the Marxist and Socialist ideas that the first pioneers espoused, for some envisioned the entire society as a network of collective agricultural and industrial association involving a minimum degree of coercion and a high degree of voluntary, reciprocal agreements. Although this vision did not materialize, belief in egalitarianism continues to this day. Voluntarism, rather than formal authority, is regarded highly throughout Israeli society, and especially so in kibbutzim and cooperative movements. Members spend a relatively large amount of time on voluntary activities, such as serving on different committees and working extra hours. Another form of voluntarism is the high percentage of kibbutzniks who serve in the elite units in the army and as officers. It is almost a social norm to volunteer for these assignments.

Furthermore, the ideological basis of the kibbutz is socialism, whose basic tenet is that the major means of production and distribution are managed and controlled by the community as a whole, and it is actively practiced in the kibbutz. Members live according to a system whereby each person works as he or she can and receives what he or she needs. Almost all needs are met by the kibbutz, including food, shelter, clothing, medical care, child rearing, and education.

A similar type of socialism exists in the Israeli society at large. The concept of national responsibility for basic health, housing, and social welfare is a given. Even the recent influx of hundreds of thousands of Ethiopian and Soviet Jews has not led to a fundamental requestioning of priorities, although the costs are enormous. And, although 25% of the population lives below the poverty line, there is not one documented case of an Israeli dying of hunger or malnutrition. If not the immediate family, then the extended family or the community at large will try to handle such a problem. Education is free, and health insurance is set at a price all people can afford.

Another key value in the kibbutz and Israeli society is the primacy of the group over the individual. From the outset of the Zionist movement until the proclamation of the state, the emphasis was consistent: The purpose of the Zionist movement was the redemption of the Jewish people. The movement, and later the state, focused on the group rather than the individual. Moreover, the early pioneers arriving in Palestine believed firmly in this socialistic approach, and they quickly realized the value of group cooperation as they attempted to make the land habitable.

Many of these pioneers were not accustomed to manual labor, were weakened by malaria and other diseases, and suffered from the hostility of the Arabs. Making the group more important than the individual to overcome such obstacles was not only desirable but absolutely necessary. This experience had the same effect on Israeli society as a whole, although to a lesser extent.

Currently, the demands made on the individual in Israel are great because of the continuing tenuous security that the nation faces, which implies that survival rests on the cohesiveness of the group. Therefore, each Israeli must sacrifice some individuality to meet these demands. Mandatory military service is required for both sexes, taxes are among the highest in the world, and Israelis can take only a small sum of money out of the country for investments elsewhere. The ultimate betrayal in the eyes of Israelis is to leave the country permanently. A similar attitude toward people who left the kibbutz to live elsewhere formerly existed. People who grew up in the kibbutz and decided to pursue a different way of life found that they were rejected by the group, although this rejection was not always conscious (Bettelheim, 1969). This reaction is much less intense than it used to be, partly because a relatively large number of young people choose to leave—between one third and one half of each age group, sometimes even more.

The relative unimportance of the individual is most apparent in an encounter with the bureaucracy, which is bothersome in most nations. However, the Israeli system presents itself to the Israeli citizen not as a guardian and servant but as a warden. The stories about the indifference and callousness of the Israeli bureaucracy are legion. Almost every dealing with a government or public agency involves standing in line for a long time, and it is quite common to have to wait in several queues in order to arrange one matter. The combination of constant demands on the individual and the unpleasant bureaucracy leads to a resistance to authority that manifests itself in the disregard to whatever seems unessential for the general safety or survival. For example, cheating on taxes is a very common practice.

Admittedly, individualism has increased significantly in recent years. Only 3% of the workforce is now in agriculture, and most Israelis live in and around cities. Erez (1986) dramatized this movement in a well-controlled study in which she manipulated leadership style across three Israeli organizational cultures. In the kibbutz, collectivism was the highest, and participative management was most effective in this setting. In the public sector, however, delegative management was most effective. But in the private sector, which was the most individualistic, directive leadership was most effective. Today, Israel is a high-tech leader, and its economy is integrated increasingly with the activities of other nations. Given this situation, we can expect to see individualism increase and conflict between groups representing different varieties of individualism and collectivism rise.

It can be seen, then, that although the instinct for self-preservation has given rise to social discipline, there is still a widespread, almost compulsive resentment of any regimentation. The result is a peculiarly Israeli mixture of self-reliant individualism and a socialistic readiness to cooperate. This interplay between individualism and collectivism is also portrayed in Hofstede's (1991) study of 53 nations, where Israelis scored near the middle on the individualism-collectivism dimension.

The deep connection to the land is another value held by both the kibbutz and the Israeli society, even though agriculture is such a small part of the economy. This connection stems partly from the knowledge that land is necessary for survival and protection, and partly from the consequence of a rebellion against generations of Jews who had no real connection to any land. The land that the Israelis inherited was poor in many ways, but the vigor of the response has been overwhelming. The people of the kibbutzim have shown their love and connection to the land through working it and making it fertile and blooming. In Israel at large, the connection was shown through the attempts to settle as much of the land as possible, even the most remote areas.

Size and Behavioral Outcomes

The kibbutz and Israel are very small, both physically and in members. Israel's population is only 6.1 million, which includes just over 1 million Arabs, and the distances between cities are very short. Driving from the Mediterranean to the border with Jordan takes an hour and a half. Both Haifa and Jerusalem are only an hour's ride from Tel Aviv. More than 80% of the population is concentrated in this small triangle. Much of the country is uninhabited desert, and consequently, it is even smaller than it appears on most maps, where it is a tiny speck about the size of New Jersey.

As a result, both in the kibbutz and in Israel, specific behavioral outcomes occur that are not common in larger organizations and societies. Relations of all kinds are much more intimate in both the kibbutz and Israel than in larger entities. In the kibbutz, a child spends almost all of his or her time with the same group of children throughout childhood. Because there are typically only a few hundred people in the kibbutz, an adult member interacts with the same people almost every day. Similarly, in the larger Israeli society, people tend to maintain a relatively steady and intimate group of friends, but with a relatively large number of acquaintances and contacts on the periphery. This results in the near certainty that when two Israelis who are strangers meet, they will find friends in common within a matter of minutes. Spending time with friends is probably the favorite pastime in Israel. People very often meet at each other's houses, without a need for an external entertainment or purpose, such as watching a video.

Families also have very close-knit ties. Small geographical distances lead to very easy access and relatively frequent visits and gatherings. This sense of closeness also manifests itself in the responsibility many parents feel toward their children even when they have become adults. When parents can afford it, buying an apartment for a son or daughter when they get married is a very common practice, and financial help frequently continues even after that stage.

Moreover, children tend to expect this help because of the high cost of living. Israel is as much, or perhaps more than, a socialistic as a capitalistic country, and approximately 40% of the industrial economy is controlled by the state or the *Histadrut*, the national labor co-operative.

Given the country's small size, maintaining anonymity and privacy requires hard work. It is extremely difficult for individuals to achieve anonymity, and intimate details about someone's past and present are common knowledge, even in the larger urban centers. There are 262 people per square kilometer in Israel, whereas the comparative figure in the United States is only 29. This intimacy and small size help to establish a strong sense of community.

Furthermore, this sense of closeness leads to a heightened intensity of experience. Tragedy rarely remains isolated within the narrow confines of family intimacy, but spreads to wider social circles. In the kibbutz, with its communal dining room and similar collective arrangements for hundreds of members, this is obvious. But it is often true also in the towns, where news travels fast and immediately affects even apparent strangers. Each death in war electrifies the country as though it were the first time, drawing strangers closer to one another. It is at such moments that a sense of cohesion is so strong that it makes the country seem more like a large village rather than a state.

Finally, the mass media powerfully dramatize this state of affairs, and Israelis are obsessive listeners of radio and TV news. No people in the entire world tunes in to the news as often, as regularly, and with such fervor.

Traumas, Worldview, and Personality

The Jews have experienced proportionately more traumas than most, if not all, major cultural groups. Two modern traumas that have had an enormous influence on the Israeli worldview and personality, both in the kibbutz and outside of it, are the Holocaust and the continuing struggle with their Arab neighbors.

More than 6 million Jews, or approximately one third of all Jews, perished in the Holocaust during World War II, and the memory of it remains vivid in Israel. Furthermore, it had an enormous impact on the process of creating the state of Israel. As Elon (1971) points out, the Holocaust

> caused the destruction of that very same Eastern European world against which the early pioneers had staged their original rebellion, but to which, nevertheless, Israel became both an outpost and heir. Because of the Holocaust there is a latent hysteria in Israeli life that . . . accounts for the prevailing sense of loneliness, a main characteristic of the Israeli personality. (p. 199)

It helps to explain the obsessive suspicions, especially of outsiders, in both the kibbutz and the society at large, and the urge for self-reliance at all costs in a world that never again can be viewed as safe and secure. Clearly, the Holocaust had left a permanent scar on

> the national psychology, the tenor and content of public life, the conduct of foreign affairs, on politics, education, literature and the arts. . . . The notoriously lively bustle . . . and seemingly endless vivacity of Israeli life merely serve as compensatory devices for a morbid melancholy and a vast, permeating sadness. . . . It crops up unexpectedly in conversation; it is noticeable in the press, in literature, in the private rituals of people. (Elon, 1971, p. 199)

It is little wonder that the term "gripe parties" is employed to describe many social gatherings.

There are countless public and private monuments to the Holocaust. Israelis do not let themselves forget. One day a year is devoted to mourning for the victims. The public commemoration serves a compulsive need to re-assert the group and demonstrate its continuing vitality. However, as the older members of society die, they are replaced by others who often do not use the Holocaust to justify questionable actions, particularly the harsh treatment of Palestinians. And the younger Israelis are focused not so much on the Holocaust as on making Israel into a modern nation that is quite comfortable with different nationalities and perspectives.

Most Israelis believe wholeheartedly that the Holocaust was possible simply because the Jews had no country of their own and consequently lacked the means of resistance. To them, it is proof that the earlier Zionist theme of a need for a land was absolutely correct. The Holocaust also explains in part why Israelis are willing to endure most hardships imposed by their government with hardly any protest.

Arab hostility has only helped to sharpen the outlines of the picture of utter loneliness drawn by the Holocaust. Since independence in 1948, Israelis have lived in a state of geographic and political isolation unusual in the modern world. Most countries today share common markets or at least open borders, a common language, or the same religion, but Israel does not. Also, it does not have any military, political, or economic alliance. This claustrophobic isolation has given rise to a pessimism that is a main feature of the Israeli personality. It is a root cause for Israeli stubbornness and largely explains why pious reprimands from other nations have little effect.

The kibbutz, although in a completely different way and for very different reasons, is also isolated in many ways from the Israeli society as a whole, choosing to keep to itself. Although egalitarian in their own society, kibbutzniks tend to view themselves as an elite, and this view about the kibbutz is also held by some Israelis. Their social systems, such as education, are almost completely separate. They are also not much influenced by criticism that comes from the outside, feeling that others who have not shared their experiences cannot judge them.

Because memories of the Holocaust are so alive, Arab threats of annihilation achieve just the opposite of their original intention. Such threats have kept Israelis wary and ready for combat long after the initial period of pioneering enthusiasm waned, and they have increased Israeli resolve, inventiveness, cohesion, vigor, and a nervous but fertile anxiety. These threats have also helped foster the sense of shared social purpose. This kind of cohesion and unity is also very strong in the kibbutz, although, like the rest of Israeli society, the members of the kibbutz are the harshest critics of their own community.

Ironically, in its early period, Zionism was predicated upon faith in peaceful change. The discovery that it was nearly impossible to achieve has affected the Israeli worldview profoundly. Redemption has become intertwined with violence on a continual basis, and the resulting dissonance is now a part of this worldview, creating an outlook that is a combination of the hopeful and the tragic.

The never-ending state of war has brought about an awareness of *Ein Brera*—there is no choice. This viewpoint reflects a fatalistic attitude. Zionists, the former rebels against their fate, have come to accept the assumption of fatalism and continual warfare. This fortress mentality was certainly not part of the original Zionist dream. Again, however, many younger Israelis are questioning the need for such constant vigilance.

Although men are subject to military service until the age of 55,

> it is the younger Israeli who must bear on . . . his shoulders the main burden of the seemingly endless emergency. One result has been a growing cult of toughness among younger people. . . . Frequent and prolonged periods of service in the army breed a stark, intensely introverted, icy matter-of-factness in the young that contrasts sharply with the externalized, rather verbose emotionalism of their elders. (Elon, 1971, p. 231)

Still, they accept their responsibility, substituting an unreflecting, elemental urge for self-preservation for the Zionistic vision of their elders. This tendency to shy away from feelings is a basic trait in the character of the new generation of Israelis, and it was also observed by Bettelheim (1969) in his classic psychological description of the children of the kibbutz. The second generation, those born in the kibbutz, are committed to "a literalness, a matter of fact objectivity which has no place for emotions" (p. 85). It seems, though, that in the past few years, people are once again more comfortable with expressing their emotions more openly.

Still, as might be expected in such a small land and organizational entity that is living constantly under a state of siege, claustrophobia has emerged as a major problem. This claustrophobia, combined with a sense of adventurism, drives many Israelis, including kibbutz members, to trips outside of Israel, ranging from the conventional 2-week tours in Europe to exotic trips that may last for months and years. Kibbutzim members, given the small size of the relatively confined society in which they exist, can experience this sense of claustrophobia even more intensely than other members of Israeli society. Many of the young people go off and explore the life outside, working and living for a year or two in the city. The sense of claustrophobia is, in part, the reason why some of them choose not to return to the kibbutz, just as it is the reason why some Israelis choose not to live in Israel.

Naturally, there are additional factors that help to form the Israeli worldview other than traumas, two of the most important of which are immigration and religion. Israel is rife with contradictions, such as pessimism and optimism, fatalism and determination, and so forth. One of the most salient of Israel's contradictions is the composition of her population. Many of her citizens are native born, but the rest are immigrants from across the world: Europe, Asia, Africa, North America, South America, and Australia. Even most of the native-born Israelis are only one or two generations removed from their immigrant past. Most immigration societies face problems resulting from serving as a melting pot for widely divergent backgrounds, but in Israel, there is a noticeable distinction between the Ashkenazi Jews and the Sepharadim or Oriental Jews. The Ashkenazim are those Jews from Eastern and Western Europe, America, and Australia. The early Zionists and the founders of the state were almost all Ashkenazim. The Sepharadic Jews, now almost half the population, are those who emigrated from the Islamic countries in the Middle East and North Africa, and who came to Israel only after the establishment of the state. The Sepharadic Jews had to enter a modern western society when many of them had significantly lower literacy rates and education, were short on professional skills, and had very little money. The largely Ashkenazi establishment, unlike the newer immigrants, was socialist and secular, and it tried to transform the mostly traditional Sepharadim into models of themselves. Although a large number of the Sepharadim prospered in their new country, many did not. By the 1960s, it became clear that a "second Israel" had emerged, and that there is a real gap between the two groups. This has resulted in a campaign aimed at improving the conditions and the opportunities of the Sepharadic Jews.

In a very definite manner, the kibbutzim represent part of this status problem. Almost all of their people are of European descent, and in many ways, they represent an Ashkenazi elite, which was unofficially reluctant to have the Oriental immigrants join its ranks. However, this is slowly changing, and there is a much higher degree of acceptance of these immigrants and their offspring in the kibbutzim.

The other major issue affecting the Israeli worldview is religion. Serious conflict exists between religious and secular Israelis, and it is an explosive issue that has not been resolved, merely shelved temporarily. In fact, it has been impossible even to reach an agreement in Israel over the most basic question: Who is a Jew?

Jews in Israel are not differentiated by synagogue affiliations as much as by the manner in which they relate to the land and state of Israel. Because of the Jewish people's reconnection with their land and their building of a modern state, there are now five main options for defining oneself as a Jew (see also Friedman, 1989). First, more than 50% of the population is secular, and they are the ones most responsible for building the new state of Israel. For the secular Zionists, being back in the land of Israel, erecting a modern society and army, and observing Jewish holidays as national holidays all became a substitute for religious observance and faith. The second group consists of religious Zionists, who make up about 25% of the population. These are traditional or modern Orthodox Jews who fully support the secular Zionist state but insist that it is not a substitute for the synagogue. The third group has about 5% of the population, and it also includes religious Zionists, but of a more messianic bent. The members of this group believe that the rebirth of the Jewish state is only the first stage in a process that will culminate with the coming of the Messiah. They form the backbone of the Gush Emunim settler movement, which acts upon the belief that every inch of the land of Israel should be settled by Jews. Furthermore, there are the ultra-orthodox, non-Zionist Jews, who constitute about 15% of the Jewish population. They believe that a Jewish state will be worth celebrating only after the Messiah comes and the rule of Jewish law is total, and that the pinnacle of Jewish life and learning was that which was achieved by the great 18th, 19th, and 20th-century yeshivas (Jewish schools for higher education) and rabbinic dynasties located in their native Eastern Europe. They have attempted to re-create that life in Israel and still dress in traditional dark coats and fur hats, naming their yeshivas after towns in Eastern Europe and preferring to speak Yiddish rather than Hebrew. They also refuse to serve in the army until they are 24 years old or celebrate Independence Day. Finally, the 800,000 secular Russians, among whom there are many atheists, who have come to Israel since the breakup of the Soviet Union constitute a powerful group, and they have created the only ethnic political party in Israel.

Given such strong opinions and points of view, it is not surprising that these groups clash fiercely over the relationship of religion to the state. Whereas the secular Jews want the state to be completely separate from religion, the religious Jews want them to be intertwined. Another serious clash is over the issue of the young men from the fourth group avoiding service in the army, which is criticized bitterly by the Zionist Jews.

Most of the kibbutzim are decidedly secular, and their founders actively rebelled against everything represented by the Judaism in their native Eastern Europe. In this sense, the worldview of the kibbutzim is similar to that held by the largest group in the population.

Thus far, we have emphasized the internal character or personality of the Israelis, but this should be related to overt behavior that Israelis manifest. The common perception is that Israelis are impolite, arrogant, and brash. A classic example of this behavior is the high-risk, macho manner in which Israelis drive. They do not keep the proper driving distance between cars because of the fear that someone will cut ahead of them. Drivers honk at each other if the car in front of them does not move within a nanosecond of the traffic light turning green. Furthermore, this arrogant behavior is exhibited in the way people cut corners in their business and personal dealings, and in the impolite manner in which customers are frequently treated. This roughness of Israeli culture is a reflection of the way Israeli society works, and it is not deliberately directed at the outside but, rather, is a spillover from the anxiety and internal frictions. Many American Jews visiting Israel experience great difficulty relating to the Israelis because of this roughness.

In part, this behavior stems from the constant feeling of insecurity, the simultaneous need to suppress it, and the need and desire to go on about daily life and behave normally. Such contradictory needs build up great repressed tensions between the desire to admit fears and worries and the belief that it is not appropriate, helpful, or masculine to do so.

Also, this behavior is partly a result of a Mediterranean influence—Italians will behave in a similar manner. Still, this is only surface behavior. Israelis are quick to react, scold, and act impolitely, but they are also quick to calm down. This harshness on the outside, combined with a soft inside, is the reason that the image of native-born Israelis is portrayed by the sabra—a cactus plant with thorns on the outside but a delicate inner part. Correspondingly, there is relatively little violence in terms of rape, murder, or extortion, and the streets are safe at night.

Generally, Israelis are very direct people. As Joyce Starr (1991) describes it,

> They are eager to get down to business, to get right to the heart of things. The little extra graces that give the Middle East its charm and style are seen by Israelis as useless decorations, impediments that only waste time. Everything is up front, without pretense, and matters are stripped down to bare essentials. Israelis almost never phrase things with "I think" or "It seems to me," the classical American way of avoiding hurting the other. They will simply attack with "you are wrong." (p. 45)

In studies of the Prisoners' Dilemma, an exercise in cooperation, Israeli men are more uncooperative at the early stages of negotiation than are most other men from other nationalities. *Dugry,* an Arabic term now part of the Israeli slang, reflects a similar orientation among Israelis, because it means,

"Don't take offense, as I am going to speak frankly and be critical, so get ready, but realize it is not personal." There are actually management programs that train Israelis to be polite to American executives, who do not enjoy a particularly high rating in this area.

In addition, informality is the norm in Israel. People introduce themselves to strangers using only first names. This behavior is repeated almost everywhere: First names are used between employees and employers, schoolchildren and their teachers, and soldiers and their commanders. As noted previously, Israelis seek to deemphasize status and power distance between individuals, and they have little patience for formality or protocol, for complicated ritual and procedure. Israeli men very rarely wear a suit and a tie. This informality is associated with a display of openness and frankness that encourages people to speak their minds and offer their opinions freely to another without feeling that they are being presumptuous for doing so. It is also associated with the way people socialize with each other—it is very common to simply drop by a friend's house without calling in advance. When someone says, "Why don't you drop by?" they actually mean it.

Both the directness and the informality are essential ingredients of the kibbutz way of life. Because status differences are greatly, if not totally, deemphasized, and all matters are subject to debate and participative decision making, the weekly meetings create a platform where opinions are usually expressed very freely, including opinions about the members themselves. Informal social relationships are very easy to maintain because the physical size of the kibbutz is so small. Informal clothing can actually be a source of pride.

Finally, Israel is a classic "doing" society in which action is taken proactively to control situations and overcome environmental problems (see the first part of this book). Although Americans like to think of themselves in a similar fashion, the Israelis far outshine them: They have an uncanny ability to improvise, and they are at their best when doing so. Israelis pride themselves on their ability to fashion solutions to both mundane and desperate problems as they occur. In part, this ability comes from their historical experience, when Jews did not have rights and the only way to survive was to look around for a shortcut. The more recent experience, when the new state of Israel had to overcome many difficult and complex problems in a very short time, has strengthened this ability. Joyce Starr (1991) gives an amusing but insightful example of this ability when she explains why an American salad bar would not work in Israel: "Israelis would bring two or three friends, all of their children, pay for one person, and send the kids to take more salad because it's 'free.' If that restaurant was in Israel, the owner would have gone bankrupt" (p. 21).

Within the kibbutz, the ability to improvise was developed to its highest form. Many of the kibbutzim possessed only scant resources, and so their members learned to use all of them in inventive ways. Without such improvisations, they might well have failed. Part of the fame that the modern and inventive Israeli agriculture has acquired worldwide can be related to the experiences the kibbutzim had to face.

Together with being an action-oriented society, Israel is also an intellectual society. There is a very high percentage of people with university degrees, and the number of books bought per capita is one of the highest in the world. This trend also exists in the kibbutz, and one way kibbutzim try to maintain a high cultural level is through special cultural events, either produced internally or brought from the outside.

As organizations change, so, too, does the culture in which they exist. The most popular model for looking at organizational change and growth is biological or evolutionary, that is, organizations go through distinct stages. Edgar Schein (1985) has described a three-stage model in which the first stage is birth and early growth, during which the main ideas and sources of inspiration come from the founders and their beliefs. These ideas serve as the glue holding the organization together. During the second stage, organizational midlife, there is a decline in the commitment that members make to the organization and the loss of key goals and values, which results in a crisis of identity. If an organization is to achieve the third stage, organizational maturity, and become even stronger, it needs to redefine its goals and values to meet the expectations of a changing world. In effect, the kibbutz is experiencing an organizational midlife crisis, and, correspondingly, Israel is as well.

In particular, most Israelis are not willing to work the long hours that each type of kibbutz requires, although they frequently feel that their children should spend at least 3 months working on it to reconnect with the country's past. The moshavim have become a popular alternative simply because of the rigidity of the life that most kibbutzniks lead, and they are characterized by a lower degree of ideological fervor, the ownership of private property, and the espousal of some rights for individuals, even to the extent of benevolently accepting that some members want to leave permanently.

Fortunately, the ideological rigidity of the founders of both Israel and the kibbutz has eased considerably, and the new generation is responding to a changing world. In the kibbutz, the rigid rules of living with only the bare essentials have changed dramatically. Life has become more prosperous, members now have all or most of the modern appliances in their own rooms, they are able to take more vacations abroad, and so on. These changes parallel those in the larger Israeli society, which has become much more materialistic.

Another dramatic shift in the kibbutzim is industrialization. Israeli agriculture has reached its upper limit, mainly because of the lack of water. By

1980, Israel was already using all of its replenishable water supply (Meyer, 1982). Today, almost all of the kibbutzim have at least one factory, employing, on average, 50% of the members. This transition occurred because of the belief that the future lies in industry rather than agriculture. Still, it has been accompanied by other changes and problems. Economic decisions in the kibbutz have become more complex, and it is harder for all members to participate in all decisions because of a lack of knowledge necessary to understand the issues.

There is also a definite shift in the kibbutzim and particularly the moshavim, from an emphasis on only group effort and collective well-being to one combining such group effort and the recognition of individual needs, privacy, and family. Many kibbutz members, and, correspondingly, many Israelis, demand more freedom for self-expression and individual preferences. One result in the kibbutz has been the decline in the practice of collective child rearing, which was once synonymous with kibbutz life and an essential part of the ideology. Another manifestation of this trend is the larger flexibility that kibbutzim show toward people who want to be able to pursue the careers of their choosing.

Although the kibbutzim are still well-represented in the Israeli parliament, or *Knesset,* their influence has declined over the past decade. This is a result of the replacement of the Labor Party by the more conservative Likud Party as the leading political party in 1977. It is probably also a result of the emphasis on the group, which resulted, in many cases, in creating people who want to adhere to group norms rather than lead. Today, the leadership of the kibbutzim is mainly in setting an example, not in being involved in politics.

Still, the kibbutzim have been an absolutely essential part of Israel's struggle to survive, and their values have been a bellwether for the country. If the kibbutzim and Israeli society are to achieve and maintain the third stage of maturity, it would probably be wise to rekindle the spiritual and moral heritage of the kibbutzim throughout Israel in some form, because their basic values were and most probably are indispensable for continued growth and success. Israel, now a global leader in high technology and other areas, is seeking to balance individual desires and national imperatives, and using the kibbutz and moshav as a starting point for discussion is probably a wise course of action.

CHAPTER 18

The Italian Opera

The only form of theatrical music that is at all controversial . . . is the operatic form.

—Copland (1957), p. 133

Italy, with a population of approximately 57 million, is about the size of Florida, but less fertile and less endowed with natural resources. The country is divided into two main regions. "Continental Italy" consists of the Alps and the northern Italian plain, and "Mediterranean Italy" encompasses the Italian peninsula and the islands. The Appenine mountains run directly down the peninsula's center, and its northern range almost completely cuts off the north from the south. This geographical division has led to extreme regionalism, and many Italians view Italy as two separate nations: the wealthier, industrial north, and the poorer, more agrarian south.

In fact, the political scientist Robert Putnam (1991) has empirically and convincingly demonstrated that the civic traditions of the north and south of Italy originated from different sources and that these traditions have persisted for centuries. In the 11th century, King Frederico established an autocratic form of government in the south that was both politically and economically successful, but over time, his successors corrupted it. The Mafia arose as the middlemen between the kings and the people, which tended to reinforce corruption. In the north, by contrast, there has been a centuries-long legacy of civic involvement through guilds and democratic elections that has held corruption in check. Today, the north of Italy is as successful as or more successful than Germany, whereas the south languishes in poverty, even though millions of dollars have been devoted to eradicating it.

There is even a group, the Northern League, that periodically seeks to create two separate nations in Italy. However, this movement is more quixotic than real, because the economically prosperous north depends heavily on emigration from the south for its workforce. Moreover, the north and south are closely linked to one another culturally, as noted below, even though there are regional differences.

Although Italian culture is justifiably renowned, it is in danger of extinction, as are the cultures of some other developed nations. It has the lowest fertility rate among nations: 1.19 children per woman. After Sweden, Italy has the oldest population among nations, with 16.1% of its population over 65. Still, the population is large, and these trends are likely to reverse. Also, there are many people who want to immigrate to Italy, and in fact, there are countless numbers of illegal aliens crossing its borders daily. Thus, although Italy will probably change, its cultural base should be relatively secure, at least for the foreseeable future.

Historically, Italy has been victimized by overwhelming natural disasters: volcanoes, floods, famines, and earthquakes. It is a geologically young country, most of which cannot be categorized as terra firma, and there have been so many mudslides resulting in great loss of property and life both in the past and in recent years that the Italians nickname the nation "landslide country" ("Hand of God, Hand of Italian Man," 1998). As a result, Italy exudes an aura of "precariousness" (Haycraft, 1985). Italians tend to accept insecurity as a fact of life. This acceptance may explain why they seem to be able to enjoy life more for the moment and why they are willing to accept events as they happen. Italians tend to feel that if something is going to happen, it will, and that not much can be done about it.

Italy's history is filled with many culturally rich and influential periods, including the Roman Empire and the Renaissance. The country emerged as a nation-state in 1861 as a result of national unification, known as the *risorgimento,* or revival. Before unification, Italians never quite identified with the many foreign bodies that conquered and ruled them. This is a possible explanation for Italians' historic contempt for the law and paying taxes; and even though Italians have been influenced overwhelmingly by foreign rule, they have managed to create a culture that is distinctly their own.

To understand Italy, it is a good idea to look at the opera, that art form that Italians invented and raised to its highest level of achievement, and that represents most, if not all, of the major features of Italian culture. The opera is a metaphor for Italy itself, because it encompasses music, dramatic action, public spectacle and pageantry, and a sense of fate. It may be tragic or comic, intensely personal or flamboyantly public, with the soloists and chorus expressing themselves through language, gesture, and music, and always through highly skilled acting. There is a larger-than-life aura surrounding operas, and the audience is vitally engaged in the opera itself, showing great emotion and love toward a singer whose talents are able to express the common feelings that Italians tend to share. Operas and operatic songs reflect the essence of Italian culture, and they are embraced by Italians with an emotional attachment that less dramatic peoples might find difficult to understand. Therefore, we chose the opera as our metaphor to understand Italian culture.

Using this metaphor, we focus on five distinctive characteristics of the opera and demonstrate how they illustrate Italian life. These characteristics are the overture; the spectacle and pageantry itself and the manner in which the operalike activities are performed in the daily life of the Italians; the use and importance of voice to express words in a musical fashion; externalization, which refers specifically to the belief that emotions and thoughts are so powerful that an individual cannot keep them within himself or herself and must express them to others; and the importance of both the chorus and the soloists, which reflects the unity of Italian culture (chorus) but also regional variations, particularly between the north and the south.

The Overture

The overture was such an influential innovation that it inspired the development of the German symphony. Essentially, the orchestra sets the mood for the opera during the overture and gives some idea as to what the audience can expect to occur. Typically, the overture is about 5 minutes in length, and it frequently includes passages that are emotionally somber, cheerful, reflective, and so forth. At various points, the overture is quick, moderate, or slow in tempo, and it employs different instruments to convey the sense of what will happen in the various acts—usually three—into which the opera is divided.

Italian culture emphasizes overtures. It stands somewhere in the middle of the continuum between American low-context culture and Asian high-context culture. Americans tend to ignore the overture and get down to business rather quickly. On the other hand, many Asians devote a significant amount of time getting to know their negotiating counterparts before doing business with them. Italians take a midway position on the issue of personal trust and knowledge, but they do tend to convey their feelings and thoughts at least partially at the beginning of the relationship. The other party has some understanding of what will unfold, but it is only a preview that is imperfect, because the unexpected frequently occurs.

There are regional differences in the manner in which the overture is performed. In Milan, which has been influenced by its proximity to Switzerland and Germany, there is a tendency to shorten the overture. Still, it occurs, even in the smallest café that has only a few tables and a modest menu featuring sandwiches. The sandwiches are presented in a colorful and appetizing manner, and *panninis*—invented in Italy—are frequently featured, as are various forms of coffee and espresso. There may be only a few moments of conversation with the owner, but they are pleasant, like the display of food. Department stores emphasize the same pattern of behavior, and the tendency to interact with the salesperson is much higher in Italy than in the United States.

In the south, the overture can be much more involved. When looking for a pair of shoes, for example, the buyer frequently visits a shop and indicates to the owner that a mutual friend suggested he make his purchase there. This information leads to a pleasant conversation and perhaps the offer of a cup of espresso. Frequently, no purchase is made, nor is it expected, on the first visit. When the buyer visits a second time, the same pleasantries occur, and he may or may not make a purchase. However, both parties expect that a purchase will occur if the buyer visits the shop for a third time. It is at this time that the real negotiations, or opera, begin. Both parties—and the audience—have a good idea about the outcome, but there will be expressions of emotion, various uses of argument and persuasion, and different tones of voice that will help to facilitate the final outcome or sale. Still, the unexpected can, and does, occur, because fate is a critical element in the mix.

Pageantry and Spectacle

By and large, Italy is a land of spectacle and pageantry. Italians tend to be more animated and expressive than most other nationalities. Many Asians, for example, attempt to minimize emotions and gestures when communicating with others. Italians, particularly those in the south, revel when communicating in an expressive manner. The level of noise in Italy tends to be high in public places, and people tend to congregate rather than be isolated from one another. Also, some bystanders do not mind becoming part of the action. For example, a driver stopped by a policeman for excessive speed may be debating the issue while a crowd, vocally supportive of the driver's plea for mercy, offers comments.

Once the overture is over and the curtain goes up, the audience is greeted by a set so visually stunning that it elicits applause. This is the beginning of the pageantry and spectacle. They play such an important role in Italian life that people and things frequently tend to be judged first and foremost on their appearances.

The surface of Italian life, playful, yet bleak and tragic at times, has many of the charactcristics of a show. It is, first of all, usually moving, entertaining, and unreservedly picturesque. Second, all of its effects are skillfully contrived and graduated to convey a certain message to, and arouse particular emotions in, the bystanders. Italians are frequently great dramatic actors, as we might expect of the creators of the opera.

The first purpose of the show is to make life acceptable and pleasant. This attitude can be explained largely by the circumstances of history, both natural and manmade, where four active volcanoes, floods, and earthquakes, as well as continuous invasions by outsiders, have created a sense of insecurity. Italians tend to make life's dull and insignificant moments exciting and significant by decorating and ritualizing them. Ugly things must be hidden, unpleasant and tragic facts are swept under the carpet whenever possible, and ordinary transactions are all embellished to make them more stimulating. This practice of embellishing everyday events was developed by a realistic group of people that tends to react cautiously because it believes that catastrophes cannot be averted, only mitigated. Italians prefer to glide elegantly over the surface of life and leave the depths unplumbed (Barzini, 1964).

The devices of spectacle do not exist because of the desire to deceive and bedazzle observers. Often, to put on a show becomes the only way to revolt against destiny and to face life's injustices with one of the few weapons available to a brave people—their imagination. To be powerful and rich, of course, is more desirable than to be weak and poor. However, it has always been extremely difficult for the Italians, both as a nation and individually, to have both power and wealth.

This eternal search for surface pleasures and distractions is accompanied by *garbo*. Although this term cannot be translated exactly, it is the finesse that Italians use to deal with situations delicately and without offense. *Garbo* turns Italian life into a work of art. Italians tend to have a very public orientation, are willing to share a lot, and are used to being on stage at all times.

As this description suggests, many Italians wish to portray a certain image to those around them. This is termed *la bella figura,* or the projection of "a confident, knowing, capable face to the world" (Brint, 1989). The importance attached to impressions is shown in the basic document of the Italian Republic, the Constitution. In the American Declaration of Independence, the first of the self-evident truths is that all men are created equal. In the Italian Constitution, the first basic principle is that "all citizens are invested with equal social dignity" (Levine, 1963). Most Italians would rather sit inside their home than go outside and make a bad impression.

A large number of Italians pursue *la bella figura* through material possessions. Giving a good impression, not only with demeanor but with material wealth, is important. Various explanations have been offered for this tendency, including years of domination by foreign nations, overcrowding in various areas, and natural disasters. Whatever the explanation, it seems that the creation of a show through an eternal search for pleasures and distractions is an attempt to deal with difficult realities of everyday life.

The Italian reliance on spectacle and *garbo* helps people solve most of their problems. Spectacle and *garbo* govern public and private life and shape policy and political designs. They constitute one of the reasons that Italians have excelled in activities in which appearance is predominant. During medieval times, Italian armor was the most beautiful in Europe: It was highly decorated, elegantly shaped, and well-designed, but too light and thin to be used in combat. In war, the Italians preferred the German armor, which was ugly but more practical. Similarly, Rome was made to appear more modern, wealthy, and powerful with the addition of whole cardboard buildings, built like film sets, on the occasion of Hitler's visit in 1938.

Italians believe that "anybody can make an omelette with eggs," but "only a true genius can make one without" (Barzini, 1964). For example, warfare during the Renaissance, as it was practiced outside of Italy, consisted of the earnest and bloody clash of vast armies. He who killed more enemies carried the day. But in Italy, it was an elegant and practically bloodless pantomime. Highly paid leaders of small companies of armed men staged the outward appearance of armed conflict, decorating the stage with beautiful props, flags, colored tents, horses, and plumes. The action was accompanied by suitable martial music, rolls of drums, heartening songs, and blood-chilling cries. The armies convincingly maneuvered their few men back and forth, pursued each other across vast provinces, and conquered each other's fortresses. However, victory was decided by secret negotiations and the offer of bribes. It was, after all, a very civilized and entertaining way of waging war. Although this approach often left matters as undecided as warfare practiced elsewhere, it cost less in money, human lives, and suffering.

The operatic pageantry of Italian life also occurs in the rituals of the Catholic Church. Italians prize these rituals for their pageantry, spectacle, and value in fostering family celebrations rather than for their religious significance. Many Italians view the Church, much like the opera, as a source of drama and ritual, but not authority. Although they do not attend church regularly, the Church still exerts a strong cultural and social influence on their behavior, and almost all Italians identify themselves as Catholics.

Furthermore, the spectacle of Italian life is quite apparent in the area of communications. Italians tend to be skilled conversationalists. Onlookers can frequently follow the conversation from a distance because of the gestures and facial expressions that are employed to convey different emotions. Similarly, one can understand many of the actions that take place in an opera without fully understanding what the actors are singing.

Although Italians tend to be emotional and dramatic, few decisions are influenced by sentiments, tastes, hazards, or hopes, but usually by a careful evaluation of the relative strength of the contending parties. This is one of the reasons that, when negotiating even the smallest deal, Italians prefer to look each other in the face. They read the opponent's expression to gauge his or her position and can thus decide when it is safe to increase demands, when to stand pat, and when to retreat.

Transparent deceptions are employed to give each person the feeling that he or she is a unique specimen of humanity, worthy of special consideration. In Italy, few confess to being "an average man." Instead, they persuade themselves that they are "one of the gods' favored sons" (Barzini, 1964).

The operatic Italians must always project a capable face to the world. Therefore, they prefer to engage only in work that will create the image of confidence and intelligence. In Italy, a middle-class person tends to work only when he or she has a profession, and not while he or she is a high school or university student. In fact, many of the lower-level jobs, such as waiting on tables, are full-time in nature and not readily available to students. In the universities, students specialize immediately in their first year and do not dabble, as is the custom in the United States. However, there is no set term for most university careers (e.g., 4 years devoted to undergraduate work and 3 years to law school), and so many Italians spend more time in school than their American counterparts.

Pageantry and spectacle also apply to business presentations and negotiations. When presenting ideas during such negotiations, a manager should ensure that the aesthetics of the presentation should be clear and exact; he should demonstrate a mastery of detail and language and be well organized. Polish and elegance count for a great deal. However, although pageantry is important in business presentations and negotiations, Italians also tend to expect good-faith bargaining.

Most, if not all, Italians feel that it is infinitely better to *be* rich than to *seem* rich. But if a person or a nation does not have the natural resources necessary to conquer and amass wealth, what is he or she to do? The art of appearing rich has been cultivated in Italy as nowhere else. Little provincial towns boast immense princely palaces, castles, and stately opera houses. Residents of some small coastal villages have completed elaborate paintings on the rocks that can be seen from the sea to give the illusion of wealth and prosperity. In spite of economic difficulties, many Italians wear good clothes, drive shining cars, and dine at expensive restaurants. However, some of these people may have only a few material possessions. Decoration and embellishment are important so that the realities of poverty, uncertainty, and a scantily endowed land can be changed into a spectacle of illusion.

The pageantry of Italian life is highlighted by its lack of a rigid social hierarchy. There is no permanent and rigid class structure in Italy. Rather, there are conditions upon which a person is judged. These include occupation and the amount of authority a person has in that role; education; ancestry; and, in most instances, wealth. However, the major focus is placed upon social behavior. The Italians term this focus *civilta,* or the extent to which someone is acculturated to the norms of the area (Keefe, 1977). These norms include styles of dress, manners, and even participation in the local community.

Position in the social hierarchy can be clearly judged by the amount of respect shown to a person and his or her family by the members of the community. However, respect is also associated with age and family position. A younger person will almost always show deference to older people, just as children show respect for parents.

Inevitably, class consciousness and the social hierarchy will change as a result of industrialization, massive migration to urban areas, low birth rates, an aging population, and the Americanization of Italian youth. However, certain titles still command much respect, such as doctor, lawyer, and professor. Many people feel honored to speak or have affiliations with someone holding such a title and will refer to him or her in a respectful, subordinate manner.

One final example of pageantry is appropriate, especially because it shows how some other cultures are similar to that of Italy (see Chapter 22, "The Spanish Bullfight"). Once a year, in every village and city, there is a celebration in honor of its patron saint (*santo patrono*) in which a parade is featured. The statue of the saint is placed in the lead position in the parade, followed by the clergy, members of the upper classes, and then all other citizens. A celebration follows in the piazza, or town center. This traditional festival and parade help to strengthen the feeling of solidarity and permit people to escape from the regular routine in a dramatic, spectacular, and fun-filled manner.

The reliance on spectacle must be clearly grasped if one wants to understand the Italians. Spectacle helps people solve most of their problems, and it governs public and private life. It is one of the reasons that Italians have always excelled in activities in which impressions are important: architecture, decoration, landscape gardening, opera, fashions, and the cinema.

Voice

Italians tend to believe that their language is the most beautiful one in the world. Much of the beauty of the Italian language derives from the fact that it has a higher proportion of vowels to consonants than all or most languages, which gives it something of a musical effect. Italians put great emotion into their language, speaking with passion, rhythm, and changing tonality. It is the quality of the way people speak that is of utmost importance, and this bias is replicated in the opera in that there are several strikingly different types of voice registers, such as the soprano and the bass. And, like the opera, the sound and cadence of the communication play a role at least equal to the content of what is said in getting the message across. Italians are often much more interested in engaging and entertaining their listeners than in conveying their thoughts accurately.

Perhaps the most difficult operatic singing is associated with bel canto, or beautiful music, introduced by the romantic Italian composer Bellini. This form of music requires extraordinary exertion and ability on the part of the singers, especially when they are singing together to express their thoughts and emotions. Bel canto is so difficult a form of opera that there is only a limited number of singers who can perform it effectively, and only Italian composers have been very successful in this area.

Italians tend to talk louder than many other nationalities, but more so in the south than in the north. At meetings or informal gatherings, individuals talk simultaneously and begin to raise their voices without realizing that they are doing so. Stories are told with passion, anger, and joy. The air in Italy is filled with so many voices that one must frequently talk in a very loud voice to be understood, thereby increasing the total uproar.

Oral communication in Italy is something of a show itself. Speaking is punctuated by elaborate gestures, befitting the Italian operatic tradition. Whatever the section of the country, Italians talk with their hands. Quick, agile, expressive movements of the hands, arms, and shoulders contribute emphasis and sincerity to the spoken words and facial expressions. For instance, a man thinking about buying fish in a market empties his imaginary waist pocket when he is told the price, and walks away without a word (Willey, 1984).

However, the gestures are not, as many believe, unrealistically exaggerated. In fact, the gestures are so realistic that they may be unapparent. The acting of the opera singers, derived directly from the Italian's natural mimicry, contributes to the erroneous impression of excessive exaggeration. In reality, Italian gestures are based on natural and instinctive movements and therefore can be understood by the inexperienced at first sight.

In addition to gestures, Italians sometimes employ flattery and polite lies to make life decorous and agreeable. The purpose is to reduce the turbulence of day-to-day living and to make life more acceptable. Flattery somehow makes the wariest of men feel bigger and more confident, similar to the larger-than-life opera singer. This perspective accounts for the fact that Italians sometimes make promises they know they cannot fulfill. Small lies can be justified in order to give pleasure, provoke emotion, or prove a point. This applies not only to the businessman who swears with soulful eyes that he will deliver his product on a certain day (and does so a month later), but also to men of government cabinet rank. Ministers will promise an appointment, will confirm it and reconfirm it, but on the appointed day, they will find an excuse for evading the appointment. Casualness toward promises is part of accepted Italian behavior.

Contentiousness is generally not far below the surface of the Italian personality. This argumentativeness surprises many because it is discordant with the usual Italian demeanor. Yet the accusatory words shouted by offended drivers, the sidewalk conversations that often sound like arguments, and the tedious monologues by Italians reciting some imagined wrong they have suffered testify to the argumentative side of Italians. For most Italians, controversy is a hobby or a sport, something in which Italians take immense pleasure (Levine, 1963).

Italians are frequently portrayed as joyful people with an operatic song on their lips. This is not completely true. They can also be rather somber, just as many of their operas can end up in death and tragedy. This dark side is emphasized through humor, which tends to be more insulting than witty. Humor generally implies the ability to detach oneself from the object of wit. However, the Italians tend to be passionate people who identify easily with what they are talking about.

Italians make up for this type of humor by analyzing everything around them through conversation. Talking is a great pastime for most Italians, who frequently meet in cafés to discuss the latest news. Privacy is frequently lacking in any Italian community, even though Italians say they mind their own business. Unlike the reserved Englishman, the Italian is apt to tell an acquaintance of a half hour's standing all about his financial status, his family's health problems, and details of his current emotional attachments. The Italian love of conversation as a pastime usually limits the chances of something secret staying so for very long, and it is this love of conversation (and voice) that is intimately related to externalization, the fourth characteristic of the opera.

Externalization

Externalization refers specifically to the fact that feelings and emotions are so overwhelming that the individual cannot keep them to himself or herself, but must express them to others. It also refers to the assumption that the event is more important than the actions of one individual, which is consistent with the Italian reaction to catastrophes and uncertainty described previously. That is, the drama is of more significance to the viewers or community than to the individuals because of its symbolism and generality. This pattern of behavior is the opposite of that of the Anglo-Saxon, which emphasizes that a person should control emotions and not express them or, as the British say, keep a stiff upper lip (see Chapter 14, "The Traditional British House"). At Italian funerals, for instance, there is no shame in showing emotions, and both women and men cry openly and profusely to express what they feel. Similarly, a major victory such as a World Cup championship is accompanied by excessive noise, large gatherings in piazzas, and communal festivities at which everyone talks excitedly and simultaneously. Although there will be some drinking, the Italians do not tend to emphasize this aspect of victory as much as do the English and Americans.

Given their emphasis on externalization, it is generally not wise to ask Italians, "How do you feel?" Unlike Anglo-Saxons, who will usually give a cursory reply, the Italians may well describe in minute detail all of their aches and pains, what the doctors have prescribed for them, and even the most intimate details of any operations they have experienced.

Because of the importance of drama in everyday life, Italians value the piazza as the center of every town and village. It is the stage on which people gather to share conversation and relate experiences. The actions that take place in the piazza are minor dramas of Italian life. Most people do not schedule meetings with others, but everyone knows that gatherings will occur at regular times at the piazza, usually around noon and at 5 or 6 p.m. after work, and it is easy to see old friends and acquaintances and to make new ones. This pattern of strolling (*fare la passeggiate*) is in sharp contrast to the German *Spatziergang*, which occurs primarily on Sunday afternoons. Even in the Italian cities where there is no central piazza, it is well-known that certain avenues serve as substitutes for them, and the villagelike behavior is replicated along them. On these avenues, there are many outdoor cafés at which people meet and greet one another, and sometimes, there are even small, open-air areas with benches that are miniature replicas of the village piazza. As might be expected, Italy has far more bars and restaurants per capita than comparable European nations: 257 inhabitants per café and restaurant in Italy versus 451 for Britain, 795 for France, 558 for Germany, and 778 for Spain (Richard, 1995). A recent Italian doctoral dissertation has emphasized the importance of externalization but changing cultural circumstances by suggesting that the large piazza is more descriptive of southern Italy, whereas bars (and the adjoining small parks) are more descriptive of northern Italy (Venezia, 1997).

Italians tend to be great spectators of life. The show at the piazza can be so engrossing that many people spend most of their lives just looking at it. There are usually café tables strategically placed in such a way that nothing of importance will escape the leisurely drinker of espresso. A remarkable result of this pastime occurred when an old woman died at her window, and 3 days passed before any of her neighbors thought that something might be wrong with the immobile figure.

Foreigners are frequently impressed by the fact that many Italians seem to be doing their jobs with whole-hearted dedication and enthusiasm. This does not mean that these Italians do everything with efficiency, speed, and thoroughness. Rather, they frequently complete their jobs with visible pleasure, as if work were not a punishment. However, when the visitors look closely at the actions of Italians, they realize that many Italians have a theatrical quality that enhances but slightly distorts the actions.

In the opera, the best example of externalization is the crowd scene. There are so many crowd scenes in Italian opera that some writers have identified them as one of its essential characteristics. Members of the crowd represent the chorus for the lead singers, and there is a dynamic interplay between the lead singers and the chorus. This interplay is analogous to the behavioral dynamics in a small village when there is a problem, and everyone comments on it in the piazza.

There is little, if any, private life for most Italians. Everything of importance occurs in public or is at least discussed in public. There is no word for privacy in the Italian language, and information is shared widely. There are some regional differences, in that northern Italians tend to be more reserved than southern Italians. However, once a person is perceived to be a member of the community, it is assumed that he or she will externalize, at least to some degree, when in public.

Business confidentiality can be a problem in Italy. Everyone discusses secret business negotiations with both friends and family as well as the press. Therefore, leaks are common for most large business deals. The media in Italy are volatile and prone to speculation because of people's interest in their neighbors' activities. Hence, ordinary business dramas become the theater with a large audience of spectators.

We have already indicated that dressing is important to Italians because it represents pageantry and spectacle in the form of *la bella figura*. Dressing is also an aspect of externalization, because it is an outward expression of the emotions that Italians feel and want to convey. Italians dress differently in public than at home at least in part because of this reason. In the business environment, clothing is well tailored and sophisticated. Through their clothing, Italians externalize the feeling of confidence.

Many aspects of daily life yield endless opportunities for drama. A well-known example of externalization is Italian driving behavior. In the larger cities, such as Rome and Naples, the drivers blow their horns impatiently, swear at one another, gesture colorfully, and drive in a dramatic and seemingly reckless manner. To an Italian, such behavior is normal because it allows him to communicate with others even when behind the wheel. Even when two drivers get out of their cars to confront one another, they rarely come to blows, although their gestures, body movements, shouts, and torrent of words would lead the onlooker to the conclusion that blood will be spilled. The drama of the occasion is what gives the Italians emotional satisfaction. There is a downside to this feature of Italian life. In 1997, Italy was a leader in road deaths per 100 million kilometers driven: 6,198. To give some perspective to this figure, the average for all nations was 541 (see "Italy's Unruly Drivers," 1999).

Even politics takes on a dramatic and entertaining edge, especially during elections. Television coverage of such events is said to have somewhat of a carnival atmosphere (Brint, 1989). Such an atmosphere reflects the Italian penchant for pageantry, voice, and externalization. And even though the Italian political system is changing radically, as discussed below, we can expect that such drama will continue to be part of the political process.

Feelings and emotions are expressed not only through direct communications but also through subtleties in Italian culture. The Italian history of natural disasters and foreign invasions has created a fear of the unpredictable. This fear can be detected behind the Italians' peculiar passion for geometric patterns and symmetry that can be destroyed easily (Barzini, 1964).

Weddings are considered the highlights of life and constitute an excellent example of externalized behavior. In fact, the wedding scene is quite common in Italian opera. Italians often save for a lifetime to marry their daughters off in an appropriate manner. Guest lists frequently include the entire village. The wedding ritual is often something of a mini-opera, beginning with the bridal party traveling in open automobiles to the church, with relatives and friends following. The success of the wedding ritual is judged by the number of cars, the size of the crowd, and the feast served. Parents are content to spend years of savings and even get into debt in order to correctly carry out the social obligations of a society that may, in the eyes of outsiders, be living at a subsistence level, but that carries on ancient traditions with real satisfaction (Willey, 1984). Throughout the wedding ritual, the emotions of sadness and joy are expressed by all. It is not uncommon for both the bride and her father to be crying while walking down the church aisle.

The family and the extended kinship group are the basic building blocks for externalization. Familial relationships tend to be close and emotional, and the behaviors found in the piazza are replicated within the family. The family is generally seen as one's greatest resource and protection against all troubles. For example, children are critically important, and normally, everything is done for them, even to the extent of satisfying their smallest wishes. Parents often go without comforts to pamper them and to see that they go to school and reach a higher rung on the social ladder. This attitude can be linked directly to the constant influx of foreigners who compete with the Italians for jobs, rapidly changing governments (56 since World War II), and the overwhelming natural disasters that have characterized Italian history. Of course, externalization plays a part in this support, because the family views its children as public expressions of its values and lifestyles.

Furthermore, family connections are often extremely important for handling problems and getting ahead. Outside the family, official and legal authority is frequently considered hostile until proven otherwise. Closeness within the family is transferred to outside relationships and brings a personal edge to most social interactions. This helps to explain why Italians are so demonstrative and why men feel almost no hesitation to show affection to one another.

In the Italian business environment, family contacts tend to be necessary to run a successful company. An example of the importance of contacts is the general lack of hiring policies. Hiring is usually accomplished through personal connections and recommendations. Many corporations select people not on the basis of their skills, but on the basis of their relationship with that person or his or her family. Bond and Smith (1998) have reviewed national preferences for various selection techniques, and Italian business is distinctive in that the interview by itself is the preferred alternative, even though this method by itself has been shown to be the least effective and biased.

The family remains the center and stronghold of Italian life, despite all modern trends, where the role of each member is understood and performed as elaborately as any Italian opera. Although men are the official leaders of the families, and women are subordinate to them, the reality of family life is much more complex. The main character in the family, who might be compared to the lead tenor, is the father. He is in charge of the family's general affairs. But although he holds center stage, his wife is an equally important figure, like the lead soprano. The Italian father may be the head of the family, but the mother is its heart. Yielding authority to the father, she traditionally assumes total control of the emotional realm of the family. The mother usually manages the family in a subtle, almost imperceptible way; she soothes the father's feelings while avoiding open conflicts. However, the woman of the house frequently has the last, unspoken word. The factors that determine the strength of the family are placed in the hands of women. Wives engineer appropriate and convenient marriages, keep track of distant relations, and see to it that everyone does the suitable thing, not for individual happiness, but for the family as a whole. The fact that women form the predominant character of Italian life can be seen through many small signs. For example, popular songs frequently highlight the role of mothers, and in some years, there are more songs devoted to her than to romance. Today, Italy ranks 20th in terms of number of men per 100 women, with a figure of 94.

However, Italy tends to be a man's world, and about 60% of the workforce is still male. When a child is born, the proud parents tie a blue ribbon to the door for a son, but only sometimes do not-quite-so-proud parents of a girl put out a pink ribbon. The principle of male superiority is enforced less strictly in the north than in the south. For example, in some Sicilian villages, unmarried women are supposed to sit indoors during the day when unchaperoned.

Divorce and abortion recently have been legalized in Italy. Legal abortion symbolizes the loosening of individual morals and the breaking of the hold of the Catholic Church over the family. In 1974, civil divorce became legal, but it seems to be more a symbol of social independence than anything else. Not many marriages have actually ended in divorce. For example, only 0.5% of marriages per 1,000 population end in divorce, whereas the comparable figure in the United States is 4.6%. However, the number of separated couples has increased significantly.

Many Italians view divorce as unacceptable because it chips away at the foundation of the family and entire clans. Others argue that it has not increased in popularity due to the fact that, without a husband, most women would be in dire financial straits. This argument is losing merit as industrialization ushers women into the workforce. Divorce, however, is still viewed seriously. If a man leaves his wife, it is not uncommon for the ex-wife to move in with the husband's family, while he is ostracized.

The family frequently extracts everyone's first loyalty. Italians raise their children to be mutually supportive and to contribute to the family. Separation from the family is generally not desired, expected, or accepted easily. Things that create conflict in Italian families may be sources of celebration in other cultures. Some normally joyful events that may cause operatic sadness are a job promotion that necessitates moving away from the family, acceptance into a prestigious university in a foreign land, and getting married (McGoldrick, 1982). Although these experiences may be sources of personal growth for the individual, they are likely to be experienced negatively if they weaken the collective sense of family.

Many Italians view education and vocational training as secondary to the security, affection, and sense of relatedness that the family has to offer. Personal identity tends to be derived primarily from affiliation with the family, not from one's occupation or personal success. One Italian father expressed these thoughts in no uncertain terms when he could not even identify a reason for his daughter's education, given his own success without having taken such seemingly irrelevant courses as calculus (McGoldrick, 1982). Learning is a threat to the family system if it means that a young person will be unduly influenced by outside authorities and perhaps accept work abroad.

Family connections are extremely important for handling problems and getting ahead. Italians, not wanting to work for outsiders, often start their own family business. The business naturally adds to the solidarity of the family. As noted previously, closeness within the family is strong, but family members tend to be much less trustful of those outside it. This helps to explain why Italians, like operatic singers, are emotionally passionate toward friends and extended family.

As noted previously, the north of Italy has been very successful economically, and most of this success is due to the existence of small firms specializing in particular products. Moreover, these firms both compete and cooperate with one another. If one firm cannot honor an order, a neighboring firm will help it produce the product so that the commitment can be kept. At the same time, firms will cut prices to move ahead of neighboring competitors. These types of close business relationships echo family and village patterns that are also expressed in the opera.

For Italians, and especially men, sex is seen as the essential life force (Newman, 1987). Although honor is a quality that all strive to have, virility and potency are still the basis upon which many men are judged. This is confirmed by the fact that an adulterous wife is considered to be a direct reflection of her husband's manliness. The ideal man is not necessarily intelligent or well off, but rather of good character and physically and sexually strong.

Most Italians do not put much faith in what others say. Everyone is considered to be an outsider except members of the family. It is not surprising that the Italians, living as they have always done with the insecurity and dangers of an unpredictable society, are among those who found their main refuge among their blood relatives. This overall fearful, suspicious attitude may be partially due to a quality upon which Italians place high value—cleverness. Because of the constant change and struggle in the country, those who can survive through enterprise, cunning, imagination, and intelligence are held in high esteem by others around them. In other words, those who can create the most imaginative show are admired by many Italians. Minor deceptions, cleverly and subtly executed, are acceptable even if not necessary. Because everyone is trying to outsmart everyone else, the population as a whole is placed on the defensive. Visitors to Italy often comment on this feature of Italian life. For example, it is common practice to shortchange customers. However, if the customer questions the transaction, the correct amount and profuse apologies will be offered immediately and without question.

Whereas the family is the group that, above all else, dramatically influences the individual, another important group, the political party, can be the difference between employment and unemployment. Italians move from group to group, feeling little remorse when doing so because they tend to be skeptical of all groups besides the family. Members of groups often create powerful coalitions that are used for gaining power and influence. These subcultures, groups, and parties allow for intergroup bargaining and dealing to gain coordination and cooperation between all involved.

Similar to Israel, Italy has a political system that, since World War II, has been based on proportional representation from many minor political parties. There are more than 40 parties in the Chamber of Deputies. This system was put into place to guard against the rise of one-party rule, as happened under Fascism. However, it tends to be extremely inefficient, as we might expect when there are 56 changes in government since World War II. Worse, the system tends to be corrupt. The worst example of corruption in Italy's history was exposed beginning in 1992 when a company in Milan refused to give a kickback, a regular business practice that is estimated to add 15% to 20% to the final price. In this instance, public officials vigorously pursued various leads involving large numbers of prominent people. More than 1,200 businesspeople were indicted, and many served prison time, as did several Mafia members and two former prime ministers; some committed suicide in prison. Although these and related activities seemed to weaken the Mafia, even more virulent and violent strains of crime became prominent in the south: the Camorra and the 'Ndranghera.

Italians of many persuasions would like to see the emergence of a genuine two-party system that is normally associated with much less corruption. Still, the sense of family and coalition behavior is so strong in Italy that we can expect many of the behaviors described in this chapter to persist. For example, we can expect that many job referrals and recommendations will still be based at least in part on family connections, much more than in the United States.

Externalization also influences the management style of Italians. There is little delegation of authority or effective communication between the different levels of management in most Italian firms. Employees have little say about decisions concerning the company or about their own work. In fact, superiors are very likely to cut off emotionally the ideas and suggestions of subordinates.

One final example of externalization is somewhat disturbing, in that Italy is experiencing difficulty integrating the large number of legal and illegal immigrants flooding into their country, particularly those from the African nations of Morocco, Nigeria, Senegal, and Tunisia. The poorest Italians are most affected in that they feel that these immigrants are taking jobs away from them. There have been some disturbing events, such as the burning of immigrants and the hanging of a 16-year-old immigrant. Many Italians are upset by this trend and, in true Italian fashion, have externalized it dramatically in newspapers, on television, and in the traditional piazza. Although such outbreaks of violence are common in many societies, these Italians are confronting the problem in an open manner involving everyone in the society, and solutions are gradually being implemented.

Externalization is directly related to the mixing and balancing of diverse elements in both the opera and Italian society. Because the entire community or audience is involved in the unfolding of the drama, several issues and factors come into play that involve numerous individuals. It is not an accident that the Italians have not specialized in one-person stage shows or dramas. Thus, Italy, although primarily stressing individualism, is very oriented toward specific aspects of groupism or collectivism. Even though individuals might not give the country as a whole much consideration, they do place great importance on local and regional affiliation. This is directly related to the next characteristic of the opera, the influence of soloists and the chorus.

Chorus and Soloists

When Italians created the opera around 1600, there were no soloists. The first great Italian composer, Claudio Monteverdi, basically used different parts of the chorus to express the ideas and emotions. However, singers vied with one another for the spotlight, and gradually, soloists became prominent. Today, it is difficult to conceive of an opera without great solo performances, which may help to explain why Monteverdi's operas are so seldom performed. The tension and balance between the chorus and soloists epitomize the struggles between the northern and southern regions, in that each region retains certain easily perceptible characteristics among its inhabitants. Most Italians define themselves by the town where they were born, and there is a sharp contrast between northern and southern Italy. These regional differences are similar to the chorus and soloists in operas. Soloists represent the regional differences in the culture, whereas the chorus is the embodiment of the overall Italian culture. In spite of the fact that there are distinct regional differences, most Italians retain the cultural characteristics described above. Even the Northern League, which for years has advocated splitting Italy into north and south, now focuses its attention on fixing the political system and eliminating corruption, because the 1992 political scandal involved all parts of the country.

The Italian word that expresses the idea of belonging first to a town, then to a region, and finally to a nation is *campanilismo,* which literally means "bell tower." It refers to the fact that people do not want to travel so far as to be out of sight of the piazza church steeple.

Because of industrialization, northern Italians have had the benefit of a thriving economy and a relatively prosperous existence. In contrast, southern Italians, who have relied on farming for their livelihood, have tended to be poorer and less educated. The people from these two regions are similar in that they love life and enjoy creating the illusion of a show. However, the difference between the people from these two regions is that southerners tend to cling to the way of living in the past, whereas many northerners look toward the future.

To most northerners, wealth is the way to ensure the lasting defense and prosperity of the family and close friends. The northerner is perpetually trying to acquire wealth in its various forms. He or she wants a job, a good job, and then a better job. He or she also wants the scientific and technical knowledge that will ensure better paid employment and advancement. On the other hand, most southerners want, above all, to be obeyed, admired, respected, and envied. They want wealth, too, but frequently as an instrument to influence people. The southerner is preoccupied with commanding the respect of the audience throughout the many operas of life. Most southerners, be they wealthy or poor, want the gratitude of powerful friends and relatives, the fear of their enemies, and the respect of everyone. The southerner seeks wealth as a means of commanding obedience and respect from others (Barzini, 1964).

In the south, the culture centers around death. The Italians worry that the operatic drama of life will fall apart when a family member dies. The experience of dying and the fear of not being able to react properly to such an event has forced the southerners to create a complex strategy to enable them to face and conquer death (Willey, 1984). The strategy encompasses hundreds of beliefs, customs, and rituals. The purpose of these rituals is to reestablish contact between the living and the dead, because according to southern beliefs, the family includes both the living and the dead. Each family member has reciprocal rights and duties. The dead have to protect the living, and the living have to keep alive the memory of the dead, and people tend to attach great value to these obligations. Thus, in the early 1980s, a parish priest in one Calabrian village thought he would discourage the long local funeral processions by levying a special fee per kilometer upon the family of the deceased. His bishop promptly transferred him to another part of Italy (Willey, 1984).

This distinction between north and south can be found easily in Italian operas that tend to depict the characteristics of one region or the other. For example, *Cavalleria Rusticana,* by Pietro Mascagni, represents a classic southern opera with its emphasis on humble folk, suspicion, and revenge. On the other hand, *Tosca,* by Giuseppe Verdi, emphasizes the north because it takes place in elegant urban settings in which important personages display more subtle and complex feelings, though no less passionate (and perhaps even more so), than those found among the southerners.

Education has been a major mechanism for bringing about the modernization of Italy and minimizing the regional differences. By diffusing the national culture through the teaching of one Italian language and by raising the literacy levels, Italians have stressed cultural unity and deemphasized regionalism to a greater degree than in the past.

Although many of the differences between "the Two Italies" have been defused and minimized through time, business dealings differ in the two regions. Working with people from northern Italy, a low-context subculture that emphasizes written rules and agreements, is much like dealing with the Americans or Germans. Negotiating effectively with northern Italians essentially means communicating with them in a straightforward, sophisticated manner. Social talk should be kept to a minimum in order to get down to business. When negotiating with people from southern Italy, a high-context subculture in which oral communication and subtle nuances are stressed, a visitor must spend time establishing rapport with his or her counterparts. Long-term relationships are important to southern Italians, and trust must be built up before business dealings become truly effective.

In spite of these subtle differences, most Italians use a collaborative style of negotiating, in that they will continue a dialogue until everyone's needs are met. Part of this style is due to the emotional nature of many Italians. Communication involves much more than words. The emotional nature of such Italians enables them to see past the words spoken to the emotions felt. This insight helps them empathize and understand the needs of those with whom they negotiate. Such aggressive yet emotional Italians want to please everyone, including themselves. Therefore, the collaborative style of negotiating is common throughout Italy.

Similar to the operatic importance of both the chorus and soloists, the regional Italian differences, combined with the overall Italian culture, helped Italy gain economic strength during the 1970s and 1980s. As noted above, this strength of Italy lies in the proliferation of small-scale commercial and industrial enterprises, which are usually run by family. People whose families used to be southern farmers brought their deep-rooted traditions to the north. Some of these traditions and skills enabled many southerners to transition their family from farming into the commercial market. The tradition of keeping ownership within the family, combined with the skills of managing a diverse product mix and a willingness to work long hours, makes the new entrepreneurs able to compete effectively with their European neighbors.

However, Italy is facing major economic problems, and its public debt is still large. Some governments in villages and even large towns do not have the money to manage critical services. To maintain a leading role in the European Union, Italy must change this situation.

The characteristics of the chorus and soloists can also be applied to other aspects of Italian culture. Italians tend to be individualistic people, yet they place importance on the group, and as we have seen, the family is the primary group that influences individuals. Whenever important decisions are made, the individual usually consults with family members to get their opinion and evaluation of the situation. Although the family's opinion is important, the final evaluation is made by the individual. This is similar to the relationship between the chorus and soloists in the opera. The chorus frequently gives the soloists the facts and opinions about the drama unfolding on stage, yet the soloists are the ones who dramatically decide how to handle the peril or situation.

The influence of the group is also felt in the business environment. In business meetings, people will externalize their feelings and opinions about a subject. They will listen to everyone's ideas and freely give their own opinions. Business meetings tend to be very productive in Italy because of the openness displayed by everyone. However, like the chorus and soloists, the decisions coming out of a meeting are frequently made by one or two dominant and/or domineering people. In spite of the influence of the group, Italians tend to be aggressive and materialistic individualists because of their bias toward spectacle and externalization.

Furthermore, the vocal sections of the chorus are directly comparable to the many regional variations of the Italian language. Although each section is important to the harmony of the chorus, each has its own melody. The Italian history of invasions has produced many dialects, each the product of the particular regional invader. The language of Italy consists of both local dialects and Italian, a derivative of the Tuscan language. Although linguistic variations are disappearing, to some extent because of the homogenizing effects of television and telecommunications, Italians still cling to the notion of having their own regional dialect.

In the opera, there is inherent inequity in the amount of fame given to each of the soloists. The same is true in the Italian economy. Today, poverty still exists in some areas, particularly in the south. Italian industry has become increasingly successful, but success is not shared equally by everyone. Because northern companies believe that there is a difference in the northern and southern work ethic, they are reluctant to locate branches in the south. The large migration of workers from the south to the north has left behind people who are not willing to give up customs and traditions that have been followed since early European civilization.

Although the Italian culture consists of many regional subcultures, the modernization of Italy has begun to unify these subcultures. The Italian culture is changing continuously into one where the melody of the regional soloists blends together into a harmonic chorus, as the political reforms described above confirm.

In this chapter, we have not explicitly treated the Italian orientation toward time, space, and the other culture-general concepts (see Chapter 1). As the discussion of the piazza suggests, Italians tend to be more polychronic than monochronic, performing many activities simultaneously. In Geert Hofstede's (1991) study of the cultural values of 53 countries, Italy clusters with those countries emphasizing a large power distance between groups in society. In other words, Italians tend to accept the fact that some groups are and perhaps should be more powerful than others, and they act accordingly. Italians also try to avoid risk and uncertainty in everyday life, preferring friends over strangers and familiar over new or strange situations, as their behavior in the piazza and externalization would confirm. And although the family and kinship are important to Italians, Italy tends to cluster with those countries that are more accepting of individualism and aggressive, materialistic behavior, all of which reflect Italians' externalized bias.

This, then, is Italy. It is still a grand and larger-than-life society whose citizens love pageantry and spectacle, emphasize a range of voices in everyday life, externalize emotions and feelings, and feel a commitment to the town and region of the country in which they were born. Italians have had a difficult history. The institutions have changed, rulers have come and gone, and people have to survive. And people do survive, thanks to their personal, unofficial relationships. In Italy, life is the theater, with each act carefully played out for everyone to witness. From this perspective, the opera is not only helpful but possibly essential for understanding Italian behavior and culture.

CHAPTER 19

Belgian Lace

It is clear that while the diversity of the cultures alive in Belgium may sometimes be a source of friction, this same diversity can and must also be, above all, a source of spiritual and material enrichment.

For this very reason, and because Belgium is the common ground where two great European cultures meet, we must continue to be what we have always been in the past: pioneers in the construction of a united Europe.

—The late King Baudouin,
1986 Christmas radio/TV message

Belgium is a small country slightly larger than the state of Maryland, with slightly more than 10 million people. The distance between its farthest points is 175 miles. Given Belgium's size and population, the casual observer should be careful not to underestimate its high degree of importance and interrelatedness in Europe and the world. Just as the gifted lacemaker takes fine threads from many spindles and weaves them into a fabric with a beautiful but strong pattern, so, too, have history, geographic position, and religion woven the Belgian culture into a diverse and complicated design. To understand Belgium, it is helpful to describe it in terms of the metaphor of lace.

Before doing so, however, let us explore its turbulent and fascinating history. For hundreds of years, the people of Belgium, both the Flemish (of Dutch ancestry) in the north and the Wallonians (of French ancestry) in the south, were ruled by a number of other nations. Over the past 500 years, at one time or another, Austria, Spain, France, and the Netherlands all ruled the area where Belgium now exists. Although there were indigenous nationalistic movements that sought to create the nation of Belgium, it was the machinations of Lord Palmerston, arguably the most influential foreign affairs minister that Britain has ever produced, that led to its establishment in 1830. He wanted to create a buffer zone between the Germans and the French in the event of war between these two nations and, in the process, to provide England with some breathing space before she was forced to enter any conflict. Lord Palmerston's instincts were unerringly correct, because Belgium was the site of some of the bloodiest battles in both World War I and World War II, and without this buffer zone, it is conceivable and even probable that Germany would have overwhelmed both the French and the English (Tuchman, 1962).

The Flemish and Wallonian cultures have existed side by side until they have developed a sense of "Belgian pride." At multinational or world-class competitions, a Belgian is a Belgian, and the entire country unites to watch the performance, regardless of the side of the language border on which the participant or team originated.

Still, it cannot be denied that there are conflicts and tensions between the Wallonians and the Flemish. Unlike many other cultural groups living in one nation or area who escalate these differences into bloody confrontations and war—for example, the fighting between the Catholics and Protestants in Northern Ireland, or that among the Croatians, Bosnians, and Serbians in the former Yugoslavia—the Wallonians and the Flemish have addressed their differences patiently and in a systematic way since 1968. In 1993, the country established three independent and separate parliaments within the three major regions of Wallonia, Flanders, and Brussels. The central government has relinquished much of its power, except in such areas as finance, defense, and international relations. Admittedly, this solution to ethnic and regional tensions is complex and has led to some bewildering outcomes. In Brussels, the capital, some streets receive only Flemish-language cable TV, whereas adjoining streets receive only French. Belgium's embassies abroad have three separate commercial attachés. And even though this solution to governing and ethnic tension may seem contrived and unduly complicated, it is far preferable than the alternative of war and destruction. As *The Economist* aptly pointed out ("Belgium: Fading Away," 1992), Belgium "deserves a clap" for avoiding the mindless ethnic wars and destruction from which other nations suffer so grievously (p. 52). Still, there is a serious movement among some prominent Wallonians to argue for national disintegration so that the Flemish region can unite with the Netherlands and possibly parts of France and Germany ("Could Flanders Be Reinvented?" 1997). Whatever the eventual outcome, Belgium serves as a very useful model that other nations with diverse cultural groups can study and at least partially follow to avoid such alternatives, and this model closely resembles our metaphor of Belgian lace.

Lace first appeared in the late 15th century in Flanders and Italy. It was originally used as a modest ornament for undergarments. By approximately 1600, lace had become a fabric of utmost luxury and a key article of trade and commerce. Nobility from all over Europe began to enhance their clothing with lappets and cuffs of lace. Dresses were soon adorned with lace overlays and shawls. Beyond clothing, lace began to drape tables, windows, and bed linens. Lace was a sign of social status and wealth. As a lacemaking center, Flanders established itself as a prominent industrial region within Europe.

Bobbin lace, first introduced in Flanders, requires the weaver to manage hundreds of bobbins in creating a single piece of lace. Systematically and rhythmically, the threads from the 10-20 sets of bobbins are braided around brass pins skillfully affixed to a cardboard pattern to form a geometric or pictorial design. The design incorporates a delicate balance of lace and space that is best exhibited when the lace is placed on a dark background fabric, such as deep-colored velvet or satin. During the Renaissance, lacemaking emerged as both an industry and an art form, as the following passage confirms:

> Form became more important than color; instead of intricate effects of limitless expansion, designers stressed clarity, symmetry, and stability. In the decorative arts, the new spirit was most noticeably expressed in sharp distinctions between pattern, background, and frame. No minor art form embodied Renaissance ideals more fully than lace. (Benton, 1970, Vol. 13, p. 85)

Traditionally, the best lacemakers were cloistered nuns. To create a square foot of lace with an intricate design may require hundreds or even thousands of hours. Legend has it that some nuns would spend their entire lives producing lace for the Pope's robes. Although lace is no longer a predominant industry in Belgium, and machine-produced lace is the norm, the Belgians still take great pride in this traditional art form; most homes have at least one piece of handwoven lace on a table or displayed in a frame.

Many Belgians can hold up a piece of lace and tell if it was handwoven or machine-made, what the relative retail value of the piece should be, and from which region of the country the piece came. The texture and pattern of the lace have regional characteristics. For instance, in Brugge and Turnhout, the texture is delicate and the patterns are ornate, whereas in St. Hubert, the thread is coarse and the design more simple. Hence, lace from Brugge might typically be used as a table runner between meals, and lace from St. Hubert might adorn the edge of the tablecloth used during a meal.

A Land of Contrasts

The beauty of lace can be appreciated fully only when the contrast of woven cloth and dark background is recognized within the overall form. Just as lace interweaves contrasting elements of a complex design into a single structure, so, too, are there many contrasting elements interwoven in Belgium, a small country that includes three recognized languages, two major cultures, three separate official regions, three flags, two major economic centers with separate industries, and three unique geographic landscapes. The starkest contrasts for Belgium are linguistic and political. In addition, other areas of contrast include the following:

- The struggle between individualism and the need to belong to a group, conform to societal rules, and have strong family ties

- The dichotomy between working and social welfare

- The stark difference between urban and rural areas

- The desire for art and beauty, but also practicality

Still, just as a lacemaker integrates contrasting designs in the masterpiece, the Belgian government attempts to integrate separate cultures into a unified republic, even when there are three separate parliaments in each of the three major regions. Linguistically, the Belgian government recognizes three native languages through regulations regarding the conduct of education and commerce within the areas populated primarily by native speakers. In Flanders, the northern portion of the country that borders the Netherlands, business and education are conducted primarily in Dutch, which is the native language of the Flemish people, and they represent about 60% of the Belgian population. In Wallonia, the southern portion of the country that borders France, business and education are conducted primarily in French, which is the native language of the Wallonian people, and they constitute about 34% of the Belgian population. In Limburg, a very small area bordering Germany with about 1% of the population, German is the native language. To be impartial and economically viable, in the capital city of Brussels, merchants, educators, government officials, and others conduct business in Dutch, French, or English, at the mutual preference of the participants.

Brussels is at the crossroads of Europe, and many multinational firms have established European offices in it in recent years because of the unification of the European Community in 1992. At any given time, about 5% of the population of Belgium are foreigners.

In Belgian schools, children are first required to study the native language of the region in which they live for at least 8 years. They are also required to study a second language, which could be Dutch, French, English, or German, for at least 4 years. It is not uncommon to meet a Belgian, usually a Fleming, who is proficient in each of the four languages and others. However, Belgians are very proud of their native languages and cultures. If two headstrong Belgians, a Fleming and a Wallonian, have to communicate, they will usually defer to English, because the Wallonian will probably not be able or want to speak Dutch, and the Fleming will not condescend to speak French to a Wallonian.

In everyday life, the impact of these linguistic differences varies significantly and may not be encountered at all by those who reside deep within Flanders or Wallonia. By contrast, Belgians living closer to the language border or in Brussels must deal with language differences daily. Belgians tend to appreciate the use of their languages and will generally warm up to outsiders more quickly if an attempt is made to learn at least one of them. Although many Belgians deal with the language differences every day, it is in poor taste for a foreigner to point out the differences or to wonder aloud why the differences cannot be resolved through diplomacy.

The oldest Catholic university in the world, the University of Leuven, located 20 miles east of Brussels in Flanders, illustrates the consequences of the language conflict. For hundreds of years, the university served both Flemish and Wallonian students and scholars, using French as the official language on campus. After World War II, linguistic tensions began to mount, causing tensions between student groups and sporadic scuffles in cafés around the university. Over a period of 20 years, the hostility evolved to the point that the university was divided into two campuses—one in Leuven (Flanders) and one on the other side of the language border in Wallonia. This separation divided not only students and faculty, but also resources, such as the library collection. Books were literally divided by title, with those in the first half of the alphabet staying in Leuven and those in the second half going to the new campus. Conducting research now necessitates visiting two campuses, but this cumbersome and inefficient solution is preferable to a long-standing linguistic conflict.

As an extension of the dual languages and cultures of the Flemish and Wallonians, the country has three prominent flags: the tricolor of black, yellow, and red, representing the Belgian country; the Flemish lion; and the Wallonian rooster. Most Belgians identify more emotionally with the flags of their respective cultures than the tricolor flag of the nation. The Flemish lion is the symbol of the Flemish resistance to French domination over hundreds of years.

Although regional and ethnic identification is clearly important, Belgians do identify themselves as Belgian when outside the nation, and they come together on critical social issues. For example, 300,000 Belgians—the equivalent of 7.7 million Americans—rallied against the seemingly careless and perhaps corrupt manner in which the judiciary handled a case involving a pedophile ring that had chillingly killed four young girls.

As we have seen, politically, Belgium is a constitutional monarchy divided into three republics: Flanders, Wallonia, and Brussels. Each republic has its own representatives in the central government, or national parliament, and its own divisions of the national political parties, which are also divided into subparties by language. Each subparty operates autonomously, yet generally follows the same political agenda as the parent party.

The two largest political parties are the Christian People's Party, whose members are primarily Flemish and Catholic, and the Socialist Party, whose members are less strict Catholics and non-Catholics and more heavily Wallonian. These two parties are also responsible for publishing most of the major newspapers in Belgium (five of seven) and supervising social facilities for youth, sports confederations, care of the aged, hospitals, savings banks, and unions. Well over 50% of all workers are union members. The successful administration of the trade unions and other social programs is heavily dependent on social stability. Because of the extensive influence of these two political parties in the life of the average Belgian, other political parties have not gained a significant foothold. Although all Belgians are required to vote in every election, they are free to vote for candidates of any political group.

Furthermore, Belgians tend to be very individualistic. Hofstede's (1991) cross-cultural study ranked Belgians as eighth out of 53 nations on this dimension. It is considered a major accomplishment for a young adult to become established in his or her own house, apart from the family. Hard work is also valued because it is seen as providing an incentive for individuals to branch away from the home. Still, even when the young leave the immediate family, they do not venture far geographically, usually living within 30 miles of their parents' home. This practice creates a strong family/community tie, essentially enhancing the family orientation of the Belgians.

Belgian individualism is also displayed in their preference for owning their homes. Despite the great expense, nearly 65% of Belgians own the place where they live, which ranges from condominiums to suburban country homes. A person's home is his or her castle, and Belgians tend to take great pride in the cleanliness of their homes. Early in the morning, it is common to see people sweeping their porches and walkways. Whereas an American might use a garden hose to wash down a sidewalk, a Belgian would typically use a bucket and a scrub brush. This preference may be traceable to the historical shortage and high cost of fresh water. Belgians also tend to take very short baths; use soapy water to wash the dishes and then wipe the soap off with a towel, rather than rinsing the dishes with water; and drink soda water, juice, beer, or wine rather than tap water or anything made with tap water.

Just as each region of Belgium has a distinctive style and texture to its lace, so, too, are condominiums and row houses often organized and decorated very distinctively, reflecting the tastes of their owners. Unlike England's traditional houses (see Chapter 14), the interior layout of a Belgian row house cannot be assumed from its exterior appearance. In Flanders, it is common for extended families to gather together to construct the exterior brick walls of a new or remodeled home.

Even though Belgians tend to be individualistic, their family orientation is strong. The family plays a central role in daily life. Family activities and meals are highly cherished. Most Belgian children go home after a long day at school, do their homework, eat dinner, help with chores, and spend time with their family. Family time often includes reading or watching television. On TV, they can see programs broadcast in French, Dutch, German, and English, usually with subtitles in a second language. Because the state owns the Belgian television stations, there are very few commercials.

On the weekends, many Belgian children participate in scouting programs. Sunday lunch is usually the biggest meal of the week. The meal will normally take place at the same relative's house every Sunday, and family from the immediate area will all attend. If a husband and wife live close to both in-laws, they will frequently rotate Sundays between the two families.

Mothers often work. Out of a total workforce of about 3 million, about 900,000 are women; however, they are typically found in traditionally female occupations, such as nursing and secretarial jobs. Few have completed a university education or occupy top management positions. Day care is subsidized heavily by the state.

Families often spend weekends and vacations together, traveling to the Belgian coast for short stays, and to Spain or the Riviera for longer stays. In the warm months, camping in the Ardennes mountains in southeast Belgium is a frequent pastime.

When a couple marry, the woman takes the name of the man and connects it with her maiden name, so that if she was a Smith and married a Jones, her married name would be Mrs. Jones-Smith. Especially in Wallonia, it is not uncommon for a couple to live together until the woman becomes pregnant with their first child, at which time the couple will revert to Catholic tradition and get married in the church. Because of the Catholic influence, divorce is rare and is recognized only after years of separation. However, the economy, more than the Catholic Church, has influenced the size of families. The socially correct family size is two children, and a family has received a perfect gift from God if the two children are a boy and a girl.

In the family, it is typical for the father and the eldest son to be the ultimate decision makers. Mothers usually administer discipline and rule household matters. Since about 1970, much has been done to emancipate women through legislation and political decision making. Although legal equality has been mostly achieved, it will take time to eradicate the convictions and prejudices that have been nurtured for so many years. Moreover, the gender-based segregation of half of the country's elementary classes (primarily in parochial schools) reinforces the traditional view of a woman's role (Verleyen, 1987, pp. 189-192).

Aside from family, over their lifetimes, the average Belgians will have only a few truly close friendships. Unlike the United States, where people tend to be very quick to establish friendships, the Belgians generally require a great deal of time before relationships mature. Most people with whom Belgians interact regularly will remain simply acquaintances, although they may have known each other for years (see also Chapter 10, "The German Symphony").

Belgians normally hold sacred their right to privacy and their own opinions. Just as lacemakers have a range of motions within which they pull from their bobbins and weave their threads around the brass pins, so, too, do the Belgians seem to have similar ranges in their varied activities. Still, a Belgian rarely strays far from the group by taking an extreme position. Generally, Belgium is a country of consensus, compromise, and cooperation. However, eccentric artists are revered as the embodiment of the eternal voice of protest, as long as they are not hostile or confrontational. For the individual, however, exclusion from the group can entail loneliness, pain, and, more often than not, material poverty (Verleyen, 1987, p. 119).

Overarching the individualism of each Belgian is a set of common political rules that has governed public policy and conduct for decades. These rules are as follows:

- The monarchy and Brussels are untouchable; in other words, all else could change, but there should still be a monarchy and Brussels should still be the capital.

- The European unification and the European Union are to be advocated without any reservation.

- The authority of NATO and the American ally may be the subject of frequent criticism, but they also enjoy the privilege of inviolability.

- Prosperity is to be shared and not to be used as a justification for confrontation or class struggle.

- Labor strikes should not be allowed to jeopardize the existing economic order.

- Privacy and personal liberty are not to be impeded in any serious ways. (Verleyen, 1987, pp. 147-150)

The varied types of occupations and pastimes enjoyed by the Belgian population present yet another area of contrast. Belgium has a long tradition of agricultural activity. The central area around Brussels has rich soil and flat terrain conducive to farming, yet only 3% of the workforce is agricultural. Also, less than 10% of the gross national product comes from farming, and the population is increasingly concentrated in the urban areas and engaged in industrial and service activities. Nevertheless, Belgians vigorously defend and subsidize their traditional agricultural base. And, although Belgium has the 16th highest population density among nations—332 per kilometer—urban planning has helped to ensure that most urban areas are pleasant.

In the past few years, a great debate has raged over national subsidies to the mining and steel industries located particularly in the Wallonian region. Many believe that there is no prospect of these industries ever regaining their former status or profitability. Many assert that governmental support should be rechanneled to help expanding industries where Belgium can compete in the EU and worldwide.

The contrasting fortunes of the north and south of Belgium have undergone a dramatic change over the past century. In 1830, French was the official language of the Belgian kingdom. The nobility spoke French; government proceedings and church services were conducted in French; and the wealthiest citizens, Wallonians, spoke French. Therefore, French came to be perceived as the cultured language. Conversely, the Flemish were perceived as the uncultured and poorer members of Belgian society. As fortunes shifted from the coal and steel industries in Wallonia to the shipping and international trade industries of Flanders, the Flemish found themselves in a position to demand recognition of their language and cultural heritage. Over the past decade, Flanders has continued to prosper, whereas most of Wallonia has been devastated by unemployment, which averages more than 15%, and depression.

Belgians must attend school from age 6 to age 18. Programs are very rigorous, and most children have at least 2 hours of homework every night after 8 hours of school. To pass from one level of education to the next, each student must take an exam. The results of the exams determine which schools the student may attend and what vocation the student may undertake. As in Germany, students begin studying for a vocation in their early teens. By the time they come out of secondary school, most begin internships in their chosen vocations or go straight into college. Belgians are highly educated and skilled craftspeople. Thus, the high rates of unemployment are very disconcerting and depressing for many of them.

In general, Belgians are very hardworking people, just like the lacemaker who may work nearly 1,000 hours on a intricate piece of lace that measures only one square foot, investing not only time but pride in the quality of her work. Because of the great pride that they take in their work and craftsmanship, regardless of how depressing the prospects of long-term unemployment might be, many Belgians would prefer to draw unemployment rather than do menial work below their level of training or skill. Therefore, immigrants from Third World countries are viewed as necessary to correct a temporary labor imbalance. Typically, immigrants are brought in from North Africa and Turkey to work in the mines and do other menial jobs that Belgians reject. These immigrants are given access to many of the social programs, such as medicine and government welfare, but they are ineligible to vote and are rarely allowed to become citizens. Although Belgians tend not to welcome Third World foreigners warmly, antiracism legislation makes discriminatory public expressions against immigrants punishable by law. Furthermore, although the Belgians feel that Third World immigrants are needed only temporarily, long-range forecasts show that the Belgian population is shrinking because of low birth rates and emigration, whereas the immigrant population is increasing. As mentioned earlier, social tradition has led most Belgian families to have two or fewer children despite the fact that the Catholic-influenced legal system prohibits abortion and most forms of birth control.

Overall, Belgians believe that people have a need and desire to work. In an effort to minimize unemployment, there has been an effort to reduce the workweek, thus allowing a few more workers into industry. Retirement age is already set at 60 years, and all Belgians have at least 4 weeks of vacation per year paid by the government. The call to reduce working hours further, and even radically, is related to a strong belief in trade union circles that the redistribution of available work will help force down unemployment rates (Verleyen, 1987, p. 231). Thus, it is not surprising that Belgium ranks 42nd of the 50 nations with the lowest percentage of the population in the workforce, at 42%; the lowest percentage is 26, in Iran.

Today, most Belgians are very forward thinking in their economic activities and are moving heavily into service and diplomatic industries in response to their native skills and worldwide economic demands.

Another sharp and abrupt contrast is between urban and rural settings. The Belgian countryside is green and lush because of the abundant rainfall and high humidity throughout the year. As one drives through Belgium, long stretches of rolling green hills with little white farmhouses can be seen. The older farmhouses have the barn on the first floor, and the family lives upstairs; the farmer with his large workhorse plowing his field is a frequent sight. At times like these, it is hard to imagine that Belgium ever entered the 20th century.

The cities typically appear as medieval fortresses, many with a wall surrounding them, preventing the gentle fall from urban to suburban to rural. There are no American-style suburbs in Belgium. An aerial view at night would show roughly circular areas of dense lights surrounded by thin networks of lights along major highways and a few spots of light in rural areas. This view might resemble the contrasting lace made around Brussels, which has densely woven patches delicately connected by threads to other densely woven patches.

Inside the cities, one finds further contrasts between the modern industrial facilities and the grandeur of the older architecture. In Brussels, the Atomium, a large structure constructed during a recent world's fair, resembles a giant silver atom. It has elevators that will take visitors up for a view around the city. The NATO buildings, among others, are modern and efficient. By contrast, the Brussels town square, The Grand Place, is surrounded by cobblestone streets and buildings with ornately carved facades, and it draws the visitor back to the city's origins in the 16th century.

A final area of contrast in Belgian culture is that between their love for art and beauty, and their sense of practicality. Obviously, most lace is beautiful and artistic, but it is also designed to adorn clothing and linens rather than to be simply admired. The artistic history of the country is evidenced by the prominence of museums, theaters, and artistic venues. In Belgium, there seems to be a museum for everything. The largest is the open-air museum at Bokrijk. Rural buildings from various centuries have been excavated from all over the Belgian area and painstakingly rebuilt here. Many retirees dress up in the authentic costumes of the times and display the tools and crafts of the era from which the buildings come.

The Rijksmuseum in Antwerp has one of the finest collections of Flemish artists in the world. Flemish art was the world standard from the 16th through the early 18th centuries. Exemplified by Brueghel, the van Eycks, and Rubens, Flemish art started with the vivid colors and figures of the Italian Renaissance, but made the people less elongated, plumper, and more realistic. Typical signs that a painting comes from the Flemish era are the presence of lace, on the clothing in portraits or on the table in a still life, and rosy red cheeks.

Inside many of the oldest churches in Belgium, one can find wonderful works of art, most with no apparent security systems attached. For example, it is not uncommon to locate a work by Rubens, van Eyck, or van Dyck hanging in an obscure village church where the doors are never locked. Some of these churches appear old and worn on the outside, but inside, they have beautifully carved vestries and pedestals for the priests to stand on while preaching. Hung around the inside walls of the church are works of art representing the 12 stations of the cross. Most of the churches were constructed so that the lighting is primarily natural and from candles. The art here was created to inspire the worshiper rather than simply to be admired, so the concept that someone might steal these works from the churches is absurd to the average Belgian. The oldest churches are all Catholic, each having a statue of the Virgin Mary with blazing little white candles all around her. When Belgians, even nonpracticing Catholics, are troubled by work or family matters, one will frequently hear them tell how many candles they have lit for Mary.

The study of art history is supported strongly by the school system. Schoolchildren flood the museums throughout the school year for lectures and sightseeing. Early lessons stress the importance of Belgian artists, nearly to the exclusion of others. This emphasis on art is initiated at a very young age and is carried forward throughout most Belgians' lives. In Belgium, painting seems to be an essential part of the culture, and many Belgians like to describe themselves as a nation of painters. Such pride is understandable, given the nation's illustrious history in this area.

Another example of Belgian practicality is the site where the Battle of the Bulge was waged in World War II. This battle was a major victory for the Allied forces and has been a major tourist attraction for many years. The site is marked by a large circular monument with pillars listing the names of the dead in that battle, resembling a modern Stonehenge. The monument is surrounded by rolling hills that, during tourist season, are meticulously covered with rows of white crosses to mark the resting places of the dead. After tourist season (September through April), the crosses are removed, and cows are pastured on the hills.

Control

Lace production requires strict and complex controls to avoid needless flaws. In addition, there must be balance between the spindles and the thread, and between the patterns in the cloth. This emphasis on controls and balance is similarly found in the Belgian preference for controlling behavior, interacting with friends and colleagues in familiar situations and surroundings, and leading balanced lives. In Hofstede's (1991) cross-cultural study of 53 nations, Belgium ranked sixth in terms of avoiding uncertainty. There are several areas where Belgians tend to exhibit this high degree of control and uncertainty avoidance, including lifestyle, transportation, social conventions, rules and procedures, and stress management. Belgians are very regulated and suspicious of anyone who would change their adopted schedule or routine. Most Belgians have a deep-rooted attachment to what is called a "3 × 8" time schedule: 8 hours for work, 8 hours for play, and 8 hours for sleep. Modern management proposals to change the organization of work so as to increase industrial output are frequently opposed. Many who own their own small businesses work longer hours, but they also tend to live over their shops, so they are never far from home and family. Most shops and businesses are closed on Sunday, but because the Catholic Church changed its policy to allow parishioners to attend high mass on Saturday evening, more Belgian businesses now have Sunday hours.

To avoid uncertainty, the political and linguistic borders are well-defined and mapped. A savvy traveler can usually determine which region he or she is in by the first reference on the city and street signs. However, this can all be very confusing to the unaware, because a sign may list two or more names for the same place, such as Antwerpen (Dutch), Anvers (French), and Antwerp (English). In the city, most maps and signs will say Antwerpen. However, if the map consulted came from Wallonia or France, the city will be marked as Anvers.

Belgium has several large ports, including Antwerp, which is the second largest port in Europe. To accommodate the huge amount of trade from its port cities, Belgium has designed the most immense transportation system in the world for a country its size. Like the threads in a piece of lace, the highways, railways, and canals in this system connect every city and village in the country, allowing goods to flow efficiently all over Belgium and into the rest of Europe.

Major roads are constructed in a hub-and-spoke fashion. There are usually roads encircling larger cities with spokes extending out toward other major cities. These highways have many signs and directions in various languages designed to accommodate industry and travelers. As one drives along the spokes from one city to another, the name of the road will change halfway between the cities. If one takes the Mechelen road from Brussels to get to Mechelen, halfway to Mechelen the name of the road will change to the Brussels road, indicating that the traveler is now closer to Mechelen than Brussels. Changing road signs can severely complicate the trip of the inexperienced traveler, especially when the languages change. However, this practice is very orderly to the Belgian mind, just as the pattern and texture of a piece of lace is set by its origin.

As one drives over the cobblestone roads of the inner city and the occasional dirt roads in the country, there are no stop signs. It is assumed at every intersection that the driver to the right has the right of way, no matter what the circumstances. Therefore, technically, at every intersection, the driver need look only to the right before proceeding, and the Belgians will sometimes grow quite impatient with a traveler who stops to look in all directions before proceeding.

One of the most interesting jobs keeping some Belgians away from the unemployment office is that of road worker. Many of the city streets are paved with cobblestones. To maintain these streets, road crews can be seen working on a small area at the side of the road, digging up the cobblestones, placing them in a pile, cleaning them carefully, and then relaying them. However, the stones are not simply replaced in a haphazard fashion. Rather, they are relayed in an orderly pattern similar to the manner in which lace is arranged, often with some artistic, geometric design. Hence, this job, although superficially menial, appeals to the Belgian sense of industry, beauty, and practicality.

In social settings, Belgians are generally very formal in their interactions with others and employ a number of explicit rules. For instance, when greeting others, the surname is the proper way to address all others except very close friends. The casual manner in which first names are used in many countries would probably offend most Belgians. This formality is common in business and social settings, even with neighbors and acquaintances.

Formal titles are used in many business and social settings in lieu of the full name; for example, Monsieur or *Mijneer* for a man, Madame or *Mevrow* for a married woman, and Mademoiselle or *Jevrow* for a single woman. Titles are also used in many subordinate-superior relationships, such as student to professor or employee to boss. Both the French and Dutch languages incorporate formal and informal manners in which a person can be addressed. Informal address is used when addressing a child, but adults generally need to know one another well before communicating in this way. Among younger people and in business with English-speaking partners, however, there is less formality, and it is common to use first names.

Greetings are also an extremely important part of the social ritual. Handshakes are the norm unless the two parties are good friends. A person will typically shake hands with everyone during the greeting and again before leaving the meeting or event. Belgians will often lament if they do not have a chance to shake hands before parting. In addition, women greeting either men or women in an informal manner will generally kiss three times on alternating cheeks.

Belgians are very conscious of social rituals, such as gift giving. Gifts are given at any type of social visit, and not to do so would be seen as rude. A typical gift when one is invited to dinner would be flowers, a small box of chocolates, or an unusual fruit, such as a pineapple. If the visit were to extend to a number of days, it would be common practice to offer a gift for each day spent. Acknowledgments and thanks are made in writing for any gift received, even birthday and holiday cards. In Belgium, New Year's cards are sent in lieu of Christmas cards.

Almost all social gatherings are somewhat formal. When alcoholic beverages are served, it is customary to wait until everyone is served and then, with some ceremony, to raise one's glass to each person in turn, catching his or her eyes and wishing him or her *gezondhiet, santé,* or the like. Similarly, it is customary to wait for everyone at the table to be served before eating. Just before taking the first bite of food, everyone says *smaaklijk,* or *bon appétit,* thus wishing everyone else a tasty meal. Invitations are frequently sent to dinner guests, even to close friends, and a formal, four-course meal is normally prepared. Afternoon tea can also be a formal event. People, including close friends and family, seldom drop by another's house without first telephoning. Neighbors also observe this protocol, maintaining a high level of formality when interacting. All of this formality, however, does not keep Belgians from visiting each other. They normally love to socialize; they just like to plan ahead when someone is coming. Their plans often include going to the bakery on the corner to get a special dessert to serve with tea, which may be traditional tea or herbal tea.

When one enters a Belgian home, there is generally an unheated entryway with stone or linoleum flooring where coats are hung and wet shoes are kept. By contrast, the living area of the house is generally warm and cozy. Thoughts of putting on a cold coat and wet shoes may explain why guests stay so long on winter nights.

Belgians tend to require certainty and privacy in social settings as well as in everyday life. In Belgium, almost every door has a lock. In a home or a business, this means that even cabinets and closets can be locked. A homeowner may need 50 keys to guarantee privacy and security. In the older buildings of the University of Leuven, there is even a light above the professor's closed office door. When a student wants to see the professor, he must ring a bell, in response to which the professor activates the light's color to indicate whether the student should come in (green), wait a few minutes (yellow), or go away (red). Although this may seem extreme, it appeals to the Belgian sense of practicality.

Certainty is also highly desirable in social agreements. For a Belgian, his word is his bond, and promises must be kept. However, beneath all of the formal rituals and procedures, the Belgian people tend to be quite friendly, laid-back, and good natured. To see this side of their personality, one can go to a local pub and observe the closeness of the relationships and abundant consumption of beer. Beer is not only a cherished drink but also a source of pride for Belgians. Most Belgian cities have at least one brewery, and the smell of the hops hangs in the damp winter air. Belgians will make beer out of almost any grain, and wine out of almost any fruit. Thus, it is not surprising that many Belgians can differentiate between many different types of beer. Like lovers of fine wine, they enjoy drinking beer immensely, not to quench their thirst, but to savor the aroma and taste of the beer itself.

Another place where Belgians are sure to congregate is at the local *frituur,* or french-fry maker's shop. In most neighborhoods, it is a place of escape from the cold weather and a place where Belgians learn all the latest gossip. Belgian french fries, *frits* (pronounced "freets"), are thickly sliced and fried once at low heat enough to soften them. Then, they are allowed to cool completely before being fried again in very hot lard. The result is a crispy outside and a soft inside, much like the bread in the bakeries. *Frits* are served in a paper cone with a choice of 20 or more toppings, including stew meat (usually horse meat with a beer gravy), curry sauce, and "sauce American," which is catsup. They are as popular in Belgium as hamburgers are in America.

Before a lacemaker arranges the spindles and thread to begin weaving a piece of lace, she first designs the pattern on cardboard and very carefully punches brass pins in the cardboard pattern to guide the thread during weaving. Similarly, one manifestation of high uncertainty avoidance is that Belgians have regulations and customs that act as brass pins to guide behavior in most situations. They tend to dislike the government and police officers but love order, so they tolerate the intrusion. Dealing with government offices is tedious. There are specific papers and experts for everything. First, one must figure out which paper to fill out for the needed service, and then the trick is to figure out which building and which window has the expert who can process the paperwork.

A foreigner moving to Belgium has 30 days to register and get a resident visa from the city that governs the area where the foreigner will be living. Then, the visa must be renewed every 3 months, and a new one must be issued whenever the foreigner changes addresses. Citizens of the EU are not required to carry visas, but most Belgians carry personal cards or business cards, with their family name, home address, and telephone number, which they can exchange or leave with a note on the back if they missed someone on whom they came to call.

As noted earlier, the complex tripartite regional governing structure of the nation, embellished by a central government, causes confusion, especially for the newly arrived foreigner. The city of Brussels, one of the two capitals of the European Parliament, is technically not equivalent to the Brussels region, although they are the same geographically. It is understandable why some visitors call Brussels the capital of confusion (Waxman, 1993).

Hofstede (1991) demonstrated that there is a strong correlation between high uncertainty avoidance and high anxiety and stress. This characteristic is manifested in Belgians in several ways. One is that they are a "doing" society: busy all day long, typically rising very early. Many Belgian sayings refer to the judicious use of time, such as "Time is money"; "Make hay while the sun shines"; and "Time heals all, so get back to business" (Verleyen, 1987, p. 55). They try to prepare for everything so that nothing can go wrong. Much of this feeling must be attributed to their geographical location and historical lack of control over invading armies. As noted earlier, modern Belgium has been a country only since 1830. The North Sea on the western coast is Belgium's only natural boundary. Therefore, any emperor conquering the continent generally started in Belgium (the Low Countries) and moved on from there, as did Bismarck and Hitler in the 20th century.

The religious orientation of the Belgians also contributes to their need to be constantly busy. Catholic doctrine places high importance on good works and personal industry in this life to ensure a comfortable station in the next. Approximately 75% of Belgians are Catholic. Historically, Belgium produced more nuns and priests per capita than any other nation in the world. Although religious intensity has declined since World War II, and most Belgians do not attend church regularly, more than 60% are still educated in Catholic schools.

Because Catholicism is the official religion of Belgium, Catholic parishes, priests, and schools are subsidized heavily by the state. Freedom of religion is guaranteed in the Belgian constitution, and most major religions can be found somewhere in Brussels. But for most Belgians, religions other than Catholicism are for foreigners.

One result of the great effort that Belgians make to follow tradition and avoid uncertainty is that they frequently have minor breakdowns. It is not uncommon to call on them for an appointment and be put off, because today they are having a *zenuw inspanning,* a Dutch phrase translated as a "nervous strain." Typically, this means they overslept, overexerted themselves, or generally are not prepared to face the world for a while.

When they feel a breakdown coming on, the average Belgian will call a doctor, who will routinely prescribe tranquilizers and bed rest. In Belgium, medicine is socialized and easily obtainable, although quality is often questionable. The health care infrastructure is immense, given the size of the population. The high number of hospital beds and doctors per 1,000 inhabitants is an unchallenged world record. Home visits by doctors and nurses are common, and paramedic support is widespread.

Cooperation and Harmony

The lacemaker's primary thoughts while weaving a strand of lace must always focus on the balance and symmetry of the design. A careful balance is maintained to ensure that neither the lace nor the linen overpowers the other. The overall effect should be one of harmony, with no stray ends or spaces to mar the unity of the structure. Each movement of the lacemaker may be quick and concise, but is always within a small range of motion. There are no extreme movements.

Furthermore, lace itself is a very subtle and unobtrusive material. Traditional lace, being all white or ivory, is used to neutralize the bold colors of background material, to soften the hardness of wooden tables, or to balance an object visually. The carefully balanced nature of lace with its neutralizing and nonextreme tone is reflected in the Belgian approach to the world, especially in continuity, statesmanship, and modesty.

Belgians exert a great deal of energy maintaining continuity, the status quo, balance, and a set standard of living for all. They normally work to ensure that their internal cultural and linguistic differences do not disrupt daily life, squelching conflicts by remaining neutral or by reaching mutual consensus among the involved parties. Throughout its existence, Belgium has had linguistic tensions of varying intensity. Yet these tensions have never mounted to violence or bloodshed. When necessary, concessions were made and tempers were defused so that tensions would be carefully balanced. In lacemaking, this means that the threads are held tightly to reduce both the slack and the potential for unnecessary gaps or holes that might weaken the durability and quality of the cloth.

Although Belgians can do little to control the weather in their country, the moderate climate seems to reflect their approach to life: the middle road between extremes. Due to the Gulf Stream off the coast, the climate is very mild, ranging from only about 35°F in the winter to about 75°F in the heat of the summer. The weather is frequently cloudy and/or rainy, with very little snow and very few fully sunny days. However, a winter day with clouds is preferable to a cloudless day, because the clouds tend to insulate the land.

The middle road between extremes is also where the Belgian manager can usually be found. Subordinates will refer to managers using formal titles and last names; however, a manager will seldom stand out because of appearance, conspicuous consumption, or attitudes that might separate management from line workers, as frequently happens in the United States. Again, to Belgians, wealth is to be shared rather than flaunted.

Furthermore, the Belgian balancing and peacemaking approach to life is replicated in their competitive (or not-so-competitive) nature. Belgians tend to be cooperative to a greater extent than they are competitive. Their social and economic structure was designed in a fashion that actually lessens the competitive drive. For instance, the socialized system for health and welfare provides full health care and monetary subsistence for all citizens. Because all those who are unemployed are eligible for welfare, receiving more than 70% of what they would have obtained if they were working, there is no major homeless problem. Furthermore, there is no time limit on eligibility for unemployment, as long as the person appears at the appointed time each week at the unemployment (labor bureau) office and regularly applies for openings in his or her stated occupation. The appointed time changes each week to prevent working around the appointment.

Recently, there has been discussion of limiting the unemployment allowance to 5 years, but as long as the government can afford it, Belgians will probably not limit this subsidy. Most citizens feel that it is a social right to have a certain standard of living regardless of a person's ability to find a job for which he or she is suited. Needless to say, the unemployment subsidy, social security/health care system, and other socialized services in Belgium are largely responsible for one of the highest tax rates in Western Europe. Although Belgian workers tend to be highly skilled and hardworking, thus creating a situation in which there is high productivity per worker, the tax rates are so high that the cost of labor almost offsets the productivity.

Another factor of Belgian society that induces a less competitive nature is that the salary earned in many jobs does not vary to reflect effort and performance. For instance, a professor who instructs classes, devotes an inordinate amount of time to research, and publishes regularly will not be paid any more than a professor who maintains a much more relaxed lifestyle. Other than personal achievement, which is not necessarily highly valued, there is little reward for working harder than the average professor or coworker. There is a greater emphasis on cooperation between colleagues rather than climbing over one another to get to the top.

Furthermore, Belgians share a great tradition of statesmanship and the ability to negotiate on behalf of others. Peter Paul Rubens, the Flemish painter, was a legendary statesman. Although he could paint, his greatest efforts were in fostering international cooperation. He was hired by royalty and wealthy merchants to paint portraits of others. While he had the subject seated for long periods of time, he was paid to put forth the philosophy or argument of his benefactor. For example, he was sent by Philip IV, King of Spain, to paint Charles I, King of England, all the while negotiating a trade agreement between the two nations. This is one reason why Rubens painted approximately 1,600 royal portraits.

Modern Belgians have carried forward this tradition. The cooperative nature of the Belgians is again apparent in their approach to the European Union and the world. Belgium's linguistic and cultural diversity made it an ideal model for the "EU 92" negotiations. Due in part to this unique status, Brussels was selected as one of the two capitals of the European Union. In 1967, for many of the same reasons, NATO moved its headquarters from Paris to Brussels. Today, of the approximately 12,800 international associations in existence, nearly 1,300 are headquartered in and around Brussels. Because of Belgium's unqualified acceptance of these organizations, its balanced nature, and its central location, Brussels has become one of the most important international areas in the world.

The Belgian propensity to overcome obstacles in negotiations and obtain a compromise is well known, frequently after bitter altercations between the parties have seemingly gone beyond the point of endurance. It is at that time that Belgians are likely to forgo the formal negotiations and adjourn to a nearby restaurant. All sorts of disputes have been resolved over glasses of beer or between the courses of a meal.

In addition, international corporations seeking expansion into European markets have flooded the Belgian borders over the past 30 years. Approximately 40% of Belgian industries are foreign-owned. The Belgian government offers international groups major tax incentives to bring central offices and/or high-tech activities into the country. Despite generous wages, high manufacturing costs, and exorbitant personal tax rates, companies have sought out manufacturing facilities in Belgium to take advantage of the transportation infrastructure and friendly economic climate. Thus, another element that the Belgians seemingly balance effortlessly is the internationalization of their small country while maintaining their own identity.

Finally, although there are obviously many reasons for the Belgians to be proud and boastful, people outside the country are rarely aware of Belgian accomplishments. For instance, many readers may not have been aware of the importance of Belgium to lace and vice versa before reading this chapter. Also, it is not generally known that Belgians produce some of the best beer and chocolates in the world. Belgium also has the 12th highest per capita gross domestic product among the world's nations ($24,757).

Despite Belgian prominence in the international circle, many people are still unfamiliar with the country. The reason underlying this lack of international recognition seems to be primarily the result of the Belgian approach to life. Belgians are not generally boastful, tending not to expound about their capabilities and accomplishments. In contrast, they act much like a small piece of lace on the collar of a garment; they bring out the best qualities of those with whom they work without being flashy or calling attention to themselves. Some view this approach as an inferiority complex of sorts, but this idea is contradicted by the definite pride that Belgians feel toward different characteristics of their country. Belgians do not typically feel they are less important or worthy of praise, as an inferiority complex would suggest; in fact, they feel quite the opposite. Belgians tend to believe that the country can and will be an integral player in the EU and the world. The typical Belgian emphasizes the role of coordinator and peacemaker among international markets, sometimes sacrificing publicity and worldwide recognition.

In short, Belgium is as complex as its renowned lace, and its citizens have learned to meet the challenges posed by the interactions that must occur among its cultural and linguistic groups. Although this country has been unified for slightly more than 160 years, its past has been rich, and its future is bright but complicated, just like the lace for which the nation is well known. Belgium adds character and richness to the European Union, just as a small piece of lace adds beauty and depth to a well-crafted garment.

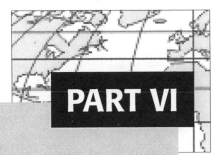

PART VI

Torn National Cultures

S ome nations have experienced major assaults on the core values of their cultures; that is, they have been torn from the cultural roots that have nourished them for decades, if not centuries. Huntington (1996) argues that these nations move from one civilizational base to another, for example, from Asiatic to Western. We provide two examples of such nations in this part of the book, Mexico and Russia.

CHAPTER 20

The Mexican Fiesta

In the North American value system are three central and inter-related assumptions about human beings. These are (1) that peo-ple, apart from social and educational influences, are basically the same.... In Mexico it is the uniqueness of the individual which is valued.

—Condon (1985), pp. 18-19

Mexico represents a classic torn culture, that is, one torn from its roots by invaders and external factors such as widespread famine that devastate it (Huntington, 1996). In Mexico's case, this process has occurred several times, most recently beginning around 1990 as this nation's leaders began the process of making it a major player in the global economy.

There are three distinctive cultures in Mexico: the Indian culture, the Spanish culture, and the mixed (Mestizo) culture derived from the marriage and sexual intercourse between the Indians and Spaniards. About 60% of the population of 91 million is Mestizo and 30% pure Indian (Amerindian) or predominantly Indian. The Indians are descendants of the Mayan and Aztec empires. Finally, about 9% are of Spanish ancestry. As might be expected, there is implicit but imperfect ordering of these three groups in terms of status: Spanish, Mestizo, and Indian. Sometimes, this ordering leads to conflicts. For example, some business firms have fallen on hard times because the Spanish and Mestizo owners and managers have found it difficult to work together, and the Indians have experienced many forms of discrimination. In more recent years, there have been attempts to alleviate the plight of the impoverished Indian groups, and the move toward globalization has helped to decrease the historical antipathy of the Spanish for the Mestizo.

Still, the threefold distinction is a critical part of Mexican culture and is celebrated at the well-known Plaza of Three Cultures in Mexico City where Cortes, the conqueror of the Indians, built an old Spanish church in 1521. The church was built on and around the site of an ancient pyramid structure built by the Indians. There is a marker at the church that frames the three-partition culture succinctly: "On August 13, 1521, heroically defended by Cuanhtemoc, Tlateloko fell into the hands of Herman Cortes. It was neither a triumph nor a defeat; it was the painful birth of the mestizo nation that is Mexico today."

Mexico, like its fiestas, is a wonderful blend of reality, tradition, art, and people. The population is growing at a 1.9% annual rate. Mexico City, the capital, has a population of more than 8 million and is the seventh largest city in the world.

Most Mexicans tend to identify with their Indian and/or Spanish heritage. Spanish is the official language of Mexico, although English is understood by many in large urban areas. As many as 100 Indian languages are still spoken in parts of Mexico. Mexico is about three times the size of Texas, or one fifth the size of the United States. The northern border is shared with the United States, and the southern border is shared with Guatemala and Belize.

Mexico is several thousand years old and is still held back by its past. Not all Mexicans of all regions have the same attitude toward the past. Mexicans in the provinces resent the Aztec-rooted Mestizo culture, whereas the middle-class minority trades off the past for a future of global economic values and rewards. Generally, however, the emotional Mexicans favor the past over the future when conflicts arise. For example, plans to build a subway line under the capital's main plaza were canceled when it was discovered that construction would destroy hidden remains of the Aztec empire.

The past is celebrated in numerous statues, in streets named after aspects of the past—including pre-Hispanic heroes and historic dates—and in the calendar. For example, the entire month of September is devoted to ceremonies commemorating Mexico's independence from Spain. This devotion to the past is also revealed in the fact that the Mexican government spends more of its budget on anthropological research of its past than does any other country.

Even the official past remains of current interest. "News" that is a half-century old is highlighted in interviews and columns. A weekly newspaper supplement was published in 1983 that reprinted selected articles from the period between 1910 and 1970. Symbols are sometimes taken from prehistoric times. A 1978 monument to policemen and firemen who died in the line of fire was a statue of Coatlicue, goddess of death, with a fallen Aztec warrior at her feet. Important figures of Mexican history have been divided into good and evil and personify concepts such as heroism, nationalism, and revolutionary ideals, or cowardice, treason, greed, and repression.

Thus, the past is important for understanding Mexican thought and action. As such, a brief review of Mexican history is essential to a comprehensive understanding of the Mexicans and their culture.

Historical Background

When Cortes arrived in 1519, ancient Mexico was populated by hundreds of indigenous tribes, including the Aztecs, the Incas, and the Mayas. Some of these were advanced societies. It took only 2 years for Cortes to conquer the indigenous people of this land in the name of Spain. Although most of the indigenous people were wiped out by the conquest and European diseases, those remaining were instructed by the Spanish in the Catholic faith during the colonial era. The silver mines and the people of Mexico were exploited for riches sent back to Spain.

After the victory over Spain in the War of Independence in 1810, Mexico began a period of independence and turmoil. By 1853, half of Mexico's territory was acquired by the United States, mostly in the Mexican war. This period was characterized by unstable leadership and exploitation of the poor peons by the elite landholders under the guise of the hacienda farms. One notable leader during this time was Benito Juarez, famous in that he was of pure Zapotec Indian.

When the Mexican Revolution ended in 1920, presidential elections began. The government attempted to break up the Catholic Church, and a Constitution was drawn separating church and state. The church was not allowed to hold land, and priests could not vote, although religion remained inseparably woven throughout the life of the Mexican. Land holdings of the church and large landholders were taken away and given to the peasants and indigenous people under the land reform measures.

In spite of the beneficial outcomes of the Mexican Revolution, many problems still remain today, including poverty, unemployment, a high birth rate, an inadequate educational system, inefficient industry and agriculture, a high foreign debt, and a variable economy lacking financing capabilities. However, the economic situation has improved markedly over the past 50 years, in large part because of the discovery of oil. Between 1985 and 1995, the yearly percentage increase in gross national product (GNP) was 2%. Currently, the average annual GNP per capita is $3,342, which is somewhat low when compared to three other major Latin American nations: Argentina ($8,048), Chile ($4,163), and Brazil ($3,646). Also, the North American Free Trade Agreement (NAFTA) has helped to increase trade between Mexico and the United States to the benefit of both sides. About 25% of the workforce is in agriculture, 21% in industry, and 54% in services.

One political party, the Partido Revolucionario Institucional (PRI) dominated politics for 71 years until the 2000 presidential election, when Vicente Fox of the Political Action Party won. Peruvian writer Mario Vargas Llosa seemed to catch the essence of the PRI when he described it as the perfect dictatorship, monopolizing power behind the trappings of democracy. The PRI had experienced several scandals in recent years and no longer had the unquestioned authority to operate as it wished. Fox waged an American-style campaign and emphasized modern economic programs and the continued need to globalize. It remains to be seen whether this election represents a decisive break with the past in the sense that the torn nature of Mexican culture is healed permanently.

Although this chapter generalizes about the culture of Mexico, in reality, it is not uniform. There are five more or less distinct regions (Kras, 1989). The northern border region has been influenced by its proximity to the United States and the presence of many foreign-owned businesses under the *maquiladora* program, in which foreign businesses ship parts into Mexico, use Mexican labor to assemble the products, and ship the products back out of Mexico free of tariffs. The northern people are more aggressive and independent than their fellow Mexicans. The central region is characterized by more traditional, conservative, autocratic, family-owned businesses. In the southeast region, people are more relaxed. There are more plantations and less industry. Business is paternalistic and autocratic. There is also a large indigenous population in this area. The capital, Mexico City, represents the fourth region, and it boasts approximately 40% of Mexico's GNP. Although it is overcrowded, it is very much a modern, cosmopolitan city. The fifth region consists of the areas along the Gulf of Mexico that are rich in oil.

The mixture of the indigenous population and the Spanish population is nearly complete, resulting in what Mexicans call mestizos. Despite the tragedy inflicted by the conquistadors, the Catholic faith helped the indigenous population assimilate into the Spanish culture. The traditional indigenous religions have blended with Catholicism, resulting in a uniquely Mexican culture that is reflected in their religious beliefs and practices. The mixing of these two cultures (Indian and Spanish) can also be seen in their distinctive architecture, their language, and many other aspects of their lives.

For example, during the fiesta of the Day of the Dead, people flock to the graveyards to put flowers and food on the tombs of their relatives. These symbolic gestures combine the Catholic concept and the ancient Indian concept of the afterlife. One day each year, people dress up like peasants and take their children to the cathedral to be blessed. In front of the church are booths where children get their pictures taken. In the backdrop of these booths and in the childrens' costumes are visible signs of the indigenous backgrounds of the Mexicans.

The Mexican Fiesta

Although there is more to life in Mexico than the fiesta, there are many aspects of the fiesta that can be related to Mexico in order to understand its culture more fully. As such, the fiesta is an appropriate metaphor through which to view Mexico. Ads that urge people to "Come to the land of the Fiesta" feature seductive girls dressed in sequins and ribbons dancing with beautiful boys to a background of romantic guitar music. This fiesta represents that of the movies, tourists, and perhaps a big town project. The real Mexican fiesta is the country fiesta—the more remote and difficult it is to get to the fiesta, the more attractive it is.

The pure pleasures of the simple life can be experienced at a fiesta: indigenous, native dances with beautiful costumes, and peasants dancing about happily. The fiesta gives Mexicans the opportunity to enliven their monotonous existence: They can see people from their neighboring towns, sell a few ornaments, and find an excuse to get drunk before the weekend. Even the most modest fiesta produces a particular mood, full of humor and energy. The fiestas are a blend of beautiful costumes, lively conversations, bustling activity, and aimless walking around.

Only in the tropical, coastal towns are the rural fiestas really gay. Although fiestas have humor, they are not good humored or consciously funny. If they are dramatic, it is unplanned. The participants may not understand the ceremonies even though they have been involved with the fiesta for years. A fiesta cannot be likened to a big block party. It is irrational, mysterious, and moving.

Generally, the state of Oaxaca has wonderful fiestas comprised of beautiful regional costumes, flower arrangements, and tall *castillos* (towers) of native fireworks. The people of Oaxaca are predominantly Indians who share good looks, grace, calm, and an un-Indian worldliness. They are quite interested in new people and new ways. The state of Chiapas, the scene of revolutionary activities in recent years, has pagan ceremonies that are alluring and frightening. Other regions only eat, sing, dance, and drink, leaving religious meanings behind. This is especially true of the tropics, which are devoted to the present.

It seems that there is always a fiesta going on in Mexico. The list of saints and revered people is extensive. There are numerous commemorative celebrations of Mexico's history that add to the fiesta. Finally, every village has its Saints Day, and the barrios of larger towns each have theirs. Carnival is celebrated in the coastal towns. The other sets of fiestas flow into each other from early in December through Epiphany. There are the dance festivals of Oaxaca in early July and Huauchinango's beautiful flower fiesta. Even the solemnity of Holy Week is broken by *fiestacitas.*

A fiesta is something that must be experienced, rather than simply observed. Those who cannot experience a Mexican fiesta firsthand can live it vicariously through an influential Mexican author and Nobel Laureate, Octavio Paz (1961, 47):

> The solitary Mexican loves fiestas and public gatherings. Any occasion for getting together will serve, any pretext to stop the flow of time and commemorate men and events with festivals and ceremonies. We are a ritual people, and this characteristic enriches both our understanding and our sensibilities, which are equally soft and alert. The art of the fiesta has been debased almost everywhere else, but not in Mexico. There are a few places in the world where it is possible to take part in a spectacle like our great religious fiestas with their violent primary colors, their bizarre costumes and dances, their fireworks and ceremonies, and their inexhaustible welter of surprises: the fruit, candy, toys, and other objects sold on these days in the plazas and open-air markets. . . . There are certain days when the whole country, from the most remote villages to the largest cities, prays, shouts, feasts, gets drunk and kills, in honor of the Virgin of Guadalupe or Benito Juarez. (p. 47)

However, in more recent years, at least some of the traditions found in fiestas have grown weak. Even the Fiesta of the Dead on November 1 is being altered. This fiesta highlights death as transformation rather than as the end of life. In this way, the importance of family history is stressed. But the American celebration of Halloween is being grafted onto the Day of the Dead, and in the process, many traditions have been discarded (see "Mexico, Haunted by New Ghosts," 1999).

There are four important aspects of Mexican culture that are revealed in the fiesta. First, the primary focus of the Mexicans is on people, and the fiesta offers them a chance to be with and enjoy the company of their family, friends, and community. Second, religion is very important throughout their lives, and the abundant religious fiestas are a chance for them to communicate with God. Third, experiencing the present is important to Mexicans, and the fiesta is an opportunity to do this. Finally, within the social order, Mexicans find freedom, and it is within the social order of the fiestas that they exhibit this freedom.

■ Primary Focus on People

People are of paramount importance to the Mexicans. A fiesta is a time to enjoy the company of family and friends. It also forms a bond between all Mexicans, uniting them into a common people. Mexico is collectivist, and there is a tight social framework in which the in-group, and particularly those in positions of authority, is expected to look after its members in exchange for their loyalty. Gabrielidis and his research team (Gabrielidis, Stephan, Ybarra, Dos Santos-Pearson, & Villareal, 1997; Triandis, in press) found that the collectivistic Mexicans display more concern for others and use accommodation and collaboration more than do the more individualistic Americans. As a whole, Mexico is a vertical collectivistic culture in which there is a good amount of social distance between superiors and subordinates, and also, as suggested earlier, a good amount of income inequality (Hofstede, 1991). But in some areas of Mexico, such as those bordering the United States, individualism is becoming stronger.

The basic building block in the society is the immediate family. In more rural areas, several generations will live together in the same house. Children are encouraged to stay dependent on the family and not leave home. The family spends most of its nonworking hours together, and the children go everywhere with the parents. Baby-sitters are rarely, if ever, used, except by a minority of the population that is rich enough to afford servants. The family is an informal welfare system in Mexico. If a cousin cannot afford to feed the children, the rest of the family will provide the groceries.

The fiesta is a chance to enjoy the company of the family. Some fiestas even extend the family. Godparents (*madrina* or *padrino*) are selected for baptisms and other important festive ceremonies in a child's life. It is an honor and a responsibility to be chosen as a godparent. A child can have different godparents for each ceremony, with the new ones adding to the existing ones rather than replacing them. Because these godparents will be present for every important occasion in the child's life, this practice actually extends the family to include the godparents and their families. *Compradazco* connotes co-parenthood shared by the parents and the godparents. A Mexican friend likened *compradazco* to a network of invisible lines connecting many houses or families in Mexico into one big family.

Friends are also very important in Mexico. Once a person becomes a friend, he or she is incorporated into the vast family network and becomes one of the trusted in-group. He or she almost becomes a part of the family, as in the case of *compradazco*. Friends of friends also become part of this network. Friends are often called by familial titles such as brother, sister, and cousin.

Mexicans are ruled much more by relationships than by abstract concepts. A Mexican will interrupt whatever he or she is doing at the sight of a friend or a relative. Diminutive endings, such as *ito* or *ita,* which mean "small," are often tacked onto the ends of names or words to suggest affection, as in "Silvita" instead of "Silvia." These endings are also used for minimizing problems and saving face.

Mexicans tend to hire relatives and friends over strangers, no matter what the qualifications or achievements are of each. In Hofstede's study of 53 nations, Mexicans tend to have a high need for uncertainty avoidance, indicating that they feel threatened by uncertain situations and strangers and try to avoid them (Hofstede, 1991). Therefore, knowing someone before hiring or doing business with him or her is important. The old adage "It's not what you know, but who you know" is taken literally. If business must be done with strangers, much time is spent getting to know the person before any deals will be made. Mexicans are not loyal to an organization, but they are committed to the people in the organization.

Considering the central role that the family plays in Mexican life, foreign executives must take the concerns of the employee's family seriously. For example, they should show interest and concern when there is illness in a family and an absence results. Understanding family ties is an excellent way for foreign managers to explain subordinates' behavior and to develop good relations with them.

Mexicans tend to view success in terms of affiliation rather than achievement; in terms of being rather than doing. It is important to be someone who is important to other people. However, achievement is more important in larger, more modern companies. The uniqueness of each person as an individual is highly valued, even though these individuals are an integral part of a collectivist culture. Mexicans refer to the soul (*alma*) or the spirit (*espiritu*) to describe this inner individual.

It is very important to protect this soul or dignity or honor. A manager should rarely, if ever, criticize a subordinate in front of his or her friends or family. Praise is very important to the Mexican. Mexicans are consensus seekers and will lie to avoid hurt feelings and confrontation. Avoiding the placement of blame on anyone is very important. In Spanish, people do not break things; instead, things just break—*se me rompio*. Lies and truth are not absolute. A Mexican will frequently say what you want to hear in order to avoid confrontation and the loss of someone's dignity, even if what is said is not the complete truth. When asked directions, Mexicans will sometimes give a false answer rather than say they do not know. When they beg one's pardon, they say, "Pretend it never happened, señor."

Michael Agar, a cross-cultural anthropologist who was asked to facilitate the relations between the Americans and Mexicans involved in a joint venture, recalls vividly how the Mexicans perceived the Americans. After working with the American businesspeople all day, the Mexican executives went out for a drink, and one of them said *el capo* as he waved an imaginary torero's cape before the bull or, metaphorically, the Americans. The Mexicans perceived themselves to be too polite and sophisticated to indicate that the Americans' behavior was boorish. However, this politeness was one of the reasons that the joint venture eventually failed, for the Americans became exasperated when the Mexicans indicated that it was "no problem" meeting a specified deadline, only to fail to do so repeatedly. The Americans bluntly told the Mexicans that they had lied, and the Mexicans were insulted. Given the communication and negotiation styles of Americans and Mexicans, such outcomes are frequent.

Mexicans tend to view humans as a mixture of good and evil. Possibly because of this perspective and the gray area between truth and lies, one can encounter occasional obstacles where someone may need to be rewarded in order to gain cooperation. Analogously, in the fiesta, one often dons a costume and a mask. This mask protects one's dignity. It allows an escape from reality without the loss of dignity. Octavio Paz (1961) even argues that the Mexican is "a person who shuts himself away to protect himself; his face is a mask and so is his smile" (p. 29).

Nonverbal communication is important in most, if not all, cultures. In Mexico, gestures, facial expressions, glances, posture, and clothing all reveal important facets of the culture. Greetings and salutations take a long time and are often full of handshakes, hugs, kisses, and pats on the back. There is more physical contact between members of the same sex in Mexico than is common in the United States. Men greet each other with an *abrazo* (embrace), whereas women may kiss. Overall, Mexicans employ more physical closeness and smaller interpersonal distances than their counterparts in North America.

Thus, a North American may withdraw from a Mexican, communicating emotional or social distance. A Mexican may seem too overbearing to the North American, when, in fact, he or she is not. Rhythms are also different between the two cultures. Mexicans tend to use more of the trunk of the body, whereas North Americans use the head and neck. Mexicans use their hands extensively in self-expression. Use of the hands helps to illustrate and emphasize what a person is saying. Many gestures used by men are charged with sexual innuendo.

Neat clothing and appearance are also important because they show respect. In Mexico, clothing and jewelry are representative of the country's great ethnic diversity. The type of dress worn indicates a person's region or ethnic background. In hats alone, the diversity is wonderful. Upper-class Mexicans distinguish their status by wearing fine clothes, expensive jewelry, and fancy hairstyles. The concern with being respectable, or *decente,* is revealed in clothing.

Conversation is an art in Mexico, and the manner in which things are said is as important as what is said. The speaker beats around the bush in a dramatic and flowery style, and often repeats things. Allusions and double meanings are a delight to the Mexican. Cultures differ in the importance they place on words in order to convey information (Hall & Hall, 1990). North Americans and Europeans place great emphasis on words. In Mexico, context is more important, and Mexicans may view a statement as honest in one situation but rude in another. Places also have meaning, for example, a man and a woman alone together in a room. Who says something and how it is said are also vital to understanding what is meant.

Meetings often become social events. The participants simply enjoy each other's company. There is a lot of emotion and passion in any conversation. When a Mexican man courts a woman, for instance, he typically produces flowery praises of her beauty. Similarly, in the fiesta, extreme joys and sorrows are exhibited.

The language often says more than it means. For example, *mi casa es su casa* literally means "my house is your house," but in reality, it means "you are welcome in my house." When Mexicans are pleased to meet you, they say they are *encantado,* that is, they are enchanted to meet you.

By and large, the emphasis in the schools has been on theoretical concepts and social competence. Intellectual pursuits such as philosophy, science, and the arts are important, whereas practical applications are largely ignored. This practice often leads to problems in business when subordinates are charged with implementing a plan but have insufficient skills to do so. Thus, international managers must realize the importance of training their subordinates, especially given their tendency not to question authority and to be agreeable. In recent years, there has been an increase in the importance of practical training. For example, Monterrey Tech (ITESM) produces a large number of first-rate business and engineering students, and some of its programs, such as the MBA program, are ranked among the best in the world.

The Emphasis on Religion

The importance of religion to life in Mexico is demonstrated by the significance and number of religious fiestas. Approximately 95% of the population of Mexico is Roman Catholic, and religion permeates many aspects of a Mexican's life, as manifested in the number and importance of the religious fiestas. The religious fiesta is a chance to communicate with God. In addition, some fiestas that are nonreligious in purpose have religious features in them.

Carnival is an important fiesta that is celebrated before Lent. Guadalupe Day is one of the more important religious holidays in which the country celebrates the anniversary of the day when the Virgin Mary, also called the Virgin of Guadalupe, appeared in Mexico City. On the nine nights before Christmas, Mexicans act out the journey of Mary and Joseph to Bethlehem. Every night after these ceremonies, or *posadas,* the children play the piñata game. Holy Week, the week before Easter, is celebrated with fiestas. In addition, each city or village has an annual fiesta for its patron saint. During the religious fiestas, Mexicans pray and light candles in the churches.

There are also family fiestas, or fiestas celebrating the traditional passages in the life of a person, and they include baptism, first communion, and weddings. The whole family, including the godparents and their families, will be present for these fiestas, which will frequently begin with a church service during which Holy Communion takes place.

Even some fiestas that are not religious in purpose have aspects of religion in them. There is a fiesta for 15 year old girls similar to the "sweet 16" party or coming-out party. It is social in origin, but it includes a service in the church with communion, a full-course meal, and dancing, preferably to a large band's music. This is one of the most important fiestas in a girl's life, and the girls wear very expensive, elaborate dresses for the occasion, whereas the boys accompanying them are in suits and ties.

Mexicans tend to believe that life is beyond their control. What God wills, happens. The common expression *si Dios nos presta el tiempo* means "if God lends us the time." The expression *ni modo* means "no way" or "tough luck." Mexicans generally consider nature to be dominant over people. When problems are encountered, the Mexican will modify the self rather than try to modify the environment. For this reason, class lines are not easily broken, and problems are often minimized. Similarly, the mask in the fiesta is a means of modifying the self in order to deal with reality. It handles reality by recognizing that nothing can be done about it, except to escape it.

The escapist attitude is also reflected in the music of the mariachis. One song's lyrics are as follows:

> Mexico beautiful and beloved
> If I die far from you
> Tell me I am sleeping
> And bring me back here

Because Mexicans tend to believe that life is beyond their control, they have a fatalistic attitude, as well as a fascination and even an obsession with death. They almost live on the edge of death. The newspapers are full of gory stories about death. This obsession is reflected in their fiestas. The Day of the Dead, also called All Souls Day, is celebrated with a fiesta to honor and remember the dead. Food and flowers are brought to the tombs of deceased relatives. Some people even set a place at the table for the dead. Candy skulls with a person's name on them are purchased and eaten or given as gifts. To the Mexican, this cheerful celebration is both for the living and the dead.

Mexicans tend to believe that death is only part of a larger picture. This belief may stem more from the indigenous religions than from Catholicism. In the circular Aztec calendar stone, the center contains the sun god with two snakes. Supposedly, human sacrifices were made on this stone in order to pay back the gods so that the continuous regeneration of life could continue. Even Christianity views death as a transition between two lives. Although some argue that to the modern Mexican, death is no longer a transition, Mexicans still tend to view death as an integral and inseparable part of life. This belief in communion with the dead is an outgrowth of the knowledge that the past is not dead.

Fiestas are also a time of death and rebirth for Mexicans in that the fiesta revitalizes and strengthens them. Thus, fiestas are a source of continual energy and renewal for the Mexican people.

The bullfight, which is clearly a ritual emphasizing bravery in the face of death rather than just a sport, is often a part of fiestas (see Chapter 22, "The Spanish Bullfight"). The Death Dance of the bullfight is an expression of the Mexican preoccupation with death. Also, bullfighting is an exhibition of machismo, in that the torero must show that he is not afraid of death. At some fiestas, there are other opportunities to show courage in the face of death, as when men hold on to the end of long poles rotating like a Ferris wheel either vertically or horizontally around a tall center pole.

Machismo is a very important concept in Mexico. Manliness and virility are greatly admired, and perhaps even more admired is authority. It is important for men to exhibit this masculinity and stoicism at all times and to show that they are not afraid of death. Male children are more exalted than their female counterparts. Boys are expected to act like little men, and they are told to look after the family when the father is away. One day each year, families take their children to the cathedral to be blessed. When they have their pictures taken outside the cathedral, they draw mustaches on the boys to make them look like men.

A Mexican male's insecurity is manifested by his fear of betrayal by women. One anthropological explanation states that because Mexican *mestizaje* began with the mating of Spanish men and Indian women, male-female relationships were based on the concepts of betrayal by women and conquest by men. The macho man must protect himself against betrayal, just as the conqueror could not fully trust the conquered.

The male worship of the female ideal is illustrated frequently by their adoration of the Virgin and their adulation of their mothers. The wife, however, is frequently viewed as a sexual object. A husband who is faithful and affectionate shows vulnerability and weakness. Mistresses let the man conquer before he is betrayed. Wives, resentful of their husbands, are sometimes too attentive to their sons. Sons, in turn, view their mothers through the feminine ideal yet adopt their fathers' ways once married.

Women, like men, spend most of their time with members of their own sex. At social gatherings, they stay close to their husbands or mingle with other women. Rarely do they spend significant time with other men. A female seeking a career runs into great pressures. The traditional role of mother and homemaker makes career choices a difficult matter. Women, however, remain central to the family, reliable in a society where illegitimate children, broken homes, and absentee fathers are common.

Although they seek security, Mexicans are introspective. Fiestas provide an emotional outlet to their solitude and self-restraint. They provide a release that is not found elsewhere.

Experiencing the Present

Although the Mexicans are very much influenced by the past, they live for the present. The fiesta allows the Mexican to stop and enjoy the moment. It is an escape from work and poverty. The fiesta is a release of the soul.

The Mexican concept of time is very relaxed, and there is always plenty of it. This is called polychronic time, meaning that more than one thing goes on at a time (Hall & Hall, 1990). Mexicans call it *la hora Mexicana* (Mexican time). Interruptions and tardiness are common, and deadlines are flexible. Absence after a long weekend is institutionalized in *San Lunes,* or Saint Monday, and this is accepted as an explanation for absence. Many projects are never seen to completion. People are expected to be late to social occasions, and hosts actually plan on this eventuality. Arriving on time is considered rude. Mexicans are dismayed over North Americans' invitations that state in advance what time a party will be over.

Even though Mexican bus or taxi drivers may have paying passengers, they will stop to give a friend a ride to an unscheduled destination. This view of time is also exhibited in communication, which is often spontaneous and simultaneous, and ideas flow from many different directions. What some term the mañana syndrome stems not from Mexican laziness or inefficiency, but rather from a different philosophy of time. Disasters are considered unavoidable—*ni modo*. This Mexican fatalism has Indian roots.

Sometimes, however, other factors, such as the importance of authority, override the cultural expression of time. One American trainer on his first trip to Mexico experienced this phenomenon. He was ready to start his class, but not one of the 50 managerial trainees was in the room. Wanting to be polite, he waited 30 minutes before starting, at which time about half of the class was present. When he complained to his Mexican superior about the lax approach of the trainees, the Mexican startled him by saying, "It is your fault." The explanation was that the American should start class on time, even if no one was in the room, and everyone would be there forthwith, because he was the figure of authority. He did so in the second class, and within 10 minutes, all of the trainees were in their seats. In all subsequent classes, the managerial trainees were in their seats when class began.

There is more pressure to be on time and to produce in larger, more modern companies. Strict adherence to time schedules is important for modern companies, and U.S. executives must be patient with the Mexican attitude toward time. They must plan for time slippage and the unanticipated.

Mexico is a country of extremes, in terms of both geography and the rigidity of the social class structure, which often makes a Mexican's life hard. However, Mexicans frequently know how to find happiness in life. They have developed the ability to find a silver lining in any cloud. The fiesta is a time for Mexicans to escape their hard life and find joy, and the mask worn at the fiesta allows them to do this. Often, these simple joys are hidden, as is the Mexican behind the mask, and not apparent to the outside observer.

Mexicans have a plethora of expressions for their displeasure with work. They say *el trabajo embrutece* or "work brutalizes," and *es la madre de una vida padre* or "idleness is the mother of the good life." Even the word for business, *negocio,* connotes the negative of leisure, that is, work is completed only for the purpose of obtaining leisure (Fisher, 1988). Although many Mexicans work hard, they do not place a high value on work. They value leisure time spent with their family and friends more highly than work. Again, they are motivated by affiliation rather than achievement, and their emphasis is on being rather than doing. Work is done only because it has to be done, a concept in stark contrast to the Protestant work ethic, which holds that work is good in and of itself. Mexicans need a balance between work and leisure, which requires them to leave some jobs until mañana. For this reason, foreigners stereotype Mexico as the land of mañana.

One reason for the deemphasis on work is that success in life is frequently based not on achievement but on personal relations. Career advancement often occurs because of personal contacts rather than achievements. Hard work does not necessarily lead to success or prosperity, and many Mexicans work hard all of their lives only to live in dire poverty.

There is no strict dichotomy between work and leisure. Mexicans like to have friends and relatives working with them in order to make work more fun. Many businesses are run by the family, and they hire family members and friends before they hire strangers.

Mexicans tend to deemphasize the future, and very little long-term planning occurs. Each day is taken as it comes. This is due in part to the unstable economy and frequent changes in governments. Follow-through on projects is often difficult to obtain. Concepts such as quality control are uncommon in all but the largest, most modern companies.

Freedom Within the Social Order

Mexican society is very hierarchical (vertical collectivism), and everyone has a role within the society. Mexico has a high score on Hofstede's power distance dimension, meaning that the society accepts without question an unequal distribution of wealth and authority (Hofstede, 1991). Thus, the distinction between the two forms of the word "you" in Spanish is noteworthy. *Tu* is informal and used between friends, and *usted* is formal and used to show respect to superiors or elders.

In the smaller villages, there are specialized roles within the community. This hierarchy can be observed clearly in the patriarchal family structure in Mexico. The father is the authority figure, and traditionally, the mother's role is to love her children and husband and to lead a life of self-sacrifice for them. Children are taught to obey their father and mother. Just as the parents take care of the children, so, too, do the more affluent members of a family take care of the poorer members. When a family holds a fiesta, the wealthier members are expected to help pay for a large part of it. It is common for a Mexican working in the United States to send money home to help pay for his or her younger sister's schooling and coming-out party. Similarly, it is expected that he or she send money to less affluent relatives to help pay for the family fiestas.

At work, there is a rigid hierarchy where the subordinates traditionally do not question the boss. A problem typical of authoritarian administrations is that Mexican subordinates tend to withhold negative information, even if important, and convey only good news. Everyone knows his or her role and conforms to it. Similarly, the government is very bureaucratic, the Roman Catholic Church is very hierarchical, and schools are traditionally structured in an authoritarian manner so that questioning is not encouraged. This stratification began before the coming of the Spaniards. Today, absolute authority within the hierarchy is beginning to break down, especially in the cities, as larger businesses are moving toward more participative management styles.

As this discussion implies, there are conflicts between traditional values and modern life. In one family, the older brother had started a promising business and hired the next oldest brother to be his chief salesperson, who complained to the father that his older brother was not paying him the promised salary but a much lower one. When the father asked the older brother about the matter, he was incensed and indicated that he would indeed pay his brother all that he owed him—to the detriment of investment in the growing business—but that he would immediately fire him, regardless of the impact on the family. When the father communicated this information to the younger brother, he withdrew his request for the promised salary until the business became more stable.

Status is important to the Mexicans. Impressive academic degrees or titles command respect. Title usage reinforces the sense of hierarchy within the Mexican society. At low levels of the bureaucracy, the use of *licienciado,* or university graduate, is common. It requires wearing a suit and tie and implies influence. The head of an office is not *Licienciado* So and So, but *El Licienciado,* as if he were the only one. Maestro is often used either for plumbers, painters, or carpenters, or for senior officials teaching at the university.

The elite was formerly drawn from purer Spanish backgrounds, and the members were very proud of their light skin and Spanish heritage. Although there are now elite members from the indigenous and *mestizo* population, there is still a preference for lighter skin and eyes. For the most part, being Indian is defined culturally, not racially, in Mexico. A person is considered Indian only if he or she speaks the language and follows the culture of the Indian. In the Revolution of 1910, the indigenous heritage of Mexico was glorified and even celebrated in an attempt to erase the stigma applied to the Indian.

Structure and security form a curious amalgam with freedom in Mexico. Everyone knows his or her role and usually will not violate it or challenge another's role; people are careful not to trammel another's dignity. Yet there is not as much pressure for conformity as there is in less hierarchical societies. Mexicans have the freedom to do what they want as long as they do not affront others and go beyond their role in society. Jobs offer security to the Mexicans, and consequently, they enjoy freedom at work. As mentioned previously, Mexicans feel free to be absent from work on Monday, the only excuse necessary being that it is "Saint Monday." Children feel very secure and warm in the family structure, yet because they are so loved and honored, they have more freedom to do what they want to do.

Mexicans as individuals can be freer from guilt and obligation than North Americans. It is not the individual that is guilty; the blame is shared by the group. The obligation is not the individual's, but the group's. Also, the Catholic religion allows Mexicans to be free from sin by asking God's forgiveness for their sins in confession. Again, friends and family usually take care of those in their group who are in need.

In a large cathedral in Mexico City, this freedom and even chaos within the structure and order could be seen clearly. Although the Roman Catholic Church is very hierarchial and structured, what went on inside this cathedral was not. People came in to pray independently and left at their leisure without any reference to leadership from the priest. This was true of the main chapel as well as the many side chapels. A woman knelt beside a priest in front of the church, apparently having her confession heard completely independently of everything else in the cathedral. The chairs, seemingly well used, were in disarray instead of in neat rows. Within the church's hierarchy, there is security and freedom.

The fiesta is a chance to observe this freedom, and even chaos. Drunkenness, promiscuity, rowdiness, violence, and reckless abandon rule the fiesta. In some ways, fiestas are a celebration of chaos. Roles, hierarchies, norms, and laws vanish. Men dress up like women, and the poor dress up like the rich. Everyone dresses up in gaudy costumes and becomes someone he or she is not. They hide behind their masks and escape from reality. During the fiesta, it is almost as if people are free to choose which mask they wear. Although they indulge in freedom and chaos during the fiesta, they return to order afterward.

The Mexicans have changed over the years and will continue to do so. In the cities and larger corporations, Western concepts such as achievement and rigid schedules are becoming more common. Larger corporations are less autocratic and paternal than the smaller businesses. This may be due in part to the fact that many of the larger corporations are owned by foreigners. Although these changes are very visible, they depict only a small part of the culture of Mexico. For the most part, Mexico is composed of smaller, more traditional businesses, with much more traditional culture. Throughout the years, the fiesta has been, and will remain, an integral part of the Mexican culture. And the fiesta will endure as a metaphor describing the importance that Mexicans place on people, religion, experiencing the present, and the freedom that exists within the social order.

CHAPTER 21

The Russian Ballet

Russia represents a classic case of a torn nation (Huntington, 1996) because it has been severed from its social, economic, and cultural roots not just once but at least three times in its tumultuous and long history, and these three pivotal periods have occurred within the past 200 years. The first period began in the early 19th century, when Peter the Great began to westernize Russia while deemphasizing its Asian influences. He defeated his chief enemy, the Swedes; created the Russian navy to facilitate trade in the largely landlocked nation; and constructed St. Petersburg (formerly Leningrad) out of swampland to connect Russia by land with the West. However, prominent Russians both in the past and currently emphasize their exceptionalism, created by their Slavic heritage and ethnicity, and they portray Russia as neither Asian nor European (see "Russian Exceptionalism," 1996).

In the second period, starting in 1917, the Russians moved away from rule by the czar to Communism, and the results were disastrous socially, economically, and culturally. Millions of people were imprisoned and died; Russia lost more soldiers and civilians in World War II than all other nations combined (an estimated 50 million of the 100 million); the economy became extremely weak after World War II because the Russian government poured most of its resources into the military and atomic weapons; priceless Christian Orthodox churches were destroyed; and religious worship was banned. Ironically, the Western press after World War II tended to picture Russia as a vibrant economy, but part of this image was based on the Iron Curtain that stood between the West and Russia. Good information was difficult to obtain.

Thus, just a few years prior to the formal dissolution of the Soviet Union in 1992, the West was ignorant of many of the realities of Russian life. During these years, former President Gorbachev led the movement toward Western capitalism, and two new words entered the English language: glasnost, or openness, and perestroika, or restructuring.

A tumultuous third period in the nation's history began in 1992 that was marked initially by optimism and hope. Economic reforms were supposedly based on Western capitalism, but they failed miserably. For example, to make Russians into capitalists, the government gave Russian citizens small shares of stock in formerly nationalized companies that were privatized as part of the largest privatization effort ever undertaken; at least 6,000 large and mid-sized firms were involved in this experiment, even though only about 8,000 firms worldwide were privatized in the 1980s. However, most of these firms failed to meet the exacting competitive standards of early-stage capitalism, at least partially because of the antiquated technology used in many industries, and most of the shares became worthless. Simultaneously, a small group of businessmen gained control, frequently in a questionable manner, over the most profitable parts of Russian industry. Corruption and crime became rampant. Some American businesspeople seeking to do business in Russia in the early 1990s were shocked at the open manner in which bribes were sought; one executive recalls an introductory dinner during which several different individuals openly bribed him. Businessmen and their businesses now have private guards because they can no longer rely on the ordinary rule of law and order. Various estimates suggest that at least 40% of the economic transactions are now based on barter, and the banking system collapsed in 1999.

To be sure, there is a debate that is likely to continue for some time about the health of Russia during this third period, especially when comparisons are made to the two earlier periods. Stephen Shenfield, an economist, presents data indicating that the Russian gross domestic product fell about 45% from 1992 to 1997, that at least 40% of the population is in serious distress and suffers from chronic malnutrition, and that life expectancy for men has fallen below what it was a century ago (see Koretz, 1998). The Economist, on the other hand, offered a much more optimistic portrayal in its articles and two major surveys of Russia published in 1992 and 1995 (see Cowley, 1995; Parker, 1992). In the 1995 survey, Andrew Cowley argued that for the first time in Russia's history, the market was more powerful than the state. More recently, The Economist has become more pessimistic; its cover for December 18, 1999 presents a portrait of "Bleak and Bloody Russia" and its involvement in its civil war with dissident Chechnya. In its editorial for this issue, this influential magazine puts the matter in this way: "What kind of a country can hold a general election without discussing a civil war whose needless brutality horrifies most decent outsiders? . . . The answer, of course, is a strange country, a uniquely strange country" (p. 15).

After the fact, it is easy to see how mistakes occurred when privatization was initiated and implemented. What is striking is that experts and policymakers devoted only a minimal amount of attention to the infrastructure required for capitalism to operate effectively, such as a strong banking system and legal system. Also, as Kashima and Callan (1994) have pointed out, it is unwise to take the entire set of practices from one culture into another without modifying it to the needs and values of the culture. This chapter focuses on the culture of Russia, with the recognition that culture influences, and is influenced by, social infrastructure and economic practices. But to disregard culture, as many economists and policymakers have in offering prescriptions for Russia and other nations, is to decrease the probability that meaningful change will occur.

We focus on Russia with its population of 149 million and a land mass that is almost double that of the United States. There is now a Commonwealth of Independent States, consisting of 12 states, that was established to reformulate the Soviet Union without the economic or political costs of union, but it has virtually disintegrated, even though politicians are seeking to revive it (see Williams, 1998). Russia's population is approximately equal to that of the other states in the Commonwealth, the largest of which is Ukraine, with a population of 52 million. Moscow is located in the western region of the nation, whereas St. Petersburg is situated to the northeast of Moscow.

Russian ballet provides an apt metaphor for Russia for several reasons. Ballet of the highest and arguably unsurpassed quality was created in Russia, as noted below. Although the Russians did not create ballet, they enriched this art form immeasurably. Also, it seems appropriate that a torn nation should be represented by a cultural metaphor that did not originate there. Furthermore, since 1992, Russian ballet has experienced political intrigue, lack of funding, and some low levels of performance, thus mirroring the nation's troubles (see Williams, 1997b). At the current time, there are attempts to reinvigorate Russian ballet, and the major ballet companies are now performing frequently outside of Russia.

To better understand Russian culture, we will take a look at three important characteristics: echelons, theatrics and realism, and the Russian soul. These elements also apply to our metaphor and help to distinguish this art form from its counterparts in other lands. With a quality larger than life, Russian ballet represents the complexities of Russian culture—the grand expression of aristocracy and the gentle beauty of a countryside.

Russian ballet means many things to many people. Some consider it to be the type of instruction given at the famous Bolshoi and Kirov academies, whereas others identify Russian ballet with specific eras and performance. Those who witnessed the sumptuous performances of Diaghilev's *Ballet Russe* in the early 20th century surely identified his productions as the Russian ballet. And audiences familiar with specific works such as *Swan Lake* and *Sleeping Beauty* proclaim these magnificent dance programs as Russian ballet. Essentially, all of these definitions are correct. As we will soon learn, the words "Russian ballet" evoke feelings of tremendous joy to anyone who is familiar with the finesse and style of the assured dancers associated with any part of this form of art.

A brief background on the evolution of ballet in Russia gives us insight as to why the ballet remains so important to Russians today, and explains why Russian ballet enjoys its excellent reputation throughout the world. Ballet in its modern form originated from court dancing in Italy during the Renaissance period. Although many Americans today think of ballet as a feminine occupation, in the 17th century, male dancers dominated the spectacles for the onlooking Italian nobility. Ballet emerged in the next century as a pantomime dance to the fascination of wealthier Europeans. In France, royalty participated in this form of entertainment by assuming starring roles. As it gained popularity throughout Europe, ballet performances became theatrical and were enjoyed by the public at opera houses. Like Louis XIV, who established an academy in France to improve the art, Peter the Great encouraged the development of social dance during the 17th century in an attempt to increase Russian awareness of the outside world. His determination to transform Russia into a powerful empire was achieved through modernization using Western Europe as a model. Russians have always had a great love of dancing, and when ballet was introduced in Russia in the 17th century, they responded enthusiastically to it. The monarchy placed emphasis on the arts by paying salaries for dancers who became known as "artists of his Imperial Majesty."

During Peter the Great's reign, one of the most significant changes in Russian ballet was the elimination of cumbersome robes to permit freer movement of dancers. In 1736, the city of St. Petersburg, also the capital of Russia at that time, became the home of the Imperial Russian ballet. Two years later, Empress Anna, who was also fond of ballet, sponsored the first school at her Winter Palace with the goal of developing professional Russian dancers.

Ballet flourished in the 18th century with the assistance of French and Italian choreographers in St. Petersburg, Moscow, and Warsaw. Perhaps the most influential of those who staged ballet compositions was French-born Marius Petipa, who, in the late 1800s, created such masterpieces as *Swan*

Lake, Sleeping Beauty, and *The Nutcracker.* Among the legacies of the Russian ballet is its tradition of brilliant composers, such as Tchaikovsky, who collaborated with Petipa to create the music of those well-known ballets, and Prokofiev, who wrote the stirring music that accompanies the ballet of *Romeo and Juliet.*

Although ballet lost much of its vitality in Western Europe during the 19th century, Russia preserved the tradition and elegance of the art form for the rest of the world. In 1909, Sergei Diaghilev revived the splendor of classical ballet with his *Ballet Russe,* or "Russian ballet" for Parisian audiences. His company was hailed as the "most exciting artistic force in Europe for the next twenty years" (Clarke & Crisp, 1976, p. 27). Sadly, Diaghilev's extraordinary *Ballet Russe* did not survive his death in 1929 because of the lack of either a school to develop new talent or a permanent theater to call home.

After the Russian Revolution in 1917, the "artists of His Imperial Majesty" in the former St. Petersburg adapted to the socialist way of life, as did the rest of the Russian citizens. Russian dancers became state employees of state-owned companies. The world-renowned Maryinsky Theatre in St. Petersburg became the famous Kirov Theatre in Leningrad. Likewise, the Petrovsky Theatre, home of the Imperial Ballet in Moscow, was renamed Bolshoi, signifying that which is big or grand.

In fact, ballet became more popular than ever as the government discovered that ballet could express the problems and ideals of a socialist state. Soviet promotion of socialist realism emphasized all types of artistic creativity, and citizens were encouraged to attend cultural events.

To match the public fervor of ballet, an infrastructure was developed for its expansion. A. Y. Vaganova, a legendary ballerina from the old Imperial Ballet, was called upon to create a training program for dancers, and it eventually produced the finest dancers in the world. She was responsible for much of the physical richness of Russian ballet, and her method of teaching is still used widely throughout Russia. Other maestros, such as George Balanchine and Mikhail Fokine, inspired eager students, including the magnificent Anna Pavlova, Vaslav Nijinsky, and Galina Ulanova. More than 40 new ballet companies were formed, and theaters were built throughout the Soviet Union. Gifted female pupils hoping to become prima ballerinas were provided with free academic and artistic support. Soviet teachers also searched for boys with strength, agility, and stamina who wished to pursue careers as members of a ballet troupe. Even today, a retired Russian male dancer usually retains his special status as premier danseur.

In spite of recent difficulties, Russian ballet serves as the standard for the rest of the world. This measurement is based on its fine traditions of classical ballet and intense national commitment to preserving and improving the art form.

Echelons of the Ballet

Clear echelons of status and privilege exist within the ballet company. At the very top is the prima ballerina, the prominent star of the troupe. Years of schooling and practice alone do not set one dancer apart from other dancers. The principal dancer must possess a natural gift of virtuosity and inner beauty. As is true in other nations around the globe, Russian citizens revere such accomplished individuals as national heroes. Russian children look up to these dancers as semigods and -goddesses, in much the same way as American children idolize Olympic champions and great sports figures. Although she is the most famous personality within her industry, the ballerina does not necessarily receive the largest salary. However, her status as number-one dancer allows the ballerina much greater privilege than almost any payment could. Similarly, the producer, choreographer, and conductor are all held in high esteem.

The next level within the ballet company consists of the director, set designer, and costume designer, revered not only for the titles they hold, but also for their personal reputations. Then, there are those who report to the director—specifically, the production, stage, company, and wardrobe managers; musical arranger/director; set design assistant; makeup director; light designer; and dance captains. Many of these individuals possess the ambition and potential to become experts or even members of the elite. Furthermore, there is the corps de ballet, or the members of the ballet company who perform dances. They constitute by far the largest of the groups. Finally, supporting musicians and various technicians, who specialize in everything from lighting to makeup, are at the bottom of the hierarchy. They sustain the other classes or groups both within and outside of our metaphor.

During the Soviet era, the government provided ample financial support for ballet, and the echelons received rewards commensurate with the rank ordering described above. In the Soviet era, privileges were awarded selectively and were given primarily to members of the Communist party, or about 20% of the total population. Many prominent members of ballet companies were in the Communist party; even if they were not members of the Communist party, they received ample rewards because of their association with ballet. Hence, being a member of the ballet was associated with privileges that were denied to most citizens. And although the echelons still exist in the ballet, the rewards are fewer, given the inability of the government to fund adequately. However, some new funding has been found in worldwide tours that have made Russian ballet much more accessible to non-Russians. Members of the Bolshoi have even performed at Las Vegas.

Currently, it is the "new rich" who are the focus of attention in Russia. Small in number, they constitute the top echelon in Russia, and biting humor is the order of the day in describing them. For example, former President Boris Yeltsin is having difficulty understanding why his scientists come to work without pay, even when there is no electricity or light, and Anatoly Chubais (the economist responsible for the ill-fated stock system discussed above) enthusiastically responds, "Maybe we can charge them admission!" (Williams, 1997a). An even more popular joke concerns a newly wealthy Russian who cries when his new Mercedes Benz is seriously damaged in an auto accident. When a passerby points out that the man's arm is missing, the rich Russian looks where his arm used to be and cries, "Oh, my Rolex is gone!"

But these jokes mask a level of understanding about Russian culture and its echelons of power and prestige that deserves attention. As the discussion of the three periods of this torn nation implies, Russia historically has been an autocratic nation in which the few at the top ruled with an iron hand. Currently, there is some concern that Russia could revert easily to its former ways and behaviors, especially if most citizens begin to feel that the costs of capitalism outweigh the benefits. A recent survey indicated that 68% of Russians favor a "firm hand," 75% want the state to bolster its economic role, and 73% want to shun Western values and money (Higgins, 1999). The basic meaning of the echelons in Russian ballet is that outstanding performance that is honest and open is rewarded. It is easy to see when a dancer performs at a superior level, and the common citizen identifies proudly with such performance and culture. But these figures suggest that most Russians are unhappy with the newly rich who are at the top of Russian society, presumably because they have obtained many of these rewards unjustifiably and at great cost to the ordinary citizen.

Russians tend to possess a strong sense of dignity and composure. Even though the lower classes may never experience the thrill of a performance, Russians share a great pride for the reputation of their form of ballet as both enchanting magic and a symbol of magnificence. The very westernness of ballet reflects Russian dignity and superiority, regardless of class status. The most prestigious of dance companies is the Bolshoi Ballet, which tours from the Bolshoi Theatre in Moscow throughout the world. The Moscow Academic Choreographic Institute, better known as the Bolshoi School, is formally affiliated with the ballet company and is located adjacent to the theater. Less famous but sharing an equally superb tradition of dancers, teachers, and choreographers is the Kirov Ballet Company. This company and its school descend directly from Empress Anna's imperial school and ballet company and still make their home in the same building in St. Petersburg today.

Drama and Realism

Audiences throughout the world recognize Russian ballet as the most spectacular form of dance. No other art form requires such a combination of elegance and simplicity—Russian ballet is distinctive from ballet of other national origins because of its singular innovations that have developed from classical ballet foundations. Although ballet stagnated for many years in the West, Russia, along with the rest of the Soviet Union, cultivated its theatrical resources to develop unimpeachable superiority over all other national ballets. Only the pageantry of the Italian opera rivals the brilliance of the Russian ballet, and only the Spanish bullfight compares with its drama. The pursuit of perfection in Russian ballet has become an inspiration to thousands of audiences and a permanent part of Russian culture and pride.

Audiences feel the vitality of the corps de ballet during the most dramatic moments of the performance. Throughout the ballet, dancers seek audience approval by delivering increasingly lofty performances. Sometimes, the audience will respond to a dance so positively that a dancer will step out of character and take a bow, something that happens rarely in the West. In the final scene, the dancers pour their remaining ounces of energy into the dance in order to make an unforgettably grand impression on every last spectator. Each member of the company strives to be remembered in the minds of the audience as a glorious image of movement. In response, the audience expresses approval in the form of applause, floral gifts, and ovations. The dancer offers his or her performance, again and again, in return for audience gratification.

Like the dancer who makes a personal attempt to appeal to people in the audience, the ordinary Russian citizen tries to make an impression on those who are in a position to help. The most efficient way to accomplish anything is through personal favors. Rather than jeopardizing careers by assuming risk or showing initiative, some Russians will avoid taking responsibility or other action that may be construed as controversial, especially when jobs are scarce.

Similarly, the interchange between the dancer and the audience is symbolic of the basic exchange between total strangers in mundane matters. Whether the dancer gives pleasure to those who watch and is rewarded with faithful appreciation from the audience, or two citizens or firms barter with one another, each participant offers the other one something that he or she desires.

Just as Mexicans tend to use the fiesta to escape a mundane existence, so, too, do Russians place great value on the theatrical component of the performing arts. Films, plays, and the ballet offer a chance for diversion. The ultimate cultural fantasy is comprised of a melodramatic storyline surrounded with extravagant scenery and fancy costumes. The greater the pull of the heartstrings, the more Russians tend to love it; this sentimentality is part of the rare self-indulgence of the culture. Like the ballet company that relies on theatrics to please the audience, the Russian shopper uses drama to persuade the clerk to decrease the price of an item. An indisputable part of Russian culture is the custom of bargaining and negotiation to beat the system. Similarly, at an early age, students learn to supply the right answer in the classroom. Sharing of answers is tolerated, and children become adept at skirting around authority with minimal confrontation.

As might be expected in an autocratic culture, favoritism and corruption have been and continue to be used extensively to get around the system. Disobeying laws is a part of Russian culture, even if for mere trifles. It is little wonder that firms must have their own private police forces. Friends and connections are important, and many Russians have developed complex networks of relationships that allow them to survive in an unpredictable world. A great deal of effort is required to create and maintain these relationships, in the hope that benefits will result. Russians are continual gift givers, hoping to influence future generosity on the part of others. Such behavior is not likely to change, even with widespread privatization of the economy.

Russians initially tend to take extreme views and offer few concessions when negotiating. If a foreign opponent makes a concession, it is perceived as a weakness. Unlike American negotiators, Russians have little authority to make on-the-spot decisions and prefer not to make decisions spontaneously. Chess is a national pastime, and much of the relative strength of the many regional and world champions from Russia comes from their ability to think ahead. Players rely on strategic planning, whether offensive or defensive, to consider potential repercussions, similar to what the Russians do when negotiating.

Furthermore, many consider drinking vodka to be a national pastime. Drunkenness is accepted as a socially approved method of entertainment and escape that is helpful in coping with years of suffering and hardship. Russians respect the need to drink thoughtfully or sorrowfully. At the same time, they join together in triumphant discovery—singing, laughing, and forgetting time. Especially in rural areas, drinking is a part of any type of festivity. Despite severe shortages, Russians manage to make a feast out of nothing. Kitchen tables are the most likely setting for sharing conversation and vodka with friends. Throughout this culture, there is a tenderness, and even an affection, shown by sober people to those who have overindulged. Everyone seems to understand the Russian need to consume vodka, although alcoholism is a widespread problem that has been linked to many social ills.

Another important difference is Russian patience in working out compromises. Whereas time is a precious resource for American negotiators, deadlines often go ignored in Russian negotiations. Budgets and production schedules traditionally have been difficult to meet, and the prevailing attitude has been "Why bother?" Within the bureaucracy, it is apparent that citizens are used to tolerating long delays and complacency.

Compromise is not always necessary for achieving goals; compassionate appeals may be equally effective. Yale Richmond (1992) describes the time that he arrived at his hotel in Moscow hungry, after a long plane flight, only to learn from the woman in charge of guest services that the currency exchange office was closed for the day. He was traveling alone, did not have any rubles, and therefore would be unable to pay for dinner. When asked, she had no suggestions to offer. Instead of retreating, Richmond chatted with this complete stranger about his trip, the weather, his family, and her children, and eventually, he returned to the subject of his hunger. This time, she reached into her own purse and lent him some rubles until the next day. Although he did not expect to bargain with the woman, he approached her as another human being, and she responded with kindness.

Haskell (1963, 1968) makes several points about the role of realism in Russian ballet. First, Russian choreography tends to emphasize realistic interpretations through the expressions of characters, as noted in the part of Albrecht in *Giselle*. Whether Nureyev or Vikulov played the role, it was played with such vivacity that the transition from self-centeredness to remorsefulness over his lover's suffering was genuinely evident to the viewer. Besides individualistic realism, the spectacle is subordinated to the human values in the story. In Russian versions of *Sleeping Beauty,* the scene in which Princess Aurora falls into her slumber is choreographed with more than 100 dancers on stage. Even in the midst of a Russian crowd, the audience can sense a very real interaction among the principal dancers. Western productions of the same scene tend to be vacuous, usually employing only Princess Aurora and four suitors at most. Another Russian contribution to the world of ballet, according to Haskell, is the reliance on experts for accurate set and costume design. Leon Bakst, famous for creating lavish sets and costumes, was the first to tie his depictions to historical information relative to the era in which a ballet took place. Thus, Russian costumes have always been able to boast a thread of truth, and sets on the Russian stage have likewise lent credibility to the ambience of the ballet.

It is well known that idealism is very important to most Russians. During Communist rule, atheism became the official policy on religious affiliation as the party ideology replaced the church. Official pressures made it risky for most of society to openly participate in religion, which led to an underground system of hidden beliefs. Since the adoption of a 1990 law allowing religious freedom, many Russians have renewed their interest in the traditional values of the Orthodox Church. In 1991, for the first time in more than 70 years, the Orthodox Christmas Day (which is celebrated not on December 25th but on January 7) was proclaimed a national holiday in Russia.

Realism also plays a role in everyday life in Russia as people attempt to survive daily obstacles. Connections, or personal contacts, are easily the most valued perquisite for the privileged. Knowing someone who is able to influence an outcome is an accepted way of life in Russia. Pulling strings is an effective way to arrange the swap of apartments between strangers and acquaintances. Procuring a single ticket to a ballet at the Bolshoi requires connections unless one is an extremely senior government official, a well-placed businessperson, or a foreign tourist.

Connections can also be serious business, as in the case of a doctor willing to recommend a surgeon to a patient who wishes to circumvent the bureaucratic health system. The ultimate accomplishment of a parent is to secure better educational opportunities for a child; special arrangements can be made outside of the formal admission system of a school. Regardless of the type of favor asked, it is understood that a return favor may be redeemed at a later date. In some cases, it can be very helpful to slip the contact a bribe of rubles, chocolates, or even a Western trinket like a felt-tip pen or a wall calendar. Building personal recognition is the first step in securing a long-term connection.

Another dramatic tool borrowed from a ballet performance is the use of *vranya,* or bluffing. *Vranya* is best characterized by the statement, "You know I'm lying, and I know that you know and you know that I know, but I go ahead with a straight face and you nod seriously." It is publicly distasteful for most Russians to admit that anything has gone wrong. Social ills have been repressed in an attempt to maintain the image of Russian superiority.

From a foreign perspective, Russians have been characterized as serious and unexpressive, betraying no emotion in public. They hold a reputation for hardiness and stoicism. Often, this external toughness comes across as coarse indifference or pushy discourtesy to the visitor. In the brusque surliness of service people, and glum faces of crowds full of impassive stares, foreigners find the gruff, cold impersonality we expect. But this exterior is *maskirovannoye,* a false front. The stereotypical demeanor is part of the drama of Russian culture. Underneath the mask is a raw humanness that could not be more real.

Ballet is much more than a dance on stage; it is a marvel of choreography, music, costumes, and lighting that creates a distinct mood for each audience. Choreographers express ideas through every dancer's movements, whether presenting a precise theme or leaving an audience free to use its imagination. Composers write scores for accompaniment to the beautiful technique of ballet, and orchestral conductors lead musicians to perform scores at the proper tempo, rhythm, and volume for dancers. Wardrobe designers and lighting experts use special knowledge of their crafts for ballet productions, and visual artists also contribute to the mood by designing sets to provide the proper backdrop for each dance. Finally, trained athletic dancers combine flexibility, strength, and balance to perform a series of dances that often tells a story for spectators of all ages.

A final consideration of this characteristic of Russian culture is the seeming contradiction of drama and realism. On the surface, these principles appear to be opposites. Herein lies one of the major dichotomies within the culture. Theatrics project a contrived atmosphere, whereas realism is rejection of visionary ideals. One of the more puzzling aspects of Russian culture is the illusion of disparity. Russians are categorized as both lazy and hard-working; they want to have money, yet they despise it. Russians are depicted as uninterested in building relationships (Adler, 1997) and, at the same time, as "warm and helpful" after new interpersonal relationships are formed (Richmond, 1992, p. 3). Russians seemingly want to *get* money rather than *earn* it. Russian people do not usually respect those who simply work hard, and yet they are willing to make sacrifices themselves. Denied religious freedom for more than 70 years, Russians still possess faith and hope. Russians tend to be both dreamy and pragmatic; they place great value on the work of writers, artists, and dancers. Like members of other cultures, Russians are faced with choices about priorities.

Conflicting roles exist between public and private relationships. In their public roles, Russians are characterized as careful, cagey, and passive; in their private lives, they are depicted as honest and direct. Foreigners describe Russians as suffering, unruly, and stoic; they are also known as cheerful, generous, obedient, and hospitable. Like other nationalities, they can be publicly pompous and privately unpretentious, caring, or unkind. Perhaps Dostoyevsky described it best as "half saint and half savage." With friends, Russians feel free to pour out woes to one another and are not burdened by the need to disguise the realities of disappointment or pain.

The Russian Soul

From the 13th century until the time of Peter the Great, and then from 1917 to 1992 during the Communist era, Russians were isolated from the rest of the world. Two events, the Tatar (Mongol) invasion and the Ottoman conquest of Constantinople, abruptly halted commercial, religious, and cultural exchanges with other nations and limited Russia's development for centuries. Russia had relatively little need for trade because it was self-sufficient in agriculture; most of its interaction with other nations related to land disputes. From the Russian perspective, territorial expansion resulted from victories over foreign invaders. At one time or another, Teutonic Knights, Lithuanians, Poles, Swedes, French, Germans, and Asian groups invaded Russia, which has no natural border defenses. On all sides, fear of invasion by neighboring adversaries led to a Russian preoccupation with state security. A tradition of serving the state, whether peasant or noble, evolved from the suspicion of the hostile powers that surrounded Russia. In subsequent centuries, Russian rulers purposely limited foreign influence on the empire, and as a result, later attempts to introduce new methods and technologies were met with skepticism by the people.

Today, Russian distrust is still prevalent, as indicated by their feelings about Western influence noted above. Also, Russia is concerned about the rising importance of China, with which it shares borders. As we might expect, Russians want to be independent of foreign influence, and this is refracted in the concept of the Russian soul, which basically reflects the desire for distance so that the culture can be preserved, as it has been for so long. Reinforcement of the idea that distance is essential for survival is a characteristic of the Russian citizen, even today. As a people, Russians are considered self-reliant, strong willed, and full of inner resources. Although it may seem that so many years of czarist regimes and the iron fist of Communism have hindered the outward use of such resources, the argument is well-supported that, in fact, individual perseverance and creativity have thrived in spite of absolute rule. Undoubtedly, many Russians have been very entrepreneurial since 1992, but the inadequacy of the infrastructure, such as effective laws and banks, has stymied their efforts.

Each member of a Russian ballet troupe must endure laborious training on a daily basis and possess unfailing discipline in order to perfect the art. Classes, rehearsals, and performances comprise an exhausting routine for Russian dancers; this cycle amounts to a dancer's complete focus on the world of dance with little time for much else. This distance or separation from everyday life allows the dancer to put all of his or her energy into the dance. Orthopedic surgeons, massage therapists, and medicine have become part of the reality of contemporary ballet; physical demands often require dancing through bodily aches and pains. Relying on Russian self-determination, each dancer is able to achieve total concentration, fueled by the passionate intensity of the Russian soul. The result is unmatched excellence, both in technical performance and in artistry.

The Russian soul is a mixture of intense feeling; it is emotion, sentiment, and sensitivity combined. It is triumph over seemingly insurmountable troubles, or sadness arising from the discovery of stark truth. Over the years, much has been written about the magic and mystic nature of the Russian soul. What is known as something mysterious seems to boil down to this: At the very core of individual Russian expression is the enigmatic principle or soul that places absolute value on decency, respect, honesty, and moral goodness. As a result partly of heredity and partly of learning, the people of Russia seem to have a stony resolve unlike any other that can be interchanged with human compassion in the blink of an eye. Creative, electrifying, and daring, the Russian soul is the source of inspiration within the dancer.

Throughout the arts, the Russian soul is the unmistakable power that compels the writer, actor, painter, or dancer to aspire to greatness. A potent force, the Russian soul shaped the insightful expression of Dostoyevsky's writings. His literature revealed the extent of responsibility that Russians feel for the afflictions and pain of the rest of the world. Company and conversations begin to matter as soon as one steps into a Russian's personal life. Among friends and family, Russians become the wonderful, flowing, emotional people of Tolstoy novels, sharing humor and sorrows and confidences. They enter a simple intimacy in which individuals are less self-centered than in the West. Russians tend to pour out their hearts in total commitment to friendships and become easygoing, affectionate, and tender.

Furthermore, intellectuals look for a spiritual compensation to escape the boredom of everyday life, whether in ballet, novels, or poems. Russian culture reveres poetry for its wit, courage, and creativity. Poets such as Pushkin are regarded as heroes for daring to use metaphor to conceal meanings in light of censorship.

Intimacy appears to be more pronounced among Russian families than elsewhere in the world. Accommodations are typically crowded, with multigenerational families living in very small spaces. Although changing, extended families have resided together in cramped situations under relentless scrutiny for decades, usually within apartments. Beds serve as couches in sitting areas, and bathroom facilities are shared among many within the apartment. Privacy is an oddity; no Russian word exists to describe isolation in positive terms.

Many Russians like to think that they have a monopoly on virtue, whether it refers to family loyalty, a sense of duty, or love of nature. Emotionality is considered a positive attribute, and some of the most convincing arguments between Russians appeal to the irrational element of human existence. Guilt is also a factor in emotionality. Similarly, the presence of guilt helps the dancer to feel more deeply. Russians feel that they can communicate emotions through their eyes, conveying love, hate, or passion. Whether emanating unbounded joy or expressing woeful melancholy, the Russian dancer performs with an inner dynamism that members of other cultures find very difficult to duplicate. The severe Russian climate is also responsible for both the resourcefulness and the strength of Russian people. For centuries, peasants have endured long winters of bitterly cold temperatures, brutal winds, and frozen grounds while longing for spring. Springtime inevitably brings the considerable work of quickly tilling soil and planting seeds so that crops may be harvested before the first frost less than 5 months later. Unpredictable weather and danger of crop failure are of great concern, yet Russians have proven able to endure hardship. Unable or, in many cases, unwilling to take risks with imported technologies, peasants rely on familiar, if primitive, tools and techniques. They are masters of patience and resolve, recognizing that they do not have control over everything in life. As Yale Richmond (1992) explains,

> In contrast to Americans, most Russians have lived, until recently, much
> as their ancestors did before them—in small villages, distant and isolated,
> their freedom of movement restricted, and without the comforts and
> labor-saving tools provided by modern society. (p. 9)

The geography contributes to feelings of powerlessness; the mountainous
terrain and desolate barren spaces outside of the cities are under continual
permafrost. Russia is one of the least densely populated nations in the world.
There are only nine inhabitants per square kilometer.

Just as Russian workers in the city or country survive harsh winters and
hot summers, children also learn to adapt to hardship. Parental indulgence is
a national cult, and toys teach meaningful lessons. Russian-made toys tend to
break easily, and when children experience the disappointment or anger of a
new or favorite toy falling apart, they learn that they have little control over
their world. Russian children learn to accept the fact that their world is not
perfect without too much bitterness. Perhaps this is why students of Russian
ballet are able to adjust without bitterness to grueling schedules of dance
instruction, traditional classroom subjects, and physical workouts that build
strength and flexibility.

At all levels of society, the device of public shaming is central to the
Russian system. There is a collective responsibility for children, exhibited
through overprotectiveness. Russian babies are traditionally wrapped in
kosinkas, a mummy-like wrapping that allows little movement. Infants are
bundled so tightly that they can barely move. Russian culture reasons that
swaddling is necessary for the first 9 months of life to protect a baby from
hurting itself. The baby is unswaddled only for nursing and bathing, at which
time he or she is showered with love and affection. A baby learns to develop
complete trust in his or her mother, who returns that trust with complete and
uncritical love. Thus, an infant is unable to explore fully his or her environment and must rely on only his or her eyes or cries to express emotions. During the period of swaddling, the baby experiences repeated feelings of both
security and anger, which are replaced with freedom and happiness when the
kosinka is removed from time to time. Besides achieving total dependence on
the part of parents, the Russian baby continually experiences polarized emotions in infancy. As a result, the Russian child grows up with the dual beliefs
of powerlessness and guilt for personal actions. Like the special relationship
between Japanese mothers and their sons that results in the creation of *amae,*
or dependency (see Chapter 3), long-lasting psychological dependency is
generally emphasized in Russian culture.

Without a doubt, Russian society has a pronounced collective emphasis.
Szalay (1993) found that Americans make almost twice as many associations
to the word "individual" than do Russians, whereas Russians make almost
three times as many associations to the word "people" as do Americans.

Young children are taught how to behave and relate to others at an early age. Respect and deference for authority figures is a norm in every classroom. Landon Pearson (1990) points out that "A respectful and, indeed, slightly fearful attitude to adult authority is inculcated into Soviet children from the moment they set foot into an educational establishment" (p. 111). From childhood on, Russians acquire an acute sense of place and propriety, of what is acceptable and what is not. They generally know what they can get away with, and what should not be attempted. Student discussion is limited, and individual thought is not encouraged. Pupils learn that supplying "official" answers ensures good grades, which can lead to admission to higher education and a good job after graduation.

Educational institutions are designed to shape young minds using structured discipline and group dynamics. Much learning is based on memory drills and the modeling of rigid prescriptions. Enormous peer pressure is exerted over children to achieve stringent expectations. Russian children learn early the futility of challenging authority; parents are often chastised by teachers and other officials for the failure of offspring to meet social norms.

One of the more remarkable new universities reflects this modeling of strict behavior, but in both a new and a traditional way that is reflective of the era of Russian royalty. The New University of the Humanities emphasizes the teaching of proper manners, particularly within the Institute for Noble Young Ladies, modeled on an imperial-era boarding school that trained the daughters of wealthy merchants and noblemen in the czar's court. Other educational groups are also stressing etiquette because it is critical in business, particularly international business. Many of the new rich are sending their children to these schools, as are many others who have difficulty paying the tuition, which is $1,500 a year at the University (see Williams, 1998).

Formal ballet productions bring together dancing, music, design, and an audience. With the exception of solos by individual dancers, the ballet troupe dances together as one large body. Even the solos are precisely "blocked," or staged, by choreographers to balance the entire performance. All members of the company are mutually dependent upon each other, and individual needs, rights, and desires are subordinated to the whole, to the company itself. It is the choreographer's job to integrate the dancer's body with the music score, the possibilities of the stage, and the mood to be conveyed. Choreographers must "explore and expand the dancer's capabilities" while ensuring that the components of the ballet production, as well as the dancers, are all in sync (Clarke & Crisp, 1976, p. 38). As a result, Russian dancers think of themselves as members of a company, and "people's artists" of the former USSR, rather than as individual dancers.

The group ethic can be traced to the mir, or the small village cooperative that made all farming decisions for the community, even through the early 1900s. Not only did the mir choose which crops to plant and when, but it also collected taxes and resolved conflicts. As Richmond (1992) notes, "Its authority, moreover, extended beyond land matters. It also disciplined members, intervened in family disputes, settled issues that affected the community as a whole, and otherwise regulated the affairs of its self-contained and isolated agricultural world" (p. 15). The mir consisted of household heads who discussed issues and reached group consensus about courses of action. Decisions based on the collective will were binding on every household. Even before the 1917 revolution, Russian czars approved of this type of informal local government because such units were capable of controlling the vast populace. The mir enforced both tax collection and military conscription, as well as other programs that influenced the lives of the peasants. In describing the mir, Richmond (1992) aptly concludes, "Because the mir affected so many people, it played a major role in forming the Soviet character" (p. 15). It is interesting to note that popular usage of the word mir refers to the definition of peace.

A few examples of collective behavior include communal seating in restaurants and group participation in attending cultural and sports events. Physical contact, such as jostling or pushing among total strangers, is typical in crowds, as is holding hands among friends of the same sex. Older Russians generally are more than happy to offer unsolicited advice, even to foreigners, and it is seldom considered impolite to drop in on friends unannounced (Richmond, 1992, pp. 17-20).

In sum, like the ballet, Russian culture can be unpredictable and enigmatic. Russian culture today fuses together the earnest elements of emotion, spirituality, and survival once found in old Russia. Echelons within Russian society, drama and realism, and the Russian soul as expressed in Russian ballet are characteristics that have made the Russian people culturally unique. Although Russia may privatize its economy significantly and become more Western in its economic orientation—and the jury is still out on this matter— the characteristics of the Russian ballet described in this chapter should be of help in understanding Russia's underlying culture for years to come.

PART VII

Same Metaphor, Different Meanings

S ometimes, what is seemingly the same cultural metaphor is interpreted in a radically different manner in different nations. For example, the symbols connected with the Spanish bullfight are radically different from those related to the Portuguese bullfight. In the Spanish bullfight, the bull is killed, whereas in the Portuguese bullfight, it is only harnessed or stopped physically. Thus, we need to be sure that the metaphor we choose to study is one for which there is no ambiguity or confusion. In this part of the book, we describe Spain and Portugal through the cultural metaphors of their respective bullfights.

CHAPTER 22

The Spanish Bullfight

The characteristic that, on the surface, best portrays Spaniards is their contagious vitality, their love of life. Therefore, it may seem paradoxical that the metaphor used in this chapter to describe Spanish culture is the bullfight, a confrontation with death. Yet this feature touches on other, less obvious qualities pervasive among Spaniards. Underlying their outer joy, or *alegría,* Spaniards tend to host a deeply ingrained sensitivity to the tragic, and an equally strong emotional pull toward the heroic. Perhaps these characteristics, more than their love of life, are what has made the bullfight *la fiesta nacional* for hundreds of years; in combination, these characteristics are manifested in a unique form of individualism emphasizing self-reliance and pride. The bullfight combines a passionate celebration of life with an elaborate system of rituals—a grandiose and artistic spectacle with blood, violence, and an all-too-real danger to the valiant performers. It exemplifies Spanish pride, individualism, emotionalism, and many other characteristics of Spanish people and culture.

As might be expected, flamenco and the bullfight are closely intertwined, and both activities highlight the proud and self-sufficient flavor of individualism unique to Spain. Whatever a Spaniard does, he or she wants it to be distinctively individualistic and a personal expression of individuality. For example, in Germany, a symphony may advertise that its program will be the same on both a Friday and a Saturday night, and in that program, there will be few, if any, differences in the performances. This is not true in Spain, for each bullfight and each flamenco dance is, or should be, unique. The following discussion will relate different aspects of Spain's culture to the many facets of the bullfight. But first, the sequence of the event itself is provided in order to establish the language and image of the bullfight.

The bullfight, or *corrida de toros,* meaning "running of the bulls" (also, *la corrida* or *los toros* for short), takes place on Sunday afternoons or on holidays, timed precisely against the setting of the sun. The corrida begins with the white handkerchief signal of the officiating president and the sounding of a trumpet. The commencement of the bullfight is celebrated with the colorful opening *paseillo,* or parade of participants that marches in hierarchical order to the upbeat tune of the *pasodoble*. Once the parade is over, the president again uses his white handkerchief to signal the entrance of the first bull, as he does to signal the beginning of each stage of the event.

There are three separate groups (cuadrillas) of principal participants in the corrida. Each group is made up of a matador and his assistants. The cuadrillas fight and kill two bulls each, for a total of six bullfights during the event. When the first bull is released into the ring, it is confronted by three of the matador's assistants, the banderilleros. These men maneuver the bull with their magenta and gold capes, revealing to the matador the bull's peculiarities of movement; sometimes, the matador participates in this stage as well.

A few minutes later, the matador enters the ring and demonstrates his bravery with his more artistic cape passes, including the classic verónica. The matador's valor, or lack thereof, often evokes emotional responses among the spectators. They applaud, cheer, and shout "Olé!" when impressed by the matador's bravery, or boo and whistle when they are displeased with his performance. In this way, the public interacts with the matador, prompting him to perform more and more dangerous and aesthetically beautiful moves. These, in turn, further arouse the audience.

After the initial demonstrations with the bull, the two picadores enter the ring on horseback. One stands by as a reserve, and the other provokes the bull into charging his own horse. This allows him to get close enough to the bull to jab it with his long, spiked pole. The picador's task is to sufficiently weaken the bull so that his speed will decrease, thus allowing the bullfighter to show his abilities.

The second stage of the bullfight allows the bull to perk up from its difficult ordeal with the picador. In this more exciting part of the fight, the banderilleros, on foot, each place two banderillas (colorfully decorated wooden sticks with barbed tips) into the bull's neck, where they should remain. At this point, the bull is rested and more ferocious than ever; it is ready to challenge the matador in the final stage of the fight.

In the final phase, the matador has 15 minutes to display his skill and build up the drama of the "moment of truth," performing dangerous passes with the much smaller red cape (muleta), which is draped over his sword.

Before beginning, he salutes the president; asks permission to kill the bull if it is his first bull of the afternoon; and may dedicate the kill to a friend, a dignitary, or the public. Once the kill is complete, the response of members of the audience determines to a large extent the level of the reward the matador is to receive. Ultimately, the president decides on the level of the reward. A brave bull, too, is applauded as it is dragged out of the arena.

The same three stages are repeated for each of the five remaining bulls in the corrida, alternating cuadrillas with each new bull. The bullfight officially ends when the president leaves his seat.

Ancient Origins of the Bullfight

The bullfight has long been a popular feature of Spanish culture. Its appearance in Spain has been attributed to a number of possible sources, including festivities of the ancient Minoan culture on the island of Crete 2000 years before Christ, Roman circus combats, and the Moors. Whichever explanation may be true, the roots of the Spanish bullfight lay buried under layers of different peoples who invaded the Iberian Peninsula (now Spain and Portugal), bringing their respective cultures with them.

The same waves of invasions that, somewhere along the way, gave birth to the bullfight also bred the uniquely Spanish blend of races. People have inhabited what is now Spain for more than 100,000 years. Traces of the peninsula's prehistoric inhabitants include the famous cave paintings of Altamira, which are at least 13,000 years old. Recorded history picks up with the migration of the Iberian people from northern Africa into the southern two thirds of the peninsula, around 3000 B.C. A series of other peoples subsequently came to Spain to conquer, trade, or settle there. The Phoenicians (a Semitic race) came first, followed by Celts (a Nordic race), Greeks, Carthaginians (from Carthage in northern Africa), Romans, Jews, Germanic tribes, and Moors. Gypsies are the most recent racial group to have taken their place in Spanish society, arriving from Egypt in the Middle Ages.

Cuadrillas

The successive waves of invasion and immigration can be likened to the repeated attacks of the fighting bull and, even more appropriately, to the series of six bulls that is released into the ring during the course of the event. In terms of this metaphor, foreign invasions were so common throughout Spain's early history that it would take two consecutive corridas for the defending toreros to experience as many attacking bulls as there were invading peoples!

The physical characteristics resulting from the coming together of these various racial groups on the Iberian Peninsula are a mixture of short, dark, Semitic types (predominant in the south) and taller, fair descendents of Celtic and Germanic ancestors (most common in the north). Frequently, combinations of these traits are seen as well, such as the large number of people with dark hair and blue eyes. Another prevalent trait among Spaniards is the classic Roman nose. In sum, there is no single image that would portray a "typical" Spaniard accurately, although certain combinations of features are notably Spanish, especially if one looks separately at the different regions of Spain. In addition, there are certain personality traits that cross tribal boundaries. Wheaton (1990) reports that "the Greek philosopher Stabo found common traits among all the isolated bands living on the peninsula: hospitality, grand manners, arrogance, indifference to privation, and hatred of outside interference in community affairs" (p. 21). These are characteristics that are still used frequently to describe the Spanish temperament.

The various invading peoples are also responsible for importing a number of prominent cultural attributes into Spain. The Romans (who ruled Spain for 400 years beginning around 200 B.C.) brought their "vulgar Latin" language with them, which evolved into today's Castilian Spanish. The Spanish word for Spain—*España*—is only a slightly modified version of the Latin name *Hispania,* which the Romans gave to the country. (Previously, Spain had been called Iberia by its Iberian inhabitants and Hesperia by the Greeks.) The Romans also constructed aqueducts, bridges, roads, and walls. The famous two-level aqueduct of Segovia stands as an impressive relic of the Roman rule. Finally, the Romans were responsible for the spread of Christianity into Spain.

Attributable to the more than 700-year presence of the Muslim Arabs, or Moors, are more than 4,000 words used in modern Spanish. Words for many agricultural products that the Moors brought with them derive from this source, as do many words beginning with *al.* Examples include the Spanish word *arroz* from the Arabic *al ruzz* (rice), *aceite* from *al zait* (olive oil), and *naranja* from *naranj* (orange)—foods that are now an intricate part of the Spanish diet (Graham, 1984). The Arabic influence in Spain is also responsible for advances in the fields of irrigation, mathematics, medicine, and, most notably, architecture, among others. The light, airy, and colorful *mezquita,* or mosque, in Córdoba and the impressive palaces Alhambra and Generalife in Granada are present-day monuments of Moorish architectural feats.

The cuadrillas in the bullfight clearly show Spaniards' attitude toward teams and collectivism. In a country with strong individualism, but a shared need for defense, association with others is sometimes necessary. Translated, cuadrilla does not mean team; the men in the cuadrilla do not work together closely. Rather, *cuadrilla* means "group, bank, or gang," reflecting the fact that there is safety in numbers and the toreros combine their distinct, individual efforts to achieve the death of the bull. Spanish history is full of heroic events when strong and proud individuals gathered to achieve some common temporary and difficult goal, such as the voluntary self-burning of the entire town of Numancia before giving up to the Romans, the conquistadors in Latin America, and the guerrilla warfare against Napoleon. In fact, the term "guerrilla warfare" was first used to describe the seemingly unorganized but systematic attacks that the Spanish used to defeat Napoleon in 1812.

The repeated invasions of the Iberian Peninsula by foreigners produced a tendency for the inhabitants to cluster together for a sense of security and control over the environment. This effect, and the lack of abundant water, is reflected in the fact that Spanish peasants on the steppes of central Spain chose to build their houses near one another, forming many small hamlets, villages, and towns. Their fear of loneliness and desire for security were so strong that they were, and still are, willing to travel great distances to work their fields just so that they may live in the vicinity of others (Crow, 1985).

The tendency for Spaniards to live close together has generalized to urban housing arrangements, which take the form of apartment living rather than isolated home owning. In Spain, as in much of Europe, it is desirable to live as close to the center of the city as possible, where the action is. Marvin (1988) writes, "It is felt that as one moves further from the centre, so the quality of life gradually diminishes, because at the far limits of the town there are few bars, shops and *plazas* [squares] where people gather" (p. 129). The effect of this sentiment can be compared to housing patterns in the United States. The middle-class American's ideal house is in the suburbs with a nice-sized yard, or, for the wealthy, a mansion in the midst of many acres of land. In Spain, the wealthiest Spaniards choose to make their urban apartments their permanent dwelling. They may, however, enjoy a country home as a secondary, weekend getaway.

The widespread insecurity among Spaniards that historically made city life so appealing may well be the reason why Spain had an above-average score on uncertainty avoidance in Hofstede's (1991) study of cultural values in 53 nations. That is, Spaniards prefer to interact with long-term friends and acquaintances rather than with outsiders. As a result, Spaniards tend to work in the same organization for many years or even their entire lifetimes. Relating the need for control over one's environment and nature to the bullfight in southern Spain, where the event first appeared, Marvin (1988) writes the following:

> Nowhere is this subordination and "culturizing" of nature, in Andalusian terms, more dramatically demonstrated than in the corrida. It is an urban event intimately linked with the country, which brings together, in

the centre of human habitation, an uncontrolled wild bull, an item from the realm of nature, and a man who represents the epitome of culture in that, more than any ordinary man, he is able to exercise control over his "natural" fear (the fear felt by the human animal), an essential prerequisite if he is to control the wild animal. . . . The corrida is constructed in such a way that the imposition of human will is extremely uncertain because of the difficult circumstances; a situation which in turn generates tension, emotion, and dramatic interest. (pp. 130-131)

However, Spaniards' true loyalty does not extend to the larger collective; it is generally directed only toward a smaller unit: family, friends, town, or region. Like the cuadrilla, the family is a large and affectionate clan whose members ferociously defend each other's honor, rights, jobs, and so on. The worst insult one can give a man is to derogate his mother, and the worst thing one can say to a woman is to insult her child (Wheaton, 1990). The protective spirit of the family also extends to the upbringing of the children. Parents dress their children well and pamper them. They bring them along wherever they go and allow them to stay up until all hours of the night. This produces children who are good-natured and outgoing, and who have a strong sense of self and of their own importance (Wheaton, 1990).

The backbone of the tribal system during Spain's history of battles and invasions was the women. Tough and resourceful, they held the group together and catered to the needs of family members (Crow, 1985). However, historically, the woman's role is more of a nurturing one than an authoritative one. Thus, it is the husband, not the wife, whose role can be compared to that of the matador, as the person who has the last word. Like the matador who adoringly dedicates the kill to his wife or sweetheart, the Spanish husband accords his wife her due respect as stronghold of the family; he thinks of her as if she were a saint. And he expects her to behave like one. Until very recently, the laws supported this expectation. However, there have been many social changes in recent years, as discussed later in this chapter.

General Francisco Franco's 36-year dictatorship, from the Spanish Civil War until his death in 1975, had more backward policies for women than any other European country. A wife had to have her husband's written permission to do many things outside the home, such as opening a bank account, obtaining a passport, or traveling abroad. Civil divorce was illegal until 1981. Abortion, homosexuality, and adultery were also punishable by law. Extramarital affairs were considered unconditionally criminal for women; men were at fault only if they tainted the family's honor by failing to keep their affairs clandestine (Wheaton, 1990). The macho "Don Juanism" is so ingrained in Spanish culture that it was considered perfectly acceptable for a husband to keep a mistress on the side. However, although the famous, nonfictional Don Juan conquered numerous women's hearts, he usually did so one at a time, keeping the women's reputations and status intact.

All this has been changing rapidly in the past 15 years. Now, several hundred thousand mothers are unmarried, and the use of contraceptives among married women is widespread. Kissing and embracing in public are common. University attendance is split equally between the sexes. However, few women in Spanish society attain high-level jobs, and Spanish heritage is, of course, still patrilineal. However, children go by both their father's and mother's last names. In addition, when a woman gets married, she keeps her name but adds her husband's name to her own, linking the two by the possessive word *de,* or "of." For example, if a woman named Maria Alberti married a man named Miguel Sanchez, her name would officially become Maria Alberti de Sanchez. If her husband then died, she would become Maria Alberti Viuda de Sanchez—literally, Maria Alberti Widow of Sanchez.

The family is only one side of the Spanish tendency to cluster into loose groups like the cuadrilla. Historically, when the people of Spain started grouping together, they did not unite under a national flag; the geographical boundaries that sliced up the country topographically and climatically also retained invaders and inhabitants within isolated regions of the peninsula. Therefore, foreign influences and native loyalties were determined by region, resulting in vastly differing cultures and distinct personal appearances. There are four different languages and many dialects spoken in Spain: Castilian, known outside of Spain as Spanish; Catalonian, Galician, and Basque. Despite the similarities, the cultural differences between these regions remain incredibly large.

The greatest geographical barriers in Spain are its mountain ranges. Although foreigners normally think of Spain's sunny beaches and flat, coastal plains, it is actually one of the most mountainous countries in Europe, second only to Switzerland. Also, Spain is the second largest country (behind France) in Western Europe and has a population of 40 million. Although Spaniards in the city live close to one another, the population density is only 79 people per kilometer versus 229 for Germany. Therefore, distance separates people and allows for great variation in culture and the look of the land.

Sol y Sombra

Seating at the bullfight is divided into three sections: sun (*sol*), shade (*sombra*), and a combination of sun and shade (*sol y sombra*). This is made possible by the previously mentioned fact that the hour at which the bullfight takes place is timed against the setting sun. Tickets for seats in the shade are the most expensive. They cost approximately double the price of seats in the sun, which are the cheapest. Because bullfight tickets are relatively expensive to begin with, the price differential in seating separates the members of the audience into wealthier and poorer groups.

With a few exceptions, Spain itself can be divided into the cooler, wet, more prosperous north and the hot, dry, lethargic south. It also has a large, central plateau area (the *meseta,* or "tableland") that undergoes extremes of both heat and cold, and poverty and wealth, making it comparable to the *sol y sombra* sections. A more detailed description of some of the better known Spanish regions will help illustrate the depth of regional differences in geography, climate, people, and culture.

There are 17 regional states in Spain, and in recent years, there has been a devolution of power from the national government to them. Given their unique languages and cultures, the Basque provinces and Catalonia are of particular interest, as noted below.

In the northwestern corner of Spain, just above Portugal, lies Galicia. Its frequent rain and drizzle, lush vegetation, and wide *rías* (fjords) simulate the Northern European landscape of the natives' Nordic ancestors who settled in the region. The Gallegans also share their fair skin, light eyes, and bagpipe music with their Celtic cousins, the Scots. Working as fishermen, shepherds, and farmers, the people in rural areas of Galicia speak their own language, a mixture of Portuguese and Castilian Spanish.

Moving eastward along the northern coastline of Spain, one eventually encounters the Basque provinces. The region is one of Spain's most prosperous. Bilbao, the nation's industrial capital, is situated on the Basque coastline. The Basque countryside is adorned with beautiful Alpine vistas of rolling hills and Swiss-style farmhouses, and it is home to the hardworking, rugged descendants of the Iberian Peninsula's earliest settlers, the Iberians. The Basque language, Euskara, bears no demonstrable relation to any known language in the world. It is thought to date back to the prehistoric Bronze Ages, thousands of years before Christ. The Basques have one of the strongest separatist movements of all of the Spanish regions. Their notorious radical, separatist organization, the ETA (an acronym for Basque Nation and Liberty), is responsible for widespread terrorist activities against the Spanish Civil Guard, Spanish civilians, and Basque Autonomous Police. However, there is only limited support for this activity.

In Spain's northeastern corner, sandwiched between the Pyrenees mountains and the Mediterranean Sea, is the other region that harbors resentment against the control of Madrid. Supported primarily by its large textile and tourist industries, Catalonia shares the prosperity of the Basque region. Its culture is more European than the rest of Spain. The Catalan language is highly related to the southern French Provençal. It is a Mediterranean development of Latin and is taught in school and spoken by most Catalans. Barcelona, the capital of Catalonia, rivals Madrid in population and is playing an increasingly central role in European life and international affairs, for example, hosting the Summer Olympics in 1992. Catalans, although often characterized by their "canny common sense," or *seny,* also demonstrate artistic capability. The region has produced a number of Spain's master artists, such as Salvador Dalí, Joan Miró, and architect Antoni Gaudí, and contributed to the artistic development of Pablo Picasso, who was born in southern Spain.

In the center of Spain, on its sparsely populated plateau, or *meseta,* at an altitude of 2,000 to 3,000 feet, lies Castile, which exerts a dominant influence on Spanish culture. It is the birthplace of Spain's official national language, known outside of Spain as Spanish, and within it as Castilian. Castile is politically dominant, too, with Spain's capital, Madrid, at its center. The landscape of this region consists of vast expanses of arid steppeland on which 10,000 castles were built during the battles of the Middle Ages (hence, the name *Castilla*). The dryness of the Castilian air allows for extremes of temperature, making the region akin to the *sol y sombra* seating at the bullfight. A Spanish proverb says, *Nueve meses de invierno y tres de infierno* ("Nine months of winter and three of hell"), and it describes the Castilian climate accurately. In Madrid, for example, even on the most treacherously hot days of August, the temperature can be deliciously cool in the shade, and one often needs a sweater in the evening.

Finally, Andalusia, in southern Spain, is home of the bullfight, Gypsies, and stereotypically dark Spaniards. The climate is relentlessly hot and dry. The peasants' parched faces mirror the parched face of the land, teaching the Andalusians how cruel yet beautiful life can be (Wheaton, 1990). Strongly influenced by the long Moorish presence in Andalusia, the natives express their intense feelings of joy and tragedy through their flamenco dancing and their lamenting, "deep song," the *cante jondo.* Andalusia's scattered towns of whitewashed houses and red-tiled roofs reveal its Mediterranean essence. The majority of Andalusian land, however, belongs to a small number of large estates, where acres and acres of irrigated, rolling hills and valleys are used to cultivate olive groves and other agricultural products.

The above descriptions only hint at the incredible variety of Spain's regions and at the harshness of life in the heat of the Spanish sun. Although Spain lies roughly between the same parallels as Cape Cod and Cape Hatteras in the United States, and Madrid is at the same latitude as New York City, the mountains around Spain's periphery keep the Atlantic and Mediterranean moisture out. The central plateau bakes like an oven. The resulting austere living conditions throughout much of Spain are what engendered that underlying Spanish sense of sadness and tragedy that seems to relate more closely to the Spanish love of the bullfight than the Spaniards' outward gaiety. It is perhaps for this reason that Spaniards do not smile quietly and peacefully, but laugh loudly and cry deeply in a land of extreme change and passion.

The Pompous Entrance Parade

A more joyful side of Spanish culture is represented by the parade, or *paseillo*, at the beginning of the bullfight. The corrida opens with the proud march of all of those individuals who appear in the arena during the course of the afternoon accompanied by the sound of the happy *pasodoble* music. Lavishly costumed, everyone from the matador to the *areneros*, who tidy up the sand, struts into the ring in descending hierarchical order according to the importance of the participant's role. Every last one proudly shows himself off to the public eye. The aristocratic opening stems from the bullfight's aristocratic past; until the late 1600s, only noblemen (hidalgos) fought bulls to prove their manhood to their ladies, peers, and underlings (Crow, 1985).

The values permeating both the *paseillo* and Spanish culture are honor, dignity, and pride, as well as a contempt for manual labor. These aristocratic values seeped into Spanish culture during its centuries of battles and heroes. The swelling of the noble class in Spain at this time was so great that even today, it has been estimated that around 50% of the Spanish population has some claim to a title (Wheaton, 1990). Together, these are the values that make up the most important of all overriding Spanish characteristics—individualism.

The pompous entrance parade highlights the individualistic, proud, and fun-loving aspects of Spanish culture. Crow (1985) eloquently describes this aspect of the Spanish mind-set in the following passage:

> The Spaniard, thus, does not feel that he is born to realize any social end, but that he is born primarily to realize himself. His sense of personal dignity is admirable at times, exasperating at others; selfhood is the center of his gravity. His individual person has a value that is sacred and irreplaceable. In the universe he may be nothing, but to himself he is everything. (p. 11)

Proud Spanish individualism produces a number of outcomes for the Spanish culture. It helps to explain the Spanish people's lack of effective collective efforts. In fact, the anarchist movement was particularly popular in Spain at the turn of the 19th century, as we might expect in a nation valuing proud and self-sufficient individualism so highly. Because Spaniards refuse to subordinate their personal beliefs to a collective goal, and because everyone has to have a say in everything, there is a tendency for nothing to ever get done. Many Spaniards who can afford it opt to hire a *gestor*, or a person who will wait in the necessary lines and wade through the bureaucracy in their place (Wheaton, 1990). As Crow (1985) observes,

> Spanish individualism is still anarchic and inorganic. The race is not cohesive except when it is unified "against someone or something." If Spaniards could only work as hard for as they do against things, their country would be one of the most dynamic and most progressive in Western Europe, perhaps in the world. (p. 361)

On top of their difficulties in cooperating, part of the problem Spaniards have had in being productive is that their culture does not teach them to view work in the same positive light in which Americans see it. Work is seen as a means to an end—survival—not an end in itself. For example, whereas American teenagers are often encouraged or forced by their parents to take summer jobs or part-time jobs during the school year even though the parents could support them easily, in Spain, families prefer to give their children educational and cultural experiences, such as sending them to France or England for the summer. The independence gained through work experience is not considered as important. In fact, one Spanish king in the 18th century issued a royal document telling his people that work is, indeed, honorable.

Further complicating the situation, jobs in some parts of Spain are often difficult to obtain and not very lucrative. As a result, Spaniards may be extremely hardworking when necessary to make ends meet (moonlighting is common in Spain), but in many regions, the economic constraints on getting ahead curb their ambition. In fact, the only Spanish word for success in business is *triunfo*, a word that Spaniards borrowed from the battlefield and the theater (Graham, 1984). The Spanish word for business, too, reveals the culture's disdain for commercial and administrative activities. The term they use is *negocio*, literally translated as "the negation of leisure" (Graham, 1984).

Many Spaniards do not mind if they accomplish little, because they value self-expression more than material success. This is why the Spaniard has to be neither a Picasso nor a successful businessperson to be self-satisfied; recall that even participants in the mundane aspects of the bullfight parade proudly around the ring. Crow (1985) quotes an Englishman he met in Spain as having said, "In this country every blessed beggar acts like a king!" (p. 362). Rather than through material goods, Spanish individuals tend to be content to express their self-sufficiency through "wit, grandiloquent phrases, appearances, courtesy, generosity, and pride" (Wheaton, 1990, p. 68). Extremely articulate and enjoying the sound of their own voices, Spaniards will often spend hours conversing in the street cafés or bars where they meet. The odd result of this manifestation of Spanish individualism is that "often the most arrogant person in a group is the most charming" (Wheaton, 1990, p. 68).

Like the bullfighters with their elaborate costumes, Spaniards tend to spend a large chunk of their monthly salary on fashionable clothes to enhance the effect of their performance. The expense is not wasted, however, because they spend much of their time under the scrutiny of the public eye, getting together in public places rather than in their homes, a situation that is partly due to their rather cramped living space.

The proud marchers of the *paseillo* adhere to a rigid hierarchical order as they file around the ring. Spaniards readily accept a certain amount of inequality in the power structure of their society. But in Hofstede's (1991) study of 53 countries' cultural values, Spain actually clustered with those nations deemphasizing power distance, ranking 31st of 53. Similarly, it ranked 20th out of 53 nations on individualism. These are predictable results, given the balance that Spaniards seek between hierarchical order and individualistic expressions, and they help to confirm the concept of proud but self-sufficient individualism found in Spain.

Finally, the pride and acceptance that Spaniards feel about everyday life have contributed to the current of realism portrayed in Spanish art. Wheaton (1990) writes, "An invitation to contemplation, careful observation of life as it is, and directness of expression are qualities that come to mind when one asks what it is that has remained consistently 'Spanish' about Spanish art" (p. 290). From ordinary scenes, like a shepherd feeding his dog, to images of Christ with streams of blood pouring from underneath His crown of thorns and Picasso's horrifying cubist depiction of the bombing of Guernica, Spanish artists concerned themselves with documenting the world around them, as each artist would uniquely see it. The same tradition has allowed Spaniards over the years to face violence and death with dignity.

Audience Involvement

The excited cheers and shouts of "Olé!" as the bull's horns whisk past the matador's gracefully leaning body highlight the strong Spanish emotionalism. The shouts and cheers are not only a form of self-expression but also a form of audience participation, affecting the matador's behavior and further performance. Furthermore, once the matador makes his kill, the public displays its judgment of his performance. The audience's judgmental response in turn indicates the appropriate salute for the matador to make. If the members of the audience are displeased, they boo and whistle, and the matador does not reenter the ring. If they are pleased, they cheer, and the matador will step back into the ring to acknowledge the applause. If the positive public response is prolonged, the matador will take a lap of honor around the ring with his banderilleros. If the matador's performance was very good, the members of the public wave handkerchiefs to request that he be honored with an ear of the bull. The president must comply if the majority of the audience members wave their handkerchiefs. It is then up to the president to decide whether or not to award two ears for an exceptional performance, or, in rare cases, even the tail. After receiving any of these rewards, the matador takes a lap of honor around the ring, during which the audience throws objects (wineskins, hats, articles of clothing, and so on) to the matador, which are then thrown back, much like autographs. Other objects are meant as gifts to the matador, such as flowers and cigars.

Likewise, the emotional nature of Spanish expression is not only a one-sided outpouring but also an interactive form of communication. Therefore, although Spaniards' emotionalism might, on one hand, reflect their proud individualism, on the other hand, its participative and empathetic qualities surpass this notion. They convey the Spanish culture's emphasis on relationships, generosity, hospitality, and recognition of social needs.

These attributes relate back to the social behavior introduced in the previous section. The Spaniards' gregarious and fun-loving nature is magnified by their uninhibited emotionalism. Spanish men are not too shy to compliment women, whether acquaintances or strangers. There is even a special name for these pleasant remarks—*piropos*. Spaniards are also not afraid to allow the conversation to move onto a personal level, which helps avoid the small talk of the American cocktail party and the shop talk between business acquaintances. Thus, Spaniards come across as genuine, interesting individuals rather than as superficial socialites or narrow-minded career people.

In allowing themselves to act on their emotions, Spaniards are incredibly generous and hospitable. Just as they enthusiastically wave their handkerchiefs in the air if they are moved by a matador's performance in order to reward him with a trophy from the bull, the Spaniards are moved by their relationships with other people to want to give them whatever they can. This takes the form of sharing food, cigarettes, or general kindness, which contributes to the upbeat social atmosphere.

The Spanish social life, for example, is often accompanied by the communal enjoyment of food and drink. To accommodate this taste, Spanish bars serve a wide variety of appetizer-sized portions of food called tapas, which groups of friends order to share. On a side note, the exotic nature of the food echoes the somewhat grotesque and exotic nature of the bullfight, as exemplified by tapas such as *pulpo* (octopus); *calamares* (squid); *morcilla* (blood sausage); *oreja de cerdo* (pig's ear); or, on the more ordinary side, *tortilla* (potato omelette), *empanadillas* (meat or seafood patties), goat cheese, olives, and ham. Overall, the loud talking, odor of food, and joviality produced from the beer and wine create a sense of vitality and life that further intensifies the emotional nature and gaiety of Spanish social interactions, much like the interactive involvement of an excited audience with a bullfighter.

Spaniards also share in their day-to-day lives outside of social gatherings. If a Spaniard brings a package of food to eat on the train, the first thing that person does after opening the packet is to offer its contents to everyone nearby. The traveler in Spain should not feel reluctant to accept a cookie or a piece of sausage (chorizo) in such a situation and should avoid hoarding his or her own food.

Spanish hospitality is primarily an outgrowth of the Arabic culture. Phrases and customs expressing courtesy, such as *esta es su casa* ("this is your home") and *buen provecho* ("enjoy your meal"), are traces of Moorish domination (Wheaton, 1990). However, Spanish hospitality is not to be mistaken for the American custom of inviting virtual strangers into one's home. In Spain (as in other Latin countries), one can know people for years without being invited into their home for a meal; if a dinner invitation is called for, it is much more likely to take place in a restaurant.

In addition, like the Arabs, Spaniards are generally relationship-oriented. So, as with their propensity toward material sharing, Spaniards' concept of time focuses on interpersonal interactions. Thus, for example, completing the natural cycle of a conversation or other human interaction takes on more importance for the Spaniards than does punctuality. In Hall and Hall's (1990) terms, Spaniards have a polychronic orientation toward time, doing several activities simultaneously while being highly involved in interactions.

Spanish emotionalism and generosity are also related to Spain's national social policies. A strong social security program, trade unions, almost totally subsidized universities, and a mandatory month's paid vacation for all workers reflect Spaniards' responsiveness to people's needs. Spain is less materialistic and aggressive than many other nations, such as Japan and the United States: In Hofstede's study (1991) of 53 nations, Spain clustered with those nations that were more "feminine," as we would expect.

One attribute of Spain's feminine orientation is an emphasis on the quality of life. For example, the workday in Spain is traditionally broken into morning (about 9:00 a.m. to 1:00 p.m.) and afternoon (about 4:00 p.m. to 8:00 p.m.) by a leisurely pause for the day's main meal. The meal may be followed by a little nap, the famous siesta. In the summertime, when the midday sun is very hot, shops and businesses conserve human energy by closing for an hour or so longer than usual and staying open later in the evening. Many offices may even have a summer schedule (*horario de verano*), entailing longer morning hours (perhaps from 8:00 a.m. until 2:00 p.m.) and taking the afternoon off altogether.

The longer lunch also pushes the whole day's schedule back, so that the lighter, evening meal is not served until 9:00 p.m. or 10:00 p.m. in most households. People then tend to stay up later than in most other countries, spending time with their families or going out with their friends. The importance of enjoying life and the company of others is punctuated by the fact reported in the Spanish newspaper, *País*, that Spaniards sleep less than any of their European neighbors (Wheaton, 1990). The ceaseless movement of pedestrians out for a stroll in the streets of Spanish cities also reflects the Spanish taste for leisure. Thus, the centrality of relationships, emotional expression, and living well, as represented by audience responsiveness in the bullfight, is a distinguishing feature of Spanish culture.

The Ritual of the Bullfight

The logical outcome of all of the overarching features of Spanish culture described above—regionalism, a sense of tragedy, proud individualism, and emotional interaction—is an attraction to the ritual, which provides an arena for all of these characteristics. The ultimate ritual in Spanish society is the bullfight. From its ritualistic handkerchief signals to its precisely regulated sequence and strictly defined roles of the matador, banderilleros, and picadores, and from the official role of the president to the sacrifice of the wild bull in the moment of truth, the corrida is permeated with rituals. Rituals define the bullfight; they make it what it is. This point is often missed by foreigners, who mistake it for some sort of cruel sport. It is not a sport. The ritual is a way of combining festivity with solemnity and life with death. These are some of the features that draw Spaniards to the bullfight, and these are the same features that draw Spaniards to a more encompassing ritual in Spanish society—religion.

Christianity entered Spain during the Roman rule in the first century after Christ. Although the Romans resisted it, Christianity was taken up by Spaniards with an unparalleled fervor. The tales of torture, martyrdom, and sainthood of the early Spanish Christians appealed highly to their sense of tragedy; the Spaniards' many hardships made them appreciate the ascetic Catholic values. At certain times in history, the Spanish zeal for Christianity went out of control, to the detriment (and death) of many. In particular, at the end of the 15th century, under the reign of the Catholic monarchs

Ferdinand and Isabella, religion sowed the seeds for the persecution and expulsion of hundreds of thousands of Jews under the auspices of the Holy Inquisition. At the same time, a large missionary effort was launched to convert the "heathen" native peoples of the recently discovered New World. Whole cultures were consequently disrupted.

In addition to its fervor, Spanish Catholicism differed from that of any other Catholic country in another way. The Spanish people preserved their pagan traditions right alongside their new Christian beliefs. Therefore, to the Spaniard, God is not an intangible, elusive concept, but rather an almost human, concrete presence. Thus, the Spaniard's relationship with God is a very personal one. Spaniards see God as patient and forgiving of human weaknesses and are not afraid to have conversations with Him, asking for personal favors.

The personal aspect of Spanish religion was enhanced by the Moors as well as by Spain's pagan past. The Moors, too, enjoyed an all-encompassing relationship with God (Allah) and left evidence of this fact in the Spanish language. The expression *si Dios quiere* ("if God wills it") is used widely, as is the phrase *ojalá,* meaning "I hope so," derived from the Arabic *wa shá' allah* ("may God will it") (Wheaton, 1990).

However, Spanish people do not always deal directly with God. Because they like religion to have a personal flavor, it is just as common, if not more so, for Spaniards to pray to the Virgin Mary and the saints. Thus, one often finds small candles lit in front of statues of the Virgin and the saints in churches, with a charitable contribution box nearby to compensate for the requested favor. However, favors are not asked randomly of any saint. When you lose something, you pray to St. Anthony; when you travel, you may wear a protective medallion with the image of St. Christopher. Many Spaniards also make pilgrimages to places where the Holy Virgin appeared. Finally, these religious references surface in everyday life, such as the common female name Maria del Pilar, usually Pilar for short, after the Virgin of the Pillar in Zaragoza, and the equally common name Conchita, a nickname for Maria de la Concepción (Mary of the Immaculate Conception).

A wilder aspect of paganism that is wound into Spanish religion is the popular celebration, or fiesta. The fiesta is a ritual like the bullfight (the bullfight is actually part of many fiestas, exemplifying their pagan nature). Each region of Spain has its most famous fiesta, like the fiesta of San Fermín in Pamplona, Las Fallas in Valencia, El Roco in Andalusia, and Holy Week celebrations throughout the country. These celebrations involve extravagant costuming, floats, processions, and drinking that stray far from piety. As a case in point, does the scene of dozens of men running in front of rushing bulls sound more Christian or more pagan? The answer is obvious, yet this ritual is observed as part of the celebration of a Christian saint in Pamplona. To the

Spaniard, religion simply does not occupy a separate compartment in life; it can be incorporated into life's most mundane and most dramatic moments (also see Chapter 20, "The Mexican Fiesta").

The pervasiveness of religion in Spanish day-to-day life would seem to work in favor of the Church, but after Franco's death in 1975, there was an anticlerical period, during which a negative reaction to conservative Catholicism occurred. Still, almost half of the population attends church regularly, and 90% of the population declares itself to be Catholic, suggesting that Catholicism as a cultural influence is very strong. In recent years, there has been a renewed interest in Catholicism, as manifested in popular recordings and films. For many years, movie directors had difficulty persuading actors to be priests and nuns in film, but this is no longer true (see "Popular Culture's Heavenly Glow," 1997).

The ritual of the classic bullfight, too, may be losing its appeal in contemporary Spanish society. It is being replaced by soccer matches and other forms of Sunday afternoon entertainment.

There are several reasons for this state of affairs, including the opposition of animal rights groups; the popularity of other forms of entertainment, such as soccer; and the lack of bullfights in several regions. In more than half of Spain, bullfighting virtually does not exist. To stem this decline, some bullfighters have turned the bullfight into stunts. Jesulin de Ubrique, for example, performs on TV in front of live, all-female crowds, and throwing bras and other accessories into the ring is common. And, although bullfighting employs more than 200,000 Spaniards, or 1% of the labor force, financial rewards tend to flow disproportionately to only a small number of matadors (approximately 200). Furthermore, although there are 324 bullrings in Spain, only 7 are deemed first class and 43 as second class. The newer forms of bullfighting, including the use of female matadors, has helped to stem the decline in popularity: In 1996, there was a record number of bullfights: 16,500 (see "Spain: Locked Horns," 1997). However, even soccer simply does not capture the essence of Spanish culture in the way that the bullfight does, probably because soccer is too universal a sport. Although soccer draws the same kinds of excited crowds as the bullfight, soccer fans have no role in the game comparable to audience participation in the bullfight, such as judging the matador. And, whereas soccer players form highly cooperative teams, bullfighters' groups are much looser. The latter reflect Spanish collective behavior more accurately. Finally, in contrast to the fact that the bullfight is an elaborate ritual, soccer is a sport, albeit a popular one. Therefore, there is little chance that soccer will ever completely replace the bullfight in Spanish culture.

An American student's experience as an exchange student living with a Spanish family helps to illustrate the importance of bullfighting in Spanish culture. One Sunday, the father turned on the televised bullfight and said to him, "I hate bullfighting, but if you want to understand the Spanish, you had better learn about it."

Still, Spain is undergoing rapid change, particularly since Franco's death in 1975. It is now a member of the European Union. After a long period of very conservative, Catholic behavior, there has been a strong movement toward freedom and creativity that has attracted worldwide attention. The *movida* (cultural movement) has been propelled forward by the activities of such artists as Barcelo (painting), Almodovar (cinema), Dominguez (clothes designer), and Mecano (pop music). Very relaxed customs can now be found in Spanish society, and some have argued that Spain is being too influenced by the United States. Although such change is real, it is difficult to imagine Spain without the rituals of the bullfight and the underlying Spanish culture that the bullfight expresses.

In summary, a passage by Crow (1985) concisely recapitulates some of the points made in this chapter:

> Spain today is a composite of all that has gone before. Her taproot reaches into the bottomless past. On several successive occasions in history she has flowered in beauty, shedding her glory over the civilization of Europe. On many other occasions she has grimly closed her door on the outside world, and retired into the gloom of fixed memories. In spite of her perennially poor government, her vitality is ever present, and appears inexhaustible. The Spanish people are among the most generous, the most noble human beings on earth. Their spontaneous art places them in a unique category among the nations of Europe, both for its quantity and for its incomparable beauty. With one foot in the present and the other in the past, Spain today stands straddling the unfathomable abyss. (p. 356)

As the people of Spain pursue an accelerated course of modernization, they are evolving into the more cosmopolitan embodiment as envisioned by the founders of the European Union. It is hoped that Spaniards will not lose their special love of life that makes Spain so unique and wonderful. Whatever the eventual outcome, the bullfight will remain as a major, if not the major, metaphor for understanding deep-seated cultural values and attitudes among the Spanish people.

CHAPTER 23

The Portuguese Bullfight

S uperficially, Spain and Portugal are very similar in many ways. As inhabitants of the Iberian Peninsula, they have experienced hundreds of years of successive invasions. Both were seafaring nations that became world powers during the era of the conquistadores. In Hofstede's (1991) study of cultural values in 53 nations, Spain was somewhat more individualistic than Portugal, with respective rankings of 20 and 34. Their scores on power distance (high), masculinity (low), and uncertainty avoidance (high) were similar. Comparing Portugal and Spain on the indexes in *The Economist Pocket World in Figures* (1997) yields many more similarities than differences. Spain, of course, is more than five times the size of Portugal, and it is wealthier ($13,434 gross domestic product per person vs. $9,851), but purchasing power parity (with the United States equaling 100) is 54 versus 47. The population in Portugal is about 10 million, whereas it is 40 million in Spain, and the languages are different. But by and large, these nations are remarkably similar in many ways, at least superficially.

Thus, it is instructive to compare the cultural metaphors for these two nations: the bullfight. In both Spain and Portugal, the bullfight celebrates emotionalism, love of life, and heroism. But the Spanish bullfight emphasizes tragedy and is a ritual of death, and there are more expressions of individualism in the Spanish version than in the Portuguese version, although such expressions are present in Portugal as well. Studying these two types of bullfights helps to sensitize us to subtle cultural differences that are often overlooked, such as assuming that all Asian nations are the same in culture. And as we will see, there are, indeed, substantive cultural differences between Spain and Portugal.

As in Spain, bullfighting in Portugal was once the sport of noblemen. In the 18th century, Marquees de Pombal, the Portuguese prime minister, prohibited the killing of bulls after the son of the Duke of Arcos was killed in a bullfight. This prohibition profoundly changed the nature of Portuguese bullfighting and, over time, led to expressions of cultural values that are, to an outsider, startling and unique. Even the Spanish marvel at the Portuguese bullfight. In this chapter, we describe the Portuguese bullfight in terms of four cultural characteristics: pride in traditions, stratification amid unity or collectivism, artistry and human gore, and profitless bravery.

Pride in Traditions

There are six separate rounds in the Portuguese bullfight, and in each of them, there is a specific *cavaleiro* (mounted horseman) and *forcados* (footmen). The bullfight spectacle begins with the grand entrance into the bullring by all of the participants. The *cavaleiros* enter the ring first; they wear the traditional costumes of the 17th century. Their embroidered vests and feathered hats clearly emphasize the cultural heritage of the Portuguese. The *forcados* are attired in more humble yet traditional brown pants and small vests. The *toreiros,* or cape men, stand out because of their embroidered pants and vests that are very similar to those worn by the Spanish matadors. Metaphorically, the *cavaleiros* stand for the noble class, with its elegance and style, whereas the *forcados* represent the common laborer of Portugal. These *forcados,* much like their ancestors, are not flashy and do not mind getting dirty while performing their task. They understand and accept their role in society and are proud to contribute in any way possible.

The bullfight begins by featuring a fast bull pitted against a graceful horse and rider. The *cavaleiro* must first demonstrate his control of the horse and his ability to avoid the charging bull, after which he faces the bull from across the ring and rides furiously toward him. At the last minute, the *cavaleiro* swerves to avoid the bull but simultaneously drives a wooden spear into his neck. The *cavaleiro* repeats this activity six or seven times, and each time is more dangerous than the previous one. Then, he exits the ring and the *forcados* enter.

The *forcados,* an eight-man team, line up as if playing leapfrog. The leader hollers *"O Toro"* continuously until the bull charges. Fortunately, the horns of the bull are covered in a leather sheath. When the bull plows into the leader, he does not get gored. But the bull easily picks up the entire eight-man team, and the action becomes furious. Finally, the group brings the bull to a standstill, and one man takes hold of the tail. It is hoped that the outcome is a successful *pega,* that is, the seven descend from the bull while the eighth man hangs onto the tail and stays upright behind the speeding beast until the bull comes to a halt. The entire process is repeated with five additional bulls. After each of the six rounds, the *cavaleiros* and *forcados* meet in the center of the ring and take a victory lap around it while the crowd shows its appreciation by throwing flowers, hats, and other accessories. Then, the *cavaleiros* and *forcados* throw these items back to the crowd as a sign of respect and appreciation for the crowd's support.

This description is a poor substitute for actually seeing a Portuguese bullfight. When the bull picks up one *forcado* or several *forcados* and hurls them into the air, the sensation is stunning. It is even more stunning to see a seemingly foolhardy *forcado* break loose of the eight-person team in his attempt to stop the bull all by himself. Sometimes, he is actually successful, but it is more likely that he will sail high into the air over the bull's back when the bull rushes into him, picks him up, and treats him with disdain. But is the *forcado* really being foolhardy? Only an understanding of Portuguese culture will help us to answer this question.

The soul of Portugal is reflected in the warmth of the people, who are spiritually connected to the land. As noted, the *forcados* represent the typical Portuguese laborers: simple and honest people who work all day and then come home at dusk to a warm supper and a carafe of homemade wine. After dinner, they tend to go to the local café to drink an espresso and talk to their friends about the local soccer team. These people are repeating the pattern of simple lifestyles that their ancestors established. They realize that they are separate from the upper class (represented by the *cavaleiros*) but are proud of their role in the bullfight and in society.

According to Hofstede (1991), Portugal is a high uncertainty avoidance country. Of the 53 countries in his study, only Greece was higher on this characteristic. One of the characteristics of a high uncertainty avoidance culture is an urge to work hard and to search for absolute truth. For this reason, it is not surprising that religion is very important in the culture; Portugal is 90% Catholic. Similarly, the *cavaleiros* bless themselves, asking God for protection while in the ring with the bull. Metaphorically, each of the participants in the bullfight seeks truth. For example, the *cavaleiros* test their control of horse and bull, each time being more daring and trying riskier moves. The *forcados* also search for truth and test their courage by facing the bull head on. For the most part, the Portuguese seek inner truth and strength, and they believe that actions speak louder than words. Given the importance of uncertainty avoidance, the Portuguese have a tremendous sense of pride, but truth is also illustrated clearly by the *pega*.

Portugal is still a Catholic nation influenced heavily by the clergy, and it did not suffer from the anticlericalism unleashed in Spain after Franco's death in 1975. As we might expect in a culture that values the search for truth, regular church attendance is widespread. As Catholics, the Portuguese believe that all of us are sinners in some way, for which we must atone. Hence, many people go to confession on a weekly basis and view this activity as important as actually attending Sunday mass.

Clergymen are considered experts, and their opinions are regarded highly. Many Portuguese use the clergy in the same way that Americans use psychologists. The ordinary citizens respect anyone who is a symbol of authority, whether it is a clergyman, a doctor, or a manager.

Authority is challenged only rarely in this hierarchical culture. Roles are defined clearly. Metaphorically, the *cavaleiro* is the authority figure in the bullfight, and the *toreiros,* the men with the capes, are used only to support him by distracting the bull long enough so that the *cavaleiro* can transition to another horse or grab another spear. (Of course, the torero is the most important person in the ring in Spain.) Although the *toreiros* are men, they play a supportive role similar to that of women in Portuguese society. In everyday life, the roles of men and women are defined clearly. The man is seen as the conqueror and hunter who provides for the family, whereas the woman is the supporter who does all the cooking and cleaning. Even though more and more women are entering the workforce, they are not usually considered the breadwinners of the household. Women who work outside of the home are still expected to come home and take care of their "womanly responsibilities," such as cooking, cleaning, and taking care of the children. Based on this pattern, one would expect Portugal to be a masculine country, but actually, it ranks 45th out of 53 nations on the masculine-feminine dimension (Hofstede, 1991), presumably because the Portuguese place great value on the land, the environment, and relationships. Hence, it is acceptable for a man to be nurturing. Just as the *cavaleiros* and *forcados* are loyal and demonstrate mutual respect for each other, so, too, do men and women. Divorce is very uncommon in Portugal and is considered a disgrace. Actually, when a husband cheats on a wife, or vice versa, they are said to be *meter os cornos,* which literally means to be "gored by the bull." When a man is gored, much like the *pega,* he is expected to try to remarry. If he is unsuccessful, family members may well experience a sense of shame and derisively call him a quitter.

Given the significance of tradition, long-term trust is important in business. Metaphorically, the bull represents an outsider trying to conduct business, and the Portuguese are very suspicious and afraid of getting "gored by the bull." Paradoxically, then, Portuguese people are both very friendly and simultaneously suspicious. Relationship building, especially outside of work, is very important in gaining the needed trust.

Although there are very few women in management roles, the Portuguese will conduct business with women if they feel that they are figures of authority. Although gender is important, authority outweighs it. Thus, at least in business, it is more important to be a person of authority first and a woman second.

Timeliness is important, and a person is viewed as disrespectful if he or she is not punctual. It is very uncommon to be late for work or a meeting. Unlike the Spanish, who are known for being tardy, the Portuguese see timeliness as extremely important and reflective of character and inner strength.

Finally, in light of the emphasis on tradition and following rules, it is easy to understand why change is slow and innovation deemphasized. Deviating from the norm is rarely accepted. In a recent bullfight, for example, one of the *forcados* decided to do a 360-degree spin while the bull was charging, but this act was not viewed favorably by the public. Although it was innovative and more exciting due to the increased risk, the traditional *pega* is still preferred by a majority of the crowd. This lack of innovation has retarded Portugal's development.

◼ Stratification Amid Unity

One of the interesting things about Portugal is that it is a collectivist society. Although it is important to define rules clearly, the most critical feature of this culture is that the group is successful. This is demonstrated clearly in the bullfight: When a *cavaleiro* enters the ring, for example, the other five *cavaleiros* shake his hand and wish him luck in the bullfight, thus signifying that it is more important to see oneself as part of a group than to win. Likewise, before the *pega*, it is customary that the lead *cavaleiro* dedicate his efforts to a spouse, teacher, or even the entire crowd. In many instances, he will give his hat to the individual to whom he is dedicating the event and collect it once his "job" has been completed. This tradition dates back to the time when soldiers would go out to battle, leaving behind a token by which their loved ones could remember them. What the *cavaleiro* asks for in return is permission to proceed, which is usually signaled by a wave, hug, or applause. After each bullfight, *cavaleiros* and *forcados* meet at the center of the ring and shake hands, which symbolizes the coming together of social classes. They explicitly recognize that it is not the nobleman or the common citizen who achieves success independently, but rather all parties working together.

Although Spain and Portugal are similar on objective measures, as noted previously, the Portuguese have developed a decidedly different character from that of the people of Spain. International travelers who mingle with the Portuguese usually return home filled with special warmth for the people. The Portuguese are easily approachable and always helpful. In Portugal, the family is perhaps the single most important institution in society. Many of the people have no close friendships outside the family unit. Although the people in the cities have become increasingly sophisticated, the more rural areas are still characterized by working families who manifest this pattern of behavior. As a result, it is common to see people marrying their neighbors. And newlyweds tend to live close to their parents, friends, and place of birth.

Similarly, it is common for the entire family to gather for lunch at home. Lunch is by far the most important meal of the day, and everything in the country shuts down between 12:00 p.m. and 2:00 p.m. in order for people to eat. At lunchtime, people do not discuss work; there is a clear separation between work and family life that is rarely crossed. Food is very important to the Portuguese, and they usually make very elaborate meals at lunchtime, whereas dinner is much lighter and less formal. Beer and wine are consumed during lunch and constitute a very important part of the culture. Many families grow their own grapes and make enough wine for the family to last an entire year.

When Portuguese children decide that they no longer want to go to school, they are expected to go out and work to help the family. For many, this means that they go out to the fields and work alongside their fathers, whereas others learn a trade such as carpentry or marble crafts work. As in other collectivist societies, employment for life is very common in Portugal, but it is largely due to the fact that the people do not have many choices. Regardless of which job they have, the money that the children make is turned over to the parents at the end of the month. The father then gives the children an allowance, and the rest is used to buy food and pay the bills of the house. This practice continues as long as the child lives with his or her parents, usually until he or she gets married. Similarly, it is the responsibility of the children to take care of aged parents. Nursing homes do not exist in Portugal, and the aged parents typically live with their children until they die. If there is more than one child, the oldest is responsible, but it is customary for the younger children to help out either by having the parents live in their homes or by providing money for food and clothing.

After dinner, there is usually a local café where everyone gathers to have an espresso and to socialize. The family will go as a group, but upon arrival, each member will join natural subgroupings. Men will sit with their friends and play cards, women will discuss the daily occurrences for an hour or two and return home to start preparing the meal for the next day, and the children will play a game of *fusebol* or watch TV with their friends. This is really the only time during the week that people socialize outside the family and spend time with their friends.

It is important to understand the stratified, collectivist norms that the Portuguese emphasize. To conduct business in Portugal, it is critical to develop a relationship. One of the best ways to establish such relationships is over lunch. One frequently repeated aphorism is that the Portuguese need 2 hours for lunch owing to the fact that one hour is for eating, and the other hour is for talking. Many business deals are finalized during lunch, and presumably, the better the lunch, the better the deal. Bribery is commonly used to get things accomplished and is an accepted way of life. If a businessperson is trying to get paperwork signed or to close a deal, he or she may want to host lunch at the most expensive restaurant in town, and by the time the dessert is served, there will probably be a successful resolution of the issue.

Artistry and Human Gore

The beauty of the Lusitano horse, the elaborate costumes worn by the *cavaleiros,* and the elegance of the opening ceremony demonstrate the artistry that is seen throughout the country. In Portugal, the performance of the horse in the bullring is perhaps one of the most important factors in the breeding and selection process of the Lusitano horse. The horses are trained by their riders and learn many things, including prancing, moving sideways, and standing on their hind legs. These skills are shown off during the bullfight and are needed in order to avoid the bull. The movements of the horse are admired by all, and the *cavaleiro* is applauded for his efforts in training the animal. It is extremely important that the *cavaleiro* demonstrates control of the bull and horse, which is done by spearing the bull repeatedly.

This artistry is also seen in music, arts and crafts, and the architecture of the country. There are fado houses throughout Portugal, where the female *fadista,* clutching a traditional black shawl, sings the sad and romantic songs of Portugal. A rough translation of fado is fate, from the Latin *fatuum,* meaning prophecy. A fado usually tells of unrequited love, jealousy, and a longing for days gone by. Fados became famous in the 19th century when Maria Severa, the beautiful daughter of a Gypsy, took Portugal by storm, singing her way into the hearts of the people, especially the Count of Vimioso, the most renowned bullfighter of his day.

Handpainted ceramics called *azuleijos* constitute an important craft in Portugal. Because of their decorative design, these tiles have been adopted by builders and are seen in almost every house. Other handpainted pottery is also seen throughout the country, especially in the northern region known for its painted *rosters,* which are an icon in the home of most Portuguese. The architecture of Portugal is visible in the cathedrals, churches, and castles spread across the country. For the most part, Portuguese architecture imitates Italian and Spanish designs. There is little, if any, uniqueness to the architecture, but its beauty is undeniable.

What we see at the bullfight is not only the artistry but also human gore. The *forcados* are often injured while trying to wrestle the bull, and it is very common to see blood on their faces and clothing. In the Spanish bullfight, the gore comes from killing the bull, but the Portuguese bullfight is said to be the "revenge of the bull." The first time that people watch the *pega,* they are amazed at the violence and the pain inflicted by the bull on the *forcados.* In an attempt to stop the charging bull, the *forcados* are often trampled, thrown, and injured. The gore, however, is experienced only by the working class (*forcados*) and not the upper class (*cavaleiros*), which is symbolic of what has occurred during wartime. The *forcados* are similar to the front line of the army, whereas the *cavaleiros* are the generals. Still, it is very rare that a *forcado* is killed (less than one every 10 years or so). The Portuguese see the bullfight as an art form rather than human gore, although international visitors frequently do not agree.

In business, much as in the bullfight, the Portuguese are perfectionists. If something goes wrong, they will try to fix the problem repeatedly until they get it right. The *cavaleiros,* for example, will sometimes change horses three or four times in order to find the one that will help them put on the best show. The Portuguese are also very detail oriented. If the bull clips the horse or the *cavaleiro* drops one of his spears, the *cavaleiro* will repeat the exercise. This level of detail is seen in business negotiations involving contracts. Unlike the Spanish, who finalize many business transactions orally, the Portuguese require that everything be in writing.

Duplication, however, is more important than innovation. The Portuguese believe in the status quo and are suspicious of those who try to do things differently. Their belief is that if they have done it a certain way successfully many times in the past, what need is there to change? This thinking is very different from the individualistic ideas that we see in the United States, which rewards creativity or thinking "outside the box." In Portugal, this type of thinking is seen as breaking tradition, so it is probably wise for foreigners to follow the maxim, "When in Portugal, do as the Portuguese."

Profitless Bravery

When Americans attend the Portuguese bullfight, they tend to focus on the *pega*, probably because they see only the violence, human triumph, and misfortune (see Chapter 13, "American Football"). But although Americans may equate the physical violence of the *pega* to that of American football, the Portuguese see the *pega* as a symbol of bravery.

In American football, stars like Dan Marino and Reggie White are role models for kids because of their athletic ability and the money they earn. A major criticism of today's football players is that they lack the love for the game that previous generations had. Presumably, the players are more interested in the money than in the game itself. The average salary for a professional football player is nearly 1 million dollars, and many players make far more than the average. On sports talk shows and in letters to the editor, fans continually complain that players have no loyalty to the teams and cities, especially since the advent of free agency. Many fans have difficulty identifying with the football players who supposedly represent their teams and cities.

Conversely, the *forcados* are amateurs and do not make any money at all, even though the *cavaleiros* are paid. How can this be? In many cases, the *forcados* are battered and bruised by the bull, and no one in his right mind would do this without getting paid, would he? But the Portuguese bullfight is not about making money, being a hero, or having your own sport. Rather, it is a joyous celebration of tradition and bravery. These *forcados* do it for the love of the ritual and the lessons that it has taught them. The bullfight forces a man to look deep within himself for a sense of pride, and it is a reminder of the hardships faced by previous generations.

It is very typical during the *pega* that a *forcado* acting as team captain is not successful in holding the bull the first time. As opposed to quitting or giving way to another *forcado,* he will go out again. Sometimes, three and four attempts must be made to grab the bull, but it is always the same brave lead *forcado* who is involved in the *pega*. Broken ribs and legs are common in the sport but are ignored until the task of capturing the bull is completed.

Saving face is a concept that is very important to the Portuguese. Regardless of how badly the *forcado* is injured, nothing can be worse than the injury to the ego. The shame that a person would bring to the family by quitting an important task before completion is unthinkable. Playing with pain is a part of the game with which Americans are familiar, but most have never witnessed it to the extent that is visible in the bullfight. Portuguese are extremely proud of the fact that the *pega* is performed only in Portugal and that it symbolizes the courage of the people.

One business implication of this pattern of behavior is that the Portuguese are stubborn but persistent. The *forcado* can be knocked down repeatedly but will get back up again no matter how badly beaten he is. Although persistency is an excellent characteristic, some people see this stubbornness as illogical beyond a reasonable point. Whether in a bullring or business environment, it is important to prepare for dealing with this extreme level of persistence.

Persistence typically leads to completion of tasks. Hence, a contract made with a Portuguese is generally ironclad. However, the Portuguese are very hard negotiators. Because they are so persistent and stubborn, negotiation is typically very difficult. The American saying when something is going to take a long time is "you'd better bring your lunch." In Portugal, it should be "you'd better buy lunch," because unless a relationship can be built outside a business setting, success will not occur. The process tends to be long and drawn out, and will normally require many lunches.

As this chapter has demonstrated, the Portuguese and Spanish bullfights are as different as the people themselves. The people of Portugal are less aggressive than those of Spain, and killing the bull is repulsive to them. One of the main characteristics of the bullfight is audience involvement. The Spanish will applaud an excellent performance by the matador or torero but will not hesitate to whistle and boo if displeased with the performance. If they boo, the torero will not reenter the ring. However, prolonged applause and the waving of handkerchiefs is a great honor, and the torero is rewarded with an ear—and in some cases, the tail—of the bull; he is also well paid. On the other hand, in the Portuguese bullfight, the audience rarely, if ever, boos a performance. Regardless of how the *cavaleiros* and *forcados* performed, they are treated with respect. This pattern reflects the origin of the Portuguese bullfight, which is a celebration of bravery and life, not death. The bullfight is symbolic of the battles that Portugal and its people faced during the invasion of the Moors. If people were to boo and whistle, it would be taken as a sign of disrespect for the soldiers who served the country. Thus, it is important that, at the end of each of the six stages or rounds, the participants gather at the center of the ring so that the audience can acknowledge and applaud their efforts.

There is also a great deal of difference in the role of hierarchy in both nations. In Spain, the participants enter the ring in descending order of importance, whereas in Portugal, all of the participants are viewed as of equal importance even though the *cavaleiros* represent the noble class and the *forcados* represent the working class. In Spain, the president determines the award given to the matador, but in Portugal, the people decide on the reward by applauding. In the bullfight and throughout Spain, the people like to show off by dressing nicely, whether rich or poor. This is clearly not the case in Portugal, as evidenced by the humble clothing worn by the *forcados*. All of these characteristics help to demonstrate that Spain is a more individualistic society than Portugal.

The biggest difference between the two bullfights, however, is deeply rooted in the meaning of the bullfight for each country. In Spain, the bullfight is about control and conquest through death. The matadors are expected to control the bull, and once this control is demonstrated, they kill it. In the Portuguese bullfight, death is not a part of the ritual. The true meaning for all Portuguese is the celebration of bravery demonstrated by the *cavaleiros* and *forcados*.

Still, similar to other nations facing globalization, Portugal is understandably concerned that its culture is not altered significantly. It is now a member of the 15-nation European Union, within which it is the poorest nation. The EU provides subsidies to its poorer members with the expectation that higher economic growth will occur and that eventually these nations will, in turn, help to subsidize other activities and nations in the confederation. In the case of Ireland, this approach has worked remarkably well, but clearly, Irish culture has been affected (see Chapter 12, "Irish Conversations"). Some Portuguese are even concerned about the symbolism found on the new European coins, where Portugal looks as if it were a part of Spain (see Trueheart, 1998). However, cultural patterns that have taken hundreds of years to develop are difficult to destroy, and we can expect that the Portuguese bullfight will continue to reflect the underlying values that the Portuguese hold dear, even if changes are introduced into this beloved activity.

PART VIII

Beyond National
Borders

Throughout the rest of the book, the basic unit of analysis was the nation. However, it is also possible to develop a cultural metaphor for an ethnic group whose members reside in either different nations or the same nation. In this part of the book, we do so for the ethnic Chinese residing in several nations. The Chinese family altar is a cultural metaphor with which ethnic Chinese identify, regardless of the nation in which they live.

419

CHAPTER 24

The Chinese
Family Altar

When a Westerner visits a traditional Buddhist temple in Asia, he or she sees different images of the Buddha, such as the reclining Buddha, the sitting Buddha, and so forth. However, in a Chinese Buddhist temple, these Buddha images are supplemented by a formidable group of statues that seems to represent warriors who are massive in size and strength. These fierce-looking warriors frequently have rough-looking beards and moustaches, and they carry large swords. It is a surprise for many Westerners, then, to learn that these warriors are actually representations of important people within extended kinship and family groups, and that they actually lived in Chinese villages 1,000 or 2,000 years ago. The position of honor that these warriors have in the temple is but one demonstration of the importance that the Chinese place on the family and kinship group, even to the extent of allowing them to be situated alongside the Buddha images.

Throughout this book, we have given prominent attention to the nation as our unit of analysis. But as Ronen and Shenkar (1985) demonstrate, it is possible to cluster countries into groups that are similar to one another in terms of language, religion, and geographical closeness.

On the other hand, the Chinese represent one ethnic group for which one metaphor is appropriate, regardless of the nation in which they reside. This does not seem to be true for other ethnic groups. Thus, Joel Kotkin (1993) has described the major ethnic groups—the expatriate Chinese, the Japanese, the Jews, the English, and the Asian Indians—who have achieved remarkable economic success outside of their homelands. However, the metaphors for the non-Chinese groups as described in this book—the kibbutzim and moshavim, the Dance of Shiva, the Japanese garden, and the traditional British house—do not apply fully when members of these groups become expatriates.

The importance of the family and kinship group cannot be overestimated for the Chinese, and the metaphor we have selected for the Chinese—the family altar—reflects this fact. One Taiwanese diplomat who lived in several countries had a family altar in Taiwan but, when traveling, carried drawings of his ancestors to whom he and his children prayed; Amy Tan's best-selling novel *The Kitchen God's Wife* (1991) includes the concept in its title; many expatriate Chinese travel to their original homeland so that they can visit the burial places of their ancestors at least once in their lives, because in Confucianism, the living relatives have the obligation to tend such places on a regular basis if at all possible, or at least to visit them; and the Chinese family name is traditionally given before the personal name, unlike the Western practice of mentioning the personal name first. These examples—and countless others could be cited—indicate the prominent place that family and kinship groups hold in Chinese society.

Of course, some may argue that other ethnic groups are also family oriented. However, Chinese society is neither individualistic nor collectivistic, as are other family-based ethnic groups; rather, it is based on relations (Bond, 1986). Confucians, for example, feel that the individual has roles to fulfill, but in doing so, his or her individualism can enlarge and enrich the self for the greater good of the family and kinship group. The relation-based system of the Chinese, in which roles are differentiated, is quite different from that of the more collectivistic and nondifferentiated system of the Japanese, as Nakane (1973) has pointed out:

> In the Japanese system all members of the household are in one group under the head, with no specific rights according to the status of individuals within the family. The Japanese family system differs from that of the Chinese system, where family ethics are always based on relationships between particular individuals such as father and son, brothers and sisters, parents and child, husband and wife, while in Japan they are always based on the collective group, i.e., members of a household, not on the relationship between individuals. (p. 14)

Hence, the Chinese tend to take seriously their relations with others, whether inside the kinship group or outside of it. They have separate words for older brother, younger sister, and each aunt or uncle from each side of the family, and they tend to make lifelong friendships that are clearly demarcated from acquaintances. Still, similar to many other high-context ethnic groups, the Chinese usually spend a long time getting to know an individual before doing business with him or her. Other unique characteristics of the Chinese family system are described below. Furthermore, like the Japanese and other group-oriented cultures, the Chinese tend to experience difficulty differentiating the individual from the group. There is no equivalent word for "privacy" in Chinese and some other languages that stress the importance of the group rather than the individual, such as Japanese and Arabic. In fact, the word "I" has negative connotations associated with it in the Chinese and Japanese languages, as do many of the other characters that are used in conjunction with it. From both the Chinese and Japanese perspectives, the individual exists or is someone only when he or she is a member of a group.

Chinese culture is closely associated with Confucianism, Taoism (pronounced "Dowism"), and, to a lesser extent, Buddhism. Because we have already highlighted Buddhism in Chapter 4 (see pp. 42-43), we will treat only Confucianism and Taoism in this chapter, after which we will describe the Chinese altar and its three dimensions: roundness, which symbolizes the continuity and structural completeness of the family; harmony within the family and the broader society; and fluidity, or the capacity to change while maintaining solid traditions. We will then briefly describe the activities of the 55 million expatriate Chinese and the countries in which they have been such an important economic driving force.

Confucianism and Taoism

Confucius died in 479 B.C., frustrated that he was never able to become a major advisor to any of the regional rulers in China. However, his ideas took hold in large part because of the vicious warfare that was occurring between these regional rulers, and his emphasis on forming tradition deliberately in accordance with China's idealized past period of Great Harmony had wide appeal.

Confucian thought is encapsulated in five terms, the first of which is *jen,* or human-heartedness, or the simultaneous feeling of humanity toward others and respect for oneself (see Smith, 1991). Second, *chuntzu,* "the superior man," is someone fully adequate and poised to accommodate others as much as possible rather than to acquire all that he or she can acquire selfishly. Third is *li,* or propriety, and it refers to the way things should be done. For example, the Five Relationships involve the appropriate conduct that should occur between father and son, older and younger siblings, husband and wife, older and younger friend, and ruler and subject. More specifically, *li* reflects the importance that Confucius attached to the family, and it evolved from the earlier era of ancestor worship to include the concepts of filial piety and veneration of age. There is a second meaning of *li*—ritual—and it is envisioned as encompassing all of a person's activities during his or her whole life.

Te is the fourth term, and it refers to the power by which men and women should be ruled, not by force but by moral example. Finally, there is *wen,* which accords a place of prominence to the arts as a means of peace and as an instrument of moral education.

The device for developing tradition deliberately was extreme social sensitivity, and this is still reflected in the Chinese concept of face. As discussed in Chapter 3, "The Japanese Garden," face is an unwritten set of rules by which people in society cooperate to avoid unduly damaging one another's prestige and self-respect. In bargaining, for example, the winner should allow the loser some minor tactical reward, especially when all of the observers can ascertain the identity of the vanquished. If a father's business becomes bankrupt and the father dies suddenly, his sons frequently will work to pay off the debt in order to maintain face for the family. When an individual loses face, he or she tends to adopt a stony or blank expression, as if nothing has happened; generally, face is forfeited through loss of self-control or a display of frustration and anger (Bonavia, 1989, pp. 73-74).

Some experts have argued that Confucianism is not a traditional religion because it has no concept of a personal God and only an amorphous concept of heaven or a shadowy netherworld in which ancestors live and help to guide the living. Thus, the Chinese tend to focus on this world and not the next. David Bonavia (1989, pp. 56-57) aptly captures the essence of being Chinese in the following description, although he was primarily discussing modern China:

> The most determining feature of the Chinese people's attitude to the world around them is their total commitment to life as it is. . . . In this world view, all human activity—religion, sex, war—consists of functional acts aimed at achieving something. Only the arts are considered to have intrinsic value, and they are chiefly reflections of the real world or an imagined world, not abstract patterns. . . . Action must have a purpose, the Chinese feel; there is nothing ennobling about pain, and death is an infernal nuisance. . . . Most Chinese, seeing a Hindu holy man stick a knife through his cheeks or walk on coals, would conclude that he was either a fool or a fraud. . . . The central concept of Chinese society is functionality. (pp. 56-57)

Usually, Taoism is considered the primary religion among the Chinese, whereas Confucianism relates to the manner in which an individual is to behave in society. This religion was supposedly created by Lao Tzu, who was born in 604 B.C., and its main tenets were outlined in one small book, *Tao Te Ching*, or "The Way and the Power."

Tao, or "the way," has three overlapping meanings, the first of which is that it can be known only through mystical insight. In the second sense, Tao refers to the ordering principle behind the universe or all life, and it represents the rhythm and driving force of nature. The third sense of Tao is the way in which a person should order his or her life to be in balance with the universe.

Power, the second part of the title of the book, refers to the belief that a person gains power by leading a life that is in harmony with the dictates of the universe. This approach continues to shape the Chinese character and is manifested in the desire to achieve a state of serenity and grace.

The basic approach of life that is consonant with the universe is *wu wei*, or creative quietude. It is simultaneous action and relaxation and letting behavior flow spontaneously. Creative quietude is never forcing or straining, but rather seeking the empty spaces in life and nature and moving quietly and without confrontation through the avenues of least resistance.

Taoists reject all forms of self-assertiveness and competition and seek more of a union with nature and a simplicity of life than materialistic possessions. There is an extreme aversion to violence that verges on pacifism. Taoism also includes the traditional Chinese symbols of yin and yang, which connote that there are no clear dichotomies, but rather that all values and concepts are relative to the mind that entertains them. Thinking in terms of yin and yang means analyzing the universe into pairs of interacting opposites, such as shadowed and bright, decaying and growing, moonlit or sunlit, earthly or heavenly, and male or female. Whether something is classified as yin or yang depends not on its intrinsic nature but on the roles it plays in relation to other things, which is consistent with the relation-based sytem of the Chinese. Clayre (1985) expands on these ideas as follows:

> In relation to Heaven man may be classified as yin, but when paired with Earth he would be seen as yang. Heaven itself is the supreme embodiment of the yang aspects of the cosmos: ethereal, bright, active, generative, initiatory and masculine. Earth is seen as deeply yin: solid, dark, cool, quiescent, growth-sustaining, responsive and feminine. (p. 201)

Men and women are not seen as exclusively yang or yin: Each has a predominance of one aspect or the other, and the balance within them and between them may change. The relation of the two elements is always changing, a continuous cycle where each may dominate in responsive sequence. This idea may have evolved from the annual cycle of growth and decay found in agricultural China, as well as in the rotation of day and night and seasons of the year.

Traditionally, Taoists had little empathy for Confucianists, whom they viewed as pompous and ritualistic. A more fundamental difference is summarized by the Chinese themselves, who say that "Confucius roams within society, Lao Tzu wanders beyond." However, in many ways, Taoism, Confucianism, and Buddhism are complementary, and it is commonly said that they are "the Three Faiths in One." Thus, many Chinese accept Confucianism as a guide to daily living, have recourse to Taoist practitioners for ritual purifications and exorcisms, and employ Buddhist priests for funerals.

We have merely sketched some of the major concepts and values that make up the Chinese value system, and there are wide divergences from it in many situations. Still, this value system has not been stamped out or radically changed for thousands of years, as Mao Tse-tung and others would have liked. Rather, it has evolved slowly over time. Ambrose King (as quoted in Kotkin, 1993) has pointed out that many of the 55 million expatriate Chinese have developed a culture of "rationalistic traditionalism, a combination of traditional filial and group virtues with a pragmatism shaped by the conditions of a new competitive environment" (p. 177). Similar to the Italian Catholics, who attend church only irregularly, these expatriate Chinese, and even those living within the confines of China, are influenced more culturally than spiritually by their three faiths.

In a similar manner, the Chinese culture is linked closely to language. People in China's various regions are actually a mix from diverse ethnic origins who speak mutually unintelligible dialects. In southeastern China, where Cantonese is the primary dialect, it is impossible to understand the dialect of northern China, which is Mandarin. Remarkably, all dialects of spoken Chinese can be written in the same way and understood by anyone, regardless of the pronunciation of words. Whereas the English language employs only 26 letters to represent all spoken sounds and written words, the Chinese language is a storehouse of more than 50,000 different symbols, or logograms, each representing a different word. Amazing feats of memory are required to master such a language, which tends to reinforce cultural values. This generalization is also valid for the Japanese language, which was derived from the Chinese (see De Mente, 1990).

Roundness, Harmony, and Fluidity

The Chinese family altar is the cornerstone of family life for Chinese in many parts of the world. It is the tie that binds a dispersed family and serves as a focal point for viewing an extended family as including the living, the dead, and those as yet unborn. Although it may be thought of as a traditional and ancient aspect of Chinese society, and even as an anchronism in present-day mainland China, the Chinese altar is helpful in providing insight into the values, attitudes, and behaviors of the Chinese.

The physical presence of the altar represents the family as a well-knit, integrated unit. A house with two altars contains two families; a household with no altar usually considers itself part of another family, and its members will go to the house in which the altar resides for important rituals. In many parts of the world, the Chinese tend to live in family or kinship compounds that have several houses, and frequently, each of them contains a family altar. Typically, the altar stands in the central room of the house, opposite the principal door. Such altars are meant to be seen publicly: Many are visible from the street, and guests usually sit in front of them. Normally, there is an incense pot on the left side of the altar, because this is the position of honor for any of the animistic gods that the Chinese revere; the ancestral tablets are placed on the right side alongside their incense pot. Most of the altars have a backdrop depicting some of the more popular deities. The newer, more prestigious backdrops are painted on glass in bright colors that glitter. Varying amounts of religious odds and ends, including written charms and souvenirs of visits to temples, also decorate the altar, and frequently, a Buddha image also stands on it. The ancestral tablets affirm the idealized picture of the Chinese family as a patrilineal kinship group and commemorate its immediate patrilineal forebears and their wives. The family may also have a larger ancestral hall housing the tablets of more distant forebears.

Many families worship at the family altar regularly, and sometimes, every day. A representative of the family, usually one of the older women, burns three sticks of incense. One stick goes into the ancestor's incense pot, another stick is positioned in the incense pot reserved for the gods that the family members revere, and a third stick is placed outside the door to welcome the gods and ancestors. As might be expected, the older members of the family tend to worship more frequently than the younger members.

Furthermore, the family tends to commemorate the death days of their closer ancestors or those whom they have known personally. On such occasions, the living members of the family serve the deceased members full meals, complete with bowls and chopsticks, rice and noodles, and some of their favorite dishes; food is also provided for the animistic gods in many instances. In this context, people treat ancestors almost as if they were still living kinsmen. Family members typically eat the food after the ancestors have supposedly eaten, that is, once the incense sticks have burned out. Ancestors also receive food offerings during major festivals for the gods; domestic worship of the gods tends to occur on the first and fifteenth of every lunar month.

Roundness, the first of the three characteristics of the family altar, stands for the continuity and structural completeness of the family; it symbolizes that the family is the basic, distinct, and enduring feature of the Chinese culture. The family altar as such represents the critical point of continuity between the natural world and the supernatural world. As indicated previously, Confucianism did not develop a Westernized conception of heaven, but it holds that the dead exist in a shadowy netherworld and can communicate with, and directly influence, the living relatives. For the Chinese, there is not a sharp demarcation between birth and death. Rather, all humankind is considered to be part of an organic system; in yin and yang fashion, individuals are continually being born into it and processed in it, but they do not experience final separation from it or death in the Westernized sense. To the Chinese, the system, life, and time itself are circular, and all are united to one another because of this circularity. This perspective is consistent with both Buddhist and Taoist beliefs.

According to this rounded viewpoint, what is crucial is that the Chinese individual has descendants who can worship him or her and provide food and sacrifices; under such conditions, he or she will lead a contented life in the netherworld. All of the efforts of the living are directed toward obtaining a rounded family in which the descent line is preserved. Thus, roundness suggests a unity of the family circle that is related to the structural ideal of flawless Chinese patrilineage. Male children, who are obligated to perform ceremonial and ancestral rites, are preferred over female children. Hence, roundness also suggests that men should have wives who can bear sons.

There are some problems with this idealization of roundness. Some women cannot bear sons. Under classical Chinese law, failure to bear a son was grounds for divorce. Some children die before they are of an age to produce offspring, and historically, it was common for them to be buried unceremoniously and unmourned. Sometimes, the father does not live to an old age, and his family does not receive the honor accorded to those who have achieved such a distinction. However, the premature death of parents does not preclude their participation in the family, because they can be enshrined in ancestral tablets; the premature death of a husband does not weaken his wife's claim to a position in the descent line; and the failure to have children is correctable by adoption.

Such a patriarchal approach has led to the inequality of the sexes. Daughters occupy an inferior position to sons in the family, as do wives to husbands, and the mother assumes a position of relative equality with her husband and authority over her adult sons only when she is old, at which point she is accorded a position of honor and prestige. In such a context, most activities are segregated by sex.

In previous eras, polygamy was common among the Chinese, and it can still be found in isolated instances in rural areas. This practice complicated the familial structure, but the first wife was usually accorded the most honor and authority. In the modern world, it is typical for a Chinese man to marry only one woman, although the practice of having a "minor wife" or mistress is common. Because of the emphasis on the family, the Chinese businessman frequently works alongside his wife, or she will handle office matters while he is in charge of external relations. This pattern has limited the growth of many Chinese businesses, because only the wife and other family members are given positions of authority. Sometimes, the husband and wife rarely see one another because of his external activities, but this is acceptable behavior provided that the husband is working hard on behalf of the family.

One Chinese family living in Thailand is typical in that every Sunday, the wife of the oldest son hosts all family members at their home, including the younger sons and their families. Even though some of the brothers are not very competent, the eldest son and chief executive officer of the family business allows them to keep their positions as vice presidents and heads of the family's factories, but non-family members actually are the key decision makers in their factories. However, these non-family members participate in the Sunday activities on only an irregular basis. Because they are excluded from becoming full members of the familial in-group and can never aspire to become owners of the factories in any real sense of the word, it is common for them to quit after a few years and establish their own businesses.

This rounded perspective leads the Chinese to take a long-term perspective on problems and issues that they face. Unlike Americans, most of whom feel that a long-term plan involves a projection into the future of 3 to 5 years, the Chinese tend to be comfortable with plans that are expressed in 10-, 20-, and even 100-year increments. Geert Hofstede (1993), whose 53-nation study of cultural values is highlighted in this book, has expanded his four-dimensional framework into five dimensions because of recent research on the Chinese. He calls this dimension "the Confucian dynamic," and it reflects a long-term rather than a short-term orientation; in some ways, it also resembles the Protestant ethic in that deferred gratification of individual needs is accepted for the purpose of long-term success that helps the family.

Louis Kraar (1994), commenting on the causes of the success of the overseas or expatriate Chinese, begins his analysis by emphasizing this Confucian ethic:

> Regardless of where they live or how rich they are, the Overseas Chinese share an abiding belief in hard work, strong family ties, frugality, and education. Yes, this same constellation of virtues defines much of what Westerners have labeled the Protestant Ethic, but for the Overseas Chinese these attributes are not musty relics from their culture's past but compelling rules to live by. (pp. 92-93)

This rounded conception of familial relationships is distinctively Chinese, and it encompasses members of the family over space and time. It is the family rather than the individual that has been the basic unit of social organization among the Chinese since the time of the Duke of Chou in the 12th century B.C. He established the system of *bao-jia,* or family/kinship rule, and divided society into units of 10, 100, 1,000, and 10,000 families arranged by neighborhoods and districts. Each unit chose a leader from its ranks who was responsible for the behavior and welfare of all of the families in that jurisdiction, and this leader in turn reported directly to the leader of the next *bao-jia* unit. If a man committed a crime, the head of his own household would be held accountable, followed by the head of his 10-family unit, the 100-family unit, and so on. As a result, minor crimes were rarely reported beyond the smallest unit, which had the authority to settle such matters. In one way or another, modern Chinese follow this pattern of collective responsibility, although practices vary widely by the nations in which they reside.

Furthermore, the concept of roundness helps to explain the well-known Chinese practice of *guanxi,* or connections. The lifeblood of a Chinese company is *guanxi.* Penetrating the layers of *guanxi* is like peeling an onion. First come connections between people and ancestors; then between people from the same village; then between members of the family; and, finally, between the family and close associates who can be trusted, such as the competent executives who are not family members but who actually run the factories. All of these relationships are considered to be continual in nature, and obligations go far beyond what can be put into a contract. For example, a Chinese businessman will help a household servant establish her own business after she has served the family faithfully for several years; he will also expect a Western colleague to help his son gain admission into a prestigious Western university after they have worked together on a joint venture for some years.

Typically, the Chinese, similar to many other high-context cultures, are less concerned with what is written in the contract than in the actions that people take to meet their obligations as they emphasize *guanxi.* For example, the American Chamber of Thailand spent 2 years identifying an American partner for a Chinese Thai businessman who was seeking to establish a joint venture. At long last, all of the principal parties were to gather for dinner in Bangkok to finalize the arrangements, but the Chinese Thai businessman stormed out of the room when the American businessman showed up with a lawyer and a written contract, thus putting an end to the potential joint venture. To the high-context Chinese, this was an affront of the highest order.

The Chinese also tend to bypass the use of banks because of this system of *guanxi.* In fact, banks were unknown in China until the 20th century. Throughout the world, the Chinese establish communal investment and credit associations. A group of friends, relatives, and colleagues pool their money to form a mutual fund from which each member may take turns borrowing, and the Chinese rely on the personal closeness of the group to inhibit fraud or default. Sometimes, these associations will lend money to other Chinese who cannot afford to contribute to the association. Furthermore, the Chinese are well known for lending their personal funds to their relatives in other nations, for example, Taiwanese investment in Malaysia, Thailand, and China.

The largest Chinese families even establish private social welfare agencies that are open to anyone from the family. For example, the Chinese Lee family—there is also a Korean Lee family—operates a social welfare agency in a large building in New York's Chinatown that helps any Lee of Chinese origin obtain employment or solve any crisis, such as dealing with immigration officials who may be trying to deport him and his family.

Even the conception of the modern Chinese businessman is related to the concept of roundness. Many Chinese businessmen fly around the world so frequently that they have been caricatured as "spacemen." They meet regularly with business associates in other nations who are united with one another through *guanxi*. If they are working with non-Chinese businessmen, they spend a great deal of time getting to know them so that the noncontractual nature of their relationships is given prominence.

As explained in Chapter 3, "The Japanese Garden," the need for harmony and its development as a cultural ideal seems to have originated in the activities surrounding wet rice farming, and this generalization is also valid for China. Given the need to cooperate closely if subsistence for all was to be provided, the Chinese accorded primacy to harmony rather than to other ideals, such as the Western conception of life, liberty, and the pursuit of happiness. When disharmony infects the relations in the family, supernatural explanations for it are frequently offered, and the support of ancestors and gods is the natural way to reestablish harmony.

Roundness is a necessary but not sufficient condition for the second characteristic of the family altar, harmony. Ideally, the harmonious family is one in which there are few, if any, quarrels, financial problems, or illnesses. The most common prayer among many devout Chinese is for harmony, and it is frequently printed on door frames, charms, wedding cakes, and even the walls of homes. It is a prayer that is directed to both ancestors and gods. And, as indicated above, the members of the living family offer food and rituals in return for the harmony that they are seeking.

People make all kinds of requests at the family altar, for example, helping a child pass an examination, curing the sick, and obtaining employment. Although the requests are not always met, devotees often feel renewed hope and comfort, in large part because of the rituals that unite deceased and living family members through the medium of the family altar. Even the skeptical carry out the rituals—just in case.

Although the Chinese seek to achieve harmony, their worldview is not nearly as comforting as that of the Christian, who can aspire to a tranquil heaven that is under the supervision of a benign and personal God. The shadowy netherworld represents a degree of uncertainty that the Christian does not have to take into account. It may be for this reason that the Chinese tend to believe in luck and fate, and that they have little, if any, control over events. In a Chinese Buddhist temple, for example, the worshiper can purchase a set of fortune sticks that he throws on the ground and then rearranges before consulting a book that predicts his future in terms of this rearrangement. Similarly, many Chinese do not use car seatbelts, because they believe that nature will take its normal course, no matter what they do.

Also, although other cultural groups like to gamble, many Chinese clearly are attracted to it, seemingly in part because of this sense of uncertainty, luck, and fate. The major sense of security and harmony comes from the rounded family and the all-encompassing family altar. Many times, gambling and games of chance reinforce both harmony and roundness. For example, large Asian families, each of which may include 30 or more individuals and several generations, go to restaurants for several hours of convivial conversation and relaxation, during which time they leisurely play cards and other games of chance. Similarly, it is not unusual for a Chinese family of 30 or more members, including several generations and close family servants, to go to the seashore for 4 or 5 days and spend most of the time inside an air-conditioned house talking to one another, drinking, eating sumptuous meals, and playing games of chance in which all participate; sometimes, no one even ventures to the beach because of the enjoyment that the family members experience interacting with one another under such circumstances.

The third characteristic of the family altar is fluidity, or the capacity to change while maintaining solid traditions. It reflects the relation-oriented approach of the Chinese, because they can be individualistic as long as they meet their many obligations to various family members, including those who are deceased.

Thus, although the Chinese tend to be conservative, they are frequently innovative and entrepreneurial. The number of Chinese inventions and scientific breakthroughs is startling, and Joseph Needham (1954) has an ongoing project describing them that, when completed, will fill 25 volumes. These include the first suspension bridge, fishing reels, rudders for ships, hand gliders, parachutes, fireworks, lacquer, wallpaper, paper, armor made from paper, wheelbarrows, and the first design for a steam engine. Similarly, as Kotkin (1993) and many others have described, the Chinese have been very successful in establishing business enterprises, and they are disproportionately successful and entrepreneurial compared to most other ethnic groups. This balanced emphasis on conservatism and innovation clearly reflects the concept of fluidity.

In traditional Chinese religion, there is a huge pantheon of gods and goddesses, most of whom are the heroes of Chinese myths, legend, and history, and deified by either imperial order or popular choice. Some communities have cult followings that have evolved around a particular historical figure who supposedly protects and guides the town, or who may have worked a miracle in it. The reputed powers of the best known deities have been confirmed by generations of Chinese over the centuries. However, devotees believe that the power of a deity tends to decline with age and eventually loses its efficacy completely. The Chinese generally pray only to gods who have answered at least some of their petitions. When the decline in power occurs, the devotees begin to worship a new god. Thus, there is fluidity in that change occurs, but devotion at the family altar continues.

Even the history of China can be interpreted in terms of the three characteristics of the family altar. Han, the largest cultural group, consists of more than 90% of the population. However, given the billion-plus people in China, it is not surprising that there are more than 60 cultural groups that range in size from millions of people to only a few thousand, and most of them have and have had harmonious relations with one another. Almost all of Chinese history can be divided into periods defined by dynasties. Families or rulers occupied the throne until another took the power away. History was viewed as endless cycles of renewal and decline, starting with the first dynasty in approximately 1953 B.C. and not ending until the retirement of the last emperor in A.D. 1911. Each ruler was considered to have a mandate bestowed on him by the gods to rule fairly and wisely. When an heir became corrupt or lazy, rebellions would break out, and a new emperor would surface. Typically, he would introduce reforms that were consistent with the underlying cultural values of roundness, harmony, and fluidity. The fact that China was the most developed civilization in the world for a significant portion of this long time period may also be attributed to the emphasis on these three characteristics. As a broad generalization, the dynastic cycle helps to explain, through the mechanism of periodic renewal, how the Chinese were able to retain a consistent and continuous pattern of government for thousands of years (Major, 1989, pp. 46-47). Thus, this cycle exemplifies all three characteristics of the family altar: roundness, or continuity and structural completeness of the family and family-based nation; harmony over thousands of years marred only by periodic revolutions; and fluidity, or maintaining the past while accepting change.

▛ The Expatriate Chinese

Today, there are more than 55 million expatriate Chinese, and many of them have been spectacularly successful in businesses throughout the world when compared to other cultural groups. Initially, these emigrants from China did not come from mainstream Chinese society, which was, at times, insular and suspicious of foreigners whose cultures they generally considered to be inferior to that of the Chinese. Rather, they originated from the peripheral southern regions of China, where control and subservience to the emperor was less rigid.

In some of the countries in which these expatriate Chinese settled, such as Thailand and the United States, they have integrated themselves effectively and have even married non-Chinese in increasingly large numbers. In other countries, such as Malaysia and Indonesia, the Chinese experience discrimination and resentment, and they tend to be less effectively integrated with the other cultural groups. In Malaysia, for example, a Chinese cannot be the chief executive officer of a company seeking government contracts. To get around this restriction, the Chinese put a native Malay into this position while retaining most of the power.

Some of this discrimination seems to be religious in nature, for example, Muslims in Malaysia and Indonesia versus Confucians. Whatever its causes, it has divided such countries into Chinese and non-Chinese groups that experience difficulty in developing harmonious relations.

Taiwan, a country of 21 million people, is an interesting example of the success that the expatriate Chinese have wrought. It was established as a separate country after World War II, when Chiang Kai-shek and his followers were driven out of China by the Communists. Its rulers realized that the most important resource of Taiwan was the Confucian dynamic of its people, and so laws were established that fostered entrepreneurship. Taiwanese businesses are generally small and family dominated, and they have been so successful that the country is now one of the richest in the world.

Hong Kong, 95% of whose citizens are Chinese, has a population of 6.1 million people. Although it occupies only a small area of 412 square miles, more than 120 million fly into Hong Kong each year, most of whom are there for the purposes of business or shopping. Business is so successful that the executives have been forced to build "vertical factories" that are housed in tall buildings, and each factory is built on top of the other.

In Singapore, with its population of 3.3 million, there are three main ethnic groups: Chinese (77%), Malays (15%), and Indians (6%). Like Taiwan and Hong Kong, this country has been resoundingly successful, in large part because of the herculean efforts of the Chinese; until recent years, the country was extremely poor. These three countries have been so successful that they, along with Korea and Thailand, are nicknamed the Five Tigers of Asia.

Thailand has a population of 58 million, and its two main ethnic groups are native Thai (75%) and Chinese (14%). These two groups are quite comfortable with one another, and, as indicated previously, intermarriage is common. Whereas the Chinese play their traditional role as businessmen, particularly small businessmen, the Thais tend to control the government, the military, and the banks. Ironically, the Thais are continually debating the merits of "Taiwanizing Thailand," because many of them prefer to keep their long-established and traditional ways of doing business and enjoying life that are frequently incompatible with modern approaches.

The expatriate Chinese are influential in most, if not all, of the countries in which they reside. Unlike the expatriate Japanese, who tend to separate themselves from the societies in which they reside and eventually want to return to Japan, the expatriate Chinese seek integration in the countries in which they reside, but they stay in contact with one another through their far-flung families and the activities of the Chinese "spacemen," who roam the world seeking business opportunities.

In short, the expatriate Chinese are similar to the traditional Chinese in the sense that the family is the basic social unit through which all are united in a relation-based system. Roundness is emphasized by these families, who form a complex but informal network throughout the world, as is harmony and fluidity. The Chinese, regardless of their country of residence, tend to exhibit conservative and high-context behavior. Even though some of the Chinese may have moved away from the practice of honoring ancestors at the family altar, they typically accept the importance that is attached to the need for roundness, harmony, and fluidity. In this sense, the family altar is not only an appropriate metaphor for the Chinese, but one that illustrates clearly the major values of this ethnic group, no matter where they settle permanently.

References

Adler, N. (1997). *International dimensions of organizational behavior* (3rd ed.). Cincinnati, OH: South-Western College Publishing.

Alotaibi, M. (1989). *Bedouin: The nomads of the desert.* Vero Beach, FL: Rourke.

Al-Zahrani, S., & Kaplowitz, S. (1993). Attributional biases in individualistic and collectivist cultures: A comparison of Americans and Saudis. *Social Psychology Quarterly, 56,* 223-233.

Arden, N. (1990, May). Searching for India along the great trunk road. *National Geographic,* pp. 177-185.

Aronson, D. R. (1978). *The city is our farm.* Cambridge, MA: Schenkman.

Axtell, R. (1990). *Dos and taboos around the world* (2nd ed.). New York: Wiley.

Banerji, P. (1983). *Erotica in Indian dance.* Atlantic Highlands, NJ: Humanities Press.

Barnlund, D. (1989). *Public and private self in Japan and the United States.* Yarmouth, ME: Intercultural Press.

Barzini, L. (1964). *The Italians.* New York: Atheneum.

Barzini, L. (1983). *The Europeans.* New York: Simon & Schuster.

Beckett, J. D. (1986). *A short history of Ireland.* London: Cresset Library.

Belgium: Fading away. (1992, October 31). *The Economist,* p. 52.

Benet, S. (1951). *Song, dance, and customs of peasant Poland.* London: Dennis Dobson.

Benton, W. (Ed.). (1970). *Encyclopedia Britannica.* Chicago: Encyclopedia Britannica.

Berry, J. (1990). Psychology of acculturation: Understanding individuals moving between cultures. In R. Brislin (Ed.), *Applied cross-cultural psychology.* Newbury Park, CA: Sage.

Bettelheim, B. (1969). *The children of the dream.* New York: Macmillan.

Bisbee, S. (1951). *The new Turks.* Philadelphia: University of Pennsylvania Press.

Bleak and bloody Russia. (1999, December 18). *The Economist,* pp. 15-16.

Bonavia, D. (1989). *The Chinese.* London: Penguin.

Bond, M. (1986). *The psychology of the Chinese people.* New York: Oxford University Press.

Bond, M., & Smith, P. (1998). *Social psychology across cultures* (2nd ed.). London: Blackwell.

Bond, M. et al. (1987). Chinese values and the search for culture-free dimensions of culture. *Journal of Cross-Cultural Psychology, 18,* 143-164.

Boorstin, D. (1965). *The Americans: The national experience.* New York: Random House.

Booth, W. (1998, February 22). One nation, indivisible: Is it history? *Washington Post,* pp. A1, A18, A19.

Boswell, T. (1990, August 12). What we are talking about when we talk about sports. *Washington Post Magazine,* pp. 22-28.

Braganti, N., & Devine, E. (1992). *European customs and manners* (2nd ed.). Minneapolis, MN: Meadowbrook.

Brint, S. (1989, July-August). Italy observed. *Society,* pp. 71-76.

Brislin, R. (1993). *Understanding culture's influence on behavior.* New York: Harcourt Brace.

Burns, A. C. (1963). *History of Nigeria.* London: Allen & Unwin.

Burr, A. (1917). *Russell H. Conwell and his work.* Philadelphia, PA: Winston.

Burtless, G., & Smeeding, T. (1995, June 25). America's tide: Lifting the yachts, swamping the rowboats. *Washington Post,* p. C3.

Busting up Sweden, Inc. (1999, February 22). *Business Week,* pp. 52-54.

Cahill, T. (1995). *How the Irish saved civilization.* New York: Doubleday, Anchor Books.

Campbell, J. (1962). *The masks of God: Oriental mythology.* New York: Penguin.

Cannadine, D. (1998). *The rise and fall of class in Britain.* New York: Columbia University Press.

Carroll, S., & Gannon, M. (1997). *Ethical dimensions of international management.* Thousand Oaks, CA: Sage.

Carson, R. (1962). *Silent spring.* Greenwich, CT: Fawcett.

Clarke, M., & Crisp, M. (1976). *Understanding ballet.* New York: Harmony.

Clayre, A. (1985). *The heart of the dragon.* Boston: Houghton Mifflin.

Condon, J. C. (1985). *Good neighbors: Communicating with Mexicans.* Yarmouth, ME: Intercultural Press.

Conty, M. (1999, Fall). Belle of the ball. *Hermes,* pp. 42-44.

Coomaraswamy, A. (1969). *The dance of Shiva.* New York: Sunwise Turn. (Original work published 1924)

Copland, A. (1957). *What to listen for in music.* New York: New American Library. (Original work published 1939)

Cottrell, J. (1986). *Library of nations: Germany.* Alexandria, VA: Time-Life Books.

Could Flanders be reinvented? (1997, September 20). *The Economist,* p. 54.

Cowley, A. (1995, April 8). A survey of Russia's emerging market: A silent revolution. *The Economist,* pp. 1-22.

Craig, J. (1979). *Culture shock: What not to do in Malaysia and Singapore.* Singapore: Times Book International.

Crook, C. (1991, May 4). A survey of India. *The Economist,* pp. 1-18.

Crow, J. A. (1985). *Spain: The root and the flower* (3rd ed.). Berkeley: University of California Press.

Culturegrams: The nations around us (Vol. 2). (1991). Garrett Park, MD: Garrett Park Press.

Daun, A. (1991). Individualism and collectivity among Swedes. *Ethnos, 56,* 165-172.

David, P. (1998, April 25). A survey of Israel: After Zionism. *The Economist,* pp. 1-18.

David, P. (1999, November 6). A survey: Undoing Britain? *The Economist,* pp. 1-18.

Death among the blossoms. (1991, May 25). *The Economist,* pp. 39-41.

Degrees of dissatisfaction. (1996, June 20). *The Economist,* p. 48.

Delany, M. (1974). *Of Irish ways.* Minneapolis, MN: Dillion.

De Mente, B. (1990). *The kata factor.* Phoenix, AZ: Phoenix Books.

Deutsch, E. (1968). *Bhagavad gita.* New York: Holt, Rinehart & Winston.

Dindi, H., & Gazur, M. (1989). *Turkish culture for Americans.* Boulder, CO: International Concepts.

Earley, C., & Laubach, M. (in press). Structural identity theory and the dynamics of cross-cultural work groups. In M. Gannon & K. Newman (Eds.), *Handbook of cross-cultural management.* London: Blackwell.

The Economist pocket world in figures, 1998 edition. (1997). New York: Wiley.

Eine kleine samba. (1995, November 4). *The Economist,* p. 49.

Elon, A. (1971). *The Israelis.* New York: Penguin.

England's shame. (1998, June 20). *The Economist,* p. 19.

Erez, M. (1986). The congruence of goal-setting strategies with sociocultural values and its effects on performance. *Journal of Management, 12,* 83-90.

Faiola, A. (1997, October 2). Priest tries to rap Brazilians back into fold. *Washington Post,* pp. A1, A18.

Fieg, J. (1976). *A common core: Thais and Americans.* Yarmouth, ME: Intercultural Press.

Fieg, J., & Mortlock, E. (1989). *A common core: Thais and Americans* (rev. ed.). Yarmouth, ME: Intercultural Press.

Fisher, G. (1988). *Mindsets: The role of culture and perception in international relations.* Yarmouth, ME: Intercultural Press.

Fisher, M. (1993, March 21). Germany's wimp complex. *Washington Post,* pp. C1-C4.

Fiske, A. (1991a). The four elementary forms of sociality: Frameworks for a unified theory of social relations. *Psychological Review, 99,* 689-723.

Fiske, A. (1991b). *Structures of social life.* New York: Free Press.

Fleckenstein, B. (1999). Germany: Forerunner of a post-national military? In C. C. Moskos, J. A. Williams, & D. R. Segal (Eds.), *The post modern military* (pp. 31-53). New York: Oxford University Press.

Flood, P., Gannon, M., & Paauwe, J. (1996). *Managing without traditional methods: International innovations in human resource management.* Wokingham, UK: Addison-Wesley.

The flowers of Kobe. (1995, January 21). *The Economist,* pp. 35-36.

Frank, R., & Cook, P. (1995). *The winner-take-all society.* New York: Free Press.

Friedman, T. L. (1989). *From Beirut to Jerusalem.* Garden City, NY: Doubleday.

Frost, E. (1987). *For richer, for poorer.* New York: Council on Foreign Relations.

Furness, N., & Tilton, T. (1979). *The case for the welfare state.* Bloomington: Indiana University Press.

Gabrielidis, C., Stephan, W., Ybarra, O., Dos Santos-Pearson, V., & Villareal, L. (1997). Preferred styles of conflict resolution. *Journal of Cross-Cultural Psychology, 28,* 661-677.

Galbraith, J. K. (1984). *The affluent society* (4th ed.). Boston: Houghton Mifflin.

Gannon, M. (1988). *Management.* Boston: Allyn & Bacon.

Gannon, M. (2001). *Working across cultures: Applications and exercises.* Thousand Oaks, CA: Sage.

Gannon, M., & Associates. (1997, August). *Cultural metaphors as frames of reference for nations: A six country study.* Paper presented at the annual meeting of the Academy of Management, Boston, MA.

Gannon, M., & Audia, P. (in press). The cultural metaphor: A grounded method for analyzing national cultures. In C. Earley & H. Singh (Eds.), *Work behavior across cultures and nations.* Thousand Oaks, CA: Sage.

Geertz, C. (1973). *The interpretation of culture.* New York: Basic Books.

Gelfand, M., & McHusker, C. (in press). Negotiation and conflict management. In M. Gannon & K. Newman (Eds.), *Handbook of cross-cultural management.* London: Blackwell.

George, P. (1987). *University teaching across cultures.* Bangkok, Thailand: U.S. Information Service.

Glain, S. (1998, April 23). Malaysia's grand social experiment may be the next casualty of Asian crisis. *Wall Street Journal,* p. A15.

Glyn, A. (1970). *The British: Portrait of a people.* New York: Putnam.

Going international: Part 2, Managing the overseas assignment. (1983). [Videotape]. (Available from Copeland Griggs Productions, San Francisco, 415-668-4200)

Gopal, R., & Dadachanji, S. (1951). *Indian dancing.* London: Phoenix House.

Gotchenour, T. (1977). The albatross. In D. Batchelder & E. Warner (Eds.), *Beyond experience* (pp. 131-136). Brattleboro, VT: The Experiment Press.

Graham, R. (1984). *Spain: Change of a nation.* London: Michael Joseph.

Grimond, J. (1999, February 6). A survey of Germany. *The Economist,* pp. 1-18.

Gross compensation: New CEO pay figures make top brass look positively piggy. (1996, March 18). *Business Week,* pp. 32-34.

Haire, M., Ghiselli, E., & Porter, L. (1966). *Managerial thinking: An international study.* New York: Wiley.

Hall, E. (1966). *The hidden dimension.* Garden City, NY: Doubleday.

Hall, E. (1983). *The dance of life.* Garden City, NY: Doubleday.

Hall, E., & Hall, M. (1990). *Understanding cultural differences.* Yarmouth, ME: Intercultural Press.

Hand of God, hand of Italian man. (1998, May 16). *The Economist,* p. 56.

Hann, C. (1985). *A village without solidarity: Polish peasants in years of crisis.* New Haven: Yale University Press.

Haskell, A. (1963). *The Russian genius in ballet.* Elmsford, NY: Pergamon.

Haskell, A. (1968). *Balletomania.* New York: AMS.

Haycraft, J. (1985). *Italian labyrinth.* New York: Penguin.

Heclo, H., & Madsen, H. (1987). *Policy and politics in Sweden*. Philadelphia: Temple University Press.

Hess, D. (1995). *The Brazilian puzzle: Culture on the borderlands of the Western world*. New York: Columbia University Press.

Higgins, A. (1999, December 17). Through prism of war in Chechnya, Russians glimpse a new identity. *Wall Street Journal*, p. A1.

História do Brasil: Curso moderno. (1971). São Paulo, Brazil: Companhia Editora Nacional.

Hofstadter, R. (1955). *Social Darwinism in American thought*. Boston: Beacon Press.

Hofstede, G. (1980a). *Culture's consequences*. Beverly Hills, CA: Sage.

Hofstede, G. (1980b). Motivation, leadership, and organization: Do American theories apply abroad? *Organizational Dynamics, 9*, 42-63.

Hofstede, G. (1991). *Cultures and organizations: Software of the mind*. New York: McGraw-Hill.

Hofstede, G. (1993). Cultural constraints in management theories. *Academy of Management Executive, 7*, 81-94.

Hofstede, G., & Bond, M. (1988). The Confucius connection: From cultural roots to economic growth. *Organizational Dynamics, 16*(4), 4-21.

Hollinger, C. (1977). *Mai pen rai means never mind*. Tokyo: John Weatherhill. (Original work published 1967)

Hughes, T. (1994). Technological momentum. In M. Smith & L. Marx (Eds.), *Does technology drive history?* (pp. 101-114). Cambridge: MIT Press.

Huntington, S. (1996). *The clash of civilizations*. New York: Touchstone.

Huxley, A. (1951). *Antic hay*. New York: Modern Library.

Integrated but unequal. (1997, February 8). *The Economist*, pp. 58-59.

Italy's unruly drivers. (1999, August 7). *The Economist*, p. 38.

Iwao, S. (1990). Recent changes in Japanese attitudes. In A. Romberg & T. Yamahoto (Eds.), *Same bed, different dreams* (pp. 55-73). New York: Council on Foreign Relations.

Jago, A., Maczynski, J., & Reber, G. (1996). Evolving leadership styles? A comparison of Polish managers before and after market economy reforms. *Polish Psychological Bulletin, 27*(2), 107-115.

Jago, A., Reber, G., Boehnish, W., Maczynski, J., Zavfel, J., & Dudorkin, J. (1993). Culture's consequences? A seven nation study of participation. In D. F. Rogers & A. S. Raturi (Eds.), *Proceedings of the 24th annual meeting of the Decision Sciences Institute* (pp. 451-454). Washington, DC: Decision Sciences Institute.

Jarvenpaa, S., Knoll, K., & Leidner, D. (1998). Is anybody out there? Antecedents of trust in global virtual teams. *Journal of Management Information Systems, 14*(4), 29-36.

Jenkins, D. (1968). *Sweden and the price of progress*. New York: Coward, McCann & Geohegan.

Jordan, M. (1997, June 7). Japan's personnel offices really personal: Company matchmakers help employees find a spouse. *Washington Post*, pp. A17, A20.

Joyce, J. (1964). *Portrait of the artist as a young man*. New York: Viking.

Kagitcibasi, C. (1990). Family and home-based intervention. In R. Brislin (Ed.), *Applied cross-cultural psychology* (pp. 121-141). Newbury Park, CA: Sage.

Kakar, S. (1978). *The inner world*. New York: Oxford University Press.

Kanter, R. (1979). Power failures in management circuits. *Harvard Business Review,* *57*(4), 65-75.

Karp, J., & Kranhold, K. (1999, February 5). Enron's plant in India was dead; this month, it will go on stream. *Wall Street Journal,* pp. A1, A6.

Karp, J., & Williams, M. (1998, April 22). Leave it to Vishnu: Gods of Indian TV are Hindu deities. *Wall Street Journal,* pp. A1, A10.

Kashima, Y., & Callan, V. (1994). The Japanese work group. In H. Triandis, M. Dunnette, & L. Hough (Eds.), *Handbook of industrial and organizational psychology* (2nd ed., Vol. 4, pp. 609-646). Palo Alto, CA: Consulting Psychologists Press.

Kaufman, J. (1999, October 22). Why doesn't business, like baseball, create improbable heroes? *Wall Street Journal,* pp. A1, A8.

Keefe, E. (1977). *Area handbook for Italy.* Washington, DC: American University Press.

Kesselman, M., Krieger, J., Allen, C., DeBardeleben, J., Hellman, S., Pontrisson, J., & Ost, D. (1987). *European politics in transition.* Lexington, MA: D. C. Heath.

Kettenacker, L. (1997). *Germany since 1945.* Oxford, UK: Oxford University Press.

Khalid, M. (1979). The sociocultural determinants of Arab diplomacy. In G. Atiyeh (Ed.), *Arabs and American cultures* (pp. 123-142). Washington, DC: American Enterprise Institute for Public Policy Research.

Kightly, C. (1986). *The customs and ceremonies of Britain.* London: Thames & Hudson.

Kluckholn, F., & Strodtbeck, F. (1961). *Variations in value orientations.* Evanston, IL: Row, Peterson.

Koretz, G. (1998, October 5). How sick is the Russian bear? *Business Week,* p. 30.

Kotkin, J. (1993). *Tribes.* New York: Random House.

Kraar, L. (1994, October 31). The overseas Chinese. *Fortune,* pp. 91-114.

Kras, E. S. (1989). *Management in two cultures.* Yarmouth, ME: Intercultural Press.

Krich, J. (1993). *Why is this country dancing?* New York: Simon & Schuster.

Lakoff, G., & Johnson, M. (1980). *Metaphors we live by.* Chicago: University of Chicago Press.

Lancaster, J. (1996, November 14). Curtains in Riyadh. *Washington Post,* pp. A1, A26.

Lannoy, R. (1971). *The speaking tree: A study of Indian culture and society.* New York: Oxford University Press.

Laurent, A. (1983). The cultural diversity of Western concepts of management. *International Studies of Management and Organization,* *13*(1-2), 75-96.

Lessem, R. (1987). *The global business.* London: Prentice Hall International.

Levine, I. (1963). *Main street, Italy.* Garden City, NY: Doubleday.

The little class game. (1992, September 12). *The Economist,* p. 64.

Mackey, S. (1987). *The Saudis: Inside the desert kingdom.* Boston: Houghton Mifflin.

Mackey, S. (1992). *Passion and politics: The turbulent world of the Arabs.* New York: Penguin.

Major, J. (1989). *The land and the people of China.* New York: J. B. Lippincott.

Marvin, G. (1988). *Bullfight.* New York: Blackwell.

McClave, D. E. (1996). The society and its environment. In E. Solsten (Ed.), *Germany: A country study* (pp. 125-156). Washington, DC: Library of Congress.

McCourt, F. (1996). *Angela's ashes.* New York: Random House.

McGoldrick, M. (1982). *Ethnicity and family therapy.* New York: Guilford.

Md. Zabid, R., Anantharaman, R., & Raveendran, J. (1997). Corporate cultures and work values in dominant ethnic organizations in Malaysia. *Journal of Transnational Management Development, 2*(4), 51-65.

Mexico, haunted by new ghosts. (1999, November 6). *The Economist,* p. 36.

Meyer, L. (1982). *Israel now: Portrait of a troubled land.* New York: Delacorte.

Michon, J. (1992, December 5). Crown and crisis. *The time machine.* New York: Arts & Entertainment.

Milbank, D. (1993, March 17). We make a bit more of St. Patrick's Day than the Irish do. *Wall Street Journal,* pp. A1, A8.

Miller, L., & Hustedde, R. (1987). Group approaches. In D. E. Johnson, L. R. Miller, & G. F. Sommers (Eds.), *Needs assessment: Theory and methods* (pp. 105-131). Ames: Iowa State University Press.

Milner, H. (1989). *Sweden: Social democracy in practice.* New York: Oxford University Press.

The Mittelstand takes a stand. (1995, April 10). *Business Week,* pp. 54-55.

A modern vogue for more than a brogue. (1996, November 2). *The Economist,* p. 52.

Moore, T. (1859). *The poetical works of Thomas Moore.* Boston: Philips, Sampson.

Morin, R. (1998, September 6). Shy nations. *Washington Post,* p. C5.

Morrison, T., Conaway, W., & Douress, J. (1995). *Dun & Bradstreet's guide to doing business around the world.* Englewood Cliffs, NJ: Prentice Hall.

Munshi, K. (1965). *Indian inheritance* (Vol. 1). Bombay: Bharatiya Vidya Bhavan.

Nakane, C. (1973). *Japanese society.* London: Penguin.

Narayana, G., & Kantner, J. (1992). *Doing the needful.* Boulder, CO: Westview.

Needham, J. (1954). *Science and civilization in China.* Cambridge, UK: Cambridge University Press.

Neff, R. (1999, October 25). An inflexible Japan? Look again. *Business Week,* p. 78.

Newman, P. (1987, December 7). A national contempt for the law. *MacLean's,* p. 40.

Norton, R. (1999, October 25). The luck of the Irish. *Fortune,* pp. 194-220.

Nydell, M. (1987). *Understanding Arabs: A guide for Westerners.* Yarmouth, ME: Intercultural Press.

O'Brien, F. (1961). *At swim-two-birds.* In U. Mercier & D. Greene (Eds.), *1000 years of Irish prose.* New York: Grossett & Dunlap.

O'Brien, F. (1974). *The poor mouth: A bad story about the hard life.* New York: Seaver. (Original work published 1940)

Oldenburg, D. (1991, November 1). The world in words: Describing global societies metaphorically. *The Washington Post,* p. B5.

Olson, M. (2000). *Power and prosperity: Outgrowing Communist and capitalist dictatorships.* New York: Basic Books.

Olson, M. (1982). *The rise and decline of nations.* New Haven, CT: Yale University Press.

Ortony, A. (1975). Why metaphors are necessary and not just nice. *Educational Theory, 25*(1), 45-53.

Osland, J., & Bird, A. (2000). Beyond sophisticated stereotyping: Cultural sense-making in context. *Academy of Management Executive, 14*(1), 65-77.

Ouchi, W. (1981). *Theory Z.* Reading, MA: Addison-Wesley.

Out of control. (1999, December 4). *The Economist,* p. 44.

Paglia, C. (1997, September 17). Gridiron feminism. *Wall Street Journal,* p. A22.

Parker, J. (1992, December 5). Russia reborn: A survey of Russia. *The Economist,* pp. 1-26.

Paz, O. (1961). *The labyrinth of solitude: Life and thought in Mexico.* New York: Grove.

Pearson, L. (1990). *Children of glasnost: Growing up Soviet.* Seattle: University of Washington Press.

Pearson, V., & Stephens, W. (1998). Preferences for styles of negotiation: A comparison of Brazil and the U.S. *International Journal of Intercultural Relations, 22,* 80-99.

Peters, S. (1980). *Bedouin.* Cambridge, MA: Harvard University Press.

Pope, H. (1997a, March 14). The new middle: Turks add their voices to contest of generals and fundamentalists. *Wall Street Journal,* pp. A1, A13.

Pope, H. (1997b, May 15). Turkish mustaches, or the lack thereof, bristle with meaning. *Wall Street Journal,* pp. A1, A10.

Popular culture's heavenly glow: Spain's newly-fashionable Catholicism. (1997, August 2). *The Economist,* pp. 57-67.

Prewo, W. (1993, February 12). The sorcery of apprenticeship. *Wall Street Journal,* p. A14.

Punctured football. (1993, January 9). *The Economist,* p. 83.

Putnam, R. (1991). *Making democracy work: Civic traditions in modern Italy.* Princeton, NJ: Princeton University Press.

Reid, T. R. (1999, January 14). The Yanks have landed. *Washington Post,* pp. A24, A26.

Reischauer, E. (1988). *The Japanese today: Change and continuity.* Cambridge, MA: Belknap.

Richard, C. (1995). *The new Italians.* New York: Penguin.

Richmond, Y. (1992). *From nyet to da.* Yarmouth, ME: Intercultural Press.

Robinson, E. (1995, December 10). Over the Brazilian rainbow. *Washington Post,* pp. C1, C8.

Robinson, E. (1997, September 28). Pulsations. *Washington Post Sunday Magazine,* pp. 13-14, 38.

Robinson, E. (1999). *Coal to cream.* New York: Free Press.

Ronen, S., & Shenkar, O. (1985). Clustering countries on attitudinal dimensions: A review and synthesis. *Academy of Management Review, 10,* 435-454.

Ross, A. (1969). *What are u?* London: Andre Deutch.

Rowland, D. (1985). *Japanese business etiquette.* New York: Warner.

Russian exceptionalism: Is Russia different? (1996, June 15). *The Economist,* pp. 19-21.

Ruth, A. (1984). The second new nation: The mythology of modern Sweden. *Daedalus, 113,* 53-96.

Samovar, L., & Porter, R. (1994). *International communication: A reader* (7th ed.). Belmont, CA: Wadsworth.

Sanford, C. (1961). *The quest for paradise.* Urbana: University of Illinois Press.

Schatz, S. (1987). *Nigerian capitalism.* Berkeley: University of California Press.

Schein, E. H. (1985). *Organizational culture and leadership.* San Francisco: Jossey-Bass.

Schneider, R. (1996). *Brazil, culture and politics in a new industrial powerhouse.* Boulder, CO: Westview.

Schulze, H. (1998). *Germany: A new history* (D. Schneider, Trans.). Cambridge, MA: Harvard University Press.

Schulze, H. W. (1938). *The story of musical instruments: From shepherd's pipe to symphony.* Elkhart, IN: Pan-American Band Instruments.

Schwartz, S. (1994). Beyond individualism and collectivism: New cultural dimensions of work values. In U. Kim, H. Triandis, C. Kagitcibasi, S. Choi, & G. Yoon (Eds.), *Individualism and collectivism: Theory, method, and applications* (pp. 19-40). Thousand Oaks, CA: Sage.

Sendut, H., Madsen, J., & Thong, G. (1989). *Managing in a plural society.* Singapore: Longman.

Shamberg, M. (Producer), & Crichton, C. (Director). (1988). *A fish called Wanda.* Hollywood, CA: Metro-Goldwyn-Mayer.

Shirouzu, N. (2000, January 5). Leaner and meaner. *Wall Street Journal,* pp. A1, A8.

Smith, H. (1958). *The religions of man.* New York: Harper & Row.

Smith, H. (1991). *The world's religions.* San Francisco: HarperCollins.

Smith, K., Grimm, C., & Gannon, M. (1992). *Dynamics of competitive strategy.* Newbury Park, CA: Sage.

Smith, L. (1990, February 26). Fear and loathing of Japan. *Fortune,* pp. 50-60.

Solomon, M. (1996). *Consumer behavior.* Englewood Cliffs, NJ: Prentice Hall.

Solsten, E. (1996). Introduction. In E. Solsten (Ed.), *Germany: A country study* (pp. 87-111). Washington, DC: Library of Congress.

South-East Asia's learning difficulties. (1997, August 16). *The Economist,* pp. 30-31.

Spain: Locked horns. (1997, March 8). *The Economist,* pp. 58-59.

Srinivas, M. (1980). *India: Social structure.* Delhi: Hindustan.

Starr, J. (1991). *Kissing through glass.* Chicago: Contemporary Books.

Stewart, E., & Bennett, M. (1991). *American cultural patterns: A cross cultural perspective* (2nd ed.). Yarmouth, ME: Intercultural Press.

Stoller, R. (1975). *Perversion: The erotic form of hatred.* New York: Pantheon.

Sugawara, S. (1998, August 21). From debt to desperation in Japan. *Washington Post,* p. G3.

Sundberg, G. (1910). *Det Svenska folklynnet.* Stockholm, Sweden: Norstedt & Soners.

A survey of the Koreas. (1999, July 10). *The Economist,* pp. 1-30.

Szalay, L. (1993). *The subjective worlds of Russians and Americans: A guide for mutual understanding.* Chevy Chase, MD: Institute of Comparative Social and Cultural Studies.

A tale of two cities. (1993, June). *Business Traveler,* pp. 25-27.

Tan, A. (1991). *The kitchen god's wife.* New York: Ballantine.

Tasker, P. (1987). *The Japanese: Portrait of a nation.* New York: Meridian.

Tornblom, K., Jonsson, D., & Foa, U. (1985). National resource, class, and preferences among three allocation rules: Sweden vs. USA. *International Journal of Intercultural Relations, 9,* 51-77.

Triandis, H. (in press). Generic individualism and collectivism. In M. Gannon & K. Newman (Eds.), *Handbook of cross-cultural management.* London: Blackwell.

Triandis, H., Brislin, R., & Hui, C. (1988). Cross-cultural training across the individualism-collectivism divide. *International Journal of Intercultural Press Relations, 12,* 269-289.

Triandis, H., & Gelfand, M. (1998). Convergent measurement of horizontal and vertical individualism and collectivism. *Journal of Personality and Social Psychology, 74,* 118-128.

Trompenaars, F., & Hampden-Turner, C. (1998). *Riding the waves of culture* (2nd ed.). New York: McGraw-Hill.

Trueheart, C. (1998, January 30). Can Portugal survive the Euro? *Washington Post,* pp. A25, A28.

Tuchman, B. (1962). *The guns of August.* New York: Macmillan.

Twitchin, J. (n.d.). Training notes for the video *Crosstalk at work: Cross cultural communication in the workplace.* London: BBC Training Videos.

Venezia, E. (1997). *Cross-cultural management: UN solo management nella differenziata realta Italiana?* Tesi di laurea, Universita Boccon: di Milano.

Verleyen, F. (1987). *Flanders today.* Tielt, Belgium: Lannoo Editions.

Vogel, E. (1979). *Japan as number one: Lessons for America.* Cambridge, MA: Harvard University Press.

Wallace, P. (1999). *The psychology of the Internet.* Cambridge, UK: Cambridge University Press.

Wang, G. (1962). *Latar belakang kebudayaan cina: Basis of Chinese culture.* Kuala Lumpur: Dewan Bahasa dan Pustaka.

Waters, M. (1984). *The comic Irishman.* Albany: State University of New York Press.

Waxman, S. (1993, June 9). Brussels, capital of confusion. *Washington Post,* pp. D1, D6.

Weber, M. (1947). *Theory of social and economic organization* (A. Henderson & T. Parsons, Trans.). New York: Free Press.

Wheaton, K. (Ed.). (1990). *Insight guide: Spain.* Singapore: APA Publications.

Where Ikea got its style. (1997, November 18). *The Economist,* pp. 108-109.

Willey, D. (1984). *Italians.* London: BBC.

Williams, C. (1998, February 23). A tough new course in Moscow schools: Manners. *Washington Post,* p. A13.

Williams, D. (1997a, August 23). All of Russia grieves for beloved comic who brought light to dark days. *Washington Post,* p. A20.

Williams, D. (1997b, February 3). Bolshoi's "Swan Lake" has been polluted, critics say. *Washington Post,* p. A12.

Wilson, P., & Graham, D. (1994). *Saudi Arabia: The coming storm.* Armonk, NY: Sharpe.

Zachary, G. (1999, March 17). Barring entry: Ireland faces a shortage of pubs, and the blame falls on old rules. *Wall Street Journal,* pp. A1, A10.

Zaman, A. (1999, December 2). Spreading faith through fashion: Turkish chain promotes Islamic clothing. *Washington Post,* p. A32.

Zetterberg, H. (1984). The rational humanitarians. *Daedalus, 113,* 72-79.

Index

About the Author

$\mathcal{M}$artin J. Gannon (PhD, Columbia University) is Professor of Management and Director of the Center for Global Business, Robert H. Smith School of Business, University of Maryland at College Park. He is also the Founding Director of the College Park Scholars Program in Business, Society, and the Economy (an undergraduate living-learning community). His previous positions at Maryland include Associate Dean for Academic Affairs, Chair of the Faculty of Management and Organization, and Co-Founder/Co-Director of the Small Business Development Center. At Maryland, he teaches in the areas of international management and behavior and business strategy. He is the author or coauthor of 85 articles and 14 books, including *Dynamics of Competitive Strategy* (Sage, 1992); *Managing Without Traditional Methods: International Innovations in Human Resource Management* (1996); *Ethical Dimensions of International Management* (Sage, 1997) and the *Handbook of Cross-Cultural Management* (in press).

Professor Gannon has served as a management consultant and trainer to a large number of private firms, federal government agencies, and labor unions. Specific organizations for which he has worked include the Strategic Forum Consulting Group in Malaysia and Indonesia; the Polish-American Center, University of Lodz, Poland; Bocconi University, Milan; Universities of Tübingen and Kassel, Germany; University College–Dublin; London Business School; Universiti Kabangsaan, Malaysia; and Thammasat University, Bangkok. Currently, he is the main external consultant to GEICO Insurance Company on the design and delivery of its Senior Management Training Program. He is also the University of Maryland Academic Director of the

Northrop Grumman Managerial IMPACT Certificate Program designed to increase international skill sets.

Professor Gannon has been Senior Research Fulbright Professor at the Center for the Study of Work and Higher Education in Germany and the John F. Kennedy/Fulbright Professor at Thammasat University in Bangkok.

Related books by Martin J. Gannon on cultural metaphors:

Cultural Metaphors: Readings, Research Translations, and Commentary (Sage, 2001)

Working Across Cultures: Applications and Exercises (Sage, 2001)

Available from:

Sage Publications
2455 Teller Road
Thousand Oaks, CA 91320

Email: order@sagepub.com
Phone: 805-499-9774

On the Web at www.sagepub.com